EARLY MISSOURIANS
AND KIN

A genealogical compilation of inter-related
early Missouri settlers, their ancestors,
descendants and other kin.

D1714137

Facsimile Reprint

Published 1991 by
HERITAGE BOOKS, INC.
1540E Pointer Ridge Place, Bowie, Maryland 20716
(301)-390-7709

ISBN 1-55613-462-2

A Complete Catalog Listing Hundreds of Titles on
History, Genealogy & Americana
Free on Request

Printed in the United States of America
P & D Printing, Venice, Fla.

C O N T E N T S

E A R L Y   M I S S O U R I A N S
THEIR ANCESTORS, DESCENDANTS
AND OTHER KIN

FOREWORD

My grandfather, Thomas Osborn, lived prior to when
Missouri was admitted to the Union more than one
hundred and sixty years ago. Although this represents an unusual combination of generation spreads
it illustrates that we, today, are not far removed
from the period when the first Americans crossed
the Mississippi River to permanently settle in
Missouri.

I was born at the turn of the century, in Joplin,
Missouri, a mining town of rough individuals, and
part of an area last to be settled in Missouri. Indians had been pushed into Oklahoma not far away,
but they resented leaving the rich hunting grounds
of the Ozarks. They, on occasions, displayed this
by making return forays. My father would not be
separated from his "six-shooter" and kept one
under his pillow at night until I was about ten.
He belonged to the "Anti-Horse Thief Association"
and wasted no time in joining a posse when called
upon.

I recall a vacation trip our family took into Arkansas in a covered wagon, not quite the "up-to-
date" mode of travel for the time, but before the
"horseless carriage" reached Joplin. I remember
the rough roads and fording streams deep enough
for the horses to be troubled as to whether they
were expected to wade or swim across. Also, the
night entertainment we had teasing the tumble
bugs.

My paternal great-grandparents are of the Burgess,
Branson, Cox and Shockley families. They followed
Daniel Boone into Missouri when he was invited by
the Spanish Governor of the Territory of Louisiana
of which Missouri was a part, to bring in one hundred Americans to establish permanent settlements
along the Missouri River.

John Burgess, my grandfather, lived at Reddings

Mill, near Joplin when the Civil War broke out, but he and his family removed to Oswego,Kansas for awhile during hostilities to avoid the unpleasant and frustrating feelings among relatives and neighbors with divided loyalities.

My parents were born in the early 1860´s,my mother in Iowa and my father in Missouri. My mother migrated to Missouri with her parents in a covered wagon train, and they were stopped enroute by the notorious Jesse James, and Younger brothers. My great-granduncle and aunt, Andrew and Mary Cox entertained them one evening at dinner, only to find out their identity as they mounted their horses to depart. Under Mary´s dinner plate was a five dollar gold piece she found while removing the dishes.

The embryo for the material used in compiling the information in this book originated when I began collecting data for my own genealogy. My trails lead me into Gasconade, Osage and Maries Counties of Missouri, and the St. Louis environs, where I found ancestors and other kin of mine there in the early part of the 19th century. I became so intrigued with the first Missouri settlers and the early history of the State that my files began to be dominated by the people and events in this stage of our American history. There was a progressive drifting away from my own direct roots to a study of families regarded as founders of Missouri.

Among these frontierpeople, isolated in small settlements, unable to travel long distances due to poor trails and modes of travel, intermarriage developed completely different from that of today. Cousins married each other, so did uncles and nieces, and families living close together matched up in wedlock as long as the correct assortment of sexes lasted.

The entanglement created a maze difficult to cope with in developing charts. An individual would often show up in a number of places on the charts I was attempting to compile.This led me to believe that perhaps about all of these newcomers to Missouri were related in some way, either by blood or marriage,and this proved to be substantially true.

2

From my collection of data, I have compiled a genealogical chart that shows just how more than 7100
individuals are related to each other. It evolves
from a nucleus of early Missourians and includes
ancestors and descendants, and other kinships
extending into the present generations. It should
prove to be of value to genealogists, particularly
those seeking data about westerners, or those ancestors who may have lived west of the Mississippi
more than a century ago.

The Mississippi River is a natural divider of the
east and the west. A chain of circumstances to be
related in detail later,made Missouri a fine hunting ground for genealogists. The opportunities to
receive land grants near St. Louis, the Indian
discouragements of crossing the Mississippi at
other places and the hiatus of frontier movements
further west out of Missouri, resulted in making
this State a graveyard for more than two generations of western migrators.

I can take credit for this book only as a compiler. Without the valued assistance I have received
from many relatives and friends, it would have
been an impossibility to assemble the voluminous
material in this book. Many individuals not
included in the list of credits shown here deserve
recognition. They have submitted a limited amount
of information, but of importance in filling in
missing data.

The following have dilgently worked with me and
have contributed a large percentage of the data
shown. They are:

No.		
C42A	Mrs.	Jackie Baker, Joplin, Mo.
E84D	Mr.	William Basnett, Jefferson City, Mo.
B26B	Mrs.	George Berry, Pine Grove, California
E86B	Mr.	Roger Branson, Edmond, Okla.
B19E	Mr.	Ray Burgess, Venice, Florida
A72C	Mr.	James Burgess, Atlanta, Georgia.
	Mr.	Michael Burgess, San Bernardino, Ca.
	Mrs.	John Burns, Ponca City, Ok.
E88A	Mr.	Virgil Carroll,Union,Mo.
C18F	Mrs.	Gertrude Cogbill, Fullerton, Ca.
	Mrs.	Bette Crouse, Burlington, N,C,
A45A	Mr.	Ira Fillingham, Venice, Fla.
	Mrs.	Ida Frank, Willows, Ca.

D79B	Mrs. Chester Gausman, Custer, So. Dak.
E75A	Mrs. Charles Hern, Anaheim, Ca.
C33A	Mrs. Russell King, Smithville Mo.
E95C	Mrs. Vernon Newman, Napa, Ca.
F39E	Mrs. Bessie Nicks, Moody, Mo.
C39A	Mr. Dee Owsley, Florissant, Mo.
	Miss Bessie Priester, Springfield,Mo.
F37A	Mrs. James Ritterbusch, Fulton, Mo
A98A	Mrs. Thomas Shockley, Nashville, Tenn
C31A	Mrs. Raymond Spainhour, Lone Jack, Mo.
	Mrs. Doyle Stacy, Richardson, Texas
F68C	Nrs. Ray Stribling, Wichita Kansas
F59Aa	Mrs. Tommy Tolbert, Chesterfield, Mo.
	Mrs. Bobbie Wilson, Fayetteville, Ark
C19D	Mrs. Gordon Winn, Salem, Oregon.

I am also thankful to the authors of the books mentioned in the bibliography, for providing me with useful essential information.

PART I

HISTORY OF FRONTIERS

PART I
HISTORY OF FRONTIERS

A review of American History, particularly that
part pertinent to our frontiers and frontier life
including events and environments responsible for
the westward migrations can be a rewarding and
worthwhile project for genealogists seeking clues
in American ancestry.

There are very logical reasons why, for example,
under a certain set of circumstances regarding our
frontiers, a westerner at our last frontier, the
Pacific Ocean, might expect to find that one or
more of his lineages passed through Missouri about
a century and a half ago. And, to find that their
ancestors came from Tennessee or Kentucky. A
frontier study might also lead the searcher successfully on back into No. Carolina, or Virginia,
or Maryland, or some other of the Colonial States.
He may also find good reason to believe that at
some stage, an ancestor came from overseas, arriv-
ing at a certain port of entry during an unusual
influx of emigrants.

The migratory patterns were shaped by the opportunities our predecessors had at various times to
penetrate westward into the domain of the redmen.

There were major frontier stages in our history
that were important factors in determining when
and where our westward migrators moved and linger-
ed perhaps long enough to leave behind telltale
evidence for the genealogists, in grave markers,
family and public records, etc.These frontiers had
their beginning when the English established their
first permanent foothold in America at Jamestown,
Va., in 1607. The ending came when the westerners
were no longer regarded as pioneers and homestead-
ing was substantially completed in about 1890.

The primary frontiers may be divided into five
stages:

         Stage One: (1607 to about 1700)
         Stage Two: (1700 to 1763)
         Stage Three: (1763 to about 1790)
         Stage Four: (1790 to 1849)
         Stage Five: (1849 to about 1890).

The Boone and Shockley Families: To illustrate the
migratory patterns, the history of these two
Missouri pioneering families will be discussed
with each stage of migration as representative of
the activities and movements of the frontiersmen.

STAGE ONE
(1607-abt.1700)

Preceding the settlement of Jamestown,Virginia in
1607 by the English, European Countries were busy
with discoveries and explorations along the Atlantic Coastal areas of the American Continent.

John Cabot, a Venetian discovered Labrador in 1497
for England; Giovanni de Verrazano, a Florentine
navigator, visited the Atlantic Coast and New York
Bay in 1526, but made no claims; and, Cartier dis-
covered the St. Lawrence River, in 1535 for the
French. They later settled in the "back lands" of
Canada, and then proceeded to claim the territory
west of the Appalachian Mountains, south to the
Gulf of Mexico. Spain claimed Florida and South
America.

The British successfully contested the right of
Spain to the Atlantic Coastal region north of Flo-
rida by establishing a settlement at Jamestown,
Virginia on the James River.

The Dutch asserted their independence from Spain
in 1602, and two years after the founding of
Jamestown, an Englishman, Henry Hudson sailed into
New York Bay and up the Hudson River to establish
"New Netherlands" for the Dutch. He laid claim to
all land between the 40th and 45th North Latitude.
In 1638, the Swedes settled in the Delaware region
and established New Sweden.

The Dutch and Swedes did not possess any of North
America for long.The Swedes were forced to surren-
der to the Dutch in 1655. And, when the Dutch began to expand into eastern Long Island, the Eng-
ish took over all their possessions in America,
by force, in 1664.

One of the reasons the first English settlers wanted to come to America was in the hope of finding
gold. This dream did not come true for them, but
it did to their descendants about 240 years later.
by those who participated in the California "gold
rush" of 1849.

The colonists were seeking an opportunity for more

7

religious freedom. They also hoped that they would be instrumental in finding a passage across the continent of America to the Indies.

The Crown wanted to establish colonies to provide an outlet for their surplus population; to find products England was purchasing from other countries such as lumber, spices, silk and mineral; and to check the expansion of the Spanish along the Atlantic.

JAMESTOWN(1607): In December 1606, three ships, the Goodspeed, Discovery and Sarah Constant with 120 emigrants left London. They made the voyage across the Atlantic in 4 months, via the Canaries and West Indies. The vessels were over-crowded, and food and drinking water were scarce. Sanitary provisions were inadequate.

They spent two weeks in the Chesapeake Bay before deciding to land on 14 May, 1607. The site selected was up the James River about 32 miles, and on a small island. There were about 100 passengers who survived the trip, consisting entirely of men and boys. The wives arrived later.

PLYMOUTH(1620): The original intent was to bring the emigrants in two ships, the Speedwell and Mayflower. However, after making two trial runs from Southhampton, England, the Speedwell was abandoned as unseaworthy. The number of emigrants was reduced to 102 and the Mayflower set sail alone from Plymouth, on 20 September, 1620. These pilgrims suffered aboard ship as did those who went to Virginia but they landed at Plymouth, Massachussets on 21 December with 100 survivors.

MASSACHUSETTS BAY COLONY(1630): Salem, the place of the first permanent settlement, grew out of a small fishing village established in 1623, about 15 miles up the coast. Most of inhabitants of the original setlement returned to England prior to the "Great Migration" to follow. The few who remained moved to the Salem area. In the Spring of 1630, eleven ships were sent to Massachusetts, and by the end of the summer there were about one thousand settlers in Salem, composed of many professional men of means and influence. During the

17th Century,the "Stage One" period, the colonists
were busy establishing small communities near the
Atlantic Coast. Many were of the sea-faring type
engaging in trade on the Atlantic. Indian hostilities, sometimes almost non-existant and sometimes
the cause of massacring raids on isolated settlements, dampened a desire to break away from more
concentrated communities, the "western" frontier
lay close to the Atlantic.

COLONIZATION

Virginia had its origin at Jamestown.Massachusetts
and Connecticut grew out of the Pilgram Colony at
Plymouth and the Puritan Colony of Salem, added by
emigrants who came directly to the Connecticut
Coast. New York and New Jersey were settled by the
Dutch and Swedes. New Hampshire was inhabited by
the English about the same time as Massachusetts,
the first documented settlement being in 1633 by
David Thompson.

Rhode Island settlers came from Massachusetts.
Roger Williams fled persecution at Salem because
he advocated a separation of church and state. He
founded Providence in 1636. A colony was established at Newport in 1639, and another at Warwick
in 1643.

The Dutch settled on the site of the present city
of Hartford, Connecticut, and the English from the
Plymouth Colony eatablished themselves at Windsor
on the Connecticut River, in 1633. The inhabitants
of three Massachusetts towns left their communities amd migrated by land in true pioneering fash-
ion into Connecticut. Some Watertown inhabitants
founded Wetherfield in 1634, and Windsor was
founded by people from Newtown, in 1635. In 1638,
a group of middleclass English landed at Boston
and proceeded along the Connecticut coast to found
New Haven.

Maryland: The patent for the land presently Maryland was granted to Cecilius Calvert(Lord Baltimore) in 1632. As a result, an expedition of about
300 emigrants in two ships, the Ark and Dove, left
England in December 1633, under the command of
Leonard Calvert. He was a brother of Cecil and be-

came the first governor of Maryland.

The ships reached the mouth of the Potomac River, 27 March, 1634, and moved up it to the St. George tributary, where the first permanent settlement of Maryland was made.

North Carolina: This State was the scene of unsuccessful attempts to colonize in the 16th Century After two previous expeditions failed, Sir Walter Raleigh established a colony on Roanoke Island off Albermarle Sound, 22 July 1587. The entire colony vanished mysteriously, perhaps due to disease or massacre by Indians. From this colony, Virginia Dare was born. Although her known life was about 9 days, she is accredited with being the first English born in America. The first permanent settlement in North Carolina was made in about 1653 by migrators from Virginia who settled on the Chowan River in Albemarle Sound.

South Carolina: In 1669, three ships sailed from England. After a stop in Barbados to pick up other emigrants, they arrived in Charleston Harbor and then moved into the Ashley River. These first permanent English settlers in South Carolina became the founders of Charleston in 1680.

Pennsylvania: The Swedish were the first to settle in Pennsylvania, coming from settlements east of the Delaware River. The land came into the possession of England in 1664, and the region was granted to William Penn in 1680, by the Crown. The Quakers were the dominant element for nearly one hundred years. A rapid influx to Pennsylvania began in 1681 when about one thousand emigrants arrived. Settlers to this State were predominately from overseas until about 1770 when a large number of people from Connecticut and New York moved into the area.

Georgia: This State was the last of the thirteen English Colonies to be established after nearly a half century hiatus. Exercising a grant, James Oglethorpe and about one hundred emigrants arrived at Charleston and then moved south to the Savannah River to found Savannah in February 1733. Other ships followed, bringing English, Scotch and Germans. A second settlement was made at Augusta in

1737.

<u>INDIANS DURING STAGE ONE</u>: Before 1700, the Indians played an important role in limiting the western movement of the colonists. Some were hostile, some friendly and others were a combination of both. Much of their attitudes were based on the behavior of the whites. When friendly, they rendered valuable assistance to the newcomers to America. They taught the colonists to grow corn, tobacco and other products; how to cultivate; how to make maple syrup and carve out canoes; how to track and trap game; and, they were excellent guides in the wilderness. The colonists taught the Indians how to use tools, work beasts of burden, and introduced the cow, bringing a new dimension to agriculture.

The Indians restricted the colonists in moving westward, delaying them in being able to use lands away from the coastal region, desired for farming, excepting along some of the rivers. The relationships of the colonists and Indians varied somewhat throughout the colonies. Much of this was due to the attitude of the new settlers. In some colonies treaties and compensation for lands resulted in friendly relations, and in other communities, the hatred between the races resulted in little or no effort to be friendly.

South Carolina:The English settlers were cordially welcomed as an ally of the natives.The Port Royal tribe was a constant threat to the old inhabitants living near the Charleston settlement, and the English assisted in the defense of the area.

North Carolina: Aside from Indian hostilities during the period of unsuccessful colonization, attempts in the late 16th Century,all was relatively peaceful until the Tusacroras War of 1711, in the second stage of frontiers.

Virginia: At Jamestown, the settlers were never safe from Indian attacks, until 1644, after the second uprising of the Indians resulted in the redmen leaving the area permanently. A massacre of whites in 1622, resulted in the death or capture of about three hundred English. A similar loss was

11

experienced in 1644.

Maryland: The Maryland settlers were fortunate in that the natives were experiencing harassments by the Susquehanna tribe. They looked to the English for help in their defense and in return assisted the colonists in getting established.

Pennsylvania: There never was serious hostility between the two races. When William Penn arrived, his friendly attitude and offer to pay for lands acquired, did much to cement good feelings.

Delaware, New Jersey, and New York: The Dutch and Swedes initiated Indian contacts and are accredited with the resultant good relations between the races.

New England:These people experienced both friendly and hostile feelings with the Indians. The first settlers who landed at Plymouth received a welcome reception from the natives, due primarily to the fact that a plague just before the English arrived nearly wiped out the local Indian tribe.

As a consequence, the Indians were the first to make friendly gestures.

Rhode Island:Roger Williams, founder of the first English settlement in this State, was able to make friends with the Naragansett tribe, but not with the Pequots.

In 1637, the Pequots attacked the Wetherfield Connecticut community, but the combined forces of Connecticut and Massachusetts completely annihilated the tribe. A second war, called the King Philip's War between the colonists and the Indians, began in 1675. It was three years later that outlying settlements in New Hampshire and Maine were safe from attacks.

At the turn of the century, in 1700, the end of Stage One of the American Frontiers, the colonists were living close to the Atlantic Ocean, or along some of the rivers. The venturous and the agriculturists had hardly begun their westward trek.

With the English settled in on the eastern front, the French on the north, the Indians and French on the west, and the Spaniards on the south, the theatre was all set for the contest to decide who would conquer the west.

The Boone Family: By the close of the 17th Century, George Boone III (Cat.No.I-10A) was living in Devonshire England. He was married to Mary Maugridge, daughter of John Maugridge. Their children were: George IV, Sarah, Squire Sr. (No. I-11C) who married Sarah Morgan, John, Joseph and James.

The Shockley Family: Richard Shockley 1st (No. D10A), was born in Britain in about 1650. He was brought to America by James Robinson, who received a 200 acre grant of land in Somerset County,Md. under the "headright" policy in 1671, for paying transportation to America for himself, his wife Barbereth, his daughter Frances and Richard Shockley.

It is probable that Richard devoted some time in working out his obligation to Robinson, and then acquired property of his own in Somerset County, Md. He married Ann Boyden there on 4 October 1674. Their children were born between 1677 and 1690. They were: Richard,Jr.,Elenor, Elizabeth, William, David, Mary and John (No. D11G).

Richard's homestead was called "The Shockley Place", acquired by patent dated 1 June 1685. The description states that it was along Dividing Creek which forms a part of the boundary between Somerset County and Worcester County, Maryland, as presently established. It was located about 18 miles south of the present city of Salisbury, Md.

John Shockley (D11G) had eight children: Isaac, Benjamin, Mary, Jonathan, Richard 2nd (D13E), John, Solomon and Sarah.

By the end of Stage One,Richard 1st. had 10 grandchildren living nearby and into the southern part of Delaware.

STAGE TWO
(1700-1763)

The second stage of the migration westward began in about 1700. The coastal areas and along the banks of some of the rivers, such as the Connecticut, Hudson, Delaware, Potomac, Rappahannock, and James, represented the frontier during the 17th Century.

There were numerous reasons for the comparative inactivity in movement. Many colonists were content with the advantage of social, political, economical and Indian-free life of well established communities.

The temptations of farmers and woodsmen were strong to move away from the coast and rivers and live in the fertile lands of the eastern valleys of the Appalachians. The increase in population and perhaps an inherent desire to move on to "greener pastures", initiated the first important migration westward.

As we move into this period, a new type of American was developing. He became known as the frontiersman. Some of his traits were inherited, but many were created as a result of the environment in which he lived. The personality lasted throughout the entire period of the westward movement,and continued to represent many of the characteristics of Americans today.

He learned to fend for himself. Government control lessened, leaving these back-woodsmen the responsibility of self government; he learned to provide his own commodities, or to do without them because of the inaccessibility to the older communities to the east; and, he learned to cope with the lonliness of the wilderness. The environment in which these people lived was so different that, as a general rule, only pioneers of one stage were of suitable personality to be the new frontiersmen. They or their descendants were usually the first to reach the next frontier.Another reason why this was a common practise, is the fact that it was logistically more feasible for settlers at a new frontier to have come only from the last frontier.

Travel was difficult and dangerous.Waterways, gen-
erally were not available.These factors are important clues to the genealogists.During this period,
the French and Indian Wars played an important
role both in the environment and movement of the
frontiersmen of this stage. Migration beyond the
mountain ranges depended very much on the outcome
of these wars, and the backwoodsmen were well
represented in the battles.

The French had built forts throughout the Ohio
Valley, and with the cooperation of the Indians,
presented a formidable deterrent to the westward
progress.

Primary migratory patterns were distinct during
the first half of the 18th Century. New Englanders
moved to New York and New Jersey and some into
Pennsylvania. Those from Maryland and Delaware
moved into Virginia and some went to Pennsylvania,
using Indian trails and waterways.

When the influx into Pennsylvania, mostly from
Europe,made a population density too great to sat-
isfy many in this State,there was a southern movement into either the older communities of Virginia
or into the virgin valleys at the mountain foot-
hills. Some continued on southward into the Carolinas and even into Georgia. Northwestern North
Carolina became the most advanced western frontier, settled primarily by Virginians. Access to
the western part of North Carolina from the east
was difficult due to the fact that many rivers and
streams emptied into the Atlantic from a north-
westerly direction. It was simpler to travel from
the coast to the west via Virginia.

The Boone and Shockley families are both excellent
examples of the routes the frontiermen traversed
during Stage Two.

The Boone Family:(1700-1763). In 1712, George
Boone(I-10A), was living in a village called
Bradninch, England. In that year, he sent his
three eldest children to America to study the fea-
sibility of the family migrating there. They were
George IV((I-11A), Sarah, and Squire, Sr.(I-11C).
His son George returned and told his father that
15

one hundred pounds would buy 5000 acres of land in Pennsylvania.

The family booked passage on a boat scheduled to sail 17 August 1717. They traveled about 70 miles to the port city of Bristol and paid 35 pounds for six full fares and two half fares. The boat was hot and over-crowded and the passengers survived on putrid salt meat and water that was barely potable.They landed at Philadelphia 10 October, 1717. In the Spring of 1718, the family excepting Squire moved northwest up the Schuýkill River to near the present city of Reading, in Burks County. It was a Quaker stronghold. George Sr. was appointed Justice of the Peace. Sarah married John Stover and they moved to the valley of Virginia. Squire Sr. married Sarah Morgan in 1720 and lived in Abington a few miles north of Philadelphia. He worked as a blacksmith and weaver, and moved to his father's tract in 1739. They had eleven children: Sarah, Israel Sr., Samuel Sr., Jonathan, Elizabeth, Daniel (I-12F), Mary, George V., Edward, Squire Jr. and Hannah.

Friction developed between the Boone family and the Quakers which influenced them to sell out and migrate. In May 1750, they set off in a caravan of one covered wagon, horses and cattle. Daniel, the hunter provided fresh meat nearly every day.

They stopped in the Virginia valley for short stays, and followed Indian trails on into North Carolina. They arrived in the Valley of the Yadkin River in late 1751. After spending the winter in a cave, they built a log cabin. The Boones moved at least twice, and records indicate they lived for awhile in Rowan County, and then moved to the mouth of Beaver Creek along the upper Yadkin River,a few miles from the present city of Wilkesboro. Daniel served under General Braddock and and Washington in the French and Indian Wars, in 1755. He married Rebecca Bryan of Rowan County on 14 August 1756.

The North Carolina frontier burst aflame under attacks by the Cherokee Indians in February 1760. The Boone family with the exception of Daniel, moved to Culpepper, Virginia. Daniel was present at a peace council on 19 November 1760, He later left North Carolina for awhile and joined his family in Virginia. The next year he left on a hunting trip into the wilderness in North Carolina and what later became Tennessee. Upon his return to Culpepper Rebecca had a new baby named Jemina. Daniel accepted her as his daughter, although his wife admitted that Daniel's brother Ned was the father. Later, the Boones returned to North Carolina and Daniel continued hunting along the frontiers of Virginia and North Carolina.

The Shockley Family:(1700-1763). The children of Richard Shockley 1st.,clustered about the Shockley homestead within a radius of about 30 miles in the eastern part of Maryland and the southern part of Delaware. This colony appears to be the entire assembly of Shockleys in America until the middle of the 18th century, based on a diligent search for this surname.

The first record found of the Shockleys in Virginia appeared in the tax lists of Lunenburg County (presently the County of Charlotte), in 1749. James, Thomas and Richard(D13E), were in the tabulation of tithables.Solomon was listed in Halifax (now Pittsylvania) in 1756. David Shockley was found in Lunenburg County in 1762. In 1753,James, Thomas and Richard were found as land owners in what is now Pittsylvania, regarded at that time to be on the western frontier. Many Missouri pioneers or their ancestors passed through Pittsylvania County in late 18th Century.

In 1763, there were about a million and a half colonists in America. They were predominately English or American born, but there was the beginning of a blending of other nationalities. Americans were dissatisfied with English rule. They resented taxation without being represented in governing matters. The British unwisely contended that their Parliament had supreme authority throughout the British Empire. The American colonists felt that they should have control of all taxations, just as the English did in their homeland. Dissatisfaction grew throughout the colonies, and laws and "Proclamations" by the British were fragrantly ignored.

The Proclamation Line of 1763: In this year, the English closed the frontiers to the colonists, forbidding further westward migration in an attempt to appease the Indians.They ordered all pioneers living west of a Proclamation Line, to "remove" themselves and return to settlements to the east. The line ran along the Blue Ridge and northerly along the mountain ranges of the Appalachians.

The Stamp Act, the Sugar Act and the Townsend Act were imposed extracting additional revenues from the colonists.

Disregarding the Proclamation Line,some Virginians moved over the Blue Ridge and established a fort and settlements along New River about thirty miles beyond the legal limits. They were in Grayson and Carroll Counties as presently established.In 1769, Virginians migrated into the present State of Tennessee and set up the first permanent English settlement along the Watauga River which is a tributary of the Holston in northeast Tennessee. They were joined two years later by North Carolinians living along the Yadkin River who were dissidents of the Government.

On 26 April 1774, Lord Dunmore, governor of the New York and Virginia colonies, issued an order for the immediate assembly of three thousand men to go against the Shawnee Indians living on the Scioto River in Ohio. One half of the force to be recruited by Colonel Andrew Lewis from the frontier settlements, and the other half by Lord Dunmore from the regulars, and the "civilized" areas of Virginia.

Lewis moved out from the New River settlements in August 1774 with about fifteen hundred men. Dunmore's army was stationed at Fort Pittsburg. The mountaineers traveled afoot along Indian trails through the wilderness towards Point Pleasant on the Ohio River in what is now West Virginia. The Dunmore troops sailed down the Ohio in a large armada of canoes and rafts.

Dunmore had two purposes in mind. He wanted to defeat the Indians, and he wanted to teach the colonists that raw, untrained troops were no match for his regulars. He hoped to maneuver Lewis' forces into an early conflict with the Indians, alone, and then, when the frontiersmen were discouraged and in many cases deserters, the experienced troops would arrive and get credit for the victory. Instead of continuing down the Ohio River to meet Lewis, he diverted his army to a position east of the Indian villages on the Scioto.

The Indians, under the command of Chief Cornstalk, had been scouting the two forces, and were able to surprise the mountaineers at Point Pleasant actually before all of Lewis' men had arrived. Cornstalks' men attacked at dawn on 10 October 1774. The battle raged in hand-to-hand fighting all day. Although Lewis' forces sustained heavy losses, they were able to force Cornstalk to retreat across the Ohio to the Pickaway Plains east of the Scioto River. Lewis also crossed the Ohio and pursued the Indians contrary to the orders from Dunmore. Lewis joined Dunmore's forces at the Indian villages and forced the Shawnees to sign a treaty, but serious friction developed between the two leaders. The Point Pleasant Battle has been regarded as the first engagement of the colonists against the Indians in the Revolution, even though it was prior to the actual commencement of the war.

The frontiersmen played an important role in the

Revolutionary War, especially against the Indians, from the first important engagement at "Bunker Hill" on 17 June 1775 to the signing of the Paris Peace Treaty on 3 September 1783.

The British encouraged the Indians to attack the frontier settlements, and supplied them with guns and ammunitions from the various British forts in the Ohio Valley. In 1778, Colonel George Rogers Clark recruited one hundred seventy five men,mostly from the advanced settlements, and lead an expedition into Ohio. They captured the British Forts, Kaskaskia and Cahokia on the Mississippi. Fort Vincenne in the present State of Indiana was captured, retaken by the British and again captured by Clarks' army.

John Sevier, who shared leadership of the Watauga colony in Tennessee with James Robertson, was a captain in the Battle of Point Pleasant, and took an active part in the Battle of Kings Mountain in South Carolina with other frontiersmen in late 1780. He also served under General Francis Marion in campaigns in Georgia and the Carolinas. The Kings Mountain battle was termed the "turning point" in the Revolution.

The western frontiers spread from Tennessee into Kentucky but not without extreme sacrifice by the pioneers. The land had been the scene of bitter wars between the Iroquois and Cherokee Indians. Both tribes laid claim to the land. The region was then declared by both tribes to be a sacred hunting ground, not to be owned by redmen or whites.

The first English settlement in Kentucky was made by James Herrod in 1774, who traveled down the Ohio River to establish a fort at Harrodsburg, in the present county of Mercer, near the Kentucky River. In 1775, Richard Henderson and Daniel Boone of North Carolina, negotiated a treaty with the Cherokees at the Watauga settlement. Henderson' firm, "The Transylvania Company" was granted all of the lands south of the Ohio River, and between the Kentucky and Cumberland Rivers, in exchange for money and gifts. Although the Virginia Government voided the treaty, Henderson and Boone pre-

pared to occupy the lands. They established Fort
Boonesboro in 1775 along the Kentucky River near
Harrod's fort. They were the first permanent
settlers in Kentucky, entering it from the south
through the Cumberland Gap. Frontiermen from the
Watauga colony were the pioneers into the central
part of Tennessee, at the site of the present city
of Nashville. In 1779, James Robertson and eight
comrades left eastern Tennessee and passed through
the Cumberland Gap into Kentucky. They crossed the
Cumberland River and then turned southward through
unbroken wilderness to a point on the Cumberland
where Nashville now stands. They built cabins and
planted corn. Later, Robertson returned to Watauga
with some of his party.

In the autumn of that year Robertson headed a
second expedition to Nashville, taking with him
some of the Watauga families. The women and
children and a few men traveled what they thought
to be a safer route via the Tennessee River even
though it was a round-about way. They had scows,
flat boats, canoes and one cannon, and all the men
carried rifles. One boat containing about 30
persons stayed behind because of smallpox aboard.
They were attacked by Indians, and those who were
not killed were taken captives. The remainder of
the expedition reached the mouth of the Cumberland
and moved up that river,arriving at the settlement
in April,1780. These settlers were the nucleus
of the Central Tennessee developments. Some moved
southeastward, merging with the easterners of the
State.

The Boone Family:(1763-1790). Daniel Boone(I-12F)
and Rebecca had nine children: James, Israel, Sus-
annah(I15C), Lavinia, Daniel Morgan(I15G),Rebecca,
Jesse, Nathaniel(I15J), and Jemima.

James was killed by the Indians in Kentucky in
October 1772, while his father was making his
first attempt to move his family to the State.
Israel was killed at the battle of Blue Licks
Bryan's Station, Kentucky in Auguat 1782; Jemima
was kidnapped by the Indians in July 1776, but was
rescued by her father: Daniel Sr. was taken by the
Indians in the early part of 1778, but by a
clever bit of trickery managed to escape. He had a

21

faculty of talking himself out of trouble with the redmen.

Daniel made his first hunting trip into Kentucky in 1764, when he reached the Cumberland River. He did some inspections for land speculators, and became quite impressed with the climate and abundance of wild game, During the 1760´s, he hunted very much alone in the wilderness, at which time he became well acquainted with frontier settlers in southwest Virginia, and northwest North Carolina. He returned again to Kentucky in the autumn of 1768 with his brother Squire and William Hill. They followed buffalo trails about one hundred miles from the Clinch and Holston Rivers to the headwaters of Big Sandy River.

On 25 September 1773, Daniel and his brother Squire with their families and some neighbors living along the Yadkin River in North Carolina, set out for Kentucky. Before reaching the Cumberland Gap, the gateway to Kentucky, they were attacked by Indians. Six of the party were killed, including Daniel´s son James. The party returned to a settlement in Virginia. While there, Governor Dunmore sent a messenger to Daniel asking him to join the force being assembled for the Point Pleasant encounter with the Indians. He volunteered and served as liaison officer between the armies of Dunmore and Lewis. When the treaty was signed between the Cherokees and Henderson representing the Transylvania Company, Boone was instructed to carve out a "Wilderness Road" through the Cumberland Gap into the heart of Kentucky.

When the road was completed to the banks of the Kentucky River, Boone and his men built Fort Boonesboro. It was a rectangular stockade about 260 feet long by 150 feet wide. At each corner stood a two story blockhouse with slits in the walls through which the settlers could observe and shoot at Indians. Cabins were built along the sides of the fort, between which were barricades of log posts sunk into the ground. There were two heavy gates on opposite sides of the fort. Boonesboro was about 30 miles east of Fort Harrodsburg, built the previous year by migrators from the northern route, down the Ohio River.

After an absence, Daniel returned to Boonesboro
in September 1775 with a little band of migrators
from North Carolina. With him, were his wife
Rebecca and children, Israel, Jesse,Daniel Morgan,
Rebecca, Lavinia and Jemima. Susannah had married
a few months before to William Hayes,Sr(I15Ca).
Daniel's son William died in infancy and Nathan
was not born until 1781. Within a few days, tne
Boones were followed into the fort by the Calla-
ways, and some of Rebecca's relatives. It was not
long before the fort was bustling with newcomers
and activities around the fort.

The Kentucky settlers experienced hard times and
attacks by the Indians, and in 1776 only about two
hundred remained at the fort of more than 500 who
had made the trek to the frontier. Many returned
to "civilization" and many died.Problems developed
when the pioneers had to leave the fort to care
for crops and travel some distance to salt beds
for sorely needed salt to cure meat.

While on a trip for salt, Edward (Ned) Boone,
brother of Daniel was attacked and killed by the
Indians, on 6 October 1780.

Bryan's Station was built in 1779, by relatives of
Daniel's wife. It was located near the present
city of Lexington. In August 1782, it was besieged
by about 600 Indians. The defenders numbered less
than two hundred. More than 60 settlers were
killed.

New settlers poured into Kentucky. They came
primarily from the southeast through the Cumberland Gap from Virginia, North Carolina and Tennessee, or down the Ohio River from Pennsylvania or
what is now West Virginia. The population soared
to nearly 25,000 by the end of the war with Britain. Daniel moved his family about, being dissatisfied with the population increase and growing scarcity of wild game. He maintained a trad-
ing post for awhile on the Ohio and lived near
Point Pleasant in the present West Virginia.

By the close of Stage Three in about 1790, Daniel
was ready to be a pioneer in new lands, with serious thoughts about Missouri.

23

The following is a list of some of the surnames of
Missouri pioneers also found in the records of
Kentucky early settlers:

Boone	Clay	Hart	Pointer	Travis
Brooks	Clements	Haynes	Poor	Tyler
Bryan	Collins	Henderson	Reynolds	Walker
Caldwell	Compton	Humphrey	Russell	
Callaway	Davis	Johnson	Stewart	
Campbell	Eads	King	Tate	
Cannon	Hall	Martin	Taylor	
Clark	Hancosk	Miller	Todd	

The Shockley Family:(1763-1790):In the mid 1700's
a Shockley colony was established in Halifax
County, Virginia, presently Pittssylvania County.
It was situated on both sides of Pigg River in the
northwestern part of the county, about fifteen
miles east of the present city of Rocky Mount.
Thomas Shockley purchased 275 acres there in
November 1750. James Shockley received land
patents from the State of Virginia for 300 acres,
on 13 November 1753, and for another 400 acres on
26 July 1765. Richard Shockley 2nd (D13E) bought
100 acres on 13 October 1753. Solomon Shockley was
shown on the Tax List in November 1756.

Thomas left the county before 1760,and indications
are that he moved to Anderson Co., So. Carolina,
and died in Jackson County Georgia. During this
period the Thomas Shockleys created somewhat of
a set of contradictory records. James Shockley did
not appear on the Tax list of Pittslvania County
during the period from 1755 to 1763, however he
died there in 1796.Richard continued in the county
records as a taxpayer between 1752 and 1766.Shock-
ley entries continued throughout the remainder of
the 18th Century.

Richard Shockley 2nd(D13E) married Elizabeth. Her
maiden name is unknown. Their children were: Thomas, Richard3rd.(D14B), Isom, Isaiah(Josiah)(D14D),
Wilson, Meredith(D14F), William and Elizabeth.When
Richard 2nd disappeared from Pittsylvania between
1766 and 1775, it appears that he defied the
Proclamation of 1763 prohibiting colonist from
moving beyond the Blue Ridge Mountains.

Later records showed him to be on New River in the

present county of Carroll,Va., where he enlisted for service at Point Pleasant fighting the Shawnees. He served under the command of James Robertson of the Watauga settlement and founder of Nashville. Richard received a grant of 500 acres of land in 1785, for his services, located in Montgomery County as established at that time, and another 360 acres by "Right of Settlement" from Virginia, described as being on Little Reed Island on Big Reed, branch of New River.

At the end of Stage Three in about 1790, the Richard Shockley 2nd family were living in what is now Carroll County, Virginia.

STAGE FOUR
(1790-1849)

Since Colonial days, Americans have divided their
lands into two geographical parts, using the terms
"The East" and "The West".In the early days, they
were separated by the Appalachian Mountain Range,
but as the frontiers line moved west, the dividing
line moved with it. When the frontiers crossed the
Mississippi River, the dividing line became permanently regarded as that river.

With the first American settlements west of the
Mississippi in the environs of St. Louis, the Indian barriers to the north and south, and the limited access offered by the Spanish Government, a
bottleneck was created making St. Louis a hub or
connecting link between the East and the West. St.
Louis became a crossroads that is true, even today, serving as a connector for important highways, railways, waterways, and airways. Much of
this is due to the "head-start" created. St. Louis
is in an ideal location which made it possible for
the development of a fast growing community.

For the genealogists, Missouri History is an important chapter in American History. Within the
bounds of this State are tell-tale evidences of
value in tracing ancestry of Americans. It is of
particular value to westerners, although many of
the ancestors of other Americans may be found to
have passed through this State in generations
back. It is an ideal "hunting ground" for genealogical data to be found in public records, county
histories, on tombstones, and in church and family
records.

When the Americans began to settle west of the
Mississippi River, they found French settlements
along the banks of the Mississippi, but little remained of Spaniards or their culture.

The western frontier advancements during the period of Stage Four from about 1790 to 1849, were
confined chiefly to the present State of Missouri,
with a minor overflow into bordering territories.

By far the safest and most used route for the

American migrators to Missouri was via the Ohio
and Mississippi Rivers. Some came by foot and
others in caravans following buffalo trails
through Kentucky and then into Indian held lands
in what is now Indiana and Illinois. Until a
series of treaties with the Chichasaw, Choctaw and
Creek Indians were signed between 1830 and 1835,
routes into Kentucky and Tennessee west of the
Tennessee River, and further south through what
are now Mississippi and Alabama were quite
prohibitive due to Indian hostilities.

The lands to the north of the Ohio River were not
safe for western migrators in the beginning of
Stage Four. In 1787, the Northwest Territory was
established by the United States Government, embracing lands north of the Ohio to the Canadian
Border, and west to the Mississippi. It stipulated
that Indian lands shall never be taken from them
without their consent, or the authorization of
Congress, and that their right to liberty shall
never be disturbed.

Kentucky settlers became incensed by this denial
of Congress for them to retaliate against the Indian attacks from the north by small bands, to
steal, burn and kill.. These frontiersmen simply
ignored this provision by Congress. Friction between the races continued well after the defeat
of Chief Tecumseh at Tippecanoe Indiana in 1811.

Even after the threat of Indian attacks subsided,
there was no great migration west through Ohio,
Indiana and Illinois until after the canals, railroads and highways were completed. The Erie Canal
was opened in October 1825, making a waterway
connection between Albany, New York and Lake Erie;
but even this event plus the opening of canals between Lake Erie and the Ohio River later, resulted
only in primarily increasing the Ohio River access
to the west.

The National Highway from Cumberland Maryland, to
Wheeling West Virginia was completed in 1818, but
its ultimate destination at Vandalia,Illinois was
not finished until 1852. Rail lines were built in
short runs near cities and then were gradually
welded into trunk lines. The first railroad to

connect the eastern seaboard with the "west" reached Dunkirk, New York on Lake Erie in 1851. Canal, highway and railroad transportation facilities came too late to be of use in bringing the easterners to Missouri prior to when the State was admitted into the Union in 1821.

Migrating through the wilderness in the late 1700's and early 1800's was difficult. To move a family more than about four hundred miles was usually accomplished by breaking up the journey into more than one stage. Because of this, the very early Missouri families were predominately from Kentucky, although their stay in that State may have been for only a short period. Some of the parents and older children remained behind and set the younger generation the task of migrating to Missouri. In a search for possible places from which a Missouri pioneer may have come, the distance factor is important. For this reason, the probabilities strongly favor the assumption that any family came from Kentucky, Tennessee, North Carolina, Virginia, Pennsylvania or West Virginia, in the absence of other information to the contrary. A few French and Spanish came up the Mississippi from settlements along the Gulf Coast.

In 1682, LaSalle explored the Mississippi River and laid claim to lands now Missouri, for the French, naming it Louisiana in honor of the French King. After the French and Indian Wars, France lost all its possessions in America in 1763. All the lands west of the Mississippi became a Spanish possession. The first Missouri settlements were by the French at Ste. Genevieve. The first Americans to permanently settle west of the Mississippi appears to be in about 1776 near a salt deposit in Jefferson County. Some of the pioneers were killed by Indians and others removed to another settlement for protection. One writer accredits John Dodge with being the first actual permanent American settler in Missouri, but the date was given as 1787, a questionable time of first arrivals.

On 9 March 1804, known as the "Day of the three flags", Spain ceded to France, lands embracing the present State of Missouri. And, on the same day France relinquished the same land to the United

States.

Daniel Boone is sometimes referred to as the "founding father of Missourians", Although he was not the first American to settle there, he did receive permission by the Spanish to establish permanent settlements along the Missouri west of St. Louis. Daniel's son Daniel Morgan built a cabin there in 1795 about fifteen miles west of the mouth of the Missouri. His father arrived a short time after.

By 1820, the American frontier extended nearly the full length of the Missouri River to the west boundary of the present State of Missouri, and along the Mississippi. By 1840, almost the entire State was dotted with pioneers.

Indians were not troublesome, excepting during the War of 1812, when the Sac and Fox Tribes from the north attacked outlying settlements along the Missouri and forced the frontierspeople to build blockhouses for protection.As a result of treaties in 1815 and 1816, the Indians agreed to leave Missouri. The Oklahoma tribes, however, resented giving up the fine hunting grounds of the Ozarks of southwest Missouri, and often staged raids on the early settlers there. As a consequence, this area was the last to be permanently settled.

Frontiersmen were always called on throughout American history to play a strong role in the American Wars, but the early 19th Century far excelled other periods in demands on them to serve their country in battle. They not only had to fight for their own protection, but also in national engagements such as: The War of 1812; The Black Hawk War; The Seminole Indian War of Florida; and the Mexican Wars. They also participated in the fight by the State of Missouri to expel the Mormons. These wars had a profound effect on the migratory patterns and establishment of new frontiers.

The War of 1812: The Proclamation of War against the British on the 19th of June 1812, was the result of dissatisfaction of the United States in Britain's interference in United States commerce. But, the western frontiermen had another reason.They resented the British cooperation with the Indians in their fight to prevent the Americans from occupying western lands, particularly in Indiana, Illinois and Wisconsin.

In 1813, there were three United States armies operating on the northern frontier. They were called The Army of the West; of the Center; and, of the North. Missourians served under General William Henry Harrison (ninth President of the U.S.)

Following a successful naval battle in which the U.S.Navy was under the command of Commodore Perry, 10 September 1813, Harrisons troops embarked on Perry's ships and crossed into Canada. The Army of the West completely routed the British. In this engagement Chief Tecumseh of the Indian warriors was slain. The recovery of Detroit and other Michigan territory, completed the campaign for Harrison's army, and they joined the Army of the Center.

The war raged until early 1815. General Jackson, with a force of about 6000 men were entrenched near New Orleans under a breastwork of earth and cotton bales,when substantially the entire British Army stormed the entrenchment. It was a great victory for Jackson's men. About two thousand British were killed or wounded, and the U.S. forces lost only eight killed and thirteen wounded. The treaty of peace was ratified on 17 February 1815.

The Black Hawk War: In 1804, five Indian leaders of the Cherokee, Sac and Fox Tribes ceded about fifty one million acres of land lying mostly in western Illinois and Wisconsin to the United States. Keokuk, Chief of the Sacs removed his tribe peacefully to the west of the Mississippi River. However, Black Hawk, a member of the tribe became enraged and refused to budge from the Illinois territory, and he and his band decided to remain and fight. He ordered the whites to leave.

A call was issued in Missouri for a volunteer force of one hundred men to serve in a war against these Indians who claimed the treaties were invalid. On 15 July 1832, a Missouri detachment

30

arrived at Fort Pike on the Des Moines River in
Clark County. They assisted in the command of the
fort until September, and then they were mustered
out of service. Engagements continued for nearly a
year, mostly in Illinois, until the Black Hawk
followers were entirely defeated.

The Seminole War: Missourians are credited with
playing a leading role in the United States war
with the Seminole and Creek Indians in Florida.

In accordance with the terms of a treaty with the
Florida Indian tribes, the United State Government
was in the process of removing the redmen to
Indian Territory west of the Mississippi River
when some of them refused to go. In 1834, one
hundred men under the command of Major Dade were
attacked by Seminoles and all of his force excepting four were killed.

Intermittent warfare continued and in the fall of
1837, Governor Boggs of Missouri was asked to re-
cruit two regiments of volunteers from his State
primarily because of their reputation and exper-
iemce as fighters.

Colonel Gentry commanded a Missouri army that dis-
embarked from ships in Tampa Bay, on 15th November
1837. He was ordered by Zachary Taylor, Commander
of US forces in Florida, to march his men to Lake
Okeechobee, where the entire Seminole forces were
encamped. Some of the Indian army consisted of
runaway slaves from Georgia. The Missouri con-
tingent was assigned the front position with the
U.S. regulars bringing up the rear.

In the initial attack, Colonel Gentry was killed
but his men fought on until the Indians were defeated. About 140 Missourians were killed.

Guerrilla fighting continued, however, operating
from hideouts in the swamps and everglades until a
treaty was signed in 1842.

The Mormons in Missouri: In 1832, Joseph Smith,
leader of the Mormons, established headquarters
for the church at Independence, Missouri. The members were called "Saints" and all others "Gentil-

es". Encounters between these two forced the Mormons to move into Caldwell County in 1836. Soon, the Mormons in this county outnumbered the "Gentiles" and held most of the county offices.Friction and skirmishes developed, and on 25 October 1838, the State militia was called out in behalf of the non-members. As a result, the Mormons were forced to leave Missouri.

The Mexican War: Stephen F. Austin received a land grant in Texas Territory from the Mexican Government in 1821, and he immediately began a colonization of Americans that expanded rapidly. The Mexican government became distrustful and friction developed between the inhabitants of the Territory and their government. In a battle fought between a Mexican force of one thousand men and half the number of insurrectionists, the Texans were victorious.In retaliation, the Mexicans besieged Fort Alamo on 6 March 1936. Colonel William B. Travis and his force of one hundred eighty seven men died fighting. However, a decisive battle at San Jacinto, on 21 April, gave Texas her freedom. Texas was admitted as a State of the United States on 29 December 1845.

In April 1846, war was declared on the United States by Mexico as a result of a dispute over boundaries. A counter-declaration was made by the U.S. Government. This war lasted two years ending in a decisive victory for the United States. A treaty was signed on 2 February 1848. Boundaries were fixed, but revised later by a purchase from Mexico establishing the present bounds, in 1858. As in past wars, Missouri volunteers responded to the call, and were well represented in Mexican-United States engagements. The First Regiment of Missourians arrived at Fort Leavenworth, Kansas on 18 June 1846. They fought in battle under General Kearney on 18 August, resulting in the complete submission of all of New Mexico. In the same summer, Hon. Sterling Price resigned from the United States Congress to take charge of another Missouri Regiment. His forces put down an uprising against American occupation on 24 January 1847. A third Missouri regiment was mustered into service in May 1847. After the war, the Missourians proudly returned home and once again proved their value as

32

fighters.

<u>The Boone Family(1790-1849)</u>: Daniel Boone left
Fayette County Kentucky, where he served as sher-
iff in 1788, and took up residence in Maysville,
Mason County on the Ohio River. In that year, he
talked of leaving Kentucky and migrating to "West
of the Mississippi". He believed that Kentucky had
become too crowded, and did not like the fact that
Maysville was not free of Indian attacks coming
from north of the Ohio.

In 1795 he sent his son Daniel Morgan to Missouri
for the purpose of studying the feasibility of the
family moving there. Upon his return, Daniel Jr.
informed his father that the Spanish Governor had
invited the "American Hero" to bring in one
hundred Americans who wished to settle permanently
along the Missouri River west of St.Louis. Daniel
was delighted, and accepted the invitation.

The exact year that Daniel Boone left Kentucky is
disputed in histories, but it was probably between
1797 and 1799. Some friends, and relatives of his
wife, Rebecca, prepared for the journey. They
carved out huge canoes measuring about sixty feet
in length from giant trees capable of carrying
five tons, each.

When the parties began their journey, the women,
children and some of the household goods were
placed in the canoes on the Ohio with Daniel
Morgan in charge. They left first, moving down the
Ohio to the Mississippi, and then up that river to
St. Louis. Daniel Boone and the older males made
the trip overland with the cattle and horses. They
followed buffalo trails to a point below
Louisville, then crossed the Ohio and went to Ft.
Vincennes in Indiana. From there, they travelled
through Indian country of Illinois to the Mississippi and then crossed over to St. Louis.

Boone received a heroes welcome by the Lt. Governor in St. Louis. The Stars and Stripes and the
Spanish flag flew over the palace.Bands played and
he was given a cannon salute.After the ceremonies,
Daniel and Rebecca rode horseback to Daniel Mor-
gan´s cabin built by him on his previous stay in

Missouri.

Until Daniel Boone's death on 26 September 1820, he lived very much as he always had. He hunted and trapped, and went on expeditions up the Missouri and Platte Rivers. He was appointed Chief Magistrate by the Spanish and given the power to assign tracts of land. His son, Daniel Morgan served as Commissioner in Gasconade County. The Boone family represented the typical frontierspeople of this Stage.

The Shockley Family(1790-1849): At the beginning of Stage Four of the American frontiers, the Shockleys living in the advance areas were represented by the Richard Shockley(D13E) family. This family was in Carroll County, Virginia. His descendants were among the Missouri pioneers. Meredith, Sr., son of Richard did not leave Virginia to live, but he visited his children in Missouri before he died. Isaiah, Wilson, Isam, Richard 3rd., Thomas and William were on the Tax Rolls of Grainger County, Tennessee between the periods 1797 and 1827, and repeated in White County, Tenn., later, beginning in 1811. At present, there is a colony of Shockleys living near Spencer,Van Buren County, Tenn. This was a part of White County in the early 1800's. Isaiah(D14D) died in Van Buren County, and his estate was administered on 1 April, 1867.

According to Goodspeed's History of Gasconade County, Missouri, the Shockleys were among the first settlers of Gasconade Co., as early as 1812. These early migrators followed routes typical of the pattern of many of the pioneer Missourians, coming from east and central Tennessee, and Virginia.

34

STAGE FIVE
(1849-1890)

Prior to 1849, when the gold rush to California
began, Americans had already settled in California
and Oregon. In California, a party led by John
Bidwell had arrived, and in 1846, George and Jacob
Donner with a party of Mississippians reached the
Sierra Nevada Range in California. They were
stranded there for the winter. Only forty out of a
total of seventy nine survived to complete the
journey.

As early as 1840, Americans were migrating to
Oregon, and in that year they were entering at an
annual rate of about one thousand.

Emigrants began the western trek at Independence,
Missouri, primarily, and travelled overland to
Grand Island, Nebraska, on the Platte River. They
followed this river to Casper, Wyoming and a junction with Sweetwater River, and along this river
to South Pass, Wyoming. The usual route then continued to Fort Bridger in southwest Wyoming. At a
later date, the "Pony Express" diverted at this
point to San Francisco. From South Pass, the trail
continued to Soda Springs, Idaho. The California
trail branched off to San Francisco, and the Oregon Trail went to Fort Hall, Idaho on Snake River,
and followed this river northwest into Oregon and
to Fort Walla on the Columbia River. The last leg
was along the Columbia to Fort Vancouver.

The treaty with Mexico,called "The Treaty of Guad-
alupe" was signed 2 February 1848, and ratified by
Congress 10 March. California was a part of the
acquistion in this treaty. It had been a "distant
region" reached primarily by sea, going around
South America. There was little realization as to
how great was the territory gained.

In 1849, a rumor reached Missouri that gold had
been found in the sands of Sacramento River, in
California. Missourians eager to be the first to
reach the sites of the finds poured west in great
numbers. It took their wagon trains about five
months to make the trip. Some of them took the
Oregon Trail, and others crossed the thousand

miles of desolate plains and mountains. In one year, about four million dollars worth of gold was mined, and in another year San Francisco had fifteen thousand inhabitants. Some of the prospectors found riches beyond their wildest dreams, while others experienced hardships and disappointment. Many returned to Missouri, meeting newcomers along the way with eagerness to see for themselves.

For about a decade, California and Oregon remained frontier islands, separated from Missouri by two thousand miles. Then, settlements began to spring up in Colorado and elsewhere.

As the emigrants moved up the Platte River on the Oregon Trail, serious disturbances developed between the Indians and the "intruders". As a consequence, the U.S. Government arranged a conference with the various Indian tribes, including the Sioux, Assinboin, Grosventres, Arikara, Crown, Arapahoe and Cheyenne. The meeting was scheduled to be held at Fort Laramie, Wyoming, on the Oregon Trail. The tribes were scattered from Canada to the Arkansas River, making it difficult to assemble. Indians drifted in during the summer of 1851. At the close of the council, the Indians recognized the rights of the United States to build roads and posts without limitations, and agreed to cease harassing the travelers. They were to be paid an annuity of $50,000 for fifty years. Tribal lands were not to be settled by whites. Indian Territory was defined as having a west boundary along territories of Oregon, Utah, New Mexico and Texas.

In preparing the treaty, the United States Government changed the figure of fifty thousand dollars to fifteen thousand. This represented a cancelation of seventy percent of the agreed price. In spite of this, the Indians in general kept the peace until later when treaty violations began to occur.

In 1855, the U.S. Government ceased to recognize the treaty and a demand was made for the Indians to cede their lands to the United States. New Territories of Kansas and Nebraska were created on 30 May 1854, embracing all of Indian Territory excepting what is now Oklahoma.

Some of the forty-niners did not give up their prospecting life even after it became less profitable. They moved about with burro and shovel and pan, hoping to "strike it rich" some day. Several hundred of them were working in the Pikes Peak area of Colorado when gold was discovered in the sand beds of streams late in 1858.

As news reached the Missourians, camps began to line the Missouri River from Independence to Council Bluffs. Winter was approaching and few dared to take the risk of travel over the plains at that time of the year. For most of the new prospector candidates the journey began in April 1859. The distance was only about 700 miles, and not the grueling type as earlier trips. Pikes Peak or Bust" became the slogan. They went in heavy and light wagons, on horseback with pack animals and in coaches of the Pikes Peak Stage. Some, even pushed their baggage along in light two-wheeled carts.

By June many were disappointed and homeward bound. Gold was not to be found in sufficient quantities to make many rich. They began to realize that it was a professional mining and smelting job.

It was not until the Colorado inhabitants turned to agriculture and considered themselves permanent settlers that Missouri lost its "frontier" status.

The Civil War(1861-1865): The primary cause for the "War of Secession" was the question of slavery. But, when South Carolina seceded from the Union in December 1860, followed quickly by Mississippi, Florida, Alabama, Georgia, Louisiana and Texas, it became a matter of grave importance to resolve the question of their rights to secede.

By May, 1861 the States of Virginia, Tennessee, Arkansas and North Carolina were added to the Confederate States of America, with Jefferson Davis as its president.

Border states with inhabitants having mixed sympathies, stood aloof. Delaware, Maryland, Kentucky and Missouri decided to remain in the Union.

The war began with the firing on Fort Sumter at
Charleston, South Carolina on 12 April 1861 by
Confederate troops. During that year the operations in the West concerning Missourians, particularly, were those in Missouri at Carthage, Wilson's Creek and Belmont. The South was victorious
in all three.

The following year, the Union was forced to abandon Kentucky, and the North suffered many reverses
until the tide began to turn in favor of them in
1863.

On 4 January 1861, Claiborne Jackson was inaugura-
ted as governor of Missouri. When President Lincoln made a request for men from that State, Jackson refused, stating that: "not one man will be
furnished by him to carry out such an unholy crus-
ade". His action resulted in a secondary civil war
in Missouri. He was forced to abandon the State
Capitol and set up his office at Neosho, Missouri.
On 31 July, a State convention was convened and
the Governors office was declared vacant. Hamilton
Gamble was made governor.

Jackson and Sterling Price recruited a force of
pro-Confederates. This army fought the Union in
some of the early engagements.

On New Years Day,1863, President Lincoln issued
the "Emancipation Proclamation", declaring that
all slaves were free. By the end of that year, the
Union held possession of the Mississippi River,
Missouri, Alabama, Kentucky and Tennessee. They
controlled a large portion of Mississippi and Florida.

In 1864, the primary operations were in Virginia,
and in 1865, the only formidable Confederate army
consisted of General Lee's forces around Peters-
burg and Richmond.His army was surrounded at Appo-
matox where Lee surrendered on 9 April. By the end
of May, all of the Confederate army had surrendered and the war was at an end.

There were twenty seven engagements in Missouri
during 1861, seventeen in 1862, three in 1863 and
eleven in 1864. As the war progressed, the victor-

ies began to swing in favor of the North.

After the Civil War ended, the railroads became a strong factor in western migration, especially. Because of thinly populated areas and rapid extension of the railroads, the U. S. was forced to subsidize them. Congress granted twenty square miles of land along the right-of-ways to companies for every mile of track laid by them. Communities began to flourish along rail lines, and others withered if they were not readily accessible.

The Union Pacific thrusted westward from Omaha, Nebraska, and the Central Pacific began from the west at Sacramento, California, crossing the Sierra Nevada Range to meet the western bound builders. The "wedding of the rails" was consummated near Ogden, Utah, on 10 May 1869. The colorful ceremonies concluded with the driving of a golden spike. The opening of railroads from the Atlantic to the Pacific paved the way for the phenomenal growth of the West that followed.

Exploitation and cheating by the Whites, and the slaughter of buffalo, confronted the Plains Indians with the grave prospect of starvation. This resulted in a series of massacres of Americans.

The U.S.Congress proposed to set up a great system of reservations for the Indians. At a general council in 1867, the southern Plains Indians agreed to take up residence in Oklahoma. The Sioux and Cheyenne tribes protested and in 1876 Chief Crazy Horse and Chief Sitting Bull launched the Sioux Wars.

Lt.Col. George A.Custer, commander of the 7th Regiment was ordered to proceed against the Sioux in Montana. He arrived at the junction of Big Horn and Little Horn Rivers on 24 June 1876. The main body was to meet him there in two days. His force was cut off by an army of twenty five thousand warriors under Sitting Bull, and not a single member of his men survived the onslaught.

The Indians were rounded up and removed from the Plains and sent to Oklahoma. In their stead, developed a "Cattle Kingdom". Vast ranges were stocked with longhorns and sheep from Texas. In 1870, grazing lands were free, and the American cowboy came into existence.

In 1890, the Director of the Census announced that "it can hardly be said that a frontier line remains in the United States." Thus, one era in United States History had drawn to a close.

The Boone and Shockley families (1849 to 1890).No serious attempt has been made to trace these families beyond Missouri. Descendants of Missouri frontiersmen continued to "go west". A number of the Boones moved to Kansas at an early date, and the Shockleys have been found in Nebraska, Utah, California and Oregon.

With the increase in transportation facilities, and industrial development, the western trend pattern so trusted by the genealogists became less pronounced and other factors needed considerations. Americans began to move in all directions as opportunities warranted.

Descendants grow at a fast rate, adding many branes to the family tree. Surnames change when females marry. Without the aid of a distinct migratory pattern, the lineage seeker would find the problem becoming increasingly difficult, were it not for other factors. Improved public records, the help of professional searchers, and the advent of the computer, are some of the many advantages searchers have today. Nothing seems to surpass the element of "pure luck". It may be more correct to call it perseverance when one discovers an old family bible in possession of a relative that "tells all".

PART II

INDEX/BIOGRAPHY

PART II

Parts II and III of this book are the primary genealogical working sections. Part IV augments them in that its use provides a better over-all scanning of the relationships when the desired information is of a broad nature. Part IV is not made a part of this discussion.

Formulating Serial Numbers: The composition of individual numbers consists of five parts, as follows:
1. Capital letter designating an arbitrary division into 22 parts.
2. Two digit number designating a Sibling Group.
3. A capital letter disignating an individual in a Sibling Group.
4. A lower case letter designating a spouse.
5. A lower case letter, f or m representing a father or mother, respectively of a spouse.

For example: A23C   One of the siblings in a Sibling Group.
               A23Cb A spouse of the above sibling
               A23Cbm Mother of spouse A23Cb.

Primary and Secondary Numbers: An individual may have more than one number, representing more than one position on the genealogical charts, appearing in any one of the three categories, Sibling, spouse or parent of a spouse.

Only the Primary number appears in Part II. To find any Secondary numbers an individual may have, refer to Part III, where these are noted in parenthesis with the individual. The Primary number is that number chosen by category rank, first as a Sibling, then a spouse and lastly if neither of the first two is represented, as a parent of a spouse.

USE OF PART II: INDEX/BIOGRAPHY
In using the book to compile a genealogical chart, Part II would normally be the first reference. A typical procedural method shown here illustrates its use.

Assume that it is desired to compile a genealogical chart showing ancestors, descendants, and other kinships of Sarah Shockley. The index contains eleven Sarah Shockleys. The selection of which one applies to the particular case must be determined by identification other than the mere name. Suppose it is known that the one desired was born in Virginia in about 1800. Only four can qualify: D15A,D16E;and, D21I and D11Da because of lack of data.

If no other data is shown in the INDEX to indicate which Sarah is the cor- rect one, then a look at Part III, explained later, might reveal the name of a husband or other kin as an aid to the proper selection. Although not consider- ed too reliable, a date of birth range is shown in PART IV, CHARTS.

Assume that Sarah Shockley D16E, has been selected as the correct Sarah. Her biographic data is shown with her name in the INDEX.

USE OF PART III: This section is a tabulation of SIBLING GROUPS. The framed
letter and a two digit number at the upper left of each group represents the
identification of the Siblings of a Family Group, not their parents. On the
same line are the Surname of the Family and the Father's Serial Number. On the
next line are the given name of the father and the maiden name of the mother.

The Siblings are tabulated with their given names indicated in capitals. Their
spouses are shown with a suffix lower case letter.The first marriage with "a".
If other marriages are shown, the letters b,c,etc. are used. Spouses parents
follow the name of the spouse.

When a Sibling Group number is shown with an individual enclosed in hyphens,
i.e. -A61-, this indicates the offspring group of that individual. Other numbers assigned to the individual are shown in parenthesis.

The following example illustrates the manner in which this section may be used
in formulating charts:

Example: Use Sarah Shockley D16E, found in PART II. Refer to Sibling Group D16
Part III, and locate SARAH D16E as a Sibling. Note that she has three Second-
ary Numbers; C11Aa, as wife of Joshua Cox, B11Bam, as mother of B11Ba, and
B11Cam, mother of B11Ca. Her parents are show on line two of Group D16,(Isaiah
Shockley,and Ruth Young, her maiden name).

Sarah's siblings are: D16A WILLIAM, D16B NELLY, D16C SAMUEL, D16D THOMAS, D16F
RICHARD. D16G URIAH, D16H ISAIAH, D16I MARY, D16J RUTHA, D16K RYE.
Their spouses and spouse's parents are also shown when available.

Ancestral knowledge may be obtained by finding the father as a SIBLING using,
in this case, the Serial Number at the upper right in Group D16. This is D14D.
See SIBLING GROUP D14 and find the name Isaiah D14D. Repeating the procedure,
the parents of Isaiah are found on line 2,(Richard 2nd and Elizabeth —).

The descendants of Sarah Shockley may be found by referring back to Group D16
and noting that she married Joshua Cox, with a Primary Number C11A. Their offspring Sibling Group is indicated along with JOSHUA C11A, Group C11, as -C12-.
SIBLING GROUP C12 lists children of Joshua as: Andrew C12A, Rutha C12B, William C12C, Matilda C12D, James C12E, John C12F, Jacob 12G. Their mother was
Sarah. Then in the second marriage of Joshua, Mary McMatt was the mother of:
Jasper, George, Henry and Joshua.

The grandchildren of Joshua and Sarah Shockley may be found by again referring
to Sibling Group C12, and noting that the children of Andrew C12A are inicated
as being Group C16, Rutha C12B by referral to those of her husband under his
Primary Number John Burgess (B11B). Then by referral to Group B11, their offspring are tabulated in Sibling Group B13.

42

The biographies of all those individuals compiled in developing a genealogical chart may be obtained by finding their names in the INDEX where the biographies are shown.

Charting aunts, uncles, cousins, nieces, nephews and other kin should not be difficult if a serious study of the composition of the Sibling Group data is made. Other ancestral lineages may be charted by establishing Sibling Primary Numbers of spouses, if available. There are too many possible uses for these tabluations to site and illustrate all of them.

NAME	NUMBER	BIRTH	COMMENTS
Abbiatti Michael	B44Aa		b.p.La/ m.1971
Abbiatti Shelly Lynn	B52A	1973Apr13	
Abbiatti Todd Michael	B52B	1975Dec30	
Ackle J. Fred	R32Ba		m.1912Oct12 of Boise Idaho
Adams C	A14Db		
Adams D	A14Dc		
Adkins Alfred	G21A		d. single
Adkins Butler	Y43Ba		m.1879Jan12
Adkins Charles	G21C		of Rolla Mo.
Adkins Edna	G21B		of Maries Co. Mo.
Adkins J.P.	J22Caf		
Adkins John Hubbard	G12Fa		
Adkins Laymon	G21E		d. Dixon Mo. Car accident
Adkins Maude	J22Ca		of Okla.
Adkins W.D.	P13Ba		of Laclede and Green Co. Mo
Adkins Wilda	B13Ia		
Agee James William	C26Ab		m.1916Jun10 d.1935Aug24
Agee W.T.	P13Ca		of Osage Co. Mo
Aher Jane	G50Ca		
Albeitz -	K28Ha		
Albright Brian Craig	F69Ba		
Alexander Cicero	B88A	1836Mar15	b.p.Ky/Clark d.1912Apr28 Mo./Monroe
Alexander Eben M	B89A	1861Dec24	b.p.Mo/Monroe m.1896Dec17 d.1935Mar25
Alexander Elizabeth	B90A	1903Aug11	b.p.Mo./Paris m.1925Dec25 d.1981Aug30
Alexander Elizabeth	A61Ca	1765ca	
Alexander John	A62Fa		
Alexander John Jr.	B87A	1800	b.p.Ky./Clark Co. d.1844 Mo/Monroe Co.
Alexander John Sr.	B86A		d.1841
Alexander John Sr. Mrs	B86Aa		
Alldridge John S	D36Aa		
Alldridge W.G.	D49A		of Rosedale, Mo.
Allen Alexander	Z32Ca		of Tacoma, Wash.
Allen Kenneth	Y53Ca		of Maries Co Mo
Allison Beulah	A74E	1909Apr11	
Allison Bird P	A73E	1865Ca	
Allison Helen	A74D	1904Sep1	
Allison John Isaac	A73C	1865Ca	
Allison John Rawleigh	A66Ba	1840Mar24	d.1913Jun6
Allison Joseph	A74C	1902Jun11	
Allison Lottie	A73D	1865Ca	
Allison Martha	A73A	1865Ca	
Allison Mattie Ethel	A74A	1897Apr7	m1922Jun8
Allison Maude	A74B	1900Jul31	d.1950
Allison Rebecca Jane	A73B	1865Ca	
Allison Ruth	A39Fa	1810Aug29	d.1865ca
Ames S	A14Da		
Ammerman -	E21Fb	1835Ca	m. In Phelps Co/Mo.
Ammerman Conrad	Y72D		m.1872Apr16
Ammerman Ida May	Y48Ca	1867	d.1927

NAME	NUMBER	BIRTH	COMMENTS
Ammerman Isaac	Y71F		of Maries Co. Mo. Of Illinois.
Ammerman Isaac	Y70A		m.Prob.Ky. Of Warren Co./Mo d.MariesMo
Ammerman James	Y72C		of Maries Co./Mo. Moved to Ark.
Ammerman Jane	Y72E		of Maries Co./Mo.
Ammerman Jennie	Y71C		
Ammerman John	Y71D		
Ammerman John Carroll	Y72F	1845Aug11	m.1867Feb14 d.Belle Mo. 1925Mar5
Ammerman Joseph	Y72B		d. Single
Ammerman Joseph	Y71H		of Maries Co/Mo. d. Idaho
Ammerman Nancy	Y71B		m.Warren Co/Mo d. Maries Co. Mo.
Ammerman Philip Hibler	Y71A	1821	b.p.Warren Co/Mo. d. Maries Co/Mo.
Ammerman Samuel	Y71E		
Ammerman Sanford	Y71I		m.1839May23 Maries Co/Mo. d.Polk Co.Mo
Ammerman Sarah Ann	Y14Fa		
Ammerman Willard B	Y72A		of Belle Mo.
Ammerman William	Y71G		of Maries Co/Mo West.Mo. after Civil W
Anderson Addie	Z24B		of New Mexico
Anderson Amanda M	D25Fam	1832Jul19	m.1853Sep20 d.1873Mar30
Anderson Delila	C36Ia		m.1866Feb4 Morgan Co/Mo
Anderson Demi	A76Na	1890Ca	
Anderson Eliza Ann	R26Db		
Anderson Elizabeth	C15Ea	1843Apr12	b.p.Tenn m.1860 d.1873Nov15 Mo.
Anderson Emeline	U11Ea		m.1834Sep30 Osage Co/Mo
Anderson Emily J.	Y23Ea	1834Apr23	b.p.Miss. m.1856Jan24 d.1875Sep17 Mo
Anderson Grace	Z24E		of Arkansas
Anderson James Monroe	V25Ea		of Vienna Mo., of St.Louis d.1898May5
Anderson John H	D77Fa		m.1902Jan8
Anderson Lois	Z24A		of Jefferson Cy./Mo
Anderson Mahala	G46Aa		m.1845Ca
Anderson Mildred	Z24D		of St. Louis
Anderson Nellie	B22Ba		m.1917Jan10
Anderson Paul	Z24C		of Pryor, Okla
Anderson Rebecca Ann	Z35Da		
Anderson Richard W	V25Ca		to Maries Co/Mo from Mississippi 1832
Anderson Thomas	V25Caf	1813Jan5	b.p.Tenn Of Miss. m.1837Nov12 d.1860Mo
Anderson Thomas B	Z17Ca		
Anderson William	Z35Daf		of Miss. m.Twice. (2) in Mo.
Anderson William	U11Ia		
Andrews Lucie	A72Da	1936Aug4	m.1951Jun3
Antrim Martha	E08Cb		m.1748Dec
Antrim Thomas	E08Cbf		
Appley William Dr.	Y61Da		no issue
Archer Elizabeth	L12Ea		m. in Osage Co/Mo of Maries Co/Mo
Arendall Alice	T18Ea	1859Mar22	m.1882Mar21
Arendall Augustan E	Y23Ha		of Belle Mo.
Arendall James	T14Ib		
Arendall Joseph Jones	Y23Haf	1812Mar22	b.p.Ky. d.1833Dec2 Miller Co/Mo
Armer Ray	E46Aa		of Freeburg Mo.
Arnett Louvica	R22Cam		m.1860

NAME	NUMBER	BIRTH	COMMENTS
Arnett Mary Lou	A79Ba		m.1902Feb2
Arnold Charles	Q46B		of Henry Co/Mo
Arnold Edward P	Q33La		m.1875Apr29
Arnold Frank	Q46C		of Henry Co/Mo
Arnold Frank	G39Fa		
Arnold Mae	Q46A		of Henry Co/Mo
Ashley Leonard	A15Aa		
Atkins Adaline	D28C	1839Oct4	m.1874Jan1 d.1927Aug14
Atkins Caswell C	D28A		
Atkins Drusa	D28E		
Atkins Elsie	G21D	1889	b.p.Vera Okla m.1908 d.1909Feb2
Atkins Emma	D45B		Moved from Mo to Okla.
Atkins John M	D45A		Never married
Atkins Lucy	D28G		
Atkins Parker	D17Ja		m.1831Jul14 Grayson Co/Va
Atkins Rachel	D45C		of Arkansas
Atkins Sallie	D28D		
Atkins Sarah	D18Aa		m/1851Nov20
Atkins Stephen	D28B		
Atkins Stephen R	D65Ca		
Atkins Thomas	D28F		
Avery Emeline	Y13Da		m.1841
Ayers William	F41Aaf		m.1653 Md. of England, Maryland,Va.
Ayres Anna	F41Aa	1637Ca	m.1658 d.1695
Backues A.J.	E46Ca		of Freeburg/Mo
Backues Adam	S22H		of Maries Co/Mo
Backues Amanda	S20H		m.1879Feb2
Backues Andrew J	S22G		of Maries Co/Mo
Backues Andrew J	S21A	1858Nov6	of Maries Co/Mo
Backues Cena O	S18G		m.1839Dec26 Of Mo. and Kansas
Backues Eliza	S20G		m.1881Jan2 Moved to southwest Mo.
Backues Eliza	S18D	1812Apr9	b.p.Va m.(1)Poe −1830(2)1849Apr19 Mo.
Backues Emeline	S22B		of Maries Co/Mo
Backues Emeline	S20A		
Backues Eve	S22J		of Maries Co/Mo
Backues Isaac C	S18C	1824Jan31	m.1845Ca Osage Co/Mo d.1910 Maries Co
Backues John	S20E		m.1872Aug1 Maries Co/Mo d. in Kans.
Backues John	S18A		of Osage Co/Mo d. young
Backues John H	S22E		of Maries Co/Mo
Backues John Keeney	S19B		
Backues Lydia	S22C		of St. Louis Mo.
Backues Malinda	S20F		m.1870sep25 Maries Co/Mo
Backues Martin	S22A		
Backues Mary A. Mrs	S17Aa	1784Jul8	b.p.Va. m. Va d.Maries Co/Mo 1870Mar11
Backues Mary Ann	S20C		
Backues Minnie	Y56Aa		
Backues Morris S	S22F		of Maries Co/Mo
Backues Pattie Mrs	S18Bb		
Backues Ray	S22D		d. single drowned.

NAME	NUMBER	BIRTH	COMMENTS
Backues Rowena	S18E		
Backues Sallie	S18F		
Backues Sandford 2nd	S19A		
Backues Sanford	S17A	1787Aug17	b.p.Va. To Maries Co/Mo 1819 d.1854Feb
Backues Sarah	S22I		of Marires Co/Mo
Backues Susan H	S20B		
Backues Susan Mrs	S18Ca	1823Jun28	m.1845ca Osage Co/Mo d.1902Nov12Maries
Backues Thomas M	S20D		of Dixon Mo
Backues Thomas Sr	S18B	1810Jun22	b.p.Va m(1)1838Dec20 Mo. d.1896Mar3
Backues Virginia	S20I		
Bacon -	L19A		of Granite City Mo
Bacon -	L19B		of Granite City Mo
Bacon James H	L16Ga		
Bacon John F	S20Fa		m.1870Sep25 Maries Co/Mo
Bacon Small	L19C		of Granite City Mo
Bade Joseph Jr	G22Ea		of Maries Co Mo
Bade Louis	G22Da		of Maries Co Mo
Bagg Eunice	A13Ha		
Bagwell Inez	Z32Ba		of Othello Washington
Bailey Alexander	H52B		d. single or childless
Bailey Allen	H52C		of Maries Co/Mo
Bailey Allen Mrs	H52Ca		of Maries Co Mo
Bailey Brownlow	H57H		of St Louis Mo
Bailey Daniel	H52G	1825Jun10	of Maries,and Phekps Co Mo d.1866Mar11
Bailey Daniel W	H56A		
Bailey Elbert	H53C		
Bailey Elizabeth Mrs	H51Aa		
Bailey Elkanah P	H53B	1842Apr25	d.1922Nov11
Bailey Etta	H57B		of Maries and Phelps Cos/Mo
Bailey George	H54D		
Bailey George	H52D		
Bailey George A	H55D		m.1879Feb17 Maries Co/Mo.,Okla,New Mex
Bailey H.T.	H56E		
Bailey Ida	H57I		of St Louis Mo
Bailey Ida	H56C		
Bailey James R Jr	H52E		
Bailey James Sr	H51A		b.p.Tenn of Maries Co/Mo
Bailey James Wiley	H55B		of Rolla Mo
Bailey Jane	H53A		
Bailey Jane	H54A		
Bailey John P	H55A		m.1880Dec13 of Maries Co/Mo
Bailey Lida	H57F		of St. Louis Mo
Bailey Luna	H57C		of Maries and Phelps Cos/Mo
Bailey Lutitia	H52I		
Bailey Margaret	H52A	1806Nov16	d.1868Oct11 To Mo with husband
Bailey Margaret	H56G		
Bailey Margaret	H54B		
Bailey Martin Alonzo	H55E		m.1881Mar16
Bailey Mary Ann	H52H		of Phelps Co/Mo

NAME	NUMBER	BIRTH	COMMENTS
Bailey Mary M	H56B		
Bailey Minnie	H57E		of St Louis Mo
Bailey Minnie	H56F		
Bailey N.B.	H56H		d.single
Bailey Nigaria A	H55F		m.1878Apr12
Bailey Ora	H57D		of Maries and Phelps Cos/Mo
Bailey Orval	H57A		of Rolla Mo
Bailey Paul	A76Mb	1900Ca	
Bailey Polly Ann	H54C		
Bailey Raymond	H57G		of St. Louis Mo
Bailey Robert L	H56D		
Bailey Tabitha	F07Fb		m1792Sep18 Rowan Co. No.Car
Bailey William	H54E		
Bailey William	H52F		
Bailey William A	H55C		m.1880Jun27
Baker Hiram	E71A	1831May	b.p.Tenn/ m.1856Aug17 d.1905Oct20Mo
Baker Jackie Clyde	C42Aa		
Baker James	E17Fa		
Baker Lidia	E63Da		m.1901
Baker Lizzie	E30Da		d.1931Dec17
Baker Louemma	Y61Fa		
Baker Martha Ellen	E72A	1872Nov7	m.1895Aug20 d.1958 College H. OsageMo
Baker Nancy	E71B		
Baker Sam	Y36Ea		
Ball Burgess	B99Aa		
Ball James Col.	B06Daf	1678	m.1706 d.1754
Ball Jeduthun	B06Da	1725	
Ball Joseph Col	B97Abf		
Ball Mary	B97Ab		
Ball Robert	A72Ga	1940Jun11	m.1962
Ballance Eliza	K32G		
Ballance George W	K32B		of Granite City Mo
Ballance John Wesley	K32E		of Maries Co Mo
Ballance Martha Ann	K32F		d. Phelps Co/Mo
Ballance Mary Jane	K32D		Entire life in Maries Co Mo
Ballance Thomas Monroe	K32C	1860Jul31	d.1930Sep17 Dixon Mo. Without issue
Ballance William D	K31Aa		Arrived in Mo. with Davis family
Ballance William E	K32A		of Maries Co/Mo
Barbarick Andrew	E51A		d. single
Barbarick Barbara	E67Cam		m.1825 Of Owensville Mo
Barbarick Bransford	E51H		of Belle Mo
Barbarick Cecil	E51B		d. single
Barbarick Clarence	E51D		d. single Drowned in Gasconade R. Mo
Barbarick Dora	E51M		of Gerald Mo
Barbarick Floyd	E51K		of Belle Mo
Barbarick Frederick	C11Gaf	1786Aug27	b.p.N.C.Mackleburg Mo.1815 d.1863Aug26
Barbarick George	E51I		of Belle Mo
Barbarick J.H.	E24Ib	1824	of Gasc.Co Mo. m1849Feb24 d.1855
Barbarick James	E48Ha		of Belle Mo

NAME	NUMBER	BIRTH	COMMENTS
Barbarick John	E51J		of Belle Mo
Barbarick Joseph	E51F		m. In Indiana
Barbarick Joseph H	E24Ba		of Gasconade Co Mo
Barbarick Logan	E51E		m. In Indiana
Barbarick Margaret	C11Ga	1812	b.p.N.C. Cabarrus Co. m1832Gasc.Co/Mo
Barbarick Matilda	D16Gb		m.1830May6 Gasc. Co Mo
Barbarick Nora	E51L		of Eldon Mo
Barbarick Rhodes	E51G		d. Jefferson Cy. Mo
Barbarick Walter	E51C		d. single
Barker Minerva	D76Cam	1816Aug7	b.p.Ind. d.1896Jan11 Gentry Co Mo
Barnes -	G35La		of Phelps Co Mo
Barnes - Dr.	I47Cbf		of Polk Co Mo
Barnes Ella	I47Cb		m.(1) Morris -
Barnes Joab	A39Ia		
Barnes Joseph	Z43Ca		
Barnes Nancy Caroline	A67Ca		d.1893Oct1
Barnes Ricy Ozina	A67Ba	1834Jun3	d.1912Feb13
Barnes Sarah J	A67Ma	1846Feb26	d. 1910Jun25
Barnett Cora	P15Ga		
Barnett Isaac	I54Ba		m/1897Aug1
Barnett Ollie	J27Ha		m.1902Apr26 of Springfield Mo
Barnhart Daisy	G19Fa		of Maries Co Mo
Barnhart E.P.	U16Da		
Barnhart Fannie	U18Aa		
Barnhart George	G51Da		
Barnhart Isaac	T21Ba		of Maries Co Mo
Barnhart James	G51Db		
Barnhart Martha S	U15Ham		m.1883Oct25
Barnhart Mary Ellen	G51Ia		d.1930Jul7
Barnhart Mat	U18Aaf		
Barnhart Monroe	E55Ea		
Barnhart Paralee	G19Ea		of Maries Co Mo
Barnhart Thomas	T24Ga		of Maries Co Mo
Barnhill James	I59Gb	1780	m.1804 d.1825
Barnwell Julian F	Q33Iaf		Father Robt. H Barnwell
Barnwell Laura	Q33Ia		m.(1) W.C.Moreland(2)R.H.Moreland Mo
Barr George	V18Ja	1852	d.1934
Barr Ida	D32Da		
Barr Warren M	D32Daf		
Barrett Kathleen	E86Bb		m.1969Apr2 Okla.City Okla
Bartel Delores	E88Ba		m 1943Aug28
Bartle Roena	Y33Ba		of Polk Co Mo
Bartle Warren	G62Fa		May be Y33Baf
Bartle Warren	Y33Baf		
Bartlett Milton	A73Aa	1865ca	
Barton Charity	C34Aa		
Bartow Doris	F37Ba		m.1960
Basemore Lamar Halley	B38Baf	1900Oct28	b.p.Ga./Screven Co Father Thomas.
Basham Edward	Y26Caf		

NAME	NUMBER	BIRTH	COMMENTS
Basham Elizabeth	Y26Ca		
Basham Nancy	T14Gb		
Basnett Betty Jean	E84F	1936Oct18	m.1953 May25
Basnett Dorothy May	E84G	1938Nov21	m.1960Apr9
Basnett Juanita Ruth	E84C	1930Oct31	d. 1930Oct31
Basnett Larry Dean	E84H	1944Mar31	m.1968Mar11
Basnett Lemuel Gerald	E84B	1929Aug17	m.1949Feb17
Basnett Lemuel Pollard	E83Da		m1926Dec23
Basnett Lillie Pearl	E84A	1928Jan29	m1942Dec26
Basnett Logan	E83Daf		
Basnett Paul Jerome	E84E	1934Dec21	m1956Jul15
Basnett William Logan	E84D	1932Nov1	Never married
Bassett Elmer	Y34Ea		of Maries Co Mo
Bassett George	J15Ea		
Bassett Lucinda	A90Ka		m.1832Dec26 Mason Co Ky
Baster George	D65Ba		
Bastian Arthur Richard	D78Ba	1881Jul1	b.p.Iowa Vincent m1915Nov25 d.1963 S.D
Bastian James Calvin	D79C	1923Aug24	b.p.Wyo. m(1)1948Aug14,(2)1962Jun17
Bastian John Milton	D78Bb		m.1968Feb4
Bastian Mary Elizabeth	D79B	1919Apr3	b.p.Colo/FtCollins m.1944Dec27 of Nebr
Bastian Metha Ellen	D79A	1916Dec25	b.p.Wyo.Platte Co m.1937Jun6
Bastian Theodore	D78Baf		
Batte Agnes	F15Da		m.1780Nov5
Batte Sarah	F15Ca		m.1787Feb3 Anne Arundel Co. Md.
Baty Daniel	E89Aaf		
Baty Ida Belle	E89Aa	1877Jan2	b.p.Mo/Keonig d.1965Jan30 OwensvilleMo
Baumgartner Elizabeth	E83Aa		m1938Jun12
Bax William	E22Ma		of Mo. Moved to Arkansas
Baxter Isaac	B08Ka		
Bazemore John Lamar	B48A	1957Nov5	b.p. Fla Miami
Bazemore William D.	B38Ba	1933Aug11	b.p.Fla. Daytona Beach m.1956Jun30 Fla
Bazemore William G.	B48B	1959May11	b.p. Fla Miami
Beard George W	B15Iaf		
Beard Lorena	B15Ia		
Beard Mary	E30Ha		m.1901Apr9 No issue
Beasley Jeanette	G42Aa		of Illinois
Beasley Jennie	G38Ba		of Henry Co Mo
Beck Celia	D47Ga		
Becker George Walter	B74Aa	1920Jan17	b.p. N.Y. Sea Cliff m.1948Aug7 WWII
Becker June Marie	B76B	1955Aug3	b.p. N.Y. Glen Cove m.1982Oct3 Fla.
Becker Linda Jane	B76A	1949Jun5	b.p.N.Y. Glen Cove m1977Jan Fla.
Beckham Anderson	G35Ia		
Beckham Arminta	G38D		m.1880Dec13 of Maries Co Mo
Beckham Caswell	G35Fa		of Phelps and Wright Cos. Mo
Beckham Dora	G38G		of Maries and Henry Cos. Mo
Beckham George M	G43Baf	1834Mar21	d. 1916
Beckham John	G38B		of Henry Co. Mo
Beckham Leonard	G38A		d. near Dillard Mo
Beckham Lucy	D28Fa		

50

NAME	NUMBER	BIRTH	COMMENTS
Beckham Martha	G38F		of Maries and Henry Cos Mo
Beckham Perry	G38C		of Maries Co Mo d. Henry Co Mo
Beckham Riley	G43Cb		
Beckham Rowena	G38E		of Maries Co Mo
Beckham Thomas	G43Ba		d. Phelps Co Mo
Beckman Dewey	M21A		
Beckman William	M13Ca		
Beckman William Jr	M21B		
Behm -	K23Fa		of Pacific Mo
Belk Amanda	U12Db		
Belk John	U12Dbf		
Belk Julia Ann	U12Dc		
Bell Alegerene	G62I		d.1938 Alberta Canada
Bell Alphia	F66Ea		
Bell C.C.	G62B		Judge
Bell Carter	G65C		d. St. Louis Mo.
Bell Charles	G63G		of Maries Co Mo
Bell Clark	G63A		of Maries Co Mo
Bell Clay	G63K		of Pulaski Co Mo
Bell Columbus	G65E		of Newburg Mo
Bell Dora E	G62K		d.1938
Bell Edward	G66E		of Dixon Mo
Bell Finis	G66G		d. No issue
Bell George W	G36Caf	1823Apr9	b.p.Mo. d.1904Feb24 of Maries Co Mo
Bell Goldie	G64D		of St Louis Mo
Bell Henry	G63F		of Maries Co Mo.
Bell Ida	G64B		of St. Louis Mo
Bell Isabelle	G63D		of Maries Co Mo
Bell James Madison	G62A	1848Feb15	d.1918Jul11 of Maries Co Mo
Bell John	G62C		
Bell John W	G66D		of Edgar Springs Mo
Bell Josephine	G62H		of Maries Co. and St. Louis Mo.
Bell Louisa J	G62F		of Rolla Mo.
Bell Martha	G63I		of Miller Co Mo
Bell Mary R	G62G		of Maries Co Mo.
Bell Melvina	G62J		of Maries Co Mo
Bell Mollie	G66F		of Dixon Mo
Bell Noah	G65B		d. single
Bell Peter	G66C		of Iowa
Bell Rachel	G66B		d. St. Louis Mo
Bell Richard T	G62E		of Rolla Mo
Bell Riley	G64A		of Dent Co Mo
Bell Roan	G65A		
Bell Rose	G63H		of Howard Co Mo
Bell Sallie	G63B		of Maries Co. Mo.
Bell Sylvia	G64C		of St. Louis Mo
Bell Thomas	G63E		of Maries Co. Mo
Bell Tine	G63J		of Sedan Kansas
Bell Wilbert	G65D		of Maries Co Mo.

NAME	NUMBER	BIRTH	COMMENTS
Bell William	G66A		Killed in R.R. machine shop in Canada
Bell William R	G62D		
Bell William R. Mrs	G62Da		
Bell William W	G63C		of Maries Co Mo
Belt Joseph Sprigg	F110a		m.1790Apr28
Benage A.L.	V140a		of Maries and Laclede Cos Mo. Teacher.
Bennett -	Z380a		of Dallas Co. Mo.
Bennett Joseph	I58Da		
Bennett Polly	M15Fam		
Bennett Sarah	Q310a		later,m.Collins-, then Josiah Carter
Berger Anna Louise	D90Cam		
Berling Gus	G63Ka		of Pulaski Co. Mo.
Berry Elizabeth Jane	P12G	1861Apr12	
Berry George Linton	B26Ba		
Berry George W	P12C	1853Nov9	
Berry James David	G37A		d.1937Oct Of Miller Co Mo.
Berry John	P11Aa		m.(1) to Martha Copeland. Of Maries Mo
Berry John Allen	B22Ha		m.1935Jun23
Berry John Jehu	P12A	1850Sep14	d. 1918Jan2
Berry Lydia Campbell	D27Ja		
Berry Margaret	P12B	1852Aug19	b.p. Mo. Maries Co
Berry Mary	P12D	1856Sep28	
Berry Nancy	P12E	1858Sep1	
Berry Sarah Ann	P12F	1860Jan3	
Berry William	G35Ga		
Berry William Matthew	G37B		d.1934Jun4
Besson Anne	B04Dam		m.(1) Watkins -
Beymer Archie	C40Aaf		
Beymer Nellie Roe	C40Aa		
Biles Charles	M14Ba		
Bilyeu -	H53Ab		
Bilyeu -	E52Aa		Welch descent
Bilyeu Cynthia Ann	Z35E		m.(1)1859ca
Bilyeu James	Z35A		Removed to Ark during Civil War
Bilyeu Monroe	Z35B		Removed to Ark. during Civil War
Bilyeu Priscilla	Z11Aa		m.Prob in Md. 1807ca. French descent
Bilyeu Ruth Ann	Z35C		Removed to Ark. during Civil War
Bilyeu Stephen	Z35D		of Maries Co Mo
Bilyeu William	Z11Fa		Removed to Ark during Civil War.Confed
Birdsong -	Y54Ka		
Birdsong Lissie	E43Aa		of Maries Co Mo.
Birdsong Malissa	Z33Aam		of Washington and Idaho.
Birdsong William N.	E43Aaf	1851Apr3	m.1881Oct16 d.1929Apr5 Maries Co. Mo.
Birkman -	E65Aa		
Birmingham C.C.	G61Ba		of Ohio
Birmingham Catherine A	S12Ea	1866	d.1919Dec22
Birmingham Thomas	U17Ga		of Franklin Co Mo
Birmingham Walter	S12Eaf		
Birmingham Walter	S14Ea		of Washington Mo

NAME	NUMBER	BIRTH	COMMENTS
Birmingham Walter	P15Ea		of Franklin Co Mo.
Bishop Adam	Y58Ga	1870	Moved to Okemah Okla
Bishop John	G20Caf	1836Apr22	b.p.Tenn/Rowan Co m.1858 d.1884May4 Mo
Bishop John Bunyan	Y58Fa	1868Mar16	of Okemah Okla
Bishop Mable	D77Ha		m.1915July
Bishop Missouri	G20Ca		m.1889Nov7
Bishop Virginia Ellen	G12Ea	1862Feb7	b.p.Mo/Maries Co
Black Joshua	F22Aa		m.1810Dec21
Black Phoebe Elizabeth	D18Gb		m.1893Jan12 Phelps Co Mo
Blackmore -	I48Ca		
Blackmore Earl	I50C		
Blackmore Grace	I50A		
Blackmore Lela	I50E		
Blackmore Lois	I50B		
Blackmore William	I50D		
Blackwell -	D56Ba		
Blackwell Ida May	F37Aam		
Blackwell Richard	G45Ea		
Blackwell Thomas	M16Eb		no issue
Blankenship Elmina	V18Cam		
Blankenship Jessee	V18Fa		
Blanton -	G48D		
Blanton -	G48C		
Blanton Amanda	G47C		of Maries Co Mo To Dallas Co. Mo 1877
Blanton Benjamin J	B95A	1838Sep20	b.p. Mo. Jefferson Cym1853Jun29 d.1915
Blanton Caroline	G47D		no issue
Blanton Daniel M	G48A		of Chilhowee Mo
Blanton Elizabeth Mrs	B93Aa		
Blanton Ezekiel	G10Eb		
Blanton Hattie Pearl	B96A	1872Aug24	m.1896Dec17 d.1922May10 Paris Mo
Blanton J.H.	G48B		of Colo. Springs Colo.
Blanton Jasper	G47B	1842Aug9	d.1931May30 Soldiers Home St.James Mo
Blanton Jasper Mrs	G47Ba		
Blanton John	G47A		moved to w. part of Mo.
Blanton Thomas	B94A		b.p. Ky. m.1827Dec26
Blanton Thompson	B93A		
Blaylock Elizabeth	A70Aa	1837	d. 1926
Blaylock Martha	A78Ca	1869Mar5	d.1943Feb14
Bledsoe Etha	R28Ea		
Blenkarn Walter A	D79Aa		m.1937Jun6
Boatwright Ada	B18Ba		d.1953Jan13 Parnell Mo
Bodendick Fred E	Z34Ea		of St. Louis Mo
Bodendick W.T.	I44Ca		of St Louis Mo
Boggs James	Q37Ia		
Bolin Mary	A79Ca	1885ca	
Bollinger Mary Ellen	B22Ea		m.1926Aug14
Bonsteel Marton D	D88Ba		d.1981May23 of Ohio
Boone -	I40C		
Boone Abigail	I58I	1732	

NAME	NUMBER	BIRTH	COMMENTS
Boone Albert	I46E		Moved to W. part of Mo.
Boone Albert G	I56B		
Boone Allison	I59I		
Boone Alonzo	I56A		
Boone Andrew	I48D		
Boone Ann	I24E		
Boone Anna	I13C		
Boone Anna	I48B		
Boone Banton	I24A		
Boone Banton Dr	I17A		d. Callaway Co. Mo
Boone Banton Jr Hon	I25A		of Henry Co Mo. Mo. Speaker of House
Boone Benjamin	I11G		
Boone ClaudeBrooks Mrs	I48H		
Boone Daniel	I12F	1734Nov2	b.p.Pa. m.1756Aug14 d.1820Sep26 Mo.
Boone Daniel	I48F		
Boone Daniel	I45B		of Tenn.
Boone Daniel Morgan	I15G	1769Dec23	d.1839Jul13 Justice Gasc Co Mo of Kan.
Boone Deborah	I58D	1720	
Boone Delinda	I57D		
Boone Diana	I58E	1722	
Boone Edward	I16D		
Boone Edward (Ned)	I12I	1740Nov30	d.1780Oct6 Killed by Indians
Boone Eliza J	I46B	1852	d. Western Mo
Boone Elizabeth	I12E	1732	b.p.Pa/Berks Co. d.1816
Boone Elizabeth	I16F		
Boone Elizabeth	I47B		
Boone Elizabeth C	I23C		
Boone Ellender Mrs	I59Ca		
Boone Emily	I56H		
Boone Eva	I48A		of Marionville Mo
Boone Frank	I48G		d1923
Boone George	I58A	1714	
Boone George	I59A		
Boone George III	I10A		b.p.Devonshire Eng.Phila.1717 d.1744
Boone George IV	I11A		b.p.Eng. of Phila. m.1713 d.1753 Pa
Boone George L	I24D		
Boone George V	I12H	1739Nov2	b.p.Pa d.1820Nov14 Shelby Co.Ky. of Va
Boone George VI	I16E		
Boone Hannah	I12K	1746	m.1765ca No.Car.
Boone Hannah	I58C	1718	
Boone Hannah	I59G	1786	m.1804 d.1862
Boone Hannah	I19B		
Boone Harriet	I56E		
Boone Hayden	I18C		
Boone Hayden	I22B		
Boone Henderson	I47C	1848Apr28	b.p.Mo/Maries Co of Hickory,Polk CosMo
Boone Hezekiah	I58J	1735Ca	
Boone Howard	I57B		

NAME	NUMBER	BIRTH	COMMENTS
Boone Isaiah	I18B		
Boone Israel	I42B		d. Maries Co/Mo
Boone Israel	I15B	1759Jan25	d.1782Aug17 Killed byIndians in Ky.
Boone Israel	I19A		b.p. No. Car near Lenoir
Boone Israel Mrs	I19Aa		
Boone Israel Sr	I12B	1726	b.p. Pa. m.1747 Pa.
Boone Israel Sr. Mrs	I12Ba		
Boone Isreal	I13B		b.p. No.Car New Lenoir
Boone James	I57A		
Boone James	I11H		
Boone James	I15A	1757May3	d.1773. Killed by Indians in Ky.
Boone James M	I56C		
Boone Jemima	I15D	1762Oct4	b.p. Va. Culpepper m.1777 Ky d.1829
Boone Jemima	I57I		
Boone Jeptha V	I23A		
Boone Jeremiah	I58H	1729	
Boone Jeremiah	I59F		
Boone Jesse	I13A	1748	of No.Car d.1829Dec In Am.Rev/No.C.
Boone Jesse	I15H	1773May23	Mem.1st Mo. Legislature d.1821
Boone Jesse	I42C		of Polk Co Mo d.1875Ca
Boone Jesse	I48E		
Boone John	I57C		
Boone John	I42A		of Mo. In Dallas Tex. before 1853
Boone John	I22E		
Boone John	I11D		
Boone John	I16B		
Boone John Mrs	I42Aa		d. in No. Car.
Boone Jonathan	I40B		In Maries Co. Mo in 1834
Boone Jonathan	I12D	1730	of Berks Co/Pa d.1816
Boone Jonathan Mrs	I40Ba		
Boone Joseph	I11F		
Boone Josiah	I58G	1726	m.1750 Exeter Berks Co Pa d.after1814
Boone Josiah Jr	I59C		
Boone Lavina	I15E	1766Mar23	of Kentucky d.1838
Boone Lavinia	I57J		of Ky.
Boone Mahaley	I57M		
Boone Malinda	I57E		
Boone Margaret I	I24G		
Boone Maria	I16J		
Boone Maria	I24H		
Boone Marion	I41A		Killed in Camden Co Mo in Civil War.
Boone Martha	I47A		d. in infancy.
Boone Martha	I16G		
Boone Martha L	I23E		
Boone Mary	I58B	1716	m.1737
Boone Mary	K25Aa	1801	b.p. Tenn. m.1830Ca d.1846 Vienna Mo.
Boone Mary	I57F		
Boone Mary	I24I		
Boone Mary	I11E		

55

NAME	NUMBER	BIRTH	COMMENTS
Boone Mary	I12G	1736	m.1754
Boone Mary	I46C		
Boone Mary	I61Ca		
Boone Mary A	I23B		
Boone Mattie	I48C		d 1899 Western Mo.
Boone Maxemille	I23D		
Boone Melcina	I57L		
Boone Milley	I24F		
Boone Milo	I22C		
Boone Minerva	I56F		
Boone Moses	I18A		
Boone Nancy	I57H		
Boone Nancy Elizabeth	I41B		of Maries Co/Mo
Boone Nathan	I15J	1781Mar2	d.1856Oct16 To Mo in 1800
Boone Noah	I59B		
Boone Oliva	I57K		
Boone Pantha	I56G		
Boone Polly	I16I		
Boone Rachel	I42D		m.No.Car or Tenn. Of Maries Co Mo
Boone Rebecca	I15F	1768May26	d. in Ky.
Boone Rehuma	I59D		
Boone Rehuma #2	I59H		
Boone Rodolph	I24B		
Boone Roy P. Mrs.	I48J		
Boone Ruth	I59E		
Boone Samuel	I22A		
Boone Samuel	I11I		
Boone Samuel Capt	I16C		
Boone Samuel Jr	I14A		
Boone Samuel Sr	I12C	1728May31	m.1748 d.1808 or 1816 In Am.Rev./Ky,Va
Boone Samuel T	I23F		
Boone Sarah	I11B		of Devonshire Eng. Of Pa.and Va.
Boone Sarah	I12A	1724	b.p.Pa m.1742 Pa d.1815
Boone Sarah	I16H		
Boone Sarah	I46A	1852	of Crowley Colo in 1935
Boone Squire	I16A		d. St. Charles Co. Mo
Boone Squire Jr	I12J	1744Oct5	m.1765 d.1815Aug5 Ky/Mo/Ind. Minister
Boone Squire Mrs	I16Aa		
Boone Squire Sr	I11C	1696	b.p. Eng m.1720/Pa d.1765 Of Va/No.Car
Boone Susan	I57G		
Boone Susannah	I15C	1760Nov2	b.p.Va/Fredericksburg m1775 d.1799 Mo
Boone Thomas	I22D		
Boone Van D	I56D		
Boone Willard	I48I		of Branson Mo
Boone William	I45A		of Tenn
Boone William	I24C		
Boone William	I58F	1724	
Boone William	I15I	1775Jun20	d. in infancy
Boone William (Babe)	I46D		Moved to w. Mo after father's death

NAME	NUMBER	BIRTH	COMMENTS
Boone William Daniel	I40A	1809	b.p.NoCar Lenoir of Tenn d1878
Booth Jonathan	A13Ea		
Borden Benjamin	E08Aaf		of Chatham N.C. about 1752
Borden Rebeckah	E08Aa		of Chatham Co N.C. about 1752
Bortree Esther A	A16Aa		
Boulware -	J21Aa		of near Albuquerque New Mex.
Bowen Thomas	Y13Fa	1806Apr10	b.p. Tenn Methodist minister.
Bowers Robert Clayton	C23B	1953Jun13	
Bowers Russell	C20Ab		m.1945Nov10 Wife's 2nd marriage
Bowers Scott Howard	C23A	1948Jun16	
Bowie William	F11Ea		
Bowman Bethel	A39Ka		
Bowman Daniel H	M15F		near Vichy Mo and Henry Co Mo
Bowman Della	M25A		of near Vienna Mo
Bowman Edward	M25D		of Maries Co Mo
Bowman Everett	M25B		of Maries Co/Mo.A world rodeo champion
Bowman Hannah	M15C		of Laclede Co Mo
Bowman John	M25E		of Maries Co Mo
Bowman John	M11Fa	1312Apr9	d.1897Jan4 of Maries Co Mo
Bowman John	M26A		
Bowman Margaret	M26B		of Henry Co Mo
Bowman Margaret E	M15B	1861Sep6	m.1882Dec10 d.1897Aug1
Bowman Mary J	M15A		of Maries Co Mo
Bowman Maud	M25F		of Maries Co Mo
Bowman Richard	M25C		of Maries Co Mo
Bowman Sarah	M15D		
Bowman William Thomas	M15E	1884	b.p.Mo/Maries Co d.1933Jun21
Bowman Wm. Thomas Mrs	M15Eb		
Boyce Sarah Frances	P12Aa		d. before 1913
Boyd Cynthia Marie	B39Ba		m.1978Apr1 Vero Beach Fla
Boyd Mary	M11Bb		
Boyden Ann	D10Aa	1636ca	m.1674Oct4 Somerset Co. Md
Boyle Edith	C18Ca		
Bradford -	Z38Da		of Greene Co Mo
Bradford David	A39Ba	1797ca	
Bradford Jacob	A39Ga		
Bradley James H. Jr	B49B	1979Feb24	b.p. Ga. Blairsville
Bradley James Harrison	B39Aa	1951Apr13	m.1973Jun10 Ft. Pierce Fla
Bradley Melanie Hope	B49A	1977Jan6	b.p. Fla. Vero Beach
Bradshaw Mart	Y45Ca		no issue
Brall Jamima Ann	C36Ha		m.1865Jul16
Branch P	A13Cd		
Brandel Mike	J23Gaf		
Brandel Sallie E	J23Ga		m.1909Jan12 of Maries Co.Mo.
Branson -	E49Da		
Branson -	E11C		
Branson -	D21Aa		
Branson -	E49Ba		of Osage Co Mo.
Branson -	E49Ca		

NAME	NUMBER	BIRTH	COMMENTS
Branson –	E23D		of Kansas City Mo.
Branson –	E23A		of Dixon Mo.
Branson –	E23C		of Springfield Mo
Branson – Mrs	E11Ca		
Branson —	E10C		
Branson Abraham	E77C	1754Oct15	d.1827Jun16
Branson Agnes	E25E		
Branson Albert E	E82C	1866	died young
Branson Alfred	E65I		of Owensville Mo.
Branson Alfred Jr	E66A		d. Owensville Mo.
Branson Alfred Mrs	E24Da		
Branson Alfred P	E24A	1838Mar15	b.p. Mo./Gasconade Co d.1909Jun7 Texas
Branson Alice	E29C		of Belle Mo.
Branson Allen G	E37C		of Little Maries R. Maries Co. Mo
Branson Amanda	E22B	1853	m.(1) Stephen Owens d.1935Nov12 of Mo
Branson Andrew	E16G		
Branson Andrew	E19G	1819Oct39	of Gasconade Co. Mo in 1847
Branson Andrew	E15A	1789	b.p. Va. m.1810ca d1835 Mo.1829 of N.C
Branson Andrew	E90B	1838	
Branson Andrew B	E17D	1807Feb9	b.p.Va
Branson Andrew J	E21A	1833Jan23	d.1915Jun27 of Rolla and Maries Co.Mo
Branson Andrew Jackson	E69A	1859Nov22	m.1880May16 d.1936 Jan 31
Branson Andrew R.	E20E	1849	b.p. Mo. Middle name Richardson
Branson Ann	E17I		m/1839Apr14/Mo To Mo. in 1821
Branson Ann	E09C		
Branson Ansley	E44B		of St. Louis Mo
Branson Archibald A	E25H		of Dixon Mo
Branson Beau Gentry	E87D	1975Nov11	b.p. Taxas/Wichita Falls
Branson Benjamin	E22N	1856	b.p. Mo.
Branson Benjamin	E78H	1797Apr30	d.1820Sep27
Branson Benjamin F	E20D	1859Feb12	b.p.Mo. m.1883Feb14 d.1935Dec31 Maries
Branson Benjamin F Jr	E25I		of Dixon Mo
Branson Benjamin J	E90F	1846	
Branson Besse	E65E		of Belle Mo
Branson Bryon	E28E		of Nebraska
Branson Buddy Orin	E85I	1922Oct23	b.p.Oklahoma/d1981 Aug1
Branson C.S. Dr.	Y46Aa		of Belle Mo
Branson Catharine	E69G	1853	m.1868Aug16
Branson Catherine	E19F	1823Dep1	m.1838Mar30 of Gasconade Co Mo
Branson Charles	E60B		
Branson Chrissa	E24J		d.young 1864Nov11 bu.Owensville Mo
Branson Clarence	E65C		d. Warrenton Mo
Branson Clyde	E66C		of Owensvlle Mo
Branson Cora	Y34Ha		m.1917May25 of St. Louis Mo
Branson Cynthia M.	E87B	1966Jun7	b.p.Okla/Okla City
Branson David	E17A	1810Jan17	m.1832Jun14/Mo(2) 1846 d.1881 RollaMo.
Branson David	P11Gaf		
Branson David	E08D		
Branson David	E90E	1844	

NAME	NUMBER	BIRTH	COMMENTS
Branson David C	E29D		d.1918Feb16 No issue
Branson Dolly	E25B		d.1937 Waynesville Mo.
Branson E.C.Jr.	E85G	1919Mar3	b.p.Okla
Branson Eli	E80A		
Branson Elijah	E90H	1849	
Branson Elizabeth	E29B		
Branson Elizabeth	E22C	1855	b.p.Mo Osage Co d. Maries Co. Mo
Branson Elizabeth	E60A		
Branson Elizabeth	E34B	1869Apr18	m.1887Dec1 Later of Maries Co/Mo
Branson Elizabeth	E08K		
Branson Elizabeth	E09D		m.about 1764
Branson Elizabeth	E82E	1870	d. young
Branson Elizabeth J	E21C	1836May8	m.1856Sep4 Osage Co Mo
Branson Elizabeth Mrs	E24Ca		
Branson Elizabeth Mrs	E08Ha		
Branson Elizabeth Ruth	E12B	1810	b.p.Va m.1828 Marion Co Tn. d. 1843Ca
Branson Ellen	D42A		no issue
Branson Emma	E22M	1849	b.p.Mo.
Branson Ethel	E25N		of Pulaski Co/Mo
Branson Eula Evelyn	E85B	1904Sep29	b.p.Okla/d.1969Nov13
Branson Everett	E66D		of Columbus Ga.
Branson Ewell C.	E25K	1881Apr1	m(2)1902Jul27 d.1958Jan2 Miami Okla.
Branson Floyd Franklin	E85A	1903May1	b.p.Okla/d.1963Jun19
Branson Galba E	E24C	1841	b.p.Mo. Gasc. Co. d.1889 Taney Co.Mo
Branson Garrett	E65H		of Overland Mo.
Branson George W.	E17C	1820ca	b.p. Tenn m.1839Mar24
Branson Gilbert	E22I	1841	of Osage Co Mo.
Branson Gladys Claudia	E85D	1909Sep22	b.p.Okla/d.1936
Branson Hanna M	E24I		d.1885
Branson Hannah M	E21F	1838ca	of Shannon Co/Mo
Branson Hannah Mrs.	E78Ha		
Branson Henry	E65Iaf		
Branson Henry	E81C	1766Jan25	b.p. N.C./Orange Co
Branson Henry Childers	E19K	1833Nov22	of Gasc. Co. Mo in 1843
Branson Hiram	E16K		
Branson Hiram	E90G	1847	
Branson Ida	E29F		of Maplewood Mo
Branson Isaac	E78E	1793Mar16	
Branson Isaac	E90A	1836	
Branson Isabelle Mrs.	E08Ca		
Branson J. Nath	D42C		of Maries Co Mo
Branson Jacob	E08B		
Branson Jacob	E77B		m.1795Dec16
Branson James	E22E	1835ca	
Branson James Marion	E69B	1840Feb9	m.1861Feb5 d.1931Jun29
Branson James T	E58B		
Branson Jane Ann	E86A	1937Jan24	b.p. Okla/Miami
Branson Jared	E28B		of Maries Co Mo
Branson Jared	E16A	1817Oct15	b.p.Tenn/Marion Co m1839Dec14 d1882 Mo

59

NAME	NUMBER	BIRTH	COMMENTS
Branson Jarret E	E15C	1785ca	m.1807Mar12(2)1851 d.1867Mar9 Mo
Branson Jarrett	E10D	1754	b.p.Va d.1831MarCa Gasc. Co Mo
Branson Jeff	E34C		of WestoverMo. and Winfield Kansas
Branson Jemina	E90C	1840	
Branson Jesse	E65B		d. Owensville Mo
Branson Jinney	E82J	1883	d. young
Branson Job Richardson	E20F	1845	
Branson Johanna	E82F	1872	m.1892Jan27
Branson John	E16H		
Branson John	E61G		
Branson John	E23E	1861Sp21	d.1911Aug15 Okla. Penitentiary guard.
Branson John	E19B		
Branson John 1st	E10A		of Va. Friend of George Washington
Branson John 1st Mrs	E10Aa		
Branson John 2nd	E11A		b.p. Va. N.W, Mo. in 1821
Branson John 2nd Mrs	E11Aa		
Branson John 3rd	E12A	1775ca	b.p.Va.m.1803Dec15Va. of N.C./Tenn/Mo.
Branson John Day	E08C		Will 1768 Sep1
Branson John L	E22L	1844	of Osage Co Mo
Branson John M	E69H	1855Oct	
Branson John M	E69Ja	1878Jun28	m.1878Jun28
Branson John N.	D27Ha		
Branson John Sevier	E17E		b.p.Tenn. d.1905Nov24 To Mo. in 1821
Branson John T	E70Aa	1869Apr4	b.p.Mo/Osage Co m.1901Mar10 d.1953Mo
Branson John W	E82K	1875	m.1916Sep14
Branson Jonathan	E08F		
Branson Joseph	E22O	1856	
Branson Joseph	E08E		
Branson Joseph	E78G	1796Jan1	d.1878Nov12
Branson Joseph	E81B	1764Mar6	b.p.N.C..Orange Co
Branson Joseph	E87C	1972Mar23	b.p. Okla/Okla City
Branson Julia Ann	E69C	1840	b.p.Tenn d.1919 Mt. Sterling Mo
Branson Julia Ann	E90D	1842	
Branson Julie Renee	E87A	1962Oct13	b.p. Okla/ Okla City
Branson Kate	E37B		of Benton Co./Mo
Branson Kitty	D42E		of near Kansas City Mo.
Branson Laura	E25L		
Branson Lavicy	E16J		
Branson Leslie	E44A		A miller in Detroit Mich
Branson Levi	E80B	1732ca	
Branson Levi	E81F	1773Sep25	b.p.N.C./Chatham Co
Branson Levi	E81G	1776Jan13	b.p. N.C./Cjatham Co
Branson Lewis F	E24E	1845	b.p.1845 Mo.Gasc.Co. of Taney Co/Mo
Branson Lillian	E30Eb		
Branson Lional	E08G		of Hardy Co/Va d.Will April 1809
Branson Louisa	E24N		d. Springfield Mo.
Branson Louisa Jane	E19J	1831Jan6	of Gasc. Co/Mo in 1843
Branson Lucy Jane	E82I	1881May18	m1902Nov18
Branson Lucy M	E58A		d. young

NAME	NUMBER	BIRTH	COMMENTS
Branson Lydia	E81E	1771Apr28	b.p. N.C./Orange Co
Branson Madison	E17L	1822Apr22	b.p.Tenn m.1842Dec25 d.1871Jan11 Mo.
Branson Mahala	E34A	1857Nov28	b.p.Mo./Woolam m.1883Feb4 d.1912Feb7
Branson Malinda	E82G	1877	m.1893Aug2
Branson Manola	E69I	1857	
Branson Margaret Eliza	E85J	1924Sep29	b.p.Okla/d.1945Nov25
Branson Marian	E15E		m.1810Nov13
Branson Martha	E65A		d. Gerald Mo.
Branson Martha	E16D		
Branson Martha	E22J	1842	b.p. Mo of Osage Co. Mo.
Branson Martha	E09E		m.1769Jan11
Branson Martha E	E69J	1864	m.1878Jun28
Branson Martha Marg.	E29A	1866Sep29	m.1885Dec23 d.1937Feb1 Belle Mo
Branson Martin V	E22K	1848	b.p.Mo. m.1869Dec9 of Osage Co/Mo.
Branson Mary	E34D		of Maries Co/Mo. of Washington State
Branson Mary	E61I	1814	
Branson Mary	E08J		
Branson Mary	E09B		
Branson Mary	E77A		m.1801Mar.
Branson Mary	E78B	1788Jul10	
Branson Mary (Margie)	E16E	1809Sep23	d.1847Oct11
Branson Mary A	E24G	1849Oct11	b.p. Mo/Gasc. Co. d.1866Oct30 Mo.
Branson Mary Ann	E17K		b.p. Tenn. m1844
Branson Mary Ann	E21D	1340	d.1899Aug.
Branson Mary E	E20C	1841Jan29	b.p.Mo. m.(2)1870Jun19 d.1871Aug8
Branson Mary Frances	E82Aa		m.1883Jan25
Branson Mary J Mrs	E17Da		d.1895
Branson Mary Jane	E69E	1849	
Branson Matilda	E16I	1824Nov15	b.p.Tenn Hancock Co d.1861Gentry Co.Mo
Branson Matilda H	E82D	1867Oct10	m.1889
Branson Maud	E25M		
Branson Melissa	E20B	1853Oct4	b.p.Mo/Gasc.Co m.1873Nov3 d.1876Jan8
Branson Millie	E61B	1810	m.1834Nov11
Branson Minerva	E24D	1843	b.p. Mo/Gasc Co. Osage Co in 1860
Branson Minerva	E22A		d. in Maries Co Mo
Branson Minnie	E25F		of Maries Co Mo
Branson Mrs	E10Ca		
Branson Nancy	E19C		
Branson Nancy	E17H		b.p. Tenn m.1836Jan10
Branson Nancy	E25C	1868	m.1885 Feb26 d.1930May14
Branson Nancy Jane	E73A	1903Jan22	b.p. Mo Osage Co. Judge
Branson Nancy Jane	E82B	1864	m.1884Feb6
Branson Nannie	E22H		d. single
Branson Nathaniel	E78D	1791Dec23	d.1817Oct25
Branson Neoma	E61F		
Branson Olivia C	E24B	1840	b.p.Mo/Gasc Co
Branson Ollie	E65D		d. in Colo.
Branson Oma	E65F		of Fulton Mo
Branson Paradine	E25J		of Miller Co Mo

NAME	NUMBER	BIRTH	COMMENTS
Branson Patsy	E19H	1826Jun10	of Gasconade Co in 1843
Branson Pereby Mrs	E15Aa		m.1810ca Will recorded 1849Nov2
Branson Polly	E19E	1821Sep19	of Gasconade Co Mo. in 1843
Branson Ramus	E28C		of Roseburg Oregon
Branson Ray	E65G		of E. Carondelet Ill.
Branson Ray	E37A		d.1937
Branson Rebecca	E61A	1809	m. in 1830´s
Branson Rebecca	E70A	1884Mar	b.p.Mo/Osage Co m1901Mar10 d1903Jan25
Branson Rebecca	E81D	1768Feb15	b.p.N.C./Orange Co
Branson Rees	E78A	1780Sep3	m.1802Mar10 d.1815Mar11
Branson Reuben	E17B	1808Mar13	Tenn/Cave Cumberland Mts Tenn Mo 1821
Branson Reuben	E13A		
Branson Reuben	E12C	1808abt.	
Branson Reuben Mrs	E13Aa		
Branson Reuben Mrs	E12Ca	1810ca	
Branson Reuben S	E24H	1853	b.p.Mo.Gasc. d1935 Founder Branson Mo
Branson Rhoda	E17J		m.1841Jun25 Mo. in 1821
Branson Richard Wm.	E85H	1920Dec23	b.p.Oklahoma
Branson Roger Wayne	E86B	1939Mar5	b.p.Okla/Miami m(1)1961Feb9(2)1969Apr2
Branson Rolla	E19I	1829Jan21	of Gasconade Co Mo in 1843
Branson Ruth	E16B	1823	b.p.Tenn m(1)Cox-m(2)1845 d.GentryCoMo
Branson Ruth Ann	E21B	1834Jan5	b.p.Mo/OsageCo m1855 d.1917Dec17
Branson Sallie	E28A		
Branson Sally	E19D		
Branson Samantha J	E22P		of Maries Co Mo Moved to Okla.
Branson Samuel K	E24M		of Dent Co Mo
Branson Sarah	E17F	1805ca	b.p. Va. To Mo in 1821 d.1900 Osage/Mo
Branson Sarah	E61H		
Branson Sarah	E08I		
Branson Sarah	E82H	1879	
Branson Sarah Ann	E22G	1846	b.p. Mo.
Branson Sarah M	E69F	1851	
Branson Sarah Mrs	E10Da	1745abt.	d. after 1830 Gasc. Co Mo
Branson Sina Perkins	E19L	1835Oct19	b.p. Gasc. Co Mo
Branson Sophia	D42D		of near Belle Mo
Branson Stella	E28D		of St. Louis Mo
Branson Stephen	E22F		
Branson Stephen	E17M		b.p.Tenn m.1842Jun9 d.1866Jul11
Branson Stephen	E49Baf		of Osage Co Mo
Branson Susan	E61C		m.1837Jun1
Branson Thelma	E65Ia		of Owensville Mo
Branson Thelma Bernice	E85C	1907Oct28	b.p.Okla
Branson Thelma Mae	E66B		of Owensville Mo
Branson Thomas	E16F		
Branson Thomas	E37D		of St. Louis Mo
Branson Thomas	E12D		Fought in battle New Orleans War 1812
Branson Thomas	E11B		Fought Indians under Cpt Robertson1771
Branson Thomas	D42B		of near Linn Mo
Branson Thomas	E23F		

NAME	NUMBER	BIRTH	COMMENTS
Branson Thomas	E61E		
Branson Thomas	E22D		
Branson Thomas	E15B	1780ca	m.1807Abt. d.1851 To Mo in 1821
Branson Thomas	E09A		To Va. Frederick Co.1703 d.1746abt.
Branson Thomas	E08A		
Branson Thomas	E78F	1794Jul13	d.1861Nov22
Branson Thomas	E81A	1762Feb15	b.p.No.Car/Oragne County
Branson Thomas Benson	E82A	1861Nov22	m.1883Jan25 d.1952Feb2
Branson Thomas F	E25D		d.1911 Owned hotel Vienna Mo.
Branson Thomas Haskell	E85E	1911Jun28	b.p.Okla
Branson Thomas J.	E24F	1847	b.p. Mo/Gasc Co Farmer Greene Co Mo
Branson Thomas Jeff.	E69D	1344Feb15	m.1864Feb25 d.1925Sep 13
Branson Thomas Jr	E17G		b.p. Tenn m.1849Feb1 To Mo in 1821
Branson Thomas Jr	E10B		He surveyed with George Wahington
Branson Thomas Mrs	E11Ba		
Branson Thomas Mrs	E09Aa		of Frederick Co/Va
Branson Thomas S	E14A		m.1837
Branson Thomas Sr	E07A		To AM. 1703.d.1744 Will prob N.J.+ Va.
Branson Valentine	E19A	1810	b.p.Va. d.1876 Gasc Co/Mo of BledsoeTn
Branson Valentine	E24K	1851	b.p.Mo/Gasc Co d.1934 bu. Bland Mo
Branson Valentine	E15D		m1807May7
Branson Wayne Gentry	E85F	1914Oct12	b.p.Okla/m.1933Sep12 Miami Oklahoma
Branson William	E22Q	1835ca	of Owensville Mo
Branson William	E25G		of Dixon Mo b. after 1365
Branson William	E16C		of Gasc Co/Mo 1835
Branson William	E61D		
Branson William	Y34Haf		of Dixon Mo.
Branson William	E08H		of Stafford Co./Va d. before 1801
Branson William "Red"	E18A	1840Jun15	b.p.Mo/Gas m.1860Jan12 d.1919Dec28
Branson William A	E82Fa		m1892Jan27
Branson William G	E20A	1842	b.p. Mo/Gasc. Co.m.1865ca Of Maries Co
Branson William H	E24L		of Springfield Mo
Branson William J	E29E		Moved to Colo.
Branson William Jr	E23B	1865ca	of Springfield Mo
Branson William M	E25A		m.1891Aug9 of Dixon Mo. Lumberman
Branson William P	E78C	1790Dec11	
Branson William R	E21E		of Maries Co/Shannon and St. Louis Mo
Brashears Flavilla M	T13Aa		m.1833Dec5 Osage Co Mo
Brashears Joseph Rev	T13Aaf		
Brasier Green M	G47Da		no issue
Brasier John Rile	G47Ca		of Maries Co/Mo and Dallas Co. in 1877
Brasier Polly	G25Ca		Moved to Vernon Co/Mo
Brasier S.T.	G25Caf		
Bray Albert	E42C		of Maries Co Mo
Bray Dora A	Q44La		m.1892Jun26
Bray Edward	Y44Aa		No issue
Bray Ellis	E42B		of Maries Co Mo
Bray Minnie	E42E		of Phelps Co Mo
Bray Seth	E42A		of Maries Co Mo

NAME	NUMBER	BIRTH	COMMENTS
Bray Stella	E42D		of Maries Co Mo
Bray T.A.	E34Aa		m/1883Feb4 Of Maries Co Mo
Bray Thomas A	Q44Laf		
Breeden –	G33Ca		
Breeden –	G33Fa		
Breeden –	E32Bb		of Union Mo
Breeden Abraham R	D25Gb	1838Feb18	b.p.Tenn/Roane Co Of Maries Co Mo
Breeden Alice	P17F		of Washington Mo.
Breeden Anna	P17G		of St. Louis Mo
Breeden Charles	P16H		of St. Louis Mo
Breeden Dora	P17H		of St. Louis Mo
Breeden Elizabeth	P16F		of Union Mo.
Breeden Ella	P16O		of near Kansas City Mo
Breeden Elmer	P16A		
Breeden Emma	P16P		of Jefferson Cy. Mo
Breeden Eunice	P16D		of Union Mo
Breeden Everett	P16C		of Union Mo
Breeden Hannah	V21C		
Breeden Hester	P16N		of Eldon Mo
Breeden Isaac	G33Daf		
Breeden J.R.	G33Caf		
Breeden Jacob	P16I		of St. Louis Mo
Breeden James R	P14Ca		
Breeden Jesse	P16K		of St. Louis Mo
Breeden John	D25Gbf		
Breeden John	V19A		Maries Co/Mo from Roane Co Tenn 1842ca
Breeden John	P16B		of Eldon Mo
Breeden John Mrs	V19Aa		
Breeden John William	V21B	1846Feb6	b.p.Mo Jasper Co m1869Nov14 Maries1854
Breeden Joseph Frost	V20A		m.Tenn. d.1875 Maries Co of Joplin Mo
Breeden Lamon	P16E		of Union Mo
Breeden Leslie	P17D		of Washington Mo
Breeden Levi	P16J		of St Louis Mo
Breeden Louis Roland	V21A	1842	
Breeden Louisa	G12Ca	1853Nov22	m.1870Jan9 d.1935
Breeden Lula	G33Da		m.1906
Breeden Marshall	P17C		of Washington Mo
Breeden Melvia	P16M		of St. Louis Mo
Breeden Nettie	P17E		of Washington Mo
Breeden Ollie	P16L		of St. Louis Mo
Breeden Sarah	V21D		
Breeden Stephen	S14Ba		
Breeden Stephen	P17A		of Washington Mo
Breeden Thomas	P17B		of Washington Mo
Breeden Willard	P16G		of Union Mo
Breeden William	P14Ea		
Breeden William	U12Aa		of Shannon and Maries Cos/Mo
Breeden William	G12Caf		
Breeden William	S14Aa		

NAME	NUMBER	BIRTH	COMMENTS
Breeding -	U12Ga		
Breeding -	T16Da		sister of Elijah Breeding
Breeding Elijah	U12Gaf	1799	b.p.Ky(Prob)Father John Mother Napper-
Breeding James	G32Caf		
Breeding Malinda Ann	G32Ca		of Maries Co. and Eldon Mo
Brewer Christiana	A15Ja	1793Sep29	b.p.NJ Patterson m.1814Jan11 d.1876Apr
Brewer Wm. Bogardus	A15Jaf		
Briggs A Moses	S12A		of Maries Co Mo
Briggs A.M.	U15Ia		
Briggs Boney	J21A		of near Albuquerque New Mexico
Briggs Charles	S13A		m.1879Feb2
Briggs Daniel Boone W.	S11G	1839	m.1860 d.1863Nov6 by bushwhackers.
Briggs Dennis	S12D		of Okla.
Briggs Effie	J21E		
Briggs Elizabeth	D15Ba	1807Nov10	b.p.Tenn m.1824Nov30 d1869Aug12 Mo
Briggs Elizabeth	D16Fa		m.1826Nov20
Briggs Emeliza	S13D		m.1896Sep19 of Okla.
Briggs Eugenia	S13C		of Okla
Briggs Eva	S16A		
Briggs Ewell	J21C		d. single
Briggs James	S12B		of Union Mo
Briggs James	J20Ba		of Maries Co Mo
Briggs James Lafayette	S11D	1840	d.1923Nov29 In Mo. Militia Civil War
Briggs James T	S13E		of Okla
Briggs James Y	S10A		b.p.No.C m.Tenn. d CivilWar Rolla Mo
Briggs John	D16Ba		m1809Feb1 of Marion Co.Tenn
Briggs John	S16E		
Briggs John Burr	S11C	1833Apr4	b.p.Tenn d.1891Dec22 Maries Co Mo
Briggs John H	S15A	1861Apr20	d.1911Jul30
Briggs Lafayette	L16Haf		of near Springfield Mo
Briggs Mabel	J21D		of near Albequerque New Mexico
Briggs Margaret	S15C		
Briggs Margaret	S13G		of California
Briggs Mary	S15B		
Briggs Mary Minerva	S11E	1858	d.1893Mar31
Briggs Mary Sharilla	Q32Ca		
Briggs Mollie	S16B		
Briggs Newton	S13F		of Oklahoma
Briggs Sarah Jane	Q31Dc		m(1)Burckhart
Briggs Scott Terry	S11A	1837Mar4	b.p.Mo.Maries Co d.1900Jan9 Maries Co
Briggs Sharilda	S11H		
Briggs Sidney	S11F		
Briggs Stephen	S13B		of New Mexico
Briggs Stephen	L16Ha		
Briggs Terry	G19Da		
Briggs Terry	S12C		of Washington Mo
Briggs Thomas	S16C		
Briggs Thomas J	S12E	1861Nov24	m.1885Nov24 d.1932Apr14 Maries Co Mo
Briggs Walter	S16D		

NAME	NUMBER	BIRTH	COMMENTS
Briggs Wherry	J21B		of near Alburquerque New Mexico
Briggs Zylphia	S11B	1831Jan7	m.1856 d.1922Feb25 Maries Co Mo
Briscoe Andrew	D38Da		went to Oregon
Briswalter Helen	B19Ca		m1917Jun17
Briswalter John	B19Caf		of Joplin Mo
Briswalter Myrtle Mrs	B19Cam		of Joplin Mo
Brittain Jennie	Y24Gb		of Maries Co Mo.
Brittain Maria	Y33Aa		d. without issue of Canyon Cy Colo.
Brittain Stella	Y62Aa		of Owensville Mo
Brocke Mary	A88Cam		
Brooks Claude	I48Ha		of Kansas City Kansas
Brooks Mary A	C37Bb		of Cross Timbers Mo
Brown -	V26Bb		
Brown Ann	Q40Aa		of Maries Co. Mo and Broken Arrow Okla
Brown Dessie	E31Ha		
Brown Dude	E54Ba		Moved from Maries Co Mo
Brown Fern	R24Ma		m.1921Jul30
Brown Francis	A76Ta	1905abt	
Brown Harriet	K30Aa		d.1888Apr16 of near Vienna Mo
Brown Lera	B19Cb		m.(1) O'Rourke
Brown Minnie	Y76Ca		m.1911Sep15 of Rector Mo
Brown Patricia Gail	D91Ba		
Brown Phebee	A76Ia	1885Apr19	d.1953Dec20
Brown Robert	Q40Aaf	1772Dec30	of Paris Ill. Maries Co Mo 1847
Brown Vallie M	A76La	1892Nov17	d.1927Jan14
Brown Walter	A76Ja	1890abt	
Brown William	C37Eb		of Mo.
Bruce Sarah E	C36Aa		m.1840Mar24 Mo. d.Pomeroy Washington
Brumble John	P11Ca		b.p. Osage Co Mo. Lived there.
Brumley John	G44Ca		of Bland Mo
Bryan B.D.	A68Ka		
Bryan David	I62A		to Warren Co Mo 1800
Bryan Eleanor	I61F		
Bryan Henry	I62E		of St. Charles Co Mo 1808
Bryan James	I61A	1723	d.1807
Bryan Jonathan	I62C		to Mo in 1800
Bryan Joseph	I61D	1735abt	
Bryan Martha	I121a		
Bryan Morgan Jr Capt	I61B		Founder Bryan's Sta. Lexington Ky.
Bryan Morgan Sr	I60A	1671	b.p.Denmark m.1719 Pa.d.1763 No.Car.
Bryan Polly	I62D		
Bryan Rebecca	I62F		
Bryan Rebecca	I12Fa	1739Jan9	m.1756Aug14 d.1813Mar18 Mo
Bryan Samuel	I61E		
Bryan Susan	I62B		
Bryan Thomas	I61G		
Bryan William	I61C	1733	
Bryan William	I12Ga		m.1754
Buck Jane	F05Ca		of Anne Arundel Co. Md

NAME	NUMBER	BIRTH	COMMENTS
Buck Willie Thurlow	A75Ba	1899Mar12	d.1973Dec20
Buckingham Roy R	A45Ba		
Buckley Mary	F43Aa		
Bullock Jackson	Q45Ca		of Maries Co Mo
Bullock James	Q45Da		
Bullock James	M14Da		of St. James Mo
Bumpass Sarah	E16Aa	1835Jan13	b.p.Mo/Gasc Co m.1839Dec14 d1907Jan15
Bumpass William	E16Aaf		of Gasc. and Maries Cos Mo. Co. Treas.
Burcham Herbert	Y36Da		
Burchard Barbara	Y66C		
Burchard Eliza Jane	E67Ca		
Burchard Fannie	Y66E		d single
Burchard Malissa J	Y66D		
Burchard Mary Ellen	Y66A		of Clebourne Texas
Burchard Nathan	Y25Faf		of Gasc and Maries Cos/Mo
Burchard Samuel	E67Caf		m.1825 d.1868 To Mo in abt. 1804 ofPa
Burchard Virginia	Y66B		m.1874Sep29 of Phelps Co Mo
Burd Ailsie	T24Ca		
Burd Anna	T24Ea	1835May20	d.1912Dec1 Maries Co Mo
Burd Mary	T24Da		
Burgess Abbie Marie	F30F	1834Nov14	
Burgess Absalom	F22J	1805Jul1	
Burgess Achsah	A90B		
Burgess Achsah	F14A		m.1781Nov27
Burgess Adolphus A	A68I		d.1879Jul2
Burgess Albert Carl Jr	B30C	1926Nov2	b.p. Mo./Joplin m.1949Jul24 Joplin
Burgess Albert Carl Sr	B19C	1895Jan9	b.p.Mo./Joplin.m(1)1917(2)1968 d.1979
Burgess Alexander	F28A		
Burgess Alexander	F17D		
Burgess Alfred	B13L	1877	b.p. Mo.(Prob. Newton Co.)
Burgess Allen	A80C		
Burgess Almeda	F56J		
Burgess Alvin Dero	A76L	1887Jan14	d.1958Jul11
Burgess Amelia	F10A	1759Oct16	b.p. Md/Prince Georges Co.
Burgess AmmonLafayette	A71B	1878Oct2	d.1934Dec10
Burgess Anderson	A39E	1808Apr24	b.p.No.Car/Rowan Co m.1830Tenn of Mo.
Burgess Andrew J	B11F	1839	of Newton Co./Mo in 1860
Burgess Ann	A64A	1743Apr	b.p.Md/Anne Arundel Co/All Hallows Par
Burgess Ann	A99B		In fathers Will Annapolis Md.1748Dec6
Burgess Ann Dorsey	F23A		
Burgess Anne	B05C	1685Dec5	b.p.Md/Anne Ar Co m/1709Oct22 d.1742Ca
Burgess Anne	B07B	1721Oct9	b.p. Md./Anne Arundel Co d. young
Burgess Anne	B04J	1680Oct7	b.p. Md/Anne Ar Co m.1697Jul25 Md.
Burgess Anne	A34C		d.1826 Spinster.
Burgess Anne	F18B	1760Jun20	b.p. Md/Anne Arundel Co
Burgess Anne	B03E		b.p.England. Early 1600's
Burgess Anne #2	B07L	1745Mar30	b.p. Md/Anne Arundel Co.All HallowsPar
Burgess Annie	A76O	1900Ca	
Burgess Arch	Z38E		of Greene Co./Mo

NAME	NUMBER	BIRTH	COMMENTS
Burgess Arlene Mrs	A75Fa	1930Nov2	
Burgess Arthur	B28F		of Upland Calif. Stockton
Burgess Avo	A76P	1895Jul5	d.1973, Oct 28
Burgess Bailey	A76Q	1900Sep15	d.1968Jul26
Burgess Barbara	F15B		
Burgess Barbara	Z33Ea		"Went West"
Burgess Barbara	B45B	1954Sep2	
Burgess Basil	F10F	1768Dec31	b.p.Md/Prince Georges Co.
Burgess Basil	F22C	1789Jun15	d.1862Nov20
Burgess Basil Capt	F14C		m1785Jan11.Served Army,Navy
Burgess Basil Capt	A99A	1741Dec20	m.1759Feb8 d.1780 of Prince Geo.Co.Md
Burgess Benedict	F33A		
Burgess Benjamin	F56G	1858	b.p.Mo
Burgess Benjamin	A88G		
Burgess Benjamin	F15D		b.p.Md/Anne Ar.Co m1780Nov5 d.1793Dec
Burgess Benjamin	B06C	1721ca	b.p.Md Anne Ar.Co christened 1721Jul9
Burgess Benjamin	B04G	1664Ca	b.p.Md/AnneAr Co. Mariner of England
Burgess Benjamin	B07O		no issue
Burgess Benjamin F.	F35G	1861Aprl	b.p. Mo/Fuersville d1924Jun10 No issue
Burgess Bert	B11I		of near Denver Colo.
Burgess Berta Lee	A77H	1917Aug9	m.1937Apr10
Burgess Bertha	A80E		
Burgess Bertha	Z38A		no issue
Burgess Bradley Carl	B42D	1962Sep6	
Burgess Bret Michael	B53C	1982Jul4	b.p. La./Sulphur
Burgess Brian David	B42C	1959Jun10	
Burgess Brice Warfield	F27F		
Burgess Caleb	B07J	1739Sep30	b.p.Md/Anne Ar Co. d1791
Burgess Caleb Ensign	F17B		b.p.Md Anne Ar Co m.1802Aug19 d.1817
Burgess Canza Well	A79A	1879Nov12	d.1967Feb23
Burgess Carl	A80I		
Burgess Carmach	A76T	1906May	
Burgess Caroline	F57C	1889Feb11	b.p.Ark/Indian Terr.
Burgess Cart	B13I	1871	b.p. Probably Kansas.
Burgess Cassandra	F11D		b.p.Md m.1781Mar9
Burgess Catherine W.P.	F28C		m. 1828Sep10
Burgess Celeste	F51A	1906	
Burgess Celina	A68D		
Burgess Cephus	F56I		"Disappeared mysteriously"
Burgess Charles	Z38B		of Calif.
Burgess Charles	F18D	1764Feb26	
Burgess Charles	A88A		b.p. Md/Prince Georges d1740 Annapolis
Burgess Charles	B04H	1670Ca	b.p.Md/Anne Ar Co. m1703Oct26
Burgess Charles	A39D	1806May16	d.1887Dec7
Burgess Charles	F11F		b.p.Md.Prince Georges Co.Alive in 1763
Burgess Charles	F10E	1767Dec18	b.p.Md/Prince Georges Co.
Burgess Charles	A76K	1885	d.1965
Burgess Charles	B13H	1869	b.p. Prob. Kansas
Burgess Charles A.	F35H	1876Mar29	b.p.Mo/Fuersville m1900Mar d1953Jun22

NAME	NUMBER	BIRTH	COMMENTS
Burgess Charles H.	A75C	1913Oct2	d.1975Jun19
Burgess Charles J	A72B	1928Sep7	m/ 1953
Burgess Charles L.	A67J	1843Sep27	m.1860Apr3 d.1915May17
Burgess Charles O	F29E		
Burgess Charles W	F30K	1849Feb26	
Burgess Charlie	A70H		
Burgess Charlotte	F21C		
Burgess Charlotte	A66E	1847May18	d. 1912Jan12
Burgess Chesley	K27C		of Granite City Mo.
Burgess Cindy Lee	B43B	1956Dec24	
Burgess Clarence Perry	B19A	1887Oct12	b.p.Mo/Joplin m(1)1907(2)1936d.1962Sep
Burgess Clemensa	A68J		
Burgess Clyde Cecil	B19D	1900Mar20	b.p.Mo/Joplin m1921Mar1(2)1941d.1982
Burgess Cora Annis	B15E	1874Aug30	b.p.Mo,Albany m1893Oct19 d1932Nov13
Burgess Cora Louise	B29C	1924Apr8	b.p.N.Y.Roslyn m.1948Feb12 of Florida
Burgess Cynthia	F20C		
Burgess Cynthia	A66F	1830Ca	
Burgess Cynthia A	F34G	1830	
Burgess Daisy	A76M	1900Ca	
Burgess Dallas	A80M		
Burgess Dan	A78F	1860Ca	
Burgess Daniel	A66K	1848Ca	
Burgess Daniel	B03H		b. early 1600´s
Burgess Daniel B	A77C	1908Dec14	m.1930Oct4
Burgess Dealia Iantha	A71G	1889Aug2	d.1969Sep5
Burgess Dorendia Susan	A71F	1886Apr17	d.1966Apr30
Burgess Dorinda	A67I	1842Jan1	d.1916Dec11
Burgess Dorothy Eliz.	A72G	1939Dec21	m1962
Burgess Dorsey Earl	F53B	1937Jun10	d.1959Jun29Topeka Kans. Bicycle acc.
Burgess Dorsey Gavon	F51B	1908Aug26	m.1936Jun22 KansCy/Mo. d1952Mar19Kans.
Burgess Dudley	B13D	1861	b.p.Mo/Newton Co
Burgess Dudley H	A68H		
Burgess Edna	B28B		
Burgess Edward	F18I	1771Jul14	b.p.Md/Anne Ar.Co. All Hallows Parish
Burgess Edward	B06A	1717ca	b.p.Md/Anne Ar Co/ch.1717Apr14
Burgess Edward	A37B	1739Nov27	b.p.Va/Stafford Co St. Pauls Parish
Burgess Edward	B05A	1686	b.p.Md/Anne Ar Co m.1713Jan12 d1715
Burgess Edward	A34D		d.1824 Montgomery Co Md.
Burgess Edward	F24A		of Montgomery Co Md.In uncles Will1824
Burgess Edward	A35B	1767Apr2	b.p.Md/Stafford Co
Burgess Edward	K27A		of Chicago,Ill
Burgess Edward Capt	B04A	1655Ca	b.p.Md/Anne Ar Co m.aft1676 d.1722Mar
Burgess Edward Capt	B07G	1733	b.p.Md d1809Dec5 of Montgomery Co.Md
Burgess Eleanor	A90G		m.1824Jun28 Mason Co Ky
Burgess Eleanor	F21A		m.1808Apr6 Montgomery Co Md
Burgess Eleanor	F20D		m.1785Jan11. Husband´s cousin
Burgess Elias	F29B	1843	
Burgess Elijah	F56F	1855	b.p. Mo
Burgess Elijah	Z36Aa		of Springfield Mo

NAME	NUMBER	BIRTH	COMMENTS
Burgess Eliza	F34C		m.1837Aug31
Burgess Elizabeth	A34B		d.1824Nov2 Prob.Montg.Co.Md. Spinster
Burgess Elizabeth	F18E	1765Nov12	
Burgess Elizabeth	B06D	1723	b.p.Md Anne Ar Co ch.1723Dec29 SoRiver
Burgess Elizabeth	F22A	1784Oct4	m.1810Dec21
Burgess Elizabeth	B07M	1751Nov26	
Burgess Elizabeth	F32C		
Burgess Elizabeth	B04I		b.p.Md Anne Ar Co/So.Par after 1670umm
Burgess Elizabeth	F27A		
Burgess Elizabeth	A88C	1714Nov15	m.1734Jan23 of Prince Georges Co/Md
Burgess Elizabeth	F13A	1714Dec20	b.p.Md/Anne Ar Co. Only child
Burgess Elizabeth	F10C	1762Dec13	b.p. Md/Prince Georges Co.
Burgess Elizabeth	F23D		
Burgess Elizabeth	B05B	1688Aug5	b.p.Md Anne Ar Co m.1704Aug15
Burgess Elizabeth	A39B	1800Ca	
Burgess Elizabeth	A67D	1834Jan9	d.1909Feb10
Burgess Elizabeth	B10B	1810	b.p.Tenn m.1830Oct14 Gasc.Co/Mo
Burgess Elizabeth	B03I		
Burgess Elizabeth	B08O	1765May25	m.1792Dec11
Burgess Elizabeth	F31C		
Burgess Elizabeth	Z38C		of Dallas Co/Mo
Burgess Elizabeth	A68F		
Burgess Elizabeth J	A70D	1849	
Burgess Elizabeth M	B11A	1829Oct20	d.1865Mar20
Burgess Elizabeth M	F34E	1839Ca	
Burgess Elizabeth M	F35E	1856Apr7	b.p.Mo/Fuersville
Burgess Elizabeth Mrs	A34Fa		of Montgomery and Alleghany Cos Md.
Burgess Elizabeth W.	F26A		
Burgess Elizer Ann	F28D		
Burgess Elma	B28A		
Burgess Elva	F57B	1887Dec10	b.p. Ark. Indian Territory
Burgess Emaline	A70B	1841	
Burgess Emma Alverda	B15C	1870Nov22	b.p.Mo.Gentry Co m.1891Feb15 d.1944Mar
Burgess Ephraim	A34F		of Mont. Co/Md Not married in 1790
Burgess Essie	A77A	1904Oct26	m.1921Dec29
Burgess Esther	B29A	1909Jun22	b.p.Kans. Greeley m.1933Aug20 of Fla
Burgess Ethel Adella	B55A	1874Sep21	b.p.Mo Newton Co
Burgess Ethel May	B19G	1909Aug17	b.p.Mo/Joplin m.1930Nov5.Of Venice Fla
Burgess Etta	Z38H		of Greene Co/Mo
Burgess Eva R	F29A	1824Nov11	m.1941Dec4
Burgess Everette	B28E		d.1968June Vernon Texas
Burgess Fancy Hill	A79K	1889Oct2	d.1972Aug19
Burgess Fannie	A76F	1878Ca	m.1901Mar1
Burgess Fate	A70E	1850Ca	
Burgess Flora Jane	B15G	1878Feb5	b.p.Mo/Albany m.1898Dec21
Burgess Foster F	A80L		
Burgess Francis	F30I	1844Nov21	
Burgess Francis F	F30E	1832Jan15	
Burgess Frank	B13J	1873	b.p.Kans

NAME	NUMBER	BIRTH	COMMENTS
Burgess Frank	Z38G		of Greene Co/Mo
Burgess Frankey	A38F		m.1800Jul11 Rowan Co/NC
Burgess Fred M	B28D		m.1953Aug6 Of Parnell Mo
Burgess Geneva	A80J		
Burgess George	F32A		
Burgess George	B04B	1657Ca	b.p.Md/Anne Ar Co m aft 1682 d1704Md
Burgess George	F18F	1767Jun12	b.p.Md/Anne Ar. Co
Burgess George	F12A		Died young or returned to England
Burgess George A	A79I	1894Jan8	m.1916Mar29
Burgess George Erwin	B15F	1876Jun23	m.1902Mar2(2)1915Jan27 d1963Albany Mo
Burgess George Milton	B32B	1930Jun5	b.p.Tex Port Arthur m1950May22 d1961La
Burgess George W	A39C	1804Jan8	d.1872Mar26 or 1873
Burgess George W	F29C	1848	
Burgess George W.	B13E	1863Jan10	b.p.Mo/Newton Co m.1885Oct11 d.1935Mo
Burgess Grace Marie	F57A	1884Dec15	b.p.Kans.LaCygne m.1902Jan20 d1968 Ok.
Burgess Guy	A91G		of St.Joseph, Mo
Burgess Harriet	F23E		
Burgess Harvey	A79E	1883Mar10	d.1930Jun5
Burgess Henry	F56A	1843	b.p. Mo/Gasconade Co
Burgess Henry	A76G	1881Dec22	d.1938May29
Burgess Henry Clay	F30J	1844Nov21	
Burgess Hershel Glenn	B25A	1906Feb14	b.p. Mo./Gentry Co. Darlington
Burgess Hetty	F23H		
Burgess Hilda Eunice	F54B	1904May29	b.p. Mo/Fuersville
Burgess Hiram	A39J	1820Ca	Nickname John
Burgess Hiram Mrs	A39Ja	1820Ca	Indian. No issue
Burgess Hiram Simpson	A78A	1859Feb8	m.1879Jan31 d.1896Jul11
Burgess Honor	B08I	1773Jul1	
Burgess Howard L.	A75D	1917Sep2	d.1961Oct22. Middle name: Lafayette
Burgess Husley	A64I		In fathers Will 1757Jul23 Anne Ar CoMd
Burgess Ibby	A66G	1828Ca	
Burgess Ida	A92C		of St. Joseph Mo.
Burgess Ida Lou	A77B	1906Apr12	m.1922Aug d1975Jan20
Burgess Irene	F57E	1893Jan7	b.p.Ark/Indian Terr.
Burgess Irvin	A79B	1880Sep29	m.1902Feb2
Burgess Isaac	B03G		b. early 1600's England
Burgess Isaac W	A66D	1844Jul6	d.1928Jan19
Burgess Isabelle	F56D	1849	b.p. Mo
Burgess Jacki Sue	B43A	1953Sep7	b.p. Mo. m1978Sep23
Burgess Jacob Isaac	A79D	1885Ca	
Burgess James	A76C	1865Feb10	d.1947Jan16
Burgess James	A69C	1835Ca	
Burgess James	A90H		
Burgess James	F56C	1847	b.p. Mo
Burgess James	B13K	1875	b.p. Newton Co Mo or Kans.
Burgess James Arthur	B18B	1880Jun7	d.1959Apr22 Parnell Mo
Burgess James B	B15H	1880Jul14	b.p. Mo Albany. d18800ct30 Albany Mo
Burgess James Crawford	A67C	1832Jul28	d.1877Jun2
Burgess James Fred.	F35F	1855Feb24	b.p.Fuersville Mo d1877Apr4 unmarried

NAME	NUMBER	BIRTH	COMMENTS
Burgess James M	B10A	1808	b.p.Tenn m(2)1845Mar16 d1851Denver Mo.
Burgess James Sr	B09A	1778Ca	b.p. No.Car
Burgess James William	A76I	1883Jun15	d.1950Jun23
Burgess James Zebedee	A72C	1930Jul28	of Atlanta Georgia
Burgess Jane	B06G		
Burgess Jane	A34G		d.1825 Single
Burgess Jane	B04Ga		b. Mid 1600's
Burgess Jane	B08P	1767Feb6	m.1786Feb1
Burgess Jane	A64C	1746Oct14	In fathers Will 1757Jul23 Anne Ar CoMd
Burgess Jane C	F34F	1828	
Burgess Jean Mrs	A80Ia		
Burgess Jefferson	A90Ga		m.1824Jun28 Mason Co/Ky
Burgess Jeremiah	B03D		b. in early 1600's In England
Burgess Jesse	B18A		of Vernon Texas
Burgess Jessie	F57F	1897Jul2	b.p.Ark/Indian Terr.
Burgess Jewell Vey	B23B	1905Aug26	d.1906 Albany Mo
Burgess Jimmie Frank	A77G	1915Oct6	
Burgess Jody	A76D	1870	d.1946
Burgess Joe	A69A	1833	d.1911Jun11
Burgess Joe	A66I	1835Ca	
Burgess Joel	A39F	1810May	d.1880May16
Burgess John	F29D	1850	
Burgess John	A34A		of Montg. Co Md m.1800Mar19 d1313Jul13
Burgess John	B04E		b.p.Md/Anne Ar Co b.aft1664 d.bef1700
Burgess John	F34A	1833Jun25	b.p.NoCar m.1853Mar10 d.1890Dec21 Mo
Burgess John	F17A		m.1798Mar14 Anne Ar. CoMd.
Burgess John	F56E	1852	b.p. Mo
Burgess John	F19A		In father's Will 10Jan1779
Burgess John	B05E	1696Aug17	b.p.Md Anne Ar Co So.Riv.Par.d.1774
Burgess John	A64F	1753May24	b.p. Md.Anne Ar Co.All Hallows d1780
Burgess John	B13F	1865	b.p. Kans or Newton Co Mo
Burgess John	A66L	1837Ca	
Burgess John	B08A	1751Nov20	d. Without issue
Burgess John	A67E	1845Ca	
Burgess John	B09C	1787	b.p.No.Car. In 1830Census Gasc Co.Mo
Burgess John	A70F		
Burgess John Brice	F16D		d.1815. Md. Anne Ar Co. Without issue
Burgess John Capt	F14D	1766Jan24	m.1785Jul27 d.1821Oct7 Mont.Co Md.
Burgess John Col	B07C	1725Jun8	b.p.Md/Anne Ar Co m.1755Ca Census 1790
Burgess John D	A90A	1798	b.p.Md.Anne ArCo.m.1822Oct17d1874Nov26
Burgess John Dorsey	F20A		of Mason Co. Ky by 1800
Burgess John E	F30G	1835Oct4	
Burgess John Franklin	A72H	1941Aug18	m.1960
Burgess John H	F21H		b.p.Md/Prob in Montgomery Co
Burgess John Linville	A79G	1887Apr15	m.1908Oct11 d.1954Feb5
Burgess John Magruder	F11G		m.1779Oct18 (2)1794Feb26
Burgess John Price B.	A35A	1764Apr5	
Burgess John R	A91E		of St. Joseph Mo
Burgess John Raymond	F54A	1901Jun4	b.p.Mo/Fuersville umm. buMarshall Mo.

NAME	NUMBER	BIRTH	COMMENTS
Burgess John Shirley	A76A	1858Jun14	d.1933Aug29
Burgess John W	B11B	1832Feb2	b.p.Tn.OfGentryCo/Mo d.1907May31Joplin
Burgess John Wesley	F35D	1871Mar17	b.p. Mo/Fuersville m.1904Mar d1927Jun9
Burgess John West	F15C		m.1787Feb3 Md/Anne Ar Co.
Burgess John William	F30H	1837Mar29	Two John siblings recorded
Burgess Joseph	B04F	1665abt	b.p.Md/Anne Ar Co So.Riv. d young
Burgess Joseph	B07D	1727Jun27	b.p. Md/Anne Ar Co m.1751Jan13 d.1806
Burgess Joseph	B08L	1780Sep2	
Burgess Joseph	F22G	1799Dec29	d. single
Burgess Joseph	B03B		b.p.Eng In Md. but returned to England
Burgess Joseph	A78G	1860Abt	
Burgess Joseph	F61C		of Sparta Ill.
Burgess Joseph Capt	B08B	1753Jan20	d.1778Nov17in Am. Rev
Burgess Joseph Charles	F56H	1860Sep15	b.p.Mo Vienna m.1880Dec16Ark d.1931Ok.
Burgess Joseph Daniel	A70A	1839Ca	d.1913
Burgess Joseph Henry	F35C	1863Oct19	unm. d.1889Apr20 Of Jewell Col.Liberty
Burgess Joseph Matson	B10G	1812	b.p. Mo. d.1854Nov25Gasc. Co/Mo
Burgess Joseph V	A90K		b.p. Ky m.1832Dec26 Mason Co/Ky
Burgess Joshua	F22I	1807Jul18	
Burgess Joshua Capt	B08G	1769Jul3	b.p. Md/Anne Ar Co. m1790 d1731Oct15Ky
Burgess Joshua Kate	F30D	1830Mar13	
Burgess Joshua Randall	B53A	1976Feb4	of Sulphur La.
Burgess Judson C	F31A		d.1894 single
Burgess Julia Lyn	B42A	1951Apr18	of Joplin Mo
Burgess Juliana	F32B		
Burgess Juliana	F21F		
Burgess Juliet	F23C		
Burgess Katherine Mrs	B04Ba		b. Mid 1600's Of Md. Returned to Eng.
Burgess Katie	A91F		of St. Joseph Mo
Burgess Kent Kenard	A80G		
Burgess Lidey	B08K	1777Dec9	
Burgess Lloyd	F61B		of Sparta Ill.
Burgess Loris Ann	B42B	1953Oct21	of Joplin Mo
Burgess Lou	Z38D		of Greene Co Mo
Burgess Louis	F29G		d. Without issue.
Burgess Lucinda	A69B	1833Aug31	d.1911May19
Burgess Lucinda	F61E		
Burgess Lucy	F57H		
Burgess Lucy	F62Aa	1774	d.1852Jan1
Burgess Lula Mae	A76S	1903	d.1958
Burgess Lunsford	A35C	1762Sep20	b.p.Va/Stafford Co St.Pauls Parish
Burgess Mabel	B19B	1891	d.1894 Death: Spinal meningitus
Burgess Malenda	F34J		b.p.Mo/Gasc. Co (now Osage)
Burgess Malissa J	A68C		of Arkansas
Burgess Margaret	A67A	1846Ca	
Burgess Margaret	A39G	1815abt.	
Burgess Margaret	A34E		m.1804Sep5
Burgess Margaret	B05G	1698Ca	b.p.Md/Anne Ar Co ch1698Nov13 m.1710
Burgess Margaret Ann	F26C		

73

NAME	NUMBER	BIRTH	COMMENTS
Burgess Margaret Ann	A72F	1938Jun9	m.1957
Burgess Margaret E.	B29B	1911Nov19	b.p.Kans, Lane m1932May10NY(2)1945Aug
Burgess Margaret L	B32A	1926Sep27	m(1)1946Dec23
Burgess Marjorie Lee	B30A	1922May19	b.p.Mo/Joplin m.1945Sep12
Burgess Mark Robert	B43D	1964Apr7	of Jefferson Cy/Mo
Burgess Martha	A77F	1914Apr6	m.1953Sep
Burgess Martha	A66A	1838Aug21	d.1872
Burgess Martha Almina	B15J	1884May9	b.p.Mo/Albany m.1906Dec23 d1956Oct27
Burgess Martha Amanda	F35A	1866Mar18	b.p.Mo/Osage Co m.1893Aug24 d.1939Aug
Burgess Martha Ameriws	A75B	1912May12	
Burgess Martha Jane	A79H	1892Jan12	m.1913Jun29
Burgess Martha Ruth A	F34H	1843	b.p. Mo/Gasc.Co(now Osage) m.1867d1878
Burgess Martin	B13M	1859	b.p.Mo/Gentry Co d.Gentry Co
Burgess Mary	A39I	1818Feb9	
Burgess Mary	B07F	1730Jan27	of Md.Anne Ar Co In father's Will 1773
Burgess Mary	B03F		b.p.Eng. In early 1600's
Burgess Mary	F31D		
Burgess Mary	C15Ha		
Burgess Mary	B07K	1743Dec25	
Burgess Mary	B13G	1867	b.p. Kans. or NewtonCo Mo
Burgess Mary	A34I		
Burgess Mary	A38D	1767Ca	b.p.Va/Stafford Co ch1767Jul7
Burgess Mary	F18J	1773Apr21	
Burgess Mary	A78H	1860abt	
Burgess Mary A	A70C	1843	
Burgess Mary Ann	F27C		
Burgess Mary Ann	F32D		
Burgess Mary Ann	A79J	1896Mar2	m.1916Apr19 d.1948Jan26
Burgess Mary Ann	A76H	1883	
Burgess Mary Ann M	B11C	1834Feb28	b.p.Tn. or Mo. d.1907Feb3 Joplin,Mo
Burgess Mary Clara	B10H	1809	
Burgess Mary E	C28Ba	1820Mar4	m.1846Sep14 d.1881Sep2 Mo.Gasc Co.
Burgess Mary E	F34D	1820	
Burgess Mary E	A66H	1841Ca	
Burgess Mary Elizabeth	A66C	1842Aug29	d.1925Jul25
Burgess Mary Elvira	B10F	1802	b.p.Tenn/ d Bay Mo after 1880
Burgess Mary Elvira	C27Aa		
Burgess Mary Evaline	F35J	1875Sep2	b.p.Mo/Fuersville unm. d.1929Jan1 Mo
Burgess Mary Hollyday	F10H	1773	b.p.Md/Prince Georges Co.
Burgess Mary Kathleen	B25D	1911Sep25	b.p. Mo/Albany
Burgess Mary Leoma	A67L	1850May	d.1926Nov3
Burgess Mary M	A91B		of St.Joseph Mo
Burgess Mary Mrs	B06Ea		of Md/Anne Ar Co
Burgess Mary Patricia	B30B	1923May13	b.p.Mo/Joplin m.1946Aug23
Burgess Mary T	F30B	1825May2	
Burgess Matilda	F15A		
Burgess Matilda Jane	B13B	1857	b.p.Mo/Newton Co d. Infant
Burgess Mattie W	A92B		of St.Joseph Mo
Burgess Mayhue Blaine	A71E	1884Jun4	d.1955Dec3

NAME	NUMBER	BIRTH	COMMENTS
Burgess Megan Eliz.	B53B	1980Nov4	b.p. La/Sulphur
Burgess Michael	F22F	1796Aug1	
Burgess Michael D	A90J		m.1839Dec4 Mason Co/Ky
Burgess Michael Ens.	B08C	1754Apr11	b.p.Md/Anne Ar Co m1783Oct22 Am.Rev.
Burgess Mildred Eliz.	B25C	1909Apr30	b.p.Mo/Albany
Burgess Milly	A38E		m(1)1787Oct9Rowan Co/N.C.There in 1826
Burgess Minnie	A91C		of St.Joseph Mo
Burgess Minnie Mrs	B28Da		
Burgess Mordecai	A88F		
Burgess Mordecai	F11A		b.p.Md d.1786 Will indicates no desc.
Burgess Mordecai	A90C		m.1820Mar20 Mason Co Ky
Burgess Mordecai	F18H	1769Nov5	b.p.Md/Anne Ar Co/All Hallows Parish
Burgess Moses	A37C	1742Dec2	b.p.Va/Stafford Co m.1762May30 Va.
Burgess Nancy	F21B		
Burgess Nancy	B08J	1775Sep15	
Burgess Nancy	F27D		
Burgess Nancy	F22D	1796Mar31	
Burgess Nancy	A76N	1890 abt	
Burgess Nancy Jane	A67G	1839Dec17	d.1891Oct16
Burgess Nancy Mrs	B10Ga		
Burgess Nathan	A77D	1909Jun4	m.1936Mar17
Burgess Nellie	F57D	1890Dec9	b.p.Ark/Indian Terr.
Burgess Nellie	A39K	1820 abt	
Burgess Octavia	K27B		of Vienna Mo
Burgess Oliver	A76R		m.1901 d.1913Dec22
Burgess Olli	A80H		
Burgess Orlando Ransom	B15A	1868Jan18	b.p.Mo/Albany m1892Mar27 d.1913Apr20
Burgess Osgood	F20B		m.1809Dec20
Burgess Otto	A80B	1915Ca	
Burgess Parisetta	A76B	1865	
Burgess Pee	A70I		
Burgess Peregrine	F23B		
Burgess Perry A	B11H	1848	b.p.Mo/Gentry Co Settled in DenverColo
Burgess Perry Andrew	B15I	1881Sep22	b.p.Mo/Albany m.1905Feb10 d1928Mar28Mo
Burgess Peyton	A67F	1845abt	
Burgess Philemon	B08M	1761Dec13	m.1800Feb18
Burgess Phoebe Dela W	F17E		m.1790Jan2
Burgess Phoebe Eliz.	B15B	1869May31	b.p.Mo/Albany m1892Jan10 d.1944Mar19Mo
Burgess Polly A	A68E		
Burgess Polly Ann	A76J	1890abt	
Burgess Pretteman P	A71D	1882Oct11	d.1944Jan21
Burgess Priscilla Mrs	B070a		of Md/Anne Ar. Co
Burgess Rachel	B06H		
Burgess Rachel	F27G		
Burgess Ralph	A80F		
Burgess Ray Elmer	B19E	1902Nov10	b.p.Mo/Joplin m1925Dec25 Paris Mo Twin
Burgess Rebecca	A66B	1838Aug21	d.1925Apr18
Burgess Rebecca	F27E		
Burgess Rebecca	F22H	1802Jun5	m.1825Dec21

NAME	NUMBER	BIRTH	COMMENTS
Burgess Rebecca Mrs	A64Fa		
Burgess Rebecca O	F23G		
Burgess Reuben Jr	A38C	1777Jun14	b.p.Va/Stafford Co of Rowan Co No.Car
Burgess Reuben Sr	A37D	1744Feb12	b.p.Va/Stafford Co m.1765Sep d1820 NC.
Burgess Richard	F31B		
Burgess Richard	F26B		
Burgess Richard	B08E	1757Sep1	b.p.Md/Anne Ar Co m.1778Feb25 daft1808
Burgess Richard	A88B		of Md/Prince Georges Co d1784 Md.
Burgess Richard	F10B	1761Mar2	b.p.Md/Prince Georges Co Queen Ann Par
Burgess Richard	A78B	1860Abt	
Burgess Richard Ens.	F11B		m.1782Sep17Md/PrinceGeo.Co In Am. Rev
Burgess Richard Herb	A71I	1895Oct17	d.1967May31
Burgess Richard Herb.	A72A	1926Dec15	m.1950
Burgess Richard Jr	F18C	1762Apr25	b.p.Md/Anne Ar Co
Burgess Richard Sr	B06E	1724Ca	b.p. Md/Anne Ar. Co
Burgess Robert E	B31A	1924Dec17	b.p.Mo/Joplin m.1949Apr16
Burgess Robin Ann	B43C	1958Oct17	m.1978Dec16
Burgess Roderick	F22B	1787Feb18	b.p.Md/Howard Co d.1852 Without issue
Burgess Roger Glenn	B45A	1951Jul31	b.p.La/Lake Charles Atty Sulphur La
Burgess Rose Lee	A80D		
Burgess Ross	A80A		
Burgess Roy Arthur	B19F	1902Nov10	b.p.Mo/Joplin m.1929Jan31 of Carmel NY
Burgess Ruth	B08F	1763May10	m.1778 d.1835
Burgess Ruth	F21D		
Burgess Ruth	F29F		
Burgess Ruth	A90F		
Burgess Sallie	A77E	1911Apr13	
Burgess Sallie Marg.	A71C	1880May15	d.1901Oct29
Burgess Sally	F32E		
Burgess Sally	A90I		
Burgess Samuel	B07H	1735Feb28	b.p.Md/Anne Ar Co d.1773Anne Ar.
Burgess Samuel	F18A	1758Sep10	b.p.Md/Anne Ar Co All Hallows Par
Burgess Samuel	F17C		m.1809Dec1
Burgess Samuel	B03C		b.p.Eng early 1600´s
Burgess Samuel	A64B	1744Jan19	d. young
Burgess Samuel	F33B		
Burgess Samuel Chew	B05F	1698	b.p.Md/Anne Ar. ch1698Nov13 m.1716Apr3
Burgess Samuel W. Mrs	F16Ca		Probably a Warfield
Burgess Samuel West	F16C		d.1815
Burgess Samuel#2	A64H		b. bet.1757-1763 Fathers Will 1757Jul
Burgess Sanders	F16B		
Burgess Sandra Sue	F53A	1937Jun10	m.1961Jun3 Topeka Kans.
Burgess Sarah	A34J		m.1787Feb19 Md/Fredericks Co.
Burgess Sarah	F14B	1762	b.p.Md/ of Mason Co./Ky
Burgess Sarah	B06B	1719Ca	b.p.Md/Anne Ar Co So.Riv Par Unmarried
Burgess Sarah	A64G	1756Oct22	b.p.Md/AnneAr Co
Burgess Sarah	F18G	1769Nov5	
Burgess Sarah	B07E	1727Feb2	
Burgess Sarah	F11C		m.1790Apr28

NAME	NUMBER	BIRTH	COMMENTS
Burgess Sarah	A68G		
Burgess Sarah	B08N	1769Jan21	
Burgess Sarah	A76E	1872abt	
Burgess Sarah Ann	F21E		m.1827Feb3
Burgess Sarah Ellen	F30A	1823Sep18	
Burgess Sarah Manerva	B10E		
Burgess Sarah Maria	B05H	1698abt	b.p.Md ch.1698Nov13 m1709Sep8 d.1750Md
Burgess Sarah Mrs	B05Aa		m.1713Jan12
Burgess Sarah Mrs	B07Aa	1725abt	
Burgess Shela Taft	A75A	1910Nov29	d.1963Nov11
Burgess Sheridan	A90E		
Burgess Simon Peter	A79F	1885Feb4	
Burgess Simpson	A80K		
Burgess Sophia	B05J		
Burgess Sophia EwenMrs	B03Ab	1635abt	of Anne Arundel Co/Md
Burgess Stella	F57G		
Burgess Susan	B10C	1301	d.1832Oct
Burgess Susan	F28B		
Burgess Susan F	B11G	1846	b.p. Mo of Gentry Co and Newton Co.Mo
Burgess Susan Mrs	F10Da		
Burgess Susanna	B05I	1699Mar14	b.p. Md/Anne Ar Co So.Riv d.bef1742
Burgess Susanna	B04K		b.p.Md/Anne Ar Co b.aft 1684 m1700Jul.
Burgess Susanna	B04C		b.p. Md/Anne Ar Co So.Riv In Will 1686
Burgess Susanna Mrs	B07Jb		m.1787Apr6 Md. J.Mercer widow d.1794Ca
Burgess Susannah	B07N	1754Feb1	b.p. Md/Anne Ar Co All Hallows Par.
Burgess Thomas	A34H		of Montgomery Co Md.1788
Burgess Thomas	F34I	1838Ca	b.p. Mo/Gasc Co(Now Osage Co)
Burgess Thomas	F22E	1784Jul1	b.p. Md/Anne Ar Co m.1820Dec1
Burgess Thomas	A39H		Went to Mo then Ark. In Indian Wars
Burgess Thomas	F19B	1775abt	In fathers Will 1779Jan10
Burgess Thomas	B13A	1855	b.p.Mo/Newton Co
Burgess Thomas	F56B	1845	b.p. Mo/Gasconade Co
Burgess Thomas	F25A		Mentioned in Edward's Will 1824
Burgess Thomas	A33A		b.p.Va/Stafford Co Of N.C.,Tenn d1830
Burgess Thomas	A66J	1834Ca	
Burgess Thomas	B28C		d.1948Aug. Modesto Calif.
Burgess Thomas A	A78C	1863Feb17	d.1927Dec11
Burgess Thomas Dorsey	F23F		
Burgess Thomas Dr	F61A		of Nashville Ill.
Burgess Thomas Edward	A72E	1936Apr7	m.1954
Burgess Thomas Erwin	B11E	1838Jan31	b.p.Tn.or Gasc Co Mo m1867Mar3 d1915
Burgess Thomas Erwin	B25B	1907Aug23	b.p.Mo/Albany
Burgess Thomas J. Jr	A92A		of St. Joseph Mo
Burgess Thomas Jeff	F30C	1828Jun15	b.p.Ky/ In St Joseph Mo/1850
Burgess Thomasine	F16A	1766Sep10	
Burgess Tom	A67H	1840abt	
Burgess Tommasin	F27B		
Burgess Tony	Z38F		of Greene Co Mo
Burgess Upton	A90D		m.1834Jan4 Mason Co/Ky

NAME	NUMBER	BIRTH	COMMENTS
Burgess Ursula	F11E		b.p. Md
Burgess Ursula	B06F	1726Ca	b.p. Md/Anne Ar Co ch.1726Dec11 d1792
Burgess Ursula	A64D	1748Nov27	
Burgess Ursula	A88D	1703ca	b.p. Md. ch.1703Aug13
Burgess Ursula	A99C		In fathers Will Annapolis Md 1748Dec6
Burgess Vachel	F23I		
Burgess Vachel Capt	B08D	b1756May9	b.p. Md/Anne Ar Co m.1782Oct1 d1824Apr
Burgess Valda Fern	F54C	1907Nov18	b.p.Mo/Fuersville d.1982 May Marshall
Burgess Valentine	A68A	1843Nov10	m.1879Oct2 Justice Peace Warren Co. Mo
Burgess Vance DeKalb	A67K	1845Oct21	d.1932Jun22
Burgess Vardry Jeff.	F35I	1868Sep7	d.1928Dec31 unmarried
Burgess Vardry Rev	F34B	1817	b.p. N.C. In Gasc.Co/Mo1840 m.1840
Burgess Viana Artella	A71H	1894Jul5	d.1895Jan6
Burgess Vicie	B11D	1840	
Burgess Vilsie Marie	B23A	1902Oct24	b.p.Mo/Albany d.Albany Mo
Burgess Vinney	A38G		m.1813Jan7 Rowan Co No.Car
Burgess Virlene	A68K		
Burgess W. Thomas	K26Aa	1850abt	of Maries Co Mo
Burgess W.M.	A91D		
Burgess Walter Smith	F10G	1771Jan21	b.p.Md/Prince Georges Co.
Burgess Washington	F21I	1779Nov28	b.p.Md/Prob Mont.Co m1824Jan17 d.1857
Burgess Waymon L	A68B		
Burgess West	B07I	1737Nov23	b.p.Md/Anne Ar Co d. In Am.Rev 1777
Burgess West Jr	F16E	1777	b.p.Md/Anne Ar Co m.1803Aug3 d1825 Md
Burgess William	B02A	1595ca	b.p.England Truro,Cornwall
Burgess William	B05D	1684Nov19	Md/Anne Ar Co.All Hallows Par No issue
Burgess William	A39A		
Burgess William	A88E		
Burgess William	F29H		
Burgess William	B13C	1858	b.p. Mo/Newton Co
Burgess William	A38B	1769Jun15	b.p.Va/Stafford Co St.Pauls Par
Burgess William	A37A		m.1755Jan19
Burgess William	B07A	1721Oct9	b.p.Md/Anne Ar Co All Hallows d1763
Burgess William	A78E	1860abt	
Burgess William	A64E	1751Jun10	
Burgess William	B08H	1771Feb9	b.p. Md/Anne Ar Co
Burgess William	F22K	1810Mar17	m.1835Sep22
Burgess William	B09B		b. bet 1780-1790 NC d.1845 Gasc Co/Mo
Burgess William	A79C	1885 abt	
Burgess William	B04D	1665 abt	b.p.Md/Anne Ar Co m1697Aug13 d1698Jun
Burgess William	B03A	1622	b.p.Eng d1687Md/ In Am.1650ca.Anne Ar.
Burgess William Burley	B10D		
Burgess William Burton	B11J	1855ca	of Newton Co/Mo
Burgess William D	A91A		of St.Joseph Mo
Burgess William Fred.	F10D	1765Jan15	b.p.Md/Prince Georges Co
Burgess William Howard	A72D	1932Aug19	m.1951Jun3
Burgess William K	A70G	1855Aug27	d.1937Feb24
Burgess William McKin.	A75E	1919Dec24	
Burgess William Mrs	B10Da		

NAME	NUMBER	BIRTH	COMMENTS
Burgess William P	F21G		m.1816Apr29
Burgess William Simp.	A67B	1830Aug20	d.1905Jul30
Burgess William Thomas	F35B	1854Jul19	d.1877Apr17 Bland Mo.unmarried
Burgess William W.	F61D	1841Jan22	d.1913Sep26
Burgess William Walter	B15D	1872Sep12	b.p.Mo/Albany d.1881 or 1891 Albany Mo
Burgess Willie Mrs	A80Ka		
Burgess Willis	A78D	1860abt	
Burgess Winfield S	A67M	1852Feb25	d.1905May2
Burgess Zebedee	A75F	1923Mar3	of Detroit Mich. 1982
Burgess Zenith Bloom.	A71A	1876Feb5	d.1876Feb24
Burks Celia	S13Dam		
Burnett James	T25Da		of Howell Co Mo
Burns Albert Taylor	G51I		
Burns Alvis	G59B		of Texas
Burns Burton	G51C	1848Apr14	m.1872Sep15(2)1883Jun29 d.1920Nov29
Burns Carney	G59A		of Maries Co Mo
Burns Charity	G57G		of Dixon Mo
Burns Dulcie	G57F		of Maries Co Mo
Burns Edith	G60A		
Burns Elizabeth	G53E		d. Miller Co Mo
Burns Eugene	G61C		of Ohio
Burns George	T28Aa		of Henry Co Mo
Burns George G	G51F		
Burns Gertie	G57H		of Rolla Mo
Burns Griselda	G57E		of Maries Co Mo
Burns Henry	G50A		b.p. Tenn.(East) of Maries Co Mo
Burns Henry	G52C		of Maries and Taney Cos/Mo
Burns Henry Carroll	G53B		d. Miller Co Mo
Burns Henry Mrs	G50Aa		m. in Tenn
Burns India	G58C		of Springfield Mo
Burns Isaac H	G51H		of Vienna Mo Surveyor,assessor,judge
Burns J. Cleve	G57J		of Franklin Co/Mo
Burns James	G51A		Captured as Conf. soldier Civil War
Burns James	G52A		of Maries and Taney Cos Mo
Burns James	G53A		d. Miller Co Mo
Burns James M	G57D		of Maries Co Mo
Burns Jeff	G57A		of Okla
Burns Jennie	G57C		m1898Mar23 of Union Mo
Burns John	G57B		of Colo.
Burns John	G49A		b.p.SoC. d Maries Co Mo of Tn. Mo 1832
Burns John Mrs	G49Aa		
Burns Julian	G50B		Moved to Taney Co after Civil War
Burns Livinia	G50E		m. Maries Co Mo
Burns Lucinda	G50D		m. Maries Co Mo d.Maries Co
Burns Mabel	G60B		of New Lexington Mo
Burns Malinda	G59D		of Okla
Burns Margery	G60D		of Dallas Texas
Burns Marie	G59E		of Union Mo
Burns Martha	G52B		of Maries and Taney Cos/Mo

NAME	NUMBER	BIRTH	COMMENTS
Burns Mary	G51D		
Burns Mary	G50F		d. single
Burns Matilda	G53D		of Binghamton NY
Burns Minerva	G51E		
Burns Pearl	G61B		of Ohio
Burns Polly	G53C		of Illinois
Burns Preston	G58B		m.Calif.
Burns Ransom	G51B		d. in Confederate Army Civil War
Burns Robert	G58A		of Laurel Montana
Burns Roland	G50C		m. in Tenn d Union Army Civil War
Burns Ruth	G61A		of Ohio
Burns Sophia	G57I		m.1909May27 of Franklin Co Mo
Burns Stella	G59C		of Maries Co Mo
Burns Thomas	G56A		d. in Okla
Burns Viola	G60C		of Topeka Kans
Burns William	G51G		
Burns William	G60E		of St. Louis Mo
Burrows Charles	G14Ba		
Burrows Susan C	C28Cb	1839Sep25	b.p. Mo/Perry Co m.1863Nov13 d1914Ark.
Burton -	J23Ca		of Pershing Mo
Burton Frank	G66Fa		of Dixon Mo
Burton Nancy	P10Aa		of McMinn Co Tn. To Mo.1830´s d1376
Burton William	D15Aa		m.1815Nov4 Tenn/Grainger Co
Bush J	A15Ka		
Bush R.T.	A76Ma	1900 abt	
Bushrod Hannah	B98Da		
Bussell Moniza Carol.	A73Ea	1865 abt	
Butcher George	G21Ba		of Maries Co Mo
Butcher Thomas	C38Ea		of Springfield Mo
Butler Jane	B97Aa		m.1715abt d1729
Butler Samuel Rev	Q32Ga		of Franklin Co Mo. In Confederate Army
Cahill -	D63C		of Owensville Mo
Cahill James	D23Ga		
Cahill John	D63A		of Gasconade Co/Mo
Cahill Walter	D63B		of near Canaan/Mo
Caldwell A	A13Ca		
Caldwell Elizabeth	A60Aa	1733	d.1818
Caldwell Jane	G56Aa		of Okla
Caldwell John	A60Aaf		
Caldwell Louisiana	D27Cam	1813Mar30	b.p.Mo/Washington Co. m1838Jan4 d1873
Caldwell Sarah	G51Cb		m.1883Jun29
Callaway Emaline	I18Ca		
Callaway Flanders	I15Da		m.1777 of Warren Co/Mo
Callaway James	I21B		d.1815 War of 1812. Of Warren Co/Mo
Callaway John B	I21A		d.1825 Of St.Chas.,Warren Cos./Mo
Callaway Richard	I15Daf		d.1780 Killed by Indians in Ky
Calvert Rodham	F32Ea		
Camden John	E31Ga		
Camp Elmer	Z34Ha		m.1899Apr23

NAME	NUMBER	BIRTH	COMMENTS
Campbell –	Y55Ca		of Ponca Cy/Okla
Campbell –	M25Fa		of Maries Co/Mo
Campbell Addie	E43Fa		of Jefferson Cy/Mo
Campbell Elizabeth	E17Ab	1811	1st Husband James Hawkinsm(2)1840Dec31
Campbell Evelyn Edith	D88C	1909Mar31	b.p.Mo/Bland of St. Louis Mo
Campbell Ida	A78Ba	1860 abt	
Campbell James	R14Da		
Campbell James McMein	D85B	1877Mar10	b.p.Mo/Fuersville m.1904Jun9 d1944Dec
Campbell Joseph	A76Ha	1880 abt	
Campbell Laura	A78Ga	1860 abt	
Campbell Malinda	D16Hb		m.1837Nov23 Gasc. Co/Mo
Campbell Malinda Eliz.	D85A		d. Springfield/Mo
Campbell Marie	D88B	1905Mar22	b.p.Mo/Bland m1960Feb20 of Ohio
Campbell Marlene	E91Aa		m.1961Aug12
Campbell Morris K	R12Fa		
Campbell Nancy	A39Jb		
Campbell Nevada C	D85C	1880Jan29	d. Marshall Mo
Campbell Olive Eliz.	D88A		Died in infancy
Campbell Precious	C11Gb		m.1837Mar23 Mo/Gasc Co
Campbell Robert	E17Abf		
Campbell Robert H.	D21Ea	1848Jan23	b.p.MO/Osage Co m(1)1370Oct12 d1915Jun
Cannon Elizabeth	D58Ca		
Cannon Grant	A76Ba	1865 abt	
Cannon John	A76Nb	1890 abt	
Cannon Joseph	A76Nc	1900 abt	
Cansler –	I40Ca		
Cansler Allie	G31Ea		of Dixon and Vienna Mo.
Cansler Anna	I42Ca		
Cansler James H	V14Aa	1843Feb8	d.1885Apr13 Rolla Mo. Sheriff ViennaMo
Cansler James Mrs	G51Aa		
Cansler John	I46Caf		Killed in Maries Co Mo in Civil War
Cansler John	G51Aaf		
Cansler Nathan H.	V14Aaf	1822Sep15	d.1879Apr24
Cansler Nathan H.	I46Ca		
Carber Alexander	Z23A		of California
Carber Anna Louise	Z23F		of California
Carber Henry Jefferson	Z23C		of California
Carber Joel	Z14Aa		b.p.Mo/Gasc Co m.1853Feb27 California
Carber John C	Z23G		of California
Carber Lucinda Jane	Z23B		of California
Carber Melvina D	Z23E		d single
Carber Rose	Z23D		of California
Carley John	C37Ga		of Hickory Co/Mo
Carnes Ann	P11E		b.p.Tenn. d.Maries Co Mo
Carnes Edith E	P11D		b.p.Tenn Mo in abt 1835 m.OsageCo Mo
Carnes Elizabeth	P13A	1856Jan31	d1896Jan1 of Maries Co Mo
Carnes Ida M	P14E	1871	d.1938Aug22 Washington Mo
Carnes Jehu	P10A		of McMinn Co Tn. Mo. in abt1835 d1860
Carnes Jennie L	P14D		Entire life in Maries Co/Mo

NAME	NUMBER	BIRTH	COMMENTS
Carnes John F	P11I	1835	d.1871 Maries Co/Mo
Carnes Josiah	P09A		b.p.Va
Carnes Josiah Dr.	P11J		d Maries Co Mo early in Civil War
Carnes Josiah Mrs	P09Aa		of Virginia
Carnes Levi	P11H		b.p.Tn/ d1365May18 Civil War.Poisoned
Carnes Louisa	P14B		of Vienna Mo
Carnes Lydia Ann	P14A		
Carnes Mary	P13B	1858Jul28	d.1932Jan15 of Laclede and GreensCosMo
Carnes Mary	P11B		b.p. Tn/ To Missouri in mid-1830's
Carnes Mary	V18Ea		
Carnes Mary	P14C		d in Union Mo. Second initial P or R
Carnes Matilda	P11A		b.p.Tn/ m 1849 To Mo in mid 1830's
Carnes Nancy	P13C	1861Mar6	d.1887Jan1 Of Osage Co/Mo
Carnes Nancy J	P11C		b.p.Tn/ To Mo. in mid 1830's Osage Co
Carnes Thomas	P11F		b.p.Tn/ Of Osage Co Mo near Linn
Carnes William P	P11G	1830Dec11	b.p.Tn/McMinn Co m.1855 d1896Mar2
Carney Edna	Y29Da		of Phelps Co/Mo
Carr Mertie	A71Da	1884Aug26	d.1960Sep19
Carrington Julie	A76Da	1870 abt	
Carrington Malinda	Q33Fa		
Carroll Charles E	E63B	1887Oct25	b.p.Mo/Woolam m1916 d.1923Mar4 Wash.Mo
Carroll Charles W	E88H	1931Sep9	b.p.Mo/Union d.1971Jan11 SanDiego Ca.
Carroll Chester E	E88D	1922Feb1	b.p.Mo/Woolam m1939
Carroll Clarence M	E88B	1918May8	b.p.Mo/Woolam m1943Aug28
Carroll Daniel	E62G	1851	d.1934 Woolam Mo
Carroll Donald D	E91A	1939Jan21	m1961Aug12
Carroll Edith E	E88F	1927Apr30	b.p.Mo/Union m1944 d.1961Nov29
Carroll Eliza	Y22C	1821Aug15	b.p.Mo/St Louis Co
Carroll Emma S	E63G	1874Apr6	b.p.Mo. Woolam
Carroll Frank E	Y41B		of Pulaski Co Mo
Carroll George	E62F	1819	of Barry Mo/1850
Carroll Humbolt	Y41F		of Stanislaus Calif.
Carroll Jacob	E61Ba		m.1834Nov11
Carroll James H	E63F	1872Feb23	d.1872Oct3 Gasconade Co Mo
Carroll James J	Y22B		of Pulaski Co/Mo
Carroll James Wiley	E62C	1837	
Carroll Jennie	Y41G		
Carroll John	Y14Ba		m. in St.Louis d. abt 1842
Carroll John	E62D	1841	In Civil War
Carroll John H	Y41H		of Vienna Mo, near Gasconade River
Carroll John Jasper	E63D	1868Aug20	d. 1938Nov24 Union Mo
Carroll Jose	Y41D		of Pulaski Co Mo
Carroll Joseph M	E63J	1884Oct23	b.p. Mo/Woolam m.1916 d.1974Oct15 Mo
Carroll Juret	E62B	1836	
Carroll Kathy D	E92B	1963Nov27	
Carroll Kelly D	E92A	1962May7	
Carroll Kenneth L	E88E	1924Dec8	b.p.Mo/St.Louis m 1942
Carroll Kevin D	E92C	1964Nov4	
Carroll Laura	Y40A		of Denver Mo d. Childless

NAME	NUMBER	BIRTH	COMMENTS
Carroll Lida	Y40B		of Maries Co/Mo
Carroll Martha A	E63E	1870Aug23	d.1888Mar18 Gasconade Co Mo
Carroll Mary	Y41E		of Pulaski Co Mo
Carroll Mary Ellen	E63A	1890May25	b.p.Mo/Woolem m.1916Feb29Hermann d1934
Carroll Philip H	Y22A	1838Jan9	d.1899Jan4 Maries Co Mo
Carroll Raymond E	E88G	1929Aug25	b.p.Mo/Union
Carroll Robert L	Y41C		of Pulaski Mo
Carroll Sarah Ann	Y22D	1323Jun1	d.1887Jul18 Maries Co Mo
Carroll Sarah Jane	E62E	1843	m.4 Sep1864
Carroll Sarah Jane	E63C	1866Dec18	d.1868Dec15 Woolam Mo
Carroll Thomas H	E63H	1876Nov27	b.p.Mo Woolam d1945Jun18 Union Mo
Carroll Virgil E	E88A	1927Jan17	b.p. Mo/Woolam m.1940 Dec15
Carroll Warren D	E93C	1968Dec12	
Carroll Wayne D	E91B	1943Apr13	b.p.Mo St Clair m1960Sep12
Carroll Wayne D Jr	E93A	1961Mar9	
Carroll Wendy D	E93D	1968Dec12	
Carroll William August	E88C	1919Jun6	b.p.Mo Woolam m.1939
Carroll William D	E93B	1962Sep27	
Carroll William Jr	E62A		
Carroll William R	Y41A		of Pulaski Co Mo
Carroll William R	Y40C		of Phelps Co Mo
Carroll William Riley	E63I	1879May29	b.p.Mo/Woolam d1951 Jan18 Union Mo
Carroll William Sr	E61Aa	1808	b.p.No.C/ m.in 1830´s
Carruthers Elayne	B32Ba		
Carter Hiram	D26Fa		
Carter Lemuel	Q32Ha		d.In Confederate Army Little Rock Ark
Carter Lorenzo	Q32Hb		of Hickory Co Mo. In Union Army CivilW
Carter Louisa M	D36A		d1928May16
Carter R	D21Ha		
Carter Ransom	Q32Jb		
Carter Sally	A76Ca	1867Jun6	d1936May23
Caruthers Julia	A73Cb	1865 abt	
Caton Elizabeth	I21Aa		
Cauthon Cordella	C36Cb		
Chambers Hester	R29B		
Chambers James	H57Ca		of Maries and Phelps Cos/ Mo
Chambers Susan	R29C		
Chambers William	R29A		d single
Chambers William	R26Fa		of Phelps Co Mo
Champs Mildred	B98Ea		
Chandler Quintilla	G40Cam		
Chappell -	Q32Ia		of Cooper Co Mo
Chew Betty Mae	C41Aa		
Chew John	F42B	1687	m1708 d.1718
Chew John Col	F40A	1590	b.p.Eng/Chewton m.Va. d1653 Md
Chew Roy Jackson	C41Aaf		
Chew Samuel Col	F41A	1634	m1658 d1676 of Va and Md
Chew Sarah	F42A		b.p.Md/Anne Ar Co m aft 1676Jul d1740
Chew Sarah Mrs	F40Aa		

NAME	NUMBER	BIRTH	COMMENTS
Chrisenbury Washington	D18Bb	1846Oct28	
Christopher -	D13Ha		
Church R	A11Fa		
Churchill Mary B	A16Da		
Cladwell -	E31Aa		
Clagett Ninian	A34Ea		m.1804 Sep5
Clark John	A76Fa		m.1901Mar1
Clark Martha A.E.	H55Ba		of Rolla Mo
Clark Mary Ann	D58Ba		
Clark Stephen	H55Baf		
Clark Susan	B63Aa		d.1916Jul16 Bloomsburg Pa
Clark William	V18Hb		
Clatterbuck Ora	G34Da		of St Louis Mo
Clay Ann	E22Ia		of Osage Co Mo
Clay William	E22Iaf		
Clayton Martha	B62Ca	1910Mar17	m.1910Mar17
Cleeton Wilma June	B31Aa		m1949Apr16
Clemens Elizabeth	R18Aa		d.Maries Co Mo at age 97
Clements Ellen	Y13Ca		
Clements Mary	Y13Eb		
Clemmons Lillie	Y76Da		m.1925Feb20 of Maries Co Mo
Clemons -	E61Ha		
Cleton Dorothy Irene	C31Ba		m1955May27 of Harrisonville Mo
Clymer George W	Q43Ca		
Coale Susannah	B08Ha		
Coates Ellen	Y32Ab		d. Childless
Cobble Elizabeth Alice	F68Aa	1933Sep22	
Cochrane Edward A	A95Aa	1799	b.p.Tn/Rutherford Co d1893Oct20
Cochrane Miranda B	A96A	1827Oct7	b.p.Tn/Rutherford Co m1855Nov7 d1856Tn
Cock John	Q37Ea		of Phelps Co Mo
Coen -	R23Ba		of Madrid New Mexico
Coffey -	K21E		of Kansas Cy/Mo
Coffey -	K21A		of Minco Okla
Coffey -	K11H		
Coffey -	K21D		of Wheatland Mo
Coffey Alexander	K12B		m.1866Oct11 d1912Sep7
Coffey Altha	K19B		
Coffey Arlie	K21B		of Duncan Okla
Coffey Arthur	K18A		of Okla Cy Okla
Coffey Arthur B	K16H		of Portland Oregon
Coffey Belvia	K20C		of Wichita Kans
Coffey Benjamin I	K14E		
Coffey Bernice	K24B		of St Louis Mo
Coffey Bertie	K19A		d in infancy
Coffey Campbell	K11C	1831Mar	b.p. Mo/Maries Co d1892May8 Maries Co
Coffey Carney	K18C		of St Louis Mo
Coffey Cecil	K21G		of Weaubleau Cy/Mo
Coffey Cellus	K24A		of St Louis Mo
Coffey Cosy	K17B		of Salt Lake Cy Utah

84

NAME	NUMBER	BIRTH	COMMENTS
Coffey Dove	K13C		of Bolivar Mo
Coffey Earl	K23A		of Vienna Mo
Coffey Elizabeth	K11E		
Coffey Elizabeth	K15B		of Big Piney Mo
Coffey Ernest	K18B		of Tuscon Ariz.
Coffey Estelle P	K16I		of Vista Mo
Coffey Florence	K20B		of Kansas Cy Kans
Coffey George	K22A		of "western" Mo
Coffey Hiram Kimzey	K14F	1862	m.1886Jun13 d1925Nov13
Coffey Irvin	K15A	1871Feb14	d1896Feb8 single
Coffey Irvin	K11A		d.Maries Co Mo early in Civil War
Coffey Irvin E	K16A		d in infancy
Coffey Isabelle	K14B		no issue. Of Dixon Mo
Coffey Isabelle	K13B		of Clinton Mo
Coffey James	K12G		m.west.Mo d1890 Vista Mo
Coffey James H	K16E		of Osceola Mo
Coffey James S	K14A		of Dixon Mo
Coffey Jesse	K23C		of Vienna Mo
Coffey Jesse	K21C		of Carrollton Mo
Coffey John	K12A	1844Dec15	m 1866Oct11 Maries Co Mo d1881Sep6 Mo
Coffey John	K14D		d single
Coffey John	K17A		of Attica Kansas
Coffey John Richard	K13G	1859Aug11	
Coffey Lavina	K11D		d before 1875
Coffey Lawrence	K20A		d in infancy
Coffey Lennie	K23E		of Vienna Mo
Coffey Lillie E	K16G		of Kansas Cy/Mo
Coffey Lizzie	K23F		of Pacfic Mo
Coffey Martha	K12E		m1875Jul25 of WeableauCy Mo.,and Texas
Coffey Martha	K13A		of Weaubleau Cy Mo
Coffey Martha R	K16B		
Coffey Marvel	K10A		m. NoCar or Tn.To Mo/Maries Co in 1834
Coffey Mary E	K16F		of Selma Calif.
Coffey Mary F	K14C		m1879Sep19 d.1930Jul3 Of Freeburg Mo
Coffey Matilda	K13D	1857	d.1929
Coffey Nancy C	K16D		d.1921Nov21. No issue
Coffey Nellie	K13F	1862Nov22	d.1930Nov12 Minden Mines Mo
Coffey Oliver	K15C		of Vista Mo
Coffey Roy	K21F		of Weaubleau Cy Mo
Coffey Samuel	K12F		d abt 1888 Texas
Coffey Sherman	K23B		of Vienna Mo
Coffey Sidney	K23G		d1922 Mar17
Coffey Smith	K09A		
Coffey Squire	K11B	1825	m.1850 Of Maries and Hickory Cos Mo
Coffey Squire	K12D		m1876Oct2Maries Co Mo dabt 1920 Okla.
Coffey Squire	K15D	1875 abt	of Wichita Kans
Coffey Temperance	K11F		of Maries and Howell Cos Mo
Coffey Thomas	K23D		of Vienna Mo
Coffey William	K08A		Lived near Boones in No Car

NAME	NUMBER	BIRTH	COMMENTS
Coffey William	K12C		d.1880 of Rich Hill Mo
Coffey William B	K11G		d abt 1863
Coffey William B Mrs	K11Ga		Moved from Maries Co Mo to Oklahoma
Coffey William D.Boone	K13E	1856Dec14	d.1933Aug8 Of Western Mo
Coffey William M	K16C		of McClave Colo.
Cogbill Brian Carl	C24B	1944Mar14	
Cogbill Deborah Dawn	C25C	1953Jan6	
Cogbill Herbert Tracy	C20D	1923Sep27	b.p.Ok/Rockerville m1947Aug17 d1948Dec
Cogbill Ina Lois	C20A	1914Jan16	b.p.Mo/Joplin m(1)1930Mar17
Cogbill James Fred	C18Fa	1891Jan2	b.p.Mo/Newton Co m.1912May3 d1943Nov8
Cogbill James Marcus	C25B	1951Jul26	
Cogbill James Quentin	C20C	1918Aug12	b.p.Mo/Newton Co Spring Cy m1944Jan5
Cogbill Kelly Ross	C24D	1951Jul14	
Cogbill Linda Jean	C25A	1946Oct31	
Cogbill Lloyd Clayton	C20B	1916May3	b.p.Mo/Joplin
Cogbill Suzanne Helen.	C24C	1946Nov1	
Cogbill Tracy Lloyd	C24A	1942Oct1	
Colbert John	Z15Ba		of Calif
Cole W.C.	T15Ga		
Coleman Mary	Z12Ca		of San Jose Calif
Coles -	I58Ea		
Collier Amos T	M23C		
Collier Byron	M23H		
Collier David D	M23J		of Jefferson Co Mo
Collier Edna	M23D		
Collier Hiram	K37Da		d. Childless
Collier John W	M23B		of Phelps Co Mo
Collier Lou	M23I		of St Louis Mo
Collier Mary A	M23A		of near Arlington Mo
Collier Randall	F36Baf		
Collier Robert	F36Ba		
Collier Sidney J	M23F		of Joplin Mo
Collier Thomas J	M23G		of Kansas
Collier William E	M15Aa	1826Oct1	b.p.Tn/ d1888Jul22 Maries Co Mo
Collier William E Jr	M23E		of near Springfield Mo
Collins -	R14Bb		
Collins Elsie	A72Ba	1935Jan26	m.1953 d1965Mar23
Collins John	G32Ga		of Phelps Co Mo
Collins Sarah Ann	G16Ba		of Westphalia Mo
Collins William	E31Ba		
Collins William	H53Aa		
Colmer Lenore	V26Ea		m1896
Colton Ephraim	A11Ia		
Colvin -	H17Aa		
Compton Cordia	B13Fa		
Compton Mary Ann	E22Iam		
Compton William	E22Ja		of Osage Co Mo
Conley L.W.	G31Aa		
Connor Edward	U17E		of Franklin Co Mo

NAME	NUMBER	BIRTH	COMMENTS
Connor James	U17B		of Franklin Co Mo
Connor James	P17Ga		of St Louis Mo
Connor John	U17D		of Franklin Co Mo
Connor John	U16Ca		of Franklin Co Mo
Connor Mary	U17G		of Franklin Co Mo
Connor Michael	U17C		of Franklin Co Mo
Connor Thomas	U17A		of Franklin Co Mo
Connor William	G19La		of Washington Mo
Connor William	U17F		of Franklin Co Mo
Constable Billy Bruce	C31Da		m1943Nov13 Lee's Summit Mo
Cook -	D43Da		
Coolidge Elizabeth	F11Gb		m1794Feb26
Coolidge Mary	F11Ba		b.p.Md m.1782Sep17 Prince Georges CoMd
Coomrod -	V26Db		
Cooper Burton	C27A	1805May11	b.p.Tn d1875Mar21 Bay Mo
Cooper Charles Scott	B46A	1953Jan16	
Cooper Charles Thomp.	B33Aa		m.1950 Jun21
Cooper Charlotte	C28J	1828	d.1877
Cooper Clifford Waldo	C31F	1922Aug30	b.p.Mo/Owensville m1944Apr2 d1978Dec17
Cooper Delores Mae	C31G	1931Oct16	d.1932Mar6
Cooper Eliza Ann	C28I	1845	
Cooper Eliza Ann	C29G	1867Jul22	b.p.Mo/Osage Co m1885Aug27 d.1939Feb19
Cooper Elizabeth Helen	C28H	1843Jul15	b.p.Mo/Bay m.1874Dec24 d1911Mar14Osage
Cooper Elizabeth S	C29E	1866Jan29	b.p.Mo/Osage Co d1870Oct11Osage Co
Cooper Ida May	C30C	1894May2	b.p.Mo/ m1912May20 d.1957May3 Nebraska
Cooper Ira Burton	C30A	1892Sep2	b.p.Mo/Byron m.1916Feb29 d1972Apr9 Mo
Cooper James Burton	C29D	1864Nov22	b.p.Mo/ m1889Mar14Linn d1894Jan8 Mo
Cooper James M	C28A	1825Sep4	b.p.Tn/ d1877Jun1 Gasconade Co Mo
Cooper James William	C31B	1934Mar23	b.p.Mo/Gasc Co m1955May27 Cass Co Mo
Cooper Jewell Ethel	C31E	1917Jan5	b.p.Mo/Bland m1935Oct15 d1979Apr18 Mo
Cooper John Burrows	C29F	1870Feb28	d.1870Sep23
Cooper John Burton	C28C	1831Nov23	b.p.Mo/Bay m1863Nov15 d1870Sep23 Osage
Cooper Lloyd Burton	C31C	1928Aug29	b.p.Mo/Pleasant Hill m1947Apr12
Cooper Lois Evelyn	C31D	1925Apr20	b.p.Mo/Harrisonville m1943Nov13
Cooper Mary T	C29C		b.p.Mo/Osage Co m1877
Cooper Mildred Irene	C31A	1918Dec9	b.p.Mo/Owensville m1948Jun5 Mo.
Cooper Oda Franklin	C30B	1890Jan13	b.o.Mo/Cooper Hill d1953Apr9 unmarried
Cooper Peter Ernest	C30D	1891Feb24	b.p.Mo/Cooper Hill d1893Sep4
Cooper Rebecca	C28E	1836	
Cooper Robert Wiley	C28D	1834	b.p.Mo/ m.1852Mar4
Cooper Ruth	C28F	1838	
Cooper Susan Barbara	B46B	1961Feb21	
Cooper Thomas McQuin	C28G	1840Nov20	b.p.Mo/Gasc Co m1882Mar4 d1917Jun27Mo
Cooper Vardry M.B.	C29A	1852Nov16	d.1870Mar23 Osage Co Mo
Cooper William A	C28B	1827Mar26	m.1846Sep12 d.1898Mar17 Gasc. Co Mo
Cooper William A	C29B	1855Jul21	d.1870Dec30 Osage Co Mo
Copeland -	G29D		d. in infancy
Copeland Albert	G41C		of Phelps Co Mo

NAME	NUMBER	BIRTH	COMMENTS
Copeland Albert	G39D		
Copeland Albert W.	G12C	1848Dec17	b.p.Mo/Maries Co m.1870Jan9 d1930Nov11
Copeland Alfred	G39E		
Copeland Alice	G45B		of Maries Co Mo
Copeland Alta	G24A		of Columbia Mo
Copeland Amanda	G15F		
Copeland Andrew J.	G29L	1847Oct2	b.p.Mo/Maries Co m.1870Nov3 d1928Apr11
Copeland Anna	G42F		of Gasconade Co Mo
Copeland Anna	G23F		
Copeland Armina A	G18B	1876Nov15	of Vienna Mo
Copeland Barbara	G36B		
Copeland Basheba	L16Ia		m.1900Aug25 d.1923Aug10 No issue
Copeland Belle	G32B		One daughter Ethel
Copeland Ben	G34D	1885Jan28	d.1932Jul31 Drowned in Osage River
Copeland Benjamin	G41J		of Phelps Co Mo
Copeland Bertie	G16F		no issue
Copeland Bertie	G33A		of Utah
Copeland Bessie	G30B		
Copeland Bettie	G20H		of Maries Co Mo. Twin of Lettie
Copeland Boley	G41Ka		of Phelps Co Mo
Copeland Callaway	G15B		
Copeland Callaway	G11C		Moved to Laclede Co Mo
Copeland Calvin C	G12D	1846Nov7	b.p.Mo/Maries Co m.1868Dec10 d1927Jun
Copeland Calvin C.	G18H	1868Oct3	of Okla
Copeland Campbell	G34C		
Copeland Cansada	G45E		d.1932Sep13
Copeland Casandra	G25B	1859Aug1	b.p.Mo/Maries Co m.1879sep21 d1929Mar
Copeland Charles	G41D		of Phelps Co Mo
Copeland Charles	G32F		of Okla
Copeland Charles	G43E		d in infancy
Copeland Charles	G17F		
Copeland Chester	G42D		of Phelps Co Mo
Copeland Clay W	G20E	1875Mar8	m.1898Mar23 of Union Mo.
Copeland Crissie C	G39B		
Copeland David	G41E		of Phelps Co Mo
Copeland David Alonzo	G18L	1870Apr21	m.1897Aug4 d.1932Aug22 of Vienna Mo
Copeland Davis	G11B		Moved to Hancock Mo in 1880´s
Copeland Della	G22E		of Maries Co Mo
Copeland Dolph	G19J		of Union Mo
Copeland Dora	E33Aa		
Copeland Edna	G19I		of Washington Mo
Copeland Edward	G30A		
Copeland Edward	G17D		
Copeland Edward A	G19G		of Maries Co Mo
Copeland Eliza	G29I	1832Aug30	m.1848Aug29Maries Co/Mo d1905May27
Copeland Eliza	G35G		d1848Dec25
Copeland Eliza J	G12H		d1870abt
Copeland Ellen	G44C		of Bland Mo
Copeland Elsia A	G20G	1888Aug10	m1906Dec27 of St. Louis Mo

NAME	NUMBER	BIRTH	COMMENTS
Copeland Emily Jane	G35I		
Copeland Emma	G33F		of Eldon Mo
Copeland Emma	G34B		of Linn Mo
Copeland Emma	G43C		of Eldon Mo
Copeland Emma	G32G		of Phelps Mo
Copeland Ethel	G44F		
Copeland Eunice	G22D		of Maries Co Mo
Copeland Eva	G34A		m1900Dec31 of near Vienna Mo.
Copeland Everett R	G19F		of Maries Co Mo
Copeland Fannie	G29O		Moved to Ark. then back to Maries CoMo
Copeland Fannie	G14A		
Copeland Felina E	G28C		
Copeland Flora L	G28A		
Copeland Frances	G35E		
Copeland Francis M.	G12A		Union soldier Civil War d W.Missouri
Copeland Francis M.	G35K	1850Jan13	d.1918Jul6 Twin of Thomas J
Copeland Frank	G42G		of Illinois
Copeland Frank	G19E		of Maries Co Mo
Copeland Freeman	G22C		of Maries Co Mo
Copeland George	G41A		of Phelps Co Mo
Copeland George	G17C		
Copeland George H	G15C		of Rich Hill Mo
Copeland Gertie	G23D		
Copeland Granville	E32Da		
Copeland Granville M	G18D		of Maries Co Mo
Copeland Hattie	G23C		
Copeland Henderson	G13C		of Maries Co Mo
Copeland Henry	G40A		of Maries Co Mo
Copeland Homer	G22B		of Maries Co Mo
Copeland Hubbard	G20D	1877Dec17	m1902Jan1
Copeland Ida	G17A		
Copeland Ida Eleanor	G18G	1873Apr5	d1874Nov20
Copeland Isaac	G41I		of Phelps Co Mo
Copeland Isaac Newton	G35L		of Phelps Co Mo
Copeland J. Ollie	G33B		Lived on Gasconade R. Maries Co Mo
Copeland James	G34E		d single
Copeland James	G16A		
Copeland James	G29A		d.bef.1874 Of Tenn. and Massac Co.,Ill
Copeland James	E33Aaf		
Copeland James	G32A		Moved to Arkansas
Copeland James	G35B		Drove ox team to Cal. gold rush 1849
Copeland James	G42A		of Illinois
Copeland James	G23A		
Copeland James	E32Aaf		
Copeland Jasper	Y61Ca		
Copeland Jasper	G32H		d single
Copeland Jehu	G29M	1845Apr11	m.1866 d1920Jul13 near Dixon Mo
Copeland John	G44G		
Copeland John	U12Iaf		

NAME	NUMBER	BIRTH	COMMENTS
Copeland John	G10D	1795Mar4	b.p.Tenn To Mo. early 1830´s. Minister
Copeland John	G43D		d. in California
Copeland John	G42C		of Phelps Co Mo
Copeland John	G41B		of Phelps Co Mo
Copeland John	G11A	1819Apr26	b.p.Tenn/Knox Co m1839 d18760ct27Mo
Copeland John	S20Ga		m.1881Jan2 Moved to sw Missouri
Copeland John	G35C		Drove ox team to Cal. gold rush 1849
Copeland John	L16Jaf		
Copeland John	G29K		Union soldier.Soldiers Home StJames Mo
Copeland John Burton	G20C	18690ct8	m1889Nov7 d1932Jan26
Copeland John Henry	G32E		d.1932 Moved to Pryor Okla
Copeland John Jr	G15A		
Copeland John Louis	G18M	1875May1	d.1933Jul2 Sheriff Maries CoMo of Okla
Copeland John Richard	G12E	1859Jan16	b.p.Mo/Maries Co m1879Aug10 Collector
Copeland John S	G36F	1870Dec14	d1920Nov20
Copeland Joseph	G36E		
Copeland Joseph	G28D		
Copeland Joseph	G41F		of Phelsps Co Mo
Copeland Joseph	G29N		Drowned Gasc. River near Hancock Mo
Copeland Joseph	G42E		of Gasconade Co Mo
Copeland Joseph A.	G20A		d. in infancy
Copeland Joseph Jr	G11F		d.West. part Maries Co Mo
Copeland Joseph Mrs	G10Ba		
Copeland Joseph Sr	G10B		
Copeland Joseph T	G35M	1840Nov16	d1923Jan4
Copeland Julia Ann	G18J	1865Nov4	m.1884Jun15 d1931Mar13 of Vienna Mo
Copeland Kenneth	G24C		
Copeland Lannie M	G18P		
Copeland Laura America	G18C	18810ct1	of Vienna Mo
Copeland Laura	G43B		of Phelps Mo
Copeland Lee	G58Aa		of Laurel Montana
Copeland Lee	G23B		
Copeland Leerva	G29E		of Western Mo
Copeland Lena	G23E		
Copeland Lettie	G40C		of Maries Co Mo
Copeland Lettis	G20I		of Maries Co Mo Twin of Bettie
Copeland Levi F	G44B		on Police force St. Louis Mo
Copeland Lizzie	G45A		of Maries Co Mo
Copeland Lorenzo Dow	G18N	1879Apr24	d.1937May21 of Granite Cy Mo
Copeland Lottie	G14B		
Copeland Lucinda	G16E		
Copeland Lucinda	G36G	1868abt	
Copeland Lucy	L16Ja		d.Monett Mo of Dixon and Springfield
Copeland Lumina Eliz.	G18I	1864Jul13	of Maries Co Mo and Hominy Okla
Copeland Mabel	G22G		of Kansas
Copeland Mamie	G45C		of Owensville Mo
Copeland Mannie	G33C		
Copeland Margaret	G44E		
Copeland Marion	G13B		

NAME	NUMBER	BIRTH	COMMENTS
Copeland Martha	G35H		of Howell Mo
Copeland Martha	G42H		of Illinois
Copeland Martha	G19D		
Copeland Martha	D25Eam		
Copeland Martha	G29H		
Copeland Martha Luella	G15G		
Copeland Martin	G36D	1847Oct20	b.p. Mo/Maries Co m1869Oct7 d1915Apr12
Copeland Martin	G32C		of Maries Co Mo d.Argyle Mo
Copeland Martin	G29G		of Western Mo
Copeland Martin	G25C		of Vernon Co Mo
Copeland Martin	G45D		
Copeland Martin M	G35O		
Copeland Mary	G19B		d in infancy
Copeland Mary	G44A		
Copeland Mary	G41K		of Phelps Co Mo
Copeland Mary	G36A		
Copeland Mary	G15E		
Copeland Mary	G16D		of Kansas Cy Mo
Copeland Mary	G35F		of Wright Mo
Copeland Mary Ann	G29J	1837Apr14	b.p. Mo/Maries Co m1857Dec27 d1917Jan
Copeland Mary Eliz.	G11H		Lived on Big Maries Maries Co Mo
Copeland Mary Ellen	G18E	1861Jul22	of Granite Cy Mo
Copeland Matilda R.	G12I		m1880
Copeland Milly Jane	G29C		of Western Mo
Copeland Minnie A	G18O		
Copeland Missouri	G59Ba		of Texas
Copeland Mollie	G33E		of Jefferson Cy. Mo
Copeland Myra Cansada	G18K	1867Apr1	of Ark. d. in Colo.
Copeland Myra D	G12G		
Copeland Myrtle	T20Ab		of Dixon Mo
Copeland Myrtle	G17E		
Copeland Nancy	G16C		
Copeland Nancy P	G28B		
Copeland Nettie	G19H		of Franklin Co Mo
Copeland Noah	G26A		d. Wayne Co Mo
Copeland Noah	G29F		of Western Mo
Copeland Oda	G41H		of Phelps Co Mo
Copeland Olive	G19C		d in infancy
Copeland Oliver	G18F	1884Mar13	of Granite Cy Mo
Copeland Oliver	G17B		
Copeland Ollie	Y54Faf		of Maries Co Mo
Copeland Peter	G11D		
Copeland Pleasant	G35A		b.p.Tenn.of Maries CoMo Gold rush 1849
Copeland Raymond	G24B		of Columbia Mo
Copeland Rebecca	G11I		m1833Aug15 Gasconade Co Mo
Copeland Rebecca	G35P		
Copeland Richard	G25A		Conf. Army d. In Alton prison
Copeland Robert	G16B		of Westphalia Mo
Copeland Robert	G39C		

91

NAME	NUMBER	BIRTH	COMMENTS
Copeland Roe	G22A		of Maries Co Mo
Copeland Rosa	G14C	1874Feb12	d.1920Nov26
Copeland Rosa	G39F		
Copeland Roy	G33D	1884Aug	m.1906 d1908Nov22 Kicked by horse
Copeland Ruby	Y54Fa		of Maries Co Mo
Copeland Sallie C	G11J	1822Apr2	b.p.Tenn d.1861Jan6 Maries Co Mo
Copeland Samuel	G41G		of Phelps Co Mo
Copeland Samuel P	G13D		
Copeland Sarah	G10E		
Copeland Sarah	G28E		
Copeland Sarah	E32Aa		Later of Callaway Co Mo
Copeland Sarah	G36C		
Copeland Sarah	G35D		
Copeland Sarah	U12Dam		
Copeland Solomon Jr	G11E		d. Maries Co Mo
Copeland Solomon MrsJr	G11Ea		
Copeland Solomon MrsSr	G10Ca		d. in Tenn
Copeland Solomon Sr	G10C	1804	b.p.Tenn.Jefferson Co Mo(1832)d1873Aug
Copeland Sterling	G22F		of Kansas
Copeland Steve	L16Ba		of Dixon Mo
Copeland Telitha Jane	G18A	1863Sep15	of Vienna Mo
Copeland Telitha T	G12F	1861Aug3	b.p.Mo/Maries Co m.1879Mar23 d1933Dec
Copeland Thomas	G40B		of Maries Co Mo
Copeland Thomas J	G35J	1850Jan13	twin of Frances Marion
Copeland Thomas J	G20B		d in infancy
Copeland Vicie	G42I		of near High Gate Mo
Copeland W Noah	G32D	1859Jul19	b.p.Mo/near Vienna Mo m1879Sep19d1930
Copeland William	G13A		
Copeland William	G29B		
Copeland William	G42B		d. in Pulaska Co Mo
Copeland William	Y34Ga		m1905abt. Of Vienna Mo
Copeland William	G43A		of St Louis Mo
Copeland William	G39A		
Copeland William J	G15D		of Rich Hill Mo
Copeland William J	G35N	1837Feb6	d1923Apr18
Copeland William M	G12B	1842Jan16	b.p.Mo/Maries Co m1860Aug19 d1918Nov18
Copeland William M	G44D		of Rolla Mo
Copeland William O	G18Q		
Copeland William Ray	G20F	1880Aug27	m(1)1909May2 of Maries Co Mo
Copeland William Riley	G11G		d1873. Thrown from horse
Copeland William Sr	G10A	1787abt	m.Tenn. d1862Maries Co Mo War 1812
Copeland Wiseman	G19A		d in infancy
Coppedge Anthony K	Q37A	1825Dec16	d.1903Apr10 Phelps Co Mo
Coppedge Belle	Q38A		no issue
Coppedge Bettie	Q39C	1866Apr29	d.1885Apr6
Coppedge Doss	Q44Eb		no issue
Coppedge Eliza Ann	Q37H	1843Apr4	m1860Mar22 d1892Sep10
Coppedge Ethel	Q39E		of Maries Co Mo
Coppedge Fielding Teed	Q37B		

NAME	NUMBER	BIRTH	COMMENTS
Coppedge George Doss	Q37C		
Coppedge George H 2nd	Q39D		of Maries Co Mo
Coppedge George H Mrs	Q36Cam		of Bradfordsville Ky
Coppedge George H Sr	Q36Caf		of Bradfordsville Ky.,Maries Co Mo1833
Coppedge James	Q38C		d in Montana
Coppedge James M	Q37D	1838Jan22	d1896Jul31 Maries Co Mo St.Legislature
Coppedge James M Jr	Q39F		of Lakewood Mo
Coppedge Jane	Q37G		
Coppedge Jane	Q38D		
Coppedge John D	Q38B		m.KansCy Mo d Long Beach Calif
Coppedge Joseph M	Q39G		of St. James Mo
Coppedge Lucinda	Q37F		of Phelps and Maries Cos Mo
Coppedge Margaret E	Q37I		
Coppedge Mary L	Q39A		
Coppedge Nancy	Q37E		of Phelps Co Mo
Coppedge Ora	Q39H		of Riverside Cal.
Coppedge Samuel H	Q39B	1872May8	d.1917Jul1 Police force St.Louis Mo
Corder —	E09Da		
Cordray Edna Pearl	E94Aa	1887May21	b.p.Ks/Concordia d.1919Apr8 Kans Cy Ks
Cordray Thomas	E94Aaf	1836	b.p.Kans/d.1888Jul20 Concordia Kansas
Cordsmeyer -	Y52Fa		
Cordsmeyer G. W.	Y52Faf		of Maries Co Mo Judge
Cordsmeyer Mary	Y62Da		m.1903Jul4 of Maries Co Mo
Corpening David J. Col	F08Hbf		
Corpening Sarah F	F08Hb	1819	d.1875
Coshow Mary	I62Ca		To Mo in 1800
Couch Dora May	B22Aa		m1922Oct9
Courtney Bathsheba	A37Aa		m1755Jan19
Courtney Louvenia	Q35Aa		m in Indiana
Courtwright John	T30Ja		
Cowan Adeline	U16E	1843	b.p.Mo Maries Co
Cowan Austin	U19A		of Maries and Crawford Cos Mo
Cowan Azariah	U18B		
Cowan David Jr	U16G		of Maries and Osage Cos Mo
Cowan David Sr	G12Baf		of Va. in 1775
Cowan Eliza	U16D		
Cowan Elizabeth	U16C		of Franklin Co Mo
Cowan Etta	U18C		
Cowan Frank	U18A		
Cowan George	U16I		of Maries and Ozark Cos Mo
Cowan John	U16F		To Ark. after Civil War
Cowan Lottie	U18D		
Cowan Louisa Evaline	U16A	1844May18	b.p.Mo Maries Co m1860Aug19 d1918Jan8
Cowan Mary Ann	U16B		
Cowan Oscar	U19B		of Maries and Crawford Cos Mo
Cowan William	U16H		of Maries and Crawford Cos Mo
Cowan William Mrs	U16Ha		of Maries and Crawford Cos Mo
Cox -	Y16Aa		
Cox -	E16Ba		

NAME	NUMBER	BIRTH	COMMENTS
Cox -	G35Nb		
Cox Albert	F34Ja		
Cox Alexander	C14C	1832	b.p.Mo Gentry Co in 1850 Farmer
Cox Andrew	C11D	1804	b.p.Va m.White Co Tn Gasc Co Mo1828
Cox Andrew Jackson	C12A	1833Dec1	b.p.Mo Gasc Co m(1)1898Jan4 d1913Nov9
Cox Bathsheba	C13I	1842	b.p.Mo Osage Co m 1860Feb2
Cox Benjamin F	C13N	1851	b.p.Mo Osage Co
Cox Betty Jean	C42A	1941Dec10	b.p.Mo/Joplin m.1962Dec1 Joplin Mo.
Cox Burton Cooper	C13C	1832Mar12	b.p.Mo Osage Co m1852May9 d1896Sep11
Cox Catherine	C15G	1849	b.p. Mo Osage Co
Cox Charles	C32D	1874after	
Cox Christopher	C15H		b.p. Mo Osage Co
Cox David	K34Da		
Cox Deala	C16E		
Cox Dora B Mrs	C32Ba	1871	d.1955 Osage Co Mo
Cox Dorsey	Z42Ca		
Cox Elizabeth Ann	C17B	1857Dec6	b.p. Mo Neosho
Cox Elizabeth Mrs	C13Aa		
Cox Elvira M	C13E	1832Mar13	b.p. Tenn of Mo Gasc Co m1949Feb1 Mo
Cox Esther Sula	C16H	1900May3	b.p. Mo Neosho m.1920Jan29 Only Child
Cox George W	C12I	1852May27	b.p.Mo Gentry Co m 1876abt
Cox Hannah	C13J	1843	b.p.Mo Osage Co
Cox Hannah Elizabeth	C26G	1861Mar7	m.1882 d1927Mar10
Cox Henry	C12J	1855	b.p. Mo m 1877 abt
Cox Henry	C11E		
Cox Henry I	C13G	1830	b.p.Mo Gasc. Co m1861Apr11
Cox Hetty Elvira	C26D	1854Jul27	m1873Jan12 d 1926ca
Cox Jacob	C12G	1846	b.p. Mo
Cox James B	C32B	1868	d.1944 Osage Co Mo
Cox James Dillard	C40A		
Cox James H	C12E	1842	b.p. Mo
Cox Jasper	C12H	1851	b.p.Mo
Cox Jasper	C14G	1832	b.p.Mo
Cox Jefferson Davis	C17E		
Cox John	A44Da		
Cox John	C11H	1810ca	
Cox John E	C16B	1858	b.p. Mo Gentry Co m1879Sep7
Cox John P	C12F	1844	b.p.Mo In Worth Co Mo Census 1850
Cox Joshua	C14D	1834Mar10	b.p.Mo Gasc Co m1855Mar1 d1893Jun9
Cox Joshua	C11A	1799	b.p. Va d1859ca Gasc and Gentry Cos Mo
Cox Joshua A	C13A	1827	b.p.Tenn
Cox Joshua J	C12K	1859	b.p. Mo
Cox Junior Jay	C41A		
Cox Lafayette	C15I		
Cox Lavina	K13Ea		of Western Mo
Cox Louisa Malinda	C26B	1867Jun19	d.1870Nov19
Cox Louise V	C13K	1846	b.p. Mo Osage Co
Cox Lucinda Ellen	C26A	1867Jun19	b.p.Mo Bryon m(1)1889(2)1916 d1945Nov
Cox Lucy	C15B	1834	b.p. Mo Gasconade Co

NAME	NUMBER	BIRTH	COMMENTS
Cox Lucy Jane	C26F	1858Aug28	d 1932Mar12
Cox Lydia	C13P	1855	b.p.Mo Osage Co
Cox Malinda	F34Ba	1825	b.p. Tenn m1840Feb6
Cox Malinda	C15D	1839	b.p.Mo Gasconade Co
Cox Manerva	C14H	1845	b.p. Mo. Gentry Co Census 1850
Cox Martha	C15A	1835	b.p. Mo Gasc. Co m1852Mar d1852Aug6 Mo
Cox Martha Annis	C16C	1862Sep19	b.p.Mo Worth Co m1879Sep21 d1937Sep5
Cox Martha Ellen	C17C	1860Jul2	b.p. Mo./Neosho
Cox Martha Jane	C13O	1852Oct26	b.p. Mo Osage Co m1882Mar4 d1922Jul29
Cox Mary	C15C	1834Nov8	b.p. Mo Osage Co m1853Mar10 d1917Sep5
Cox Mary	C14E	1837	b.p. Mo In Gentry Co Census 1850
Cox Mary Ann	C17A	1857Dec6	b.p. Mo Neosho m(2)1898Jan4 d1940May16
Cox Mary Ann	C13B	1829	b.p. Mo Gasc Co m.1848Nov5 d1875 abt
Cox Mary Emily	C26E	1856Mar11	d1928May17
Cox Matilda	C12D	1842	b.p. Mo Worth Co Census 1850
Cox Nelly Semantha	C14I	1849	b.p. Mo of Gentry Co Bogle Twp
Cox Nic	M20Da		of Montana
Cox Preston	C16D	1850	b.p. Mo Gentry Co d1886 unmarried
Cox Rachel	C16G		m1886Jul28
Cox Rachel Elizabeth	C13H	1857	b.p. Mo Osage Co. Prob. dau. 2nd marr.
Cox Rafe	S22Ba		of Maries Co Mo
Cox Rebecca	C11F		m.1827 Tn White Co d.1829 Mo
Cox Reuben B	C11B	1800	b.p. Va m(2)1841 d1376 Mo Osage Co
Cox Robert Bradford H	C16F	1867Jul28	m.1897Apr4 d1917Oct2
Cox Roxanna	C26H	1863Jun11	d1870Sep28
Cox Rutha	C12B	1836Mar18	b.p.Mo Gasc Co d1892Jun21Joplin
Cox Sarah	C14B	1830	b.p. Mo Gentry Co Bogle Twp Census1850
Cox Sarah Elizabeth	C16A	1854May10	b.p.Mo Gentry Co m1871May6 d1929
Cox Sarah Malinda	C13D	1827Jan5	b.p. Tenn m1846May12 d1876Aug27 Mo
Cox Susan	C14A	1828	b.p.Mo In Census Gentry Co 1850
Cox Susannah	C15F	1846	b.p. Mo Osage Co
Cox Sydrie	C13F		b.p. Mo Gasconade Co
Cox Theodore B	C26I		
Cox Thomas	C11C		Tax list Gasc Co Mo 1828
Cox Thomas	C32C		
Cox Thomas Jefferson	C26C	1853Feb25	d1853Mar11
Cox Thomas Jefferson	C15E	1841Aug22	b.p. Mo Osage Co m(1)1860(2)1874 d1908
Cox Wesley	C32A		
Cox William	C11G	1811Jun5	b.p.Va d1857Mar29 Gasc Co Mo
Cox William	C14F	1839	b.p. Mo In Gentry Co Census 1850
Cox William (Cocks)	C10A		b.p. Maryland In Va 1811 dTenn 1814
Cox William Dillard	C17D		
Cox William Ray	C12C	1840	of Gentry Co Mo Allen Twp Census 1850
Cox Winfield Scott	C13M	1849	b.p.Mo Osage Co
Cox Zachariah T	C13L	1847	b.p.Mo Osage Co
Coyle James	Y13Ba		
Crabtree -	M23Ba		
Crafton Maggie	K12Ga		
Craig John R	Q37Fa		of Phelps and Maries Cos Mo

NAME	NUMBER	BIRTH	COMMENTS
Crane Anna	E88Da		m1939
Crane Larkin	Z13Aa		of Phelps Co Mo
Crane Lorraine	E88Ea		m1942
Crawford -	E55Ba		
Crawley Mary	D58Da		
Crawley Mary	D16Aa		m1810Dec29
Creekpaum Telitha E	R13Ca		
Crider A.J. Dr	E41A		of Dixon Mo
Crider Ann	K37Fa		of Gasconade Co Mo
Crider Daniel	D17Haf		
Crider Daniel	D28Da		
Crider Daniel B	D47B		of near Belle Mo
Crider David	D22Da		
Crider Drusa	D47F		
Crider Ed	Y35Ba		
Crider Eliza	D47D		of Arkansas
Crider Eva L	E41G		
Crider Florence	E41C		of Maries Co Mo
Crider George	D47C		of near Chamois Mo
Crider George W	Z32D		of Pomeroy Washington
Crider John R	R15Ba		of Vienna Mo
Crider John R	Z32B		
Crider Julia Ann	R26Ca	1828Dec22	d.1873Jan5
Crider Margaret	E41D		of Maries Co Mo
Crider Martin Jackson	Z27Ba	1848	m. Maries Co Mo d1911June6
Crider Mary	E41F		of St. Louis Mo
Crider Mary Ann	C36Fa		m1852Jan9 Gasconade Co Mo
Crider Mary Jane	D22Ea		m1865Jul13 Gasconade Co Mo
Crider Monroe	D47G		
Crider Myrtle	Z32C		of Tacoma Washington
Crider Nancy	D47E		d St. Clair Co Mo
Crider Nancy Jane	Z32E		of Alberta Canada
Crider Newton M	Z32A		of Thornton Washington
Crider Oliver B	Z32G		
Crider Ollie	E41B		of St Louis Mo
Crider Rachel	D21Da		
Crider Rachel	D17Ha	1314	b.p.NoCar m1829Mar26 Gasc Co Mo d1887
Crider Thomas R	E41E		of St Louis Mo
Crider Thurman	Y56A		
Crider Tom Rush	E29Ba		
Crider Ulysses	D47A		of near Belle Mo
Crider William H	Z32F		
Crismon -	T12B		
Crismon Amanda	T14A		
Crismon Arch	T13D		In wagon train to Oregon 1852
Crismon Augusta	J16E		of Maries Co Mo
Crismon Ben	J16A		of Plato Mo
Crismon Benjamin F	T15C	1860Jul29	m1879Aug13 d1916Dec Maries Co Mo
Crismon Betsey	T13H		

NAME	NUMBER	BIRTH	COMMENTS
Crismon Campbell	T11A		On Gasc Co Mo tax list 1828
Crismon Campbell Mrs	T11Aa		Half-blood Cherokee Indian
Crismon Dow	J16C		of Cooksville Mo
Crismon Elise	J16F		of Pulaski Co Mo
Crismon Eliza E	T16F	1855Jun27	m1872Nov5 d1882Feb24
Crismon Gabriel	T16E		
Crismon George	T10A		of No Car and Mo
Crismon George Mrs	T10Aa		
Crismon Gilbert	T12A		Wagon train to Ore.1852 Returned to Mo
Crismon Gilbert	T16A	1840Jan14	d1917Mar31
Crismon Gilbert Jr	T14C		to California
Crismon Gilbert Mrs	T12Aa		
Crismon Gilbert O	T15D	1862Oct10	d1938Jan26
Crismon Hugh	T14D		
Crismon Ike	S13Baf		
Crismon Isaac	T16C		Conf Army. Arm shot off Alton Prison
Crismon Isaac	T13B		of Mo and Oregon
Crismon James	T13C	1325Aug10	b.p. Mo Osage Co d.1895Dec16Maries Co
Crismon James Munro	T15B	1855Aug20	m1873Oct2 d1878Oct17 No issue
Crismon Jeff	J16B		of Plato Mo
Crismon Jesse H	T15A	1843Dec23	d1917Feb9 Vienna merchant Judge
Crismon John	T13A		m1833Dec5 Osage Co Mo of Maries Co
Crismon Joseph	T14E	1843Apr24	m1866Nov30 d1936Oct15 Mo Union Cavalry
Crismon Judith	K26Cam		d.1883abt
Crismon Louisa J	T15F	1845Jan10	d1863Apr23 single
Crismon Mahala	T13L		m1834Feb20 Gasc Co Mo(orJan111848)
Crismon Malinda	T15I		of Maries Co Mo
Crismon Malinda	S13Ba		of New Mexico
Crismon Margaret	T15H		
Crismon Mark	T14F		
Crismon Martha J	U13Aa		
Crismon Mary	T14B		
Crismon Mary	T16H		
Crismon Mary	T15K		m1879Mar15
Crismon Mary	J16G		of Webb Cy Mo
Crismon Mary	J27Gam	1866Sep27	d1932Jul23 of Maries Co Mo
Crismon Matilda	T15J		
Crismon Monroe	J16H		of Tacoma Washington
Crismon Moses	T13F		to Oregon 1852
Crismon Myra	T14H		
Crismon Nancy	T14I		
Crismon Nancy J	T15G	1367Nov22	d.1878Aug18 Pulaski Co Mo
Crismon Nora	J16D		of Briarton Okla
Crismon Pleasant	T13E		of Oregon 1852
Crismon Polly	T13M		of Oregon
Crismon Rachel	T16G		
Crismon Rachel	L15Aam		of Maries Co Mo
Crismon Robert E	T15E		
Crismon Sallie(Cumile)	T13I		of Miller Co Mo

NAME	NUMBER	BIRTH	COMMENTS
Crismon Sarah	T13K	1818	b.p.Tenn
Crismon Stephen	T16D		ofMaries and Franklin Cos Mo Conf.Army
Crismon Stephen	T13G		to Oregon 1852
Crismon William W	T13J	1800abt	m1824Jan8Osage Co Mo d1876Dec18Maries
Crismon William W Jr	T16B		of Maries Co Mo and Arkansas
Crismon William W Jr	T14G		
Crismon William W Mrs	T14Ga		
Croft Recie	A79Ka	1892Aug17	
Cross Isaac A	G63Ja		of Sedan Kansas
Cross Lena	J27Ia		m1919Aug16 of Warrensburg Mo
Cross Martha A	C12Ja		
Crouch E	A13Cc		
Crow Mary	E25Bam		of Franklin Co Mo
Crow R	A12Bb		
Crowley Robert	A66Ha	1840abt	
Crum Edward	G14Ca		
Crum George Washington	Q44Ja	1860Jun22	m.1888 Of Maries Co Mo.
Crum John	G14Caf		
Crum Mary E	G16Aa		
Crum Rachel Jane	Y31Aa	1853Jun2	b.p.Tenn m1870Dec3 d1928Jun20 Mo
Crum Robert Sevier	G16Aaf	1828Sep9	b.p.Tenn/Greene Co mTenn1852Aug12d1838
Crutts Jacob	H56Ga		
Cummings Mildred	E34Cam	1841Feb10	d1922Oct15 Maries Co and Steelville Mo
Curtis -	K28Ia		
Curtis Betsey	D17Ia		m1835Mar26 or 1835Jan25
Curtis Jacob	Z33Ba		Father may have been Cocero Curtis
Curtis W.A.	J19Ba		m1908June28
Curtis William	D75Aa		m1830Dec5
Curtman Agnes	E39H		of Maries Co Mo
Curtman Charles Otto	U12Haf		m1858Oct21 of Maries Co and St Louis
Curtman Clyde	E39B		of near Russellville Mo
Curtman Elmer	E25Ma		
Curtman Ethel	E39E		of Maries Co Mo
Curtman Floyd	E39A		of near Russellville Mo
Curtman George Dr	U12Ha		of Maries Co Mo
Curtman Gladys	E39F		of Maries Co Mo
Curtman Lorene	E39G		of Maries Co Mo
Curtman Mabel	E39C		
Curtman May	E39D		
Daingerfield Mary C	B06Dam	1686	d1730
Dake Josephine	E23Fa		
Daley Deborah E	E20Bam	1817Oct2	b.p.Indiana m in Indiana
Damback Albert	Y53Ba		of Maries Co Mo
Dandridge Martha	B98Aa	1732	m(1)Custis (m2)1759Jan
Daniel France	A78Da	1860abt	
Daniel Vicinda	E71Aam		
Daniels Julia Ann	Y15Eb	1831	b.p.Mo Maries Co
Daniels Moses	A14Ia		
Daniels Thomas	Y15Ebf		of Tenn, Indiana, Maries Co Mo

NAME	NUMBER	BIRTH	COMMENTS
Danuser Katherine	F35Da	1879Jul13	b.p. Switzerland m1904Mar d1977Nov5Tex
Daugherty Gracie May	F68Cam		
David -	Z42Da		
David Ann Florence	D77A	1868Oct1	b.p.Mo Gentry Co m1902Feb26 d1942Jul13
David Calvin L	D75F	1826	b.p.Mo Gasc Co m1846Jan8 d1861GentryCo
David Calvin Luther	D76F	1850Sep25	b.p.Mo Gentry Co m1873Sep1 d1935JanKan
David Charles Marion	D77C	1873Apr3	b.p.Mo Gentry Co Disappeared Aug 1903
David Elizabeth	D76B	1843abt	b.p.Mo
David Elizabeth	D75D	1819abt	m1837Jul29
David Elizabeth	D16Da	1797	b.p.Va
David Elizabeth Mrs	D75Bb		
David Frank Clinton	D77J	1891Apr23	b.p.Mo/Stanberry m1928Jul27 d1976
David Hannah	D75A	1813abt	b.p.Ky m1830Dec5
David Hiram Luntsford	D76G	1852May8	b.p.Mo/Gentry Co d1916Jan10
David Hiram Thomas	D77E	1878Feb21	b.p.Mo/Hugginsville d1880Jun21
David James Monroe	D75M		
David Jeremiah	D75G	1828	b.p. Mo/Gasc Co m1848May18 d Gasc Co
David John McClure	D77G	1883Nov16	b.p.Mo/Hugginsville m1916Jan27d1865Mar
David John R	D75E	1824	b.p. Mo/Gasc Co m1845Feb15 to Texas
David Levisa Ann	D76D		b.p. Mo died at age 3
David Lewis	D74A	1794abt	b.p.Md.orVa.m1812ca d1858 Mo in 1819
David Louise Mrs	D77La		
David Lula Elizabeth	D77F	1880Sep26	b.p.Mo/Hugginsville m1902Jan8 d1939Dec
David Manerva Caroline	D75L		
David Martha Emeline	D75K		
David Martha Roseann	D76I	1857Apr1	b.p.Mo/Gentry Co
David Mary Jane	D77D	1875Nov19	b.p.Mo/Hugginsville m1898Mar27d1963Feb
David Matilda Ann	D76K	1861Jul23	b.p.Mo/Gentry Co m1879Feb23 d1928Feb13
David Michael E. Mrs	D73Aa		
David Michael Edward	D73A		b.p.Ireland of Maryland near Wash.D.C.
David Minerva Ellen	D77B	1871Mar31	b.p.Iowa/Page Co m1891Dec31 d1904Nov23
David Morgan G	D75I	1833	b.p.Mo/Gasc Co m(1)1864(2)1878d1887Dec
David Richard H	D75H	1832	b.p. Mo/Gasc Co unmarried
David Ruth C	D77K	1893Aug12	b.p.Mo/Stanberry d1893Aug12
David Ruth Jane	D75J		
David Rutha Catherine	D76H	1854Oct9	b.p.Mo/Gentry Co
David Sampson Marion	D76C	1845Mar27	b.p.Mo/Gasc Co m1867Sep15 d1907Jan28
David Sarah Ann	E17Aa		b.p.Tenn m1832Jun14 d1843
David Sarah Jane	D76A	1841Dec25	b.p.Mo
David Seth Ray	D77I	1888Nov1	b.p.Mo/Hugginsville d Argonne France
David Thomas Shockley	D75C	1817Jun5	b.p.Ky/Greenbrier m1840Aug20 d1885Jul9
David Virginia	D76J	1858	b.p.Mo/Gentry Co
David Walter Festus	D77H	1886Apr11	b.p.Mo/Hugginsville m1915Jul d1948May
David William	Z41Ba		of Tenn. To Maries Co Mo by 1837
David William	D75B	1814	b.p.Ky d.Franklin Grove Iowa
David William Mrs	D75Ba		
David William Roy	D77L	1894Aug28	b.p.Mo/Stanberry d1950
David William Wesley	D76E		b.p. Mo d in infancy
Davidson Elizabeth E	Z12Aa		of Maries Co Mo

NAME	NUMBER	BIRTH	COMMENTS
Davidson Harriett	G54C		d single Disappeared in cyclone 1883
Davidson James	G54F		of Taney Co Mo
Davidson John Perryman	G54E		of Taney Co Mo
Davidson Joseph	G54G		of Taney Co Mo
Davidson Margaret	G54A		m.in New York Lived and died there
Davidson Mary	Y30A		
Davidson Matilda	G54B		of Taney Co Mo
Davidson Nancy	G54D		of western Mo
Davidson Richard R	G50Da		m. in Maries Co Mo
Davidson Tabitha	V18Ba		of Strang Okla
Davidson William	Y15Fa		
Davies Harry	E30Gb		
Davis –	Y75Da		of Okla Cy Okla
Davis –	Y18Fa		of Maries Co Mo Spring Creek
Davis Adeline	Y54Aa		of Maries Co Mo
Davis Andy J	K33B	1866Octl	b.p.Mo Maries Co
Davis Catherime Ellen	K33F	1857Jul19	d1940Jan23 Licking Mo
Davis Clara H	K33E	1865Aug29	d1939 Maries Co Mo
Davis Elizabeth	K33A	1859Nov23	b.p. Mo/Maries Co
Davis Elizabeth Ann	Z26Aa		
Davis Ellen	Q45Ba		m1868Crawford Co d18856abt of Kansas
Davis Frederick	K31B	1830Nov15	d1872May12
Davis Grant	G63Ba		of Maries Co Mo
Davis Henry	Z16Ba		of Maries and Wright Cos Mo
Davis James	Z26Caf		of Maries Co Mo
Davis James	I20Ba		
Davis James	Y61Ba		d.1858Nov30 of Maries Co Mo
Davis Janet Louis	B41B	1950Nov7	
Davis John	K13Ca		of Bolivar Mo
Davis John	Z26Aaf		
Davis John	G12Gaf		d before 1873
Davis Jonathan	I20Baf		
Davis Joseph	Y54Aaf		
Davis Landon D	G12Ga		
Davis Lewis E	K33G	1871Aprl	
Davis Lucy	Z26Ca		of Maries Co Mo Lanes Prairie
Davis Martha	K31A		
Davis Martha C	K33D	1868Jun25	
Davis Mary	B07Ga	1730abt	
Davis Mary Elizabeth	C38Cam	1870Apr22	b.p.Iowa/Union Co d1952Nov2 Jeff.Cy Mo
Davis Meredith	A88Da		
Davis Perry E	Y34Ba		of Nevada Mo
Davis Polly Ann	Q37Ca		
Davis Rachel	G62Db		d St Louis Mo
Davis Sarah J Mrs	K31Ba		moved to Texas after death of husband
Davis Sarah Josephine	K33C	1861Oct5	m1878
Davis Thomas	B07Gaf		
Davis Thomas Sr	K31D	1830Sepl	of Maries Co Mo
Davis William	G62Dbf	1797Nov17	b.p.Prob Tenn d1882Oct2 of Osage Co Mo

NAME	NUMBER	BIRTH	COMMENTS
Davis William	Y18Faf		of Maries Co Mo
Davis William Jeffrey	B41A	1948May28	b.p.Mo Joplin
Davis William Jr	K31C	1844Jan18	d.1898Jul12 Maries Co Mo
Davis William Sr	K30A	1804	b.p.NoCar of Maries Co Mo d1864Mar13
Davis William Weaver	B30Ba		m1946Aug23
Daws Josie	A76Ga	1882Jul8	d1953Apr6
Dawson –	G60Da		of Dallas Texas
Day Elizabeth	E07Aa		
Day John	E07Aaf		
Day Martin	A15Da		
Day Sarah	I12Ca		m1748 d after Oct 1815
Deatherage Rebecca	Q33Dam	1819Jan22	m1838Mar21
Deckard Thomas	E41Bb		of St. Louis Mo
Deering America	A67Ja	1853July7	m.1870Apr3 d1904Sep17
Deering Susan F	A67Ka	1845Oct17	d.1921Apr21
DeHaven Drusilla	D17Ca		m1824May6
Dehn Julius A	Y75Ca		of Maries Co Mo
Dehn William	Q39Ea		of Maries Co Mo
DeJarnette Grover B	C39Aaf		
DeJarnette Marguerite	C39Aa	1915Feb26	b.p.Mo Hannibal m1950Sept30 HannibalMo
Delaney Robert	A74Ea	1906abt	
Denham Virginia Mrs	C12Ha		
Denman Chappell	A62Ea		
Denton –	Y41Ga		
Denton Emily R	G51Ca	1848Dec17	m.1872Sep15 d.1882Jun25
Denton Jane	G51Ba		
DePriest Andrew J	D76Caf	1816ca	b.pTennWilliamson Co m1838Nov15 d.Ind.
DePriest Sarah Ellen	D76Ca	1852May23	b.p.Ind.Gibron Co m1867Sep15 d1903Mo.
DeShields Glenn	A77Eb	1910 abt	
Dessieux Josephine	D65Ea		of Linn Mo
Dewey Elizabeth	A11Ca		
Dewey Hannah	A11Da		
DeWhitt Davetta Eloise	B26D	1916Jul6	b.p.California Sacramento m.1937Nov7
DeWhitt Delmar	B26G	1924Jun29	b.p.California Stockton m1948Mar20
DeWhitt Dorothy M. Mrs	B26Ca		m1940Jun22
DeWhitt Gertrude Mrs	B26Ga		m.1948Mar20
DeWhitt LaFaye	B26A	1907Oct19	b.p.Mo/Kansas Cy m1928Mar30 d1946Aug17
DeWhitt Loretta	B26B	1910Aug18	b.p.Mo.Kansas City m1924July
DeWhitt Willard Elmo	B26C	1914Dec24	b.p.California Sacramento m1940June
DeWhitt Willema Aurel	B26F	1922Sep21	b.p.California m1945Oct7
DeWhitt William C	B26E	1918Feb21	b.p.Calif/Sacramento m1946May15
DeWhitt William W	B15Ja		
DeWitt Ines	B19Da		m.1921March
Diehl J.M.	E30Ca		no issue
Diestelkamp Augusta	D40Da		m1895Jan20
Dillard Mary	C10Aa		of Va.,White CoTenn., d Gasc Co Mo1846
Dillard Sarah M	E12Aa	1780ca	m.1803Dec15 Patrick CoVa d.1849Jun15Mo
Dillard Thomas	C10Aaf		
Dillard Thomas	E12Aaf		of Montgomery Co Va

NAME	NUMBER	BIRTH	COMMENTS
Diller Fred	G59Cb		
Dillon Lola B	Q39Ba	1874Sep25	of Salem Mo
Dillon William A.J.	Q39Baf	1840Jul13	m.1865 d1919Dec23
Disney James	B06Ha		
Disney William	B07Ea		
Dittman Fritz	D42Da		of near Belle Mo
Dixon Pansey Edith	A75Ca	1920 abt	m.(1)Slagle —
Dobbertine Edward	F55Ca		
Dodds Ben	I44Da		of Dixon Mo
Dodds John	J27Ja		m1913Sep17 of Dixon Mo
Doerr Janet	E88Ga		
Dollarhide Grace	C38Fa		
Dorsey Anne	F14Cam		
Dorsey Basil Capt	B07Caf		
Dorsey Eleanor	F14Ca		
Dorsey Elizabeth	B07Da	1735Dec3	m.1751Jan13
Dorsey Honor	F22Ea	1802	m.1820Dec1 d1872
Dorsey John	F14Caf		
Dorsey Lloyd	F22Eaf		
Dorsey Mary Ridgely	B08Ma		m1800Feb18
Dorsey Michael	B07Daf		
Dorsey Rebecca	B08Da		m1782Oct1 Annapolis,Md.
Dorsey Sarah	B07Ca	1730abt.	d. 1768Dec
Dotson —	H14Fa		
Dotson Thomas	H14La		of Phelps Co Mo
Doty Pearl	B62Aa	1884Feb25	b.p.Pa/ m1906Apr24
Downing Ruth	E78Aa		m.1802Mar10
Doyel Mary	E23Eam	1843May3	Father: Farmer Doyel
Doyle Florida	R24Ga		m1910Nov3 Of Porterville Calif.
Doyle Hugh L.M.	G29Ea		of western Mo.
Doyle Leander	G29Cb		of western Mo.
Doyle Martha Ann	K12Ba		m.1866Oct11 d1918Sep25
Doyle Nancy	G29Ka		
Doyle Ruth	G29Fa		of western Mo
Dozier Barclay E. Dr	F58Ba		m1938Apr20
Drake Hannah	A11Hbm	1653	d1694 Par: John and Hannah(Moore)Drake
Duckworth John	E09Ba		
Duffin F.M.	J25Da		of Maries Co Mo
Duffin Hugh	J25Fa		of Maries Co Mo
Duffin Rosa	G18Ma		
Duke Isaac	D31Aaf		
Duke Jennie	D31Aa		
Duke Mary M	H55Ca		m.1880Jun27
Duncan Alice	E25Da		
Duncan Alvis	E54Aaf		
Duncan Alvis	G37Aaf		
Duncan Amanda	J14Da		m1878Dec11
Duncan Bland	E38A		of Detroit Mich.
Duncan Burl	P16Eaf		of Union Mo

NAME	NUMBER	BIRTH	COMMENTS
Duncan D.C.	C28Ja		
Duncan Edward	Y36Ba		of Iberia, Ill
Duncan Elizabeth	P16Ea		of Union Mo
Duncan John	M18Ca		d. in Arkansas
Duncan Lucy Merrill	B77Aa		m1972Dec8
Duncan Mary	G37Aa		
Duncan Milford	E25La		
Duncan Milford	G59Ca		of Maries Co Mo. May be E25La
Duncan Paralee S	E20Da	1864Dec19	m.1883Feb14 d1891Mar30
Duncan Riley	J14Daf		
Duncan Russell	E20Daf		
Duncan Sarah	E54Aa		
Duncan Thomas B	Y36Baf	1852Sep29	b.p.Mo/Maries Co
Duncan William	E38B		d. In infancy
Dunduvant Charles K	E84Fa		m/1952May25
Dunham Calvin	A14Aa		
Dunivin Didamia E	Y13Dc		
Dunlap -	T21Aa		of Maries Co Mo
Dunn Betty Jean	B40Ba	1971May11	
Dunnivan -	M11Ba		
Dupnak Linda	B38Aa	1934Jun11	b.p. Ill/Chicago
Dupnak Michael	B38Aaf		
Durbin -	C26Fa		
Durbin Julia	D27Aa		b.p.Mo/Osage Co m1851Feb20 Of Belle Mo
Durbin Malissa	K36Aa		m.1839Nov12 Gasc. Co/Mo
Durbin Philip	D39B		
Durbin Riley	D39C		
Durbin Samuel Jr	D39A		of Wood River Illinois
Durbin Samuel Sr	D27Ba		
Durnell Everett	K21Da		of Wheatland Mo
Duvall Ephraim	B06Ga		
Eads -	E16Aan		
Eads Alice	J25A		of Miller Co/Mo
Eads Amanda	J25F		of Maries Co Mo
Eads Amanda	J12J	1853Jul31	m1880abt d1917Mar1
Eads B.F. Jr	J20C		
Eads Benjamin	J11A	1807Sep16	b.p.Ky m Mo.(1)1824Jul1 d1880Dec7 Mo
Eads Benjamin F	J14D	1860Jan31	m.1878Dec11 d1929May29 of Mo. and Tex.
Eads Benjamin S	J12I		of Union Mo
Eads Bunyan	J22B		of Maries Co Mo
Eads Caroline	J12F	1831Mar1	b.p.Mo/Maries Co d.1900Sep11 Maries Co
Eads Charles	J23D		of El Dorado Kansas
Eads Cora	J25D		of Maries Co Mo
Eads Della	J23E	1880ca	d.1927
Eads Elizabeth S	J15E	1869Sep26	
Eads Ellora	J24E		of Iberia Mo
Eads Eugene	J25II		of Maries Co Mo
Eads Everett E	J22C		of Oklahoma
Eads Frances	J12A	1825May28	b.p.Mo/Osage Co d.1894Apr2 Maries Co

NAME	NUMBER	BIRTH	COMMENTS
Eads G.S.	G31Ca		
Eads George L	J24B		of Iberia Mo
Eads George Washington	J12D	1832Nov20	m.Frances Simpson,cousin d1914Nov17
Eads Gertrude	J25G		of Maries Co Mo
Eads Gus	J15C	1875Feb4	of Maries Co Mo. Near Vienna
Eads J. Alpha	J24A		of Iberia Mo
Eads J. Mick	J20F		
Eads James C	J15F	1858Jun12	of Oklahoma d1922Nov18
Eads Jennie	J12K		d Polk Co Mo. Near Humansville
Eads John	J10A		of Hagerstown Md,Ky, Moabt18180sageCo
Eads Joseph T	J15G	1864Nov25	d.1926Nov9
Eads Josephine	J20A		of Maries Co Mo
Eads Kate	J25C		of DenverMo
Eads Lewis	J12B	1827Mar1	b.p.Mo/Osage Co of Texas d.Mo1902Oct13
Eads Lewis Jefferson	J20E		d.1937
Eads Lorenzo Dow	J12G	1846Oct1	m.1883Dec2 d1911Sep9 Sheriff MariesCo
Eads Louis J	J22A		of Maries Co Mo
Eads Louisa	J12L	1856abt	d1907Mar31
Eads Louisa	J20B		of Maries Co Mo
Eads Lula	J23B		of Moffat Mo
Eads Lydia	J14C	1865Jun13	d.1931Jun3
Eads Lydia	J25E		of Maries Co Mo
Eads Malinda	J14F		of near Albuquerque, New Mexico
Eads Marion A	J15D	1872Mar4	of Springfield Mo.
Eads Mary	J23C		of Pershing Mo
Eads Mary A	J15A	1860Jan25	
Eads Mary Alice	J11B		m1823Sep30 Gasconade Co Mo
Eads Mary Sarah F.	J14B	1853Feb26	m1873Jun26 Maries Co Mo d.1889Jan8
Eads Maude M	J22D	1892May13	d.1917Mar16
Eads Milford	J25B		of St.Louis Mo
Eads Moses W	J14G	1855	b.p.Mo/mear Vienna d.1923
Eads Myra	J12H	1848Feb8	d.1925Feb11
Eads Myrtle	J24D		of Springfield Mo
Eads Perry F	J12C		
Eads Polly	Z41Ab		of Osage Co Mo
Eads Rachel	C11Bb	1813	b.p.Mo m1841May20 d1856Sep1
Eads Ray	J23A		of Pryor Mo
Eads Samuel P	J15B	1862May20	
Eads Serena	J14A		d1902Feb23
Eads Stella	J24C		of Maries Co Mo
Eads Thomas Washington	J23G	1883Juk15	m1909Jan12 1933Dec10 Of Maries Co Mo
Eads Walter	J23F		d1930
Eads Weldon W	J20D		of Denver Mo
Eads William M	J12E		d.1874
Eads William S	J14E	1851Jan25	d1915Apr5
Eagle Lester	E85Da		
East Frances	E15Ca		m1807Mar12 Va
East Susannah	E15Da		m.1807May7
Edgman Eva	A51A	1867Oct2	b.p.Ark/Newton Co m.1884Jan9 d.1940Ark

NAME	NUMBER	BIRTH	COMMENTS
Edgman Samuel Jr	A50A	1831Mar23	b.p.Tenn Roane Co m1852 d1891Mar13
Edgman Samuel Sr	A49A	1792Aug8	b.p.Tenn/Roane Co d1876Jul23 Tenn.
Edgman William	A48A	1742 abt	b.p. New Jersey
Edmunds Dixie Jean	C22B	1934Jun1	
Edmunds Ethel Lela	C22A	1932Apr5	
Edmunds Jesse	C20Aa		m.1930Mar17
Edmunds Jesse Louis	C22C	1937Aug23	
Edwards Arnold	A77Ha	1915Aug15	m.1937Apr10
Edwards Emilene	A79Ga		m.1908Oct11
Edwards G.W.	Y66Da		
Edwards N	A11Bb		
Edwards Nellie	G19Jb		
Ehrhardt Susan	Q33Ea	1832Jan16	d.1893Feb4 Maries Co Mo
Eidson Grace	C38Da		of Preston Mo
Elder Lizzie	H15Aa		of Maries Co Mo and Boston Mts. Ark.
Elder Rebecca	Y29Ham		m1867Jan24
Eldridge George	A15Na		
Elkins Bathsheba P	T15Ba		d.1878Oct15 No issue
Elkins Bettie	G58Cam		1878Aug30
Elkins L.C.	Y41Da		of Pulaski Co Mo
Ellen Mary	D91Ab		
Elliot D	B26Aa		
Elliott William	Y64Aa		of Maries Co Mo
Ellis Allan	I52C		of Knoxville Tennessee
Ellis Arthur Claude	F57Da		
Ellis Austin R	I55B		d. In infancy
Ellis Don M	I55E		m1894Oct14 Vienna Mo. of Pelham N.Y.
Ellis Edna	R24Ab		of Joplin Mo
Ellis Eliza N	E62Ga	1863	d.1941
Ellis George	I52G	1828Jul1	d. single
Ellis George G (Buddy)	I53B		of Bates Co Mo. Of Colorado
Ellis Harriet N	I55A		d. In infancy
Ellis James	I52E		of Maries Co Mo. d. Bates Co Mo
Ellis James M	I55G	1879Jan15	d.1934Dec20 Rolla Mo. Never married
Ellis John E	I55H	1881Apr8	m.1908Nov25 d1921Jun2 Oklahoma
Ellis John G	I52A		of Tenn., Mo. Crawford and Maries Cos
Ellis Judson	I54D	1877Dec3	m.1904Jan28 of Maries Co Mo
Ellis Louis Frank	I52F	1837Jul25	b.p.Tenn/McMinn Co m1867Jun27Mo d.1908
Ellis Lucretia	I52D		to Mo in about 1850
Ellis Lucretia A	I55I		of Rolla Mo
Ellis Martha	I52H		no issue
Ellis Mary E	I54B	1872Sep16	m.1897Aug1 d1899Jul1
Ellis Millie L	I55C		m1894Nov28 Vienna Mo of Denver Colo.
Ellis Ollie B	I55F		m Rolla Mo
Ellis Ora Almetta	I54A	1868May16	m1889Oct20(or1899) d1934Apr12
Ellis Phillip	I52B		of Tenn. and Mo.,Crawford and Maries.
Ellis Ramer	I54C	1875Jul1	m1896sep27 Of Maplewood Mo
Ellis Sarah Esther	I52I	1848Feb7	d.1896Aug22
Ellis T. Jeff	I52J	1843Mar21	b.p.Tenn. m1868Feb12 d1922Jun26RollaMo

NAME	NUMBER	BIRTH	COMMENTS
Ellis Thomas G	I53A		of Rich Hill Mo
Ellis William	I51A		from Tenn. Of Mo Crawford and Maries
Ellis William R	I55D	1870Nov8	m1905Apr11Rolla Mo d1922Dec23 PhelpsCo
Elrod -	S22Ha		of Maries Co Mo
Elrod Bessie	G27G		
Elrod C. Jackie	G25Baf		b.p.Prob Ind. m1855Feb2Maries Co Mo
Elrod Clara	G27B		
Elrod Colonel	Y59Aa		of Maries Co Mo
Elrod Edgar	G27E		
Elrod Epley	G27D		
Elrod Isaac Ephram	A67Aa	1857Dec22	d.1932Feb18
Elrod Leona	G27A		
Elrod Lucinda	G27I		of Maries Co Mo
Elrod Martha Serilda	G20Cam	1840Oct30	b.p.Ind/Lawrence Co. d1921Nov12
Elrod Mary E	G27F	1388	m.1902Feb15 d1918Dec17
Elrod Nancy	G27H		
Elrod Thomas Benton Jr	G25Ba	1855Dec18	b.p.Mo/Maries Co d1926Oct6 Minister
Elrod Tony	G27C		of Maries Co Mo
Elrod W.H.	E46Ea		of Summerfield Mo
Elsey John	T15Aaf		
Elsey Margaret L	T15Aa	1844Jun4	d.1917May26
Elzey John	V12Fa		
Emmons -	G42Fa		of Gasconade Co Mo
Emory Laura	J20Fa		
Emory Lewis	J20Faf		
Engle Ann	M16Db		
Engram Jacob	D12Ca		
Enochs Rebecca	I61Aa		
Erickson Edward	C37Ma		of Hickory Co. Mo
Erwin Catherine Reese	F08Aa	1800May3	m1828Mar7 d.1866Jan7
Erwin Elizbeth S	F08Ha	1804Oct17	d.1859May
Erwin William W	F08Aaf		
Essman August	D25Ca		
Etter Uva	B16Da		
Evans Jesse	K14Faf		
Evans John	Y36Ca		of St. Louis Mo
Evans Mary Ann	K14Fa	1861Jun26	m.1886Jun13 d.1931Feb9
Evans Nellie	R15Fc		of Kansas City Missouri
Evans Rose	Y64Ca		of Phelps Co Mo
Exum Cee	A73Ba	1865 abt	
Ezell Sallie	T16Dc		
Fabrette -	Z15Bb		of California
Fanbush Anna	G29Mam		
Fann -	K28Ga		
Fann Bertha	Y59B		
Fann Claude	Y59E		of St. Louis Mo
Fann Clayton	Y59C		of Maries Co Mo
Fann George	Y42Daf		Probably from Tenn
Fann Gertrude	Y59A		of Maries Co Mo.

106

NAME	NUMBER	BIRTH	COMMENTS
Fann Joseph M	Y42Da		d.1917
Fann Rainey	Y59D		of Maries Co Mo
Farmer Elizabeth	D17Ca		m.1822Oct13
Farmer John	D17Ea		
Farrell Mattie Lee	A74Ca	1901Jun25	
Farris William	A39Kb		
Fawcett Hannah	E79A		m.1796Mar16
Fawcett Joseph	E78Ba		
Fawcett Thomas	E09Ea		
Feagan Frank Andy	E82Da		m. 1889
Fearsley William	E79Aa		m.1796Mar10
Featherstone Donnie	B19Db		m.1941Feb d.1945
Feeler Benjamin	E26A		of Belt, Montana
Feeler Jackson	Y29Haf	1840Aug10	m1867Jan24 d1910Jan6
Feeler James Arthur	Y52Aa	1883Jul29	m1906Sep16 d1923Oct11
Feeler Jane	G31Gam		
Feeler Mary	Y29Ha		of Maries Co Mo
Feeler Michael Sr	E20Ba		m(1)1873Nov3(To Melissa Branson)
Feeler Simon	E20Cb	1808Apr13	b.p.Tenn m(1)Ind(2)1870Jun19 d1872Dec
Felker Harriet M.	G31Fa		m1891June20 d1914Jan11 of Carthage Mo
Felker Herman	D25Fa		
Felker Jennie	V13Da		of California
Felker John	D25Faf	1830Apr8	b.p.Germany m1853Sep20 d1889Feb6
Felker John	V13Daf		
Felker Missouri A	G31Da	1862Sep24	m1884Jul2 d1913Jan29 of Carthage Mp
Fennessey Andy	S14D		of Granite City Mo
Fennessey Bridget	S11Aa	1830Feb1	b.p.Ireland d1917Mar20 Maries Co Mo
Fennessey Dennis	S11Ea		
Fennessey Eva	S14F		of Maries Co Mo
Fennessey Kate	S14B		
Fennessey Margaret	S14E		of Washington Mo
Fennessey Mary	S14A		
Fennessey Thomas	S14C		of Meta Mo
Fenton Sarah	K32Ca		m(1) Wakefield-
Ferrell Amanda	Y64E		
Ferrell Angirona	Y61J		
Ferrell Carrie	Y64D		
Ferrell Catherine	Y62B		of Chicago, Ill
Ferrell Catherine	Y61B	1837Sep24	m Maries Co Mo d1858Jun27
Ferrell Emma	Y65C		of Springfield Mo
Ferrell Enoch Parker	Y61H	1837	of Phelps Co Mo State Leg.Cpt UnionArm
Ferrell Enoch Sr	Y60A		b.p.Va of Ind d. Maries Co Mo
Ferrell Eunice	Y65D		of Bland Mo
Ferrell Huston E. Dr	Y62D		m1903July4 of Mt.View/Mo Dentist
Ferrell Huston L	Y61L	1845Jan11	d1891Apr19 of Lanes Prairie Maries Co
Ferrell John Appley	Y63E	1865Sep23	m1887Jun8Ind. State Senator Kan,d.1922
Ferrell John J Dr	Y62A		of Owensville Mo
Ferrell John Meade	Y61G		d1911
Ferrell Lou	Y64B		of Phelps Co Mo

NAME	NUMBER	BIRTH	COMMENTS
Ferrell Lucinda	Y61C		
Ferrell Lyda	Y64A		of Mo. Maries and Phelps Counties
Ferrell Malissa	G35Na		
Ferrell Nancy Caroline	Y61K		
Ferrell Olivia	Y63D	1855Jun17	d.1876Nov4. No issoue
Ferrell Ollie	Y65B		of Bland Mo
Ferrell Ophelia	Y63B		d. single
Ferrell Polly Harriett	Y61D		d.1864abt. No issue
Ferrell Rhodes	Y61I		d single
Ferrell Robert	Y61E		d single
Ferrell Thomas	Y63A		d single
Ferrell Thomas Enoch	Y62C		of Mountain View Mo
Ferrell Thomas J	Y64F		d1937Feb6 City Supervisor Landers Wyo.
Ferrell Thomas Jeff	Y61F		
Ferrell Warren	Y63C		d single
Ferrell William	Y64C	1866	of Phelps Co Mo
Ferrell William Rhodes	Y65A		of Belle Mo
Ferrell William Rowan	Y61A		d.abt1911 Of Maries Co Mo
Ferrier Elizabeth	L15Iam		m. Osage Co/Mo Moved to Maries Co Mo
Fields John	K13Ba		of Clinton Mo
Fillingham Barbara J.	B33A	1931Nov5	b.p.Mo/Joplin m1950Jun21
Fillingham Charles F	A44E	1894Dec2	b.p.Ark/Newton Co m1922May10 d1980Jan2
Fillingham Clara May	A44C	1888Feb22	b.p.Ark/Newton Co m1911Jan15 d1975Nov
Fillingham David	A42A	1834	b.p.Ark m1854Nov15 d1868Aug14 Ark
Fillingham Grace M	A44D	1890May18	b.p.Ark/Newton Co m1914Sep27 d1976Feb
Fillingham Gustavus	A44G	1902Sep19	b.p.Ark/Newton Co Never married
Fillingham Ira Wallace	A45A	1909Jan13	b.p. Ark Harrison m1930Nov5 Joplin Mo
Fillingham James E	A43A	1859Apr15	b.p.Ark/Newton Co m1884Jan4 d1907Apr12
Fillingham Jessie Mrs	A44Ea		
Fillingham Muriel E	A45B	1912Sep1	b.p. Ark/Boone Co m1934Nov22 Joplin Mo
Fillingham Myrtle	A44B	1886Oct19	b.p.Ark/Newton Co d.1888Apr12 Ark
Fillingham Nancy Ethel	A44F	1897Apr15	b.p.Ark/Newton Co m1915May1 d1976Nov6
Fillingham Samuel E.	A45C	1914Feb25	b.p.Mo Joplin m1933Feb28 Kansas
Fillingham Samuel R	A44A	1884Oct3	b.p.ArkNewton Co m1908Feb9 d1962Mar3
Fillingham Vitge E	A44H	1907Jan12	b.p.Ark/Boone d1976May16 Barton Mo
Fillingim Samuel	A40A	1760abt	d.1829 abt
Fillingim Samuel Jr	A41A	1785abt	b.p. NoCar/Craven Co
Fillingim Sarah Mrs	A40Aa	1765abt	d1831abt Ark/St.Froncois Co
Finn Barnett	E20Aaf		b.p.Ky m(2)1864 d1895Feb28 Vienna Mo
Finn Belma	K28A		d1931
Finn Burgess	K28C		
Finn Charles H	G34Aa	1879May17	b.p. Mo Near Vienna m31Dec1900
Finn Edna	K28G		
Finn Elizabeth	J12Ea	1838Jul18	d.1918Apr2
Finn George Wesley	K27Ba	1870Mar9	b.p. Mo Near Vienna d20Feb1934
Finn Gladys	K28F		
Finn Jessie	K28I		
Finn Lee	K28B		
Finn Leona	U120a		

NAME	NUMBER	BIRTH	COMMENTS
Finn Malinda	K28H		
Finn Martha A	E20Aa	1842Jul21	b.p. Mo/Maries Co m abt1865
Finn Mary	G32Eb		of near Pryor Okla
Finn Robert	K28D		
Finn Ruth	K28E		
Finn William D	G32Ebf	1847Nov30	m(1)Malinda Russell d1903Oct5
Fisher Emma Dell	B64A	1861Sep20	b.p.Ill/Jericho m1882Feb22 d1883
Fisher Jacob	B63A		
Fisher Joyce Ann	E84Ha		m1968Mar11
Fisher William	Q33Jb		of Maries Co Mo
Fisk Oleta	R32Ga		of Los Angeles California
Fitzgerald Elvira	Y61Ga		d.1901
Fitzpatrick Bernard	U12Ka		of Maries Co Mo
Flatt Haskel	A77Aa		m.1921Dec29
Fleischmann Christ	F55Aa		
Fleischmann William	F55Da		
Fleming Naomi O	Y17Aa		
Flinn Nancy Mary	C41Aam	1900May28	b.p.Kans/KansCy d.1976Jul4Jasper Co Mo
Fly Elma	R24Ha		m.1910Nov24 Granby Mo
Fogerson W.E.	F51Aa		
Followill Milton	Y19Aa		
Followill Rob	I55Fa		m. Rolla Mo
Followill William	Y31Ba		
Followill William Jr	Y28Ba		
Foote June Ellen	C33A		of Smithville Mo
Foote Leslie Lloyd	C31Ea		m.1935Oct15 Pleasant Hill Mo
Forbush -	I61Ba		
Ford Mary	H15Ba		of Maries Co Mo. No issue
Forester -	G32Ba		
Forester Lula	G32Fa		of Okla
Forester Mary	Y61Aa		d.abt1914 Of Maries Co Mo
Forrester Elizabeth M.	V21Aa		
Forrester Thomas	V21Aaf		
Fortner Mildred	B62Da		m1912May28 d.1961
Fortune Alva	E45B		of Washington State
Fortune Ida	E45C		of Washington State
Fortune John	E34Da		d. Central Idaho
Fortune Walter	E45A		of Washington State
Foster Lula	B63Ha		
Fowler Beatrice	F38Ba		
Fowler Elizabeth	A87A		
Fowler Henry	E69Aaf	1827ca	m.1854Jun11
Fowler Phyllis Jeanne	F37Bb	1937May23	b.p.Kans/ m.1969Nov Cole Co Mo
Fowler Ruth Jane	E69Aa		m.1889May
Fowler Thomas	B05Faf		
Fowler William	A87B	1700Julca	b.p.Md/Anne ArundelCo/SoR.ch.1700Jul26
Fox I J	A13Ia		
Francher Dr	H15Da		of Kansas
Francis Almedia	F55C		

NAME	NUMBER	BIRTH	COMMENTS
Francis Annie	F55I		
Francis Biddie	F55E		
Francis Edward	F55H		
Francis Eva	F55D		
Francis Fanny Mrs	F55Fa		
Francis Gus	F55G		
Francis Logue	F55F		
Francis Marcus D.	F35Ea		d. Osage Co Mo
Francis Martha	F55B		
Francis Melissia Mary	F55A		-
Francis W.R.	Q45Ga		no issue
Franklin -	E46A		of Freeburg Mo
Franklin -	E46B		of Freeburg Mo
Franklin -	S22Ga		, of Maries Co Mo
Franklin -	E46C		of Freeburg Mo
Franklin -	E46D		of Belle Mo
Franklin -	E46E		of Summerfield Mo
Franklin -	E46F		of Freeburg Mo
Franklin -	E46G		of St. Louis Mo
Franklin -	E46H		of Belle Mo
Franklin Jemima	D17Da		m1823Jan16
Franklin Robert	S22Gaf		
Franklin Robert	E29Aa		m1885Dec23 d1930Oct3
Franks Lucinda P	F39Aa	1898Mar27	m1918Jul14 d1982
Franz John F	A72Fa	1936Dec1	m1957
Freeman Jean	D79Ca		m1962Aug14
Freese R.L.	G63Ha		of Howard Co Mo
Frey P.C.	J17Ba		of Maries Co Mo
Fritts Arletha	G35Ja		
Fritts Frances A	G35Ka	1847Aug18	d1924Jun23
Fritts Marion F	R21Ca		of Maries Co Mo Mercantile business
Fritts Philip	R21Aaf		
Fritts Phillip	G35Jaf		could be R21Aaf
Fritts Robert W	R21Aa	1835Jul11	d1917Mar20 Maries Co. School teacher
Fulton Frank	M13Da		
Fuort John	A68Ca		Farmer of Arkansas
Gabriel John	D35Aa		
Gaddy Harm	K32Fa		d. Phelps Co Mo
Gaines -	Y18Ca		of Maries Co Mo and west coast
Gaines Susan	Z27Aa		Maries Co Mo d.Washington State
Gaines Thomas	Z27Fa		
Gaines William	Z27Aaf		
Gaither Alfred Haywood	F09B		b.p. No.Car. Morganton
Gaither Alfred Moore	F08A	1793	b.p.No.Car m1828Mar7 d1829Apr Burke Co
Gaither Anne	F06A	1729Feb25	b.p.Md Anne Ar. Co d1802 N.C./Rowan Co
Gaither Basil	F47B		
Gaither Basil	F07B		d N.C.Rowan 1802 House Commons 1792-02
Gaither Basil Mrs	F07Ba		
Gaither Benjamin	F46B		b.p.Md/Anne Ar Co In fathers will 1739

NAME	NUMBER	BIRTH	COMMENTS
Gaither Benjamin	F05A	1681Feb20	b.p.Md/AnneAr Co So.R m1709Sep8 d1741
Gaither Benjamin	F06B	1710Jul16	b.p.Md/AnneAr Co dN.C.Rowan Co 1783
Gaither Benjamin	F07D		In Will of father 1777Mar26
Gaither Betsey	F47C		Will of Basil 1802Dec8 N.C. Rowan Co
Gaither Brice	F07C		In Will of Edw.F06D 1777 Md MontgomCo
Gaither Burgess	F07A	1757Jul16	b.p. Md. d1819 of N.C.Rowan,IredellCos
Gaither Burgess Sidney	F08H	1807	b.p.N.C.Iredell Co dMorganton N.C.1892
Gaither Burgess Sidney	F09D	1872Jun14	b.p.N.C.Morganton m1899Jan25 d1942Mar.
Gaither Cassandra	F06C	1734Mar23	b.p. Md. Anne Arundel Co. So.River
Gaither Charles C.P.	F08J		
Gaither Delia E	F09C		
Gaither Edward	F45C		In Nicholas Will1793Jan4 Iredell CoN.C
Gaither Edward	F46A		b.p.Md/AnneAr Co In Will father 1739
Gaither Edward	F06D	1714Dec20	b.p.Md/AnneAr d1777 Md/Montgomery Co
Gaither Edward	F05B	1689Sep28	b.p.Md/Anne Arundel Co. So River
Gaither Eleanor E	F08I		
Gaither Elizabeth	F06E	1711Oct14	b.p. Md/Anne Arundel Co So. River
Gaither Elizabeth	B07Gam		
Gaither Ellen	F47A	1769Jul7	b.p.Md/Prince Georges Co
Gaither Elvira	F08D		
Gaither Forrest	F08E		
Gaither Gassaway	F47F		In Will Basil 1802Dec8 Rowan Co N.C.
Gaither George Mrs	F02Aa		
Gaither George R	F02A		b.pEngland Original name Gater
Gaither Henry	F06F	1724May24	b.p.Md/Anne Ar Co So River Parish
Gaither Horatio	F45A		In Nicholas Will 1793Jan4 N.C.Iredell
Gaither John	F05C	1677Jan15	b.p.Md/Anne Arundel Co So. River Par
Gaither John	F03A	1599 ca	b.p.England m In Eng d. in Va. Of Md.
Gaither John	F06G	1713Apr24	b.p. Md/Anne Ar Co So River Parish
Gaither John Jr	F04A		b.p.Eng. mEng To Va1635/Ship Assurance
Gaither John Mrs	F05Ca		
Gaither Johnsey	F07E		In fathers Will 1777Mar24Montg.Co/Md.
Gaither Joseph	F06M	1722Sep18	b.p. Md/Anne Arundel Co. So River Par.
Gaither Joshua	F46C		b.p. Md/Anne Arundel Co In Will 1739
Gaither Libetious	F45D		In Will Nicholas 1793Jan4 N.C.Iredell
Gaither Mahala	E29Cam	1839Jan29	d1909 Jul15 Vichy Mo
Gaither Maria	F08G		
Gaither Martin	F08B		
Gaither Mary	F06L	1732Mar17	b.p. Md/Anne Arundel Co So River Par.
Gaither Mary	F05D	1682Apr13	b.p.Md/Anne Arundel Co So River
Gaither Mary Mrs	F03Aa	1605abt	of England
Gaither Millie	F08F		
Gaither Nathan	F47D		
Gaither Neley	F47E		
Gaither Nicholas	F07F		m(1)1779Oct26Md(2)1792Sep18 d.N.C.1793
Gaither Rebecca	F05E	1695May24	b.p. Md/Anne Arundel Co So River Par.
Gaither Ruth	F06H	1719Oct23	b.p.M.D./ Anne Arundel Co So River Par
Gaither Ruth	F05F	1679Sep8	b.p.M.D./Anne Arundel Co m1703Jan13Md
Gaither Samuel	F06I	1718Jan19	b.p. Md/ Anne Arundel Co So River Par

NAME	NUMBER	BIRTH	COMMENTS
Gaither Sarah	F06J	1726Mar19	b.p. Md/Anne Arundel Co So River Par.
Gaither Sarah	F08C		
Gaither Susan	F05G	1697	b.p. Md/Anne Arundel Co
Gaither Walter	F45B		In Will Nicholas(F07F)1793Jan4 N.C.
Gaither William	F06K	1728Jul11	b.p.Md/Anne Arundel Co So River Parish
Gaither William	F09A		b.p. N.C, Morganton
Gardner John	U14Da		of Iberia Mo
Garner Margaret	B06Aa	1720abt	
Garrett George	B16Ca		
Garrett Juanita	B27A		
Garrett Ledfrow	B27C		
Garrett Leland	B27B		
Gassaway Anne	B04Da		m1697Aug13
Gassaway Mary	B08Ea		Parents probably Thomas and Sarah
Gassaway Nicholas	B04Daf		
Gassaway Thomas	B08Eaf		
Gates Evaline	B81A	1821Aug31	b.p.N.Y./Wash.Co m1845Oct18NY dMo1896
Gates H	A14Ea		
Gates Lydia Mrs	B80Aa		of Washington Co N.Y. 1821
Gates William	B80A		of Washington Co/N.Y. in 1821
Gausman Chester H	D79Ba	1920ca	m1944Dec27 Pres Central Comm CollegeNe
Gausman Darlene Bertha	D79Cb		m1962Jun17
Gausman Harold	D80C	1954Aug1	Architecture Univ Oregon
Gausman John	D80A	1946Oct7	of So.D/Custer Co In Peace Corp
Gausman Kristine	D80B	1949Jul8	of Nebraska, Nebr.City
Gelette Julia Ann	I42Ba		of Polk Co/Maries Co/Mo Of Alabama
Gentry R Hazel	C39Aam		
German Zachariah	Y15Fd		
Gibbons Martha	M23Ca		
Gibson Anna B	Q44Ka		
Gibson James	G65Aa		
Gibson Jane	K12Da		m1876Oct2 Maries Co/Mo
Gibson Mary J	Q44Gc		of Maries Co Mo
Gibson Robert	Q44Gcf		
Giddens Elizabeth	C35Aam		
Giesler Acy	Q34Ba		no issue
Giesler Carrie L	M24B		
Giesler David	M15Da		b.p. Tenn
Giesler Edward Lee	M24A		of Northeastern Maries Co Mo
Giesler Ely	M15Caf	1818	b.p.Tenn m(1)1839Mar28 Arrived Mo 1835
Giesler John	M15Daf	1800abt	d1876Dec13 of Tenn and Mo.
Giesler John Henry	M15Ca		of Laclede Co Mo
Giesler Mary	M24C		
Giesler Nancy L	K32Eb		
Giesler Noah	Q42Da		
Giesler Waldo	D63Ca		of Owensville Mo
Gile Thomas	D77Aa		m1902Feb26
Gill John	F32Ca		
Gillispie Charles J.	D55B		

NAME	NUMBER	BIRTH	COMMENTS
Gillispie Jesse	D50Aa		
Gillispie Jesse	Y52Ab		
Gillispie Lillian	D55A		
Gillispie Malissa	Y41Ha		of Vienna Mo
Gillispie Tillie	Y57Ca		of Phelps Co Mo
Gillispie William B	E22Ca		
Gilmore Robert	E17Ja		m1841Jun25
Gilstrap Alonzo	C18B	1885Jul5	b.p. Mo/Newton Co m1909 Feb21
Gilstrap Clarence E.	C18H	1900Sep4	b.p. Mo/Newton Co d1951Apr2
Gilstrap Doris	C20Ca		m1944 Jan5
Gilstrap Edith Ray	C18G	1896Mar22	b.p. Mo/Newton Co d1897Jul3
Gilstrap Edna Lorene	C18I	1903Dec13	b.p.Mo/Newton Co m1922Oct18 d1939Oct30
Gilstrap Gertrude L	C18F	1894Aug23	b.p. Mo/Newton Co m1912May5
Gilstrap Lewis	C18C	1887Jan22	b.p.Mo/Newton Co
Gilstrap Mary Elma	C18E	1890Sep22	b.p. Mo/Newton Co m1909Mar13 d1930Jun
Gilstrap Maude M	C18D	1889Jan23	b.p.Mo/Newton Co d1890Mar16
Gilstrap Peter G	C16Caf		
Gilstrap Tabitha	C16Ba		
Gilstrap Wilbert A	C18A	1881Dec22	b.p.Mo/Newton Co m1907Dec22
Gilstrap William Henry	C16Ca	1857Sep19	b.p.Mo/Newton Co m1879Sep21 d1944Jan4
Ginn George	G15Fa		of Oklahoma
Girardin David	B76Aa	1943Oct19	m(2)1977Jan Jacksonville Fla.
Girton Alfred Franklin	B67A	1863Mar21	b.p.Pa/Espy m1882Feb22 d1942Feb13
Girton Jessie S.	B68A	1883Fab17	b.p.Pa/Luzerne Co m1903Sep3 d1966May2
Girton John K	B65A	1805Mar10	d1875May27 Bloomsburg Pa
Girton Margaret Mrs	B65Aa	1804Jan29	d.1890Mar14 Bloomsburg Pa
Girton William G	B66A	1830Apr2	d1897May14 Pa Cabinet maker
Given Angeline	V13Fa	1867Aug25	d.1908Nov11. No issue
Given Benjamin F	R12Ga		of Maries Co Mo
Given H.E.	V13Faf		
Glasby Minnie Bell	C40Aam	1868Jul3	b.p.Mo.St.Louis d.1894Mar26NewtonCo,Mo
Glenn Carl	Y76Ga		m1922Apr8 Of Vichy Mo
Glenn L.A.	Y47Ba		of Phelps Co Mo
Goe Philip	I15Fa		d.Kentucky
Goggin Charles	Y29Fa		of Maries and Phelps Cos Mo
Gojeski Carolyn Ann L	C20Ba		Parents born in Germany
Good Claude	B34B		
Good Dale	B36A		
Good Donald	B36B		
Good Francis	B35B		
Good Fred	B37A		
Good George Ulysses	B15Ea		m1893Oct19 d.1932Apr22
Good Herbert Ulysses G	B22G	1906Oct23	b.p. Mo Albany m1945May d.1949Aug19
Good John Earl	B22D	1900May1	b.p. Okla/Stillwater m1925Feb22
Good Lawrence	B35A		
Good Lloyd	B36C		
Good Loren	B34A		
Good Oran D	B22F	1904Nov11	b.p. Mo Albany m1934May27
Good Paul Woodson	B22E	1902May4	b.p. Mo/Albany m1926Aug16 d1956Jun25

NAME	NUMBER	BIRTH	COMMENTS
Good Reva Berthena	B22I	1911Aug8	b.p. Mo/Darlington m1936Oct1
Good Roy Elvis	B22A	1894Nov29	b.p. Mo Albany m1922Oct9
Good Ruby Marie	B22H	1908Jul10	b.p. Mo Albany m1935Jun23
Good Thomas Wade	B22C	1897Jan27	b.o. Mo/Gentry Co m1921Jul13
Good William Ray	B22B	1895Dec11	b.p.Mo Gentry Co m1917Jan10
Goodman Alfred	Y41Ea		of Pulaski Mo
Goodman David M	V24Aa		of Maries Co Mo
Goodman J	A11Ba		
Goodman M	A11Ab		
Goodman William	R30Fa		of Belle Mo
Goodnight Bud	H14Da		of Maries Co Mo No issue
Goodwin Margaret	A77Da	1913Nov27	m1936Mar17
Goolsby Nathalie	A75Aa	1926May30	
Gorsig Laura	Z14Ca		
Gosch William	D80Ba		of Nebraska City Nebr.
Gosney Alice	R24Na		m1923 Of Kansas City Mo
Gove William	G16Fa		no issue
Grady -	G50Ba		of Maries and Taney Cos Mo
Grady Mary Elizabeth	B44Ba		m1970
Graham -	H54Ca		
Graham Clorah Belle	J27A	1866July9	m1892Aug28 d.1906May10
Graham Eliza	J26C	1847Nov13	b.p. Tenn/Knox Co m1867Jun27 Mo d.192_
Graham George Emerson	J27H	1885Mar28	m1906Apr26 Springfield Mo
Graham George Wash.	J12Jaf	1826Dec31	b.p.Tn/Knox Co d1891Apr3 Maries Co Mo
Graham Harriet M.	J27C	1891Aug7	d.1898Aug7
Graham J.W.	L19Ba		of Granite City Mo
Graham James Wade	J27I	1889Mar29	m.1919Aug16 WWI of Warrensburg Mo
Graham John Calvin	J26A	1838Aug15	b.p.Tn/Knox Co d.Civil War 1863Feb20
Graham John Clemens	J27G	1883Jul1	m1907Apr18 Vienna Mo County Clerk
Graham Katherine	Y73Ba		m.Warren Co Mo Of Maries Co
Graham Leona May	J27E	1887Apr23	m1904Jul7 d1930Nov7
Graham Marusia	J27B		d in infancy
Graham Mary Jane	J26D	1840Dec24	b.p. Tn/Knox Co mTn1855Sep18 d1874Mo.
Graham Michael S.	J26B	1844Sep23	m(1)1865Sep26(2)1880ca d1914Jul10Mo
Graham Orleana	J27D	1896Jul26	d 1898Sep10
Graham Sarah Neppie	J27J	1893Nov11	m1913Sep17 Of Dixon Mo.
Graham William P.	J27F	1881May30	m.1900Dec30 Of Washington Mo
Granaman Dora	E31A		b.p. Mo/Maries Co d Maries Co.
Granaman Eva	E31D		of Maries Co Mo
Granaman Fritz	E22Aa		d. Maries Co Mo
Granaman Laura	E31G		
Granaman Louie	E31F		of St. Louis Mo
Granaman Lula	E31B		of Union Mo
Granaman Sophia	E31C		No issue
Granaman Waymon	E31E		of St. Louis Mo
Granaman William	E31H		
Grant Joe	P160a		of Kansas City Mo
Grant William	I12Ea		
Gray Elmer	G59Da		of Oklahoma

NAME	NUMBER	BIRTH	COMMENTS
Green "Doc"	T24Ha		
Green -	Z41F		Moved to far west. Probably Oregon
Green Anna	F22Eam		
Green Barbara	Z42H		of Maries Co Mo
Green Bee Ann	Z42B		of Colorado
Green Caroline	Z42E		
Green Clarcie	F39Ca		d1973Jul2 California
Green David	Z41E		left Maries Co Mo Single
Green Dillard	Z41A		In Maries Co Mo before 1844 from Tenn.
Green Dillard Mrs	Z41Aa		d. in Tennessee
Green Elisha	Z40A		
Green Elisha Mrs	Z40Aa		
Green Elizabeth Ann	D75Fa		m1846Jan8
Green Harriet	Z42G		
Green Henry	Z41C		of Maries Co Mo
Green Jane	Z42C		
Green John	R27Ja		
Green John	F14Aa		m1781Nov27
Green John Erwin	B20A	1892Nov17	b.p. Mo/Albany d1962Oct10
Green John Francis	B15Ba		b.p. Mo/Albany m1892Jan10 d1915Sep7 Mo
Green Mary Jane	Z42I		
Green Mary Jane	Z41D	1835Jun11	b.p. Tenn m1855Mar1 d1912May25JoplinMo
Green Sarah	Z42D		
Green Sarah Ann	Z41B		
Green Sarah Jane	Z42F		
Green Thomas Rev	F21Ea		m1827Feb3
Green Verna J	B20C	1897Oct2	b.p.Mo/Albany d1901Jan16
Green Vesta Alverda	B20B	1895Mar13	d1957Apr
Green Wesley	Z42A		of Cole Co Mo
Greenfield Eleanor	F07Fa		m1779Oct26 Md/Anne Arundel Co
Greenstreet Elizabeth	K36Ab		
Greenstreet Jane S	C36Ea		m1851Aug9 Morgan Co Mo
Greenstreet Vergie E	D29Fa		m1903
Greever Emma L	V12Bb		To Mo 1853 1st m.Hutchison- of DixonMo
Gregg Samuel Benjamin	F66Fa	1880Feb3	d.1961Jul11
Gregory Cornelia	B69Aa	1906Oct19	b.p. Tex/Austin m1940Sep19 d1976Apr27
Gregory Thomas W	B69Aaf		Atty Gen.U,S, Wilson Administration
Gremp -	G31A		
Gremp Christian C	G31F	1867Jun5	m1891Jun20 d1899Feb2 Of Carthage Mo.
Gremp Fannie Isabelle	G31B	1865Jul29	d1900Dec28 Form.Gremp von Freudenstein
Gremp Henry J Dr.	G31E	1863Mar30	m.1887Feb d1930Aug15
Gremp Karl Ludwig	G29Ia	1831Jul22	m1848Aug29 Maries Co/Mo d1903Sep5
Gremp Mary	G31C		
Gremp Solomon A Dr	G31D	1859Oct5	m1884Jul2 d1900Aug15
Gremp William A Dr	G31G	1869Jun22	d1833Jul15 of Vienna and Iberia Mo
Griffeth Mary	A62Ca	1804	m1822 d1886
Griffey Beckey	F35Ga		d Mt Zion Mo
Griffin Henry Coleman	C18Ia		
Griffith David	E41Ca		of Maries Co Mo

NAME	NUMBER	BIRTH	COMMENTS
Griffith Dorcas Ann	R30Aa		of Belle Mo
Griffith Eleanor	F14Da	1766Mar9	m1785Jul27
Griffith Henry	F14Daf		of Montgomery Co Md
Griffith Ida	S22Fa		of Maries Co Mo
Griffith William	R30Da		of Belle Mo
Groff Belle	R28Da		
Groff Chester A	J24Ea		
Groff James	R30Ia		of Kansas City Mo
Groff Rachel	R26Da		no issue
Grummond Sarah	A15Ba		
Guffey -	H57Ia		of St. Louis Mo
Guffey H.B.	Y51Da		of Rolla Mo
Gwatney Donnie	B45Ba		
Gwatney Eric	B54A	1976Mar16	b.p. Louisiana
Hadley Sam	Y37Aa		Cousin of form Gov Hadley Loveland Co.
Haggerty Tom	G16Da		of Kansas City Mo.
Hairfield Barbara	E86Ba		of Okla City, Okla.
Haislip Della	Z28Ac		
Hale Elizabeth	A70Ga	1855Aug3	d.1927Nov20
Hale Martha	A70Ha		
Hale Rhoda	A70Ia		
Hall Benjamin E	C37Cbf	1808Mar19	b.p.Tenn/Carrol Co mTenn d1872Oct28Mo
Hall Mary Emily	C37Cb	1853Dec13	b.p.Ark/Carroll Co d1942Aug1 PrestonMo
Hall Mott	A15Ib		
Hall William	J24Da		of Springfield Mo
Halslip-	Y27Ca		
Hamblatt Theresa	E85Ea		
Hamilton Frank	C16Ea		
Hamilton Raymond	A77Ea	1910abt	
Hamm -	D76Ha		
Hammond Bert	Y73Aa		of Maries Co Mo and Colorado
Hammond Nathan	F21Ca		
Hammond Ruth	F14Dam		
Hammond Vachel	F21Caf		
Hancock -	G29Ca		
Hancock Elizabeth C	B75B	1971Feb16	b.p.Italy Pozzuali
Hancock George Gray	B75A	1974Jan17	b.p.Texas/Houston
Hancock George II Dr.	B73Ba	1942Dec8	b.p.Miss/Taylorsville
Hancock Gilbert	S13Eaf		
Hancock Malinda	S13Ea		of Oklahoma
Hanes Luster	E15Ea	1810Nov13	
Hankley Thomas	G44Fa		
Hannah Margaret	V11Aa		d1873Aug11 Vienna Mo
Harberger Eliza	A15Ea		
Hardesly Francis	F05Fa		m1703Jan13 Md/Anne Arundel Co So.River
Hardin Matilda	G51Fa		
Hardwick Marilyn	A72Ea	1935Nov8	m1954
Harlan J.V.	F53Aa	1929Mar23	b.p. Kans Wichita m1961Jun3 Topeka Kan
Harmon Richard Clark	B76Ba	1958May24	b.p. Mass/Bourne

NAME	NUMBER	BIRTH	COMMENTS
Harmon Windell	B76Baf		
Harness Benton M	A76Pa	1888Apr23	
Harris B.F.	V13Ea		
Harris Belle	R28Aa		
Harris Jesse	D75Da	1837Jul29	
Harris John Roberts	A66Aa	1835abt	
Harris Luvicey	I47Ca		m1867 Conway Mo d30Mar1881
Harris Nathan	I47Caf		
Harris William H	S20Ca		
Harrison Adolpheus	Y50B		of Belle Mo
Harrison Alice	Q43F		m1878Nov21
Harrison Arminta	Q45G		d1935 Gasconade Co Mo No issue
Harrison Benjamin F	Q44I		d in infancy
Harrison Cecil	Y50D		of Belle Mo
Harrison Clark Monroe	Q44B		d early single
Harrison Eliza	Q42D		
Harrison Eliza M	Q43E		
Harrison Elizabeth	F42Ba		
Harrison Elizabeth	Q45E		
Harrison Emeline	Q45C		of Maries Co Mo
Harrison Francis M	Q45B	1845	m1868 d1935 Of Kansas and St. Louis Mo
Harrison Grace	Y50C		of Belle Mo
Harrison John Henry	Q44C	1847Apr17	d 1867 on way to Texas
Harrison John Milton	Q43B		
Harrison John Tyree	Q45A		of Purcell Jasper Co Mo
Harrison Joseph Albert	Q44L	1865Mar25	m1892Jun26 d1915Feb24
Harrison Lavina	Q45F	1838Mar13	of Maries Co Mo
Harrison Lewis Harvey	Q44H	1857Jan13	d.1936Apr5 Of Maries Co and St LouisMo
Harrison Lewis Sr	Q42B	1812Aug6	b.p.N.C. m(2)1856 d1879Dec28 Mo/Maries
Harrison Loadicea N	Q44D	1839Mar18	d.1923Dec19
Harrison Malissa Jane	Q44E	1341Apr27	d1932June
Harrison Marshall C	Q44G	1853Jan11	m(1)1880Feb1 d.1930Dec14 Of Cadmus Mo
Harrison Marshall Mrs	Q44Gb		
Harrison Mary J	Q43C	1838abt	1916May10
Harrison Matilda	Q42E		of Rolla Mo
Harrison Olive Medora	Q44J	1867Jun30	m1888 d.1931Feb10
Harrison Permelia	Q43D	1842Mar4	b.p.Mo/Maries Co
Harrison Sarah Jane	Q45D		
Harrison Sterling P	Q44K	1863Apr17	d1890Mar4
Harrison Thomas Jeff.	Q44F	1850Apr6	m1873Apr27 d1930Nov29 Maries Co/Mo
Harrison Tyree	Q42C		m.Va or NoCar d1892 Maries Co Mo
Harrison William	Q42A	1807Dec17	b.p.N.C. Sura River Maries Co/Mo 1826
Harrison William Alex.	Q44A		d early single
Harrison William H	Y50A		of Belle Mo
Harrison Willian J.	Q43A		m1871Dec31 Of Maries Co Mo
Hart Adam	Q33Caf		b.p.Tenn/Knox Co Of Maries Co/Mo
Hart Clarence	Y54Ea		of Maries Co Mo
Hart Dennis	Q33Ba	1822Feb12	b.p.Tenn d1890May12 Maries Co Mo
Hart Ethel	Y52Db		First marriage to Charles Hale

NAME	NUMBER	BIRTH	COMMENTS
Hart Everett	Y54Ia		of Bland Mo
Hart J. Bert	H56Fa		
Hart John	Y54Eaf		of Maries Co Mo
Hart John Avery	Y52Dbf		
Hart Louisa J	H53Ba	1844May3	d.1930Aug11
Hart Lovick	Q33Ca	1825abt	of Maries Co Mo To Texas after Civil W
Hartley Thomas	A38Ea		m1787Oct9 Rowan Co No Car
Hartman Catherine	B62E	1879	b.p. Pa/Danville d1891 bu.Grovania Pa
Hartman Daniel H.	B73A	1949Feb27	b.p.Texas Houston
Hartman Daniel H.	B62F	1884Jun4	b.p.Pa/Montour Co m1903Sep3 d1962Dec24
Hartman Emanuel W	B62C	1886Aug9	b.p.Pa/Montour Co m1910Mar17
Hartman Harry Franklin	B69A	1905Jan8	b.p.Pa/Bloomsburg m1940Sep19 Texas
Hartman Helen Viola	B69C	1908Aug20	b.p.Pa/Bloomsburg m1929Jan31 Roslyn NY
Hartman Isaac	B61C		no issue. Of Three Rivers Michigan
Hartman Jacob	B60A		USA of British Stock d1907 Grovania Pa
Hartman Julia Nalle	B73B	1942Nov19	b.p. Texas/Houston
Hartman Leander	B61B		
Hartman Lloyd Franklin	B62A	1881Nov25	b.p.Pa/Danville m1906Apr24 d1935Aug Pa
Hartman Ruth Rebecca	B69B	1906Nov2	b.p.Pa m1925Jun6 Roslyn NY d1970Oct13
Hartman Stella Viola	B62B	1888Nov1	b.p. Pa/Lightstreet m1909Nov18 d1951
Hartman Wellington	B61A		
Hartman William Alfred	B61D	1856	b.p.Pa m1878June d1889Nov Danville Pa
Hartman William Alfred	B62D	1890Jan27	b.p./Pa/Grovania m1912May28 d. Pa.
Hartnett Eva Clare	C38Ca	1895Jun16	b.p.Mo/Preston m1914Dec23 d1969Jan1 Mo
Hartnett Thomas F.	C38Caf	1865Jan30	b.p.Iowa/Monroe Co m1890Feb10 d1936 Mo
Haskell Charles W	V26Aa		no issue
Hassler Basil R	E73A	1895Aug8	Mo/Osage Co m.1919Aug13 d.1980May10 Mo
Hassler Lee Kenneth	E74A	1922Jun3	b.p.Mo/Osage Co m.1941Sep17
Hassler Pleasant A	E71Ba		
Hassler Sherley Jean	E75A	1942Apr3	b.p.Mo.Freedom Osage Co m.1968Apr6
Hassler Thomas Jeffer.	E72Aa		
Hastings S.E.	G20Ga		m1906Dec27 Of St Louis Mo
Hatfield Myrtle	D77Ca		
Hatmaker -	M27Fa		of St. Louis Mo
Hawes Cora Eva	C18Ba		m1909Feb21
Hawes David E	C18Ea		m1909Mar13
Hawes Emma Mae	C18Aa		m1907Dec22
Hawkins Anna	Y38B		of St Louis Mo
Hawkins Barney	J12Ka		
Hawkins Beditha Ellen	G37Ba	1852Oct13	d1912May19
Hawkins Bertha	Y36C		of St Louis Mo
Hawkins Beulah	E43Ja		of Jefferson City Mo
Hawkins Dora	Y36A		of Iberia Mo
Hawkins Elsie Mae	E88Aa	1916Apr16	b.p.Mo./St.Clair
Hawkins George P	R24Caf	1848Feb26	m.1868Apr6 d1924Aug2 Maries Co. Mo
Hawkins Jesse F	E88Aaf	1889Feb4	b.p.Mo Union m1912Nov23
Hawkins John	G37Baf		of Osage Co Mo Sheriff
Hawkins Lou	R24Ca		m1903Dec24 Of Pineville Mo
Hawkins Lucy	Y36E		

NAME	NUMBER	BIRTH	COMMENTS
Hawkins Mabel	Y36F		
Hawkins Mary E	Y20B		
Hawkins Obedience	Y36D		
Hawkins Oma	Y36B		of Anna Illinois
Hawkins Permelia	R22Aa	1852Oct4	m1867Nov11 d1896Aug29
Hawkins Price	Z34Da		of Kansas City Mo
Hawkins Ray	Y36G		d single
Hawkins Robert	R22Aaf		Moved "west"
Hawkins Sallie	Y20D		
Hawkins Samuel H	R26Ga		of Belle Mo and Franklin Co Mo
Hawkins Sarah	Q39Bam	1846Aug11	m1865 d1929Apr13 Father Perry E
Hawkins Thomas A	Y38A		of Vienna Mo
Hawkins Thomas R	Y20C		d 1936 Vienna Mo
Hawkins William	R26Gaf		of Mt Sterling Mo Militia Mormon War
Hawkins William L	Y20A		of Maries Co Mo
Hawkins Zion R	Y13Ha		mabt1845 d.1866
Hayden Mary Angeline	F56Ha	1854Aug22	b.p.Ark m1880Dec16 d1943Jul6 Okla
Hayes Jemima	I20B		
Hayes Martha	H53Ca		
Hayes William	I20A		born before 1800
Hayes William Sr	I15Ca		m1775 d1804Dec13 Murdered
Haynes -	E61Fa		
Haynes Caroline	D81D	1850	
Haynes Cornelius F	D81I	1868	b.p. Mo Gasconade Co
Haynes David	D81E	1852	b.p. Mo Gasconade Co
Haynes Eliza	Q45Aa		of Purcell Mo
Haynes Elmira	D81F	1854	b.p. Mo Gasconade Co
Haynes Hiram	D81A	1843	b.p. Mo Gasconade Co
Haynes Jefferson	D81C	1848	b.p. Mo Gasconade Co
Haynes John M	D81J	1875	b.p. Mo Gasconade Co
Haynes Luster	E61Ca		m1837Jun1
Haynes Manerva	D81B	1846	b.p. Mo Gasconade Co
Haynes Mary	D81G	1856	b.p. Mo Gasconade Co
Haynes Olive	D81H	1867	b.p. Mo Gasconade Co
Haynes Richard	D21Ca		
Haynes Wesley	D81K		
Haynes William	Y43Aa		
Haynes William	Z27Ca		of Maries Co Mo
Haynes William	D22La	1824	b.p. Tenn
Hazzard Livonia	G35Oa		
Headman Charles	R27Ka		
Healey Thomas	V18Fb		
Heaton Lula	B13Ca		
Hedge -	T25Ba		of Iberia Mo
Hegeman Grace	A15Ma		
Heide Charles	Y65Da		of Bland Mo
Heimbach Emma	B58Aa	1831	d. 1908
Helbert Charles E	E47C		of Shannon Co Mo
Helbert Eva	E47A		of Shannon Co Mo

NAME	NUMBER	BIRTH	COMMENTS
Helbert John T	E21Fa		of Maries Co Mo. Oper. Threshing Mach
Helbert Maud	E47B		of Shannon Co Mo
Helton Amanda	U12M		m1871 Jul9
Helton Ben	U15C		
Helton Bertie	U15G		
Helton Charles	U12O	1870Jun15	m1891Feb10 d1925Feb10
Helton Crismon	U11C		of Maries Co Mo
Helton David	U12I		m1880 of Cole Co Mo
Helton Elizabeth	U11H		m1827Feb11 Osage Co Mo
Helton Elizabeth	U13G		m1877Jun3
Helton Elmeda	U15I		
Helton Eunice	E36B		
Helton George	U15D		
Helton Gib	G19Ha		of Maries and Franklin Cos Mo
Helton Gordon	E36A		
Helton Henry	U14B		
Helton Isaac	U14A		d single
Helton Isaac C	U12G	1837Apr2	b.p. Mo Osage Co d1930Mar18 Union Sol.
Helton Isaac Sr	U11A	1811	m1828Oct2 Osage Mo. Of Maries Co Mo
Helton James	U10A		
Helton James	U11D		
Helton James	J14Eaf		m(1)Vaughan Bursetta Of Maries Co Mo
Helton James	U12D	1835abt	m Maries Co Mo
Helton James C	G62Ha		of Maries Co Mo and St Louis
Helton James Reuben	U13A	1852May15	b.p. Mo Maries Co m1870Sep22 d1935Nov
Helton Jane	U11G		
Helton Jesse Jr	U15E		
Helton Jesse Sr	U12E		m1870Sep22
Helton John	U14C		of Garden City Kansas
Helton John	U13B		
Helton John	E54Eb		
Helton Judith	U12K		of Maries Co Mo
Helton Louisa	U11I		
Helton Louisa	U15H		
Helton Louisa J	U12A		of Vienna Mo and Shannon Co Mo
Helton Lydia	J14Ea	1854May23	
Helton Margaret J	U13F		of Pulaski Mo
Helton Martin	U12N		m1885Feb26
Helton Mary	U14D		of Iberia Mo
Helton Mary	U12L		
Helton Mary	U13D	1845Apr9	b.p. Mo/Maries Co m1860Jan12 d1916Jul
Helton Moses	U15A		
Helton Nancy	U12B		
Helton Nancy	U13E		
Helton Oliver	U15B		
Helton Perry	U12C		m1872Feb4 Of Maries Co Mo and Texas
Helton Peter	U11E		
Helton Polly	U11F		twin of William Todd Helton
Helton Rachel	U12H		

NAME	NUMBER	BIRTH	COMMENTS
Helton Richard	U13C	1860Jan27	d1925Jan18
Helton Robert	U12J		m1894Sep9 Of Oklahoma
Helton Stephen	U12F		m1867Feb13 Of Maries Co Mo. Okla 1893
Helton William	G62Haf		
Helton William	U15F		
Helton William T	J18Ba		of Adair Oklahoma
Helton William Todd	U11B	1823Aug17	m1842 d1881Aug9 Maries Co Mo
Henderson Abiel	V24Cam		of Reynolds Co and Maries Co Mo
Henderson Albert Smith	Z30Aa	1841Jul11	m1867Aug15 d1918Dec25 Vienna Mo
Henderson Charles	Z34B		of Vienna Mo
Henderson Dora	Z34D		of Kansas City Mo
Henderson Florence	Z34H	1875Dec22	m1899Apr23 d1932Oct26
Henderson Helen A	Z34F	1869Oct22	m1892Oct23 d1921Feb20
Henderson James Alton	Z34G	1899Oct29	m1920Apr1 Killed by train 1921Sep25
Henderson Jane	Y72Fa	1850Oct10	b.p.Mo/Jackson Co dMaries Co1934Jul19
Henderson Lillie	Z34E		of St Louis Mo
Henderson Mary Lee	Z34C		of Vienna Mo
Henderson Victor	Z34A		1899Aug25 near Houston Texas
Henderson William W Dr	Y72Faf	1810Apr28	b.p. Mo/Iron Co m1836Jan28 Maries Co
Henley -	E46Ha		
Henry Patrick	J16Ga		of Webb City Mo
Henson Emily	G29Ma	1840Feb29	d.1925May21 Maries Co Mo
Henson George	G29Maf		
Henson William	G29Oa		of Maries Co Mo and Arkansas
Hern Charles Lynn	E75Aa	1942Oct20	b.p.Miss/Hattiesbburg Forest m1968Apr6
Herren Vester H Gen	A77Fa	1900Jul17	
Hiatt Abigail	F20Ba		m1809Dec20
Hiatt Stephen	F20Baf		
Hibler Dorothy	E66Ca		of Owensville Mo
Hibler Logan	E66Caf		
Hickam Elizabeth	G29Na		
Hickam Robert	G12Ha		
Hickle Harriett	J12Jam	1822Jun3	b.pTenn/Knox Co m GraingerCo Tn1837Nov
Hicks Elizabeth Jane	G62Dbm		b.p. Tennessee
Highbarger Orpha A.	F67Ea	1910Jun26	
Highley John Capt	A11Hbf	1649	m1671 d1714 of Conn Simsbury
Highley Katherine	A11Hb	1679Aug7	d.after1740
Hight -	I48Aa		of Marionville Mo
Hildebrand Mollie	Q44Ga		m1880Feb1 d1880
Hildebrand William W	Q44Gaf		
Hill Bettie Sue	F59Aa	1934Jun20	b.p. Okla/Okla. City m.1955Nov19
Hill Catherine	V12Ba	1824Dec18	d.1867Nov27
Hill Elizabeth	V12Dam	1812Jan29	m1828Jan10 Mo Maries and Gasc. Cos Mo
Hill George	V12Baf		
Hill Homer Austin	F58Aa		m1926Nov6
Hill Malinda	P14Aam		dau of George Hill
Hill Samuel Franklin	F59Aaf		
Hill William	A80Ga		
Hines William	F23Da		

NAME	NUMBER	BIRTH	COMMENTS
Hinkle John	A38Ga		m1813Jan7 Rowan Co N.C.
Hinton Mary	P12Bam	1803Jul28	d1867Feb8 Maries Co Mo
Hite Hannah	I58Ga		d before 1814
Hobbs John	B08La		
Hodges -	F52Ba		
Hodges Kerry Lee	B30Ca		m1949Jul24 Joplin Mo
Hoey C	F09Ba		
Hoey James J	R32Ea		m1920Nov15 Of Porterville California
Hogue John	Y61Ja		
Holladay Lucinda A	F30Da		
Hollenbeck Homer	Z34Ca		of Vienna Mo
Holloman Fruza	C13Ca		b.p.Tenn m1852May9 d1900Sep15 Bryon Mo
Holloway Mary	E77Ba		m.1796Dec16
Holloway Zilphia Ann	G51Gam		
Holman Alta	E43Ea		of Maries Co Mo
Holman David	D28Ca	1830Mar9	m1874Jan1 d1901Dec9 Maries Co Mo
Holman J.A.	G29Laf		
Holman James	D46B		
Holman Lyda	D46C		of Maries Co Mo
Holman Mary Susannah	R22Dam	1828Jun9	m1851Nov20 d1886Nov26
Holman Newton	D46D		born after 1874 Of Jackson Co Mo
Holman Newton	D32Ca		m Jackson Co Mo Probably (D46D)
Holman Rachel C.	G29La		m1870Nov3 Of Dixon Mo
Holman Samuel	D28Caf		From Germany Of N.C./Tenn/Carthage Mo
Holman T.D.	D33Ga		
Holman Thomas	D46A		
Holmes Albert	T30Ga		died after service in Cofederate Army
Holmes John O	E27Aa		
Holmes Lucy	T24Fa	1841Dec1	b.p. Mo Osage Co m1861Jul25 d1879Feb3
Holmes Mary Mrs	T30Cam		m. Illinois Of Westphalia Mo
Holmes Oliver	T24Faf		In gold rush to California in 1849
Holmes Oliver Perry	T30Caf		b.p. New Hamp. m.Ill. Of Wesphalia Mo
Holmes William W	T30Ca		
Holzschuh -	E51Ma		
Home Mary Mable	F51Ba	1913Dec3	
Honse Lottie	K32Ba		of Granite City Mo
Honse Mayme	Z34Ga		m1920Apr1
Hood John	H15Ea		of Maries Co Mo
Hook Daniel	A34Ja		m1787Feb19 Md/Frederick Co
Hoops Amanda M	V24B	1838Apr11	b.p. Mo/Maries Co m1857Sep d1903Dec
Hoops David	V24D		
Hoops David	V22A		To Osage Co/Mo from Va1818 dabt 1845
Hoops David	V23C		m1833Aug22(2)1845 d Maries Co Mo
Hoops Elizabeth	V25B	1839Feb8	
Hoops Frances	V27E		
Hoops George	V23A		m1836Jun23 Mo
Hoops George	V25A		
Hoops Harriett E	V25C		
Hoops Ida E	V27B		

NAME	NUMBER	BIRTH	COMMENTS
Hoops John	V23B		
Hoops John	V27A		
Hoops Louisiana	V24A		of Maries Co Mo
Hoops Lucy Ann Mrs	V22Aa		To Mo in 1818 from Va. Of Osage Co Mo
Hoops Martha	V23D		m1833Sep23 Of near Vienna Mo in 1838
Hoops Martha	V24C	1843Jun6	m1865Mar23 Maries Co Mo d1900Nov6Texas
Hoops Mary Ann	V23E		m1835Aug20
Hoops Nancy A	V25E	1850Mar19	d1923Feb3 St Louis Mo
Hoops Rachel	V23F		m1860Jul10 d1899 No issue Of Vienna Mo
Hoops Rachel A	V27C		
Hoops Susan N	V25D	1351Jul26	b.p. Mo/Maries Co d1923Apr11
Hoops Virginia	V27D		
Hope Thomas	I58Ba		m1737
Hopkins Mercy	C28Da		m1852Mar4
Horn Mildred	E85Ha		
Horn Samuel W	E19Fa		m1838Mar30 Gasconade Co Mo
Horton Jane Eliza	F08Hbm		
Howard Jeremiah Brice	F23Eb		
Howard Jesse	G33Aa		
Howard Mayme R	A77Ca	1909Sep2	m1930Oct4
Howard Minerva Jane	B11Ja		
Howard Stella	F36Ca		
Howard William	F36Caf		
Howell Deborah	I11Aa	1691	m1713 d1759 Of Phila. Pa
Howell William	I11Aaf	1650abt	d1710 Of Pa.
Hoyt Jesse	A15Fa		
Hubbard Fred	A79Ja	1916Apr19	
Hudgens Catherine	A84H		
Hudgens Crockett	A84A		
Hudgens Didley	A84C		
Hudgens Hampton	A84E		
Hudgens James	A83Ba		
Hudgens John	A84F		
Hudgens Joseph	A84G		
Hudgens Shelby	A84D		
Hudgens William	A34B		
Huffman -	Z26F		of Maries Co Mo
Huffman -	Z25A		of Kentucky
Huffman -	Z26G		
Huffman - Mrs	Z25Aa		of Kentucky
Huffman Anna Elizabeth	Z27B	1849Aug13	m Maries Co Mo. Moved to Thornton Wash
Huffman Barbara	Z26E		
Huffman Caroline	D18Ea		
Huffman Charles	Z33H		
Huffman Delila	Z28B		Probably moved to Oregon or Washington
Huffman Elizabeth	Z26D		
Huffman Frances	Z27C		of Maries Co Mo
Huffman Henry	Z26A	1818Feb6	b.p.Kentucky Moved to Maries Co Mo
Huffman Jacob	Z26B		d1862abt of Long Creek Maries Co Mo

NAME	NUMBER	BIRTH	COMMENTS
Huffman Jacob Mrs	Z26Ba		
Huffman James	Z26C		In Bloomgarden Maries Co Mo 1845Aug8
Huffman James	Z33E		"went west"
Huffman James T	Y66Ca		
Huffman James T	Z28D		
Huffman Jane	D18Da		
Huffman Jefferson D	Z29B		d single Sheriff Maries Co Mo
Huffman John	Z33F		d single
Huffman John H	Z29A		d single
Huffman John N	Z28C		
Huffman L.L.	Z28E		
Huffman Louis	Z33D		"went west"
Huffman Malissa	Z27F		of Trail Oregon
Huffman Margaret Mary	Z27D		of Maries Co Mo
Huffman Mary	Z33B		
Huffman Mary E	Z29C		m1875Sep5 Maries Co Mo
Huffman Nelson	Z33A		of Oregon
Huffman Phillip Newton	Z27A		d. In Washington State
Huffman Rowena Ann	Z33C		
Huffman Will	Z33G		of Dixon Mo
Huffman William	Z27E		of Maries and Phelps Cos Mo
Huffman William R	Z28A		Probably went to Oregon or Washington
Huffman William R Mrs	Z28Ab		
Hughes -	I58Ca		
Hughes -	E55A		of Iberia Mo
Hughes A.B.	J18D		of Moriarty New Mexico
Hughes Anna	E57G		
Hughes Bettie Jane	J18A		of Adair Oklahoma
Hughes Clay	E57C		
Hughes Daniel	E54C		
Hughes David T	Z12D		d single To California in 1850
Hughes Elisha	Z12C		
Hughes Elisha D	Z13G		d1925 Of Maries Co and St Louis Mo
Hughes Elizabeth	Z12H		
Hughes Elizabeth	E53B		
Hughes Elizabeth Ann	Q38Aam		m1845Mar20 Washington Co Mo
Hughes Ellen	E55D	1866Sep6	d1911Dec11
Hughes Elvira	Z12I	1812	b.p. Mo/Gasconade Co d1844Oct29
Hughes Etta	Z22B		of Wagoner Oklahoma
Hughes Flora	E55B		of Florida Mo
Hughes Frances	Z15B		of California
Hughes George H	Z13E		of New Mexico
Hughes Hannah	E57B		
Hughes Harriett E	Z13A	1838Nov17	of Phelps Co Mo
Hughes Hiram	Z13H		m1873Jun26 Maries Co Mo
Hughes Hiram	Z12B	1810Mar18	b.p.Ky m1838Jul22 Mo. d1891Dec21 Calif
Hughes James	Z11B		
Hughes James	E25Fa		
Hughes James E	E54A		d1877Oct1 MillerCo Mo

NAME	NUMBER	BIRTH	COMMENTS
Hughes James E Jr	E55C		
Hughes James Newton	J18C		of Center Colorado
Hughes John	Z15A		d single
Hughes John	U11Fa		
Hughes John	Z11E		
Hughes John	E52A		Welch descent
Hughes John	Z12F		of Grayson Co Texas
Hughes John P	Z13F	1852May3	m1875Jun15 d1925Jan29
Hughes Joseph	Z11D		d single
Hughes Lewis	E56C		
Hughes Lewis	E54G		
Hughes Lewis Jr	E57E		
Hughes Louisa Jane	Z14A	1839Dec2	m1853Feb27 California.
Hughes Lucinda C	Z13C		no issue
Hughes Margaret A	E55E		
Hughes Mary	E53C	1806Oct	b.p.Ky m1824Jul1 Mo d1845Mar29
Hughes Mary	Z11F		Moved to Ark during Civil War
Hughes Mary Ann	E55F	1862Dec16	m1879Dec14 d1938Dec17 Miller Co Mo
Hughes May	E57D		
Hughes McKamy Wilson	Z12A	1808Apr18	b.p.Tenn m Maries Co Mo d1887Sep13
Hughes Melvin	Z12J		d single
Hughes Melvina Jane	Z13B	1845Apr30	m1860
Hughes Minnie	E57A		
Hughes Moses	E54F		
Hughes Nancy	K11Aa		
Hughes Nancy E	J18B		of Adair Oklahoma
Hughes Nancy Priscilla	Z13D		
Hughes Napoleon B	Z14C		d 1897 Jan4
Hughes Newton	Z24Ba		of New Mexico
Hughes Oliver	Z22A		of Taney Co Mo
Hughes Polly	E54B		of Maries Co Mo
Hughes Priscilla	Z12K		d single
Hughes Rachel	E54E		
Hughes Rachel	U13Bc		m(1) Thompson - m(2)1894Apr4
Hughes Rebecca	Z12G		b.p.MoWright Co m1848
Hughes Roland	Z11C		
Hughes Ross	E56A		
Hughes Stephen	Z12E		
Hughes Stephen	E53A		
Hughes Stephen	U13Ea		
Hughes Stephen (Tebe)	E54D		d single Waynesville Mo. Drowned
Hughes Tebe	E57F		
Hughes Tebe	E56D		
Hughes Thomas	Z14B	1842	d1844
Hughes Walter	E56B		
Hughes William	Z11A		Emigrant to Md. m1807 OfKy,Tn Mo1813
Hughes William	Z10A		Welch descent Migrant to Md. d Tenn
Hughes William Mrs	Z10Aa		
Huhtala Oscar	R32Da		m1916Jul26 Of Porterville California

NAME	NUMBER	BIRTH	COMMENTS
Hull C.A.	Y64Da		
Hull Elizabeth A	D71Aa		m1867Nov27 Maries Co Mo Dry Fork
Humphrey Manley M	G57Ga		of Dixon Mo
Humphrey Mike	G63Ia		of Miller Co Mo
Humphrey Paris	Y36Aa		of Iberia Mo
Hunt -	M26Ba		
Hunt Sarah	I61Ga		
Hunter Didley	A83A		
Hunter James	A83C		
Hunter John	A38Aaf	1745abt	
Hunter John Mrs	A38Aam		
Hunter Mary (Polly)	A81A		of No.Car d Putnam Co Tenn
Hunter Mary (Polly)	A83B		
Hunter William	A81B		of probably Richmond Co N.C.
Husbands Herman	Q31Gbf		
Husbands Joseph	Q31Gb		
Huskey -			Erroneously shown as T15Iam1stPrinting
Hutchison Alexander H	S20Bb		
Hutchison Benjamin	G36Eaf		of Maries Co Mo
Hutchison Delila	Y42Dam		dau. of Joseph Hutchison Sr
Hutchison Elizabeth	Y14Fb		
Hutchison Elizabeth	G16Aam		m1852Aug12 Tenn
Hutchison Ellen	G36Ea		of Maries Co Mo
Hutchison Esther G	Q42Ba	1816May1	d1855May16
Hutchison Harrison	E31Da		of Maries Co Mo
Hutchison Henry	S22Ja		of Maries Co Mo
Hutchison James	Q42baf		
Hutchison John	S20Bbf		mTenn Of Maries Co Mo Father Joseph Sr
Hutchison L.B. Jr	G61Aa		of Ohio
Hutchison Laura I	E43Aam		m1881Oct16 d1936
Hutchison Luther	Y42Ea		
Hutchison Mat	E48Ea		
Hutchison Perry	S22Jaf		of Maries Co Mo. Father Benjamin
Hutchison William	Y42Eaf		Parents Joseph and Rachel In Civil War
Hutchison William	E48Eaf		
Hutson Della	Y54Da		of Maries Co Mo
Hutson Pat	R29Ba		
Hutton Frances	E17La		m1842Dec25
Hyatt Margaret	F21Ha		of Frederick Co Md
Ijams Susan	B05Fam		m1696Oct15 Md Anne Arundel Co So River
Imboden George Sr	Q38Aaf	1821Mar20	b.p.Va To Mo 1325 mWashington Co 1845
Imboden George W	Q38Aa	1851Jun14	d1888Aug11 No issue
Ingham Alexander	A13Da		
Innes Nannie	F30Ga		
Innes Sue	F30Ha		
Irick -	G66Ba		of St Louis Mo
Irwin Beulah	T20Aa		
Isler Grace	A45Ca		
Jackson Elizabeth	M17C		

NAME	NUMBER	BIRTH	COMMENTS
Jackson Francis	M17B		
Jackson Henry	M17A		
Jackson Jesse L	C37Ja		m1883Aug16 Of Hickory Co Mo
Jackson Spencer	M11Ha		
Jaeger Ermil	D46Ca		
James Alonzo	Z31E	1841Mar24	d1870Jan20
James Alonzo	Y52Ba		
James Americus	Z31C		d single Joined Conf Army then MoGuard
James Catherine	Z31B		d in infancy
James Columbus	Z31A		d in infancy
James Damarius	Q33Ka		of Stone Co Mo
James David	Z26Ea		of Maries Co Mo Lived on Gasc. River
James Elizabeth	Q31Ba		of Maries Co Mo
James Elizabeth	Y54Eam		of Maries Co Mo
James J.D.	E55Aa		
James John	Q31Baf		m in Tenn Of Maries Co and St Louis Mo
James John Burton Jr	D37Ca		
James John Burton Sr	Z31F		
James Leona	D50A	1902Feb14	d.1925Apr5
James Mary A	Z31G		of Osage Co Mo
James Richard	Y54Ca		of Maries Co Mo
James Thomas	Y54Ba		of Maries Co Mo
James Thomas P	Z31D	1834Jun22	d1870Nov25
Jamison Nancy Jane	Q42Bc	1836Mar1	d1902Feb22 Of Callaway Co Mo
Jarvis John	E82Ga		m.1893Aug2
Jarvis Martha F	Y61La		of Lanes Prairie, Maries Co Mo
Jenkins Sarah C.	E24Ka		
Jennings Hettie	G62Bb		
Jett -	D27Bc		
Jett Chester	E33Da		of Maries Co Mo
Jett James	E17Caf	1801	b.p Ky d1855Apr Osage Co Mo
Jett Joan	E17Ca	1821ca	b.p.Mo m1839Mar24 d1887 Osage Co Mo
Jett William	E17Ka		m1844
John Cynthia	Q33Ha		
John E.L.	D72Aa		of Maries Co Mo
John Marcus E Sr	Q33Da	1839Jan3	b.p. Tenn Conf.Army Judge Maries Co Mo
John Rebecca	Q36Da		First husband Moreland -
John William	Q33Daf	1806Aug25	m(1)1830Sept30(2)1838Mar21 d1838Sep24
Johnson -	U14Ca		of Garden City Kansas
Johnson -	Y12D		Killed in Maries Co Mo by Indians
Johnson -	G42Ia		of near High Gate Maries Co Mo
Johnson -	Y12C		
Johnson Abraham	Y13D	1817	b.p. Mo/St Louis Mo in 1823
Johnson Alfred B	Y25I	1859Sep1	of Vienna Mo Sheriff. Of Phelps Co Mo
Johnson Amanda	Y55F		of Kansas City Mo
Johnson Anna	G31Gb		m1900 Of Iberia Mo
Johnson Austin L	Y47D		of St. Louis Mo Street car conductor
Johnson Avery N	Y34H	1891Dec28	m1917May25 Of St Louis Mo Dentist
Johnson Bardney	Y18B		

NAME	NUMBER	BIRTH	COMMENTS
Johnson Cal F	Y24H	1850Jan14	d1013Dec26
Johnson Catherine	J15Fam		m in Kentucky Of Maries Co Mo
Johnson Charles	Y33A		"moved to west coast" No issue
Johnson Charles	Y55D		of Kansas City Mo
Johnson Charles Myscal	Y18E		"moved to west coast" Of Maries Co Mo
Johnson Charles W	Y47C		of Phelps Co Mo
Johnson Clarence	Y34D	1878May26	m1902Nov2 Of St Louis Mo
Johnson Clay	Y51A		of Holiness Camp Ground Maries Co Mo
Johnson Clyde	Y51E		d single Of Maries Co Mo
Johnson Cora E	Y34E	1855Feb20	ofMaries Co Mo
Johnson David	Y33B		of Maries and Polk Cos Mo
Johnson Disbury	R19Caf	1799Nov1	Welch descent To Maries Co Mo 1821
Johnson Don	C39Fa		m1949Mar13 New York City NY
Johnson Earl	Y51C		of St Louis Mo
Johnson Edgar	D53Aa		of Washington Mo
Johnson Edna F	Y34G	1888Feb15	m1905 abt Of Vienna Mo
Johnson Edward	Y49C		of Vienna Mo
Johnson Edward	Y55B		of Eminence Mo
Johnson Eliza Jane	Y26D	1852Jul4	d1923Dec4
Johnson Elizabeth	Y33C		of Pulaski Co Mo
Johnson Elizabeth	Y13H	1824Aug24	b.pWMo/Maries Co m1845abt
Johnson Elizabeth	Y14B		m in St Louis Co Mo
Johnson Elizabeth M.	Y25E		
Johnson Ella	Y49E		of Maries Co Mo
Johnson Emily C	Y16B		of Maries Co Mo and Texas early 1870's
Johnson Francis	Y55A		of Canyon City Colorado
Johnson Freda	E43Da		of Maries Co Mo
Johnson George	Y21A		
Johnson Grover C Dr	Y49F		m1921Sep28 Of Marthasville Mo
Johnson Harriet	Y18A		d1873Oct20 Of Maries Co Mo and Texas
Johnson Isaac N	Y16A		
Johnson James	Y51B		of Belle Mo
Johnson James	Y12B		ofKy In Mo 1811 Many trips back to Ky
Johnson James	Y13A	1812Dec26	b.p.Mo/St.Louis Co d1873Apr20 MariesCo
Johnson James	Y24C		d. young Of Maries Co Mo
Johnson James Mrs	Y26Ba		
Johnson James Harrison	Y25F	1851May13	of Maries Co Mo To Johnson Co Tex 1878
Johnson James K Polk	Y26B		
Johnson James Mrs	Y12Ba		
Johnson James Oliver	Y34A	1872Jan7	d1887May1
Johnson Jane	Y39B		
Johnson Jane	Y24E		of Maries Co Mo
Johnson Jane	Y70Aa		m.Prob in Ky d Maries Co Mo
Johnson John	Y24A		of Maries Co Mo Killed in early life
Johnson John	Y14A		of St Louis Mo
Johnson John Bunyan	Y18C		of Maries Co Mo. To west coast
Johnson John M. Mrs	Y13Ea		
Johnson John Marion	Y25C	1843Sep12	d1915Mar7 Entire life Maries Co Mo
Johnson John Mrs	Y14Aa		of St Louis Co Mo

NAME	NUMBER	BIRTH	COMMENTS
Johnson John Myscal	Y13E	1827Aug7	b.p.Mo/Maries Co Newspaper Vienna 1872
Johnson John Sanford	Y26C		
Johnson Julia A	Y25A	1839Jul27	d1927Sep1
Johnson Lee	Y49D		of Newburg Mo
Johnson Louisa	Y39C		
Johnson Lucinda	Y13F	1810Sep11	b.p.Tn m(1)Bowen(2)1829Jul11 d1905
Johnson Lucinda C.	Y25D	1846Jan23	b.p.Mo/Maries Co m1861Dec12 d1923May9
Johnson Lula	Y55E		of Kansas City Mo
Johnson Lydia	Y24D		of Maries Co Mo
Johnson Mabel	Y55G		of Kansas City Mo
Johnson Marie	Y55C		of Ponca City Oklahoma
Johnson Martha Mrs	Y25Ca		of Maries Co Mo
Johnson Martin V	D72Ga		
Johnson Mary	R19Ca	1827Nov17	of Maries co Mo
Johnson Mary	Y13B		
Johnson Mary	B97Abm		
Johnson Mary Belle	Y18D		of Maries Co Mo. "to west coast"
Johnson Mary E	Y34B	1873Oct18	of Nevada Mo
Johnson Mary E	Y25G	1854May19	d1912Aug23 Of Maries Co Mo
Johnson Mary E	Y39A		of Maries Co Mo Bloomgarden
Johnson Mary J Mrs	Y24Ha	1352Dec23	d1932Sep20
Johnson Mollie	Y49A		of Belle Mo
Johnson Monroe	Y17A	1347Aug31	m1870Nov23 Of Maries Co Mo
Johnson Myrtle	Y51D		of Rolla Mo
Johnson Myscal	K34Ea		
Johnson Naomi E	Y34F	1881Apr1	d1888Mar3
Johnson Narcissus	Y24F		of Maries Co Mo
Johnson Octavia	Y47B		of Phelps Mo
Johnson Peter	Z42Ba		of Colorado
Johnson Philip	Y71Ca		First wife Jennie Ammerman
Johnson Phillip	Y14F		
Johnson Ray	Y55H		d single
Johnson Robert	Y70Aaf		of Ky To Warren Co Mo 1310 In Am Rev
Johnson Robert	Y11B		From Eng with brother Thomas Am Rev.
Johnson Samuel	D71Da		
Johnson Samuel	E30Ga		m1889Jul2 d1892Jul21
Johnson Sarah	Y25B		d in California
Johnson Sarah	Y13G		m1838Feb15
Johnson Sarah	Y14C		of Maries Co Mo
Johnson T Francis	Y18F		of near Rolla Mo
Johnson Thomas	Y24G		of Maries Co Mo
Johnson Thomas J	Y14D	1810Sep18	b.p.Ky Of Tenn and Mo. Mo.Legislature
Johnson Thomas Jr	Y12A	1782abt	b.p.Tenn east Mo in 1811 Maries Co1823
Johnson Thomas Jr Mrs	Y12Aa		
Johnson Thomas L	Y47E		of St Louis Mo Real estate
Johnson Thomas Sr	Y11A		From Eng to Am with brother Robert
Johnson Thomas Sr Mrs	Y11Aa		
Johnson W.D.P.	Y39D	1352Jul29	m1874Sep29 d1919Jun14 Phelps Co Mo
Johnson Waldo P	Y47F		Of St Louis Mo Founder Webster Pub Co

NAME	NUMBER	BIRTH	COMMENTS
Johnson William	Y47A		of St Louis Mo
Johnson William	Y24B		of Maries Co Mo. No issue
Johnson William	Y34C	1877Jun17	d1877Jul10
Johnson William	Y13C		m1825
Johnson William	Y21B		of Bloomgarden Mo "Threshin' Billy"
Johnson William E Dr	Y49B	1873Dec26	m1902Apr7 d1928Mar16 Belle Mo
Johnson William Henry	Y25H	1857Jan23	of Phelps Co Mo
Johnson William J	Y26A		
Johnson William S	Y14E	1818Mar1	b.p.Mo/ m abt1837 d1871Aug2 Maries Co
Johnson William S	Y23Daf		
Johnson William S	Y14E		
Johnson William S	Y73Caf		
Johnston Martha Jane	D89Aam	1849Jul15	d1914Mar26
Joice A.L.	H14Ja		of Maries Co Mo Judge
Jones Alfred Burton	Y58C		of Maries Co Mo Pea Vine
Jones Alfred H	A57A	1843Apr22	b.pGa/Gilmer Co m1879Dec27Ark d1922Mar
Jones Amanda	Y43A	1859Aug26	m1878Dec29 d1880Nov6
Jones Benjamin	B13Ga	1854	
Jones Betty Lucille	C31Fa		m1944Apr2 Of Lees Summit Mo
Jones Boley Anderson	Y58D		of Long Creek Maries Co Mo
Jones Claude O	Y45D		of Lindell Mo
Jones Clayton D.P.	Y23D	1827	b.p.Mo St Louis d1910Jan14Ca
Jones Effie	Y58F		of Okemah Oklahoma
Jones Elijah	Y14Ca	1806Jul31	b.p.Tenn To Maries Co Mo abt1834 d1881
Jones Elizabeth	Y23I		of Bloomgarden Maries Co Mo
Jones Elizabeth Jane	Y42E		of Lanes Prairie Maries Co Mo
Jones Francis Marion	Y23G	1841Feb15	m1861Dec12 d1919Sep1 Minister,farmer
Jones Gabrilla	Y23A	1845Sep8	d1863Jul1 Single
Jones George Wash.	Y23F	1842Aug4	b.p.Mo/Maries Co d1909Feb5 Merchant
Jones Georgia Ann	Y43B	1862May24	m1879Jan12 d1880Nov3
Jones Gertrude	Y44B		no issue
Jones Ida	Y44A		no issue
Jones Ida	Y58E		of Vienna Mo
Jones Ida I	Y43C	1864May19	d1888Jan19
Jones Irvine Jackson	Y23E	1832Nov3	b.p. Mo St Louis Co m1856Jan24 d1909Mo
Jones James A	Y23B	1825Mar1	d1861Dec5
Jones James A Jr	Y42C	1859Jul27	m1881Dec12 d1903Apr24
Jones James Edgar	Y58A		of Rolla Mo
Jones Jerry	Y42B		
Jones Jerry Mrs	Y42Ba		
Jones Joan	Y45C		no issue
Jones John C Thurman	Y58B		of St Louis Mo
Jones Laura	Y45A	1862	d1916 Of Maries Co Mo
Jones Leona F	Y42D	1852Mar	
Jones Lydia	Y45B		d single
Jones Lydia Ann	Y23J		of Pulaski Mo
Jones Maria Lila	F65Aa	1850Sep23	d.1935Feb19
Jones Maud	Y58G		
Jones Myrtle	Y46B		of Maries Co Mo

NAME	NUMBER	BIRTH	COMMENTS
Jones Nancy	T14Ca		to California
Jones Napoleon B Dr	Y23H	1848Sep8	b.p.Mo/Lindell d1900Dec12 smallpox
Jones Ollie	Y46A		of Belle Mo
Jones Omer H Dr	Y45E		of Vienna Mo
Jones Pearl Ann	A58A		
Jones Ralph Dr	Y45F		of Pawnee Oklahoma
Jones Samuel	A56A	1797	b.pS.C.Pendleton Co m1818Feb25 d1871
Jones Thomas J Dr	Y23C		b.p.Mo St Louis Of Maries Co Mo
Jones William	D45Ca		Lived in Arkansas
Jones William Clayton	Y42A	1849Jun10	m1873Mar15 d1913May21
Jones William T	Y43D		of Maries Co Mo Bloomgarden
Jones Willis	A55A	1760abt	d abt 1805 Pendleton S.C.
Jones Willis Mrs	A55Aa	1780abt	dabt1880 Gilmer Co Ga
Jordan Archibald	A62Aa		
Joyce Hezekiah	M15Db		
Joyce Hezekiak	M28Fb		Prob M15Db
Juergens Herman	S13Ca		of Oklahoma
Juergens John Adam	J22Da		of Maries Co Mo
Juergens Laura	T15Da		of Maries Co Mo
Juergens Laura	T15Da		of Maries Co Mo
Keaton George M	L16Fa		
Keaton Grace	L18C		d single
Keaton Nora	L18B		
Keaton Samuel	L18A		d 1926 single
Keeler Nathan	A15Ia		
Keeney -	S13Aa		of Osage Co Mo
Keeney -	J15Aa		
Keeney Barbara	R30Ja		of Maries Co Mo
Keeney Hannah M	D65Ga	1856Feb19	b.p.Mo/Osage Co d1924Jan19
Keeney Malinda	S18Ba		m1833Dec20 Osage Co Mo of Dixon Mo
Keeney Mary	R24Ia		m1910Nov6 of Diamond Mo
Keeney Michael	S18Ga		m1839Dec26 Moved to Kansas
Keeney Sylvester	D65Gaf		
Keeney Sylvester	E46Ba		of Freeburg Mo
Keerigan -	E29Fb		
Kehr Luellen	E54Fa		
Keith William	T30Ha		
Kellis -	J25Ga		of Maries Co Mo
Kelsey Stephen	A12Ca		
Kelton Dana Jean	B26Ea		m1946May15
Kendrick -	G42Ha		of Illinois
Kennett Margaret	Q37Da	1842Nov30	d1918Jun15
Kimble Elizabeth	A48Aa		
Kimsey Solomon	G51Eaf		
Kimsey William	G51Ea		
King Frances	B24Da		m1926Feb1
King Myrtle Minerva	E25Ka	1884May24	d.1971Oct15 Miami, Oklahoma
King Russell	C33Aa		of Smithville Mo
King William Alfred	B05Ja	1685	d1739

131

NAME	NUMBER	BIRTH	COMMENTS
King William Riley	E25Kaf		
Kinion Charles B	J18Aa		of Adair Okla
Kinkeade Elizabeth	Y19Ba		m(1)Clements(2)1865Jan15
Kinnard John R	P13Ab		of Maries Co Mo
Kinsey -	V23Bb		no issue
Kinsey Elizabeth	D17Ka		m1848Jan11 Gasconade Co Mo
Kinsey W.T.	G15Ea		
Kischer Juanita C	E84Ea		m.1956Jul15
Klenke Eugene	E88Fa		m1944
Klenke Sharon	E91Ba		m1960Sep17
Kline Elizabeth	B66Aa	1831Dec22	d.1921Nov19 buried Bloomsburg Pa
Klosner John I	D18Ca		
Kloth Gary Lee	F69Aa	1956Dec27	
Kluner Amanda	G51Ga	1861Aug16	d1909Oct29
Kluner Herman	G51Gaf		
Kluner Mary A	G51Ha		
Knight -	K16Ga		of Kansas City Mo
Knight J.M.	Z13Ca		no issue
Knight James M	Y43Ca		May be Knight J.M. Z13Ca
Knight William	Y53Aa		of Maries Co Mo
Koenig Chris	R31Fa		of Belle Mo
Kokenberger Sam	R27Ea		
Kokensparger -	G60Ba		of New Lexington Mo
Korn Anna	B17A		
Korn Charles	B12Aa	1852Feb22	of Gentry Co Mo Huggins Twp.
Korn Edna L	B16C	1883Sep11	1969Nov7
Korn Homer	B17B		
Korn James	B12Ba		
Korn Pruda N	B16B		d1890
Korn Robert Wade	B16D		
Korn Walter L	B16A	1876	d1957Jan9
Korte Patricia Ann	B77Ab		m1977Sep23
Krause Bruce Harton	B40B	1948Aug27	b.p.Mich.Lansing m1971May11 Army1971-3
Krause Cherl Ann	B40A	1947Mar12	b.p.Mich.Lansing m1969June6
Krause Floyd	B30Aa		m1945Sep12
Krewson Jacob	S22Eaf		of Maries Co Mo
Krewson Josephine	S22Jam		of Maries Co Mo dua of Cpt C.W.Krewson
Krewson Nora	S22Ea		of Maries Co Mo
Krill Rose E	C16Fa		m1897Apr4
Krone Jack	M25Aa		of near Vienna Mo
Krone Mabel	J18Ca		of Center Colo.
Krone Monroe	U12La		
Krone Robert	V16Ba		
Krone Sat	E27Ba		
Krone William	G21Ca		of Rolla Mo
Krueger Theresa D.M.	D85Ba	1884Apr24	b.p. Mo Osage Co m1904Jun9 d1918Sep14
Krum Lydia	B60Aa	1823	b.p.Pa/Grovania d1884
Krum Rebecca	B57Aa		
Krunenberg Ida	E30Ea		

NAME	NUMBER	BIRTH	COMMENTS
LaSalle Enola	B13Eb		m(1) Hickman
Lacy Frances	R12Aa		d1920Aug22 Of Va. and Maries Co Mo
Lacy Lucretia	R11Aa	1806Sep4	b.p.Va d1877Oct10 Maries Co Mo
Lacy Phoebe	I51Aa		of Tenn, and Crawford and Maries Co Mo
Lafaver Margaret B	C39Ba		m1945Aug5 Wheatland Mo
Lainhart Wilbert D.	B21Ba		m1917May27
Laird -	A92Ca		of St Joseph Mo
Laird Jack I	C39Da		m1946Dec20 Sweet Springs Mo
Lam Jane	D75Ga		m1848May18
Lamar Isham	C17Eaf		
Lamar Syrilda Alamae	C17Ea		
Lambert Elizabeth	A76Aa	1855Jan25	d1926May9
Lambeth Daisy Eva	F52G	1912Mar26	
Lambeth Bessie Mae	F39E	1905Aug2	m1935Jul25
Lambeth Calvin Charley	F52C	1900Dec18	
Lambeth Dena Albert	F39F	1914Nov29	m1939Nov18 d1940Nov10 also McLambeth
Lambeth DoVada	F52B	1898Feb11	d.1952Jun19
Lambeth Dollie Ina	F52F	1906Dec11	
Lambeth Ella Lee	F52A	1896Mar19	
Lambeth Lucinda Jane	T13Aa	1853	b.p.Mo/Mareis Co d1920Jun27
Lambeth Lytle	G11Ja	1806Sep14	b.p.NoCar/ d1833Mar31MariesCo Mo
Lambeth Mary	J12Ca		
Lambeth Pierce Fathin	F39B	1898Oct30	m1916Sep17 buried S.Fork Mo =McLambeth
Lambeth Robert Pierce	F52D	1903Oct22	
Lambeth Roy Leander	F39C	1900Jun16	m1921Jun12 d1977Jul11 California
Lambeth Samuel	G11Jaf		of N.C.until 1825,E.Tenn1837Mo1844
Lambeth Tony Alfred	F39D	1902Aug19	m1925ca of So.Fork Mo also McLambeth
Lambeth Virgil Ernest	F39A	1897Sep6	m1918Jul14 d1975Jan5 So Fork Mo
Lambeth Zeno Mack	F52E	1905Feb17	d.1906Aug
Lance Betty	A75Da	1920abt	
Land Della	G36Eam		of Phelps Co Mo
Landers Opal	F39Da		
Lane Artellia Vermel	F57Aam		
Lane Catherine	Y28A		of MariesCo Mo
Lane Charles C	Y15Da		of Maries Co Mo 1826
Lane Mahala	Y28B		
Langenberg Victor H.	D88Ca	1907Dec4	of Belle Mo
Lankenau Charles Edwin	F36C	1895Oct8	b.p.Mo/Bem d1965Sep22 Colorado
Lankenau Elsie May	F36E	1901Dec23	b.p. Mo/Bem d Bem Mo
Lankenau Henry	F35Aaf		
Lankenau John Henry	F35Aa	1862Jan27	b.p.Mo.Gasc Co m1893Aug24 d1934Apr25Mo
Lankenau Mary Zelma	F36A	1898Aug1	b.p.Mo/Gasc.Co m1919Dec3 d1975Aug26 Mo
Lankenau Nora Ethel	F36B	1894Jul9	b.p.Mo/Gasc Co d1970Mar23 Illinois
Lankenau Ola Eva	F36F	1906Jun11	b.p.Mo/Bem Gasc. Co d1975Apr9
Lankenau William Ira	F36D	1900May26	b.p.Mo/Bem d Bem/Gasconade Co
Lankford -	E23Aa		of Dixon Mo
Laraway Linda	A72Ha	1940Mar13	m1960
Lare Mary	F29Ca		
Lark Michael	F21Fa		

NAME	NUMBER	BIRTH	COMMENTS
Larrick -	Z26Ga		
Laughlin Thomas N	P11Da		mOsage Co Mo. Of Maries d.PulaskiCo Mo
Laughlin William	J11Ba		m1823Sep30 Gasconade Co Mo
Laughlin William Silas	F34Hb		
Lawson Andrew	T14Eaf		
Lawson Caroline	T14Ea		
Lawson Dalilah Ann	V18Ca	1861Feb16	d.1884Jun17 No issue
Lawson George	V18Caf		In Missouri St. Guard Killed Civil War
Lawson Gordon	G57Ea		of Maries Co Mo
Lawson Margaret	V17Da	1818Apr16	b.p.Tenn d1899Jul20 In Mo 1839
Lawson Nathan S	V17Daf		
Lawson Patience	F63Ca	1800Sep13	d.1848Feb16
Lawson Polly Ann	T15Eam		
Lazarus Emanuel	B58A	1831	d1915 Grovania Pa. Blacksmith,farmer
Lazarus Lydia Rebecca	B59A	1859Dec12	b.p. Pa Grovania m1878Jun d1930Oct22Pa
Lazarus Samuel Jr	B57A		b. U.S.A.
Lazarus Samuel Sr	B56A		b.p.Germany
Lazarus Samuel Sr Mrs	B56Aa		
Leach Edward S	C29Ga	1862Nov12	m1885Aug27
Leach Levi	K21Aa		of Minco Okla
Leake Lulu Mabel	F66Da		
Leden Marjorie Jane	B74Ba	1926Nov24	b.p. NY/Greenport m1948Oct30
Lee -	E54Gb		
Lee Cynthia	U12Gb		of Maries and Pulaski Cos Mo
Lee Drury Owen	D18Ba		m1845Dec25(2)1846Oct28
Lee Louis	L15Fa		to Blanco Texas about 1880
Lee Mary	K32Aa		of MariesCo Mo
Lemons Telitha	R14Aa		of Colorado
Letterman James	Y40Ba		of Maries Co Mo
Letterman Peter F	Y40Aa		of Denver Mo d without issue
Leverich George Thomas	C16Aa		m1871May6
Lewis -	I43Ba		
Lewis Alva	D52Da		of Rector Mo
Lewis Elizabeth Jane	D18Ga		m1867May12
Lewis Emma Alice	C37Ia		m1883Nov27 Of Hickory Co Mo
Lewis Sarah	I15Ga		
Lewis Stella Lou	A79Ia		m1916Mar29
Light Allen	H14C		d single
Light Caroline	H14J		of near Veto Maries Co Mo
Light Catherine	H13E		m1876Oct15
Light Della	H19E		of California
Light Elbin K	H14F		d near Newburg Mo
Light Ellen	H15D		of Maries Co Mo and Kansas
Light Ellen	H14L		of Phelps Co Mo
Light Enoch	H14G		of Phelps Co Mo
Light Enoch	H12A		of Tenn In Maries Co Mo by 1834
Light Enoch Mrs	H12Aa		
Light Flower	H12C		d Vichy Mo Jockey Spencer Hill Track
Light George	H15C		of Texas

NAME	NUMBER	BIRTH	COMMENTS
Light George	H14B		d single
Light Georgia	H19B		of St Louis Mo
Light James	H19G		
Light Jane	H15E		of Maries Co Mo
Light John	H13A		d single
Light John	H15A		of Maries Co Mo and Boston Mts Ark
Light John	H11A		d.in Tenn
Light John Mrs	H11Aa		of Tenn
Light John Stacy	E82Ba		m.1884Feb6
Light Libbie	H14K		of Texas Co Mo
Light Love	H18B		of California
Light Lutita Melvina	H14D		of Maries Co Mo No issue
Light Maud	H18C		of California
Light Nancy	H13D		
Light Nellie	H19F		
Light Obadiah	H12D		of Tenn. Never came to Mo
Light Otto	H19A		of St Louis Mo
Light Roy	H18A		of California
Light Sadie	H19D		of California
Light Sarah	H13C		
Light Sarah	H14E		of Maries Co Mo No issue
Light Temperance C.	H13B	1830	of Maries Co Mo
Light Val S	H14I		of Rolla Mo. City Marshal
Light Virgil	H19C		of California .
Light William	H14A		d single
Light William Henson	H15B		of Maries Co Mo Sprg Crk Twp No issue
Light Wright	H12B		of Maries Co Mo Sprg Cr Twp In Mo 1339
Light Zebedee D	H14H		of Phelps Co Mo
Likings Bonnie	A77Ga	1915abt	
Lindsey Leonida L	A66Ca		
Lingell Nancy	I12Ha		
Linn Eleanor	A90Da		m1834Jan4 Mason Co Kentucky
Linville William	I61Fa		
Liston Isaac	K37Ba		
Little Dorothy Mae	A71Ia	1906Apr17	
Livingston -	T25Ea		of Miller Co Mo
Lloyd Ernest	E24Na		of Springfield Mo
Lock Jack	P17Ea		of Washington Mo
Lockwood Luther	D86B		
Lockwood Meredith C Jr	D87B		
Lockwood Meredith C Sr	D86A		
Lockwood Meredith Mrs	D86Aa		
Lockwood Wayne Edward	D87A		
Lockwood William D.D.S	D85Aa		d Springfield Mo
Log Francis	A68Aaf		
Log Frankie	A68Aa		
Logan -	H54Ba		
Logan Enos S	Z17Fa		
Logan George Lyons	B32Aa		m1946Dec23

NAME	NUMBER	BIRTH	COMMENTS
Logan Katherine H.	B44A	1948Oct18	m1971
Logan Lawrence Lyons	B44B	1951May18	m1970
Logan Thomas Burgess	B44C	1953Sep16	
Lollar Corder	A39Ib		
Lollar Isaac E	A67Ia	1842Feb23	d1870May20
Lollar John Jefferson	A67La	1846Dec5	d.1918May22
Longhead Wesley	F50Aa		m1973
Loomis Abigail	A12Ea	1711Apr30	b.p.Conn/Simsbury m1731May7 d1802abtN˙
Loomis Philip	A12Eaf		
Loomis S	A11Fb		
Loomis Samuel	A11Ja		
Lore Daniel	E48C		d single
Lore David	E48B		d single
Lore James E	E21Da		d1872abt
Lore John	E48A		of Belle Mo Employed Rock Is RR
Lore Lyda	E48F		
Lore Martha	E48D		d single
Lore Minerva	E48G		
Lore Ruth	E48H		of Belle Mo
Lore Sarah	E48E		
Loupe "Babe"	G14Aa		of near Vienna Mo
Love Clara H	K33Ga		
Love Elnore I	Y34Da		m1902Nov2 St Louis Mo
Love James	K33Gaf		
Love Jasper	D66Da		ot Kansas City Mo
Love John	Q33Gaf		of Maries Co Mo Father Isaac Love
Love John E	R21Ba	1844Jul2	b.p. Mo Maries Co d1922Oct22 Vichy Mo
Love Margaret E	Q33Ga		d1859Jun14 Of Maries Co Mo
Love W.E.	L19Aa		of Granite City Mo
Lovelace James A.	R22Da	1856Jan14	m1884Jun3
Lovelace Thomas Jones	R22Daf	1824Dec24	m1851Nov20 d1897Nov11
Lowder Duncan M	T15Ha		
Lucas Alpha May	B21Ca		m1923May3
Lueckenhoff Herman	G34Ba		of Osage Co Mo County Clerk
Lugabill Emma	Y63Ea		of Bluffton Ohio m1887Jun8 Indiana
Lusby –	B07Fa		
Lusk William H	F30Fa		
Luster Mary	Y23Ca		of Maries Co Mo
Lynch Helen Elisabeth	B74A	1926Apr19	b.p.NY m1948Aug7 Roslyn NY Reg.nurse
Lynch Megan Brianne	B78B	1980Jan25	b.p.NY Glenhead
Lynch Peter Elmer Jr	B74B	1927Aug3	b.p.NY/Mineola m1948Oct30 WW2 Navy
Lynch Peter Elmer Sr	B69Ba	1901Jul10	b.p.NY/Roslyn m1925Jun6 Fire Marshall
Lynch Peter Gregory	B77A	1951Jul20	b.p. NY/Glen Cove m1972Oct8(2)1977Sep
Lynch Richard Thomas	B77B	1953Apr20	b.p.NY/Glen Cove d1970Dec19
Lynch Shaun Peter	B78A	1978Sep7	b.p. NY/Glen Cove
Lyons –	G60Ca		of Topeka Kansas
Lyons Robert	E30Fa		ofSpringfield Mo
Maccubin Helen	A34Aa		m1800Mar19 Montgomery Co Md
Macgruder Sarah Ellen	E84Ba		m1949Feb17

NAME	NUMBER	BIRTH	COMMENTS
Macklefresh David	B05Eaf		Will probated 1711Aug15 Inn keeper
Macklefresh Jane	B05Ea	1700abt	d1733Mar bu.Md/Anne Arundel Co.
Magruder Amy	F11Fa		
Magruder Eleanor	F11Ga		
Magruder Elizabeth	A88Ba	1715abt	d Will prob 1794Oct20
Mahan Fannie	V24Da		
Mahan John	V24Daf		
Mahaney -	K16Da		of Texas
Mahaney E.P.	K12Ea		m1875Jul29 of Gasc. Co Mo and Texas
Mahon Malinda	Y52Dam		d1921Jul13 Father: George Mahon
Mahon Sarah Ann R.	R26Ha		of Maries Co Mo
Mahoney Alverta L	D76Ga		
Mahoney Nancy Jane	B11Ea	1844Mar28	b.p.Ind/Ripley Co d1929May12Albany Mo
Maidwell Ethel	A77Gb	1922Jul27	
Malone Frances	Q42Ca		m In Virginia or No.Car
Malone George W	Z24Aa		of Jefferson CityMo
Malone Hannah	Y31B		
Malone James	Y31A	1842May20	b.p.Mo/Maries Co m1870Dec3 d1913Feb14
Malone William	Y15Fb		
Malson James William	D76Ka		m1879Feb23
Manicke John C	Y76Ba		m1906Jul16 Of Belle Mo Merchant
Manier Julia Ann	A76Ka	1890	1937
Manning Lillian	E88Aam	1896Apr30	b.p.Mo/Villa Ridge d1978Dec23StClairMo
Maples Joe	A44Ca		
Maples Samuel	E69Ea		
Marcee Susan A.H.	H52Ga	1831Mar17	d1877Mar2 Father W. Maurice Marces
Marcee William	H52Gaf		
Markham Mike	A72Fb		
Marshall Mary	A11Ea		
Martin "Cad"	G36Faf		
Martin -	R23Aa		m1885Aug20 Of Glen Rio New Mexico
Martin -	U16Fa		Probably moved to Ark. after Civil War
Martin -	G11Ca		
Martin Benjamin	J27Ea		m1904Jul7
Martin Cleo	E85Aa		
Martin Ella	P15F		d Denver Mo
Martin George	P15D		of Maries Co Mo
Martin Ida	P15E		of Franklin Co Mo
Martin Irvin	P15A		of Maries Co Mo
Martin James	V18Ia		m1880Nov14 Of St. Louis Mo
Martin James O	V15Ba		In Union Army
Martin John	V15Baf		
Martin John	P14Aaf	1814abt	d about 1898
Martin John Y	U16Faf		
Martin John Y	G11Caf		
Martin Louisa M	I54Ca		m1896Sep27 Of Maplewood Mo
Martin Lumina	G36Fa	1876Mar9	d1903Oct5
Martin Mary	G18Eam		of Maries Co Mo
Martin Mary	J20Fam		Parents John Martin/Malinda Hill

NAME	NUMBER	BIRTH	COMMENTS
Martin Milly	F07Aa		
Martin Moses	P15C		of Maries Co Mo
Martin Oliver	P15G		d1932
Martin Ollie	Y76Ea		m1913Jul8 Of Lodi California
Martin S	A13Ib		
Martin Sallie Louise	R24Cam	1847Nov18	m1868Apr6 d1925Jan26 Of Vienna Mo
Martin Telitha	G12Bam		
Martin Walter	P15B		of Maries Co Mo
Martin William C	P14Aa		
Mason Emily	M28Aa		
Mason Gus	R31Ha		of Belle Mo
Mason Hank	M28Ea		of Owensville Mo
Mason Lucinda	G13Cam		m1875Mar21
Massa Andrew	A67Da	1842Apr4	d1915Jan31
Massa William	A67Ib	1831	d1891Jan31
Massey Mary (Polly)	V12Da	1831Mar23	
Massey William			First Printing Error: T16Fa incorrect
Massey William	V12Daf	1805Apr5	m1828Jan10 Mo Father David
Mathers Harry	F66Ba		
Mathews Della	D29Ga		m1904
Matlock –	G35Aa		of Maries Co Mo. (Medlock same family)
Matlock Edna J	G43Bam	1844Feb22	d1864Feb27 Father Wash Matlock(G35Ba)
Matlock G.W.	Q45Ea		
Matlock G.W. (Wash)	G35Da		of Maries Co Mo also spelled Medlock
Matlock Sophronia A	M11Ca	1849Dec9	b.p. Mo Maries Co d1932Sep15 Mo.
Matlock Wesley R	Z32Ea		
Matson Ruth	B09Aa		of N.C. and Tenn
Matthews Amanda C	D27Da	1841May6	b.p. Mo Gasconade Co d1916Jul19 Maries
Matthews Bartlett G	D27Gaf		
Matthews Elizabeth	C28Ga		
Matthews Leonard	F36Fa		
Matthews Mattie	R15Ea		of Brinktown and Meta Mo
Matthews Pet	F36Faf		
Matthews Polly Lavinia	D27Ga	1848Jan12	d1922Mar3
Matthews Samuel J	C13Ia		m1860Feb2
Mattox Betty Jane	C31Ca		m1947Apr12 Of Pleasant Hill Mo
Maugridge John	I10Aaf		
Maugridge Mary	I10Aa		Sailed for America 1717Aug17
Maxwell Cordella	G35Lb		of Phelps Co Mo
Maxwell Ella Mae	A75Ea	1926Mar12	
Maxwell John	C26Ga		m1882
Maxwell William	B08Kb		
Mayfield Ernest	G45Ba		of Maries Co Mo
Maynard A.K.	A17Eaf		
Maynard Lulie E	A17Ea	1862Nov27	b.p.Ind/JacksonCo m1883Nov18 d1940Apr
Maynor Mary	E80Ba		
McAfee George	G62Ib		
McAfee Michael	G62Ga		of Maries Co Mo
McAndrew Susan	I40Ab		

NAME	NUMBER	BIRTH	COMMENTS
McBride Charlotta	A39Ca	1803Jul18	d1880Dec24
McBride Ebenezer	B91A		
McBride Eliza	B92A		d1875
McBride Harry	D34Ea		of near Marionville Mo
McBride Margaret	A39Da	1808Feb25	d1891Dec22
McCabe Iva P	Z32Aa		of Gentry Co Mo
McCabe Lula	Z32Fa		
McCann -	Q31Fa		
McCann John	F21Aa		m1808Apr6
McCarthy Angelia	E83Dam		
McCarty Lee	C37Ka		of California
McCormack Enoch	C36Bb		of Washington State
McCrary Nancy	B94Aa		m1827Dec26 d1889Aug12
McCrory Nan	G34Ca		
McCune Cora Frances	F67H	1912Mar1	b.p.Ks/Benton m1933Aug16 Marion Ks
McCune Elsie Edna	F67F	1908Jan14	b.p.Ks/Benton m1930Apr20 Eureka Ks
McCune Laura Gladys	F67B	1899Apr15	b.p.Ks/Benton d.1900Apr9 Benton Kansas
McCune Leander Burgess	F67G	1910Jan7	b.p.Ks/Benton m1935Apr20 Canton Ks
McCune Lewis Obadian	F66Aa		
McCune Lila Susan	F67D	1903Dec3	b.p.Ks/Benton m1917Jul3 Furley Kansas
McCune Ralph Lewis	F67E	1906Apr22	b.p.Ks/Benton m1941Jun7 Wichita Kansas
McCune Vesta Marie	F67A	1897Mar20	b.p.KansBenton d1938Feb3 BolengeAfrica
McCune Zola Ruth	F67C	1901Jun15	b.p.Ks/Benton m1924May11 d1984Jan29Ks
McCutcheon Nora B	R32Ca		m1914Dec8 Of Porterville California
McDaniel Emma	Z27Ea		d Phelps Co Mo
McDaniel J.A.	G18Ca	1880abt	of Vienna Mo
McDaniel Samuel	Y33Ca		of Pulaski Mo
McDaniel Zetta	V28Aa		
McDaniels Frank	P16Na		of Eldon Mo
McFarland Rebecca	C17Eam		
McGee Edna J	Y35B		also McGhee
McGee Elizabeth	Y19E	1849Mar17	d1868Mar8 Also McGhee
McGee Elizabeth	Y14Ea	1818Oct1	m1837abt d1897Aug29 Also McGhee
McGee Henry	Y13Dbf		Also McGhee
McGee Henry	Y19C	1843Aug23	d1851Sep7 Also McGhee
McGee J Ellen	Y19I	1860Mar26	Also McGhee
McGee James B	Y19H	1857Feb10	d1868Dec11 Also McGhee
McGee John	Y13Ga	1817	m1838Feb15 Father Henry McGee(McGhee)
McGee Leona	Y19F	1851Sep13	Also McGhee
McGee Lucinda	Y19A	1839Jan31	died "early in life" Also McGhee
McGee Nancy	Y13Db		m1843
McGee Sarah Jane	Y19G	1854Mar2	m1874Mar29 d1923Aug22 Also McGhee
McGee Thomas	Y19D	1846Jun13	Also McGhee
McGee Thomas S	Y35A		Also McGhee
McGee William Riley	Y19B	1841Apr27	m1865Jan15 d1870Nov5
McGowan Anna Susan	E15Ba		m1807
McGraw Harry	E30Ja		m1902Dec25 Of Rolla Mo
McGriff Martha	I43B		of Iberia Mo
McGriff William	I41Ba		d young Of Bradley Co Tn/Maries Co Mo

NAME	NUMBER	BIRTH	COMMENTS
McGriff William D	I43A		of St Elizabeth Miller Co Mo
McIntyre M	F09Aa		
McKamy Fannie	Z14Cb		
McKay Dora	B14A		
McKay Duncan	B14C		
McKay George	B14B		
McKay Jack	B11Da		
McKay Jasper	B14E		
McKay John	B14D		
McKee Albert	C16Ga		
McKenney –	E68Aa		
McKenzie James	F11Da		b.p. Md m1781Mar9
McKinney Leslie	M28Fa		of Joplin Mo
McKinney Loyd	E43Ha		of Jefferson City Mo
McKissack Nancy	A52Aa	1778ca	b.p.Va d1825 Caswell Co No.Car
McKnight –	P11Fa		of near Linn Osage Co Mo
McKnight Pattie Mrs	S18Bb		m(1) James Pattie
McKnight Sarah Mrs	V23Cb		of Osage Mo m(1)1838 T.Pattie(2)1845ca
McLambeth Eli	F34Ha		b.p.Mo Gasc Co m1867abt d1877
McLambeth Leander P.	F38B	1872Sep11	b.p.Mo Osage Co m1895Mar10 d1934Nov11
McLambeth Valverva M	F38A	1875Sep24	m1896Dec6 d1964Nov7
McMahan Sarah	I13Aa		of No. Carolina
McMatt Mary	C11Ab		b.p.Tenn 1822 or 1831
McMilliam –	E16Da		
McMilliam Daniel	E67C	1819	to Missouri in early 1830´s
McMilliam Edward	E67B	1812	to Missouri in early 1830´s
McMilliam T.J.	E68A		
McMilliam Thomas	E67A		of PatrickCoVa to Mo in 1820´s
McMilliam William	E16Eaf		of Wales.Came to Patrick Co Va
McMillian John M	C15Aa		
McMillian Mary Adeline	F35Aam		
McMillian William Mrs	E16Eam		
McNaghten Frank M	V26Ba		m1885
McQueen Emma	R30Ka		
McQueen James	S18Db	1824Feb17	m1849Apr19
McQueen James J	K37Aa		
McQueen James J	R30Kaf		
McQueen Mary Amelia	E82Iam		
McWhorter –	T29Ba		of Springfield Mo
Meade Belinda	Q44Dam		m Ill Mo abt1844
Meade Katherine	Y60Aa		
Meadows Lenora	A76Db	1875abt	
Medlock Harriet	Y13Ab	1828May10	d1870Nov23 Also Matlock
Medlock John	Z41Fa		Moved probably to Oregon Also Matlock
Meltabarger James	J26Da	1836Oct8	m1855Sep18Tn/KnoxCo In Mo 1866 d.1911
Meltabarger Josie	T15Eb		
Meltabarger Lafayette	T15Ebf	1861Jan16	b.p.Tn/Knox Co d1882Jan16
Mercer Elizabeth	F22Ia		
Merriwether Belle	Y52Dbm	1863May9	d1916Jan5

NAME	NUMBER	BIRTH	COMMENTS
Messersmith Montgomery	G48Ca		
Metz Charles	Y55Ea		of Kansas City Mo
Mikkelson Clarence	R24Ja		m1911Sep6 of Niangua Mo
Milan -	R31Da		of Oklahoma
Milan -	E5ILa		of Eldon Mo
Miller -	T13Ba		d. in Wagon Train Nebraska
Miller A Britton	B62Ba		m1909Nov18 Traveling salesman
Miller Alma	V13Aa		m1889Nov24 Of California
Miller Charles	D29Ea		
Miller Chris Ann F.	F50A	1955May23	m1973
Miller David	U11Ha		m1827Feb11 Osage Co Mo Penn German
Miller Edna Mrs	M13Aa		
Miller Eliza	H12Cb		m(1) Jacob Love No issue
Miller Elizabeth	J26Aa		of Knox Co Tenn. Did not come to Mo
Miller Emma Mrs	Y61Ha		
Miller Fern Eleanor	F37A	1922Feb5	b.p.MoOwensville m1942Aug30 Jeff.Cy Mo
Miller Henry B	Y18Aa		d 1873Aug26 Gainesville Texas
Miller Jane	T16Db		
Miller Jesse	D77Da		m188Mar27
Miller John	G62Kb		
Miller Joseph	L15Ha		to Blanco Texas about 1880
Miller Lucinda	G32Cam		Father: David Miller
Miller Malinda	G11Bb		m(1) Woolsey -
Miller Martin	H12Cbf		
Miller Martin	C35Aaf		
Miller Nancy Elizabeth	C35Aa	1803ca	b.p.Tenn m1818 E.Tenn d1387 Mo
Miller Nelson	Z26Da		
Miller Robert Lee	F37B	1933Jun18	b.p.Mo/Owensville m(1)1960(2)1969Nov
Miller Sarah E	Z30A	1852Jan15	d1907Jan22 Maries Co Mo
Miller Susanne Kay	F50B	1969Aug24	b.p.Mo/Jefferson City
Miller William Fred.	F36Aa	1892Feb7	m1919Dec3 Hermann Mo d1965Jul22Jeff.Cy
Mills Maud	G51Hb		of Vienna Mo m(1)North -
Minnear Essie	A76Qa	1897Jun	d1953
Minnear George	A76Sa	1900abt	
Misel C.W.	E28Aa		
Mitchell John	B04Ka		m1700Jul14
Mitchell Luvicia	R26Cb		
Mitchell Margaret E	D82Aa	1821Nov21	b.p.Tenn/White Co d1891Aug9 White Co
Mitchem Blanche	D62A		
Mitchem Chesley	D62C		
Mitchem Gerthalene	D62D		
Mitchem Homer	D62B		
Mitchem Mollie	M24Aa		of Northeast Maries Co Mo
Mitchem William	D47Fb		
Mizell -	G43Da		
Mizell C.W.	M14Fa		of Heavener Oklahoma
Mizell James	G43Daf		
Moman Hiram J	Y26Da		
Moman Mary J	H14Ib		of Rolla Mo

NAME	NUMBER	BIRTH	COMMENTS
Moman Mary Jane	Y26Aa		Could be H14Ib
Moon Elwood	G27Ha		
Moon Scianna	G25Bam	1838Aug29	b.p. Ind m1855Feb2 d1919Nov28 Mo.
Moon Wood	Z42Ha		of Maries Co Mo
Moone Belle	B13Ha		Could possibly be Moore
Moore Nancy	D83Aa		m(1)Brewster- d1936Apr22Tn/White Co
Moore Ophelia	D69Ca		of St. Louis Mo
Moreland -	Y21Aa		
Moreland Anderson	Q31D	1813abt	b.p.Tn. m1839Aug8Gasc.CoMo Crawford Co
Moreland Anderson Mrs	Q31Db		
Moreland Andrew J	Q34K	1873Aug30	of CleburneTexas and Los Angeles Calif
Moreland Ann	Q34A		d single
Moreland Ann	Q31E		of Tenn., and Howell and Maries Cos Mo
Moreland Avery	Q33K		d1939 Of Stone Co Mo
Moreland Elias	Y24Ea		
Moreland Elias	Y21Aaf		
Moreland Elias Jr	Q32A		
Moreland Elias Sr	Q31A		13 in family in Civil War Both sides
Moreland Eliza C	Q32E	1850Dec15	m1865abt d1932Dec16
Moreland Elizabeth	Q34B		no issue
Moreland George	Q32B		Minister. Went to Ill after Civil War
Moreland George	Q30A		To Mo "very early" b.prob in 1760´s
Moreland George	Q34D		"moved westward from Missouri"
Moreland George Mrs	Q30Aa		
Moreland Hannah	Q33C	1837	d1862
Moreland Irby	Q32K		
Moreland J.R. (Shack)	Q33G	1838	d1898Feb17 Of Maries Co Mo
Moreland Jacob	Q33E	1825Dec28	d1878Apr5 Of Maries Co Mo
Moreland James E	Q33H		
Moreland Jane	Q32H		
Moreland Jeff	H56Ca		Prob son of Thomas H Moreland
Moreland Jerry N	R22Ea		
Moreland John	Q34C		"moved westward from Mo"
Moreland John (Jack)	Q31C		
Moreland John P	Q40A	1845abt	of Maries Co Mo and Broken Arrow Okla
Moreland Malinda	Q33J		of Maries Co Mo
Moreland Malissa	Q34F		"Moved westward from Mo"
Moreland Margaret	Q34G		"Moved westward from Mo"
Moreland Margaret E	Q33L		m1875Apr29 Of Maries and Henry Cos Mo
Moreland Mary	H55Ea		of Vichy and Henry Co Mo
Moreland Mary A	Q33D		
Moreland Mary Caroline	Q32J		of Texas
Moreland Mattie	Q34I		of Texas
Moreland Miriam	Q32F		of Maries Co Mo
Moreland Nancy	Q32G		of Franklin Co Mo
Moreland Nancy	Q34H		of Texas
Moreland Nancy	Q31G	1811	b.p.Tenn d1907
Moreland Ollie	Q34J		of Texas
Moreland Pleasant	Q32D		d1862

NAME	NUMBER	BIRTH	COMMENTS
Moreland Pleasant Mrs	Q32Da		
Moreland R.H.	Q33I		
Moreland Rachel H	Q33M	1849	m1871Dec18 d1923
Moreland Rebecca Jane	Q33B		
Moreland Samantha	Q32I		b.p. Mo Maries Co dCooper Co Mo
Moreland Sarah	Q31F		
Moreland Sarah E	Q33A	1823Sep22	m1846Oct1 Mo/Maries Co d1963Mar27
Moreland Thomas	Q32C		
Moreland Thomas	Q31B		of Maries Co Mo
Moreland Thomas H	Q33F	1833Apr8	d1904Apr16 Civil War 32nd Mo Infantry
Moreland W.W.	Y24Da		
Moreland Walter	H57Ba		of Maries and Phelps Cos Mo
Moreland William	Q34E		"Moved westward from Missouri"
Moreland William M	Q32L		"Bucky Bill"
Moreland William W Sr	H55Eaf		of Maries Co Mo
Morgan Don C	E86Aa		
Morgan Sarah	I11Ca	1700	m1720 near Phila Pa
Morhaus Emily	Y49Fa		m1921Sep22 Of Marthasville Mo
Morley Joan	F03Ab		of Lamberhurst Co England
Morley Ruth	F04Aa	1635abt	
Morris Lawrence M	B40Aa		m1969Jun6
Morris Richard	B50A		
Morrison McClure	D76Aa		
Morrison Wynema	F58Fa		m1943Aug6
Morrow Eliza	T16Ba		
Morrow Frances Ann	C13Ga		m1861Aug11
Morrow James	T16Baf		
Morton Susannah	R10Aa	1786May20	m1805Sep11 d1854Jan28 Maries Co Mo
Mosby Anna	V28F		of Arizona
Mosby Bettie	V28C		d1927 Arizona
Mosby David S	V28E		of Granite City Mo
Mosby George	V28D		of Dixon Mo
Mosby Joseph	V25Ba		b.p.Ky of Callaway and Osage Cos Mo
Mosby Joseph H	V28A		d1910
Mosby Samuel L	V28B		d1935 single. With U.S. Weather Bureau
Mosby Williamson	V25Baf		of Ky Came to Callaway and MariesCo Mo
Mosier Anna	Q43Aa	1871Dec31	
Mosier Daniel	Q43Aaf		
Moss Edward	Y58Gb		of Forest City Mo
Moss Edward Rev	K25A	1800Apr18	b.p.Tn/McMinn Co d 1892Jan19Vienna Mo
Moss Eliza	U14Ba		
Moss James	K26B	1851	d1915
Moss Johnathan	U14Baf		d1873
Moss Lucinda	K26A	1848abt	
Moss Martha	K26C	1853Oct19	m(1)1873Mar30(2)1882after d1922Jul13
Moss Sybilla	G11Ba		
Moss William	K11Ha		
Moulder Martha E	A57Aa	1850Jul28	b.p.Tn/ m Harrison Ark d1894Jul8Ark
Moulder Samuel	A57Aaf	1802	b.p.Tn d abt1881 Boone Co Arkansas

NAME	NUMBER	BIRTH	COMMENTS
Mueller Louis	F36Aaf		
Muller Sophia	D41Ca		of Owensville Mo
Murphy Joseph	Z29Ca		m1875Sep5
Murphy Kelley	T30Ea		of Maries and Wright Cos Mo
Murphy L.J.	Y58Ea		of Vienna Mo
Murphy Louisiana K	T30Da		m(1) Woods-
Murphy Nancy	S11Da		
Murphy T.A.	T18Ha		of Dixon Mo
Murphy Thomas Dale	B21Fa		m1930Dec25
Murphy W.A. (Lannie)	K26Caf		m. sometime after Civil War
Murphy William C	K26Ca		m1873Mar30 d1882 Sheriff Maries Co Mo
Murry Lafayette	Q43Da		
Murry Thomas	Q43Daf		
Mustain John Rev	G35Ha		of Howell Co Mo Methodist minister
Myers C.C.	Y32A		of Vienna Mo from Tenn.(Prob GreeneCo)
Myers C.C. Mrs	Y32Aa		
Myers Cera	A79Da	1885abt	
Myers Gabriel	Y15Fc		b.p.Tn/ of Maries Co Mo bef.1830 AmRev
Myers George	Y15Fcf		
Myers John	E23Ca		of Springfield Mo
Myers Joseph	K34Fa		
Myers Joseph S	G27Fa		of Oregon
Myers Martha	A70Ea	1850abt	
Myers W.C.	V16Bb		
Myers William	Y30Aa		
Nanney Lucy	S20Bbm		m in Tenn Of Maries Co Mo
Nanney Martha E	Y42Eam		d1870 Of Coyle Hollow Maries Co Mo
Neidert George	E42Ea		of Phelps Co Mo
Neil Leroy	B24Fa		m1933Mar10
Nelson Elsie Marie	B22Ga		m1945May
Nelson James S	J14Aa		
Nelson Anna Mrs	D77Ga		m1916Jan27
Nelson Ebenezer	A38Fa		m1800Jul11(or Nov1820)Rowan Co No.Car
Nelson George	V18Ga		
Nelson John	G44Ea		
Nelson Joseph	E85Faf		
Nelson Margaret Ellen	E85Fa	1913Nov29	b.p.Okla/Chelsea
Nelson Nancy	C12Ia		m1876abt
Nelson William H	H13Ea		d1941
Nevell Joyce	I59Fa		
Newberry Harmon H	H52Ia		
Newberry Lydia	Y71Ga		of Maries Co Mo to w.Mo after Civil W.
Newberry Susan Rebecca	Y71Ia		m1839May23 Maries Co Mo d in Polk Co
Newbound -	D42Aa		No issue
Newman Heber John	E95Caf		
Newman Vernon Clifford	E95Ca	1909Dec18	b.p. Utah Ogden m.1947Jul3
Newton Clemm	F32Da		
Newton Merle Arthur	B22Ia		m1936Oct1
Nichols Abraham	C26Da		m1873Jan12

144

NAME	NUMBER	BIRTH	COMMENTS
Nichols Cletus	E43Ga		of Jefferson City Mo
Nichols Ida Ellen	F38Aa	1879	d1964Dec29
Nichols Iva	B13La		
Nichols Maggie	B13Ka		
Nicholson William	B05Ba		m1704Aug15 d1719 Anne Arundel Co Md
Nickell Nancy Jean	F70Aa	1956Jun13	m.1975Jul22 Ky/Hazel Green
Nicks Lloyd	E83Ca		m1926Dec23
Nicks Walter	F39Ea	1901Apr21	d1979Mar29 So Fork Mo
Nielson Alice	A78Ea	1860abt	
Nieweg August	Y45Aa	1860	b.p. Mo/Maries Co d1934
Nieweg Minnie	Y25Ha	1865	d1905 Of Phelps Co Mo
Nipp W.R.	Q33Ma		
Nisley James Jackie	F68Da	1940Jan24	d.1970May16
Nisley Meaji Lynn	F71A	1969Apr4	b.p. Tenn/Nashville
Noble Aaron	A13H	1748Nov25	b.p.Conn/Hebron
Noble Abigail	A13G	1745Feb16	b.p. Conn/Hebron
Noble Albert Jackson	A16B	1816Sep30	b.p.NY/NY m1848Feb20 d1883Sep18 Mo.
Noble Asiel	A15E	1782Aug7	
Noble Carlton Monroe	A16D	1821Jan27	
Noble Catherine Sophia	A16G	1827Aug25	
Noble Charles Albert	A17A	1851Nov11	b.p.Mo St. Louis
Noble Charles Harris	A16J	1834Jun30	
Noble Clarissa	A15N	1803May18	of Red Bank New Jersey
Noble Daniel	A12B	1700Nov25	
Noble Daniel	A14F	1768Oct1	
Noble David	A12E	1709Mar3	b.p. Mass/Westfield m1731May7 d1761Feb
Noble David	A14B	1755Mar19	b.p.Conn/Hebron m1774Nov23 d1820Nov25
Noble David	A15B	1778Jun26	
Noble David Capt.	A13A	1732Jan25	b.p.Mass/Westfield m1753Feb21 d1776Aug
Noble David William	A16A	1814Oct29	
Noble Electa	A15I	1789Apr5	d Ohio
Noble Elizabeth	A11F	1673Feb9	
Noble Enoch	A13F	1742Dec25	b.p.Conn/Hebron d young
Noble Enoch	A14D	1763Jan14	
Noble Enoch George	A16H	1829Sep25	
Noble Ernest Wheeler	A17D	1856Dec20	
Noble Esther	A15F	1784Feb6	of Norwalk Conn
Noble Ezekiel	A14E	1767abt	
Noble Hannah	A11B	1664Feb24	
Noble Hannah	A13J	1752May15	b.p. Conn/Hebron
Noble Helen Grace	A17C	1854Nov5	
Noble Helen L	A18B	1888Jul18	b.p.Kansas m1907Dec24 Joplin Mo d1964
Noble Henry Orville	A17E	1860May31	b.p. Mo/St Louis m1883Nov18 d1934JanNY
Noble James	A11H	1677Oct1	m1698abt(2)1704Feb24 d1712Apr22 Mass
Noble James	A12A	1697Mar29	d1700Jan1
Noble James	A12D	1707Jan12	
Noble James	A13C	1736Jul19	b.p.Conn Hebron
Noble James	A15G	1735May16	d1794Feb8
Noble James	A15M	1796Apr3	

NAME	NUMBER	BIRTH	COMMENTS
Noble James Taylor	A16I	1832May15	b.p.Penn/Sterling
Noble John	A13K	1755Mar17	d1755Mar17
Noble John	A11A		
Noble Katherine	A13D	1738Jul5	b.p.Conn/Hebron
Noble Lucy	A14I	1774Oct	
Noble Luke	A11G	1675Jul15	
Noble Lydia	A12C	1704Dec7	
Noble Lydia	A13I		b.p. Conn Hebron bapt 1750Mar29
Noble Lydia Mrs	A14Fa		
Noble Mark	A11E		
Noble Mary	A11I	1680Jun29	
Noble Mary	A15D	1781May7	
Noble Matthew	A11D		
Noble Miranda	A15K	1793Feb4	
Noble Norman Wheeler	A18D	1902Jun29	b.p. Mo Joplin m1926Jan26
Noble Olive Blanch	A18C	1891Feb3	b.p. Kans/Galena d1965Dec5 Fla
Noble Oliver	A13B	1734Mar3	b.p.Conn/Hebron
Noble Orville M	A18A	1885Mar4	b.p.Kansas/Galena d1888Oct25
Noble Polly	A14H	1772Jun15	
Noble Rebecca	A11J	1683Jan4	
Noble Rebecca	A14C		bapt1760 d1777Oct19
Noble Roswell	A15H	1787Oct3	d1825abt of Baltimore Md
Noble Ruth	A13Aa	1732Mar6	b.p. Mass/Westfield m1753Feb21 d1817
Noble Ruth	A14A	1753Aug12	
Noble Ruth Mrs	A11Ha		
Noble Sallie	A15A	1776Jan26	
Noble Sarah	A16C	1818Nov13	d1820Aug22
Noble Sarah Maria	A16F	1825Aug22	
Noble Sophia	A15L	1794Dec3	d Monmouth N.J.
Noble Thirza	A13E	1740Jul27	b.p. Conn/Hebron
Noble Thirza	A14G		d.about 1771
Noble Thirza	A15C	1779Nov3	d Williamsburg NY
Noble Thomas	A10A	1632abt	b.p. England m1660Nov1 d1704Jan20 Mass
Noble Thomas	A11C	1666Jan14	
Noble Truman Wilgus	A17B	1853Jul11	
Noble Washington A	A16E	1823Mar3	
Noble William Taylor	A15J	1791Jun16	b.p.Mass/Pittsfield m1814Jan1I d1861NY
Noblett – Mrs	M10Aa		
Noblett Angeline	M11G		of Maries Co Mo
Noblett Barbara A	M14F		of Heavener Okla.
Noblett Chester	M22C		of Kansas City Mo
Noblett Clarence	M22B		of Kansas City Mo
Noblett Claude	M20C		of Montana
Noblett Clay	M22A		of Louisiana
Noblett Edna	M13E		
Noblett Eleanor	M11I		m1839Aug8 Gasconade Co Mo
Noblett Elizabeth Ann	M12A	1855Jan22	m1874May d1924May12 Of Maries Co Mo
Noblett Ellie	M20F		of Maries Co Mo
Noblett Frank	M11D		In California gold rush

146

NAME	NUMBER	BIRTH	COMMENTS
Noblett Henry Clay	M11C		m1864Mar29 d St James Maries Co Mo
Noblett Ida	M14B		
Noblett Ira	M11A	1825	b.p. Tn. or No Car m1853abt d1871Apr11
Noblett Ira Jr	M12D		d1875Jul25 Drowned at Indian Ford
Noblett Jeff	M12B		b.p. California Of near Vienna Mo
Noblett John	M20B		of Montana
Noblett John A	M11B		d1898Feb1 of Maries Co Mo In Civil War
Noblett John W	M14C		of St James Mo
Noblett Julia	M13D		
Noblett L.E.	M13A		
Noblett Leo	M20G		d1862. Train wreck Wyoming
Noblett Margaret Ann	M11F	1816Nov19	d1881Aug22 Of Maries Co Mo
Noblett Mary J	M14D		of St James Mo
Noblett Minnie	M13C		
Noblett Myra Jane	M11H		of Maries and Pulaski Cos Mo
Noblett Oliver	M13B		d single
Noblett Raymond	M20A		of Montana
Noblett Rhea	M20D		of Montana
Noblett Sarah E	M14E		of Tacoma Washington
Noblett T.J.	G18Aa	1863abt	of Vienna Mo
Noblett Vera	M20E		of Montana
Noblett Will	M12C		b.p. California Of near Vienna Mo
Noblett William	M14A		d1916Aug13 Shannon Co Mo
Noblett William	M10A		
Noblett William Berry	M11E		In California gold rush
Nolen Edward Langley	A97A	1856Sep30	b.p. Tn/Williamson Co m1886Nov4 d1917
Nolen Kate	A98A	1900	b.p.Tn/Williamson Co Of Nashville
Nolen William Martin	A96Aa	1817Apr26	b.p. Tn/Williamson Co d1897Nov7
Norman Mary J	C37Aa		of Mounds Okla
Norris –	T29Ea		of Tennessee
Norris Katherine	A70Fa		
Null –	E54Ga		
O'Neill James H	M23Ia		of St Louis Mo
Odom Isaac W	K11Da	1824	b.p. Miss d. before 1875 Howell Co Mo
Odom Jacob	K11Daf		b.p.Scotland America in 1812 Of Miss.
Offutt Elizabeth	A94A		m1731 Md d1835 Rutherford Co Tenn
Offutt Jane	A93Aa		d1810
Offutt MordecaiBurgess	A93A	1744Jan25	b.p.Md/ d1814 Mar7 Md
Offutt Samuel	A38Ca	1712Apr19	m1734Jan23 d1761May15
Offutt William	A88Caf		
Ogle Polly	D17Ba		m1815
Ogle William	V18Ha		
Ohmart William Frank	F67Ca	1901Feb20	d.1980Jul14
Oliphant Anne S	A61Aa	1768	m.1790Oct11 d1841
Oliver Martha Ellen	R22Ba		m1866 d1383Feb
Oram John	F22Ha		m1825Dec21
Orr Elzey	G57Fa		of Maries Co Mo
Orr James	K11Fa		"moved to Howell Co. Mo"
Orr Mertie	R15Eb		of Meta Mo

NAME	NUMBER	BIRTH	COMMENTS
Orton Malinda	K27Bam		b.p.Ill/Belleville m(1)Benton-
Osborn Agnes E	B72D	1854	b.p.Ill Twin of William
Osborn Alice C	B72G		
Osborn Berta A	A82B	1889Aug	b.p. Mo
Osborn Charles T	B72E		
Osborn Charley T	A82C	1883Mar	b.p.Mo
Osborn Cora Evaline	B72F	1864Sep5	b.p. Iowa/Cedar Co m1886Oct10 d1918Apr
Osborn Earl H	A82E	1894Apr	b.p.Mo
Osborn Frances Amelia	B72B		
Osborn Harry	A82D	1884Oct	b.p.Mo
Osborn Mary J Mrs	B72Ca	1859Apr	b.p.Indiana
Osborn Scott H	A82A	1876Jan	b.p.Kansas
Osborn Thomas	B71J	1819Dec12	b.p.NY/Thompkins Co m1845Oct18 d1910Mo
Osborn Wesley	D35Ba		of Stanberry Mo
Osborn William	B70A		b.p. Prob. N.J. or Cayuga Co NY
Osborn Willis	B72C	1854Sep	b.p.Ill m1875 Twin of Agnes
Osborn Winfield Scott	B72A		
Ousley -	G33Ea		Also Owsley
Ousley Dena	D21Fa		
Ousley Martha	E17Ea		Also Owsley
Ousley Virgil	D68Ca		of Eldon Mo Also Owsley
Overlease Jane	H14Ha		of Phelps Co Mo
Owens A Dolph	E49D		
Owens Bernice	E50D		of Rolla Mo
Owens Burr	E49C		
Owens Corrine	D90E		
Owens Cyrus	D90B		
Owens Daniel	E32A		of Maries Co Mo/ Later of Callaway Co
Owens Della	E50B		of Rolla Mo
Owens Don Mack	D90C	1905Aug7	b.p.Mo FranklinCo m1933Sep21 d1978Nov
Owens Elija	D21Ga		
Owens Elijah	D27Bb		
Owens Francis C.W.	E21Ca	1822May6	b.p.Tn/Denman m1856Sep4 of Osage Co Mo
Owens Gladys	D90G		
Owens Guy	E50A		of Rolla Mo
Owens Helene	E50C		of Rolla Mo
Owens Herbert	D90F		
Owens Ida May	E30I	1876Mar18	m(1)1899Jan19 (2)1939Jan5
Owens Isaac Mack MD	D89A		dOwensville Mo
Owens James	E50E		of Rolla Mo
Owens James	E49A		d single Of Belle Mo
Owens James	C30Ca		
Owens James C	E48Fa		
Owens Jesse	E30D	1863Dec14	m1916Jul9 Of Cooper Hill Mo
Owens Jessie	E32B		
Owens John Robert	E30B	1859Aug24	d1887Sep29 d single
Owens Joseph Reed	E30H	1873May24	m1901Apr9 No issue
Owens Laura Belle	E30G	1871May22	m1889Jul2
Owens Lucille	D90D		

NAME	NUMBER	BIRTH	COMMENTS
Owens Mary	E50F		of Rolla Mo
Owens Mary Frances	E30C	1861Oct4	m1884Dec23 d1898Feb20 No issue
Owens Mary P	F30Ca		
Owens Nancy Ann	E30A	1857Jun29	m1376Dec19 d1373Jul10
Owens Oliver	E49B		of Rolla Mo
Owens Pearl	E32D		
Owens Robert	E32C		
Owens Robert Mack	D91A	1937Dec21	of Deluth Minn.
Owens Sarah	E30F	1868Aug3	m1887Oct Of Springfield Mo
Owens Stephen	E22Ba		
Owens Susan Blanche	E30J	1879Oct16	m1902Dec25
Owens Waldo	D90A		
Owens William C Dr	E30E	1865Nov10	m1893Oct1(2)1922Aug26 Of St Louis Mo
Owens William Don	D91B	1939Dec12	
Owsley Crawford	C15Da	1836Feb11	d1908Dec5
Owsley David A	C36H	1844Feb25	b.p.Mo/Morgan Co m1865Jul16 d1915Mar3
Owsley David Ray	C38B	1887Nov12	b.p.Mo/Almon m1912Nov9Cross Timbers Mo
Owsley Dee Kemp	C39A	1916Mar21	b.p.Mp/Preston m1950Sep30Mo In WWII
Owsley Elias H	C36I	1846	b.p.Mo/Morgan Co d1866Feb4 In Civil W.
Owsley Elihu (Hugh)	C38C	1889Jun24	b.p.Mo/Almon m1914Dec23 d1981Aprl Mo
Owsley Elijah Bunton	C37H	1859Sep5	b.p.Mo m1883Mar31 d1950Feb27 HickoryCo
Owsley Elijah Bunton	C36G	1836Jan2	b.p.Iowa m1857Feb3 Mo d1914Mar3 Okla
Owsley Emma E	C37M	1868Dec26	b.p.Mo/Hickory Co d1922 Twin:George
Owsley Emma Mrs	C37Da		of Washington State
Owsley Emmanuel M	C36C	1826Oct9	b.p.Tn/Claiborne Co m1846Mar12 d1892Mo
Owsley Ethel Fern	C39E	1923Sep20	b.p.Mo/Wheatland m19460ct17 New Mexico
Owsley Flora J Mrs	C37La		of Jackson Co Mo
Owsley George A	C37L	1868Dec26	Mo/Putnam Co d1936May30 Jackson Co Mo
Owsley George Wash.	C38D	1891Jul7	b.p.Mo/Almon d1938Jan8 Preston Mo
Owsley Hannah	C36D	1839	b.p.Ind/Putnam Co m Morgan Co Mo
Owsley Henry A	C36A	1818Mar12	b.p.Tenn/Claiborne Co m1340Mar24 d1905
Owsley Homer Allen	C38F	1896Jul11	b.p. Mo/Almon
Owsley Ila Mary	C39C	1919Dec16	b.p.Mo/Almon
Owsley James Irving	C37A	1847	b.p.Mo/Osage Co m1868Mar17 Of MoundsOk
Owsley John	C34A		
Owsley John Whiteley	C37I	1860Jun8	b.p.Mo m1883Nov27 Osage Mo d1953Oct12
Owsley Leconsul	C37F	1855	b.p.Mo m1884Jul17 Hickory Co d1842Okla
Owsley Leta May	C39D	1921Nov30	b.p.Mo/Almon m1946Dec20 Sweet Sprgs Mo
Owsley Louisa	C36B	1814	d1911Jul24 Spokane Wash.
Owsley Martha A	C37J	1863	b.p.Mo/Putnam Co m1883Aug16 Hickory Co
Owsley Martin Miller	C36E	1832	b.p. Ind/Putnam Co m1851Aug9 Mo CivilW
Owsley Mary Susan	C37K	1865	b.p.Mo/Putnam Co m1886Sep14 d Calif.
Owsley Merle Inolee	C39G	1930Jul6	b.p.Mo Wheatland m1947Jul27 Wheatland
Owsley Nancy Elizabeth	C37E	1854	b.p. Mo
Owsley Nellie May	C38E	1895Feb16	b.p.Mo/Almon d1934Jul18
Owsley Nora Jane	C38A	1886Jan16	b.p.Mo/Almon d1978Dec16 Buffalo Mo
Owsley Reuben	C37D	1852	b.p.Mo Of Washington State
Owsley Robert	C35A	1802ca	b.p.Tenn/Claiborne Co m1818 dMorgan Co M
Owsley Robert Hoyt	C39B	1917Nov19	m1945Aug5 Wheatland Mo

NAME	NUMBER	BIRTH	COMMENTS
Owsley Robert Rainey	C37C	1849Dec27	b.p.Mo/Osage Co m1876Apr16 d1920Oct4Mo
Owsley Ruby Clare	C39F	1925Jan19	b.p.Mo/Wheatland m1949Mar13 NY NY
Owsley Sarah Frances	C37G	1857Jul10	b.p.Mo m1877Dec2 d1895Sep28 Hickory Co
Owsley William	C36F	1834	b.p.Ind/Putnam Co m1852Jan9 Mo d1864
Owsley William Burton	C37B	1848	b.p.Mo Osage Co d1923 Cross Timbers Mo
Paddock Roy	I48Ja		
Painter Ursula	B03Ac		d.1700 Father Dr Nicholas Painter
Palmer C.O.	E41Ga		
Palmer Joseph	D22Fa		m1867Sep17 Bland Mo
Palmer Sarah A	D20Fa		In Howell Co, Olden Twp, Mo 1879
Pankey Caroline	R12Cb		
Pankey Mack	R12Cbf		
Parker –	B03Ia		of Anne Arundel Co Md
Parker Addie	I54Da		m1904Jan28 Of Maries Co Mo
Parker Amanda	K35A		of Wright Co Mo
Parker Carrol	A80Ha		
Parker Drusilla	K34C		of Maries and Hickory Cos Mo
Parker Eliza	G62Aa	1843Nov13	b.p.Mo/Polk Co d1926Nov15
Parker Emeline	K34D		
Parker Henry	K11Baf		of Bloomgarden Mo
Parker James	K34A		
Parker John F	Y54Gaf		
Parker Malinda	K34G	1849Aug9	m1865Jul3 d1918Aug6
Parker Marion	G36Aa		
Parker Martha Mrs	K11Bam		or Matilda
Parker Mary	G36Da	1849Jan26	m1869Oct7
Parker Myra	K35B		of Wright Co Mo
Parker Myscal Mrs	K34E		m(1)Johnson
Parker Olive	Y54Ga		of Maries Co Mo
Parker Polly	K34F		
Parker Rainey	G57Ia		m1909May27 Of Franklin Co Mo
Parker Ruth Mrs	D17Fb		
Parker W.C.	Z17Ea		
Parker Wesley	G36Daf		
Parker William	K34B		
Parks Amanda	C37Fa		of Stillwater Okla
Parks Sindrella	C37Ca		of Almon Mo
Parrish Temperance	C37Cbm	1811Apr9	b.p. N.C. d1892Nov17 Almon Mo
Passons Thomas L	A74Aa	1889Jun28	m1922Jun8 d1957Mar20
Patterson Edward	E47Ba		of Shannon Co Mo
Patton J.E.R.	A16Fa		
Pearson –	T25Aa		of Vienna Mo
Pearson –	I52Ea		
Pearson Arizona	G19Ja		of Union Mo
Pearson Charles	G20Faf		
Pearson Griselda	G20Fa		of Maries Co Mo
Pearson Robert Dr	F09Ca		
Pease David Lawrence	F49Aaf		
Pease Linda Susan	F49Aa	1955Sep25	b.p.Minn/Minneapolis

NAME	NUMBER	BIRTH	COMMENTS
Peek Robert	A67Ga	1836Mar26	d1919Aug11
Peggs J.D.	V28Ca		of Arizona
Pelikan Frank T	M13Ea		
Pelikan Julius	K33Fa		d1930Oct
Pendleton Eliza	U16Ga		of Maries and Osage Cos Mo
Pendleton George	U16Gaf		
Pendleton Irenah	G21Ea		
Pendleton John Riley	G21Eaf		
Pendleton Ollie	G59Aa		of Maries Co Mo
Penn Elizabeth	A53Aa	1800	b.p. No.Carolina
Penn John	A53Aaf	1775abt	b.p.Va. d about 1845 Arkansas
Perkins Isaac	T24Fbf		of Maries Co Mo
Perkins Isabelle	T24Fb		of Maries Co
Perkins John	F34Ca		m1837Aug31
Perrin Alonzo	R27La		
Peters Edwin	Y65Ca		of Springfield Mo Instr. Drury College
Peters Jeff	M28Ca		of Maries Co Mo
Peters Lrone Ann	A72Aa	1930Oct6	m1950
Peth John	F55Ia		
Petty William	K11Ea		of Maries Co Mo Farmer Fly Creek
Phelps Cordella	E22La		of Osage Co Mo
Phelps D	A15Kb		
Phelps John	C13Ja		
Phelps Laura Jane	E69Da		m1864Feb25
Phelps Lee Rev.	E22Pa		
Phelps Sallie	E22Na		
Phelps Tilman	E69Ga		m.1868Aug 16
Phillips -	E25Ja		of Miller Co Mo
Phillips Florence	E63Ia		
Picker Adolph	G20Ia		of Maries Co Mo
Pickering Alex	T29Ca		of Tulsa Okla
Pickering Belle	G31Ga		d1899Sep25
Pickering George	G31Gaf		
Pierce Jenness	G35Ea		
Pierce Mary E	F66Ca	1378	d.1904
Pierce Sarah	A49Aa	1798May2	b.p.Tn. Roane Co. d1874Jul23In/MeigsCo
Pierce Walter	H57Ea		of St Louis Mo
Pierson William A	V26Ca		m1885
Pigg Agnes	G12Gam		
Pinnell Asa	R18A	1772Dec12	b.p. N.C. m Ky Mo in 1813 d1871May27
Pinnell Asa D	R22A	1845Jul20	m1867Nov11 d1931Mar30
Pinnell Augustus	R19B	1318Jun3	b.p.Mo/Maries Co d1900Feb21 Maries Co
Pinnell Bluford	R24A	1867Oct14	m1890Dec24 Of Maries Co Mo and Ark.
Pinnell Carrie M.	R24B	1870Aug2	of Centertown Ark.
Pinnell Claude	R24F		Killed by lightning
Pinnell Cynthia E	R21B	1848May8	d1930Nov22
Pinnell Della Ferol	R24J	1892Aug9	m1911Sep6 of Niangua Mo
Pinnell Elizabeth	R21A	1839Sep1	d1917Mar17 Of Maries Co Mp
Pinnell Ella E	R21C	1843Aug30	d1900May4 of Maries Co Mo and Kansas

NAME	NUMBER	BIRTH	COMMENTS
Pinnell Elsie Maud	R24E		
Pinnell Elvin Cecil	R32A		d1897Jul15 single
Pinnell Ernest	R23G	1887Feb9	m1911Dec d1918Sep21
Pinnell Everett	R23E	1879Oct6	of Grandfield Okla
Pinnell George Louis	R24H	1888Jun3	m1910Nov24 of Granby Mo
Pinnell Gladys	R32D	1897Sep12	m1916Jul26 of Porterville Calif.
Pinnell Gregory	R23C	1873Nov11	of Pampa Texas
Pinnell Gretchen	R32E	1902Sep11	m1920Nov15 Of Porterville Calif.
Pinnell Halley Hunter	R24M	1901Sep17	m1921Jul30 of Marshfield Mo Minister
Pinnell Ida Leora May	R22D	1861May19	m1884Jun3
Pinnell Ira Martin	R24I	1890Aug27	m1910Nov6 of Diamond Mo
Pinnell James Tilden	R24C	1876Nov14	m1903Dec24 Pineville Mo Pros. atty.
Pinnell Leila	R23F	1887Oct6	d1907Oct3 single
Pinnell Lessie Lavina	R24K	1896May28	of Okla City Okla
Pinnell Lester Lee	R24N	1903Jan18	m1923 Of Kansas Cy Mo
Pinnell Lester W	R32F	1910Feb4	of Porterville Calif
Pinnell Lida	R23B	1870Dec4	m1898Jun6 Of Madrid New Mexico
Pinnell Lunsford L Mrs	R19Aa		d St Louis Mo
Pinnell Lunsford Lane	R22B	1848Feb3	m1866(2)1885Mar1 d1931Feb1 Mo UnionArm
Pinnell Lunsford Lane	R19A	1813Mar23	b.p.Probably Ky d1865Aug9 St Louis Mo
Pinnell Lunsford S	R24G	1886Aug1	m1910Nov3 Of Porterville Calif
Pinnell Mary E	R22E		
Pinnell Muriel E	R32B	1895Jan9	m1912Oct12 d1924May18
Pinnell Peter	R16A		b.p.Wales To Va early 1700´s Am,Rev
Pinnell Peter Mrs	R16Aa		
Pinnell Ralph E	R32C	1891Jul26	m1914Dec8 Of Porterville Calif
Pinnell Richard	R17A		b.p.Va Moved to S.Car. before 1772
Pinnell Richard Mrs	R17Aa		of Virginia
Pinnell Rosalia	R23A	1869Feb14	m1885Aug20 Of Glen Rio New Mexico
Pinnell Walter	R23D	1876Oct14	of Blair Okla
Pinnell Wheeler Ward	R24L	1899Aug22	of Kansas City Mo
Pinnell William B	R20A		of Washington Co and St Louis Mo
Pinnell William Bowles	R22C	1866Jan29	m1887Dec24 Maries Co Mo Of California
Pinnell William L	R32G	1905Jun26	b.p. Calif/Los Angeles
Pinnell William L	R24D		
Pinnell William Lewis	R19C	1824Jan27	b.p. Mo/Maries Co m1844Aug12 d1887Jul1
Plummer Lydia G	F21Ga		m1816Apr29
Poe Andrew	D41Ba	1876Apr3	of Belle Mo
Poe Annis	D54Ba		of Bland Mo m(2) to Gus Baumann
Poe Barnabas Madison	S18Da		m1830Jan27 Osage Co Mo d abt1847
Poe Robert I	D41Aa	1866Jan16	of Belle Mo
Poe William Pike	D41Aaf	1842Jun21	d1935May4 Belle Mo
Pohl Joseph	G27Ga		
Pointer "Cap"	R27Ma		
Pointer -	R31Ca		
Pointer -	R31Aa		
Pointer Angie	E33C		of near Meta Mo
Pointer Charles	R31Aaf		
Pointer Daniel	E22Bb		

NAME	NUMBER	BIRTH	COMMENTS
Pointer Elizabeth	E17Cam		
Pointer Elizabeth Ann	E71Aa	1835Dec14	b.p. Mo/Osage Co
Pointer Florence	E29Da		
Pointer Forest	E33B		Never married
Pointer Fred	E33E		m in Colo. d Carrigo Sprgs Texas
Pointer James	E17Ha		m1836Jan10
Pointer Louisa	E33F		d single
Pointer Minnie	E33D		of Maries Co Mo
Pointer Nancy	E17Ma		m1842Jun9
Pointer Nancy Ann	E220a		
Pointer Polly	R28Ca		
Pointer Sheldon	E33A		moved to Okle
Pointer William	E71Aaf	1808	b.p. Ky/ m.1835Jan8
Pool -	D35A		of Gentry Co Mo
Pool -	D35B		of Stanberry Mo
Pool Elisha	D26Ba		in Gentry Co Mo 1850 census
Pool R.G.	D35C		of Agra Oklahoma
Poor Barton	Y29Ga		
Poor Mary	I62Aa		to Warren Co Mo 1800
Poppell Calvin	B29Bb		
Poppell Edgar Broward	B29Aa	1910	b.p.Fla/Winter Park m1935Aug20 d1959
Posey Allen A	E39A	1875Jan29	b.p.Mo/Osage Co. m1898 d1960Nov17 Mo
Posey Humphrey	E69Ca	1841Feb22	b.p.Ga/ m1862Apr10 d1915Jan28 Mo
Posey Ladoiska Ann	E63Ba	1901May16	b.p.Mo/Koenig m 1916 d.1960Aug4Wash.Mo
Powers Emeline	V12Ea		
Powers John Dr	V12Eaf		
Powers John Thompson	L15Iaf	1806Sep22	of Osage Co Mo before 1831
Powers Lydia	T16Bam		
Powers Lydia Angeline	L15La		of Blanco Tex abt1880, of Maries Co Mo
Powers Melissa	S11Ca		
Prater Richard	P15Fa		
Pratt Gladstone C	F57Ea		
Prescott Avaline	B15Ib		
Prewett James	G36Ab		of Shannon Co Mo
Prewett John	Y31Bb		
Prewett Moses (Doc)	U13Fa		of Pulaski Mo
Prewett Roena	G36Cam	1832Apr20	b.p.Kentucky d1903Nov9 Maries Co Mo
Price -	R13Da		of Nebraska
Price Elizabeth	A37Ca		m1762May30 Stafford Co Va St Pauls Par
Price Elizabeth	D27Fa		"moved to Ozarks, later to Oklahoma"
Price Jack	Y74Faf		
Price Linda	Y74Fa		m1881Oct24
Price Nellie	R30La		of Osage Co Mo
Pruitt Robert A	B43Ca		
Pryor John	D18Ha		m1859Apr3
Pryor Lottie	U13Ba		
Pryor Louisa Jane	U11Ca		
Pryor Nancy	G35Ab		m(1)Prewett. Of Maries Co Mo d Maries
Pryor Robert F	D18La		

NAME	NUMBER	BIRTH	COMMENTS
Pryor Stephen	U11Caf		
Pryor William T	D18Fa		m1857Apr30
Puckett Carl Dr.	F57Ba		
Purcell Frank	D56F		of Salem Mo
Purcell George	D56C		of Rector Mo
Purcell Helen	D56D		of Rector Mo
Purcell Isolene	D56B		
Purcell Lester	D56G		of Chicago Ill
Purcell Oren	D52Fa		
Purcell Shockley	D56A		of Chicago Ill
Purcell Velma	D56E		of Salem Mo
Putnam –	Z38Aa		no issue
Quisenberry William	R11Da		
Raaf Caroline Lena	D90Ca	1907Nov29	b.p.Mo/Gerald m1933Sep21
Raaf William Henry	D90Caf		
Ragan Charles	Y57B		of Phelps Co Mo d single
Ragan Dolph	Y57A		of Phelps Co Mo
Ragan George M	Y39Ba		
Ragan John	Y57C		of Phekps Co Mo
Ragan Leona	G44Ga		
Ragan Maud	Y57D		of Phelps Co Mo
Ragland Elizabeth J	B87Aa		
Ramey Amy Edna	F66A	1875Apr16	b.p.Ill m1895Jan27 Ks d1961Nov15 Kans
Ramey Amy Frances	F65C	1856Jul18	b.p.Ohio d1875Feb5 Ill
Ramey Charles Walter	F66C	1879May3	b.p.Ill m1900Sep13 Ks d1934 KansCy Mo
Ramey Edgar Clement	F65F	1863Apr1	b.p.Ohio Georgetown d1875Feb17 Ill
Ramey George Emer	F66D	1882May9	b.p.Ks m KansCy Mo d1974Mar6 Ca.
Ramey George Neyman	F65E	1861Feb11	b.p.Ohio d.1862Jun17 Georgetown Ohio
Ramey John Waterfield	F65B	1854Jun22	
Ramey Lucretia C.	F66F	1890May10	b.p.Ks m1908Aug9 d.1962Mar31Olathe Ks
Ramey Mary Susan	F66E	1886Mar13	b.p.Ks Benton mKans Cy Mo dHouston Tx
Ramey Minnie Edith	F66B	1877Apr24	b.p.Ill m.1900 Ill 1902 Benton Kans.
Ramey Robert	Y74Ca		no issue
Ramey Samuel	F64Fa	1828Jun7	d.1864Mar30
Ramey Thomas Costello	F65D	1858Oct19	b.p.Ohio d.1875Feb28 Iuka Ill
Ramey William Burgess	F65A	1852Nov16	b.p.Ohio m1871Dec17 Ill d1900May13 Kan
Ramsey –	Z20A		m(1)Nancy Hughes Springfield Mo Of La.
Ramsey Charles	I48Ba		of Huntington Park California
Ramsey DeLafayette			Incorrectly shown as T15Iaf 1stPrint.
Ramsey Diana	L14Aa		
Ramsey James K.P.	T15Ia		of Maries Co Mo
Ramsey Mrs	Z20Ab		second wife of Ramsey –
Ramsey Robert L	L14Aaf		
Ramsey Rutherford	Z21A		of Joplin Mo
Ranyon Sarah Ann	A90Ja		m1839Dec4 Mason Co Kentucky
Rathbone Emmely	D12L		mother unwed
Rathbone Love	D12K		mother unwed
Rathbone Mary	D11Eb		unwed mother of Love and Emmely
Ray –	H14Ka		of Texas Co Mo

154

NAME	NUMBER	BIRTH	COMMENTS
Ready Martha J	U12Ca		m1872Feb4 of Maries Co Mo and Texas
Ready Richard	R28Ba		
Ready Thomas	U12Caf		of Maries Co Mo
Redcliff Jean	E66Da		of England
Redd Annis Almina	B24F	1912Jun29	b.p.Mo/Albany m1933Mar10
Redd Charles E	B15Ga		m1898Dec21
Redd Charles Jr	B24A	1899Nov5	b.p.Mo/Chillicothe
Redd Elizabeth N.	B24E	1909Jun30	b.p. Mo/Albany m1928Mar27
Redd George William	B24B	1901Jul5	b.p. Mo/Chillicothe m1921Sep4
Redd Lee Thomas	B24D	1907Jan17	b.p.Mo/Albany m1926Feb1
Redd Oland Dorsel	B24C	1905Nov5	b.p. Mo/Albany m1924Jan27
Reed -	D28Aa		
Reed Adele D	V26A	1858Aug23	d1890Sep25 Grand Junction Colorado
Reed Anna M	V26C	1861Nov20	b.p.Mo/Vienna m1885 Of Burlington Kan.
Reed Austin M	V26E	1868Dec22	m1896 Of Sepulveda California
Reed Bertie R	V26D	1866Nov17	m1889 Of Van Nuye California
Reed Cassius M	V26G	1865Jul4	b.p.Pa/Darlington d1883 single
Reed Elizabeth	R25Aa	1800Nov30	b.p.Mo/ Franklin Co d1872Jun2 MariesCo
Reed Lucinda Penelope	J12Ga	1853Feb27	m1883Dec2 d1920Apr23 Of Miller Co Mo
Reed Samuel B	V26F	1870Mar5	m1894 Of Ellinwood Kansas
Reed Samuel W	V24Ba	1832Feb4	b.p.Pa/Darlington m1857Sep Mo d1892Kam
Reed Therese H	V26B	1860Jan24	m1885 Of Folsom New Mexico
Reese Catharine	E77Ca		m1779Oct22
Reeves -	Q42Ea		of Rolla Mo
Reeves Joseph	H13Ca		
Reeves Tony	H16A		of Maries Co Mo d elsewhere
Reichel Ulrich	S14Fa		of Maries Co Mo
Reid Walker G	F30Aa		.
Renfro -	Q31Ea		m probably in Tennessee
Renfrow Fred	G20Ha		of Maries Co Mo
Renick Ann	Y24Ga		of Maries Co Mo
Renick Felix	E29Fa		
Reynolds -	T23Ba		of Miller Co Mo
Reynolds Hannah C	V14Aam	1823Nov15	
Reynolds William J	K32Da		of Maries Co Mo
Rhodes Ida	H17B		
Rhodes Isaac	Q32Jc		
Rhodes Isaac	H13Da		
Rhodes Lucy	H17A		
Rhodes Mary	B15Fa		m1902Mar2
Rice -	H12Ca		
Rice -	K28Aa		
Rice Catherine	L15Ea		"to Blance Tex. about 1880 d.there"
Rich Marge	E88Ha		
Richa Mary Adaline	D41Aam		of Gasconade Co Mo
Richardson Anne Belle	A97Aa	1859May6	b.p.Tenn/Williamson Co m1886Nov4 d1937
Richardson Benjamin P	D89Aaf	1849Nov21	d1878Jun2
Richardson Diana Lisa	F70Ba		m1983Apr23 Phoenix Oregon
Richardson Mollie M.	D89Aa		d. Owensville Mo

NAME	NUMBER	BIRTH	COMMENTS
Richardson Thomas	B05Ia	1700 abt	
Richay Melvin Duane	F68A	1931May7	b.p.Ks/Benton m1954Oct10 Chanute Ks
Richey Bethine	F68B	1933Aug2	b.p.ElDorado Ks Lived a few hours
Richey Byron Eugene	F67Fa	1908Nov17	
Richey Duane Albert	F70B	1958Oct7	b.p. Ark/Eureka Springs m1983Apr23 Ore
Richey Janet	F70E	1969Dec16	b.p.Africa Kitwe Zambia d1970Apr30 Afr
Richey Larry Allen	F70D	1968Sep10	b.p. Africa Kitwe Zambia
Richey Michelle	F70F	1970Aug15	b.p. Ind/Indianapolis
Richey Miriam	F70C	1960Feb20	b.p. Conn/Hartford d1963Nov7 Africa
Richey Renetta Dorene	F68C	1934Jul6	b.p.Ks ElDorado m1955Jun18 ElDorado Ks
Richey Robin Eugene	F70A	1955Nov28	b.p.Okla/Drummond m1975Jul22 Ky.
Richey Vesta Ruth	F68D	1938Jul29	b.p.Ks ElDorado m1968Sept SpringfeldTn
Richmond Joseph	T15Ka		m1879Mar15
Ricker -	K34Fam		
Ricketts Elizabeth	F22Ka		m1835Sep22
Ridenhour Adam	R26D		
Ridenhour Adam Louis	R30L		d1937 Of Osage Co Mo
Ridenhour Albert A	R27H		
Ridenhour Alexander	R28D		
Ridenhour Amelia	R26A		d single
Ridenhour Bruce	R31D		of Oklahoma
Ridenhour Charles	R31B		d1911Aug31
Ridenhour Cora	R31H		of Belle Mo
Ridenhour David Jasper	R30K		
Ridenhour Decatur	R31C		of Oklahoma
Ridenhour Elizabeth	D64Aa	1813Aug1	m1839May2
Ridenhour Elizabeth	R26G		of Belle Mo and Franklin Co Mo
Ridenhour Ella	R31F		of Belle Mo
Ridenhour Elvira	R26F		of Phelps Co Mo
Ridenhour Fred M	R27F		
Ridenhour James L	R27I		
Ridenhour John	R25A	1802Oct31	b.p. Mo/Franklin Co d Belle Mo 1852Aug
Ridenhour John A	R27A		
Ridenhour John Clark	Z27Da		of Maries Co Mo and Wash. St d1919Jan8
Ridenhour John O	R31A		of Maries Co Mo Postmaster Belle Mo
Ridenhour John S Mrs	Z27Dam		of Maries Co Mo died after husband
Ridenhour John Sartain	Z27Daf	1815Apr1	b.p. Mo/Maries Co d1897Apr25
Ridenhour John Shep.	R30A		of Belle Mo Store and Post Office
Ridenhour John W	R28A		
Ridenhour Lennie F	R27K		
Ridenhour Lewis J	R27G		
Ridenhour Louis H	R28C		
Ridenhour Margaret A	R27D		
Ridenhour Margaret C	R26B	1846Mar11	d1909Apr11 of near Belle Mo
Ridenhour Martha L.	R30D	1854Nov28	d1882May28 Belle Mo
Ridenhour Martin	R26H		of Maries Co Mo
Ridenhour Martin A.J.	R30H		b.p. Mo/ Near Belle Mo
Ridenhour Mary E	R27E		
Ridenhour Mary Jane	R30C		

NAME	NUMBER	BIRTH	COMMENTS
Ridenhour Mollie	R28B		
Ridenhour Nancy Eliz.	R30B		of Dixon Mo
Ridenhour Polly	R27M		
Ridenhour Rainey	R31E		of Belle Mo
Ridenhour Reuben J	R26E		d1850abt Gasconade Co Mo
Ridenhour Rhoda J	R27N		
Ridenhour Robert R	R28E		
Ridenhour Sarah F	R27L		
Ridenhour Sarah F.	R30G	1852Sep12	m1880Nov28 d1924Aug17 of Maries Co Mo
Ridenhour Sophia	R31G		of Belle Mo
Ridenhour Susan M	R27J		
Ridenhour Susan M. C.	R30F		of Belle Mo
Ridenhour Thomas B.	R26C	1842Jun20	d1927Jan5
Ridenhour Thomas H.	R30J		of Maries Co Mo
Ridenhour Thomas M	R27B		
Ridenhour Virginia H	R30I		of Kansas City Mo
Ridenhour William A	R27C		
Ridenhour William A	R30E		d in infancy
Rigby John	E25Aaf		
Rigsby Emma	E25Aa		m1891Aug9
Riley James	H54Aa		
Riley Mildred Eliz.	F59Aam		
Ringeison Charlotte	F36Aam		Father: Frederick Ringeison
Rinks Mattie	H14Ga		of Phelps Co Mo
Ritterbusch James K.Jr	F49A	1955Feb18	b.p.Mo/St. Louis m1980Jun28
Ritterbusch James Karl	F37Aa	1921Oct27	b.p. Mo/Bland d1983Aug7 of Fulton Mo
Ritterbusch Louis C.F.	F37Aaf		
Roach Rachel J	Z13Ga		of Maries Co Mo and St. Louis
Roark Prentice	A74Da	1904Sep3	d1967Mar17
Roark Raymond Paul	E84Aa		m.1942Dec26
Roberds Catherine	G19Ga		of Maries Co Mo
Roberds Charles	J16Ea		of Maries Co Mo
Roberson "Bud"	G45Aa		of Maries Co Mo
Roberson -	Q37Ba		
Roberson -	K25Ab		m(1)Hutton -
Roberson Dollie	G13Ca		of Maries Co Mo
Roberson Dollie	G36Fb		
Roberson Glen	J24Ca		of Maries Co Mo
Roberson Jane	J14Dam		
Roberson Lucinda	Q33Gb		Her maiden name may not be Roberson
Roberson Pleas	G36Fbf		
Roberson T.H.B.	Q33Ja		of Maries Co Mo
Roberson William (Wid)	G13Caf	1838Feb5	m(1)1858Mar7(2)Bullock Of MariesCoMo
Roberts James H	L16Aa		of St.James Mo
Roberts John	A66Ea	1829Feb11	d1904Aug13
Roberts Lanora	A76Oa	1900 abt	
Robins Edward Col	F44A	1602	b.p. England d1653Md Va in 1615
Robins Elizabeth	B03Aa		d.Md/Anne Arundel Co Of Virginia
Robins Jane Mrs	F44Aa		b.p. Eng d Northampton Va

NAME	NUMBER	BIRTH	COMMENTS
Robins Obedience	F44B		
Robins Thomas	F43A		
Robins Zachariah	E08Ja		
Robinson Alice	Y37A		of Loveland Colo.
Robinson Ison H	Y20Ba		
Robinson Mattie	A73Ca	1865 abt	
Robinson Obedience	Y37B		of "Denver" prob Denver, Mo.
Rodgers David Sylvanus	D77Ba	1870Oct7	b.p. Iowa/Lucas Co m1891Dec31 d1903Mo
Rodgers Ethel Opal	D78A	1892Oct	b.p. Mo/Stanberry d at 8 days of age
Rodgers Eva Fern	D78B	1394Jan7	b.p. Mo/Stanberry m1915Nov25 of So.Dak
Rodgers Gladys Mrs	D78Ca		
Rodgers John Bennett	D77Baf	1833Dec25	b.p.Ohio d Iowa bet.1880-1885
Rodgers Paul David	D78C	1902May26	b.p.Mo/Maryville d1956Oct28
Rogers Abigail	E76A		born before 1744
Rogers Alex M	K37G		of Kansas
Rogers Alexander S	D71Baf	1804Nov19	d1873Sep24 Osage Co Mo Presiding Judge
Rogers Betsy	C11Gc	1847	b.p. Va d1847 Osage Co Mo
Rogers Cynthia	K37E		
Rogers Elisha	Y42Aaf		d1874Mar of Long Creek Maries Co Mo
Rogers Emeline	K37D		No issue
Rogers Ernie	Z24Da		of St Louis Mo
Rogers Isaac D	K37C		of Wright Co Mo
Rogers John A	E34Caf	1840Mar11	d1909Jul3 Of Maries,Crawford Cos Mo
Rogers John C	K37F		of Gasconade Co Mo
Rogers John D	E29Ca		of Belle Mo
Rogers Joseph H	K37H		d Gasconade Co Mo
Rogers Louemma	Z33Aa		of Oregon
Rogers Louisa	R30Cam		
Rogers Lucy	K37B		
Rogers Malissa	K37A		
Rogers Martha	D38Aa		
Rogers Martin L	E29Caf	1838Feb23	d1916Jan19 Vichy Mo Farmer
Rogers Melcena	E34Ca		to Steelville Mo after husbands death
Rogers Morgan	Z33Aaf		of Washington and Idaho
Rogers Oscar	R27Na		
Rogers Rachel M	Y42Aa	1354Jul23	m1873Mar15 d1922May22
Rogers Susan	Y42Ca	1862Jun26	m1881Dec12 d1902Nov9
Rogers Susannah	D71Ba	1843Dec18	m1869Sep12 d1935Jan31
Rogers Valentine	K36A		m(1)1839Nov12(2)1886 d1886Jul9Bland Mo
Rogers William	D38Aaf		d in Bland Mo
Rogers William	E08Ka		
Romine Jane	D65Fa		of Shannon Co Mo
Romine Lee	Y39Ca		of Maries Co Mo
Root Howard	Y37Ba		"of Denver" Assumed Denver Mo
Rose Marion	S13Faf		of Oklahoma
Rose Missouri	S13Fa		of Oklahoma
Ross Fred	A80Jb		
Ross Thorton Delbert	B21Ea		m1937Jul31
Rothwell Mary	T27Fa		

158

NAME	NUMBER	BIRTH	COMMENTS
Rowan William A	I55Ea		m 1894Oct14 Vienna Mo Of NY
Rowden -	G57Ja		d1934Dec13
Rowden -	G51Ab		m(1)McKee
Rowden Abram	V10A		b.p.Va or NC of Tenn d1840 Alabama
Rowden Abram E	V18C	1845Sep29	b.p. Mo/Maries Co d1918Jun9 Maries C
Rowden Abram Mrs	V10Aa		
Rowden Ake E	V12B	1818Jan25	b.p. Tn/E.Tenn Of Maries Co Mo.
Rowden Almon	E39Ca		
Rowden Alonzo(Lonnie)	V17E		
Rowden Andrew	V17G		
Rowden Ann	T14Da		
Rowden Ann Clark	V17O		
Rowden Arthur M	V26Da		m1889
Rowden Asa	V15D		m1871Jul9
Rowden Asa	V11A	1792	b.p.N.C. Maries CoMo 1842 Of Osage C
Rowden Benton	V14D		"moved to SW Mo or Arkansas"
Rowden Caroline H	V17J		
Rowden Charlotte	V15A	1853Jul31	d1873Sep12 single
Rowden Cordelia	V13B	1851Dec28	m1869Nov14 d1933Aug17
Rowden Elizabeth	V18G		of Miller Co Mo
Rowden Elizabeth	V16B		
Rowden Emeline	V18H		
Rowden George	V15C		
Rowden H Benton	V11C		
Rowden Harrison	V17B		
Rowden Isaac D	V17A		
Rowden Isaac N	P11Ba		of Maries Co Mo
Rowden Jacob	V17F		
Rowden James	V18A		of Miller Co Mo
Rowden James	P11Haf		
Rowden James E	V17D	1811Jun26	d1889Apr21 In Mo 1839
Rowden James H	V12E	1830 abt	of Maries Co Mo
Rowden John	V18D		d Union Army Civil War single
Rowden John	V17H		
Rowden John	V18B		of Strang Oklahoma
Rowden John Hardin	T14Daf		
Rowden Linda Branham	V17I		
Rowden Louis A	S20Ia		
Rowden Louis Clinton	V13D	1856Jan16	d1888Apr13 Maries Co Mo Circuit Cler┤
Rowden Malinda	V18I		m1880Nov14 Of St Louis Mo
Rowden Malinda	V14A	1843Oct31	d1879Jan9
Rowden Margaret	P11Ha		
Rowden Margaret	V15B		
Rowden Margaret	V14C		of Maries,Miller,Laclede Cos Mo.
Rowden Martha Parks	V17L		
Rowden Mary	V14B	1848Jun4	d1885Dec14
Rowden Mary	V18J	1859Jun22	d1882Jun21
Rowden Nancy	V18F		
Rowden Nancy Dial	V17M		

NAME	NUMBER	BIRTH	COMMENTS
Rowden Nathaniel	V11B		of Weakley Co Tn,Ill.,Maries Co Mo
Rowden Nathaniel Mrs	V11Ba		
Rowden Nina Ann	V13E	1867Mar5	m1896Feb d1900Sep30
Rowden Rachel	V12F		
Rowden Robert	V12A	1819Oct18	b.p.Tn/East d1888 Of Ala.,Osage Co Mo
Rowden Robert	V16A		
Rowden Robert L	V13F	1864Jun25	d1915Oct22 No issue
Rowden Rufus	V12D	1826Sep9	d1888Dec7
Rowden Sally	V17K		
Rowden Sarah C.	V13C		m1867Feb13 Of Maries Co Mo,, Oklahoma
Rowden Sarah Susan	V12G		
Rowden Satterwaite	V13A	1850Mar17	m1889Nov24 d1934Jul21 Maries Co Mo
Rowden Susan Lawson	V17N		
Rowden Wiley	V17C		
Rowden William A	V12C		of Maries Co Mo First County Clerk
Rowden William D	V14E		of Maries Co Mo
Rowden William N	V18E		
Rowland Robert F	F58Da		m1932Nov23
Rucker Mamie	Z33Da		"went west"
Rucker William	D47Da		of Arkansas
Russell –	G53Da		of Binghamton NY
Russell Joseph	G29Haf		
Russell Levi M (Lee)	G29Ha		
Russell Malinda	G32Ebm		
Russell Malinda	U120am		
Russell Nancy	D25Ea	1841Apr27	b.p. Mo/Maries Co d1922Jan10 Waynes Co
Ryan Maggie	Y47Aa		of St Louis Mo
Ryan Sarah	A90Ca		m1820Mar20 Mason Co Ky
Ryno George	Z42Ea		
Sackett A	A11Aa		
Salley Zadie	C38Ba		m1912Nov9 of Cross Timbers Mo
Sample Malinda	G10Cb		
Samples Chester A	D60F		
Samples George Robert	D47Ea		
Samples Jessie L	D60B		
Samples Martha A	D60A		
Samples Maud Marian	D60D		
Samples Nancy	D60E		
Samples Nellie C	D60C		
Sanders –	G53Ea		of Miller Co Mo
Sands Isaac	H52Ha		of Phelps Co Mo
Santee Nancy	S20Ea		m1872Aug1 Of Maries Co Mo and Kansas
Satterfield Ollie	Y52Ca		
Sauls –	G62Ba		
Sauls George W	G62Ka		
Scantlin Henry M	R13Ba		m1878Apr7
Schneider Frank	Y44Bb		no issue
Schneider Martin	Y61Jb		
Scholl Joseph	I15Ea		of Kentucky St Charles Mo 1795

NAME	NUMBER	BIRTH	COMMENTS
Schram Sallie	M16Da		
Schrimsher Arlonzo	F58Caf		
Schrimsher Trula	F58Ca	1908Nov24	b.p.Ok/Frederick m1928Aug31 Minco Okla
Schue Charles	E31Ca		no issue
Schultz John	F55Ea		
Schupp John Louis	F67Ha	1911Jul7	d.1969Feb22
Schupp Oscar Valmer	F67Da	1905Mar30	d.1978 Apr15
Schweigler Julius	R30Ga		m1880Nov28 Of Maries Co Mo
Schwenck Metha	D78Bam		
Scott -	C13Pa		
Scott -	C13Fa		
Scott B.F. Jr	E40C		of Pulaski Co and St Louis Mo
Scott B.F. Sr	E25Na		of Pulaski Mo
Scott Catharine	D75Ia		m1864Apr28
Scott Dora	E23Ea		of Texas
Scott Dorsey	E40A		of Pulaski Co and St Louis Co Mo
Scott Ethel	E40G		of Pulaski and St Louis Cos Mo
Scott George	E23Eaf		
Scott Henry	L15Ga		no issue
Scott Henry	L16Ea		d near Richland Mo
Scott Irene	F39Fa		
Scott Lula	E40D		of Pulaski and St Louis Cos Mo
Scott Maud	E40H		of Pulaski and St Louis Cos Mo
Scott May	E40F		of Pulaski and St Louis Cos Mo
Scott Rosa	G20Da		m1902Jan1 No issue
Scott Rosa	E40E		of Pulaski and St Louis Cos Mo
Scott Sarah Mrs	D74Ac		
Scott Savannah	L17B		·of California
Scott Thomas	G20Daf		
Scott Thomas	L17A		of California
Scott Wayne	E40B		of Pulaski and St Louis Cos Mo
Scott Will J	A77Ec	1910 abt	
Searcy -	Z42Aa		of Cole Co Mo
Sears S	A14Eb		
Seda -	E65Ea		
Sellers Elizabeth Ann	Q42Bb	1838Jan21	m1856 d1857eb6
Sellers Leslie M	F58Ga		m1948Aug17 Of Midland Texas
Selvidge Homer	K21Ea		of Kansas City Mo
Senne John Christian	G29Ja	1830Apr27	b.p. Germany US 1849 m1857 d1906May24
Sewell -	E65Da		
Sewell -	G10Da		
Sewell Anna	G10Db	1813	b.p. Tenn d1889Aug7 Maries Co Mo
Sewell John B	D65Da		
Sewell Martin	D65Daf		
Sewell Miriam	Q31Aa		
Sewell Nicholas Maj.	B04Ca		Sec of State Md under Lord Baltimore
Sewell Tina	G38Aa		
Shackleford -	K28Fa		
Shackleford -	K28Ea		

NAME	NUMBER	BIRTH	COMMENTS
Shackleford C. Arthur	A44Fa		
Shanks Arnold David	E83G	1917	d.1917 Osage Co Mo
Shanks Bertha Cyrilla	E83D	1909Dec8	m.1926Dec23
Shanks Crave	A66Cb		
Shanks Emery Franklin	E83E	1911	d.1920 Osage Co Mo
Shanks Gladys Irene	E83C	1908Jan1	m1926May d.1969Jul17
Shanks James	E46Da		of Belle Mo
Shanks James	E82Iaf		
Shanks James Andrew	E83B	1906Aug17	d.1975 Never married
Shanks John	Q34Ga		"moved westward from Mo"
Shanks Lula Mae	E83F	1913	d.1920 Osage Co Mo
Shanks Martha	S22Aa		
Shanks Ray Oscar	E83A	1903Sep12	m.1938Jun12 d.1979Aug 7
Shanks Syl	E41Ba		
Shanks Thomas	G27Aa		
Shanks William Vance	E82Ia	1881Feb	b.p.Mo/Osage Co d.1917Apr4 Osage Co
Sharp -	K16Fa		of Selma California
Sharp Joseph K	R29Ca		
Sharpe Matilda	F08Aam		
Shaver Robert M	E30Ia		m1899Jan19
Shaw George W	T30Fa		of Dixon and Wright Co Mo
Shekell John	A34Ia		
Shelton George	S13Daf		m(1)(2)Tn/McMinnCo Miller,MariesCos Mo
Shelton James	J16Da		of Briarton Oklahoma
Shelton Jesse	S13Da		m(2)1886Sep19 of Ok m(1)Laura Brannam
Shelton John	I52Ha		no issue
Shelton Josie	T15Ea		
Shelton Lee	I52Ia		
Shelton Mary O	T27Da		of Miller Co Mo No issue
Shelton Mrs	T13Cb		
Shelton William	T15Eaf		
Shelton William	T27Daf		
Shephard Millie	R19Ba	1817	d1903Feb13 Maries Co Mo
Shephard Nancy	Q42Aa		of Madison Co Ky. To Mo in about 1833
Sherman Charles W	Y71Ba		m Warren Co Mo d Maries Co Mo
Sherman James M	Y73C		d1931 abt
Sherman Joseph	Y73B		m Warren Co Mo.Of Maries Co In ConfArm
Sherman Margaret	Y73A		of Maries Co Mo and Colorado
Sherrill Alpha M	E19Aa	1820	b.p.Tn of Bledsoe Co 1850 Gasc. CoMo
Sherrill George	T29Aa		of Arlington Mo
Sherrill Matilda	U12Ea		m1870Sep22
Shinkle Cynthia	Q32Ba		
Shinkle George W	Q36A		of Maries Co Mo County Judge
Shinkle James Stephen	Q36C	1838Jan6	m1860Mar22 d1893Aug10
Shinkle John	Q36D	1840	d1908
Shinkle Leonard	Q36B		of Texas Killed in Union Army
Shinkle Samuel	Q35A	1806Oct13	b.p. Tenn(probably) m in Indiana
Shinn —	E09Ca		
Shinneman Bert	Y64Ea		

162

NAME	NUMBER	BIRTH	COMMENTS
Shobe –	Z12Ha		
Shobe Mary Jane	Z18A		m(1)Hull–
Shockley –	D34F		of near Marionville Mo
Shockley –	E24Ia		
Shockley –	D59A	1871Feb2	b.p. Osage Co Mo Lynn Twp
Shockley Agnes	D12C	1711 abt	b.p. Md/Worcester Co
Shockley Albert	R27Da		
Shockley Alexander	D22G	1346	b.p. Mo In Gasconade Co Mo census 1850
Shockley America A	D23E	1841	b.p. Va/Carroll Co
Shockley Amos	D27F	1843	In Osage Co Mo 1850 Of "Ozarks", of Ok
Shockley Amos	D17D	1799	b.p. Va m1823Jan16
Shockley Amos	D25I		b.p. Mo/Maries Co d1921Dec11 Neosho Mo
Shockley Amos M.V.	D40E	1873Oct13	m1903Jan18 d1935Jul19
Shockley Andrew J	D18A	1826Oct8	b.p.Tn m1851Nov20 In Gasc. Co Mo 1850
Shockley Andrew Jack.	D27I		b.after1829 m1873Apr8 Gasconade Co Mo
Shockley Andrew James	B12D	1845Mar1	b.p. Mo/Albany In Gentry Co Census1850
Shockley Ann Eliza	D38D		"moved to Oregon"
Shockley Anna Lee	D33G	1882Oct12	b.p.Mo/Vienna In Will Thos Holman 1902
Shockley Aquilla	D58B	1793Mar27	Twin of Thomas
Shockley Asberry	D23B	1831	b.p.Va/Carroll Co
Shockley Barbara	D22D	1838	of Gasconade Co Mo in 1850
Shockley Benjamin	D12I	1731Jul4	b.p.Md/Worcester Co Stepney Parish
Shockley Benjamin	D13B	1717abt	b.p.Md/Worcester Co d1791abt Worcester
Shockley Bettie	D32B		of near Vienna Mo
Shockley Beulah	D53A		of near Washington Mo
Shockley Bloomfield	D26G		d Hamburg Iowa
Shockley Candis A	D23A	1825	b.p. Va/Carroll Co(Form.Grayson Co.
Shockley Caroline	D21B	1835	b.p.Mo/Osage Co In Gasc Co 1850
Shockley Caswell F	D26A	1834	b.p.Va In Gentry Co Mo Census 1850
Shockley Catharine Mrs	D19Da	1836	b.p.Tn In Van Buren Co Tn 1860
Shockley Cathran Mrs	D13Fa		
Shockley Celeah(Celia)	D27C	1837	b.p.Mo In Osage Co Mo Census 1850
Shockley Charles W	D33B		of near Vienna, Maries Co Mo
Shockley Charlotte J.	D26B	1836	b.p.Va In Gentry Co Mo 1350 (Sharlot)
Shockley Charlotte M	D29A	1868Mar8	b.p. Mo/Gasconade Co d1868Apr8
Shockley Charlotte M	D17J	1812Apr18	b.p.Va m1831Jul14Gasc. Co Mo d1875Feb4
Shockley Clara E	D33A	1878Feb5	d1912Jan21
Shockley Claude	D52B		of Dixon,Wyoming
Shockley Claude M	D29J	1890Feb21	b.p.Mo/Pulaski d1890Apr15
Shockley Clifford	D53C		of near Owensville Mo
Shockley Cora	D29D	1873Feb27	b.p.Mo/Gasc Co m1891Jan12 d1970Aug27
Shockley Darcus	D19C	1839	b.p.Tenn In VanBuren Co Tn 1850 Census
Shockley Darcus C	D30B	1856	b.p. Tenn In 1850 Census Van Buren Co
Shockley Darcus Mrs	D16Ca	1796	b.p. No Car
Shockley David	D22B	1834	b.p. Mo In Gasconade Co Census 1850
Shockley David	D11E	1686abt	b.p.Md/Somerset Co d Will pr.1754Nov22
Shockley David Jr	D12B	1709abt	b.p. Md/Worcester Co
Shockley David P	D30D	1860	b.p.Tenn Van Buren Co
Shockley Dena Rebecca	D40B	1866Aug6	m1885Sep24 d1935Jul9

NAME	NUMBER	BIRTH	COMMENTS
Shockley Dewey	D43A		of Shannon Co Mo
Shockley Earl	D34B		of near Marionville Mo
Shockley Edward	D51A		of Maries Co Mo
Shockley Elenor	D11B	1680Apr23	b.p. Md/Somerset Co
Shockley Eliza	D41A		of Belle Mo Father born 1845
Shockley Eliza Jane	D21G	1833	b.p. Mo/1833 In Gasconade Co 1850
Shockley Elizabeth	D11C	1682abt	b.p. Md/Somerset Co
Shockley Elizabeth	D14H	1768Jun17	b.p.Va/now Carroll Co d1848Jun10 Tenn
Shockley Elizabeth	D29E	1876Mar16	b.p.Mo Pulaski Co d1919Dec27
Shockley Elizabeth	D26C	1842	In Gasconade Co Census 1850
Shockley Elizabeth	D27H	1847	b.p. Missouri
Shockley Elizabeth	D38C		Third wife of D38Ca
Shockley Elizabeth	D20D	1845abt	b.p.Mo Osage Co Mo 1850
Shockley Elizabeth Ann	E69Ba		m.1861Feb4
Shockley Elizabeth J	D21C	1835abt	b.p. Mo/Osage Co In Gasc Co 1850
Shockley Elizabeth Mrs	D11Aa		
Shockley Elizabeth Mrs	D13Ea		
Shockley Elizabeth(Het	D22A	1831	In Gasc CoMo 1850 Later "southern Mo"
Shockley Ellen	D52D		of Rector Mo
Shockley Emmett Oscar	D29G	1881Sep20	b.p.Mo/Pulaski Co m1904
Shockley Esau	D17C	1797abt	b.p.Va m1822Oct31 d1850Feb VaCarrollCo
Shockley Flora Mrs	D33Fa	1890abt	Wife of Maries Co Mo Historian
Shockley Florence	D43B		Drowned in Maries Co Mo
Shockley Floyd	D34C		of near Marionville Mo
Shockley Francis Ausb.	D27D	1839Feb18	b.p. Mo d1923Feb4
Shockley FrancisMarion	D20F	1848Nov20	b.p.Mo/Linn Gasc Co 1879 of Howell Co
Shockley Frederick	D22J	1855	b.p.Mo/Gasconade Co There in 1860
Shockley Gidian	D58A	1791Jan10	
Shockley Gilbert	D26Ca		In Gasconade Co Census 1850
Shockley Glenn	D34A		of near Marionville Mo Engr. Frisco RR
Shockley Grace Mrs	D11Ea	1690abt	
Shockley Hannah	D19A	1833	b.p.Tenn In Van Buren Co Tenn 1850
Shockley Harriett	D21A		born before 1830
Shockley Harriett A	D26F		m.1844(probably)Gasconade Co Mo
Shockley Henry	D17L	1814abt	b.p.Va m1848Jan11 (or name "Daniel"
Shockley Henry	D40D	1871Apr2	m1895Jan20 d1920Jan8
Shockley Henry	D27A	1830	b.p. Mo/Maries Co m1851Feb20 dMariesCo
Shockley Isaac	D12J	1736Nov1	Md/Worcester Co Stepney Parish
Shockley Isaac	D13A	1715abt	b.p. Md/Worcester Co
Shockley Isaac Andrew	D29F	1879Jan14	b.p. Mo/Pulaski Co m1903 d1918Jan21
Shockley Isaiah	D21D	1841	b.p. Mo/Osage Co In Gasc.Co 1850Census
Shockley Isaiah	D22I	1850	b.p.Mo In Gasconade Co Mo Census 1850
Shockley Isaiah	E48Gb		
Shockley Isaiah Jr	D16H	1806abt	b.p.Tn/Grainger Co m1837Nov23 d1849Mo
Shockley Isaiah(Josiah	D14D	1765abt	b.p.Va m1787abt dVan Buren Co Tn 1867
Shockley Isom(Isham)	D14C	1770 abt	b.p. Virginia
Shockley J. Mack	D41C		m. Gasc Co Mo of Owensville Mo
Shockley James	D12D	1714abt	b.p. Md/Worcester Co d.will p 1796Apr
Shockley James	D17B	1794abt	m1815

NAME	NUMBER	BIRTH	COMMENTS
Shockley James G	D26H		m1869 d1899 Of Maries Co Mo Conf.Army
Shockley James H	D25B	1849	b.p. Mo Never m. In Osage Co 1850
Shockley James M.H.	D18E	1836Jul1	b.p. Mo/Gasconade Co m1855May20
Shockley James Milton	D33C		of Jefferson City Mo Lawyer
Shockley James Monroe	D27G	1845Feb9	b.p. Mo m1866Nov29 d1925Apr18 Osage Co
Shockley Jane	D75Ea		m1845Feb15
Shockley Jesse	D26E		Never married
Shockley Jessie	D52G		d Dent Co Missouri
Shockley Joanna R	D24B	1838	b.p. Virginia
Shockley John	D12A	1707abt	b.p. Md/Worcester Co d1761abt
Shockley John	D13F	1725abt	b.p. Md/Wprcester Co
Shockley John	D20G	1850	b.p. Mo In Gasconade Co. Mo. 1850
Shockley John	D11G	1690	b.p.Md/Somerset Co d.will p. 1766Jun19
Shockley John	D17A	1793	b.p. Na d. will p.1963AprVa. of Mo.
Shockley John F	D23F	1844	b.p.Virginia
Shockley John Lunce	D59B	1873Sep12	b.p.Mo/Osage Co Lynn Twp
Shockley John Marvin	D33D	1885abt	of Maries Co Mo Farmer
Shockley John McMein	D21F	1848	b.p. Mo In Gasconade Co Mo Census 1350
Shockley John O	D29C	1871Mar31	b.p. Mo/Gasconade Co d1871Jun7
Shockley Jonathan	D13D	I721abt	b.p. Md/Worcester Co
Shockley Joseph	D25E		born after 1833 Of Maries Co Mo
Shockley Joseph	D22H	1848	b.p. Mo In Gasconade Co Mo Census 1850
Shockley Joseph H Sr	D37A		of near Vienna Mo
Shockley JosephMillard	D33F		d1976Octl Asst.Hist.MariesCo Mo(King)
Shockley Joshua	D22E	1840	b.p. Mo m1855Jul3 Gasconade Co
Shockley Josie	D52C		of Webster Oklahoma
Shockley Juliet C	D26D	1842 abt	never married Of Gentry Co Mo 1850
Shockley Lafayett	D30A	1853	b.p.Tenn. In VanBuren Co 1860 Census
Shockley Leona	D32C		m Jackson Co Missouri
Shockley LeonardMered.	D43B		of Springfield Mo and Oklahoma
Shockley Lina	D52F		
Shockley Lloyd	D34D		of near Marionville Mo
Shockley Lottie	D25F		b.p. Mo/Maries Co
Shockley Louisa	D25C	1839	of Maries, Osage Cos Mo Of Arkansas
Shockley Lucy	D52E		of NW Colorado
Shockley Lucy A	D59C	1875Sep13	b.p.Mo/Howell Co Olden Twp
Shockley Lucy J	D40I		
Shockley Lunsford L.L.	D20I	1326Dec21	b.p.Mo/Gasc Co m1343Dec8 d1899Dec5
Shockley Mahaley	D18I	1846Dec14	b.p. Mo/Gasconade Co m1860Dec2
Shockley Malinda	D18C	1832Octl	b.p. Mo/Gasconade Co (birth 1832or1331
Shockley Mansfield	D43C		never married
Shockley Manuel H	D40H		
Shockley Margaret Mrs	D12Da		
Shockley Martha	D40F		d.in infancy Martha and Mary, twins
Shockley Martha	D15C	1806Sep8	b.p. Tn m Tenn d1883Jan8 To Mo afoot
Shockley Martha A	B12A	1852Mar1	b.p. Mo/Gentry Co m1875Aug15 d1916Jan4
Shockley Martha E	D44A	1880Feb25	b.p. Mo/Gasc Co Bland
Shockley Martin V	D23C	1835	b.p. Virginia Carroll Co
Shockley Mary	D11F	1688abt	Md/Somerset Co

NAME	NUMBER	BIRTH	COMMENTS
Shockley Mary	D12F	1723Nov30	Md/Worcester Co Stephany Parish
Shockley Mary	D13C	1719abt	b.p.Md/Worcester Co
Shockley Mary	D34E		of near Marionville Mo
Shockley Mary	D40G		d in infancy Twin of Martha
Shockley Mary A	D24A	1833	b.p.Virginia
Shockley Mary Ann	D16I	1807	b.p. Tn/Grainger Co mWhite Co Mo 1828
Shockley Mary E	D25D	1841	of Osage Co Mo 1850 2nd wife of D25Da
Shockley Mary E	B12E	1855Apr7	d1860 bu. OldBrick Cem Albany Mo
Shockley Matilda	D32A		born after 1860 Of St Louis Mo
Shockley Matilda	D18B	1829Jan31	b.p. Mo/Gasc.Co m1845Dec25(2)1846Oct28
Shockley Maud	D52A		of Rector Mo
Shockley Meredith Jr	D17G	1802	b.p. Va m1824May6 Arr. Mo early 1820´s
Shockley Meredith Sr	D14F	1770	b.p. Va/Grayson Co(now Carroll)d1856ca
Shockley Merida	D27E	1841	b.p. Mo In Osage Co Mo Census 1850
Shockley Millie O	D33H		of Jefferson City Mo
Shockley Minerva	B12C	1849	b.p. Mo/Gentry Co.
Shockley Nancy	D25G		m(1) to Peter Copeland
Shockley Nancy	D17E	1804abt	b.p.Va m1826Jun1
Shockley Nancy	D20H	1820	In Gasconade Co Mo Census 1850
Shockley Nelley	D18H	1844May15	b.p.Mo/Gasc Co m1859Apr3(or "Milly")
Shockley Nelly	D16B	1788abt	b.p.Va/Carroll Co(present) m1809Feb1Tn
Shockley Nevada P	B12B		
Shockley Oliver C	D23D	1838	Va/Carroll Co
Shockley Oliver Jr	D29H	1888Apr9	b.p.Mo/Pulaski Co d1888 Jun29 Twin
Shockley Oliver Wesley	D18G	1841Jun22	b.p.Mo/Gasc Co m1867May12(2)1893Jan12
Shockley Ollie	D29I	1888Apr9	Mo/Pulaski Co d 1888Jun30 Twin
Shockley Orland	D23G	1845	b.p.Va
Shockley Owen	D15B	1801Dec3	b.p.Tn/Grainger Co m1824Nov30 d1855Mo
Shockley Patrick	D38A		
Shockley Perry	D54B		
Shockley Perry	D20B	1837	b.p.Mo
Shockley Peter	D19B	1836	b.p.Tenn In Van Buren Co Tn Census1850
Shockley Phebe Mrs	D17Aa		
Shockley Prilla Lexie	D59E	1881Feb22	b.p. Mo/Howell Co Lynn Twp
Shockley Rachel M	D40C		
Shockley Raymond	D54A		of Bland Mo
Shockley Rebecca	D22L	1829Oct20	b.p. Mo/ near Woolen m1844 d1910Jun9
Shockley Rebecca I.	D38B		
Shockley Reuben S	D17K	1812abt	b.p.Va m1848Jan11 Gasc Co Mo("Richard"
Shockley Richard	D16F	1800	b.p.Va/Carroll Co m(1)1826(2)1830d1851
Shockley Richard 1st	D10A	1650ca	b.p.Britain m1674Oct4 Md d1716Aug23 Md
Shockley Richard 2nd	D13E	1728abt	Md/Worcester dabt1798Va In Amer Rev
Shockley Richard 3rd	D14B	1760	b.p.Va d after 1832 Marion Co Tenn
Shockley Richard Jr	D11A	1677Jun1	b.p. Md/Manokin d aft 1741 of Del1722
Shockley Richard Mrs	D14Ba		d bet 1840-1850 Marion Co Tenn
Shockley Robert F	D40J	1883Feb16	d1897Jul7 Never married
Shockley Robert Frank.	D29B	1869Dec2	b.p. Mo/Gasconade Co d1897Oct11
Shockley Rosa	D51B		of Maries Co Mo
Shockley Rubin	D20E	1846	b.p.Mo In GasconadeCo 1850 Census

166

NAME	NUMBER	BIRTH	COMMENTS
Shockley Ruth	D21H	1832	b.p. Mo/Osage Co
Shockley Rutha	D18J	1849Nov13	b.p.Mo/Gasconade Co d1849Dec8 Mo
Shockley Rutha S	D16J	1793abt	b.p.Tn/Grainger Co d abt1834Gasc Co Mo
Shockley Rye	D16K		
Shockley Samantha	D30C	1858	b.p. Tenn/Van Buren Co
Shockley Samuel	D16C	1791	b.p.Va/CarrollCo of Van Buren Co Tn
Shockley Samuel	D22K	1856	b.p.Mo/Gasconade Co In 1860 Census
Shockley Samuel	D18D	1834Feb25	b.p.Mo/Gasconade Co m1855May20
Shockley Sarah	D12H	1728Jan13	Md/Worcester Co Stepney Parish
Shockley Sarah	D27B	1832	In Osage Co Mo Census 1850
Shockley Sarah	D13H	1729abt	b.p.Md/Worcester Co
Shockley Sarah	D15A	1794abt	b.p.Va m1815Nov4
Shockley Sarah (Sally)	D22F	1844	b.p.Mo m1867Sep19 Bland Mo
Shockley Sarah (Sally)	D18F	1839Feb12	m.1857Apr30. Of Gasconade Co Mo 1850
Shockley Sarah (Sally)	D16E	1797abt	b.p. Va/Carroll Co (formerly Grayson)
Shockley Sarah A	R22Ca	1868Nov5	b.p.Mo/Maries Co Of Porterville Calif.
Shockley Sarah Manerva	D21I		
Shockley Sarah Mrs	D11Da		
Shockley Sarah Mrs	D11Ga	1694abt	
Shockley Serena	D25A		of Missouri Never married
Shockley Sidney Clyde	D48A		of Springfield Mo and Oklahoma
Shockley Snoden Earl	D29K	1894Aug17	b.p.Mo/Waynesville d1904Mar16 Mo
Shockley Sollomon	D12G	1726Dec6	b.p.Md/Worcester Co Stepney Parish
Shockley Solomon	D13G	1727abt	b.p. Md/Worcester Co
Shockley Sophia	D41B		of Belle Mo
Shockley Susan	D37C		
Shockley Tennessee Ann	D21E	1345Octl8	b.p.Mo/Gasconade Co d1927Aprl Mo
Shockley Thomas	D14A		b.p. Va/ before 1765
Shockley Thomas	D14Ha	1755Sep15	b.p.Va/Pittsylvania m 1787 dTn1843Sep
Shockley Thomas	D16D	1797	b.p.Va/Carroll Co Mo abt 1830 Gasc Co
Shockley Thomas	D22C	1336	b.p.Mo In Census Gasc. Co 1850
Shockley Thomas	D43D		
Shockley Thomas	D58C	1793Mar27	Twin of Aquilla
Shockley Thomas Atkin.	D33E	1877ca	State Rep.Pulaski Co Mo Attorney
Shockley Thomas B	D20C	1842	b.p.Mo In Gasconade Co Census 1850
Shockley Thomas Bartl.	D40A	1861Aug4	d1926Nov2 Of Shannon and Dent Cos Mo
Shockley Thomas Barton	R14Ca		
Shockley Thomas Benton	D27J		"moved to Colorado"
Shockley Thomas J	D19D	1831	b.p.Tenn In Van Buren Co Tn Census1860
Shockley Thomas Jeff.	D82A	1818Aug4	b.p. Tenn/White Co d1886Jun30 White Co
Shockley Thomas Jeff.	D84A	1892Mar18	b.p. Tenn/White Co d1917Apr18
Shockley Thomas Rich.	D25H	1852Sep27	b.p.Mo/Vienna m1874Mar29 d1921Sep29 Mo
Shockley Thomas Vinc.	D17H	1808Octl8	b.p. Va. m1829Mar26Mo d1890Dec25
Shockley Thomas Y	D20A	1832	b.p.Mo In Gasconade Co Mo Census 1850
Shockley Tressie	D34G		
Shockley Uriah	D16G	1804	b.p. Tn/Grainger Co m(1)Tn(2)1830 Mo
Shockley Victoria	B12F		
Shockley Vincent	R22Caf		m1860 d abt1875 Union Army Civil War
Shockley Wainwright	D83A	1842Sep30	b.p.Tn/White Co m1880Sep20 d1921Feb21

167

NAME	NUMBER	BIRTH	COMMENTS
Shockley Wesley	D17I	1810abt	b.p.Va m1835 Gasconade Co Mo
Shockley Wilbur Gray	D48C		of Springfield Mo and Oklahoma
Shockley William	D11D	1684abt	b.p.Md/Somerset Co d Will adm 1735 Del
Shockley William	D12E	1719Sep4	b.p.Md/Worcester Co Stepney Parish
Shockley William	D26I	1839	b.p. Mo/Gentry Co
Shockley William	D14G	1775abt	b.p.Va
Shockley William	D53B		ofOwensville. Born after 1903
Shockley William	D16A	1785abt	b.p.Va/Carroll Co m1810Dec29Tn d1860Tn
Shockley William M	D37B		of near Vienna Mo.Born after 1869
Shockley William M.	D32D	1867Oct6	of Maries and Shannon Cos Mo
Shockley William R	D17F	1805	b.p.Va m1833Aug15 Gasconade Co Mo
Shockley William R	D59D	1879Mar17	b.p.Mo/HowellCo Lynn Twp
Shockley William S	D58D	1795Jun16	
Shockley Wilson	D14E	1770ca	b.p.Virginia
Sholl –	T19Ea		of St Louis Mo
Short –	Z35Ea		m abt 1859 Killed Civil War Confed.
Short Mary	Z36A		of Springfield Mo
Shulta –	F52Fa		of Sullivan Mo Minister
Siddens Charles Edgar	B21A	1892Mar8	b.p.Mo/Albany m1915Dec22
Siddens Golda Julia J	B21E	1907May1	b.p.Mo/Albany m1937Jul31
Siddens Jim	D76Ba		
Siddens Lola Elizabeth	B21B	1896Mar2	b.p.Mo/Albany m1917May27
Siddens Ralph Leland	B21C	1902Apr15	b.p.Mo/Albany m1923May5
Siddens Retha Lemora	B21F	1911Dec10	b.p.Mo/Albany m1930Dec25
Siddens Sylvania M	B21D	1907Dec12	b.p.Mo/Albany d1923Dec24
Siddens William Joseph	B15Ca		m1891Feb15
Sieber –	F52Aa		
Sigler James	H56Ba		
Simmons Sarah	F15Cb		
Simpson –	L20B		
Simpson Angeline	L20A		
Simpson Anna	I16Ca		of Kentucky
Simpson Anna Minerva	E94C	1889Aug1	b.p. Mo/Belle
Simpson Barney H	L15D		"to Blanco Tex abt 1880" m His cousin
Simpson Basheba	L21C		of near Springfield Mo
Simpson Benjamin	E17Ia		m1839Apr14
Simpson Benjamin	L12C		of Osage Co Mo
Simpson Blanche	L21E		of Springfield Mo
Simpson Bryan	L21I		of near Springfield Mo
Simpson Bunyan	L21F		of near Springfield Mo
Simpson Callie	L16E		d. near Richland Mo
Simpson Caroline	L15G		"moved to Blanco Texas" No issue
Simpson Carrett	E94I	1901Apr26	b.p. Mo/Bland
Simpson Carrie Olive	E94E	1895Mar22	b.p.Mo/Belle
Simpson Cecil Shockley	E94J	1909Mar2	b.p. Mo/Bland
Simpson Charles	E94H	1900	b.p. Mo/Belle
Simpson Clara	E94G	1899Apr22	b.p. Mo/Belle
Simpson Daniel	L12B		of Pulaski Mo
Simpson Daniel Mrs	L12Ba		of Pulaski Mo

NAME	NUMBER	BIRTH	COMMENTS
Simpson Dee	E94F	1896May3	b.p. Mo/Bland
Simpson Diora	L16C		m1899Aug25 Of near Houston Texas
Simpson Dorcas	I16Da		of Kentucky m(1)White –
Simpson Edna	L21B		of near Springfield Mo
Simpson Effie	L21A		of near Springfield Mo
Simpson Eva May	E95B	1914Sep9	b.p. Kansas/Kansas City
Simpson Frances	L15C	1833	d1905Aug9
Simpson George Wilson	E95D	1917Aug14	b.p. Kans/Kansas City d.1961Aug14
Simpson Hannah	E14Aa	1819Jan1	b.p.Mo/ m1837 d1890May3 Maries Co Mo
Simpson James	L12D		of Osage Co Mo
Simpson Jane	L15B	1829Oct13	of Tx.Birth and death in covered wagon
Simpson John	E48Ga		Father Benjamin. May be L12C
Simpson John W	L16I		m(1)1900Aug25
Simpson Josephine	L16H		
Simpson Kathryn Pearl	E95C	1916Feb12	b.p.Kansas/Kansas City
Simpson Leonard	L21G		of near Springfield Mo
Simpson Leora Delpha	E94D	1891Mar22	b.p. Mo/Belle
Simpson Louisa	L15H		to Blanco Texas about 1880
Simpson Lydia Angeline	L16G		d1930May21 Granite City Mo
Simpson Mahala	L15A		died in childbirth
Simpson Mahala Emeline	L16F	1862	d1931Jun19
Simpson Mallie Ruth	E94B	1883Feb22	b.p. Mo/Belle
Simpson Martha	L13A		
Simpson Mary	L15F		to Blanco Texas about 1880
Simpson Matilda	L16A		
Simpson Moses L	L15E		to Blanco Texas about 1880
Simpson Nancy	L11B		
Simpson Oscar Stanford	E94A	1386May1	b.p.Mo/Belle d1941Jan23 Kansas Cy Ks
Simpson Rezin	B08Pa		m1786Feb1
Simpson Ruth Naomi	E95A	1912Jan21	b.p. Kansas /Kansas City d1975Sep26
Simpson Samuel	L15I		Blanco Texas then Maries Co Mo d1905
Simpson Samuel	L12A		m Osage Co Mo. Of Vernon Co Mo
Simpson Samuel Mrs	L12Aa		m Osage Co Mo Of Vernon Co Mo
Simpson Thomas	L16D		of Granite City Mo
Simpson Tine	L16B		
Simpson Victoria	L21D		of near Springfield Mo
Simpson William	L21H		of near Springfield Mo
Simpson William Jr	L12E	1808	b.p.Ky Of Maries Co Mo
Simpson William Sr	L11A		
Simpson William Sr Mrs	L11Aa		
Simpson William T	L16J		of Dixon and Springfield Mo
Simpson William(Snurl)	L14A		
Sisk Pluright	I59Ea		
Skaggs –	T18H		of Dixon Mo
Skaggs Alice	T19C		of Pueblo Colo
Skaggs Asa	M11Ga		
Skaggs Bennett	T20A		of Eldorado Sprgs Mo Owned ice plants
Skaggs Bettie	M16E		
Skaggs Charlotte	M15Cam		m1339Mar28 Gasconade Co Mo

169

NAME	NUMBER	BIRTH	COMMENTS
Skaggs Eli	M16C		d single
Skaggs Freeman	T17A		b.p.Tenn/East To Mo after Civil War
Skaggs Freeman Mrs	T17Aa		of Tenn and Maries Co Mo
Skaggs George	R22Bbf		
Skaggs George W	T19D		of Pueblo Colorado
Skaggs Gideon P	T18A	1848	b.p.Tenn Maries Co Mo 1865 d1927
Skaggs Gordon	T18D		
Skaggs Harvey	M16B		d single
Skaggs James	T18F		
Skaggs Jane	T18B		m1865Sep26Knox Co Tenn d1874Nov8
Skaggs Jefferson D	T18E		m1882Apr21 of Ibernia Mo
Skaggs John	M16D		
Skaggs Julia	R24Aa		m1890Dec24 d1909Nov14
Skaggs Laura J	T19E		of St Louis Co Mo
Skaggs Louis J	R24Ba		d1937 Centertown Ark
Skaggs Margaret	M16A		d single
Skaggs Mary	T19B		of Pueblo Colorado
Skaggs Matilda E	T19F		of Maries Co Mo
Skaggs Minnie	T19A		of near Pueblo Colorado
Skaggs Newton	T18G		
Skaggs Sallie	T19G	1875Jun27	d1918Nov2
Skaggs Vina	R22Bb	1859Jul14	m1885Mar1 d1923Feb27
Skaggs W.P.	T18C		
Skaggs William	T27Ha		"moved to Arkansas"
Skeen Walter	D25Da		
Skeen William	D31A	1880Sep26	d1918Dec26
Skelton Emmett	T19Ba		of Pueblo Colorado
Skelton Perry	T19Ca		of Pueblo Colorado
Skidmore Joseph	A15Ca	1781May7	
Skouby Leanora	Y49Ba		of Belle Mo
Skyles -	Y18Ba		
Slagle Erastus	A71Fa	1884Feb13	d1958Jun10
Slagle Howard	A71Ga	1885Sep1	d1966Sep15
Slater Hariett	Y27Ba		
Slater Harriett	E17Bb		
Slater Silas	Y61Ka		
Slats -	P16Fa		of Union Mo
Slone Charles	E23Da		of Kansas City Mo
Smallwood John	M12Aa		m1874May d abt 1939 of Gasconade Co M
Smiley Dora	Z32Ga		
Smith -	H19Fa		
Smith -	E65Fa		
Smith A	A13Cb		
Smith Abraham	F63E	1804	m.1826Oct8 Brown Co Ohio
Smith Alfred	V23Ea		m1835Aug20
Smith Amos L	D40Ia		
Smith Anna	F62D		b.p. Md m.1778Dec23 Md
Smith Anne	A99Aa		m1759Feb8 Md. Prince Georges Co
Smith Basil Burgess	F64E	1829Jun27	b.p. Ohio m1857Feb10 Ill d1884Sep23Il

NAME	NUMBER	BIRTH	COMMENTS
Smith Benjamin	V23Da		m1833Sep24 of Vienna Mo 1838
Smith Charles	F63I		
Smith Charles Burgess	F62A	1765Nov25	b.p.Md/Prince Georges Co
Smith Charlotta	Y72Fam		m1836Jan26 To Maries Co Mo by 1835
Smith David W	E30Aa		
Smith Eleanor	F62G		
Smith Elizabeth	E62Aa		
Smith Elizabeth	F62F		b.p. Md m.1788Sep22 Md
Smith Ellen Frances	E24Kc	1870	b.p.Mo/Canaan bu. Bland Mo
Smith Esther	F62I		m.1804Jan23 Md
Smith Frances Adaliza	F64G	1834Feb19	b.p.Ohio m1855Sep16 Xenia Ill d1873Jan
Smith George	F63H		
Smith Harriet	F62J	1782	b.p. Md m.1802Jun21 Md d 1854 Md
Smith Hays	F63F		m1834Dec27 Highland Co Ohio
Smith Isabella	F64J	1841Sep2	b.p.Ohio m1860Aug25 d1918Nov12
Smith James	Z33Ca		
Smith James E	Q39Ha		of Riverside California
Smith James H	D40Ca		
Smith James Haddock	A99Ba	1733	d.1806
Smith James Haddock	F64B	1822Nov6	b.p.Ohio Adams Co m1848Sep16 d1862 Feb
Smith James Samuel	E62Aaf		
Smith Jane	D74Ab		
Smith Jennie	H14Ia		of Rolla Mo
Smith Josephine	I55Da		m1905Apr11 Rolla Mo
Smith Lucretia	F64F	1832Feb19	b.p.Ohio m1852Feb19GOhiod.1913Jan10Ill
Smith Lucy	F63D		m.1837Nov10 Brown Co Ohio
Smith Lucy	F64D	1827	b.p. Ohio m.1850Oct23 d1902Jan30Oregon
Smith Martha	F62C	1756Jun20	b.p.Md m.1778Jan20 d.1843Oct13
Smith Mary	F63B	1798ca	
Smith Mary Elizabeth	E24Kb		
Smith Mary Jane	F64A	1820Mar13	b.p.Ohio Adams Co m.1851Dec25 Ohio
Smith Moses	V23Fa	1818Jun23	m1840Jul10 d1899 Vienna Mo No issue
Smith Patience	F64H	1836Oct30	b.p.Ohio m1858Marl Xenia Ill d1873Jan
Smith Sarah Ann	F63G		
Smith Sophia Ann	F64C	1825Jan1	b.p.Ohio m1845Jun17 Ohio d.1854Jun24
Smith Stephen	F62B		
Smith Susanna	F62H		m.1782Feb13 Md
Smith Susanne Claramon	D76Fa		m1873Sep1
Smith Ursula	F62E		b.p.Md m.1780 Sep20 Md
Smith Walter	F62Ja		
Smith Walter	F63A	1790	d.1846Nov17 Highland Co Ohio
Smith William	R14Ba		of Maries Co Mo and Oklahoma
Smith William	Y74Bb		m1885Apr26 No issue
Smith William	F63C	1800Jan11	b.p.Ky. m.1819May13 Ohio d1855Feb Ill.
Smith Wyatt	V23Daf		
Smith Zerelda	F64I	1839May2	b.p.Ohio m1856Dec10 Ill d1873Jan5
Smitherman G. Scott	B32Ab		
Smithers "Cad"	Y14Bb		
Smithers –	Q44Ea		

NAME	NUMBER	BIRTH	COMMENTS
Smithers -	Y71Ea		
Smythe Mary Elma	C20Da		m1947Aug17
Sneed W.D.	G44Aa		
Sneed William	G45Ca		of Owensville Mo
Snell Julia	B91Aa		
Snodgrass -	K32Ea		(possibly Maria)
Snodgrass Arch	Y15B		
Snodgrass Archibald	Y29C		
Snodgrass Bessie	Y53E		of Maries Co Mo
Snodgrass Charles D	Y52F		of Miller Co Mo Supt. of Schools Atty
Snodgrass Chester	Y54F		of Maries Co Mo
Snodgrass Clara	Y53B		of Maries Co Mo
Snodgrass Clarice	Y54C		of Maries Co Mo
Snodgrass Cleve	Y53D		of Maries Co Mo
Snodgrass Ebenezer	Y52C		
Snodgrass Ebenezer J	Y29B	1856Sep5	d1907Mar17 Of Maries Co Mo
Snodgrass Ernestine	Y54I		of Bland Mo
Snodgrass George Mrs	Y15Ea		
Snodgrass George Sr	Y12Ca		of Ky, Tenn and Mo
Snodgrass George W	Y52E		
Snodgrass George W Jr	Y29E		
Snodgrass George Wash.	Y15E		b.p. Ky m(1) No issue d1887Nov5
Snodgrass Harry	Y54L		m Columbia Mo of Maries Co Mo
Snodgrass Holly	Y54H		d single
Snodgrass Ina	Y54B		of Maries Co Mo
Snodgrass J.S.	K23Ea		of Vienna Mo
Snodgrass James	Y15A		
Snodgrass James David	Y29A	1853Mar27	m(2) 1878Sep1 d1910Jan18
Snodgrass Jesse J	Y52D		
Snodgrass Julia A	Y29G		
Snodgrass Lela	Y54E		of Maries Co Mo
Snodgrass Leslie	Y54K		of Maries Co Mo LumberYard
Snodgrass Lola	Y53C		of Maries Co Mo
Snodgrass Louis	Y53F		of Maries Co Mo
Snodgrass Loyd	Y54A		of Maries Co Mo
Snodgrass Maria E	Y29I		
Snodgrass Matilda	Y15D		
Snodgrass Nannie	Y52B		
Snodgrass Nellie	Y57Aa		of Phelps Co Mo
Snodgrass Olivia	Y52A		m1906Sep16
Snodgrass Oma	Y53A		of Maries Co Mo
Snodgrass Polly	Y15C		
Snodgrass Raymond	Y54J		of Paducah Kentucky Teacher
Snodgrass Roy	Y54D		of Maries Co Mo
Snodgrass Sarah	Y15F		of Maries Co Mo and Texas
Snodgrass Sarah A	Y29F		of Maries and Phelps Cos Mo
Snodgrass Simon	Y29D		of Maries Co Mo
Snodgrass Thomas Edw.	Y52G		d1910Jan23
Snodgrass Wash	Y54G		of Maries Co Mo

NAME	NUMBER	BIRTH	COMMENTS
Snodgrass William R	Y29H		
Sollenberger -	J25Ca		of Denver Mo
Sorrell Martha	Y25Fam		of near Bland Mo
Sorrell Virginia	R11Ba		m1839Oct15 Maries Co Mo Of Texas
Soudermeyer Henry	E20Ca		
Soudermeyer M.E.	E27B		
Soudermeyer Sarah M	E27A		
Southard Edward	Q33Aa	1823Mar22	b.p. Tn/m1846Oct1 Maries Co Mo d1900
Southard Sherman	G40Ca		of Maries Co Mo
Southard William A	G40Caf	1859Apr18	Father:William born Tenn 1814Dec10
Southerland -	T30Hb		
Spainhour Raymond Wm.	C31Aa		of Lone Jack Mo
Sparks Elizabeth	I62Ea		In St Charles Co Mo 1808
Sparlin Elma	B13Aa		
Sparrow Matilda	B05Eb		m1734 abt
Sparrow Thomas	B04Ja		m1697Jul25
Spaulding -	E16Ja		
Spencer Elizabeth	Q31Bb		m(1) Chambers -
Spencer Nancy	D80Aa		of Custer So. Dakota Teacher
Spessard Blanche	B15Fb		m1915Jan27
Spratley Edward	G18Ba		of Vienna Mo
Spratley James H	Z34Fa		m1892Oct23
Spratley William H	K34Ga		m1865Jul3 d1929abt Granite City Mo
Sprewell -	Y72Ca		
Spurrier Rezin	F17Ea		m1790Jan2
Stanford Elizabeth	V12Aam		m in Kentucky
Stanton Julia	C11Ge		m1853Feb6
Stark James E	C37Ea		of Missouri
Stark Virginia	C37Ha		m1883Mar11 Of Hickory Co Missouri
Stebbins Hannah	A11Ga		
Stebbins R	A12Ba		
Steir Henry	F21Ba		also "Stier"
Steir Mary Ann	F21Ia		m1824Jan17 also "Stier"
Stephenson -	Q44Ec		
Stevenson Robert	Y38Ba		of St Louis Mo
Stewart Alva	Z37A		of Springfield Mo
Stewart Alva	D52Ga		
Stewart Ben	Z37C		of Rolla Mo
Stewart Bert	Z37B		of Rolla Mo
Stewart Charles Edward	D29Da		m1891Jan12
Stewart Claude	D57A		of Salem Mo
Stewart Cora	Z37F		d Greene Co Mo
Stewart Georgia	Z39C		of Springfield Mo
Stewart Gertrude	Y52Da	1890Aug20	d1930Jul12
Stewart Irene	Z39A		of Springfield Mo
Stewart James	Z35Eb		of Maries Co Mo d1833Ca
Stewart Jane	Z37D		d single
Stewart John	I12Ka		m1765abt No Car d 1770 by Indians
Stewart Joseph	Z37E		d Springfield Mo

NAME	NUMBER	BIRTH	COMMENTS
Stewart Lazarus	Y52Daf	1861Aug25	d1930Apr18 Cole Co Mo
Stewart Marie	Z39B		of Springfield Mo
Stewart Olive May	D57B		of Salem Mo
Stewart Vince Jr	G16Ca		of Kansas City Mo
Stewart Vincent	Z31Ga		of Osage Co Mo
Stewart Wilbur	D52Ea		of NW Colorado
Stites John	J25Aa		of Miller Co Mo
Stock Fern Opal	E74Aa	1926Mar6	b.p.Mo/Freedom, Osage Co
Stockton Bettie	R12Ca		
Stockton James M	D38Ca		m(1)Julia Powell(2)Emma Montgomery
Stockton Jane	Y40Ca		of Phelps Co Mo
Stockton JohnHenderson	D27Caf	1808Dec23	b.p.Va(prob) m(2)1838 d1874Mar
Stockton Joseph	D71Ea	1841Nov7	d1917Apr2 In Union Army Civil War
Stockton Orrisemus	D27Ca	1834May6	d1900 Maries Co Mo Union Army Civil W.
Stockton Paul	G27Ba		
Stockton Richard	E42Da		of Maries Co Mo
Stockton Sarah Ann	D26Ha		d1932Mar29
Stockton William	D42Ea		of near Kansas City Mo
Stokes James	Q43Fa		m1878Nov21
Stokes Mina	U12Ja		m1894Sep9
Stoltz Bona Jean M	A72Ca	1934May15	
Stovall John	E61Ia		
Stover Jacob (John)	I11Ba		of Pa In Va before 1748
Stratman Henry	E41Da		of Maries Co Mo
Street Hugh	G24Aa		of Columbia Mo
Street Richard A	T29Fa	1851Nov29	b.p.Ind/ d1923Sep30 Vienna Mo
Stribling Anne	A86E	1741abt	b.p.Va/Stafford Co ch.1741Jan18
Stribling Deborah Ruth	F69B	1959Oct25	b.p.Ks/Kingman m1976Aug28 Kansas Cy Mo
Stribling Donald Ray	F69C	1961Jan4	b.p.Ks/ElDorado
Stribling Elizabeth	A86D	1739abt	b.p. Va/Stafford Co ch.1739Sep18 Va
Stribling Frances	A86B	1734abt	b.p. Va/Stafford Co ch1734 StPauls Par
Stribling Jane	A86C	1736abt	b.p.Va/Stafford Co ch/1736Jan21 Va
Stribling Jane Mrs	A85Aa		of Stafford Co Va St Pauls Parish
Stribling Joel	A86J	1756abt	b.p. Va/Stafford Co ch..1756Aug17 Va
Stribling Margaret	A86F	1743abt	b.p.Va/Stafford Co m1765Sep1
Stribling Mary	A86H	1750abt	b.p.Va/Stafford Co. ch1750Sep17
Stribling Milly	A86G	1747abt	b.p.Va/Stafford Co ch1747Jan28 Va
Stribling Pearl Martin	F68Caf		
Stribling Ray Eugene	F68Ca	1936Jan5	b.p.Mo/Joplin m1955Jun18 ElDorado Kans
Stribling Sarah	A86I	1753abt	b.p.Va/Stafford Co ch1753May17
Stribling Teresa Rene´	F69D	1968Feb16	b.p.Mo/Kansas City
Stribling Thomas	A85A		of Stafford Co Va St Pauls Parish
Stribling Tina Marie	F69A	1957Oct24	b.p.Ks/Wichita m1973Jan2 Kansas Cy Mo
Stribling William	A86A	1730abt	b.p.Va/Stafford Co ch1730Jan20
Stricker Joan	F49Aam		
Strickland Joseph	L15Aa	1844Sep1	b.p.Mo/Reynolds Co Mail carrier
Strickland Samual	L15Aaf	1837	d1918Jan8 Of Maries Co Mo
Strickland William	V24Ca	1836Jan9	b.p. Mo/Washington Co
Strode Martha	I60Aa		b.p. Holland d1748 Winchester Va

NAME	NUMBER	BIRTH	COMMENTS
Strong J.R.	I55Ca		m1894Nov28 d1921Aug3 Minister
Strong King	A13Ja		
Stroud Robert	Y16Ba		of Maries Co Mo and Texas
Stumpf Mary Jane	D27Ia		m1873Apr8 Gasconade Co Mo
Sudheimer William	K15Ba		of Big Piney Mo
Sughrue George	Y62Ba		of Chicago Ill
Sullins P	A68Ja		
Sullivan -	D34Ga		
Sullivan Mary	B13Ja		or "May"
Sullivant Sophronia	D65Dam		
Summers -	Y74Aa		of Dent Co Mo
Sundwall Billy H	C39Ga		m1947Jul27 Wheatland Mo
Sutter Burga	F35Dam		of Switzerland
Swafford -	P17Fa		of Washington Mo
Swanard Ralph	E41Fa		
Swicegood John	K13Aa		of Weableau City Mo
Swim John	Z35Ca		Fled to Arkansas during Civil War
Tackett Bertha	J17B		of Maries Co Mo
Tackett Ella	J17A		d single
Tackett Fielding	Y49Aa		of Belle Mo
Tackett Frank	J17C		of Maries Co Mo
Tackett G.H.	J20Aa		of Maries Co Mo
Tackett J Perry	J12La		
Tackett J.I.	J14Ca		m1884Feb24
Tackett John	S11Baf		Father believed to be Philip Tackett
Tackett Leona	J19C		m1909Mar21 Of Maries Co Mo
Tackett Louisa	Z22Aa		of Elijah Mo
Tackett Lucy	J19B		m1908Jun28
Tackett Martin M	J19A		of Vienna Mo In hardware business
Tackett Mary M	Z13Fa		m1375Jun15
Tackett Willis M	S11Ba		m1856 d1909Aug9 Of Maries Co Mo
Taff -	U12Daf		no issue
Taff -	G10Ea		
Taff Amanda	T15Ca		d1917Jul31 Also "Annette"
Taff David N	G18Ea	1860abt	of Granite City Mo
Taff James	G18Eaf		of Maries Co Mo
Taff Jeanette	U12Da		mMaries Co Mo No issue
Taff John	G46A	1819Feb7	b.p.Tn/East To Maries Co Mo 1831 m1345
Taff Mahala	J11Ab	1816May1	b.p. Kentucky d1876Nov9 Mo abt 1832
Taff Malinda	G50Ab		m In Missouri
Taff Martha	G10Aa		mTenn d after 1862 Of Maries Co Mo
Taff Minerva	I42Ab		
Taff Minnie Lee	Y25Ia		d abt 1899 Of Maries and Phelps Cos Mo
Taff Peter	G10Aaf		d1870's Maries Co Mo
Talbot John M	F30Bb		
Talbot Theodora	E15Cb		m1851 d Owensville Mo Gasconade Co
Talbot William H	F30Ba		
Talley Marion	G36Ba		of South Missouri and Arkansas
Tate Catherine	A61G		

NAME	NUMBER	BIRTH	COMMENTS
Tate David	A61F	1770	
Tate Elizabeth	A61H		
Tate Elizabeth	A62F	1803	
Tate Farabuy	A62G	1806	
Tate Hugh	A61E	1772	Ancestor of Sam Ervin Senator No Car.
Tate John	A61A	1758	m1790Oct11 d1837
Tate John O	A62B	1795	
Tate Laura Ophelia	F09Dam		Father: Dr Wm Caldwell Tate
Tate Lucinda	A62A	1794	
Tate Margaret	A61I		
Tate Martha	A62E	1801	
Tate Narcissa	A52D	1800	b.p. Georgia
Tate Robert	A61B		
Tate Samuel	A60A	1730	d1813
Tate Samuel	A61C	1765abt	
Tate Samuel	A62C	1797	m1822 d1366
Tate William	A61D	1765	
Taylor -	G54Ba		of Taney Co Mo
Taylor Asabel	A14Baf		
Taylor J.W.	Z42Ia		of Maries Co Mo
Taylor Sarah	A14Ba	1757Oct8	b.p. Mass/Springfield m1774Nov23 d1821
Teague Harry W	B23Aa		
Tennison -	Y15Aa		
Tennison William G	Y24Fa		
Tennyson Eliza Ann	K31Ca	1842Jan16	d1938Apr9 Of Spring Cr Maries Co Mo
Tennyson William B	K31Caf		
Terrill A Jack Dr	R15F	1879Sep26	m(1)1908 d1921Jun4 Of Vera Oklahoma
Terrill A.J. Mrs	R15Fb		
Terrill Amanda A	D40Aa		
Terrill Betsey	R12G		of Maries Co Mo
Terrill Carlos I	R15G	1833	d1920Nov15 d single
Terrill Charles	R14A		of Colorado
Terrill Charles M	R13H		m1885Sep24 Of California
Terrill DeWitt C	R15C		of Belle Mo
Terrill Edward	R15D		
Terrill Eliza C	R13B	1858Apr30	m1878Aug7 d1937Apr20
Terrill Eliza C	R15H	1887Jan8	
Terrill Ellen	R14D		
Terrill Frances	R14B		of Maries Co Mo and Oklahoma
Terrill George	R13G		of Grove Dale Mo
Terrill George	R11C	1816Dec14	d single Of Maries Co Mo
Terrill Hamilton	R12B		of Maries and Shannon Cos Mo
Terrill Jackson	R11E		
Terrill Jackson	R12D	1841Jun23	m1865abt d1899Dec14 Surveyor Conf.Army
Terrill James	R12Baf		of Virginia
Terrill James O	R13C		
Terrill John	R12C		
Terrill John R	R13E		of Grove Dale Mo
Terrill John R	M14Aaf		

176

NAME	NUMBER	BIRTH	COMMENTS
Terrill John W	R15A		of Belle Mo Probate Judge Pros. Atty.
Terrill Keturah	R11D	1808May4	m1832Oct29 d1843Octl6
Terrill Keturah	R13A		
Terrill Keturah	R12E		
Terrill Lucy	R15B		of Vienna Mo
Terrill Martha	R12Ba		of Maries Co Mo Cousin of husband
Terrill Mary	R13D		of Nebraska
Terrill Mary	R14C		
Terrill Millard	R13J		of Oklahoma
Terrill Nancy	R12F	1833Oct10	d1864Sep11
Terrill Nellie	M14Aa		
Terrill Reuben 1st	R10A	1784Dec7	b.p.Va/m1805Sep11 d1829Oct22 Va
Terrill Reuben 2nd	R11A	1806Aug12	b.p. Va/ m1825Aug11 Va d1356Jun6 Mo
Terrill Reuben 3rd	R12A	1830Nov15	b.p.Mo/St Louis Of Maries Co Mo
Terrill Robert W	R13I		of Oklahoma
Terrill Samuel J Dr	R15E	1877Feb15	d1912Sep13 Brinktown Mo
Terrill William	R11B	1812Jan12	b.p.Va/ m1839Oct13 Maries Co Mo
Terrill William	R13F		of Grove Dale mo
Terry Floyd	J19Ca		m1909Mar21 Of Maries Co Mo
Terry Frank M	G18Ia	1857	d1935Jun5 Of Maries Co Mo and Okla.
Terry George W	G18Ja		m1884 Jun15 dMeta Mo Of Vienna
Terry Peter	G36Ga	1866May22	d1919Feb17 Of Stickney Mo
Terwilliger Byrd	G18Ka		
Thomas Elizabeth	B04Ha		of Md m(1)1991Hanslap m(2)1703Oct26
Thomas Litton	A80Ja		
Thomas Mary	I11Aam	1661	
Thomas Olive Mrs	L16Ib		
Thomas Rachel	F17Aa		m1798Mar14 Anne Arundel Co Md
Thomas Richard W	F57Ca		
Thompson -	E54Ea		
Thompson Daniel R	D61G		
Thompson Eliza A	D61E		
Thompson Flem	T13Ia		of Miller Co Mo
Thompson Gilbert N	D61F		
Thompson Israel	Y14Daf		
Thompson J.D.	D47Fa		
Thompson James Robert	D61B		
Thompson Lucy Jane	D61D		
Thompson Lula	K37Ha		of Gasconade Co Mo
Thompson Mamie	Z37Ea		of Springfield and Oldfield Mo
Thompson Mariah	B15Aa		m1892Mar27
Thompson Martha	Y14Da	1812Jun15	d1382Jul22 Of Maries Co Mo
Thompson Nancy Y	T26Aa		
Thompson Peggy Jane	T25Fa		d1898
Thompson Rilda S	D61C		
Thompson Sarah E	D61A		
Thompson Vernie	D51Ba		of Maries Co Mo
Thompson William	D38Ba		
Thompson William S	T25Faf		of Maries Co Mo

NAME	NUMBER	BIRTH	COMMENTS
Thornton –	F52Ga		
Thorton John	H14Ea		of Maries Co Mo No issue
Threewit Charles	Y76Ha		m1924Sep29 Of Canon City Colorado
Tice N.C.	A68Ea		
Tinslar F.S. Dr	E30Ib		m1939Jun5 Of Lebanon Mo
Tipton Fannie	E43Ca		of Maries Co Mo
Tipton Parazetta	E21Ab		of St James Mo m(1)Brown(3)S. Atkins
Todd Roxie	B16Aa		
Todd Ruth	B07Dam		
Todd William	E63Ga		
Tolbert Allen S	F57Aaf		
Tolbert Elizabeth Lyn	F60A	1964Jul6	b.p. No.Car Chapel Hill
Tolbert Evelyn Irene	F58E	1913Aug13	b.p.Ok/Pryor m1931Apr6 Of Dewey Ok1983
Tolbert Helen Denise	F59B	1936Feb5	b.p. Oklahoma Shidler
Tolbert Helen Louise	F60B	1966Dec8	b.p. Mo/St Louis
Tolbert Jack Burgess	F58F	1918Nov3	b.p. Ok/Pryor m1943Aug6 Of MtView Okla
Tolbert Lee Andrew H	F57Aa	1872Apr20	b.p. Georgia/m1902Jan20 d1943Aug21Okla
Tolbert Lyle Hayden	F58C	1907Jul14	m1928Aug31 d1966Mar6 Minco Oklahoma
Tolbert Marjorie Leone	F58A	1902Dec19	b.p.Ok/Pryor m1926Nov6 Of Okla City
Tolbert Mary Patricia	F58G	1927Mar29	b.p.Ok/Pryor m1948Aug17 Of Midland Tx
Tolbert Neva Helen	F58B	1904Feb19	b.p. Ok/Pryor m1938Apr20 of Shidler Ok
Tolbert Nina Carolyn	F58D	1910Aug22	b.p. Ok/Pryor m1932Nov23 Of Dewey Okla
Tolbert Tommy Lyle	F59A	1933Apr15	b.p. Ok/Webb City m1955Nov19
Tone Margaret	B70Aa	1782	b.p.N.J. Middlesex Co. Of Cayuga Co.NY
Travis Clinton Dr	D72E		of Chickasha Oklahoma
Travis Della May	Y62Ca		of Mountain View Mo
Travis Eliza	D71E	1846Jun30	d1877Jul20
Travis Ella	D72F		d at age 9
Travis Ina Frances	D72G		
Travis Jesse	D72C		of Maries Co Mo
Travis John J	D71C	1850Feb12	d single Post Master Steens Prairie Mo
Travis Malissa	D72B		of Maries Co Mo
Travis Mary E	D71D	1840Dec2	d1906Nov27
Travis Minnie	D72H		of Maries Co Mo
Travis Oliver	Y50Ca	1877	d1938Apr1 County Judge Belle Mo
Travis Ollie	D72A		of Maries co Mo
Travis Thomas L	D71B	1844Nov9	m1869Sep12 d1928Dec14 Of Maries Co Mo
Travis Walter	D72D		of Maries Co Mo
Travis William H	D70A	1813Sep17	b.p.Th/ d1877Feb16 Maries Co Mo
Travis William James	D71A	1842Mar13	b.p.Tenn/ m1867Nov27 Maries Co Mo
Trego –	D76Ia		
Triplett Millie	I40Aa		m in No Car
Truman Kizziah	A46Aa	1810	b.p.Kentucky
Tucker –	Z12Ga		of Wright Co Mo
Tucker Fannie	Z16A		d in infancy
Tucker Myra	Z16B		of Maries and Wright Cos Mo
Tune David	Y57Da		of Phelps Co Mo
Turney Cora Louise	B19Ab	1910Jul6	b.p. Oh/Cleveland m(2)1936 d1962Jun10
Turpin Paralee	G42Ba		of Pulaski Mo

NAME	NUMBER	BIRTH	COMMENTS
Twitchell Loraine	B76Bam		
Tylar Cynthia A	Z17C		of Jefferson City Mo
Tyler Arizona	Z17E	1859	
Tyler Elisha	Z17B	1851Dec23	d1933Aug7 single
Tyler John	H54Cb		
Tyler John Hunter	Z12Gb		m1848 Wright co Mo
Tyler Nancy	Z17A	1849Sep20	d1928Jan2 single
Tyler Ruth	Z17F	1850Jul20	m1874Jul30
Tyler Thomas	Z17D	1853Sep23	
Tyner Cora B	V26Fa		m1894 Of Ellinwood Kansas
Tynes Ernest	R31Ga		of Belle Mo
Tynes Thomas J	M23Aa		of near Arlington Mo
Tyre Pearl	A41Aa	1805 abt	
Tyre Wright	A41Aaf		
Tyree Helen	E88Ca		m 1939
Tyree Mary D	U14Bam		
Tyree Nancy	V12Aa	1829Nov29	d1888Dec19
Tyree Satterthwaite	V12Aaf		of Kentucky In Mo Maries Co 1342
Valentine Ethel	A18Da		m1926Jan26
VanBeekum John Rodney	B41Ba		
VanBibber Cloe	I15Ha		to Missouri 1819
VanBibber Olive	I15Ja	1784	d1858Nov12
Vance Catherine	D70Aa	1820Mar4	d1888Jun27 Of Phelps and Maries Cos Mo
VanCleve Jane	I12Ja		m1765 Also VanCleft
Vanderpool Susan	K12Aa		m(1)1866Oct11(2)Sudheimer Fritz
VanKirk -	E39Da		
Vanoster Charles	E46Fa		of Freeburg Mo
Vaughan "Cat"	I47Baf		
Vaughan A.C. "Brud"	I47Ba		
Vaughan Alice	I44C		of St Louis Mo
Vaughan Amanda	I44D		of Dixon Mo
Vaughan Bettie	T15Ebm		
Vaughan Bursetta	J14Eam		Father: Cat Vaughan
Vaughan George	U15Ga		
Vaughan Herod	I41Bb	1313Jun30	(I41B his 2nd marriage)
Vaughan Jennette	G20Dam	1967Aug4	d1912Jun23 Father:Hood VaughanT14Aa
Vaughan Jesse	G58Ca		of Springfield Mo
Vaughan John	Y52Gaf		
Vaughan John W	T14Ba	1342Jan16	m(1)Mary Crismon1860Jul26(2)1873Aug30
Vaughan Margaret Mrs	I14Aam		of Kentucky To Missouri in 1831
Vaughan Mariona	I44A		of Ray Co Mo
Vaughan Mark	I54Aa	1869Sep10	m1899Oct20(or 1889)
Vaughan Nancy	G35Ma	1843	d1903Jan21
Vaughan Nancy E	I44E		m1900Dec30 Of Washington Mo
Vaughan Rachel	G11Ga		
Vaughan Richard W	J27Gaf	1861Sep18	d abt 1913 Of Maries Co Mo
Vaughan Roberta	J27Ga		m1907Apr18 Of Vienna Mo
Vaughan Sarah	G29Gam		m in Kentucky d about 1876
Vaughan Sarah	K12Fa		"Moved to Texas"

NAME	NUMBER	BIRTH	COMMENTS
Vaughan William	T14Aaf		of Kentucky
Vaughan William Hood	T14Aa	1816Jun5	His 2nd marriage Of Maries Co Mo
Vaughan William Sr	I41Bbf		of Kentucky
Vaughan William(PeeWee	G11Gaf		of Maries Co Mo Owned water power mill
Vaughan Wilson	I44B		of Kansas City Mo
Vaughan Zaddie	Y52Ga		
Veasman Edward	E25Ea		
Veasman Joseph	J25Ea		of Maries Co Mo
Veteto Mary Elizabeth	A69Aa	1822Dec	d.1871
Veteto Nancy	A69Ab	1864	d1938
Viemann William	F55Ba		
Villines Abraham	A52A	1775abt	b.p.Va/Nausemond Co d1860Dec Ark
Villines Hezekiah	A53A	1801	b.p.N.C./Caswell Co d1844Ark CarrollCo
Villines Nancy	A54A	1829Mar1	b.p.N.C./Persons Co d1900May18 Ark.
Vinson Arnold	A77Ba		m1922Aug
VonDanuser Hans	F35Daf		ofSwitzerland
VonWinkle Berch	A80Ea		
VonWinkle Brown	A80Da		
VonWinkle Sarah	A78Gb	1860abt	
Vurger George	I59Ga		
Waddle Jennie	Y20Ca		of Vienna Mo
Wade Clifton A	F58Ea		m1931Apr6
Wade Elizabeth	A95A	1904	m1825Jul17 d1886Oct21Tm/Williamson Co
Wade John	A94Aa	1760	b.p.Md d1840 Rutherford Co Tennessee
Waggoner Otis	Y76Fa		m1918May29 Of Pine Lawn Mo
Wagner Emily	Q36Aa		of Maries Co Mo
Wagner Emma	Y64Fa		of Denver Colorado Teacher
Wakefield Cora	G18La		of Vienna Mo
Wakefield Harris	G18Laf		
Walker A.C.	E43J		of Jefferson City Mo
Walker Abel	E77Aa		m1801Mar5
Walker Alonzo D	Q39Ca		of Maries Co Mo
Walker Anna	A79Aa	1880abt	
Walker Blanche	E43B		of Maries Co Mo
Walker Charles	E32Ba		
Walker Eliza L	Y36Bam	1854Oct20	b.p.Mo(Prob. in Phelps Cp) d1912Nov21
Walker Ellis	Y64Ab		of Rolla Mo
Walker Floyd L	E43F		of Jefferson City Mo
Walker Hadley	E43C		of Maries Co Mo
Walker Jemima	Q40Aam	1771Jun29	sister of Moses Walker
Walker Lora	E43H		of Jefferson City Mo
Walker Marlan	E43D		of Maries Co Mo
Walker Moses	Q44Daf		of Ky and Danville Ill m Ill Mo 1844
Walker Myrtle	E43G		of Jefferson City Mo
Walker Pauline	C37Ba		of Cross Timbers Mo
Walker Randal	E43I		of Jefferson City Mo
Walker Robert	K32Ga		
Walker Robert J	Q44Da	1836Sep11	b.p.Ill/Vermillion d1897Mar16 Vicky Mo
Walker Rudy	E43K		of Dent Co Mo

NAME	NUMBER	BIRTH	COMMENTS
Walker Russell	E43E		of Maries Co Mo
Walker Thomas	C15Fa		
Walker Thomassin R	E78Fa		
Walker W.A.	S22Ia		of Maries Co Mo May be E34Ba
Walker W.A.	E34Ba		May be S22Ia
Walker William P	E43A		of Maries Co Mo
Wallace -	Y42Aam		
Wallace Alva	Y75B		of Maries Co Mo
Wallace Angeline	D69B		
Wallace Arminta	Y75E		of Ponca CityOkla d single
Wallace Austin Dr	Y75A		of Chickasha Oklahoma
Wallace Belinda	D71Bam	1809Dec11	of Osage Co Mo
Wallace Belle	D68C		of Eldon Mo
Wallace Belle Mrs	Y74Ab		of Dent Co Mo
Wallace Bernice	D69A		
Wallace Blanche	D68D		of Burbank California
Wallace Charles	Y74E		pf Maries Co Mo
Wallace Charles	D68A		of Belle Mo
Wallace Clarence	D67D		of Idaho
Wallace Claude	D66A		d single
Wallace David	D65H		of Red Bird Mo
Wallace E.A. (Gus)	D66C		
Wallace Edith	Y75D		of Okla City Okla
Wallace Edward Douglas	Y74F	1862May14	m1881Oct24 d1920Jan17
Wallace Elizabeth	C11Gd		m1840Oct29Cox Wm Gasc Co Mo d1849
Wallace Emma	Y74D		no issue
Wallace Ethel	Y75C		of Maries Co Mo
Wallace Eunice	Y74C		no issue
Wallace F Barney	D65E		
Wallace Frank	D68B		of Belle Mo
Wallace Garrett	D66E		
Wallace Irene	Y74B		m1872Apr16(2)1835Apr2 No issue
Wallace James	D65F		of Shannon Co Mo
Wallace Jewel	Y76I		m1922Aug16 Maries Co Mo
Wallace John	D65G		
Wallace John	D67F		of California
Wallace John G	Y72Daf	1820Aug4	d1886Jul3 Maries Co Mo
Wallace John O	Y76C	1889Jan29	m1911Sep15 Of Rector Mo
Wallace Julia	D65B		
Wallace Laura L	D66D		of Kansas City Mo
Wallace Lewis	D66F		
Wallace Lillie	Y76A	1882Sep2	d1887Nov14
Wallace Lucy	C28Ca		
Wallace Martelia	D65A		
Wallace Melcena	D65C		
Wallace Minnie	Y76B	1885Jan21	m1906Jul16 Of Belle Mo
Wallace Nellie	Y76F	1896Oct11	m1918May29 Of Pine Lawn Mo
Wallace Oma	Y76G	1899Aug22	m1922Apr8 Of Vichy Mo Twin
Wallace Ony W	D66H		

NAME	NUMBER	BIRTH	COMMENTS
Wallace Ora	Y76H	1899Aug22	m1924Sep29 d1925Jul26 Canon Cy Colo
Wallace Robert	D66G		
Wallace Robert L	Y74A	1864Oct22	d1931Oct29
Wallace Roy	D67A		of Ink Mo
Wallace Roy	D69C		of St Louis Mo
Wallace Ruth	Y76E	1893May28	m1913Jul8 Of Lodi California
Wallace Sallie May	D66I		m1903Jan18
Wallace Sarah E	D65D		
Wallace Thomas	D66B		
Wallace Walker	D67C		of Oklahoma
Wallace William	R24Ka		of Oklahoma City Okla
Wallace William	D67E		of Idaho
Wallace William J	Y76D	1891Nov12	m1925Feb20 Of Maries Co Mo
Wallace William C	D64A		b.p.Tenn m1839May2 ofCrawford Co Mo
Wallace Zella	D67B		
Wallen Jack	C39Ea		m1946Oct17 Raton New Mexico
Waller Eliza	A84Ea		
Walls Phoebe	Y52Ea		
Walls Thomas	Y52Eaf		
Walter Elizabeth	C11Gam	1790	b.p. N.C./Cabarrus Co
Walton -	V23Ba		
Walton Amanda	V23Aa		m1836Jun23
Walton Louisiana	V23Ca		m1833Aug22d about 1843
Ware William	B05Ga		m1710Dec21 Anne Arundel Co Md
Warfield Alexander	B07Jaf		
Warfield Anne	F17Ba		m1802Aug17
Warfield Brice	F16Eaf		of Montgomary Co Md
Warfield Clara J	A16Ha		
Warfield Deborah	B07Ja		m prior to 1769Nov
Warfield Elisha	B08Fa	1741	m1778 d1818
Warfield Elizabeth	B07Ia		m(2) 1780April 11 Anne Ar. Co Md
Warfield Elizabeth	F17Ca		m1809Dec1
Warfield Nathan	F28Ca		m1828Sep10
Warfield Nicholas	F23Ga		
Warfield Rachel	F16Ea		m1903Aug3
Warfield Sarah	B08Ca	1755abt	Will dated 1823Sep23
Waring Basil	A88Aaf		
Waring Martha	A88Aa	1715Abt	b.p. Md/Prince Georges Co
Warringer Hannah	A10Aa	1643Aug17	d before 1721May12
Warringer William	A10Aaf		
Washam Julia Ann	U11Ba		
Washam Nancy Mrs	U11Bam	1827Sep7	b.p.Tenn/ m1842 d 1910Aug13 MariesCoMo
Washington Augustine	B97A	1694	m(1)1715abt
Washington Charles	B98E	1738May1	
Washington Elizabeth	B98B	1733Jun20	
Washington Frances	B99A		
Washington George	B98A	1732Feb22	b.p.Va/ m1759Jan d1799Dec14 Pres. U.S.
Washington John Aug.	B98D	1735Jan13	
Washington Mildred	B98F		d in infancy

NAME	NUMBER	BIRTH	COMMENTS
Washington Samuel	B98C	1734Nov16	
Waters Henry	A62Ga		or "Walters"
Watkins Bird T	E55Fa		of Miller Co Mo
Watkins William	F23Ea		
Watson -	Y55Ga		of Kansas City Mo
Watson -	Y55Fa		of Kansas City Mo
Weathers-	C17Aa		
Weathersby -	J23Ba		of Moffat Mo
Webb Bertha Mae	F39Ba	1900Sep17	d1972Nov14
Webb Joseph	A74Ba		1967Feb
Webb Maud Wilma	I55Ha		m1908Nov25 Of Oklahoma
Weeks Thomas M	A15La		
Weidinger Kate	K23Ga		
Welch Fount	D52Ca		
Welch Louisiana	D77Bam	1837Jan10	b.p.Ind./d1886caIowa Father Richard Ky
Weld Lucy	A13Ba		
Wells Hodge	K13Ga		
Wells J.S.	E47Aa		of Shannon Co Mo
Wells Jerry	K13Fa		of Minden Mines Mo
Wendt George	S22Ca		of St Louis Mo
Wendt John H 2nd	C26Ea		of Mercer Mo
Wentzel Frederick	H55Daf		
Wentzel L.R.	H55Fa		m1878Apr12 Of Maries Co Mo and Ill.
Wentzel Minnie	H55Da		m1879Feb17
Wertenbaker Anne	F21Ib	1808	m1857Dec12 d1886Jul30
West "Dee"	T24K		b.p. Mo/ "moved to Texas"
West "Doc"	T24M		b.p. Mo/ "Moved to Texas"
West -	Z28Aa		
West -	Z43C		
West -	T25D		of Howell Co Mo
West A.C. (Boy)	T29G		of Arlington Mo
West Alfred	M29A		of Owensville Mo
West Andy	T31A		
West Angeline	T24I		never married
West Arzilla	T25B		of Iberia Mo
West Balis	C13Ba		m1848Nov5 Osage Co Mo
West Caroline	T29A		of Arlington Mo
West Caroline	V14Ea		of Maries Co Mo
West Clarence	T21C		of Memphis Tennessee
West Cynthia	M28C		of Maries Co Mo
West Daniel M (Doc)	T28B	1870Feb10	d1915Jul27
West David	T24B		d single
West David H	T29D		of Maries and Osage Cos Mo., Colo.
West Della	M28F		of Joplin Missouri
West Delmar	M29B		of Owensville Mo
West Dillard	Z43B		
West Elijah M	M15Ba		of Gasconade Co Mo
West Ella	T29C		of Tulsa Oklahoma
West Elsie	T31F		

NAME	NUMBER	BIRTH	COMMENTS
West Emeline	T24J		
West Francis	T31C		
West George	M28B		
West Gordon	T21D		of Indiana
West Hardin	T23A		of Gasconade Co Mo "Went to Texas"
West Harriet	T29B		of Springfield Mo
West Henry	M27C		of Maries Co Mo
West Iva	T21B		of Maries Co Mo
West Jacob H	M24Ca		
West James	Y27B		
West Jane	T29E		of Tenn and Maries Co Mo
West Jane	T24G		of Maries Co Mo
West Jesse	M27B		d single Of Maries Co Mo
West Joe	E82Ha		
West John	T24D	1835Nov15	d1914Mar28.Of Maries Co.Mo.Of Colorado
West John	M27D		of Maries Co Mo
West John H	T25F		d abt 1893 Of Maries Co Mo
West Joseph	Z43A		
West Kate	F30Ka		
West Kate	T28A		of Henry Co Mo
West Lena	T31E		
West Lettie	T31G		
West Logan	M28A		
West Lucy	T24N		b.p. Texas
West Mamie	M27F		of St Louis Mo
West Marion	T24L		b.p. Mo/ "Moved to Texas"
West Mark	T24F	1839Jan11	m1861Jul25 d1912Nov29Of Maries Co Mo
West Mark	T25E		of Miller Co Mo
West Mary	M27G		of Lanes Prairie Maries Co Mo
West Mary	T29F	1862Apr15	b.p.Mo Maries Co m1887Jun7 d1924Mar27
West Mary	E82Ka		m.1916Sep14
West Nancy E	E22Ka		m1869Dec9 Osage Co Mo
West Newman	Z42Ga		
West Oliver	M27A		d single Of Maries Co Mo
West Oliver	T31B		
West Paul	T21E		of Kansas City Mo
West Richard	T24C		of Dallas Co Mo
West Roby	M28D		of Jefferson City Mo
West Rosa	M28E		of Owensville Mo
West Rose	T31D		
West Roy	E33Ca		
West Sallie	T24H		
West Sarah	T25A		of Vienna Mo
West Sarah	T23D		
West Sarah Mrs	T23Ab		"moved to near Grapevine Texas"
West Thomas	Y15Ca		
West Thomas	Y27C		
West Thomas	T25C		d in infancy
West Thomas	T24E	1837	d1908Apr18 Of Maries Co Mo Union Army

NAME	NUMBER	BIRTH	COMMENTS
West Veva	T21A		of Maries Co Mo
West Viola	M27E		of Maries Co Mo
West Warren A (Doc)	T26A		
West William	T24A		
West William	M16Ea		
West William	Y27A		of Maries Co Mo
West William	Z42Fa		of Maries Co Mo
West William	T22A		
West William Jr	T23C		of Maries Co Mo and Texas Mill owner
West William Jr Mrs	T23Ca		
West William Mrs	T22Aa		
West Woodson	T23B		of Miller Co Mo
Westphalen Charles	Y44Ba		no issue
Wheeler Helen Hannah	A16Ba	1819Oct12	b.p.Pa/Mt Pleasant m1848Feb20 d1894Dec
Wheeler Heman	A16Baf		
Wheeler Simon	A14Ha		
Wherry Daniel Boone	V20Abf		d1850 Maries Co Mo Arr. Mo mid 1830´s
Wherry Mary	V20Ab		
Whisenant Marion	Z22Ba		of Wagoner Oklahoma
Whitaker "Babe"	T27H		"moved to Arkansas"
Whitaker -	T23Cb		"moved to Texas"
Whitaker Archelaus	T27A		
Whitaker Gay	T27D		of Miller Co Mo No issue
Whitaker Hardin	G57Ha		of Rolla Mo
Whitaker James	T27B		m and d in Oswego Kansas
Whitaker John	T27E		of Miller Co Mo d single
Whitaker Margaret J	V18Cb		m1889
Whitaker Mark	T27F		
Whitaker Matilda	T27G		of Miller Co Mo
Whitaker Thomas Benton	T23Da		of Va/ To Miller Co Mo
Whitaker William	T27C		"moved to Arkansas m. and died there"
White -	P16Ma		of St Louis Mo
White Edgarda Irene	B22Ca		m1921Jul12 d1955Jan3
White Elizabeth	A71Ba	1890Jun14	d1969Feb9
White Ephraim	C36Da		m Morgan Co Mo
White James	C36Ba		of Spokane Washington
White Robert	B05Ca		m1709Oct22 d1768
White Sarah	E77Cb		m1786Jan12
Whiteason Elizabeth	A39Ea		of Warren Co Mo in 1831
Whiteason William	A39Eaf		
Whitman Allie Kath.	B21Aa		m1915Dec22
Whittle Eleanor	F06Da		
Whittle Mackel Edward	E84Ga		m1960Apr9
Whitton Belle	K12Ca		
Whrattles Margaret	T13Ja		m1824Jan8 Fourth Indian
Wideman Alice	D65Ha		of Red Bird Mo
Wilcox J.W.	Z46Ga		of St Louis Mo
Wilcox Steven	B42Ba		
Wilcoxen -	I12Aa		

NAME	NUMBER	BIRTH	COMMENTS
Wild John	G12Daf		
Wild Paulina	G12Da	1852Aug4	of Maries Co Mo
Wilder William	L18Ba		
Wiles George	T14Ha		
Wiles James	U13Ga		m1877Jun3
Wiles Jane	U13Ca	1860Dec9	d1935Jan23
Wiles Sarah (Sallie)	J15Fa		of Oklahoma
Wiles Thomas L	J15Faf	1818	b.p.N.C./To Osage Co Mo young d1905
Wilkerson John Fred.	A68Ga		
Willard Betty Jean	C19D	1927May10	m1948Dec22 Salem Oregon
Willard Ebbin Chester	C16Ha	1894May14	b.p. Kans/Medicine Lodge m1920 d1968
Willard Elnora Louise	C19A	1920Dec10	b.p.Oregon/Salem
Willard Robert Chester	C19B	1922Apr25	b.p. Oregon/Salem
Willard Ruthita	C19C	1924Aug7	b.p.Oregon/Salem
Willey Helen Candace	B39A	1952Oct24	b.p. Fla/Ft Pierce m1973Jun10 Fla
Willey Lawrence	B29Ca	1921Jun23	m1948Feb12
Willey Lawrence Edgar	B39B	1955May16	m1978Apr1 Vero Beach Florida
Williams -	T29Da		of Maries Co Mo and Colo. No issue
Williams A.J.	G62Ia		may be E21Db
Williams A.J.	E21Db		may be G62Ia
Williams Ashley G	E25Ba		d 1912 Waynesville Mo Surveyor
Williams DeWitt	A79Ha	1890abt	
Williams Dot	E35B		of Waterloo Michigan
Williams Elizabeth	C36Ga		of Hartborne Okla m1857Feb3
Williams Frank	I50Ea		
Williams Henry	G17Aa		
Williams James	Y74Da		no issue
Williams James	G62Ja		of Maries Co Mo
Williams John J	P12Ba		
Williams John W	P12Baf	1795Sep17	b.p.Mo/St Louis Co d1869Apr21Maries Co
Williams Joseph	J16Fa		of Pulaski Co Mo
Williams Katherine	T23Aa		
Williams Laura	E25Aam		
Williams Lawrence	E35C		of Lansing Michigan
Williams Margaret	D38Aam		d Bland Missouri
Williams Margaret	V20Aa		m in Tennessee
Williams Mary A	E21Aa	1844Jan26	d1899Dec7 of Rolla and Maries Co Mo
Williams Micaiah	E25Baf	1829	b.p. Mo/Franklin Co
Williams Minnie	B28Da	1907Nov9	b.p. Mo/Rodaway Co m1953Aug6
Williams Sarah J	A16Ea		
Williams Sterling	E35A		of Waynesville Mo
Williamson Kay	B45Aa		
Willis John	D52Aa		
Willoughby Thomas	D65Aa		
Wills Jack	D68Da		of Burbank California
Wilson Elizabeth Jane	U12Ham	1834Sep30	b.p.Tenn/McMinn Co m1858Oct21 Of Mo
Wilson G.W.	T19Aa		of near Puebla Colorado
Wilson Garnette Ruth	F67Ga	1912Aug12	
Wilson Herod	K37Ea		

186

NAME	NUMBER	BIRTH	COMMENTS
Wilson J. Freeman	D34Fa		of near Marionville Mo
Wilson J.H.	G48Da		
Wilson John	G50Ea		m Maries Co Mo
Wilson Lee	G55A		of Windsor Mo
Wilson Len	M27Ga		of Lanes Prairie Maries Co Mo
Wilson Nancy Rebecca B	F58Cam		
Wilson Pleasant	G55B		of near Crocker Mo
Wilson Thomas	L16Daf		
Wilson William Jr	R30Ca		
Wilson William Sr	R30Caf		
Wilson Zilphia	L16Da		of Granite City Mo
Winn Gordon Dail	C19Da		m1948Dec22 Salem Oregon
Winn Gordon Scott	C21C	1958Sep26	b.p. Oregon/Salem
Winn Mark Dail	C21B	1952Jun16	b.p. Oregon/Salem
Winn Melody Jean	C21A	1951Jul11	b.p.Oregon Salem
Winston Elvira Eliz.	Y23Ham	1821	b.p.Va/(Probably) d1912Belle Mo
Winston Laura	Y72Dam		
Wisdom Elizabeth Larue	B22Fa		m1934May27
Wise Anthony John 3rd	B38A	1933Nov5	b.p.NYPennYan m1956Dec26 Pittsburgh Pa
Wise Anthony John Jr	B29Ba	1908Dec19	b.pPa/Avelon m1932May10 Watkins GlenNY
Wise Claire	B47D	1966Jan29	b.p.Fla/Pensacola
Wise Gretchen Nicole P	B47C	1959Jan11	b.p.Maine Bath (Possibly "Gretchen")
Wise Lydia M	A90Aa	1803	m1822Oct17 d1865Oct22 St.Joseph Mo
Wise Michael Anthony	B47A	1957Dec29	b.p.Maine/Bath
Wise Patricia Eliza.	B38B	1934Oct29	b.p.Pa/Pittsburgh m1956Jun30
Wise Valerie	B47B	1963Jul13	b.p.Florida/Milton
Wiseman Davenport	G11Aaf		names "Oliver" and "Porty"
Wiseman Mary America	G11Aa	1823Feb6	b.p. Tenn/Knox Co m1839 d1895Aug25 Mo
Wiseman Matilda	V12Ca		
Wiseman Myra	V25Cam		m1837Nov12 Maries Co Mo
Wiseman Thomas D	V12Caf		
Wiser Ann	A39Eam		
Witt Ronald	B43Aa		m1978Sep23
Wittkop Kate	U13Bb		1886Jun2
Wofford Alexander	Y25Aa	1830Jun11	d1918Mar25 Of Tennessee and Dent Co Mo
Wofford Andrew J	Y48A		of Belle Mo Insurance agent
Wofford Charles Perry	Y48C	1865	d1933 Of Spartanburg N.C. and Tenn
Wofford Clay	E43Ba		of Maries Co Mo
Wofford John	Y48B		of Dry Fork Maries Co Mo
Wofford Stella	E43Ka		of Dent Co Mo
Wolever Hazel	E22Da		m1925Feb22
Wood -	F15Ba		
Wood Coffil	A13Ga		
Wood Henry	G38Ea		of Maries Co Mo
Wood John Rev	F21Da		
Wood Joseph	F29Aa		m1841Dec4
Woodruff Dow	Y76Ia		of Maries Co Mo m.1922 Aug16
Woodruff Lillie	E43Ia		of Jefferson City Mo
Woods Amanda	T30B		d single

NAME	NUMBER	BIRTH	COMMENTS
Woods Elizabeth	T30F		of Dixon and Wright Co Mo
Woods John Henry	T30A		d 1848 "on the Plains, single"
Woods Lucinda	T30I		
Woods Myra	T30G		
Woods Nancy	T30H	1843abt	d1937
Woods Richard	T30D		d "early in life"
Woods Samuel Maj.	G29Gaf		b.p. England m in Ky d1856Maries Co Mo
Woods Sarah	T30E		of Maries and Wright Cos Mo
Woods Sophia	T30C		
Woods Virginia	T30J		
Woody Archie D	U15Ha	1884	d1922
Woody Fannie	G21Eam		Parents:John H Woody b1830, Irena Burd
Woody John Jefferson	U15Haf	1864Sep8	b.p.Mo/Osage Co m1883Oct25 d1936May4
Workman John	G63Da		of Maries Co Mo
Worley Helen	D77Ja		m1928Jul27
Worrell Sarah	D14Fa	1774abt	b.p.Va/Carroll Co d after 1856 Va
Worth O.K.	H57Da		of Maries and Phelps Cos Mo
Worthington Sarah	B07Cam		
Worthington Thomasine	B07Jam		
Wright -	Z12Hb		
Wright James	M11Hb		of Pulaski Co Mo
Wright John	M18B		of Putnam Oklahoma
Wright Lydia	M18C		d in Arkansas
Wright Sarah E	C37Fb		of Stillwater Oklahoma
Wright Tacy	E78Ga		
Wright William	M18A		of Dixon Mo
Wyatt Annie	A68Aam		
Wyatt Jedo	A80Ba		
Wyatt Lena	A80Aa		
Wyatt Louise	A78Eb	1860abt	
Wyatt Mary Emily	A78Aa	1857Jun10	m1879Jan31
Wynn Lee	Y64Ba		of Phelps Co Mo
Wyrick Ellen	G49Ab		
Wyvill Jane	B07Ha		d1776Anne Ar.Co Md
Yaryan Amy Lyn	B51A	1974Aug20	
Yaryan Malcolm	B42Aa		
York -	L17Ba		
Young Etta	D75Ib		m1878Sep19
Young Harriett	B95Aa	1840Nov10	b.p. Mo/Howard Co d1915Feb10 Paris Mo
Young James	A46A	1810	b.p. Tennessee
Young Joseph	M11Aaf		
Young Joseph Alphonso	F09Daf		of Charlotte North Carolina
Young Loraine	E85Ga		
Young Mahulda	A47A	1837	b.p.Ark/NewtonCo m1854Nov15 d abt1894
Young Mary Elizabeth	F09Da	1876Mar7	m1899Jan25 d1940Dec17of Morganton N.C.
Young Nicholas	E24Ga	1846Mar6	d1925Jun2
Young Rebecca	M11Aa		m abt1853 Of Maries Co Mo Vienna
Young Rosanna	Y23Ba		
Young Ruth	D14Da	1770abt	b.p.N.C. m1788ca d Van Buren Co Tenn

NAME	NUMBER	BIRTH	COMMENTS
Zeusch -	Y36Fa		Professor Rolla Mo. School of Mines

PART III

SIBLING GROUPS

[A-10] NOBLE unknown
  unknown/unknown
A10A THOMAS -A11-
A10Aa Warringer Hannah
A10Aaf Warringer William

[A-11] NOBLE A10A
  Thomas/Hannah Warringer
A11A JOHN
A11Aa Sackett A
A11Ab Goodman M
A11B HANNAH
A11Ba Goodman J
A11Bb Edwards N
A11C THOMAS
A11Ca Dewey Elizabeth
A11D MATTHEW
A11Da Dewey Hannah
A11E MARK
A11Ea Marshall Mary
A11F ELIZABETH
A11Fa Church R
A11Fb Loomis S
A11G LUKE
A11Ga Stebbins Hannah
A11H JAMES -A12-
A11Ha — Ruth
A11Hb Highley Katherine
A11Hbf Highley John
A11Hbm Drake Hannah
A11I MARY
A11Ia Colton Ephraim
A11J REBECCA
A11Ja Loomis Samuel

[A-12] NOBLE A11H
  James/Ruth —
A12A JAMES
A12B DANIEL (A13Aaf)
A12Ba Stebbins R
A12Bb Crow R
A12C LYDIA
A12Ca Kelsey Stephen
A12D JAMES

A12E DAVID -A13-
A12Ea Loomis Abigail
A12Eaf Loomis Philip

[A-13] NOBLE A12E
  David/Abigail Loomis
A13A DAVID -A14-
A13Aa Noble Ruth
A13Aaf Noble Daniel (A12B)
A13B OLIVER
A13Ba Weld Lucy
A13C JAMES
A13Ca Caldwell A
A13Cb Smith A
A13Cc Crouch E
A13Cd Branch P
A13D KATHERINE
A13Da Ingham Alexander
A13E THIRZA
A13Ea Booth Jonathan
A13F ENOCH
A13G ABIGAIL
A13Ga Wood Coffil
A13H AARON
A13Ha Bagg Eunice
A13I LYDIA
A13Ia Fox I.J.
A13Ib Martin S
A13J HANNAH
A13Ja Strong King
A13K JOHN

[A-14] NOBLE A13A
  David/Ruth Noble
A14A RUTH
A14Aa Dunham Calvin
A14B DAVID -A15-
A14Ba Taylor Sarah
A14Baf Taylor Asabel
A14C REBECCA
A14D ENOCH
A14Da Ames S
A14Db Adams C
A14Dc Adams D

A14E   EZEKIEL
A14Ea   Gates H
A14Eb   Sears S
A14F   DANIEL
A14Fa   — Lydia
A14G   THIRZA
A14H   POLLY
A14Ha   Wheeler Simon
A14I   LUCY
A14Ia   Daniels Moses

[A-15] NOBLE A14B
        David/Sarah Taylor
A15A   SALLIE
A15Aa   Ashley Leonard
A15B   DAVID
A15Ba   Grummond Sarah
A15C   THIRZA
A15Ca   Skidmore Joseph
A15D   MARY
A15Da   Day Martin
A15E   ASIEL
A15Ea   Harberger Eliza
A15F   ESTHER
A15Fa   Hoyt Jesse
A15G   JAMES
A15H   ROSWELL
A15I   ELECTA
A15Ia   Keeler Nathan
A15Ib   Hall Mott
A15J   WILLIAM TAYLOR —A16—
A15Ja   Brewer Christiana
A15Jaf Brewer William Borardus
A15K   MIRANDA
A15Ka   Bush J
A15Kb   Phelps D
A15L   SOPHIA
A15La   Weeks Thomas M
A15M   JAMES
A15Ma   Hegeman Grace
A15N   CLARISSA
A15Na   Eldridge George

[A-16] NOBLE A15J
        William Taylor/Christiana Brewer
A16A   DAVID WILLIAM
A16Aa   Bortree Esther A
A16B   ALBERT J —A17—
A16Ba   Wheeler Helen H
A16Baf Wheeler Heman
A16C   SARAH
A16D   CARLTON M
A16Da   Churchill Mary B
A16E   WASHINGTON A
A16Ea   Williams Sarah J
A16F   SARAH MARIA
A16Fa   Patton J.E.R.
A16G   CATHERINE S
A16H   ENOCH GEORGE
A16Ha   Warfield Clara J
A16I   JAMES TAYLOR
A16J   CHARLES H

[A-17] NOBLE A16B
        Albert J/Helen H Wheeler
A17A   CHARLES A
A17B   TRUMAN W
A17C   HELEN GRACE
A17D   ERNEST WHEELER
A17E   HENRY O —A18— (B19Aaf)
A17Ea   Maynard Lulie E (B19Aam)
A17Eaf Maynard A.K.

[A-18] NOBLE A17E
        Henry O/Lulie E Maynard
A18A   ORVILLE M
A18B   HELEN L (B19Aa)
A18Ba   Burgess C Perry —B29— (B19A)
A18C   OLIVE BLANCH
A18D   NORMAN W
A18Da   Valentine Ethel

[A-34] BURGESS B07G
   Edward/Mary Davis
A34A   JOHN -F24-
A34Aa   Maccubin Helen
A34B   ELIZABETH
A34C   ANNE
A34D   EDWARD
A34E   MARGARET
A34Ea   Clagett Ninien
A34F   EPHRAIM -F25-
A34Fa   — Elizabeth
A34G   JANE
A34H   THOMAS
A34I   MARY
A34Ia   Shekell John
A34J   SARAH
A34Ja   Hook Daniel

[A-35] BURGESS A37C
   Moses/Elizabeth Price
A35A   JOHN PRICE BUCKNER
A35B   EDWARD
A35C   LUNSFORD

[A-37] BURGESS B6A
   Edward/Margaret Garner
A37A   WILLIAM
A37Aa   Courtney Bethsheba
A37B   EDWARD
A37C   MOSES -A35-
A37Ca   Price Elizabeth
A37D   REUBEN -A38- (A86Fa)
A37Da   Stribling Margaret (A86F)

[A-38] BURGESS A37D
   Reuben/Margaret Stribling
A38A   THOMAS -A39- (A81Aa)
A38Aa   Hunter Mary (A81A)
A38Aaf Hunter John -A81-
A38Aam unknown
A38B   WILLIAM
A38C   REUBEN Jr
A38D   MARY
A38E   MILLY

A38Ea   Hartley Thomas
A38F   FRANKEY
A38Fa   Nelson Ebenezer
A38G   VINNEY
A38Ga   Hinkle John

[A-39] BURGESS A38A
   Thomas/Mary Hunter
A39A   WILLIAM
A39B   ELIZABETH
A39Ba   Bradford David
A39C   GEORGE W -A66-
A39Ca   McBride Charlotte
A39D   CHARLES -A67-
A39Da   McBride Margaret
A39E   ANDERSON -A68-
A39Ea   Whiteason Elizabeth
A39Eaf Whiteason William
A39Eam Wiser Ann
A39F   JOEL -A69-
A39Fa   Allison Ruth
A39G   MARGARET
A39Ga   Bradford Jacob
A39H   THOMAS
A39I   MARY
A39Ia   Barnes Joab
A39Ib   Lollar Corder
A39J   HIRAM (John) -A70-
A39Ja   unknown
A39Jb   Campbell Nancy
A39K   NELLIE
A39Ka   Bowman Bethel
A39Kb   Farris William

[A-40] FILLINGIM unknown
   unknown/unknown
A40A   SAMUEL Sr -A41-
A40Aa   — Sarah

[A-41] FILLINGIM A40A
   Samuel/Sarah —
A41A   SAMUEL Jr -A42-
A41Aa   Tyre Pearl
A41Aaf Tyre Wright

SIBLING GROUP A

[A-42] FILLINGHAM A41A
  Samuel Jr/Pearl Tyre
A42A   DAVID -A43- (A47Aa)
A42Aa   Young Mahulda (A47A)

[A-43] FILLINGHAM A42A
  David/Mahulda Young
A43A   JAMES -A44- (A51Aa)
A43Aa   Edgman Eva (A51A)

[A-44] FILLINGHAM A43A
  James/Eva Edgman
A44A   SAMUEL -A45-(A58Aa,B19Gaf)
A44Aa   Jones Pearl A (A58A,B19Gam)
A44B   MYRTLE
A44C   CLARA MAY
A44Ca   Maples Joe
A44D   GRACE M
A44Da   Cox John
A44E   CHARLES F
A44Ea   — Jessie
A44F   NANCY ETHEL
A44Fa   Shackleford C Arthur
A44G   GUSTAVUS
A44H   VITGE E

[A-45] FILLINGHAM A44A
  Samuel/Pearl A Jones
A45A   IRA WALLACE -B33- (B19Ga)
A45Aa   Burgess Ethel May (B19G)
A45B   MURIEL E
A45Ba   Buckingham Roy R
A45C   SAMUEL E
A45Ca   Isler Grace

[A-46] YOUNG unknown
  unknown/unknown
A46A   JAMES -A47-
A46Aa   Truman Kissiah

[A-47] YOUNG A46A
  James/Kissiah Truman
A47A   MAHULDA (A42Aa)
A47Aa   Fillinghim Davis (A42A)

[A-48] EDGMAN unknown
  unknown/unknown
A48A   WILLIAM -A49-
A48Aa   Kimble Elizabeth

[A-49] EDGMAN A48A
  William/Elizabeth Kimble
A49A   SAMUEL -A50-
A49Aa   Pierce Sarah

[A-50] EDGMAN A49A
  Samuel/Sarah Pierce
A50A   SAMUEL -A51- (A54Aa)
A50Aa   Villines Nancy (A54A)

[A-51] EDGMAN A50A
  Samuel/Nancy Villines
A51A   EVA (A43Aa)
A51Aa   Fillingham James E (A43A)

[A-52] VILLINES unknown
  unknown/unknown
A52A   ABRAHAM -A53-
A52Aa   McKissack Nancy

[A-53] VILLINES A52A
  Abraham/Nancy McKissack
A53A   HEZEKIAH -A54-
A53Aa   Penn Elizabeth
A53Aaf Penn John

[A-54] VILLINES A53A
  Hezekiah/Elizabeth Penn
A54A   NANCY (A50Aa)
A54Aa   Edgman Samuel Jr (A50A)

[A-55] JONES unknown
  unknown/unknown
A55A   WILLIS -A56-
A55Aa   unknown

193

[A-56] JONES A55A
  Willis/unknown
A56A   SAMUEL -A57- (A62Da)
A56Aa Tate Narcissa (A62D)

[A-57] JONES A56A
  Samuel/Narcissa Tate
A57A   ALFRED H -A58-
A57Aa Moulder Martha E
A57Aaf Moulder Samuel

[A-58] JONES A57A
  Alfred H/Martha E Moulder
A58A   PEARL (A44Aa,B19Gam)
A58Aa Fillingham Samuel (A44A,B19Gaf)

[A-60] TATE unknown
  unknown/unknown
A60A   SAMUEL -A61-
A60Aa Caldwell Elizabeth
A60Aaf Caldwell John

[A-61] TATE A60A
  Samuel/Elizabeth Caldwell
A61A   JOHN -A62-
A61Aa Oliphant Anne S
A61B   ROBERT
A61C   SAMUEL
A61Ca Alexander Elizabeth
A61D   WILLIAM
A61E   HUGH
A61F   DAVID
A61G   CATHERINE
A61H   ELIZABETH
A61I   MARGARET

[A-62] TATE A61A
  John/Anne S Oliphant
A62A   LUCINDA
A62Aa Jordan Archibald
A62B   JOHN O
A62C   SAMUEL
A62Ca Griffeth Mary
A62D   NARCISSA (A56Aa)

A62Da Jones Samuel (A56A)
A62E   MARTHA
A62Ea Denman Chappell
A62F   ELIZABETH
A62Fa Alexander John
A62G   FARABUY
A62Ga Waters Henry

[A-64] BURGESS B7A
  William/Sarah —
A64A   ANN
A64B   SAMUEL
A64C   JANE
A64D   URSULA
A64E   WILLIAM
A64F   JOHN -F19-
A64Fa — Rebecca
A64G   SARAH
A64H   SAMUEL#2
A64I   HUSLEY

[A-66] BURGESS A39C
  George W/Charlotte McBride
A66A   MARTHA
A66Aa Harris John Roberts
A66B   REBECCA
A66Ba Allison John R -A73-
A66C   MARY ELIZABETH
A66Ca Lindsey Leonida L
A66Cb Shanks Crave
A66D   ISAAC W
A66E   CHARLOTTE
A66Ea Roberts John
A66F   CYNTHIA
A66G   IBBY
A66H   MARY E
A66Ha Crowley Robert
A66I   JOE
A66J   THOMAS
A66K   DANIEL
A66L   JOHN

[A-67] BURGESS A39D
  Charles/Margaret McBride
A67A   MARGARET
A67Aa   Elrod Isaac E
A67B   WILLIAM SIMPSON
A67Ba   Barnes Ricy Ozina
A67C   JAMES CRAWFORD
A67Ca   Barnes Nancy C
A67D   ELIZABETH
A67Da   Massa Andrew
A67E   JOHN
A67F   PEYTON
A67G   NANCY JANE
A67Ga   Peek Robert
A67H   TOM
A67I   DORINDA
A67Ia   Lollar Isaac E
A67Ib   Massa William
A67J   CHARLES L -A71-
A67Ja   Deering America
A67K   VANCE DeKALB
A67Ka   Deering Susan F
A67L   MARY LEOMA
A67La   Lollar John J
A67M   WINFIELD S
A67Ma   Barnes Sarah J

[A-68] BURGESS A39E
  Anderson/Elizabeth Whiteason
A68A   VALENTINE
A68Aa   Log Frankie
A68Aaf Log Francis
A68Aam Wyatt Annie
A68B   WAYMON L
A68C   MALISSA J
A68Ca   Fuort John
A68D   CELINA
A68E   POLLY A
A68Ea   Tice N.C.
A68F   ELIZABETH
A68G   SARAH
A68Ga   Wilkerson John F
A68H   DUDLEY H
A68I   ADOLPHUS A

A68J   CLEMENSA
A68Ja   Sullins P
A68K   VIRLENE
A68Ka   Bryan B.D.

[A-69] BURGESS A39F
  Joel/Ruth Allison
A69A   JOE -A76-
A69Aa   Veteto Mary Elizabeth
A69Ab   Veteto Nancy
A69B   LUCINDA
A69C   JAMES

[A-70] BURGESS A39J
  Hiram/unknown
A70A   JOSEPH DANIEL -A78-
A70Aa   Blaylock Elizabeth
A70B   EMALINE
A70C   MARY A
A70D   ELIZABETH J
A70E   FATE
A70Ea   Myers Martha
A70F   JOHN
A70Fa   Norris Katherine
A70G   WILLIAM K
A70Ga   Hale Elizabeth
A70H   CHARLIE
A70Ha   Hale Martha
A70I   PEE
A70Ia   Hale Rhoda

[A-71] BURGESS A67J
  Charles L/America Deering
A71A   ZENITH BLOOMINGTON
A71B   AMMON LAFAYETTE -A75-
A71Ba   White Elizabeth
A71C   SALLIE MARGARET
A71D   PRETTEMAN P
A71Da   Carr Mertie
A71E   MAYHUE BLAINE
A71F   DORENDIA SUSAN
A71Fa   Slagle Erastus
A71G   DEALIA IANTHA
A71Ga   Slagle Howard

A71H   VIANA ARTELLA
A71I   RICHARD HERBERT −A72−
A71Ia Little Dorothy Mae

[A-72] BURGESS A71I
    Richard H/Dorothy Mae Little
A72A   RICHARD HERBERT Jr
A72Aa Peters Lrone Ann
A72B   CHARLES JARVIS
A72Ba Collins Elsie
A72C   JAMES ZEBEDEE
A72Ca Stoltz Bona Jean M
A72D   WILLIAM HOWARD
A72Da Andrews Lucie
A72E   THOMAS EDWARD
A72Ea Hardwick Marilyn
A72F   MARGARET ANN
A72Fa Franz John F
A72Fb Markham Mike
A72G   DOROTHY ELIZABETH
A72Ga Ball Robert
A72H   JOHN FRANKLIN
A72Ha Laraway Linda

[A-73] ALLISON A66Ba
    John R/Rebecca Burgess
A73A   MARTHA
A73Aa Bartlett Milton
A73B   REBECCA JANE
A73Ba Exum Cee
A73C   JOHN ISAAC −A74−
A73Ca Robinson Mattie
A73Cb Caruthers Julie
A73D   LOTTIE
A73E   BIRD P
A73Ea Bussell Moniza Caroline

[A-74] ALLISON A73C
    John Isaac/Mattie Robinson
A74A   MATTIE ETHEL
A74Aa Passons Thomas L
A74B   MAUDE
A74Ba Webb Joseph
A74C   JOSEPH

A74Ca Farrell Mattie Lee
A74D   HELEN
A74Da Roark Prentice
A74E   BEULAH
A74Ea Delaney Robert

[A-75] BURGESS A71B
    Ammon L/Elizabeth White
A75A   SHELA TAFT
A75Aa Goolsby Nathalie
A75B   MARTHA AMERIWS
A75Ba Buck Willie Thurlow
A75C   CHARLES HOOPER
A75Ca Dixon Pansey
A75D   HOWARD LAFAYETTE
A75Da Lance Betty
A75E   WILLIAM McKINLEY
A75Ea Maxwell Ella Mae
A75F   ZEBEDEE
A75Fa — Arlene

[A-76] BURGESS A69A
    Joe/Mary Elizabeth Veteto
A76A   JOHN SHIRLEY
A76Aa Lambert Elizabeth
A76B   PARISETTA
A76Ba Cannon Grant
A76C   JAMES
A76Ca Carter Sally
A76D   JODY
A76Da Carrington Julie
A76Db Meadows Lenora
A76E   SARAH
A76F   FANNIE
A76Fa Clark John
A76G   HENRY −A77−
A78Ga Daws Josie
A76H   MARY ANN
A76Ha Campbell Joseph
A76I   JAMES WILLIAM
A76Ia Brown Phebee
A76J   POLLY ANN
A76Ja Brown Walter
A76K   CHARLES

A76Ka   Manier Julia Ann
A76L   ALVIN DERO
A76La   Brown Vallie M
A76M   DAISY
A76Ma   Bush R.T.
A76Mb   Bailey Paul
A76N   NANCY
A76Na   Anderson Demi
A76Nb   Cannon John
A76Nc   Cannon Joseph
A76O   ANNIE
A76Oa   Roberts Lanora
A76P   AVO
A76Pa   Harness Benton M
A76Q   BAILEY
A76Qa   Minnear Essie
A76R   OLIVER
A76S   LULA MAE
A76Sa   Minnear George
A76T   CARMACH
A76Ta   Brown Francis

[A77] BURGESS A76G
    Henry/Josie Daws
A77A   ESSIE
A77Aa   Flatt Haskel
A77B   IDA LOU
A77Ba   Vinson Arnold
A77C   DANIEL B
A77Ca   Howard Mayme R
A77D   NATHAN
A77Da   Goodwin Margaret
A77E   SALLIE
A77Ea   Hamilton Raymond
A77Eb   Deshields Glenn
A77Ec   Scott Will J
A77F   MARTHA
A77Fa   Herren Vester H. Gen
A77G   JIMMIE FRANK
A77Ga   Likings Bonnie
A77Gb   Maidwell Ethel
A77H   BERTA LEE
A77Ha   Edwards Arnold

[A-78] BURGESS A70A
    Joseph D/Elizabeth Blaylock
A78A   HIRAM SIMPSON -A79-
A78Aa   Wyatt Mary Emily
A78B   RICHARD
A78Ba   Campbell Ida
A78C   THOMAS A
A78Ca   Blaylock Martha
A78D   WILLIS
A78Da   Daniel France
A78E   WILLIAM
A78Ea   Nielson Alice
A78Eb   Wyatt Louise
A78F   DAN
A78G   JOSEPH
A78Ga   Campbell Laura
A78Gb   VonWinkle Sarah
A78H   MARY

[A-79] BURGESS A78A
    Hiram Simpson/Mary Emily Wyatt
A79A   CANZA WELL
A79Aa   Walker Anna
A79B   IRVIN
A79Ba   Arnett Mary Lou
A79C   WILLIAM
A79Ca   Bolin Mary
A79D   JACOB ISAAC
A79Da   Myers Cera
A79E   HARVEY
A79F   SIMON PETER
A79G   JOHN LINVILLE
A79Ga   Edwards Emilene
A79H   MARTHA JANE
A79Ha   Williams DeWitt
A79I   GEORGE ANDERSON
A79Ia   Lewis Stella Lou
A79J   MARY ANN
A79Ja   Hubbard Fred
A79K   FANCY HILL -A80-
A79Ka   Croft Recie

[A-80] BURGESS A79K
  Fancy Hill/Recie Croft
A80A   ROSS
A80Aa   Wyatt Lena
A80B   OTTO
A80Ba   Wyatt Jedo
A80C   ALLEN
A80D   ROSE LEE
A80Da   VonWinkle Brown
A80E   BERTHA
A80Ea   VonWinkle Berch
A80F   RALPH
A80G   KENT KENARD
A80Ga   Hill William
A80H   OLLI
A80Ha   Parker Carrol
A80I   CARL
A80Ia   — Jean
A80J   GENEVA
A80Ja   Thomas Litton
A80Jb   Ross Fred
A80K   SIMPSON
A80Ka   — Willie
A80L   FOSTER F
A80M   DALLAS

[A-81] HUNTER A38Aaf
  John/unknown
A81A   MARY (Polly) (A38Aa)
A81Aa   Burgess Thomas (A38A)
A81B   WILLIAM -A83- (I16Ha)
A81Ba   Boone Sarah (I16H)

[A-82] OSBORN B72C
  William D/Mary J —
A82A   SCOTT H
A82B   BERTA A
A82C   CHARLEY T
A82D   HARRY
A82E   EARL H

[A-83] HUNTER A81B
  William/Sarah Boone
A83A   DIDLEY

A83B   MARY (Polly)
A83Ba   Hudgens James -A84-
A83C   JAMES

[A-84] HUDGENS A83Ba
  James/Mary Hunter
A84A   CROCKETT
A84B   WILLIAM
A84C   DIDLEY
A84D   SHELBY
A84E   HAMPTON
A84Ea   Waller Eliza
A84F   JOHN
A84G   JOSEPH
A84H   CATHERINE

[A-85] STRIBLING unknown
  unknown/unknown
A85A   THOMAS -A86-
A85Aa   — Jane

[A-86] STRIBLING A85A
  Thomas/Jane —
A86A   WILLIAM
A86B   FRANCES
A86C   JANE
A86D   ELIZABETH
A86E   ANNE
A86F   MARGARET (A37Da)
A86Fa   Burgess Reuben (A37D)
A86G   MILLY
A86H   MARY
A86I   SARAH
A86J   JOEL

[A-87] FOWLER B5Faf
  Thomas/Susan Ijams
A87A   ELIZABETH (B5Fa)
A87Aa   Burgess Samuel (B5F)
A87B   WILLIAM

[A-88] BURGESS B4H
  Charles/Elizabeth Thomas
A38A   CHARLES -A99-

A88Aa Waring Martha
A88Aaf Waring Basil
A88B   RICHARD -F11-
A88Ba Magruder Elizabeth
A88C   ELIZABETH
A88Ca Offutt Samuel -A93-
A88Caf Offutt William
A88Cam Brocke Mary
A88D   URSULA
A88Da Davis Meredith
A88E   WILLIAM
A88F   MORDECAI
A88G   BENJAMIN

[A-90] BURGESS B8G
       Joshua/Sarah Burgess
A90A   JOHN D -F30-
A90Aa Wise Lydia M
A90B   ACHSAH
A90C   MORDECAI
A90Ca Ryan Sarah
A90D   UPTON
A90Da Linn Eleanor
A90E   SHERIDAN
A90F   RUTH
A90G   ELEANOR
A90Ga Burgess Jefferson
A90H   JAMES
A90I   SALLY
A90J   MICHAEL D
A90Ja Ranyon Sarah Ann
A90K   JOSEPH V
A90Ka Bassett Lucinda

[A-91] BURGESS F30D
       Joshua Kate/Lucuida A Holliday
A91A   WILLIAM D
A91B   MARY M
A91C   MINNIE
A91D   W.M.
A91E   JOHN R
A91F   KATIE
A91G   GUY

[A-92] BURGESS F30C
       Thomas Jefferson/Mary P Owens
A92A   THOMAS JEFFERSON Jr
A92B   MATTIE W
A92C   IDA
A92Ca Laird —

[A-93] OFFUTT A88Ca
       Samuel/Elizabeth Burgess
A93A   MORDECAI BURGESS -A94-
A93Aa Offutt Jane

[A-94] OFFUTT A93A
       Mordecai Burgess/Jane Offutt
A94A   ELIZABETH
A94Aa Wade John -A95-

[A-95] WADE A94Aa
       John/Elizabeth Offutt
A95A   ELIZABETH
A95Aa Cochrane Edward Alexander -A96-

[A-96] COCHRANE A95Aa
       Edward Alexander/Elizabeth Wade
A96A   MIRANDA BLANCHE
A96Aa Nolen William Martin -A97-

[A-97] NOLEN A96Aa
       William Martin/Miranda B Cochrane
A97A   EDWARD LANGLEY -A98-
A97Aa Richardson Anne Belle

[A-98] NOLEN A97A
       Edward Langley/Anne B Richardson
A98A   KATE (D84Aa)
A98Aa Shockley Thomas J (D84A)

[A-99] BURGESS A88A
       Charles/Martha Waring
A99A   BASIL Capt -F10-
A99Aa Smith Anne
A99B   ANN
A99Ba Smith James Haddock-F62-
A99C   URSULA

199

[B-03] BURGESS B02A
  William/unknown
B03A   WILLIAM Col -B4-
B03Aa Robins Elizabeth
B03Aaf Robins Edward (F44A)
B03Aam — Jane (F44Aa)
B03Ab — Sophia
B03Ac Painter Ursula
B03B   JOSEPH
B03C   SAMUEL
B03D   JEREMIAH
B03E   ANNE
B03F   MARY
B03G   ISAAC
B03H   DANIEL
B03I   ELIZABETH
B03Ia Parker —

[B-04] BURGESS B3A
  William/ Elizabeth Robins
B04A   EDWARD Capt -B5- (F42Aa)
B04Aa Chew Sarah (F42A)
B04Aaf Chew Samuel Col -F42- (F41A)
B04Aam Ayers Anna F41Aa)
B04B   GEORGE -F12-
B04Ba — Katherine
   (2)Sophia —
B04C   SUSANNA
B04Ca Sewell Nicholas Maj
   (3)Ursula Painter
B04D   WILLIAM
B04Da Gassaway Anne
B04Daf Gassaway Nicholas
B04Dam Besson Anne
B04E   JOHN
B04F   JOSEPH
B04G   BENJAMIN
B04Ga — Jane
B04H   CHARLES -A88-
B04Ha Thomas Elizabeth
B04I   ELIZABETH
B04J   ANNE (B5Ebm)
B04Ja Sparrow Thomas (B5Ebf)
B04K   SUSANNA

B04Ka Mitchell John

[B-05] BURGESS B04A
  Edward/Sarah Chew
B05A   EDWARD -F13-
B05Aa — Sarah
B05B   ELIZABETH
B05Ba Nicholson William
B05C   ANNE
B05Ca White Robert
B05D   WILLIAM
B05E   JOHN -B7-
B05Ea Macklefresh Jane
B05Eaf Macklefresh David
B05Eb Sparrow Matilda
B05Ebf Sparrow Thomas (B4Ja)
B05Ebm Burgess Anne (B4J)
B05F   SAMUEL CHEW -B6- (A87Aa)
B05Fa Fowler Elizabeth (A87A)
B05Faf Fowler Thomas -A87-
B05Fam Ijams Susan
B05G   MARGARET
B05Ga Ware William
B05H   SARAH MARIA (F5Aa)
B05Ha Gaither Benjamin (F5A)
B05I   SUSANNA
B05Ia Richardson Thomas
B05J   SOPHIA
B05Ja King William Alfred

[B-06] BURGESS B05F
  Samuel Chew/Elizabeth Fowler
B06A   EDWARD -A37-
B06Aa Garner Margaret
B06B   SARAH
B06C   BENJAMIN
B06D   ELIZABETH (B99Aam)
B06Da Ball Jeduthun (B99Aaf)
B06Daf Ball James Col
B06Dam Daingerfield Mary Conway
B06E   RICHARD -F18-
B06Ea — Mary
B06F   URSULA
B06G   JANE

200

B06Ga   Duvall Ephraim
B06H   RACHEL
B06Ha   Disney James

[B-07]   BURGESS B05E
        John/Jane Macklefresh
B07A   WILLIAM -A64-
B07Aa   — Sarah
B07B   ANNE
B07C   JOHN Col -F14-
B07Ca   Dorsey Sarah
B07Caf Dorsey Basil
B07Cam Worthington Sarah
B07D   JOSEPH -B8-
B07Da   Dorsey Elizabeth
B07Daf Dorsey Michael
B07Dam Todd Ruth
B07E   SARAH
B07Ea   Disney William
B07F   MARY
B07Fa   Lusby —
B07G   EDWARD Capt -A34-
B07Ga   Davis Mary
B07Gaf Davis Thomas
B07Gam Gaither Elizabeth
        (2)Matilda Sparrow
B07H   SAMUEL -F15-
B07Ha   Wyvill Jane
B07I   WEST -F16-
B07Ia   Warfield Elizabeth
B07J   CALEB -F17-
B07Ja   Warfield Deborah
B07Jaf Warfield Alexander
B07Jam Worthington Thomasine
B07Jb   — Susanna
B07K   MARY
B07L   ANNE
B07M   ELIZABETH
B07N   SUSANNA
B07O   BENJAMIN
B07Oa   — Priscilla

[B-08]   BURGESS B07D
        Joseph/Elizabeth Dorsey
B08A   JOHN
B08B   JOSEPH
B08C   MICHAEL -F22-
B08Ca   Warfield Sarah
B08D   VACHEL -F23-
B08Da   Dorsey Rebecca
B08E   RICHARD
B08Ea   Gassaway Mary
B08Eaf Gassaway Thomas
B08F   RUTH
B08Fa   Warfield Elisha
B08G   JOSHUA -A90- (F14Ba)
B08Ga   Burgess Sarah (F14B)
B08H   WILLIAM
B08Ha   Coale Susannah
B08I   HONOR
B08Ia   Hobbs John
B08J   NANCY
B08K   LIDEY
B08Ka   Baxter Isaac
B08Kb   Maxwell William
B08L   JOSEPH
B08M   PHILEMON
B08Ma   Dorsey Mary Ridgely
B08N   SARAH
B08O   ELIZABETH
B08P   JANE
B08Pa   Simpson Rezin

[B-09]   BURGESS F18C
        Richard/unknown
B09A   JAMES Sr -B10-
B09Aa   Matson Ruth
B09B   WILLIAM
B09C   JOHN

[B-10]   BURGESS B09A
        James Sr/Ruth Matson
B10A   JAMES M -B11- (E12Ba,E16Bb,
                C12Aaf,C12Baf,C12Eaf)
B10Aa   Branson Elizabeth (E12B,C12Bam)
B10Aaf Branson John 2nd (E11A)

B10Ab   Branson Ruth (E16B)
B10Abf   Branson John 3rd (E12A)
B10Abm   Dillard Sarah (E12Aa)
B10B   ELIZABETH (D16Fb)
B10Ba   Shockley Richard (D16F)
B10Baf   Shockley Isaiah (D14D,C11Aaf,
                          C11Daf,C11Faf)
B10Bam   Young Ruth (D14Da,C11Aam,
                          C11Dam,C11Fam)
B10C   SUSAN (C11Ba,C36Cam))
B10Ca   Cox Reuben B (C11B)
B10Caf   Cocks(Cox) William (C10A,D16Gaf,
                          D16Iaf)
B10Cam   Dillard Mary (C10Aa,D16Gam,
                          D16Iam)
B10D   WILLIAM BURLEY -F34- (C15Caf)
B10Da   unknown
B10E   SARAH MANERVA
B10F   MARY ELVIRA (C15Ebm,C27Aa)
B10Fa   Cooper Burton (C15Ebf,C27A)
B10G   JOSEPH MATSON
B10Ga   — Nancy
B10H   MARY CLARA

[B-11]   BURGESS B10A
    James M/Elizabeth Branson
B11A   ELIZABETH M (D20Ia)
B11Aa   Shockley Lunsford L.L. -B12-
                          (D20I)
B11Aaf   Shockley Thomas (D16D)
B11Aam   David Elizabeth (D16Da)
B11B   JOHN W -B13- (C12Ba,B72Faf)
B11Ba   Cox Rutha (C12B)
B11Baf   Cox Joshua —C12- (C11A,D16Ea,
                          B11Caf)
B11Bam   Shockley Sarah (D16E,C11Aa,
                          B11Cam)
B11C   MARY ANN (C12Aa)
B11Ca   Cox Andrew Jackson (C12A,C17Aa)
B11Caf   Cox Joshua —C12- (C11A,D16Ea,
                          B11Baf)
B11Cam   Shockley Sarah (D16E,C11Aa,
                          B11Bam)
B11D   VICIE

B11Da   McKay Jack -B14-
B11E   THOMAS ERWIN -B15-
B11Ea   Mahoney Nancy Jane
B11F   ANDREW J
    (2)Ruth Branson
B11G   SUSAN F
B11H   PERRY A
B11I   BERT
B11J   WILLIAM BURTON -B55-
         B11Ja Howard Minerva Jane

[B-12]   SHOCKLEY B11Aa-
    Lunsford/Elizabeth M Burgess
B12A   MARTHA A
B12Aa   Korn Charles -B16-
B12B   NEVADA P
B12Ba   Korn James -B17-
B12C   MINERVA
B12D   ANDREW JAMES
B12E   MARY E
B12F   VICTORIA

[B-13]   BURGESS B11B
    John W/Rutha Cox
B13A   THOMAS -B18-
B13Aa   Sparlin Elma
B13B   MATILDA JANE
B13C   WILLIAM
B13Ca   Heston Lula S
B13D   DUDLY
B13E   GEORGE WASHINGTON -B19- (B72Fa)
B13Ea   Osborn Cora Evaline (B72F)
B13Eaf   Osborn Thomas (B71J,B81Aa)
B13Eam   Gale Evaline (B81A,B71Ja)
B13Eb   LaSalle Enola
B13F   JOHN
B13Fa   Compton Cordia
B13G   MARY
B13Ga   Jones Benjamin
B13H   CHARLES
B13Ha   Moone Belle
B13I   CART
B13Ia   Adkins Wilda
B13J   FRANK

B13Ja Sullivan Mary
B13K   JAMES
B13Ka Nichols Maggie
B13L   ALFRED
B13La Nichols Iva
B13M   MARTIN

[B-14] MCKAY B11Da
   Jack/Vicie Burgess
B14A   CORA
B14B   GEORGE
B14C   DUNCAN
B14D   JOHN
B14E   JASPER

[B-15] BURGESS B11E
   Thomas Erwin/Nancy Jane Mahoney
B15A   ORLANDO RANSOM
B15Aa Thompson Mariah
B15B   PHOEBE ELIZABETH
B15Ba Green John Francis -B20-
B15C   EMMA ALVARDA
B15Ca Siddens William -B21-
B15D   WILLIAM WALTER
B15E   CORA ANNIS
B15Ea Good George Ulysses -B22-
B15F   GEORGE ERWIN -B23-
B15Fa Rhodes Mary
B15Fb Spessard Blanche
B15G   FLORA JANE
B15Ga Redd Charles E -B24-
B15H   JAMES B
B15I   PERRY ANDREW -B25-
B15Ia Beard Lorena
B15Iaf Beard George W
B15Ib Prescott Avaline
B15J   MARTHA ALMINA
B15Ja DeWhitt William Willard -B26-

[B-16] KORN B12Aa
   Charles/Martha A Shockley
B16A   WALTER L
B16Aa Todd Roxie
B16B   PRUDA N

B16C   EDNA L
B16Ca Garrett George -B27-
B16D   ROBERT WADE
B16Da Etter Uva

[B-17] KORN B12Ba
   James/Nevada P Shockley
B17A   ANNA
B17B   HOMER

[B-18] BURGESS B13A
   Thomas/Elma Sparlin
B18A   JESSE
B18B   JAMES ARTHUR -B28-
B18Ba Boatright Ada

[B-19] BURGESS B13E
   George Washington/Cora E Osborn)
B19A   CLARENCE PERRY -B29- (A18Ba)
B19Aa Noble Helen L (A18B)
B19Aaf Noble Henry Orville (A17E)
B19Aam Maynard Lulie E (A17Ea)
B19Ab Turney Cora Louise
B19B   MABEL
B19C   ALBERT CARL Sr -B30-
B19Ca Briswalter Helen
B19Caf Briswalter John
B19Cam — Myrtle
B19Cb Brown Lera
B19D   CLYDE CECIL -B31-
B19Da DeWitt Ines
B19Db Weatherstone Donnie
B19E   RAY ELMER -B32- (B90Aa)
B19Ea Alexander Elizabeth (B90A))
B19Eaf Alexander Eben (B89A,B96Aa)
B19Eam Blanton Hattie P (B96A,B89Aa)
B19F   ROY ARTHUR (B69Ca)
B19Fa Hartman Helen Viola (B69C)
B19Faf Hartman Daniel H (B62F,B68Aa)
B19Fam Girton Jessie S (B68A,B62Fa)
B19G   ETHEL MAY (A45Aa)
B19Ga Fillingham Ira W -B33- (A45A))
B19Gaf Fillingham Samuel Rufus (A44A)
B19Gam Jones Pearl Anne (A44Aa)

SIBLING GROUP B

[B-20] GREEN B15Ba
John Francis/Phoebe E. Burgess
B20A JOHN ERWIN
B20B VESTA ALVERDA
B20C VERNA J

[B-21] SIDDENS B15Ca
William/Emma Alverda Burgess
B21A CHARLES EDGAR
B21Aa Whitman Allie Katherine
B21B LOLA ELIZABETH
B21Ba Lainhart Wilbert Daniel
B21C RALPH LELAND
B21Ca Lucas Alpha May
B21D SYLVANIA MALINDA
B21E GOLDA J
B21Ea Ross Thorton Delbert
B21F RETHA LENORA
B21Fa Murphy Thomas Dale

[B-22] GOOD B15Ea
George Ulysses/Cora Annis Burgess
B22A ROY ELVIS -B34-
B22Aa Couch Dora May
B22B WILLIAM RAY
B22Ba Anderson Nellie
B22C THOMAS WADE -B35-
B22Ca White Edgarda Irene
B22D JOHN EARL -B36-
B22Da Wolever Hazel
B22E PAUL WOODSON
B22Ea Bollinger Mary Ellen
B22F ORAN D -B37-
B22Fa Wisdom Elizabeth Larue
B22G HERBERT ULYSSES
B22Ga Nelson Elsie Marie
B22H RUBY MARIE
B22Ha Berry John Allen
B22I REVA BERTHENE
B22Ia Newton Merle Arthur

[B-23] BURGESS B15F
George Erwin/Mary Rhodes
B23A VILSIE MARIE
B23Aa Teague Harry W
B23B JEWELL VEY

[B-24] REDD B15Ga
Charles E/Flora Jane Burgess
B24A CHARLES Jr
B24B GEORGE WILLIAM
B24C OLAND DORSEL
B24D LEE THOMAS
B24Da King Frances
B24E ELIZABETH NARCISSA
B24F ANNIS ALMINA
B24Fa Neil Leroy

[B-25] BURGESS B15I
Perry Andrew/Lorena Beard
B25A HERSHEL GLENN
B25B THOMAS ERWIN
B25C MILDRED ELIZABETH
B25D MARY KATHLEEN

[B-26] DeWHITT B15Ja
William Willard/Martha A Burgess
B26A LaFAYE (See revision
B26Aa Elliot D Vol.II)
B26B LORETTA
B26Ba Berry George Linton
B26C WILLARD ELMO
B26Ca W— Dorothy
B26D DAVETTA ELOISE
B26E WILLIAM CLEDITH
B26Ea Kelton Dana Jean
B26F WILLEMA AUREL
B26G DELMAR
B26Ga — Gertrude Mrs

[B-27] GARRETT B16Ca
George/Edna L Korn
B27A JUANITA
B27B LELAND
B27C LEDFROW

[B-28] BURGESS B18B
James Arthur/Ada Boatright
B28A   ELMA
B28B   EDNA
B28C   THOMAS
B28D   FRED M
B28Da Williams Minnie
B28E   EVERETTE
B28F   ARTHUR

[B-29] BURGESS B19A
Clarence Perry/Helen L Noble
B29A   ESTHER
B29Aa Poppell Edgar Broward
B29B   MARGARET ELIZABETH
B29Ba Wise Anthony John Jr -B38-
B29Bb Poppell Calvin
B29C   CORA LOUISE
B29Ca Willey Lawrence -B39-

[B-30] BURGESS B19C
Albert Carl Sr/Helen Briswalter
B30A   MARJORIE LEE
B30Aa Krause Floyd -B40-
B30B   MARY PATRICIA
B30Ba Davis William Weaver Jr -B41-
B30C   ALBERT CARL Jr -B42-
B30Ca Hodges Kerry Lee

[B-31] BURGESS B19D
Clyde Cecil/Ines DeWitt
B31A   ROBERT E -B43-
B31Aa Cleeton Wilma June

[B-32] BURGESS B19E
Ray Elmer/Elizabeth Alexander
B32A   MARGARET LOUISE
B32Aa Logan George Lyons -B44-
B32Ab Smitherman G Scott
B32B   GEORGE MILTON -B45-
B32Ba Carruthers Elayne

[B-33] FILLINGHAM A45A
Ira Wallace/Ethel May Burgess
B33A   BARBARA JEAN
B33Aa Cooper Charles Thomas -B45-

[B-34] Good B22A
Roy Elvis/Dora May Couch
B34A   LOREN
B34B   CLAUDE

[B-35] GOOD B22C
Thomas Wade/Edgarda Irene White
B35A   LAWRENCE
B35B   FRANCIS

[B-36] GOOD B22D
John Earl/Hazel Wolever
B36A   DALE
B36B   DONALD
B36C   LLOYD

[B-37] GOOD B22F
Oran D/Elizabeth Larue Wisdom
B37A   FRED

[B-38] WISE B29Ba
Anthony John Jr/Margaret E Burgess
B38A   ANTHONY JOHN III -B47-
B38Aa Dupnak Linda
B38Aaf Dupnak Michael
B38B   PATRICIA ELIZABETH
B38Ba Bazemore William Donald -B48-
B38Baf Bazemore Lamar Halley

[B-39] WILLEY B29Ca
Lawrence/Cora Louise Burgess
B39A   HELEN CANDACE
B39Aa Bradley James Harrison -B49-
B39B   LAWRENCE EDGAR
B39Ba Boyd Cynthia Marie

[B-40] KRAUSE B30Aa
Floyd/Marjorie Lee Burgess
B40A   CHERL ANN

B40Aa   Morris Lawrence M -B50-
B40B   BRUCE HARTON
B40Ba   Dunn Betty Jean

[B-41] DAVIS B30Ba
    William W Jr/Mary Patricia Burgess
B41A   WILLIAM JEFFREY
B41B   JANET LOUIS
B41Ba   VanBeekum John Rodney

[B-42] BURGESS B30C
    Albert Carl Jr/Karry Lee Hodges
B42A   JULIA LYN
B42Aa   Yaryan Malcolm -B51-
B42B   LORIA ANN
B42Ba   Wilcox Steven
B42C   BRIAN DAVID
B42D   BRADLEY CARL

[B-43] BURGESS B31A
    Robert E/Wilma June Cleeton
B43A   JACKI SUE
B43Aa   Witt Ronald
B43B   CINDY LEE
B43C   ROBIN ANN
B43Ca   Pruitt Robert A
B43D   MARK ROBERT

[B-44] LOGAN B32Aa
    George Lyons/Margaret Louise Burgess
B44A   KATHERINE
B44Aa   Abbiatti Michael -B52-
B44B   LAWRENCE LYONS
B44Ba   Grady Mary Elizabeth
B44C   THOMAS BURGESS

[B-45] BURGESS B32B
    George Milton/Elayne Carruthers
B45A   ROGER GLENN -B53-
B45Aa   Williamson Kay
B45B   BARBARA
B45Ba   Gwatney Donnie -B54-

[B-46] COOPER B33Aa
    Charles Thompson/Barbara Fillingham
B46A   CHARLES SCOTT
B46B   SUSAN BARBARA

[B-47] WISE B38A
    Anthony John III/Linda Dupnak
B47A   MICHAEL ANTHONY
B47B   VALERIE
B47C   GRETCHEN NICOLE PATRICIA
B47D   CLAIRE

[B-48] BAZEMORE B38Ba.
    William Donald/Patricia E Wise
B48A   JOHN LAMAR
B48B   WILLIAM GREGORY

[B-49] BRADLEY B39Aa
    James Harrispn/Helen Candice Willey
B49A   MELANIE HOPE
B49B   JAMES HARRISON JR

[B-50] MORRIS B40Aa
    Lawrence M/Cherl Ann Krause
B50A   RICHARD

[B-51] YARYAN B42Aa
    Malcolm/Julia Lyn Burgess
B51A   AMY LYN

[B-52] ABBIATTI B44Aa
    Michael/Katherine Logan
B52A   SHELLY LYNN
B52B   TODD MICHAEL

[B-53] BURGESS B45A
    Roger Glenn/Kay Williamson
B53A   JOSHUA RANDALL
B53B   MEGAN ELIZABETH
B53C   BRET MICHAEL

[B-54] GWATNEY B45Ba
    Donnie/Barbara Burgess
B54A   ERIC

SIBLING GROUP B

[B-55] BURGESS B11J
    William Burton/Minerva Jane Howard
B55A   ETHEL ADELLA

[B-56] LAZARUS unknown
    unknown/unknown
B56A   SAMUEL Sr -B57-
B56Aa unknown

[B-57] LAZARUS B56A
    Samuel Sr/unknown
B57A   SAMUEL Jr -B58-
B57Aa Krum Rebecca

[B-58] LAZARUS B57A
    Samuel Jr/Rebecca Krum
B58A   EMANUEL -B59-
B58Aa Heimbach Emma

[B-59] LAZARUS B58A
    Emanuel/Emma Heimbach
B59A   LYDIA REBECCA (B61Da)
B59Aa Hartman William Alfred (B61D)

[B-60] HARTMAN unknown
    unknown/unknown
B60A   JACOB -B61-
B60Aa Krum Lydia

[B-61] HARTMAN B60A
    Jacob/Lydia Krum
B61A   WELLINGTON
B61B   LEANDER
B61C   ISAAC
B61D   WILLIAM ALFRED -B62- (B59Aa)
B61Da Lazarus Lydia Rebecca (B59A)

[B-62] HARTMAN B61D
    Alfred/Lydia Rebecca Lazarus
B62A   LLOYD FRANKLIN
B62Aa Doty Pearl
B62B   STELLA VIOLA
B62Ba Miller A Britton
B62C   EMANUEL WELLINGTON

B62Ca Clayton Martha
B62D   WILLIAM ALFRED 2nd
B62Da Fortner Mildred
B62E   CATHERINE
B62F   DANIEL -B69- (B68Aa,B19Faf)
B62Fa Girton Jessie (B68A,B19Fam)

[B-63] FISHER unknown
    unknown/unknown
B63A   JACOB -B64-
B63Aa Clark Susan

[B-64] FISHER B63A
    Jacob/Susan Clark
B64A   EMMA DELL (B67Aa)
B64Aa Girton Alfred Franklin (B67A)

[B-65] GIRTON unknown
    unknown/unknown
B65A   JOHN K -B66-
B65Aa — Margaret

[B-66] GIRTON B65A
    John K/Margaret —
B66A   WILLIAM G -B67-
B66Aa Kline Elizabeth

[B-67] GIRTON B66A
    William G/Elizabeth Kline
B67A   ALFRED F -B68- (B64Aa)
B67Aa Fisher Emma Dell (B64A)

[B-68] GIRTON B67A
    Alfred F/Emma Dell Fisher
B68A   JESSIE S (B62Fa,B19Fam)
B68Aa Hartman Daniel (B62F,B19Faf)

[B-69] HARTMAN B62F
    Daniel/Jessie Girton
B69A   HARRY FRANKLIN -B73-
B69Aa Gregory Cornelia
B69Aaf Gregory Thomas W
B69B   RUTH REBECCA
B69Ba Lynch Peter Elmer -B74-

B69C   HELEN VIOLA (B19Fa)
B69Ca Burgess Roy Arthur (B19F)

[B-70] OSBORN unknown
  unknown/unknown
B70A   WILLIAM -B71- (B81Aaf)
B70Aa Tone Margaret

[B-71] OSBORN B70A
  William/Margaret Tone
B71J   THOMAS -B72- (B81Aa,B13Eaf)
B71Ja Gates Evaline(B81A,B13Eam)

[B-72] OSBORN B71J
  Thomas/Evaline Gates
B72A   WINFIELD SCOTT
B72B   FRANCES AMELIA
B72C   WILLIS D -A82-
B72Ca — Mary J
B72D   AGNES E
B72E   CHARLES T
B72F   CORA EVALINE (B13Ea)
B72Fa Burgess George W (B13E)
B72Faf Burgess John W (B11B,C12Ba)
B72Fam Cox Rutha (C12B,B11Ba)
B72G   ALICE C

[B-73] HARTMAN B69A
  Harry Franklin/Cornelia Gregory
B73A   DANIEL HARRISON
B73B   JULIA NALLE
B73Ba Hancock George 2nd -B75-

[B-74] LYNCH B69Ba
  Peter Elmer/Ruth Rebecca Hartman
B74A   HELEN ELISABETH
B74Aa Becker George Walter -B76-
B74B   PETER ELMER Jr -B77-
B74Ba Leden Marjorie Jane

[B-75] HANCOCK B73Ba
  George 2nd/Julia Nalle Hartman
B75A   GEORGE GRAY

B75B   ELIZABETH CORNELIA

[B-76] BECKER B74Aa
  George Walter/Helen Elisabeth Lynch
B76A   LINDA JANE
B76Aa Girardin David
B76B   JUNE MARIE
B76Ba Harmon Richard Clark
B76Baf Harmon Windell
B76Bam Twitchell Loraine

[B-77] LYNCH B74B
  Peter Elmer Jr/Marjorie J Leden
B77A   PETER GREGORY -B78-
B77Aa Duncan Lucy Merrill
B77Ab Korte Patricia Ann
B77B   RICHARD THOMAS

[B-78] LYNCH B77A
  Peter Gregory/Patricia Ann Korte
B78A   SHAUN PETER
B78B   MEGAN BRIANNE

[B-80] GATES unknown
  unknown/unknown
B80A   WILLIAM -B81-
B80Aa — Lydia

[B-81] GATES B80A
  William/Lydia —
B81A   EVALINE (B71Ja,B13Eam)
B81Aa Osborn Thomas (B71J,B13Eaf)
B81Aaf Osborn William (B70A)

[B-86] ALEXANDER unknown
  unknown/unknown
B86A   JOHN Sr -B87-
B86Aa unknown

[B-87] ALEXANDER B86A
  John Sr/unknown
B87A   JOHN Jr -B88
B87Aa Ragland Elizabeth

SIBLING GROUP B

[B-88] ALEXANDER B87A
  John Jr/Elizabeth Ragland
B88A   CICERO −B89− (B92Aa)
B88Aa McBride Eliza (B92A)

[B-89] ALEXANDER B88A
  Cicero/Eliza McBride
B89A   EBEN M −B90− (B96Aa,B19Eaf)
B89Aa Blanton Hattie (B96A,B19Eam)

[B-90] ALEXANDER B89A
  Eben M/Hattie Blanton
B90A   ELIZABETH (B19Ea)
B90Aa Burgess Ray Elmer (B19E)

[B-91] McBRIDE unknown
  unknown/unknown
B91A   EBENEZER −B92−
B91Aa Snell Julia

[B-92] McBRIDE B91A
  Ebenezer/Julia Snell
B92A   ELIZA (B88Aa)
B92Aa Alexander Cicero (B88A)

[B-93] BLANTON unknown
  unknown/unknown
B93A   THOMPSON −B94−
B93Aa — Elizabeth

[B-94] BLANTON B93A
  Thompson/Elizabeth —
B94A   THOMAS −B95−
B94Aa McCrary Nancy

[B-95] BLANTON B94A
  Thomas/Nancy McCrary
B95A   BENJAMIN −B96−
B95Aa Young Harriett

[B-96] BLANTON B95A
  Benjamin/Harriett Young
B96A   HATTIE (B89Aa,B19Eam)
B96Aa Alexander Eben (B89A,B19Eaf)

[B-97] WASHINGTON unknown
  unknown/unknown
B97A   AUGUSTINE −B98−
B97Aa Butler Jane
B97Ab Ball Mary
B97Abf Ball Joseph Col
B97Abm Johnson Mary

[B-98] WASHINGTON B97A
  Augustine/Jane Butler
B98A   GEORGE
B98Aa Dandridge Martha
B98B   ELIZABETH
B98C   SAMUEL
B98D   JOHN AUGUSTINE
B98Da Bushrod Hannah
B98E   CHARLES −B99−
B98Ea Champs Mildred
B98F   MILDRED

[B-99] WASHINGTON B98E
  Charles/Champs Mildred
B99A   FRANCES
B99Aa Ball Burgess
B99Aaf Ball Jeduthun (B6Da)
B99Aam Burgess Elizabeth (B6D)

[C-10] COX(COCKS) unknown
  unknown/unknown
C10A   WILLIAM —C11— (B10Caf,D16Gaf,
                        D16Iaf)
C10Aa   Dillard Mary (B10Cam,D16Gam,
                        D16Iam)
C10Aaf Dillard Thomas

[C-11] COX C10A
  William/Mary Dillard
C11A   JOSHUA —C12— (D16Ea,B11Baf,
                        B11Caf)
C11Aa   Shockley Sarah (D16E,B11Baf,
                        B11Cam)
C11Aaf Shockley Isaiah (D14D,B10Baf,
                        C11Daf,C11Faf)
C11Aam Young Ruth (D14Da,B10Bam,C11Dam,
                        C11Fam)
C11Ab   McMatt Mary
C11B   REUBEN —C13— (B10Ca,C36Caf)
C11Ba   Burgess Susan (B10C,C36Cam)
C11Bb   Eads Rachel
C11C   THOMAS
C11D   ANDREW —C14— (D16Ia,Z41Daf)
C11Da   Shockley Mary Ann (D16I)
C11Daf Shockley Isaiah (D14D,B10Baf,
                        C11Aaf,C11Faf)
C11Dam Young Ruth (D14Da,B10Bam,C11Aam,
                        C11Fam)
C11E   HENRY
C11F   REBECCA (D16Ga)
C11Fa   Shockley Uriah (D16G,R26Baf,
                        R26Eaf)
C11Faf Shockley Isaiah (D14D,B10Baf,
                        C11Aaf,C11Daf)
C11Fam Young Ruth (D14Da,B10Bam,C11Aam,
                        C11Dam)
C11G   WILLIAM —C15— (F34Aaf)
C11Ga   Barbarick Margaret (F34Aam)
C11Gaf Barbarick Frederick
C11Gam Walter Elizabeth
C11Gb   Campbell Precious
C11Gc   Rogers Betsy
C11Gd   Wallace Elizabeth
C11Ge   Stanton Julia

C11H   JOHN

[C-12] COX C11A
  Joshua/Sarah Shockley
C12A   ANDREW JACKSON —C16— B11Ca,C17Ab
C12Aa   Burgess Mary Ann M (B11C)
C12Aaf Burgess James M (B10A,E12Ba,
                        E16Bb,C12Baf)
C12Aam Branson Elizabeth (E12B,B10Aa
                        C12Bam)
C12Ab   Cox Mary Ann (C17A)
C12B   RUTHA (B11Ba,B72Fam)
C12Ba   Burgess John W (B11B,B72Faf)
C12Baf Burgess James M (B10A,E12Ba,
                        E16Bb,C12Aaf)
C12Bam Branson Elizabeth (E12B,B10Aa,
                        C12Aam)
C12C   WILLIAM RAY
C12D   MATILDA
C12E   JAMES
C12F   JOHN
C12G   JACOB
      (2)Mary McMatt
C12H   JASPER
C12Ha   Denham Virginia Mrs
C12I   GEORGE W
C12Ia   Nelson Nancy
C12J   HENRY
C12Ja   Cross Martha A
C12K   JOSHUA

[C-13] COX C11B
  Reuben/Susan Burgess
C13A   JOSHUA A
C13Aa   — Elizabeth
C13B   MARY ANN
C13Ba   West Balis
C13C   BURTON COOPER —C26—
C13Ca   Holloman Fruza
C13D   SARAH MALINDA (C36Ca)
C13Da   Owsley Emanuel (C36C)
C13E   ELVIRA M (E17Ga)
C13Ea   Branson Thomas (E17G)
C13F   SYDRIE—

C13Fa Scott —
C13G   HENRY I
C13Ga Morrow Frances Ann
   (2)Rachel Eads
C13H   RACHEL ELIZABETH
C13I   BATHSHEBA
C13Ia Matthews Samuel J
C13J   HANNAH
C13Ja Phelps John
C13K   LOUISE V
C13L   ZACHARIAH T
C13M   WINFIELD SCOTT
C13N   BENJAMIN F
C13O   MARTHA JANE (C28Gb)
C13Oa Cooper Thomas McQuin (C28G)
C13P   LYDIA A
C13Pa Scott —

[G-14] COX C11D
   Andrew/Mary Ann Shockley
C14A   SUSAN
C14B   SARAH
C14C   ALEXANDER
C14D   JOSHUA —C17— (Z41Da)
C14Da Green Mary Jane (Z41D)
C14Daf Green Elisha (Z40A)
C14E   MARY
C14F   WILLIAM
C14G   JASPER
C14H   MANERVA
C14I   NELLY SEMANTHA

[G-15] COX C11G
   William/Margaret Barbarick
C15A   MARTHA
C15Aa McMillian John M
C15B   LUCY
C15C   MARY (F34Aa)
C15Ca Burgess John (F34A)
C15Caf Burgess William Burley (B10D)
C15D   MALINDA
C15Da Owsley Crawford (C15Ga)
C15E   THOMAS JEFFERSON —C32— (C28Ha)
C15Ea Anderson Elizabeth

C15Eb Cooper Elizabeth Helen (C28H)
C15Ebf Cooper Burton (C27A,B10Fa)
C15Ebm Burgess Mary Elvira (B10F,C27Aa)
C15F   SUSANNAH
C15Fa Walker Thomas
C15G   CATHERINE
C15Ga Owsley Crawford (C15Da)
C15H   CHRISTOPHER
C15Ha Burgess Mary
C15I   LaFAYETTE

[G-16] COX C12A
   Andrew Jackson/Mary Ann Burgess
C16A   SARAH ELIZABETH
C16Aa Leverich George Thomas
C16B   JOHN E
C16Ba Gilstrap Tabitha
C16C   MARTHA ANNIS
C16Ca Gilstrap William Henry —C18—
C16Caf Gilstrap Peter B
C16D   PRESTON
C16E   DEALA
C16Ea Hamilton Frank
C16F   ROBERT BRADFORD H
C16Fa Krill Rose E
C16G   RACHEL
C16Ga McKee Albert
   (2)Mary Ann Cox
C16H   ESTHER SULA
C16Ha Willard Ebbin Chester —C19—

[G-17] COX C14D
   Joshua/Mary Jane Green
C17A   MARY ANN (C12Ab)
C17Aa Weathers —
C17Ab Cox Andrew Jackson (C12A,B11Ca)
C17B   ELIZABETH ANN
C17C   MARTHA ELLEN
C17D   WILLIAM DILLARD
C17E   JEFFERSON DAVIS —C40—
C17Ea Lamar Syrilda Alamae
C17Eaf Lamar Isham
C17Eam McFarlamd Rebecca

211

[C-18] GILSTRAP C16Ca
  William Henry/Martha Annie Cox
C18A   WILBERT A
C18Aa Hawes Emma Mae
C18B   ALONZO
C18Ba Hawes Cora Eva
C18C   LEWIS
C18Ca Boyle Edith
C18D   MAUDE M
C18E   MARY ELMA
C18Ea Hawes David E
C18F   GERTRUDE L
C18Fa Cogbill James Fred −C20−
C18G   EDITH RAY
C18H   CLARENCE
C18I   EDNA LORENE
C18Ia Griffin Henry Coleman

[C-19] WILLARD C16Ha
  Ebbin Chester/Esther Sula Cox
C19A   ELNORA LOUISE
C19B   ROBERT CHESTER
C19C   RUTHITA
C19D   BETTY JEAN
C19Da Winn Gordon Dail −C21−

[C-20] COGBILL C18Fa
  James Fred/Gertrude L Gilstrap
C20A   INA LOIS
C20Aa Edmunds Jesse Louis −C22−
C20Ab Bowers Russell −C23−
C20B   LLOYD CLAYTON −C24−
C20Ba Gojeski Carolyn Anna L
C20C   JAMES QUENTIN −C25−
C20Ca Gilstrap Doris
C20D   HERBERT TRACY
C20Da Smythe Mary Elma

[C-21] WINN C19Da
  Gordon Dail/Betty Jean Willard
C21A   MELODY JEAN
C21B   MARK DAIL
C21C   GORDON SCOTT

[C-22] EDMUNDS C20Aa
  Jess Louis/Ina Lois Cogbill
C22A   ETHEL LELA
C22B   DIXIE JEAN
C22C   JESSE L

[C-23] BOWERS C20Ab
  Russell/Ina Lois Cogbill
C23A   SCOTT HOWARD
C23B   ROBERT CLAYTON

[C-24] COGBILL C20B
  Lloyd Clayton/Carolyn Anna Gojeski
C24A   TRACY LLOYD
C24B   BRIAN CARL
C24C   SUSANNE HELENNA
C24D   KELLY ROSS

[C-25] COGBILL C20C
  James Quentin/Doris Gilstrap
C25A   LINDA JEAN
C25B   JAMES MARCUS
C25C   DEBORAH DAWN

[C-26] COX C13C
  Burton Cooper/Fruza Holloman
C26A   LUCINDA ELLEN (C29Da)
C26Aa Cooper James Burton (C29D)
C26Aaf Cooper John Burton (C28C)
C26Aam Burrows Susan C (C28Cb)
C26Ab Agee James Wallace
C26B   LOUISA MALINDA
C26C   THOMAS JEFFERSON
C26D   HETTY ELVIRA (F38Aam)
C26Da Nichols Abraham (F38Aaf)
C26E   MARY EMILY
C26Ea Wendt John H
C26F   LUCY JANE
C26Fa Durbin —
C26G   HANNAH ELIZABETH
C26Ga Maxwell John
C26H   ROXANNA
C26I   THEODORE B

SIBLING GROUP C

[G-27] COOPER Unknown
  unknown/unknown
C27A   BURTON -C28- (B10Fa,C15Ebf)
C27Aa Burgess Mary Elvira(B10F,C15Ebm)

[G-28] COOPER C27A
  Burton/Mary Elvira Burgess
C28A   JAMES M
C28B   WILLIAM A
C28Ba Burgess Mary E
C28C   JOHN B -C29- (C26Aaf)
C28Ca Wallace Lucy
C28Cb Burrows Susan C (C26Aam)
C28D   ROBERT WILEY
C28Da Hopkins Mercy
C28E   REBECCA
C28F   RUTH
C28G   THOMAS McCUIN (C130a)
C28Ga Matthews Elizabeth
C28Gb Cox Martha Jane (C130)
C28H   ELIZABETH H (C15Eb)
C28Ha Cox Thomas Jefferson (C15E)
C28I   ELIZA ANN
C28J   CHARLOTTE
C28Ja Duncan D.C.

[G-29] COOPER C28C
  John B/Lucy Wallace
C29A   VARDRY M.B.
C29B   WILLIAM A
C29C   MARY T (E24Ha)
C29Ca Branson Reuben S (E24H)
  (2)Susan C Burrows
C29D   JAMES BURTON -C30- (C26Aa)
C29Da Cox Lucinda Ellen (C26A)
C29E   ELIZABETH S
C29F   JOHN BURROWS
C29G   ELIZA ANN
C29Ga Leach Edward S

[G-30] COOPER C29D
  James Burton/Lucinda Ellen Cox
C30A   IRA BURTON -C31- (E63Aa)
C30Aa Carroll Mary Ellen (E63A)

C30Aaf Carroll William (E62A)
C30Aam Smith Elizabeth (E62Aa)
C30B   ODA FRANKLIN
C30C   IDA MAY
C30Ca Owens James
C30D   PETER ERNEST

[G-31] COOPER C30A
  Ira Burton/Mary Ellen Carroll
C31A   MILDRED IRENE
C31Aa Spainhour Raymond W
C31B   JAMES WILLIAM
C31Ba Cleton Dorothy Irene
C31C   LLOYD BURTON
C31Ca Mattox Betty Jane
C31D   LOIS EVELYN
C31Da Constable Billy Bruce
C31E   JEWELL ETHEL
C31Ea Foote Leslie Lloyd -C33-
C31F   CLIFFORD WALDO
C31Fa Jones Bettie Lucille
C31G   DOLORES MAE

[G-32] COX C15E
  Thomas Jefferson/Elizabeth Anderson
C32A   WESLEY
C32B   JAMES B
C32Ba — Dora B
  (2)Elizabeth Helen Cooper
C32C   THOMAS B
C32D   CHARLES

[G-33] FOOTE C31Ea
  Leslie Lloyd/Jewell Ethel Cooper
C33A   JUNE ELLEN
C33Aa King Russell

[G-34] OWSLEY(Ousley) unknown
  unknown/unknown
C34A   JOHN -C35-
C34Aa Barton Charity

213

[O-35] OWSLEY C34A
  John/Charity Barton
C35A   ROBERT —C36—
C35Aa   Miller Nancy Elizabeth
C35Aaf Miller Martin
C35Aam Giddens Elizabeth

[O-36] OWSLEY C35A
  Robert/Nancy Elizabeth Miller
C36A   HENRY A
C36Aa   Bruce Sarah E
C36B   LOUISA
C36Ba   White James
C36Bb   McCormack Enoch
C36C   EMMANUEL —C37— (C13Da)
C36Ca   Cox Sarah Malinda (C13D)
C36Caf Cox Reuben B (C11B,B10Ca)
C36Cam Burgess Susan (B10C,C11Ba)
C36Cb   Cauthon Cordelia
C36D   HANNAH
C36Da   White Ephraim E
C36E   MARTIN MILLER
C36Ea   Greenstreet Jane S
C36F   WILLIAM
C36Fa   Crider Mary Ann
C36G   ELIJAH BUNTON
C36Ga   Williams Elizabeth
C36H   DAVID A
C36Ha   Brall Jamima Ann
C36I   ELIAS H
C36Ia   Anderson Delila

[O-37] OWSLEY C36C
  Emmanuel/Sarah Malinda Cox
C37A   JAMES IRVING
C37Aa   Norman Mary J
C37B   WILLIAM BURTON
C37Ba   Walker Pauline
C37Bb   Brooks Mary A
C37C   ROBERT RAINEY —C38—
C37Ca   Parks Sindrella

C37Cb   Hall Mary Emily
C37Cbf Hall Benjamin E
C37Cbm Parrish Temperance
C37D   REUBEN
C37Da   — Emma
C37E   NANCY ELIZABETH
C37Ea   Stark James E
C37Eb   Brown William
C37F   LECONSUL
C37Fa   Parks Amanda
C37Fb   Wright Sarah E
C37G   SARAH FRANCES
C37Ga   Carley John
C37H   ELIJAH BUNTON
C37Ha   Stark Virginia
C37I   JOHN WHITELEY
C37Ia   Lewis Emma Alice
C37J   MARTHA A
C37Ja   Jackson Jesse L
C37K   MARY SUSAN
C37Ka   McCarty Lee
C37L   GEORGE A
C37La   — Flora J
C37M   EMMA E
C37Ma   Erickson Edward

[O-38] OWSLEY C37C
  Robert Rainey/Sindrella Parks
C38A   NORA JANE
C38B   DAVID RAY
C38Ba   Salley Zadie
C38C   ELIHU (Hugh) —C39—
C38Ca   Hartnett Eva Clare
C38Caf Hartnett Thomas Francis
C38Cam Davis Mary Elizabeth
C38D   GEORGE WASHINGTON
C38Da   Eidson Grace
C38E   NELLIE MAY
C38Ea   Butcher Thomas
C38F   HOMER ALLEN
C38Fa   Dollarhide Grace

[C-39] OWSLEY C38C
   Elihu/Eva Clare Hartnett
C39A   DEE KEMP
C39Aa DeJarnette Marguerite
C39Aaf DeJarnette Grover B
C39Aam Gentry R Hazel
C39B   ROBERT HOYT
C39Ba Lafaver Margaret B
C39C   ILA MARY
C39D   LETA MAY
C39Da Laird Jack I
C39E   ETHEL FERN
C39Ea Wallen Jack
C39F   RUBY CLARE
C39Fa Johnson Don
C39G   MERLE INOLEE
C39Ga Sundwall Billy H

[C-40] COX C17E
   Jefferson Davis/Syrilda A Lamar
C40A   JAMES DILLARD -C41-
C40Aa Beymer Nellie Roe
C40Aaf Beymer Archie
C40Aam Glasby Minnie Bell

[C-41] COX C40A
   James Dillard/Nellie Roe Beymer
C41A   JUNIOR JAY
C41Aa Chew Betty Mae
C41Aaf Chew Roy Jackson
C41Aam Flinn Nancy Mary

[C-42] COX C41A
   Junior Jay/Betty Mae Chew
C42A   BETTY JEAN
C42Aa Baker Jackie Clyde

[D-10] SHOCKLEY unknown
  unknown/unknown
D10A RICHARD 1st −D11−
D10Aa Boyden Ann

[D-11] SHOCKLEY D10A
  Richard 1st/Ann Boyden
D11A RICHARD Jr
D11Aa — Elizabeth
D11B ELENOR
D11C ELIZABETH
D11D WILLIAM
D11Da — Sarah
D11E DAVID −D12−
D11Ea — Grace
D11Eb Rathbone Mary
D11F MARY
D11G JOHN −D13−
D11Ga — Sarah

[D-12] SHOCKLEY D11E
  David/Grace —
D12A JOHN
D12B DAVID Jr
D12C AGNES
D12Ca Engram Jacob
D12D JAMES
D12Da — Margaret
D12E WILLIAM
D12F MARY
D12G SOLLOMON
D12H SARAH
D12I BENJAMIN
D12J ISAAC
    (2)Mary Rathbone
D12K RATHBONE LOVE
D12L RATHBONE EMMELY

[D-13] SHOCKLEY D11G
  John/Sarah —
D13A ISAAC
D13B BENJAMIN
D13C MARY
D13D JONATHAN

D13E RICHARD 2nd −D14−
D13Ea — Elizabeth
D13F JOHN
D13Fa — Cathran
D13G SOLOMON
D13H SARAH
D13Ha Christopher —

[D-14] SHOCKLEY D13E
  Richard 2nd/Elizabeth —
D14A THOMAS
D14B RICHARD 3rd −D15−
D14Ba unknown
D14C ISOM (ISHAM)
D14D ISAIAH −D16−(B10Baf,C11Aaf,
                    C11Daf,C11Faf)
D14Da Young Ruth (B10Bam,C11Aam,
          C11Dam,C11Fam)
D14E WILSON
D14F MEREDITH Sr −D17−(G11Iaf,T13Laf)
D14Fa Worrell Sarah (G11Iam,T13Lam)
D14G WILLIAM
D14H ELIZABETH
D14Ha Shockley Thomas −D58−

[D-15] SHOCKLEY D14B
  Richard 3rd/unknown
D15A SARAH
D15Aa Burton William
D15B OWEN −D18−
D15Ba Briggs Elizabeth
D15C MARTHA (S10Aa,Q32Cam,Z13Bam)
D15Ca Briggs James Y (S10A,Q32Caf,
                    Z13Baf)

[D-16] SHOCKLEY D14D
  Isaiah/Ruth Young
D16A WILLIAM
D16Aa Crawley Mary
D16B NELLY
D16Ba Briggs John
D16C SAMUEL −D19−
D16Ca — Darcus
D16D THOMAS J −D20− (B11Aaf)

D16Da   David Elizabeth (B11Aam)
D16E   SARAH (C11Aa,B11Bam,B11Cam)
D16Ea   Cox Joshua —C12— (C11A,B11Baf,
                              C11Caf)
D16F   RICHARD —D21— (B10Ba)
D16Fa   Briggs Elizabeth
D16Fb   Burgess Elizabeth (B10B)
D16G   URIAH —D22—(C11Fa,R26Baf,R26Eaf)
D16Ga   Cox Rebecca (C11F)
D16Gaf Cox (Cocks)William (C10A,B10Caf)
D16Gam Branson Mary (C10Aa,B10Cam)
D16Gb   Barbarick Matilda(R26Bam,R26Eam)
D16Gbf Barbarick Fred
D16H   ISAIAH Jr (E48Gb)
D16Ha   Lore Manerva (E48G)
D16Hb   Campbell Malinda
D16I   MARY ANN (C11Da)
D16Ia   Cox Andrew (C11D,Z41Daf)
D16Iaf Cox(Cocks) William (C10A,B10Caf)
D16Iam Dillard Mary (C10Aa,B10Cam)
D16J   RUTHA S (D74Aa)
D16Ja   David Lewis (D74A)
D16Jaf David Michael Edward (D73A)
D16Jam unknown (D73Aa)
D16K   RYE

[D-17] SHOCKLEY D14F
    Meredith Sr/Sarah Worrell
D17A   JOHN —D23—
D17Aa   — Phebe
D17B   JAMES
D17Ba   Ogle Polly
D17C   ESAU
D17Ca   Farmer Elizabeth
D17D   AMOS —D24—
D17Da   Franklin Jemima
D17E   NANCY
D17Ea   Farmer John
D17F   WILLIAM R —D25— (G11Ia,G11Daf,
                              Y19Gaf,Y19Iaf)
D17Fa   Copeland Rebecca (G11I)
D17Faf Copeland William M Sr (G10A)
            D25Gaf,P11Eaf,P11Iaf)

D17Fam Taff Martha (G10Aa,D25Gam,
                         (P11Eam,P11Iam)
D17Fb   — Ruth (G11Dam,Y19Gam,Y19Iam)
D17G   MEREDITH Jr —D26—
D17Ga   DeHaven Drusilla
D17H   THOMAS VINCENT —D27—
D17Ha   Crider Rachel
D17Haf Crider Daniel
D17I   WESLEY
D17Ia   Curtis Betsey
D17J   CHARLOTTE MATILDA
D17Ja   Atkins Parker —D28—
D17K   REUBEN S
D17Ka   Kinsey Elizabeth
D17L   HENRY (T13La)
D17La   Crismon Mahaly (T13L)
D17Laf Crismon Gilbert (T12A,E17Baf)

[D-18] SHOCKLEY D15B
    Owen/Elizabeth Briggs
D18A   ANDREW J
D18Aa   Atkins Sarah
D18B   MATILDA
D18Ba   Lee Owen
D18Bb   Chrisenbury Washington
D18C   MALINDA
D18Ca   Klosner John I
D18D   SAMUEL
D18Da   Huffman Jane
D18E   JAMES M. H.
D18Ea   Huffman Caroline
D18F   SARAH
D18Fa   Pryor William T
D18G   OLIVER WESLEY —D29—
D18Ga   Lewis Elizabeth Jane
D18Gb   Black Phoebe Elizabeth
D18H   NELLEY
D18Ha   Pryor John
D18I   MAHALEY
D18Ia   Pryor Robert F
D18J   RUTHA

[D-19] SHOCKLEY D16C
   Samuel/Darcus —
D19A HANNAH
D19B PETER
D19C DARCUS
D19D THOMAS J —D30—
D19Da — Catherine

[D-20] SHOCKLEY D16D
   Thomas J/Elizabeth David
D20A THOMAS Y
D20B PERRY
D20C THOMAS B
D20D ELIZABETH
D20E RUBIN
D20F FRANCIS MARION —D59—
D20Fa Palmer Sarah A
D20G JOHN
D20H NANCY
D20I LUNSFORD L.L. (B11Aa)
D20Ia Burgess Elizabeth (B11A)

[D-21] SHOCKLEY D16F
   Richard/Elizabeth Briggs
D21A HARRIETT
D21Aa Branson —
   (2)Elizabeth Burgess
D21B CAROLINE
D21C ELIZABETH
D21Ca Haynes Richard
D21D ISAIAH
D21Da Crider Rachel
D21E TENNESSEE ANN (F35Ham)
D21Ea Campbell Robert H —D85— (F35Haf)
D21F JOHN McMEIN
D21Fa Ousley Dena
D21G ELIZA J
D21Ga Owens Elija —D89—
D21H RUTH
D21Ha Carter R
D21I SARAH MANERVA

[D-22] SHOCKLEY D16G
   Uriah/(2)Matilda Barbarick
D22A ELIZABETH (R26Ea)
D22Aa Ridenhour Reuben J (R26E)
D22Aaf Ridenhour John (R25A,D22Gaf)
D22Aam Reed Elizabeth (R25Aa,D22Gam)
D22B DAVID
D22C THOMAS
D22D BARBARA
D22Da Crider David
D22E JOSHUA
D22Ea Crider Mary Jane
D22F SARAH
D22Fa Palmer Joseph
D22G ALEXANDER (R26Ba)
D22Ga Ridenhour Margaret C ((R26B)
D22Gaf Ridenhour John (R25A,D22Aaf)
D22Gam Reed Elizabeth (R25Aa,D22Aam)
D22H JOSEPH
D22I ISAIAH
D22J FREDERICK
D22K SAMUEL
   (1)Rebecca Cox
D22L REBECCA
D22La Haynes William —D81—

[D-23] SHOCKLEY D17A
   John/Phebe —
D23A CANDIS A
D23B ASBERRY
D23C MARTIN V
D23D OLIVER C
D23E AMERICA A
D23F JOHN F
D23G ORLAND

[D-24] SHOCKLEY D17D
   Amos/Jemima Franklin
D24A MARY A
D24B JOANNA R

[D-25] SHOCKLEY D17F
   William/Rebecca Copeland
D25A SERENA

D25B   JAMES H
D25C   LOUISA
D25Ca   Essman August
D25D   MARY E
D25Da   Skeen Walter -D31-
D25E   JOSEPH -D32- (J15Caf)
D25Ea   Russell Nancy (J15Cam,G25Aa)
D25Eaf Russell Levi (G29Ha)
D25Eam Copeland Martha (G29H)
   (2)Ruth —
D25F   LOTTIE
D25Fa   Felker Herman
D25Faf Felker John (G31Daf,G31Faf)
D25Fam Anderson Amanda (G31Dam,G31Fam)
D25G   NANCY (G11Da)
D25Ga   Copeland Peter (G11D)
D25Gaf Copeland William (G10A,D17Faf.
                       P11Eaf,P11Iaf)
D25Gam Taff Martha (G10Aa D17Fam,
                       P11Eam,P11Iam)
D25Gb   Breeden Abraham R (U12Ba)
D25Gbf Breeden John (U12Aaf,U12Baf)
D25H   THOMAS R-D33-(Y19Ga,J20Caf)
D25Ha   McGee Sarah Jane (Y19G,J20Cam)
D25Haf McGee John (Y13Ga,D25Iaf)
D25Ham Johnson Sarah (Y13G,D25Iam)
D25I   AMOS -D34- (Y19Ia)
D25Ia   McGee J. Ellen (Y19I)
D25Iaf McGee John (Y13Ga,D25Haf)
D25Iam Johnson Sarah (Y13G,D25Ham)

[D-26] SHOCKLEY D17G
   Meredith Jr/Drusilla DeHaven
D26A   CASWELL F
D26B   CHARLOTTE JANE
D26Ba   Pool Elisha -D35-
D26C   ELIZABETH
D26Ca   Shockley Gilbert
D26D   JULIET C
D26E   JESSE
D26F   HARRIETT AMANDA
D26Fa   Carter Hiram-D36-
D26G   BLOOMFIELD
D26H   JAMES G -D37-

D26Ha   Stockton Sarah Ann
D26Haf Stockton Joseph (D71Ea,Y40Caf)
D25Ham Travis Eliza (D71E,Y40Cam)
D26I   WILLIAM

[D-27] SHOCKLEY D17H
   Thomas Vincent/Rachel Crider
D27A   HENRY -D38-
D27Aa   Durbin Julia
D27B   SARAH
D27Ba   Durbin Samuel Sr -D39-
D27Bb   Owens Elijah
D27Bc   Jett —
D27C   CELEAH (Celia)
D27Ca   Stockton Orrisemus
D27Caf Stockton John H (D38Caf,D71Eaf)
D27Cam Caldwell L (D38Cam,D71Eam)
D27D   FRANCIS A.-D40- (D66Iaf,R13Haf)
D27Da   Matthews Amanda (D66Iam,R13Ham)
D27Daf Matthews Bartlett G (D27Gaf)
D27E   MERIDA
D27F   AMOS
D27Fa   Price Elizabeth
D27G   JAMES MONROE -D41-
D27Ga   Matthews Polly Lavinia
D27Gaf Matthews Bartlett G (D27Daf)
D27H   ELIZABETH
D27Ha   Branson John N -D42-
D27I   ANDREW JACKSON -D43-
D27Ia   Stumpf Mary Jane
D27J   THOMAS BENTON -D44-
D27Ja   Berry Lydia Campbell

[D-28] ATKINS D17Ja
   Parker/Charlotte M Shockley
D28A   CASWELL C -D45-
D28Aa   Reed —
D28B   STEPHEN
D28C   ADALINE
D28Ca   Holman David -D46-
D28Caf Holman Samuel
D28D   SALLIE
D28Da   Crider Daniel -D47-
D28E   DRUSA

D28F   THOMAS
D28Fa   Beckham Lucy
D28G   LUCY
D28Ga   Cahill James –D63–

[D-29] SHOCKLEY D18G
    Oliver Wesley/Elizabeth Jane Lewis
D29A   CHARLOTTE M
D29B   ROBERT FRANKLIN
D29C   JOHN O
D29D   CORA
D29Da   Stewart Charles Edward
D29E   ELIZABETH
D29Ea   Miller Charles
D29F   ISAAC ANDREW
D29Fa   Greenstreet Vergie E
D29G   EMMETT OSCAR
D29Ga   Mathews Della
D29H   OLIVER Jr
D29I   OLLIE
D29J   CLAUDE M
    (2)Phoebe Elizabeth Black
D29K   SNODEN EARL

[D-30] SHOCKLEY D19D
    Thomas J/Catherine —
D30A   LAFAYETT
D30B   DARCUS C
D30C   SAMANTHA C
D30D   DAVID P

[D-31] SKEEN D25Da
    Walter/Mary E Shockley
D31A   WILLIAM
D31Aa   Duke Jennie
D31Aaf   Duke Isaac

[D-32] SHOCKLEY D25E
    Joseph/Nancy Russell
D32A   MATILDA
D32B   BETTIE (J15Ca)
D32Ba   Eads Gus (J15C)

D32Baf   Eads George W (J12D,L15Ca,G31Baf
D32Bam   SimpsonFrances(J12Da,L15C,G31Bam
D32C   LEONA
D32Ca   Holman Newton
D32D   WILLIAM MEREDITH –D48–
D32Da   Barr Ida
D32Daf   Barr Warren

[D-33] SHOCKLEY D25H
    Thomas R/Sarah Jane McGee
D33A   CLARA E
D33B   CHARLES W
D33C   JAMES MILTON
D33D   JOHN MARVIN
D33E   THOMAS ATKINSON
D33F   JOSEPH MILLARD
D33Fa   — Flora
D33G   ANNA LEE
D33Ga   Holman T.D.
D33H   MILLIE O (J20Ca)
D33Ha   Eads B.F. Jr (J20C)
D33Haf   Eads William S (J14E,P14Daf)
D33Ham   Helton Lydia (J14Ea,P14Dam)

[D-34] SHOCKLEY D25I
    Amos/J. Ellen McGee
D34A   GLENN
D34B   EARL
D34C   FLOYD
D34D   LLOYD
D34E   MARY
D34Ea   McBride Harry
D34F   UNKNOWN
D34Fa   Wilson J Freeman
D34G   TRESSIE
D34Ga   Sullivan —

[D-35] POOL D26Ba
    Elisha/Jane Charlotte Shockley
D35A   UNKNOWN
D35Aa   Gabriel John
D35B   UNKNOWN
D35Ba   Osborn Wesley
D35C   R. G.

[D-36] CARTER D26Fa
  Hiram/Harriett Shockley
D36A   LOUISA M
D36Aa   Alldridge John S -D49-

[D-37] SHOCKLEY D26H
  James G/Sarah Ann Stockton
D37A   JOSEPH H Sr
D37B   WILLIAM M
D37C   SUSAN
D37Ca   James John Burton Jr -D50-
D37Caf James John Burton Sr(Z31F,Y19Fa)
D37Cam McGee Leona (Y19F,Z31Fa)

[D-38] SHOCKLEY D27A
  Henry/Julia Durbin
D38A   PATRICK -D51-
D38Aa   Rogers Martha
D38Aaf Rogers William
D38Aam Williams Margaret
D38B   REBECCA ISABELLE
D38Ba   Thompson William
D38C   ELIZABETH
D38Ca   Stockton James M
D38Caf Stockton John H (D27Caf,D71Eaf)
D38Cam Caldwell Louisiana (D27Cam,
                          D71Eam)
D38D   ANN ELIZA
D38Da   Briscoe Andrew

[D-39] DURBIN D27Ba
  Samuel/Sarah Shockley
D39A   SAMUEL Jr
D39B   PHILIP
D39C   RILEY

[D-40] SHOCKLEY D27D
  Francis A/Amanda Matthews
D40A   THOMAS BARTLETT -D52-
D40Aa   Terrill Amanda A
D40Aaf Terrill Hamilton (R12B)
D40Aam Terrill Martha (R12Ba)
D40B   DENA REBECCA (R13Ha)
D40Ba   Terrill Charles M (R13H)

D40Baf Terrill Reuben (R12A,R20Aaf)
D40Bam Lacy Frances (R12Aa,R20Aam
D40C   RACHEL M
D40Ca   Smith James H
D40D   HENRY
D40Da   Diestelkamp Augusta
D40E   AMOS M V -D53- (D66Ia)
D40Ea   Wallace Sallie May (D66I)
D40Eaf Wallace F Barney (D65E)
D40Eam Dessieux Josephine (D65Ea)
D40F   MARTHA
D40G   MARY
D40H   MANUEL H
D40I   LUCY J
D40Ia   Smith Amos L
D40J   ROBERT F

[D-41] SHOCKLEY D27G
  James Monroe/Polly Lavinia Matthews
D41A   ELIZA
D41Aa   Poe Robert I
D41Aaf Poe William Pike
D41Aam Richa Mary Adaline
D41B   SOPHIA
D41Ba   Poe Andrew
D41C   J. MACK
D41Ca   Muller Sophia

[D-42] BRANSON D27Ha
  John N/Elizabeth Shockley
D42A   ELLEN
D42Aa   Newbound —
D42B   THOMAS
D42C   J. NATH
D42D   SOPHIA
D42Da   Dittman Fritz
D42E   KITTY
D42Ea   Stockton William

[D-43] SHOCKLEY D27I
  Andrew Jackson/Mary J Stumpf
D43A   DEWEY
D43B   FLORENCE

D43C   MANSFIELD
D43D   THOMAS −D54−
D43Da   Cook —

[D-44] SHOCKLEY D27J
    Thomas B/Lydia C Berry
D44A   MARTHA E

[D-45] ATKINS D28A
    Caswell C/— Reed
D45A   JOHN M
D45B   EMMA
D45C   RACHEL
D45Ca   Jones William

[D-46] HOLMAN D28Ca
    David/Adaline Atkins
D46A   THOMAS
D46B   JAMES
D46C   LYDA
D46Ca   Jaeger Ermil
D46D   NEWTON

[D-47] CRIDER D28Da
    Daniel/Sallie Atkins
D47A   ULYSSES
D47B   DANIEL B
D47C   GEORGE
D47D   ELIZA
D47Da   Rucker William
D47E   NANCY
D47Ea   Samples George Robert −D60−
D47F   DRUSA
D47Fa   Thompson J.D. −D61−
D47Fb   Mitchem William −D62−
D47G   MONROE
D47Ga   Beck Celia

[D-48] SHOCKLEY D32D
    William Meredith/Ida Barr
D48A   SIDNEY CLYDE
D48B   LEONARD MEREDITH
D48C   WILBUR GRAY

[D-49] ALLDRIDGE D36Aa
    John S/Louise Carter
D49A   W.G.

[D-50] JAMES D37Ca
    John Burton Jr/Susan Shockley
D50A   LEONA
D50Aa   Gillispie Jesse −D55−

[D-51] SHOCKLEY D38A
    Patrick/Martha Rogers
D51A   EDWARD
D51B   ROSA
D51Ba   Thompson Vernie

[D-52] SHOCKLEY D40A
    Thomas Bartlett/Amanda Terrill
D52A   MAUD
D52Aa   Willis John
D52B   CLAUDE
D52C   JOSIE
D52Ca   Welch Fount
D52D   ELLEN
D52Da   Lewis Alva
D52E   LUCY
D52Ea   Stewart Wilbur
D52F   LINA
D52Fa   Purcell Oren −D56−
D52G   JESSIE
D52Ga   Stewart Alva −D57−

[D-53] SHOCKLEY D40E
    Amos/Sallie M Wallace
D53A   BEULAH
D53Aa   Johnson Edgar
D53B   WILLIAM
D53C   CLIFFORD

[D-54] SHOCKLEY D43D
    Thomas/— Cook
D54A   RAYMOND
D54B   PERRY
D54Ba   Poe Annis

[D-55] GILLISPIE D50Aa
  Jesse/Leona James
D55A   LILLIAM
D55B   CHARLES JAMES

[D-56] PURCELL D52Fa
  Oren/Lina Shockley
D56A   SHOCKLEY
D56B   ISOLENE
D56Ba Blackwell —
D56C   GEORGE
D56D   HELEN
D56E   VELMA
D56F   FRANK
D56G   LESTER

[D-57] STEWART D52Ga
  Alva/Jessie Shockley
D57A   CLAUDE
D57B   OLIVE MAY

[D-58] SHOCKLEY D14Ha
  Thomas/Elizabeth Shockley
D58A   GIDIAN
D58B   AQUILLA
D58Ba Clark May Ann
D58C   THOMAS
D53Ca Cannon Elizabeth
D58D   WILLIAM S −D82−
D58Da Crawley Mary

[D-59] SHOCKLEY D20F
  Francis Marion/Sarah Palmer
D59A   UNKNOWN
D59B   JOHN LUNCE
D59C   LUCY A
D59D   WILLIAM R
D59E   PRILLA LEXIE

[D-60] SAMPLES D47Ea
  George Robert/Nancy Crider
D60A   MARTHA A
D60B   JESSIE L

D60C   NELLIE C
D60D   MAUD MARIAN
D60E   NANCY
D60F   CHESTER A

[D-61] THOMPSON D47Fa
  J.D./Drusa Crider
D61A   SARAH E
D61B   JAMES ROBERT
D61C   RILDA S
D61D   LUCY JANE
D61E   ELIZA A
D61F   GILBERT N
D61G   DANIEL R

[D-62] MITCHEM D47Fb
  William/Drusa Crider
D62A   BLANCHE
D62B   HOMER
D62C   CHESLEY
D62D   GERTHALENE

[D-63] CAHILL D28Ga
  James/Lucy Atkins
D63A   JOHN
D63B   WALTER
D63C   UNKNOWN
D63Ca Giesler Waldo

[D-64] WALLACE unknown
  unknown/unknown
D64A   WILLIAM C −D65−
D64Aa Ridenhour Elizabeth

[D-65] WALLACE D64A
  William C/Elizabeth Ridenhour
D65A   MARTELIA
D65Aa Willoughby Thomas
D65B   JULIA
D65Ba Baster George
D65C   MELCENA
D65Ca Atkins Stephen R
D65D   SARAH E
D65Da Sewell John B

D65Daf Sewell Martin
D65Dam Sullivant Sophronia
D65E   F BARNEY -D66- (D40Eaf)
D65Ea Dessieux Josephine (D40Eam)
D65F   JAMES -D67-
D65Fa Romine Jane
D65G   JOHN -D68-
D65Ga Keeney Hannah M (S21Aa)
D65Gaf Keeney Sylvester (S21Aaf)
D65H   DAVID -D69-
D65Ha Wideman Alice

[D-66] WALLACE D65E
   F. Barney/Josephine Dessieux
D66A   CLAUDE
D66B   THOMAS
D66C   E. A. (Gus)
D66D   LAURA L
D66Da Love Jasper
D66E   GARRETT
D66F   LEWIS
D66G   ROBERT
D66H   ONY
D66I   SALLIE MAY (D40Ea)
D66Ia Shockley Amos M.V. (D40E)
D66Iaf Shockley Francis A (D27D,R13Haf)
D66Iam Matthews Amanda (D27Da,R13Ham)

[D-67] WALLACE D65F
   James/Jane Romine
D67A   ROY
D67B   ZELLA
D67C   WALTER
D67D   CLARENCE
D67E   WILLIAM
D67F   JOHN

[D-68] WALLACE D65G
   John/Hannah M Keeney
D68A   CHARLES
D68B   FRANK
D68C   BELLE
D68Ca Ousley Virgil
D68D   BLANCHE

D68Da Wills Jack

[D-69] WALLACE D65H
   David/Alice Wideman
D69A   BERNICE
D69B   ANGELINE
D69C   ROY
D69Ca Moore Ophelia

[D-70] TRAVIS unknown
   unknown/unknown
D70A   WILLIAM H -D71-
D70Aa Vance Catherine

[D-71] TRAVIS D70A
   William H/Catherine Vance
D71A   WILLIAM JAMES-D72-(Y62Caf,Y74Eaf)
D71Aa Hull Elizabeth (Y62Cam,Y74Eam)
D71B   THOMAS L
D71Ba Rogers Susannah
D71Baf Rogers Alexander S
D71Bam Wallace Belinda
D71C   JOHN J
D71D   MARY E
D71Da Johnson Samuel
D71E   ELIZA J (D26Ham,Y40Cam)
D71Ea Stockton Joseph (D26Haf,Y40Caf)
D71Eaf Stockton John Henderson (D27Caf, D38Caf)
D71Eam Caldwell Louisiana(D27Cam,D38Cam)

[D-72] TRAVIS D71A
   William James/Elizabeth A Hull
D72A   OLLIE
D72Aa John E.L.
D72B   MALISSA
D72C   JESSE
D72D   WALTER
D72E   CLINTON Dr
D72F   ELLA
D72G   INA FRANCES
D72Ga Johnson Martin V
D72H   MINNIE (Y74Ea)
D72Ha Wallace Charles (Y74E)

[D-73] DAVID unknown
    unknown/unknown
D73A   MICHAEL EDWARD -D74- (D16Jaf)
D73Aa   unknown (D16Jam)

[D-74] DAVID D73A
    Michael Edward/unknown
D74A   LEWIS -D75- (D16Ja)
D74Aa   Shockley Rutha S (D16J)
D74Ab   Smith Jane
D74Ac   — Sarah

[D-75] DAVID D74A
    Lewis/Rutha S Shockley
D75A   HANNAH
D75Aa   Curtis William
D75B   WILLIAM
D75Ba   unknown
D75Bb   — Elizabeth
D75C   THOMAS SHOCKLEY -D76- (E16Ia)
D75Ca   Branson Matilda (E16I)
D75D   ELIZABETH
D75Da   Harris Jesse
D75E   JOHN R
D75Ea   Shockley Jane
D75F   CALVIN L
D75Fa   Green Elizabeth Ann
D75G   JEREMIAH
D75Ga   Lam Jane
D75H   RICHARD H
D75I   MORGAN G
D75Ia   Scott Catharine
D75Ib   Young Etta
    (2)Jane Smith
D75J   RUTH JANE
    (3) Sarah Scott
D75K   MARTHA EMELINE
D75L   MANERVA CAROLINE
D75M   JAMES MONROE

[D-76] DAVID D75C
    Thomas S/Matilda Branson
D76A   SARAH JANE

D76Aa   Morrison McClure
D76B   ELIZABETH
D76Ba   Siddens Jim
D76C   SAMPSON MARION -D77-
D76Ca   DePriest Sarah Ellen
D76Caf DePriest Andrew J
D76Cam Barker Minerva
D76D   LEVISA ANN
D76E   WILLIAM WESLEY
D76F   CALVIN LUTHER
D76Fa   Smith Susanna Claramon
D76G   HIRAM LUNTSFORD
D76Ga   Mahoney Alverta L
D76H   RUTHA CATHERINE
D76Ha   Hamm —
D76I   MARTHA ROSEANN
D76Ia   Trego —
D76J   VIRGINIA
D76K   MATILDA ANN
D76Ka   Malson James William

[D-77] DAVID D76C
    Sampson Marion/Sarah Ellen DePriest
D77A   ANNA FLORENCE
D77Aa   Gile Thomas
D77B   MINERVA ELLEN
D77Ba   Rodgers David Sylvanus -D78-
D77Baf Rodgers John Bennett
D77Bam Welch Louisiana
D77C   CHARLES MARION
D77Ca   Hatfield Myrtle
D77D   MARY JANE
D77Da   Miller Jesse
D77E   HIRAM THOMAS
D77F   LULA ELIZABETH
D77Fa   Anderson John H
D77G   JOHN McCLURE
D77Ga   — Anna
D77H   WALTER FESTUS
D77Ha   Bishop Mable
D77I   SETH RAY
D77J   FRANK CLINTON
D77Ja   Worley Helen
D77K   RUTH C

D77L   WILLIAM ROY
D77La   — Louise

[D-78] RODGERS D77Ba
   David Sylvanus/Minerva E David
D78A   ETHEL OPAL
D78B   EVA FERN
D78Ba   Bastian Arthur Richard —D79—
D78Baf Bastian Theodore
D78Bam Schwenck Metha
D78Bb   Bastian John Milton
D78C   PAUL DAVID
D78Ca   — Gladys

[D-79] BASTIAN D78Ba
   Arthur Richard/Eva Fern Rodgers
D79A   METHA ELLEN
D79Aa   Blenkarn Walter A
D79B   MARY ELIZABETH
D79Ba   Gausman Chester H —D80—
D79C   JAMES CALVIN
D79Ca   Freeman Jean
D79Cb   Gausman Darlene Bertha

[D-80] GAUSMAN D79Ba
   Chester H/Mary Elizabeth Bastian
D80A   JOHN
D80Aa   Spencer Nancy
D80B   KRISTINE
D80Ba   Gosch William
D80C   HAROLD

[D-81] HAYNES D22La
   William/Rebecca Shockley
D81A   HIRAM
D81B   MANERVA
D81C   JEFFERSON
D81D   CAROLINE
D81E   DAVID
D81F   ELMIRA
D81G   MARY
D81H   OLIVE

D81I   CORNELIUS F
D81J   JOHN M
D81K   WESLEY

[D-82] SHOCKLEY D58D
   William S/Mary Crawley
D82A   THOMAS JEFFERSON —D83—
D82Aa   Mitchell Margaret Emalene

[D-83] SHOCKLEY D82A
   Thomas Jefferson/Margaret Mitchell
D83A   WAINRIGHT —D84—
D83Aa   Moore Nancy

[D-84] SHOCKLEY D83A
   Wainright/Nancy Moore
D84A   THOMAS JEFFERSON (A98Aa)
D84Aa   Nolen Kate (A98A)

[D-85] CAMPBELL D21Ea
   Robert H/Tennessee Shockley
D85A   MALINDA ELIZABETH
D85Aa   Lockwood William E —D86—
D85B   JAMES McMEIN —D88—
D85Ba   Krueger Theresa D.M.
D85C   NEVADA CLARISSA (F35Ha)
D85Ca   Burgess Charles Albert (F35H)
D85Caf Burgess John (F34A,C15Ca)
D85Cam Cox Ruth (C15C,F34Aa)

[D-86] LOCKWOOD D85Aa
   WilliamE/Malinda E Campbell
D86A   MEREDITH C —D87—
D86Aa   unknown
D86B   LUTHER

[D-87] LOCKWOOD D86A
   Meredith/unknown
D87A   WAYNE EDWARD
D87B   MEREDITH C Jr

[D-88] CAMPBELL D85B
   James M/Theresa Krueger
D88A   OLIVE ELIZABETH
D88B   MARIE
D88Ba Bonsteel Merton D
D88C   EVELYN EDITH
D88Ca Langenberg Victor Henry

[D-89] OWENS D21Ga
   Elija/Eliza Shockley
D89A   ISAAC MACK -D90-
D89Aa Richardson Mollie Melissa
D89Aaf Richardson Benjamin Pettus
D89Aam Johnston Martha Jane

[D-90] OWENS D89A
   Isaac M/Mollie M Richardson
D90A   WALDO
D90B   CYRUS
D90C   DON MACK -D91-
D90Ca Raaf Caroline Lena
D90Caf Raaf William Henry
D90Cam Berger Anna Louise
D90D   LUCILLE
D90E   CORRINE
D90F   HERBERT
D90G   GLADYS

[D-91] OWENS D90C
   Don Mack/Caroline L Raaf
D91A   ROBERT MACK
D91Ab Ellen Mary
D91B   WILLIAM DON
D91Ba Brown Patricia Gail

[E-07] BRANSON unknown
  unknown/unknown
E07A   THOMAS SR
E07Aa   Day Elizabeth
E07Aaf Day John

[E-08] BRANSON E07A
  Thomas Sr./Elizabeth Day
E08A   THOMAS -E80-
E08Aa   Borden Rebeckah
E08Aaf Borden Benjamin
E08B   JACOB
E08C   JOHN DAY -E9-
E08Ca   — Isabella
E08Cb   Antrim Martha
E08Cbf Antrim Thomas
E08D   DAVID
E08E   JOSEPH
E08F   JONATHAN
E08G   LIONEL
E08H   WILLIAM -E77-
E08Ha   — Elizabeth
E08I   SARAH
E08J   MARY
E08Ja   Robins Zachariah
E08K   ELIZABETH
E08Ka   Rogers William -E76-

[E-09] BRANSON E08C
  John Day/Isabella —
E09A   THOMAS -E10-
E09Aa   unknown
E09B   MARY
E09Ba   Duckworth John
E09C   ANN
E09Ca   Shinn —H
E09D   ELIZABETH
E09Da   Corder —
   (2)Martha Antrim
E09E   MARTHA
E09Ea   Fawcett Thomas -E79-

[E-10] BRANSON E9A
  Thomas/unknown
E10A   JOHN 1st -E11-
E10Aa   unknown
E10B   THOMAS JR
E10C   UNKNOWN
E10Ca   unknown
E10D   JARRETT -E15-
E10Da   — Sarah

[E-11] BRANSON E10A
  John 1st/unknown
E11A   JOHN 2nd -E12-(B10Aaf)
E11Aa   unknown
E11B   THOMAS -E14-
E11Ba   unknown
E11C   UNKNOWN -E13-
E11Ca   unknown

[E-12] BRANSON E11A
  John 2nd/unknown
E12A   JOHN 3rd -E16- (B10Abf,E67Aaf)
E12Aa   Dillard Sarah (B10Abm.E67Aam)
E12Aaf Dillard Thomas
E12B   ELIZABETH (B10Aa,C12Aam,C12Bam)
E12Ba   Burgess James M (B10A,E16Bb,
                        C12Aaf,C12Baf)
E12C   REUBEN
E12Ca   unknown
E12D   THOMAS

[E-13] BRANSON E11C
  unknown,unknown
E13A   REUBEN
E13Aa   unknown

[E-14] BRANSON E11B
  Thomas/unknown
E14A   THOMAS -E18-
E14Aa   Simpson Hannah (E53Ab)

[E-15] BRANSON E10D
   Jarrett/Sarah —
E15A   ANDREW -E19-
E15Aa   — Pereby
E15B   THOMAS -E17-
E15Ba   McGowan Anna
E15C   JARRETT -E61-
E15Ca   East Frances (C35Aa)
E15Cb   Talbot Theodora
E15D   VALENTINE -E90-
E15Da   East Susannah
E15E   MARIAN
E15Ea   Hanes Luster

[E-16] BRANSON E12A
   John 3rd/Sarah Dillard
E16A   JARED -E20-(E55Daf)
E16Aa   Bumpass Sarah (E55Dam)
E16Aaf Bumpass William
E16Aam Eads —
E16B   RUTH (B10Ab)
E16Ba   Cox —
E16Bb   Burgess James (B10A,E12Ba,C12Aaf E17I
E16C   WILLIAM
E16D   MARTHA
E16Da   McMilliam —
E16E   MARY (E67Aa)
E16Ea   McMilliam Thomas (E67A)
E16Eaf McMilliam William -E67-
E16Eam unknown
E16F   THOMAS
E16G   ANDREW
E16H   JOHN
E16I   MATILDA (D75Ca)
E16Ia   David Thomas Shockley (D75C)
E16J   LAVICY
E16Ja   Spaulding —
E16K   HIRAM

[E-17] BRANSON E15B
   Thomas/Anna McGowan
E17A   DAVID -E21-
E17Aa   David Sarah Ann
E17Aaf David William (Z41Ba)

E17Aam Green Sarah Ann (Z41B)
E17Ab   Campbell Elizabeth
E17Abf Campbell Robert
E17B   REUBEN -E22- (T13Ka)
E17Ba   Crismon Sarah (T13K)
E17Baf Crismon Gilbert (D17Laf,T12A)
E17Bb   Slater Harriett (E17Eb)
E17C   GEORGE WASHINGTON -E69-
E17Ca   Jett Joan
E17Caf Jett James
E17Cam Pointer Elizabeth
E17D   ANDREW B
E17Da   — Mary J
E17E   JOHN SEVIER
E17Ea   Ousley Martha
E17Eb   Slater Harriett (E17Bb)
E17F   SARAH
E17Fa   Baker James -E71-
E17G   THOMAS Jr (C13Ea)
E17Ga   Cox Elvira (C13E)
E17H   NANCY
E17Ha   Pointer James
E17I   ANN
E17Ia   Simpson Benjamin
E17J   RHODA
E17Ja   Gilmore Robert
E17K   MARY ANN
E17Ka   Jett William
E17L   MADISON
E17La   Hutton Frances
E17M   STEPHEN
E17Ma   Pointer Nancy

[E-18] BRANSON E14A
   Thomas/Simpson Hannah
E18A   WILLIAM "Red Head" -E23- (U13Da)
E18Aa   Helton Mary (U13D)
E18Aaf Helton William Todd (U11B)
E18Aam Washam Julia Ann (U11Ba)

[E-19] BRANSON E15A
   Andrew/— Pereby
E19A   VALENTINE -E24-
E19Aa   Sherrill Alpha M

E19B   JOHN
E19C   NANCY
E19D   SALLY
E19E   POLLY
E19F   CATHERINE
E19Fa   Horn Samuel W
E19G   ANDREW
E19H   PATSY
E19I   ROLLA
E19J   LOUISA JANE
E19K   HENRY CHILDERS
E19L   SINA PERKINS

[E-20] BRANSON E16A
   Jared/Sarah Bumpass
E20A   WILLIAM G -E25- (T15Hb,U12Naf)
E20Aa   Finn Martha A (U12Nam)
E20Aaf Finn Barnett (G34Aaf,J12Eaf,
                      K27Baf)
E20Ab   Crismon Margaret (T15H)
E20Abf Crismon James (T13C,J12Aa,J27Aaf
E20Abm Eads Frances (J12A,T13Ca,J27Aam)
E20B   MELISSA
E20Ba   Feeler Michael Sr -E26- (K33Ea)
E20Baf Feeler Simon (E20Cb,K33Eaf)
E20Bam Daley Deborah E (K33Eam)
E20C   MARY E
E20Ca   Soudermeyer Henry -E27-
E20Cb   Feeler Simon (E20Baf,K33Eaf)
E20D   BENJAMIN -E28- (E55Da)
E20Da   Duncan Paralee S
E20Daf Duncan Russell (E25Daf)
E20Db   Hughes Ellen (E55D)
E20Dbf Hughes James E (E54A)
E20Dbm Duncan Sarah (E54Aa)
E20E   ANDREW RICHARDSON
E20F   JOB RICHARDSON

[E-21] BRANSON E17A
   David/Sarah Ann David
E21A   ANDREW J -E29-
E21Aa   Williams Mary A
E21Ab   Tipton Parazetta
E21B   RUTH ANN (P11Ga,M15Eam)

E21Ba   Carnes William P (P11G,M15Eaf)
E21Baf Carnes John (P10A,G11Faf,G11Haf)
E21Bam Burton Nancy (P10Aa,G11Fam,
                        G11Ham)
E21C   ELIZABETH J
E21Ca   Owens Francis C.W. -E30-
E21D   MARY ANN
E21Da   Lore James E -E48-
E21Db   Williams A.J.
E21E   WILLIAM R
E21F   HANNAH M
E21Fa   Helbert John T -E47-
E21Fb   Ammerman —

[E-22] BRANSON E17B
   Reuben/Sarah Crismon
E22A   MINERVA
E22Aa   Granaman Frits -E31-
E22B   AMANDA
E22Ba   Owens Stephen -E32-
E22Bb   Pointer Daniel -E33-
E22C   ELIZABETH
E22Ca   Gillispie William Breckenridge
E22D   THOMAS
E22E   JAMES
E22F   STEPHEN
E22G   SARAH ANN
E22H   NANNIE
E22I   GILBERT (E70Aaf)
E22Ia   Clay Ann
E22Iaf Clay William
E22Iam Compton Mary Ann
E22J   MARTHA
E22Ja   Compton William
E22K   MARTIN V
E22Ka   West Nancy E
E22L   JOHN L
E22La   Phelps Cordella
E22M   EMMA
E22Ma   Bax William
E22N   BENJAMIN
E22Na   Phelps Sallie
E22O   JOSEPH
E22Oa   Pointer Nancy Ann

(2)Harriet Slater
E22P   SAMANTHA J
E22Pa Phelps Lee Rev
E22Q   WILLIAM

[E-23] BRANSON E18A
   William/Mary Helton
E23A   UNKNOWN
E23Aa Lankford —
E23B   WILLIAM Jr
E23C   UNKNOWN
E23Ca Myers John
E23D   UNKNOWN
E23Da Slone Charles
E23E   JOHN
E23Ea Scott Dora
E23Eaf Scott George (L15Gaf)
E23Eam Doyel Mary (L15Gam)
E23F   THOMAS
E23Fa Dake Josephine

[E-24] BRANSON E19A
   Valentine/Alpha M Sherrill
E24A   ALFRED P —E34—
E24Aa unknown
E24B   OLIVIA C
E24Ba Barbarick Joseph H
E24C   GALBA E —E60—
E24Ca — Elizabeth´
E24D   MINERVA
E24E   LEWIS F
E24F   THOMAS JEFFERSON
E24G   MARY A
E24Ga Young Nicholas
E24H   REUBEN S —E58— (C29Ca)
E24Ha Cooper Mary T (C29C)
E24I   HANNAH M
E24Ia Shockley —
E24Ib Barbarick J.H.
E24J   CHRISSA
E24K   VALENTINE —E65—
E24Ka Jenkins Sarah Catherine
E24Kb Smith Mary Elizabeth
E24Kc Smith Ellen Frances

E24L   WILLIAM H
E24M   SAMUEL K
E24N   LOUISA
E24Na Lloyd Ernest

[E-25] BRANSON E20A
   William G/Martha A Finn
E25A   WILLIAM M
E25Aa Rigsby Emma
E25Aaf Rigsby John
E25Aam Williams Laura
E25B   DOLLY
E25Ba Williams Ashley G —E35—
E25Baf Williams Micaiah
E25Bam Crow Mary
E25C   NANCY (U12Na)
E25Ca Helton Martin —E36— (U12N)
E25Caf Helton Isaac Sr (U11A,E53Ba,
       U16Ba,G12Iaf,V13Caf,V15Daf)
E25Cam Cowan Mary Ann (U16B,U11Ab,
             G12Iam)
E25D   THOMAS F —E37—
E25Da Duncan Alice
E25Daf Duncan Russell (E20Daf)
   (2)Margaret Crismon
E25E   AGNES
E25Ea Veasman Edward
E25F   MINNIE
E25Fa Hughes James
E25G   WILLIAM
E25H   ARCHIBALD A
E25I   BENJAMIN F
E25J   PARADINE
E25Ja Phillips —
E25K   EWELL CRITTINGTON —E85—
E25Ka King Myrtle Minerva
E25Kaf King William Wiley
E25L   LAURA
E25La Duncan Milford —E38—
E25M   MAUD
E25Ma Curtman Elmer —E39—
E25Maf Curtman George Dr (U12Ha)
E25N   ETHEL
E25Na Scott B.F. Sr —E40—

[E-26] FEELER E20Ba
  Michael Sr/Melissa Branson
E26A BENJAMIN

[E-27] SOUDERMEYER E20Ca
  Henry/Mary E Branson
E27A SARAH M
E27Aa Holmes John O
E27Aaf Holmes William W (T30Ca)
E27Aam Woods Sophia (T30C)
E27B M.E.
E27Ba Krone Sat

[E-28] BRANSON E20D
  Benjamin/Paralee Duncan
E28A SALLIE
E28Aa Misel C.W.
E28B JARED
  (2)Ellen Hughes
E28C RAMUS
E28D STELLA
E28E BRYON

[E-29] BRANSON E21A
  Andrew J/Mary A Williams
E29A MARTHA MARGARET
E29Aa Franklin Robert -E46-
E29B ELIZABETH
E29Ba Crider Tom Rush -E41-
E29C ALICE
E29Ca Rogers John D
E29Caf Rogers Martin L
E29Cam Gaither Mahala
E29D DAVID
E29Da Pointer Florence
E31E WILLIAM J
E29F IDA
E29Fa Renick Felix
E29Fb Keerigan —

[E-30] OWENS E21Ca
  Francis C.W./Elizabeth T Branson
E30A NANCY ANN
E30Aa Smith David W

E30B JOHN ROBERT
E30C MARY FRANCES
E30Ca Diehl J.M.
E30D JESSE
E30Da Baker Lizzie
E30E WILLIAM C Dr
E30Ea Krunenberg Ida
E30Eb Branson Lillian
E30F SARAH
E30Fa Lyons Robert
E30G LAURA BELLE
E30Ga Johnson Samuel
E30Gb Davies Harry
E30H JOSEPH REED
E30Ha Beard Mary
E30I IDA MAY
E30Ia Shaver Robert M
E30Ib Tinslar F.S. Dr
E30J SUSAN BLANCHE
E30Ja McGraw Harry

[E-31] GRANAMAN E22Aa
  Fritz/Minerva Branson
E31A DORA
E31Aa Cladwell —
E31B LULA
E31Ba Collins William
E31C SOPHIE
E31Ca Schue Charles
E31D EVA
E31Da Hutchison Harrison
E31E WAYMON
E31F LOUIS
E31G LAURA
E31Ga Camden John
E31H WILLIAM
E31Ha Brown Dessie

[E-32] OWENS E22Ba
  Stephen/Amanda Branson
E32A DANIEL
E32Aa Copeland Sarah
E32Aaf Copeland James
E32B JESSIE

SIBLING GROUP E

E32Ba Walker Charles
E32Bb Breeden —
E32C ROBERT
E32D PEARL
E32Da Copeland Granville

[E-33] POINTER E22Bb
Daniel/Amanda Branson
E33A SHELDON
E33Aa Copeland Dora
E33Aaf Copeland James
E33B FOREST
E33C ANGIE
E33Ca West Roy
E33D MINNIE
E33Da Jett Chester
E33E FRED
E33F LOUISA

[E-34] BRANSON E24A
Alfred P/unknown
E34A MAHALA
E34Aa Bray T.A. —E42—
E34B ELIZABETH
E34Ba Walker W.A. —E43—
E34C JEFF —E44—
E34Ca Rogers Melcena
E34Caf Rogers John A (Y42Caf)
E34Cam Cummings Mildred (Y42Cam)
E34D MARY
E34Da Fortune John —E45—

[E-35] WILLIAMS E25Ba
Ashley G/Dolly Branson
E35A STERLING
E35B DOT
E35C LAWRENCE

[E-36] HELTON E25Ca
Martin/Nancy Branson
E36A GORDON
E36B EUNICE

[E-37] BRANSON E25D
Thomas F/Alice Duncan
E37A RAY
E37B KATE
E37C ALLEN G
E37D THOMAS

[E-38] DUNCAN E25La
Milford/Laura Branson
E38A BLAND
E38B WILLIAM

[E-39] CURTMAN E25Ma
Elmer/Maud Branson
E39A FLOYD
E39B CLYDE
E39C MABEL
E39Ca Rowden Almon
E39D MAY
E39Da Van Kirk —
E39E ETHEL
E39F GLADYS
E39G LORENE
E39H AGNES

[E-40] SCOTT E25Na
B.F.Sr/Ethel Branson
E40A DORSEY
E40B WAYNE
E40C B.F. Jr.
E40D LULA
E40E ROSA
E40F MAY
E40G ETHEL
E40H MAUD

[E-41] CRIDER E29Ba
Tom Rush/Elizabeth Branson
E41A A.J. Dr
E41B OLLIE
E41Ba Shanks Syl
E41Bb Deckard Thomas
E41C FLORENCE
E41Ca Griffith David

E41D   MARGARET
E41Da   Stratman Henry
E41E   THOMAS R
E41F   MARY
E41Fa   Swanard Ralph
E41G   EVA L
E41Ga   Palmer C.O.

[E-42] BRAY E34Aa
    T.A./Mahala Branson
E42A   SETH
E42B   ELLIS
E42C   ALBERT
E42D   STELLA
E42Da   Stockton Richard
E42E   MINNIE
E42Ea   Neidert George

[E-43] WALKER E34Ba
    W.A./Elizabeth Branson
E43A   WILLIAM P
E43Aa   Birdsong Lizzie
E43Aaf Birdsong William Newton
E43Aam Hutchison Laura I
E43B   BLANCHE
E43Ba   Wofford Clay
E43Baf Wofford Charles P (Y48C,Y25Aaf)
E43Bam Ammerman Ida May (Y48Ca,Y25Aam)
E43C   HADLEY
E43Ca   Tipton Fannie
E43D   MARLAN
E43Da   Johnson Freda
E43E   RUSSELL
E43Ea   Holman Alta
E43F   FLOYD L
E43Fa   Campbell Addie
E43G   MYRTLE
E43Ga   Nichols Cletus
E43H   LORA
E43Ha   McKinney Loyd
E43I   RANDAL
E43Ia   Woodruff Lillie
E43J   A.C.
E43Ja   Hawkins Beulah

E43K   RUDY
E43Ka   Wofford Stella

[E-44] BRANSON E34C
    Jeff/Melcena Rogers
E44A   LESLIE
E44B   ANSLEY

[E-45] FORTUNE E34Da
    John/Mary Branson
E45A   WALTER
E45B   ALVA
E45C   IDA

[E-46] FRANKLIN E29Aa
    Robert/Martha M Branson
E46A   UNKNOWN
E46Aa   Armer Ray
E46B   UNKNOWN
E46Ba   Keeney Sylvester
E46C   UNKNOWN
E46Ca   Backues A.J.
E46D   UNKNOWN
E46Da   Shanks James
E46E   UNKNOWN
E46Ea   Elrod W.H.
E46F   UNKNOWN
E46Fa   Vanoster Charles
E46G   UNKNOWN
E46Ga   Wilcox J.W.
E46H   UNKNOWN
E46Ha   Henley —

[E-47] HELBERT E21Fa
    John T/Hannah M Branson
E47A   EVA
E47Aa   Wells J.S.
E47B   MAUD
E47Ba   Patterson Edward
E47C   CHARLES E

[E-48] LORE E21Da
    James E/Mary Ann Branson
E48A   JOHN

E48B   DAVID
E48C   DANIEL
E48D   MARTHA
E48E   SARAH
E48Ea   Hutchison Mat
E48Eaf Hutchison William
E48F   LYDA
E48Fa   Owens James C -E49-
E48G   MINERVA (D16Ha)
E48Ga   Simpson John -E94-
F48Gb   Shockley Isaiah
E48H   RUTH
E48Ha   Barbarick James -E51-

[E-49] OWENS E48Fa
    James C/Lyda Lore
E49A   JAMES
E49B   OLIVER
E49Ba   Branson —
E49Baf Branson Stephen (E49Caf,E49Daf)
E49C   BURR
E49Ca   Branson —
E49Caf Branson Stephen (E49Baf,E49Daf)
E49D   A Dolph -E50-
E49Da   Branson —
E49Daf Branson Stephen (E49Baf,E49Caf)

[E-50] OWENS E49D
    A Dolph/— Branson
E50A   GUY
E50B   DELLA
E50C   HELENE
E50D   BERNICE
E50E   JAMES
E50F   MARY

[E-51] BARBARICK E48Ha
    James/Ruth Lore
E51A   ANDREW
E51B   CECIL
E51C   WALTER
E51D   CLARENCE
E51E   LOGAN
E51F   JOSEPH

E51G   RHODES
E51H   BRANSFORD
E51I   GEORGE
E51J   JOHN
E51K   FLOYD
E51L   NORA
E51La   Milan --
E51M   DORA
E51Ma   Holzschuh

[E-52] HUGHES unknown
    unknown/unknown
E52A   JOHN -E53- (U11Gaf)
E52Aa   Bilyeu — (U11Gam)

[E-53] HUGHES E52A
    John/ — Bilyeu
E53A   STEPHEN -E54- (U11Ga)
E53Aa   Helton Jane (U11G)
E53Aaf Helton James Sr (U10A,T12Ba,
                    E53Aaf,U16Baf)
E53Aam Crismon — (T12B,U10Aa,E53Aam,
                    U16Bam)
E53Ab   Simpson Hannah (E14Aa)
E53B   ELIZABETH (U11Aa,V13Cam,V15Dam)
E53Ba   Helton Isaac (U11A,U16Ba,E25Caf,
                    G12Iaf,V13Caf,V15Daf)
E53Baf Helton James Sr (U10A,T12Ba,
                    E53Aaf,U16Baf)
E53Bam Crismon — (T12B,U10Aa,E53Aam,
                    U16Bam)
E53C   MARY(J11Aa,K11Cam,T13Cam,J11Aa)
E53Ca   Eads Benjamin (J11A,J26Bbf,
                    K11Caf,T13Caf,T16Aaf)
E53Caf Eads(Edds) John (J10A,L11Ba)
E53Cam Simpson Nancy (J10Aa,L11B)

[E-54] HUGHES E53A
    Stephen/Jane Helton
E54A   JAMES E -E55- (E20Dbf)
E54Aa   Duncan Sarah (E20Dbm)
E54Aaf Duncan Alvis
E54B   POLLY
E54Ba   Brown "Dude"

(2)Hannah Simpson
E54C   DANIEL
E54D   STEPHEN (Tebe)
E54E   RACHEL
E54Ea   Thompson —
E54Eb   Helton John
E54F   MOSES —E56—
E54Fa   Kehr Luellen
E54G   LEWIS —E57—
E54Ga   Null —
E54Gb   Lee —

[E-55] HUGHES E54A
   James E/Sarah Duncan
E55A   UNKNOWN
E55Aa   James J.D.
E55B   FLORA
E55Ba   Crawford —
E55C   JAMES E Jr
E55D   ELLEN (E20Db)
E55Da   Branson Benjamin F (E20D)
E55Daf   Branson Jared (E16A)
E55Dam   Bumpass Sallie (E16Aa)
E55E   MARGARET A
E55Ea   Barnhart Monroe
E55F   MARY ANN
E55Fa   Watkins Bird T

[E-56] HUGHES E54F
   Moses/Luellen Kehr
E56A   ROSS
E56B   WALTER
E56C   LEWIS
E56D   TEBE

[E-57] HUGHES E54G
   Lewis/— Null
E57A   MINNIE
E57B   HANNAH
E57C   CLAY
    (2)— Lee
E57D   MAY
E57E   LEWIS Jr
E57F   TEBE

E57G   ANNA

[E-58] BRANSON E24H
   Reuben S/Mary T Cooper
E58A   LUCY M
E58B   JAMES T

[E-60] BRANSON E24C
   Galba E/Elizabeth —
E60A   ELIZABETH
E60B   CHARLES

[E-61] BRANSON E15C
   Jarret/Frances East
E61A   REBECCA
E61Aa   Carroll William —E62—
E61B   MILLIE
E61Ba   Carroll Jacob
E61C   SUSAN
E61Ca   Haynes Luster
E61D   WILLIAM
E61E   THOMAS
E61F   NEOMA
E61Fa   Haynes —
E61G   JOHN
E61H   SARAH
E61Ha   Clemons —
E61I   MARY
E61Ia   Stovall John

[E-62] CARROLL E61Aa
   William/Rebecca Branson
E62A   WILLIAM JR.—E63— (C30Aaf)
E62Aa   Smith Elizabeth (C30Aam)
E62Aaf   Smith James Samuel
E62B   JURET
E62C   JAMES WILEY
E62D   JOHN
E62E   SARAH JANE
E62F   GEORGE
E62G   DANIEL
E62Ga   Ellis Eliza N

[E-63] CARROLL E62A
  William Jr./Elizabeth Smith
E63A   MARY ELLEN (C30Aa)
E63Aa   Cooper Ira Burton (C30A)
E63B   CHARLES E -E88-
E63Ba   Posey Ladoisha Ann
E63Baf Posey Allen A (E89A)
E63Bam Baty Ida Belle (E89Aa)
E63C   SARAH JANE
E63D   JOHN JASPER
E63Da   Baker Lidia
E63E   MARTHA A
E63F   JAMES H
E63G   EMMA S
E63Ga   Todd William
E63H   THOMAS H
E63Ha   Foster Lula
E63I   WILLIAM RILEY
E63Ia   Phillips Florence
E63J   JOSEPH M

[E-65] BRANSON E24K
  Valentine/Ellen Frances Smith
E65A   MARTHA
E65Aa   Birkman —
E65B   JESSE
E65C   CLARENCE
E65D   OLLIE
E65Da   Sewell —
E65E   BESSE
E65Ea   Seda —
E65F   OMA
E65Fa   Smith —
E65G   RAY
E65H   GARRETT
E65I   ALFRED -E66-
E65Ia   Branson Thelma
E65Iaf Branson Henry

[E-66] BRANSON E65I
  Alfred/Thelma Branson
E66A   ALFRED
E66B   THELMA MAE
E66C   CLYDE

E66Ca   Hibler Dorothy
E66Caf Hibler Logan
E66D   EVERETT
E66Da   Redcliff Jean

[E-67] McMILLIAM E16Eaf
  William/unknown
E67A   THOMAS (E16Ea)
E67Aa   Branson Mary (E16E)
E67Aaf Branson John (E12A,B10Abf)
E67Aam Dillard Sarah (E12Aa)
E67B   EDWARD
E67C   DANIEL -E68-
E67Ca   Burchard Eliza Jane
E67Caf Burchard Samuel
E67Cam Barbarick Barbara

[E-68] McMILLIAM E67C
  Daniel/Eliza Burchard
E68A   T.J.
E68Aa   McKenney

[E-69] BRANSON E17C
  George Washington/Joan Jett
E69A   ANDREW JACKSON -E70-
E69Aa   Fowler Ruth Jane
E69Aaf Fowler Henry
E69B   JAMES MARION -E82-
E69Ba   Shockley Elizabeth Ann
E69C   JULIA ANN
E69Ca   Posey Humphrey -E89-
E69D   THOMAS JEFFERSON
E69Da   Phelps Laura Jane
E69E   MARY JANE
E69Ea   Maples Samuel
E69F   SARAH M
E69G   CATHARINE
E69Ga   Phelps Tilman
E69H   JOHN M
E69I   MANOLA
E69J   MARTHA E
E69Ja   Branson John M

STIBLING GROUP E

[E-70] BRANSON E69A
  Andrew Jackson/Ruth Fowler
E70A REBECCA
E70Aa Branson John T -E73-
E70Aaf Branson Gilbert (E22I)

[E-71] BAKER E17Fa
  James/Sarah Branson
E71A HIRAM -E72-
E71Aa Pointer Elizabeth Ann
E71Aaf Pointer William
E71Aam Daniel Vicinda
E71B NANCY
E71Ba Hassler Pleasant A

[E-72] BAKER E71A
  Hiram/Elizabeth Ann Pointer
E72A MARTHA ELLEN
E72Aa Hassler Thomas Jefferson

[E-73] BRANSON E70Aa
  John T/Rebecca Branson
E73A NANCY JANE
E73Aa Hassler Basil R

[E-74] HASSLER E73Aa
  Basil R/Nancy Jane Branson
E74A LEE KENNETH -E75-
E74Aa Stock Fern Opal

[E-75] HASSLER E74A
  Lee Kenneth/Fern Opal Stock
E75A SHIRLEY JEAN
E75Aa Hern Charles Lynn

[E-76] ROGERS E08Ka
  William/Elizabeth Branson
E76A ABIGAIL

[E-77] BRANSON E08H
  William/Elizabeth —
E77A MARY
E77Aa Walker Abel

E77B JACOB
E77Ba Holloway Mary
E77C ABRAHAM -E78-
E77Ca Reese Catherine
E77Cb White Sarah

[E-78] BRANSON E77C
  Abraham/Catherine Reese
E78A REES
E78Aa Downing Ruth
   (2)Sarah White
E78B MARY
E78Ba Fawcett Joseph
E78C WILLIAM P
E78D NATHANIEL
E78E ISAAC
E78F THOMAS
E78Fa Walker Thomassin R
E78G JOSEPH
E78Ga Wright Tacy
E78H BENJAMIN
E78Ha — Hannah

[E-79] FAWCETT E09Ea
  Thomas/Martha Branson
E79A HANNAH H
E79Aa Fearsley William

[E-80] BRANSON E08A
  Thomas/Rebeccah Borden
E80A ELI
E80B LEVI -E81-
E80Ba Maynor Mary

[E-81] BRANSON E80B
  Levi/Mary Maynor
E81A THOMAS
E81B JOSEPH
E81C HENRY
E81D REBECCA
E81E LYDIA
E81F LEVI
E81G ELI

238

[E-82] BRANSON E69B
  James Marion/Elizabeth Ann Shockley
E82A   THOMAS BENSON
E82Aa   Branson Mary Frances
E82B   NANCY JANE
E82Ba   Light John Stacy
E82C   ALBERT E
E82D   MATILDA HARRIETT
E82Da   Feagan Frank Andy
E82E   ELIZABETH
E82F   JOHANNA
E82Fa   Branson William A
E82G   MALINDA
E82Ga   Jarvis John
E82H   SARAH
E82Ha   West Joe
E82I   LUCY JANE
E82Ia   Shanks William Vance -E83-
E82Iaf Shanks James
E82Iam McQueen Mary Amelia
E82J   JINNEY
E82K   JOHN W
E82Ka   West Mary

[E-83] SHANKS E82Ia
  William Vance/Lucy Jane Branson
E83A   RAY OSCAR
E83Aa   Baumgartner Elizabeth J
E83B   JAMES ANDREW
E83C   GLADYS IRENE
E83Ca   Nicks Lloyd
E83D   BERTHA CYRILLA
E83Da   Basnett Lemuel Pollard -E84-
E83Daf Basnett Logan
E83Dam McCarthy Angelia
E83E   EMERY FRANKLIN
E83F   LULA MAE
E83G   ARNOLD DAVID

[E-84] BASNETT E83Da
  Lemuel P/Bertha Cyrilla Shanks
E84A   LILLIE PEARL
E84Aa   Roark Raymond Paul
E84B   LEMUEL GERALD

E84Ba   Macgruder Sarah Ellen
E84C   JUANITA RUTH
E84D   WILLIAM LOGAN
E84E   PAUL JEROME
E84Ea   Kischer Juanita C
E84F   BETTY JEAN
E84Fa   Dunduvant Cjarles Kenneth
E84G   DOROTHY MAY
E84Ga   Whittle Mackel Edward
E84H   LARRY DEAN
E84Ha   Fisher Joyce Ann

[E-85] BRANSON E25K
  Ewell C/Myrtle M King
E85A   FLOYD FRANKLIN
E85Aa   Martin Cleo
E85B   EULA EVELYN
E85C   THELMA BERNICE
E85D   GLADYS CLAUDIA
E85Da   Eagle Lester
E85E   THOMAS HASKELL
E85Ea   Hamblatt Theresa Annette
E85F   WAYNE GENTRY -E36-
E85Fa   Nelson Margaret Ellen
E85Faf Nelson Joseph
E85G   E.C. Jr.
E85Ga   Young Loraine
E85H   RICHARD WILLIAM
E85Ha   Horn Mildred
E85I   BUDDY ORIN
E85J   MARGARET ELIZA M

[E-86] BRANSON E35F
  Wayne Gentry/Margaret E Nelson
E86A   JANE ANN
E86Aa   Morgan Don C
E86B   ROGER WAYNE -E87-
E86Ba   Hairfield Barbara
E86Bb   Barrett Kathleen

[E-87] BRANSON E86B
  Roger Wayne/Barbara Hairfield
E87A   JULIE RENEE
E87B   CYNTHIA MICHELLE

(2)Kathleen Barrett
E87C BENJAMIN JOSEPH
E87D BEAU GENTRY

[E-88] CARROLL E63B
  Charles E/Ladoisha Posey
E88A VIRGIL E -E91-
E88Aa Hawkins Elsie Mae
E88Aaf Hawkins Jesse F
E88Aam Manning Lillian
E88B CLARENCE M
E88Ba Bartel Delores
E88C WILLIAM AUGUST
E88Ca Tyree Helen
E88D CHESTER E
E88Da Crane Anna
E88E KENNETH L
E88Ea Crane Lorraine
E88F EDITH E
E88Fa Klenke Eugene
E88G RAYMOND E
E88Ga Doerr Janet
E88H CHARLES W
E88Ha Rich Marge

[E-89] POSEY E69Ca
  Humphrey/Julia Ann Branson
E89A ALLEN A (E63Baf)
E89Aa Baty Ida Belle (E63Bam)
E89Aaf Baty Daniel

[E-90] BRANSON E15D
  Valentine/Susannah East
E90A ISAAC
E90B ANDREW
E90C JEMIMA
E90D JULIA ANN
E90E DAVID
E90F JOSEPH
E90G HIRAM
E90H ELIJAH

[E-91] CARROLL E88A
  Virgil E/Elsie Mae Hawkins
E91A DONALD D -E92-
E91Aa Campbell Marlene
E91B WAYNE D -E93-
E91Ba Klenke Sharon

[E-92] CARROLL E91A
  Donald D/Marlene Campbell
E92A KELLY D
E92B KATHY D
E92C KEVIN D

[E-93] CARROLL E91B
  Wayne D/Sharon Klenke
E93A WAYNE D,Jr
E93B WILLIAM D
E93C WARREN D
E93D WENDY D

[E-94] SIMPSON E48Ga
  John C.F./Minerva Frances Lore
E94A OSCAR STANFORD -E95-
E94Aa Cordray Edna Pearl
E94Aaf Cordray Thmoas
E94B MALLIE RUTH
E94C ANNIE MINERVA
E94D LEORA DELPHA
E94E CARRIE OLIVE
E94F DEE
E94G CLARA
E94H CHARLES
E94I CARRETT
E94J CECIL SHOCKLEY

[E-95] SIMPSON E94A
  Oscar Stanford/Edna Pearl Cordray
E95A RUTH NAOMI
E95B EVA MAY
E95C KATHRYN PEARL
E95Ca Newman Vernon Clifford
E95Caf Newman Heber John
E95D GEORGE WILSON

[F-02] GAITHER(GATER) unknown
  unknown/unknown
F02A GEORGE R -F3-
F82Aa unknown

[F-03] GAITHER F02A
  George R/unknown
F03A JOHN -F4-
F03Aa — Mary
F03Ab Morley Joan

[F-04] GAITHER F03A
  John/Mary —
F04A JOHN Jr -F5-
F04Aa Morley Ruth

[F-05] GAITHER F04A
  John Jr/Ruth Morley
F05A BENJAMIN -F6- (B5Ha)
F05Aa Burgess Sarah (B5H)
F05B EDWARD
F05C JOHN -F46-
F05Ca Buck Jane
F05D MARY
F05E REBECCA
F05F RUTH
F05Fa Hardesly Francis
F05G SUSAN

[F-06] GAITHER F05A
  Benjamin/Sarah Burgess
F06A ANNE
F06B BENJAMIN
F06C CASSANDRA
F06D EDWARD -F7-
F06Da Whittle Eleanor
F06E ELIZABETH
F06F HENRY
F06G JOHN
F06H RUTH
F06I SAMUEL
F06J SARAH
F06K WILLIAM
F06L MARY

F06M JOSEPH

[F-07] GAITHER F06D
  Edward/Eleanor Whittle
F07A BURGESS -F8-
F07Aa Martin Milly
F07B BASIL
F07Ba unknown
F07C BRICE
F07D BENJAMIN
F07E JOHNSEY
F07F NICHOLAS -F45-
F07Fa Greenfield Eleanor
F07Fb Baley Tabitha

[F-08] GAITHER F07A
  Burgess/Milly Martin
F08A ALFRED MOORE
F08Aa Erwin Catherine Reese
F08Aaf Erwin William Willoughby
F08Aam Sharpe Matilda
F08B MARTIN
F08C SARAH
F08D ELVIRA
F08E FORREST
F08F MILLIE
F08G MARIA
F08H BURGESS SIDNEY Sr -F9-
F08Ha Erwin Elizabeth S
F08Hb Corpening Sarah F
F08Hbf Corpening David Jackson Col.
F08Hbm Horton Jane Eliza
F08I ELEANOR E
F08J CHARLES C.P.

[F-09] GAITHER F8H
  Burgess Sidney Sr/Elizabeth S Erwin
F09A WILLIAM
F09Aa McIntyre M
F09B ALFRED HAYWOOD
F09Ba Hoey C
F09C DELIA E
F09Ca Pearson Robert Dr
    (2)Sarah F Corpening

F09D   BURGESS SIDNEY Jr
F09Da Young Mary Elizabeth
F09Daf Young Joseph Alphonso Col
F09Dam Tate Laura Ophelia

[F-10] BURGESS A99A
   Basil Capt/Anne Smith
F10A   AMELIA
F10B   RICHARD
F10C   ELIZABETH
F10D   WILLIAM FREDERICK -F32-
F10Da — Susan
F10E   CHARLES
F10F   BASIL
F10G   WALTER SMITH
F10H   MARY HOLLYDAY

[F-11] BURGESS A88B
   Richard/Elizabeth Magruder
F11A   MORDECAI
F11B   RICHARD -F31-
F11Ba Coolidge Mary
F11C   SARAH
F11Ca Belt Joseph Sprigg
F11D   CASSANDRA
F11Da McKenzie James
F11E   URSULA
F11Ea Bowie William
F11F   CHARLES
F11Fa Magruder Amy
F11G   JOHN MAGRUDER
F11Ga Magruder Eleanor
F11Gb Coolidge Elizabeth

[F-12] BURGESS B04B
   George/Katherine —
F12A   GEORGE

[F-13] BURGESS B05A
   Edward/Sarah —
F13A   ELIZABETH

[F-14] BURGESS B07C
   John Col/Sarah Dorsey
F14A   ACHSAH
F14Aa Green John
F14B   SARAH (B8Ga)
F14Ba Burgess Joshua (B8G)
F14C   BASIL Capt -F20-
F14Ca Dorsey Eleanor
F14Caf Dorsey John
F14Cam Dorsey Anne
F14D   JOHN -F21-
F14Da Griffith Eleanor
F14Daf Griffith Henry
F14Dam Hammond Ruth

[F-15] BURGESS B07H
   Samuel/Jane Wyvill
F15A   MATILDA
F15B   BARBARA
F15Ba Wood —
F15C   JOHN WEST
F15Ca Batte Sarah
F15Cb Simmons Sarah
F15D   BENJAMIN -F33-
F15Da Batte Agnes

[F-16] BURGESS B07I
   West/Elizabeth Warfield
F16A   THOMASINE
F16B   SANDERS
F16C   SAMUEL WEST -F26-
F16Ca unknown
F16D   JOHN BRICE
F16E   WEST Jr -F27-
F16Ea Warfield Rachel
F16Eaf Warfield Brice

[F-17] BURGESS B07J
   Caleb/Deborah Warfield
F17A   JOHN
F17Aa Thomas Rachel
F17B   CALEB -F28-
F17Ba Warfield Anne
F17C   SAMUEL

F17Ca   Warfield Elizabeth
F17D   ALEXANDER
F17E   PHOEBE DELA W
F17Ea   Spurrier Rezin

[F-18]   BURGESS B06E
  Richard/Mary —
F18A   SAMUEL
F18B   ANNE
F18C   RICHARD Jr -B9-
F18D   CHARLES
F18E   ELIZABETH
F18F   GEORGE
F18G   SARAH
F18H   MORDECAI
F18I   EDWARD
F18J   MARY

[F-19]   BURGESS A64F
  John/Rebecca —
F19A   JOHN
F19B   THOMAS

[F-20]   BURGESS F14C
  Basil/Eleanor Dorsey
F20A   JOHN DORSEY
F20B   OSGOOD
F20Ba   Hiatt Abigail
F20Baf Hiatt Stephen
F20C   CYNTHIA
F20D   ELEANOR

[F-21]   BURGESS F14D
  John/Eleanor Griffith
F21A   ELEANOR
F21Aa   McCann John
F21B   NANCY
F21Ba   Steir Henry
F21C   CHARLOTTE
F21Ca   Hammond Nathan
F21Caf Hammond Vachel
F21D   RUTH (F29Aam)
F21Da   Wood John Rev (F29Aaf)
F21E   SARAH ANN DORSEY

F21Ea   Green Thomas Rev
F21F   JULIANA
F21Fa   Lark Michael
F21G   WILLIAM P
F21Ga   Plummer Lydia G
F21H   JOHN H
F21Ha   Hyatt Margaret
F21I   WASHINGTON -F29-
F21Ia   Steir Mary Ann
F21Ib   Wertenbaker Anne

[F-22]   BURGESS B08C
  Michael/Sarah Warfield
F22A   ELIZABETH
F22Aa   Black Joshua
F22B   RODERICK
F22C   BASIL
F22D   NANCY
F22E   THOMAS -F61-
F22Ea   Dorsey Honor
F22Eaf Dorsey Lloyd
F22Eam Green Anna
F22F   MICHAEL
F22G   JOSEPH
F22H   REBECCA
F22Ha   Oram John
F22I   JOSHUA
F22Ia   Mercer Elizabeth
F22J   ABSALOM
F22K   WILLIAM
F22Ka   Ricketts Elizabeth

[F-23]   BURGESS B08D
  Vachel/Rebecca Dorsey
F23A   ANN DORSEY
F23B   PEREGRINE
F23C   JULIET
F23D   ELIZABETH
F23Da   Hines William
F23E   HARRIET
F23Ea   Watkins William
F23Eb   Howard Jeremiah Brice
F23F   THOMAS DORSEY
F23G   REBECCA O

F23Ga   Warfield Nicholas
F23H   HETTY W
F23I   VACHEL

[F-24] BURGESS A34A
    John/Helen Maccubin
F24A   EDWARD

[F-25] BURGESS A34F
    Ephraim/Elizabeth —
F25A   THOMAS

[F-26] BURGESS F16C
    Samuel West/unknown
F26A   ELIZABETH WARFIELD
F26B   RICHARD
F26C   MARGARET ANN

[F-27] BURGESS F16E
    WestJr/Rachel Warfield
F27A   ELIZABETH
F27B   TOMMASIN
F27C   MARY ANN
F27D   NANCY
F27E   REBECCA
F27F   BRICE WARFIELD
F27G   RACHEL

[F-28] BURGESS F17B
    Caleb/Anne Warfield
F28A   ALEXANDER
F28B   SUSAN
F28C   CATHERINE W.P.
F28Ca   Warfield Nathan
F28D   ELIZER ANN

[F-29] BURGESS F21I
    Washington/Mary Ann Steir
F29A   EVA R
F29Aa   Wood Joseph
F29Aaf Wood John Rev (F21Da)
F29Aam Burgess Ruth (F21D)
    (2)Anne Wertenbaker
F29B   ELIAS

F29C   GEORGE W
F29Ca   Lare Mary
F29D   JOHN
F29E   CHARLES O
F29F   RUTH
F29G   LOUIS
F29H   WILLIAM

[F-30] BURGESS A90A
    John D/Lydia M Wise
F30A   SARAH ELLEN
F30Aa   Reid Walter G
F30B   MARY T
F30Ba   Talbot William H
F30Bb   Talbot John M
F30C   THOMAS JEFFERSON -A92-
F30Ca   Owens Mary P
F30D   JOSHUA KATE -A91-
F30Da   Holladay Lucinda A
F30E   FRANCIS F
F30F   ABBIE MARIE
F30Fa   Lusk William H
F30G   JOHN E
F30Ga   Innes Nannie
F30H   JOHN WILLIAM
F30Ha   Innes Sue
F30I   FRANCIS
F30J   HENRY CLAY
F30K   CHARLES W
F30Ka   West Kate

[F-31] BURGESS F11B
    Richard/Mary Coolidge
F31A   JUDSON COOLIDGE
F31B   RICHARD
F31C   ELIZABETH
F31D   MARY

[F-32] BURGESS F10D
    William Frederick/Susan —
F32A   GEORGE
F32B   JULIANA
F32C   ELIZABETH
F32Ca   Gill John

F32D   MARY ANN
F32Da Newton Clemm
F32E   SALLY
F32Ea Calvert Rodham

[F-33] BURGESS F15D
       Benjamin/Agnes Batte
F33A   BENEDICT
F33B   SAMUEL

[F-34] BURGESS B10D
       William Burley/unknown
F34A   JOHN -F35- (C15Ca,D85Caf)
F34Aa Cox Mary (C15C.D85Cam)
F34Aaf Cox William (C11G)
F34Aam Barbarick Margaret (C11Ga)
F34B   VARDRY -F56-
F34Ba Cox Malinda
F34C   ELIZA
F34Ca Perkins John
F34D   MARY E
F34E   ELIZABETH M
F34F   JANE C
F34G   CYNTHIA A
F34H   MARTHA RUTH A
F34Ha McLambeth Eli -F38-
F34Hb Laughlin William Silas
F34I   THOMAS
F34J   MALENDA
F34Ja Cox Albert

[F-35] BURGESS F34A
       John/Mary Cox
F35A   MARTHA AMANDA
F35Aa Lankenau John Henry -F36-
F35Aaf Lankenau Henry
F35Aam McMilliam Mary Adeline
F35B   WILLIAM THOMAS
F35C   JOSEPH HENRY
F35D   JOHN WESLEY -F51-
F35Da Danuser Katherine
F35Daf VonDanuser Hans
F35Dam Sutter Burga
F35E   ELIZABETH M

F35Ea Francis Marcus D -F55-
F35F   JAMES FREDERICK
F35G   BENJAMIN FRANKLIN
F35Ga Griffey Beckey
F35H   CHARLES ALBERT -F54-(D85Ca)
F35Ha Campbell Nevada C (D85C)
F35Haf Campbell Robert H (D21Ea)
F35Ham Shockley Tennessee Ann (D21E)
F35I   VARDRY JEFFERSON
F35J   MARY EVALINE

[F-36] LANKENAU F35Aa
       John Henry/Martha Amanda Burgess
F36A   MARY ZELMA
F36Aa Miller William Frederick -F37-
F36Aaf Mueller Louis
F36Aam Ringeison Charlotte
F36B   NORA ETHEL
F36Ba Collier Robert
F36Baf Collier Randall
F36C   CHARLES EDWIN
F36Ca Howard Stella
F36Caf Howard William
F36D   WILLIAM IRA
F36E   ELSIE MAY
F36F   OLA EVA
F36Fa Matthews Leonard
F36Faf Matthews Pet

[F-37] MILLER F36Aa
       William Frederick/Mary Z Lankenau
F37A   FERN ELEANOR
F37Aa Ritterbusch James Karl -F49-
F37Aaf Ritterbusch Louis C.F.
F37Aam Blackwell Ida May
F37B   ROBERT LEE -F50-
F37Ba Bartow Doris
F37Bb Fowler Phyllis Jeanne

[F-38] McLAMBETH F34Ha
       Eli/Martha Ruth Burgess
F38A   McLAMBETH VALDERUS MACK -F39-
F38Aa Nichols Ida Ellen
F38Aaf Nichols Abraham (C26Da)

F38Aam Cox Hetty Elvira (C26D)
F38B   LEANDER PIERCE -F52-
F38Ba   Fowler Beatrice

[P-39] LAMBETH(McLambeth) F38A
    Valderus Mack/Ida Ellen Nichols
F39A   VIRGIL ERNEST
F39Aa   Franks Lucinda P
F39B   PIERCE EATHIN
F39Ba   Webb Bertha Mae
F39C   ROY LEANDER
F39Ca   Green Clarcie
F39D   TONY ALFRED
F39Da   Landers Opal
F39E   BESSIE MAE
F39Ea   Nicks Walter
F39F   DENA ALBERT
F39Fa   Scott Irene

[P-40] CHEW unknown
    unknown/unknown
F40A   JOHN Col. -F41-
F40Aa   — Sarah

[P-41] CHEW F40A
    John/Sarah —
F41A   SAMUEL -F42- (B4Aaf)
F41Aa   Ayers Anna (B4Aam)
F41Aaf Ayers William

[P-42] CHEW F41A
    Samuel/Anna Ayers
F42A   SARAH (B4Aa)
F42Aa   Burgess Edward Capt. -B5- (B4A)
F42B   JOHN
F42Ba   Harrison Elizabeth

[P-43] ROBINS unknown
    unknown/unknown
F43A   THOMAS -F44-
F43Aa   Buckley Mary

[P-44] ROBINS F43A
    Thomas/Mary Buckley
F44A   EDWARD COL. (B3Aaf)
F44Aa   — Jane (B3Aam)
F44B   OBEDIENCE

[P-45] GAITHER F07F
    Nicholas/Eleanor Greenfield
F45A   HORATIO
F45B   WALTER
F45C   EDWARD
F45D   LIBETIOUS

[P-46] GAITHER F05C
    John/Jane Buck
F46A   EDWARD
F46B   BENJAMIN
F46C   JOSHUA

[P-47] GAITHER F07B
    Basil/unknown
F47A   ELLEN
F47B   BASIL
F47C   BETSEY
F47D   NATHAN
F47E   NELEY
F47F   GASSAWAY

[P-49] RITTERBUSCH F37Aa
    James Karl/Fern Eleanor Miller
F49A   JAMES KARL Jr
F49Aa   Pease Linda Susan
F49Aaf Pease David Lawrence
F49Aam Stricker Joan

[P-50] MILLER F37B
    Robert Lee/Phyllis Fowler
F50A   CHRIS ANN FOWLER
F50Aa   Longhead Wesley
F50B   SUSANNE KAY

[P-51] BURGESS F35D
    John Wesley/Katerine Danuser
F51A   CELESTE L

246

F51Aa Fogerson W.E.

F51B   DORSEY GAVON -F53-

F51Ba Home Mary Mable

[P-52] LAMBETH F38B
    Leander Pierce/Beatrice Fowler

F52A   ELLA LEE

F52Aa Sieber —

F52B   DeVADA

F52Ba Hodges —

F52C   CALVIN CHARLEY

F52D   ROBERT PIERCE

F52E   ZENO MACK

F52F   DOLLIE INA

F52Fa Shultz —

F52G   DAISY EVA

F52Ga Thornton —

[P-53] BURGESS F51B
    Dorsey G/Mary Mable Home

F53A   SANDRA SUE

F53Aa Harlan J.V.

F53B   DORSEY EARL

[P-54] BURGESS F35H
    Charles Albert/Nevada C Campbell

F54A   JOHN RAYMOND

F54B   HILDA EUNICE

F54C   VALDA FERN

[P-55] FRANCIS F35Ea
    Marcus/Elizabeth Burgess

F55A   MELISSA MARY

F55Aa Fleischmann Christ

F55B   MARTHA

F55Ba Viemann William

F55C   ALMEDIA

F55Ca Dobbertine Edward

F55D   EVA

F55Da Fleischmann William

F55E   BIDDIE

F55Ea Schultz John

F55F   LOGUE

F55Fa — Fanny

F55G   GUS

F55H   EDWARD

F55I   ANNIE

F55Ia Peth John

[P-56] BURGESS F34B
    Vardry/Malinda Cox

F56A   HENRY

F56B   THOMAS

F56C   JAMES

F56D   ISABELLE

F56E   JOHN

F56F   ELIJAH

F56G   BENJAMIN

F56H   JOSEPH CHARLES -F57-

F56Ha Hayden Mary Angeline

F56I   CEPHUS

F56J   ALMEDA

[P-57] BURGESS F56H
    Joseph Charles/Mary A Hayden

F57A   GRACE MARIE

F57Aa Tolbert Lee Andrew H -F58-

F57Aaf Tolbert Allen S

F57Aam Lane Artellia Vermel

F57B   ELVA

F57Ba Puckett Carl Dr

F57C   CAROLINE

F57Ca Thomas Richard W

F57D   NELLIE

F57Da Ellis Arthur Claude

F57E   IRENE

F57Ea Pratt Gladstone C

F57F   JESSIE

F57G   STELLA

F57H   LUCY

[P-58] TOLBERT F57Aa
    Lee Andrew/Grace Marie Burgess

F58A   MARJORIE LEONE

F58Aa Hill Homer Austin

F58B   NEVA HELEN

F58Ba Dozier Barclay E Dr

F58C   LYLE HAYDEN -F59-

F58Ca   Schrimsher Trula
F58Caf   Schrimsher Arlonzo
F58Cam   Wilson Nancy Rebecca B
F58D   NINA CAROLYN
F58Da   Rowland Robert F
F58E   EVELYN IRENE
F58Ea   Wade Clifton A
F58F   JACK BURGESS
F58Fa   Morrison Wynema
F58G   MARY PATRICIA
F58Ga   Sellers Leslie M

[P-59] TOLBERT F58C
        Lyle Hayden/Trula Schrimsher
F59A   TOMMY LYLE -F60-
F59Aa   Hill Bettie Sue
F59Aaf   Hill Samuel Franklin
F59Aam   Riley Mildred Elizabeth
F59B   HELEN DENISE

[P-60] TOLBERT F59A
        Tommy Lyle/Bettie Sue Hill
F60A   ELIZABETH LYN
F60B   HELEN LOUISE

[P-61] BURGESS F22E
        Thomas/Honor Dorsey
F61A   THOMAS
F61B   LLOYD
F61C   JOSEPH
F61D   WILLIAM WALLACE
F61E   LUCINDA

[P-62] SMITH A99Ba
        James Haddock/Ann Burgess
F62A   CHARLES BURGESS-F63-
F62Aa   Burgess Lucy
F62B   STEPHEN
F62C   MARTHA
F62D   ANNA
F62E   URSULA
F62F   ELIZABETH
F62G   ELEANOR
F62H   SUSANNA

F62I   ESTHER
F62J   HARRIET
F62Ja   Smith Walter

[P-63] SMITH F62A
        Charles Burgess/Lucy Burgess
F63A   WALTER
F63B   MARY
F63C   WILLIAM -F64-
F63Ca   Lawson Patience
F63D   LUCY
F63E   ABRAHAM
F63F   HAYS
F63G   SARAH ANN
F63H   GEORGE
F63I   CHARLES

[P-64] SMITH F63C
        William/Patience Lawson
F64A   MARY JANE
F64B   JAMES HADDOCK
F64C   SOPHIA ANN
F64D   LUCY
F64E   BASIL BURGESS
F64F   LUCRETIA
F64Fa   Ramey Samuel -F65-
F64G   FRANCES ADALIZA
F64H   PATIENCE
F64I   ZERELDA
F64J   ISABELLA

[P-65] RAMEY F64Fa
        Samuel/Lucretia Smith
F65A   WILLIAM BURGESS -F66-
F65Aa   Jones Maria Lila
F65B   JOHN WATERFIELD
F65C   AMY FRANCES
F65D   THOMAS COSTELLO A
F65E   GEORGE NEYMAN
F65F   EDGAR CLEMENT

SIBLING GROUP F

[F-66] RAMEY F65A
  William Burgess/Maria Lila Jones
F66A   AMY EDNA
F66Aa   McCune Lewis Obadian -F67-
F66B   MINNIE EDITH
F66Ba   Mathers Harry
F66C   CHARLES WALTER
F66Ca   Pierce Mary E
F66D   GEORGE EMER
F66Da   Leake Lulu Mabel
F66E   MARY SUSAN
F66Ea   Bell Alphia
F66F   LUCRETIA CATHERINE
F66Fa   Gregg Samuel Benjamin

[F-67] McCUNE F66Aa
  Lewis Obadian/Amy Edna Ramey
F67A   VESTA MARIE
F67B   LAURA GLADYS
F67C   ZOLA RUTH
F67Ca   Ohmart William Frank
F67D   LILA SUSAN
F67Da   Schupp Oscar Valmer
F67E   RALPH LEWIS
F67Ea   Highbarger Orpha Amelia
F67F   ELSIE EDNA
F67Fa   Richey Byron Eugene -F68-
F67G   LEANDER BURGESS
F67Ga   Wilson Garnette Ruth
F67H   CORA FRANCES
F67Ha   Schupp John Louis

[F-68] RICHEY F67Fa
  Byron Eugene/Elsie Edna McCune
F68A   MELVIN DUANE -F70-
F68Aa   Cobble Elizabeth Alice
F68B   BETHINE
F68C   RENETTA DORENE
F68Ca   Stribling Ray Eugene-F69-
F68Caf Stribling Pearl Martin
F68Cam Daugherty Gracie May
F68D   VESTA RUTH
F68Da   Nisley James Jackie -F71-

[F-69] STRIBLING F68Ca
  Ray Eugene/Renetta Dorene Richey
F69A   TINA MARIE
F69Aa   Kloth Gary Lee
F69B   DEBORAH RUTH
F69Ba   Albright Brian Craig
F69C   DONALD RAY
F69D   TERESA RENE

[F-70] RICHEY F68A
  Melvin Duana/Elizabeth A Cobble
F70A   ROBIN EUGENE
F70Aa   Nickell Nancy Jean
F70B   DUANE ALBERT
F70Ba   Richardson Diana Lisa
F70C   MIRIAM
F70D   LARRY ALLEN
F70E   JANET
F70F   MICHELLE

[F-71] NISLEY F68Da
  James Jackie/Vesta Ruth Richey
F71A   MEAJI LYNN

[G-10] COPELAND UNKN
unknown/unknown
G10A   WILLIAM Sr. —G11— (D17Faf,
        D25Gaf,P11Eaf,P11Iaf)
G10Aa   Taff Martha   (D17Fam,
        G25Gam,P11Eam,P11Iam)
G10Aaf Taff Peter(J11Abf,I42Abf,G50Abf)
G10B   JOSEPH Sr. —G25—
G10Ba   unknown
G10C   SOLOMON Sr. —G29—
G10Ca   unknown
G10Cb   Sample Malinda
G10D   JOHN —G35—
G10Da   Sewell —
G10Db   Sewell Anna
G10E   SARAH
G10Ea   Taff —G46—
G10Eb   Blanton Ezekial —G47—

[G-11] COPELAND G10A
William Sr/Martha Taff
G11A   JOHN —G12— (I46Baf,U16Aaf)
G11Aa   Wiseman Mary A (I46Bam,U16Aam)
G11Aaf Wiseman Davenport Oliver T
G11B   DAVIS —G13—
G11Ba   Moss Sybilla
G11Bb   Miller Malinda
G11C   CALLAWAY
G11Ca   Martin —
G11Caf Martin John Y
G11D   PETER —G14— (D25Ga)
G11Da   Shockley Nancy (D25G)
G11Daf Shockley Wm. R (D17F,G11Ia)
G11Dam Parker Mrs Ruth (D17Fb)
G11E   SOLOMON Jr. —G15— (I53Aaf)
G11Ea   unknown
G11F   JOSEPH Jr. (P11Ea)
G11Fa   Carnes Ann (P11E)
G11Faf Carnes Jehu(P10A,E21Baf,G11Haf)
G11Fam BurtonNancy(P10Aa,E21Bam,G11Ham)
G11G   WILLIAM RILEY —G16—
G11Ga   Vaughan Rachel
G11Gaf Vaughn William
G11H   MARY E (P11Ia,J14Gam,J20Eam)
G11Ha   Carnes John (P11I,J14Gaf,J20Eaf)
G11Haf Carnes Jehu(P10A,E21Baf,G11Faf)
G11Ham BurtonNancy(P10Aa,E21Bam.G11Fam)
G11I   REBECCA (D17Fa)
G11Ia   Shockley Wm Sr, (D17F,G11Daf)
G11Iaf Shockley Meredith (D14F,T13Laf)
G11Iam Worrell Sarah (D14Fa,T13Lam)
G11J   SALLIE C (J12Cam,T18Aam)
G11Ja   Lambeth Lytle (I52Da,J12Caf,
                    T18Aaf)
G11Jaf Lambeth Samuel (I52Daf)

[G-12] COPELAND G11A
John/Mary Wiseman
G12A   FRANCIS MARION —G17— (I46Ba)
G12Aa   Boone Eliza J (I46B)
G12Aaf Boone Israel (I42B,I53Baf)
G12Aam Gelette Julia(I42Ba,I42Cb,I53Bam)
G12B   WILLIAM M —G18— (U16Aa)
G12Ba   Cowan Louisa Evaline (U16A)
G12Baf Cowan David Sr (U11Abf)
G12Bam Martin Telitha (U11Abm)
G12C   ALBERT WISEMAN —G19—
G12Ca   Breedem Louisa
G12Caf Breeden William
G12D   CALVIN C —G20—
G12Da   Wild Paulina
G12Daf Wild John
G12E   JOHN RICHARD
G12Ea   Bishop Virginia Ellen
G12Eaf Bishop John(G20Caf,Y58Faf,Y58Gaf
G12Eam ElrodMartha(G20Cam,Y58Fam.Y58Gam
G12F   TELITHA T (R15Fam)
G12Fa   Adkins John H —G21— (R15Faf)
G12G   MYRA D
G12Ga   Davis Landon D
G12Gaf Davis John (G37Caf))
G12Gam Piggs Agnes (Q37Cam)
G12H   ELIZA J
G12Ha   Hickam Robert
G12I   MATILDA ROBERTS (U12Ia)
G12Ia   Helton David (U12I)
G12Iaf Helton Isaac Sr (U11A,E53Ba,
                U16Ba,E25Caf,V13Caf,V15Daf)

250

G12Iam Cowan Mary A (U16B,U11Ab,E25Cam)

[G-13] COPELAND G11B
  Davis/Sybilla Moss
G13A WILLIAM
G13B MARION
G13C HENDERSON –G22–
G13Ca Roberson Dollie
G13Caf Roberson William
G13Cam Mason Lucinda
    (2)Malinda Miller
G13D SAMUEL P

[G-14] COPELAND G11D
  Peter/Nancy Shockley
G14A FANNIE
G14Aa Loupe "Babe"
G14B LOTTIE
G14Ba Burrows Charles
G14C ROSA
G14Ca Crum Edward
G14Caf Crum John

[G-15] COPELAND G11E
  Solomon Jr/ unk
G15A JOHN Jr.
G15B CALLAWAY
G15C GEORGE H
G15D WILLIAM J
G15E MARY
G15Ea Kinsey W. T.
G15F AMANDA
G15Fa Ginn George
G15G MARTHA LUELLA (I53Aa)
G15Ga Ellis Thomas G (I53A)
G15Gaf Ellis James (I52E,I46Aam)
G15Gam Pearson – (I52Ea,I46Aam)

[G-16] COPELAND G11G
  William Riley/Rachel Vaughan
G16A JAMES
G16Aa Crum Mary E
G16Aaf Crum Robert S.(Y31Aaf,Q44Jaf)
G16Aam Hutchison E.(Y31Aam,Q44Jam)

G16B ROBERT –G23–
G16Ba Collins Sarah Ann
G16C NANCY
G16Ca Stewart Vince Jr
G16D MARY
G16Da Haggerty Tom
G16E LUCINDA
G16F BERTIE
G16Fa Gove William

[G-17] COPELAND G12A
  Francis M/Eliza Boone
G17A IDA
G17Aa Williams Henry
G17B OLIVER
G17C GEORGE
G17D EDWARD
G17E MYRTLE
G17F CHARLES

[G-18] COPELAND G12B
  William M/Louisa E Cowan
G18A TELITHA JANE
G18Aa Noblett T.J.
G18B ARMINA AUGUSTA
G18Ba Spratley Edward
G18Baf Spratley William H (K34Ga)
G18Bam Parker Malinda (K34G)
G18C LAUNA AMERICA
G18Ca McDaniel J.A.
G18D GRANVILLE M
G18E MARY ELLEN
G18Ea Taff David N
G18Eaf Taff James
G18Eam Martin Mary
G18F OLIVER
G18G IDA ELEANOR
G18H CALVIN COLUMBUS
G18I LUMINA ELIZABETH
G18Ia Terry Frank M
G18J JULIA ANN
G18Ja Terry George W
G18K MYRA CANSADA
G18Ka Terwilliger Byrd

G18L   DAVID ALONZO —G24—
G18La   Wakefield Cora
G18Laf Wakefield Harris
G18M   JOHN LOUIS
G18Ma   Duffin Rosa
G18N   LORENZO DOW
G18O   MINNIE A
G18P   LANNIE M
G18Q   WILLIAM O

[G-19] COPELAND G12C
   Albert W/Louisa Breeden
G19A   WISEMAN
G19B   MARY
G19C   OLIVE
G19D   MARTHA
G19Da   Briggs Terry
G19Daf Briggs Scott Terry (S11A)
G19Dam Fennessey Bridget (S11Aa)
G19E   FRANK
G19Ea   Barnhart Paralee
G19F   EVERETT R
G19Fa   Barnhart Daisy
G19G   EDWARD A
G19Ga   Roberds Catherine
G19H   NETTIE
G19Ha   Helton Gib
G19Haf Helton Crismon (U11C)
G19Ham Pryor Louisa Jane (U11Ca)
G19I   EDNA
G19Ia   Connor William
G19J   DOLPH
G19Ja   Pearson Arizona
G19Jaf Pearson Charles (G20Faf)
G19Jb   Edwards Nellie

[G-20] COPELAND G12D
   Calvin C/Paulina Wild
G20A   JOSEPH AMERICUS
G20B   THOMAS J
G20C   JOHN BURTON
G20Ca   Bishop Missouri
G20Caf Bishop John(G12Eaf,Y58Faf,Y58Gaf
G20Cam Elrod M.S.(G12Eam,Y58Fam,Y58Gam)

G20D   HUBBARD (G58Aaf)
G20Da   Scott Rosa (G58Aam)
G20Daf Scott Thomas
G20Dam Vaughan Jennette
G20E   CLAY W (G57Ca)
G20Ea   Burns Jennie (G57C)
G20Eaf Burns Burton (G51C)
G20Eam Denton Emily R (G51Ca)
G20F   WILLIAM RAY
G20Fa   Pearson Griselda
G20Faf Pearson Charles (G19Jaf)
G20G   ELSIA A
G20Ga   Hastings S.E.
G20H   BETTIE
G20Ha   Renfrow Fred
G20I   LETTIE
G20Ia   Picker Adolph

[G-21] ADKINS G12Fa
   John H/Telitha Copeland
G21A   ALFRED
G21B   EDNA
G21Ba   Butcher George
G21C   CHARLES
G21Ca   Krone William
G21D   ELSIE (R15Fa)
G21Da   Terrill A (Jack) Dr (R15F)
G21Daf TerrillJackson(R12D,Q32Ea,R31Baf)
G21Dam Moreland Eliza(Q32E,R12Da,R31Bam)
G21E   LAYMON
G21Ea   Pendleton Irenah
G21Eaf Pendleton John Riley
G21Eam Woody Fannie

[G-22] COPELAND G13C
   Henderson/Dollie Roberson
G22A   ROE
G22B   HOMER
G22C   FREEMAN
G22D   EUNICE
G22Da   Bade Louis
G22E   DELLA
G22Ea   Bade Joseph Jr.
G22F   STERLING

G22G   MABEL

[G-23] COPELAND G16B
   Robert/Sarah A Collins
G23A   JAMES
G23B   LEE
G23C   HATTIE
G23D   GERTIE
G23E   LENA
G23F   ANNA

[G-24] COPELAND G18L
   David A/Cora Wakefield
G24A   ALTA
G24Aa   Street Hugh
G24B   RAYMOND
G24C   KENNETH

[G-25] COPELAND G10B
   Joseph Sr./unk
G25A   RICHARD -G26-
G25Aa   Russell Nancy (D25Ea,J15Cam)
G25B   CASANDRA (Y27Aam)
G25Ba   Elrod Thomas B. -G27- (Y27Aaf)
G25Baf Elrod C. Jackie
G25Bam Moon Scianna
G25C   MARTIN -G28-
G25Ca   Brasier Polly
G25Caf Brasier S.T.

[G-26] COPELAND G25A
   Richard/ Nancy Russell
G26A   NOAH

[G-27] ELROD G25Ba
   Thomas B Jr/Casandra Copeland
G27A   LEONA
G27Aa   Shanks Thomas
G27B   CLARA
G27Ba   Stockton Paul
G27C   TONY (Y59Ba)
G27Ca   Farm Bertha (Y59B)
G27Caf Farm Joseph M (Y42Da)
G27Cam Jones Leona F (Y42D)

G27D   EPLEY
G27E   EDGAR
G27F   MARY E
G27Fa   Myers Joseph S
G27Faf Myers C.C. (Y32A)
G27G   BESSIE
G27Ga   Pohl Joseph
G27H   NANCY (Z42Ham)
G27Ha   Moon Elwwod (Z42Haf)
G27I   LUCINDA (Y27Aa)
G27Ia   West William (Y27A)

[G-28] COPELAND G25C
   Martin/Polly Brasier
G28A   FLORA L
G28B   NANCY P
G28C   FELINA E
G28D   JOSEPH
G28E   SARAH

[G-29] COPELAND G10C
   Solomon Sr/unk
G29A   JAMES
G29B   WILLIAM
G29C   MILLY JANE
G29Ca   Hancock —
G29Cb   Doyle Leander
G29D   UNKNOWN
   (2)Malinda Sample
G29E   LEERVA
G29Ea   Doyle Hugh L.M.
G29F   NOAH
G29Fa   Doyle Ruth
G25G   MARTIN -G30- (T30Ia)
G25Ga   Woods Lucinda (T30I)
G29Gaf Woods Samuel Major (T14Faf)
G29Gan Vaughan Sarah (T14Fam)
G29H   MARTHA (D25Eam)
G29Ha   Russell Levi M (D25Eaf)
G29Haf Russell Joseph
G29I   ELIZA
G29Ia   Gremp Karl Ludwig -G31- (J15Gaf)
G29J   MARY ANN
G29Ja   Senne John Christian

253

G29K   JOHN -G32- (K14Caf,K14Bbf)
G29Ka   Doyle Nancy (K14Cam,K14Bbm)
G29L   ANDREW JACKSON
G29La   Holman Rachel Charlotte
G29Laf Holman J.A.
G29M   JEHU (L16Iaf)
G29Ma   Henson Emily
G29Maf Henson George
G29Mam Fanbush Anna
G29N   JOSEPH
G29Na   Hickam Elizabeth
G29O   FANNIE
G29Oa   Henson William

[G-30] COPELAND G29G
    Martin/Lucinda Woods
G30A   EDWARD
G30B   BESSIE

[G-31] GREMP G29Ia
    Karl L/Eliza Copeland
G31A   UNKNOWN
G31Aa   Conley L.W.
G31B   FANNIE ISABELLE (J15Ga)
G31Ba   Eads Joseph T (J15G)
G31Baf Eads Geo.Wash(J12D,L15Ca,D32Baf)
G31Bam Simpson F.(L15C,J12Da,D32Bam)
G31C   MARY
G31Ca   Eads G.S.
G31D   SOLOMON A Dr.
G31Da   Felker Missouri Annette
G31Daf Felker John (D25Faf,G31Faf)
G31Dam Anderson Amanda(D25Fam,G31Fam)
G31E   HENRY J Dr.
G31Ea   Cansler Allie
G31Eaf Cansler James H (V14Aa)
G31Eam Rowden Malinda (V14A)
G31F   CHRISTIAN C
G31Fa   Felker Harriet Mary
G31Faf Felker John (D25Faf,G31Daf)
G31Fam Anderson Amanda (D25Fam,G31Dam)
G31G   WILLIAM A Dr
G31Ga   Pickering Belle
G31Gaf Pickering George

G31Gam Feeler Jane
G31Gb   Johnson Anna

[G-32] COPELAND G29K
    John/Nancy Doyle
G32A   JAMES
G32B   BELLE
G32Ba   Forester -
G32C   MARTIN N -G33-
G32Ca   Breeding Malinda Ann
G32Caf Breeding James
G32Cam Miller Lucinda
G32D   W NOAH -G34- (K14Ca)
G32Da   Coffey Mary F (K14C)
G32Daf Coffey Campbell (K11C,J12Fa,
            G32Eaf,K26Cbf,K32Cbf)
G32Dam Eads Caroline J12F,K11Ca,G32Eam,
            K26Cbm,K32Cbm)
G32E   JOHN HENRY (K14Bb)
G32Ea   Coffey Isabelle (K14B,K32Cb)
G32Eaf Coffey Campbell (K11C,J12Fa,
            G32Daf,K26Cbf,K32Cbf)
G32Eam Eads Caroline (J12F,K11Ca,
            G32Dam,K26Cbm,K32Cbm)
G32Eb   Finn Mary
G32Ebf Finn William D (U120af)
G32Ebm Russell Malinda (U120am)
G32F   CHARLES
G32Fa   Forester Lula
G32G   EMMA
G32Ga   Collins John
G32H   JASPER

[G-33] COPELAND G32C
    Martin N/Malinda Breeding
G33A   BERTIE
G33Aa   Howard Jesse
G33B   J. OLLIE
G33C   "MANNIE"
G33Ca   Breeden -
G33Caf Breeden J.R. (G33Faf)
G33D   ROY
G33Da   Breeden Lula
G33Daf Breeden Isaac

G33E   MOLLIE
G33Ea   Ousley —
G33F   EMMA
G33Fa   Breeden —
G33Faf Breeden J.R. (G33Caf)

[G-34] COPELAND G32D
        W. Noah/Mary Coffey
G34A   EVA
G34Aa   Finn Charles H
G34Aaf FinnBarnett(J12Eaf,K27Baf,E20Aaf)
G34B   EMMA
G34Ba   Lueckenhoff Herman
G34C   CAMPBELL
G34Ca   McCrory Nan
G34D   BEN
G34Da   Clatterbuck Ora
G34E   JAMES

[G-35] COPELAND G10D
        John/ — Sewell
G35A   PLEASANT —G36— (G62Caf)
G35Aa   Matlock - (G62Cam)
G35Ab   Pryor Nancy
G35B   JAMES
G35C   JOHN
G35D   SARAH (M11Cam,Y13Abm)
G35Da   Matlock G.W. (M11Caf,Y13Abf)
G35E   FRANCES
G35Ea   Pierce Jenness
G35F   MARY
G35Fa   Beckham Caswell
G35G   ELIZA
G35Ga   Berry William —G37—
        (2)Anne Sewell
G35H   MARTHA
G35Ha   Mustain John, Rev
G35I   EMILY JANE (H55Aam)
G35Ia   Beckham Anderson —G38— (H55Aaf)
G35J   THOMAS J —G39—
G35Ja   Fritts Arletha
G35Jaf Fritts Phillip (G35Kaf)
G35K   FRANCIS MARION —G40—
G35Ka   Fritts Frances A

G35Kaf Fritts Phillip (G35Jaf)
G35L   ISAAC NEWTON —G41—
G35La   Barnes —
G35Lb   Maxwell Cordella
G35M   JOSEPH I —G42—
G35Ma   Vaughan Nancy
G35N   WILLIAM JASPER
G35Na   Ferrell Malissa
G35Nb   Cox -
G35O   MARTIN M —G43— (P16Baf)
G35Oa   Hazzard Livonia (P16Bam)
G35P   REBECCA

[G-36] COPELAND G35A
        Pleasant/ — Matlock
G36A   MARY
G36Aa   Parker Marion
G36Ab   Prewett James
G36B   BARBARA
G36Ba   Talley Marion
G36C   SARAH (G62Ca)
G36Ca   Bell John (G62C
G36Caf Bell George W —G62—
G36Cam Prewett Roena
G36D   MARTIN —G44—
G36Da   Parker Mary
G36Daf Parker Wesley
G36E   JOSEPH —G45—
G36Ea   Hutchison Ellen
G36Eaf Hutchison Benjamin
G36Eam Land Della
        (2)Nancy Pryor
G36F   JOHN S
G36Fa   Martin Lumina
G36Faf Martin "Cad"
G36Fb   Roberson Dollie
G36Fbf Roberson Pleas
G36G   LUCINDA
G36Ga   Terry Peter

[G-37] BERRY G35Ga
        William/Eliza Copeland
G37A   JAMES DAVID
G37Aa   Duncan Mary

G37Aaf Duncan Alvis
G37B   WILLIAM MATTHEW
G37Ba Hawkins Beditha Ellen
G37Baf Hawkins John

[G-38] BECKHAM G35Ia
   Anderson/ Emily Copeland
G38A   LEONARD
G38Aa Sewell Tina
G38B   JOHN
G38Ba Beasley Jennie
G38C   PERRY
G38D   ARMINTA (H55Aa)
G38Da Bailey John P (H55A)
G38Daf Bailey Daniel (H52G)
G38Dam Marcee Susan A. H. (H52Ga)
G38E   ROWENA
G38Ea Wood Henry
G38F   MARTHA
G38G   DORA

[G-39] COPELAND G35J
   Thomas J/Arletha Fritts
G39A   WILLIAM
G39B   CRISSIE C
G39C   ROBERT
G39D   ALBERT
G39E   ALFRED
G39F   ROSA
G39Fa Arnold Frank

[G-40] COPELAND G35K
   Francis Marion/Frances Fritts
G40A   HENRY
G40B   THOMAS
G40C   LETTIE
G40Ca Southard Sherman
G40Caf Southard William A
G40Cam Chandler Quintilla

[G-41] COPELAND G35L
   Isaac N/ — Barnes
G41A   GEORGE
G41B   JOHN

G41C   ALBERT
G41D   CHARLES
G41E   DAVID
G41F   JOSEPH
G41G   SAMUEL
G41H   ODA
   (2)Cordella Maxwell
G41I   ISAAC
G41J   BENJAMIN
G41K   MARY
G41Ka Copeland Boley

[G-42] COPELAND G35M
   Joseph T/Nancy Vaughan
G42A   JAMES
G42Aa Beasley Jeanette
G42B   WILLIAM
G42Ba Turpin Paralee
G42C   JOHN
G42D   CHESTER
G42E   JOSEPH
G42F   ANNA
G42Fa Emmons M.
G42G   FRANK
G42H   MARTHA
G42Ha Kendrick —
G42I   VICIE
G42Ia Johnson —

[G-43] COPELAND G35O
   Martin M/Livonia Hazzard
G43A   WILLIAM
G43B   LAURA
G43Ba Beckham Thomas
G43Baf Beckham George M
G43Bam Matlock Edna J
G43C   EMMA (P16Ba)
G43Ca Breeden John (P16B)
G43Caf Breeden James R (P14Ca,G60Aaf)
G43Cam Carnes Mary (P14C,G60Aam)
G43Cb Beckham Riley
G43D   JOHN
G43Da Mizell —
G43Daf Mizell James

SIBLING GROUP G

G43E   CHARLES

[G-44] COPELAND G36D
   Martin/Mary Parker
G44A   MARY
G44Aa   Sneed W.D.
G44B   LEVI F
G44C   ELLEN
G44Ca   Brumley John
G44D   WILLIAM M
414E   MARGARET
G44Ea   Nelson John
G44F   ETHEL
G44Fa   Hankley Thomas
G44G   JOHN
G44Ga   Ragan Leona

[G-45] COPELAND G36E
   Joseph/Ellen Hutchison
G45A   LIZZIE
G45Aa   Roberson "Bud"
G45B   ALICE
G45Ba   Mayfield Ernest
G45C   MAMIE
G45Ca   Sneed William
G45D   MARTIN
G45E   CANSADA
G45Ea   Blackwell Richard

[G-46] TAFF G10Ea
   unknown/Sarah Copeland
G46A   JOHN (T15Caf,Y25Iaf)
G46Aa   Anderson Mahala (T15Cam,Y25Iam)

[G-47] BLANTON G10Eb
   Ezekial/Sarah Copeland
G47A   JOHN
G47B   JASPER -G48-
G47Ba   unknown
G47C   AMANDA
G47Ca   Brasier John Rile
G47D   CAROLINE
G47Da   Brasier Green M

[G-48] BLANTON G47B
   Jasper/Unknown
G48A   DANIEL M
G48B   J.H.
G48C   UNKNOWN
G48Ca   Messersmith Montgomery
G48D   UNKNOWN
G48Da   Wilson J.H.

[G-49] BURNS Unknown
   Unknown/Unknown
G49A   JOHN -G50-
G49Aa   Unknown
G49Ab   Wyrick Ellen

[G-50] BURNS G49A
   John/Unknown
G50A   HENRY -G51-
G50Aa   Unknown
G50Ab   Taff Malinda
G50Abf   Taff Peter(G10Aaf,I42Abf,J11Abf)
G50B   JULIAN -G52-
G50Ba   Grady —
G50C   ROLAND -G53-
G50Ca   Aher Jane
G50D   LUCINDA
G50Da   Davidson Richard R -G54-
G50E   LIVINIA
G50Ea   Wilson John -G55-
G50F   MARY

[G-51] BURNS G50A
   Henry/unknown
G51A   JAMES
G51Aa   Cansler —
G51Aaf   Cansler John
G51Ab   Rowden —
    (2)Malinda Taff
G51B   RANSOM -G56-
G51Ba   Denton Jane
G51C   BURTON -G57- (G20Eaf)
G51Ca   Denton Emily R (G20Eam)
G51Cb   Caldwell Sarah
G51D   MARY

G51Da Barnhart George
G51Db Barnhart James
G51E   MINERVA
G51Ea Kimsey William
G51Eaf Kimsey Solomon
G51F   GEORGE G -G58-
G51Fa Hardin Matilda
G51G   WILLIAM -G59-
G51Ga Kluner Amanda
G51Gaf Kluner Herman (G51Haf)
G51Gam Holloway Zilphia Ann (G51Ham)
G51H   ISAAC H -G60-
G51Ha Kluner Mary A
G51Haf Kluner Herman (G51Gaf)
G51Ham Holloway Zilphia Ann (G51Gam)
G51Hb Mills Maud
G51I   ALBERT TAYLOR -G61-
G51Ia Barnhart Mary Ellen
G51Iaf Barnhart E.P. (U16Da)
G51Iam Cowan Eliza (U16D)

[G-52] BURNS G50B
  Julian/ — Grady
G52A   JAMES
G52B   MARTHA
G52C   HENRY

[G-53] BURNS G50C
  Roland/Jane Aher
G53A   JAMES
G53B   HENRY CARROLL
G53C   POLLY
G53D   MATILDA
G53Da Russell —
G53E   ELIZABETH
G53Ea Sanders —

[G-54] DAVIDSON G50Da
  Richard/Lucinda Burns
G54A   MARGARET
G54B   MATILDA
G53Ba Taylor —

G54C   HARRIETT
G54D   NANCY
G54E   JOHN PERRYMAN
G54F   JAMES
G54G   JOSEPH

[G-55] WILSON G50Ea
  John/Livinia Burns
G55A   LEE
G55B   PLEASANT

[G-56] BURNS G51B
  Ransom/Jane Denton
G56A   THOMAS
G56Aa Caldwell Jane

[G-57] BURNS G51C
  Burton/Emily Denton
G57A   JEFF
G57B   JOHN
G57C   JENNIE (G20Ea)
G57Ca Copeland Clay (G20E)
    (2)Sarah Caldwell
G57D   JAMES M
G57E   GRISELDA
G57Ea Lawson Gordon
G57F   DULCIE
G57Fa Orr Elzey
G57G   CHARITY
G57Ga Humphrey Manley M
G57H   GERTIE
G57Ha Whitaker Hardin
G57I   SOPHIA
G57Ia Parker Rainey
G57J   J. CLEVE
G57Ja Rowden -
G57Jaf Rowden William N (V18E)
G57Jam Carnes Mary (V18Ea)

[G-58] BURNS G51F
  George/Matilda Hardin
G58A   ROBERT
G58Aa Copeland Lee
G58Aaf Copeland Hubbard (G20D)

G58Aam Scott Rosa (G20Da)
G58B   PRESTON
G58C   INDIA
G58Ca   Vaughan Jesse
G58Caf Vaughan John W (T14Ba,I54Aaf)
G58Cam Elkins Bettie

[G-59] BURNS G51G
    William/Amanda Kluner
G59A   CARNEY
G59Aa   Pendleton Ollie
G59B   ALVIS
G59Ba   Copeland Missouri
G59C   STELLA
G59Ca   Duncan Milford
G59Cb   Diller Fred
G59D   MALINDA
G59Da   Gray Elmer
G59E   MARIE

[G-60] BURNS G51H
    Isaac/Mary Kluner
G60A   EDITH (P16Aa)
G60Aa   Breeden Elmer (P16A)
G60Aaf Breeden James R (P14Ca,G43Caf)
G60Aam Carnes Mary (P14C,G43Cam)
G60B   MABEL
G60Ba   Kokensparger -
G60C   VIOLA
G60Ca   Lyons -
G60D   MARGERY
G60Da   Dawson -
G60E   WILLIAM

[G-61] BURNS G51I
    Albert/Mary Barnhart
G61A   RUTH
G61Aa   Hutchison L.B. Jr.
G61B   PEARL
G61Ba   Birmingham C.C.
G61C   EUGENE

[G-62] BELL G36Caf
    George W/Roena Prewett
G62A   JAMES MADISON -G63-
G62Aa   Parker Eliza
G62B   C.C. -G64-
G62Ba   Sauls -
G62Bb   Jennings Hettie
G62C   JOHN -G65- (G56Ca)
G62Ca   Copeland Sarah (G36C)
G62Caf Copeland Pleasant (G35A)
G62Cam Matlock - (G35Aa)
G62D   WILLIAM R -G66-
G62Da   Unknown
G62Db   Davis Rachel
G62Dbf Davis William
G62Dbm Hicks Elizabeth
G62E   RICHARD T
G62F   LOUISA J
G62Fa   Bartle Warren
G62G   MARY R
G62Ga   McAfee Michael
G62H   JOSEPHINE
G62Ha   Helton James C
G62Haf Helton William
G62I   ALEGERENE
G62Ia   Williams A.J.
G62Ib   McAfee George
G62J   MELVINA
G62Ja   Williams James
G62K   DORA E
G62Ka   Sauls George W
G62Kb   Miller John

[G-63] BELL G62A
    James/Eliza Parker
G63A   CLARK
G63B   SALLIE
G63Ba   Davis Grant
G63C   WILLIAM W
G63D   ISABELLE
G63Da   Workman John
G63E   THOMAS
G63F   HENRY
G63G   CHARLES

G63H   ROSE
G63Ha   Freeze R.L.
G63I   MARTHA
G63Ia   Humphrey Mike
G63J   TINE
G63Ja   Cross Isaac A
G63K   CLAY
G63Ka   Berling Gus

[G-64] BELL G62B
   C.C./— Sauls
G64A   RILEY
     (2)Hettie Jennings
G64B   IDA
G64C   SYLVIA
G64D   GOLDIE

[G-65] BELL G62C
   John/Sarah Copeland
G65A   ROAN
G65Aa   Gibson James
G65B   NOAH
G65C   CARTER
G65D   WILBERT
G65E   COLUMBUS

[G-66] BELL G62D
   William R/unknown
G66A   WILLIAM
G66B   RACHEL
G66Ba   Irick —
     (2)Rachel Davis
G66C   PETER
G66D   JOHN W
G66E   EDWARD
G66F   MOLLIE
G66Fa   Burton Frank
G66G   FINIS

[H-11] LIGHT unknown
    unknown/unknown
H11A   JOHN -H12-
H11Aa unknown

[H-12] LIGHT H11A
    John/ Unknown
H12A   ENOCH -H13- (K31Daf)
H12Aa unknown (K31Dam)
H12B   WRIGHT -H14- (H52Aa)
H12Ba Bailey Margaret (H52A)
H12Baf Bailey James Sr (H51A)
H12Bam Bailey Elizabeth Mrs (H51Aa)
H12C   FLOWER -H15-
H12Ca Rice —
H12Cb Miller Eliza
H12Cbf Miller Martin
H12D   OBADIAH

[H-13] LIGHT H12A
    Enoch/unknown
H13A   JOHN
H13B   TEMPERANCE (K31Da,Y29Bam,Y29Cam)
H13Ba Davis Thomas(K31D,Y29Baf,Y29Caf)
H13Baf Davis William (K31C,Y34Baf)
H13Bam Tennyson Eliza (K31Ca,Y34Bam)
H13C   SARAH
H13Ca Reeves Joseph -H16-
H13D   NANCY
H13Da Rhodes Isaac -H17-
H13E   CATHERINE
H13Ea Nelson William H

[H-14] LIGHT H12B
    Wright/Margaret Bailey
H14A   WILLIAM
H14B   GEORGE
H14C   ALLEN
H14D   LUTITIA MELVINA
H14Da Goodnight Bud
H14E   SARAH
H14Ea Thorton John
H14F   ELBIN K
H14Fa Dotson -

H14G   ENOCH -H18-
H14Ga Rinks Mattie
H14H   ZEBEDEE D -H19-
H14Ha Overlease Jane
H14I   VAL S
H14Ia Smith Jennie
H14Ib Moman Mary J
H14J   CAROLINE
H14Ja Joice A. L.
H14K   LIBBIE
H14Ka Ray —
H14L   ELLEN
H14La Dotson Thomas

[H-15] LIGHT H12C
    Flower/— Rice
H15A   JOHN
H15Aa Elder Lizzie
H15B   WILLIAM HENSON
H15Ba Ford Mary
H15C   GEORGE
H15D   ELLEN
H15Da Francher Dr
H15E   JANE
H15Ea Hood John

[H-16] REEVES H13Ca
    Joseph/Sarah Light
H16A   TONY

[H-17] RHODES H13Da
    Isaac/Nancy Light
H17A   LUCY
H17Aa Colvin —
H17B   IDA

[H-18] LIGHT H14G
    Enoch/Mattie Rinks
H18A   ROY
H18B   LOVE
H18C   MAUD

[H-19] LIGHT H14H
  Zebedee/Jane Overlease
H19A   OTTO
H19B   GEORGIA
H19C   VIRGIL
H19D   SADIE
H19E   DELLA
H19F   NELLIE
H19Fa Smith —
H19G   JAMES

[H-51] BAILEY unknown
  unknown/unknown
H51A   JAMES SR —H52— (H12Baf,Q31Gaf)
H51Aa — Elizabeth (H12Bam)

[H-52] BAILEY H51A
  James Sr/ Elizabeth —
H52A   MARGARET (H12Ba)
H52Aa Light Wright (H12B
H52B   ALEXANDER
H52C   ALLEN —H53—
H52Ca unk
H52D   GEORGE
H52E   JAMES R —H54— (Q31Ga)
H52Ea Moreland Nancy (Q31G)
H52Eaf Moreland George (Q30A,M11Ia)
H52F   WILLIAM
H52G   DANIEL —H55— (G38Daf)
H52Ga Marcee Susan A.H. (G38Dam)
H52Gaf Marcee William
H52H   MARY ANN
H52Ha Sands Isaac
H52I   LUTITIA
H52Ia Newberry Harmon H

[H-53] BAILEY H52C
  Allen/ unknown
H53A   JANE
H53Aa Collins William
H53Ab Bilyeu —
H53B   ELKANAH P —H56—
H53Ba Hart Louisa J
H53C   ELBERT

H53Ca Hayes Martha

[H-54] BAILEY H52E
  James R/Nancy Moreland
H54A   JANE
H54Aa Riley James
H54B   MARGARET
H54Ba Logan —
H54C   POLLY ANN
H54Ca Graham —
H54Cb Tyler John
H54D   GEORGE
H54E   WILLIAM

[H-55] BAILEY H52G
  Daniel/Susan A.H. Marcee
H55A   JOHN P (G38Da)
H55Aa Beckham Arminta (G38D)
H55Aaf Beckham Anderson (G35Ia)
H55Aam Copeland Emily Jane (G35I)
H55B   JAMES WILEY
H55Ba Clark Martha A.E.
H55Baf Clark Stephen
H55C   WILLIAM A
H55Ca Duke Mary
H55D   GEORGE A
H55Da Wentzel Minnie
H55Daf Wentzel Frederick
H55E   MARTIN ALONZO —H57—
H55Ea Moreland Mary (M15Fa)
H55Eaf Moreland William W Sr (M15Faf)
H55Eam Bennett Polly (M15Fam)
H55F   NIAGARIA A
H55Fa Wentzel L.R.

[H-56] BAILEY H53B
  Elkanah P/Louisa J Hart
H56A   DANIEL W
H56B   MARY M
H56Ba Sigler James
H56C   IDA
H56Ca Moreland Jeff
H56D   ROBERT L
H56E   H. T.

H56F   MINNIE
H56Fa Hart J. Bert
H56G   MARGARET
H56Ga Crutts Jacob
H56H   N.B.

[H-57] BAILEY H55E
   Martin Alonzo/Mary Moreland
H57A   ORVAL
H57B   ETTA
H57Ba Moreland Walter
H57C   LUNA
H57Ca Chambers James
H57D   ORA
H57Da Worth O.K.
H57E   MINNIE
H57Ea Pierce Walter
H57F   LIDA
H57G   RAYMOND
H57H   BROWNLOW
H57I   IDA
H57Ia Guffey —

[I-10] BOONE Unknown
  unknown/unknown
I10A   George III -I11-
I10Aa Maugridge Mary
I10Aaf Maugridge John

[I-11] BOONE I10A
  George III/Mary Maugridge
I11A   GEORGE IV -I58-
I11Aa Howell Deborah
I11Aaf Howell William
I11Aam Thomas Mary
I11B   SARAH
I11Ba Stover Jacob (John)
I11C   SQUIRE Sr. -I12-
I11Ca Morgan Sarah
I11D   JOHN
I11E   MARY
I11F   JOSEPH
I11G   BENJAMIN
I11H   JAMES
I11I   SAMUEL

[I-12] BOONE I11C
  Squire Sr./Sarah Morgan
I12A   SARAH
I12Aa Wilcoxen —
I12B   ISRAEL Sr. -I13-
I12Ba unknown
I12C   SAMUEL Sr -I14-
I12Ca Day Sarah
I12D   JONATHAN
I12E   ELIZABETH
I12Ea Grant William
I12F   DANIEL -I15- (I62Fa)
I12Fa Bryan Rebecca (I62F)
I12Faf Bryan Joseph (I61D)
I12G   MARY
I12Ga Bryan William
I12H   GEORGE V -I16-
I12Ha Lingell Nancy
I12I   EDWARD (NED)-I17- (I23Caf)
I12Ia Bryan Martha (I23Cam)
I12J   SQUIRE Jr -I18-

I12Ja Van Cleve Jane
I12K   HANNAH
I12Ka Stewart John

[I-13] BOONE I12B
  Israel Sr/unknown
I13A   JESSE -I19- (K9Aaf)
I13Aa McMahan Sarah (K9Aam)
I13B   ISRAEL Jr
I13C   ANNA (K8Aa,I19Bam)
I13Ca Coffey William (K8A)

[I-14] BOONE I12C
  Samuel Sr/Sarah Day
I14A   SAMUEL Jr

[I-15] BOONE I12F
  Daniel/Rebecca Bryan
I15A   JAMES
I15B   ISRAEL
I15C   SUSANNAH
I15Ca Hayes William Sr -I20-
I15D   JEMIMA
I15Da Callaway Flanders -I21-
I15Daf Callaway Richard
I15E   LAVINA
I15Ea Scholl Joseph
I15F   REBECCA
I15Fa Goe Philip
I15G   DANIEL MORGAN
I15Ga Lewis Sarah
I15H   JESSE -I56-
I15Ha VanBibber Cloe
I15I   WILLIAM
I15J   NATHAN -I57-
I15Ja VanBibber Olive

[I-16] BOONE I12H
  George V/Nancy Lingell
I16A   SQUIRE -I22-
I16Aa unknown
I16B   JOHN
I16C   SAMUEL Capt -I23- (I17Aaf)
I16Ca Simpson Anna (I17Aam)

264

SIBLING GROUP I

I16D   EDWARD -I24-
I16Da   Simpson Dorcas
I16E   GEORGE VI
I16F   ELIZABETH
I16G   MARTHA
I16H   SARAH (A81Ba)
I16Ha   Hunter William -A83- (A81B)
I16I   POLLY
I16J   MARIA

[I-17] BOONE I12I
        Edward/Martha Bryan
I17A   BANTON Sr Dr -I25- (I23Ca)
I17Aa   Boone Elizabeth C (I23C)
I17Aaf SAMUEL Capt (I16C)
I17Aam Simpson Anna (I16Ca)

[I-18] BOONE I12J
        Squire Jr./Jane Van Cleve
I18A   MOSES
I18B   ISAIAH
I18C   HAYDEN
I18Ca   Callaway Emaline

[I-19] BOONE I13A
        Jesse/Sarah McMahan
I19A   ISRAEL -I40-
I19Aa   unknown
I19B   HANNAH (K9Aa,I42Dam)
I19Ba   Coffey Smith (K9A,I42Daf)
I19Baf Coffey William (K8A,I13Ca)
I19Bam Boone Anna (K8Aa,I13C)

[I-20] HAYES I15Ca
        William Sr/Susannah Boone
I20A   WILLIAM Jr
I20B   JEMIMA
I20Ba   Davis James
I20Baf Davis Jonathan

[I-21] CALLAWAY I15Da
        Flanders/Jemima Boone
I21A   JOHN B
I21Aa   Caton Elizabeth

I21B   JAMES

[I-22] BOONE I16A
        Squire/unknown
I22A   SAMUEL
I22B   HAYDEN
I22C   MILO
I22D   THOMAS
I22E   JOHN

[I-23] BOONE I16C
        Samuel/Anna Simpson
I23A   JEPTHA
I23B   MARY A
I23C   ELIZABETH C (I17Aa)
I23Ca   Boone Banton Sr (I17A)
I23Caf Boone Edward (I12I)
I23Cam Bryan Martha (I12Ia)
I23D   MAXEMILLE
I23E   MARTHA L
I23F   SAMUEL T

[I-24] BOONE I16D
        Edward/Dorcas Simpson
I24A   BANTON
I24B   RODOLPH
I24C   WILLIAM
I24D   GEORGE L
I24E   ANN
I24F   MILLEY
I24G   MARGARET
I24H   MARIA
I24I   MARY

[I-25] BOONE I17A
        Banton Sr./Elizabeth C Boone
I25A   BANTON Jr. Hon

[I-40] BOONE I19A
        Israel/ unknown
I40A   WILLIAM DANIEL -I41-
I40Aa   Triplett Millie
I40Ab   McAndrew Susan
I40B   JONATHAN -I42- (K10Aaf)

SIBLING GROUP I

I40Ba unknown
I40C   UNKNOWN
I40Ca Cansler —

[I-41] BOONE I40A
  William Daniel/Millie Triplett
I41A   MARION
I41B   NANCY ELIZABETH
I41Ba McGriff William —I43—
I41Bb Vaughan Herod —I44—
I41Bbf Vaughan William Sr (T14Aaf)
I41Bbm — Margaret (T14Aam)

[I-42] BOONE I40B
  Jonathan/unknown
I42A   JOHN —I45—
I42Aa unknown
I42Ab Taff Minerva
I42Abf Taff Peter(G10Aaf,G50Abf,J11Abf
I42B   ISRAEL—I46—(G12Aaf,I53Baf)
I42Ba Gelette J (I42Cb,G12Aam,I53Bam)
I42C   JESSE —I47—
I42Ca Cansler Anna
I42Cb Gelette J (I42Ba,G12Aam,I53Bam)
I42D   RACHEL (K10Aa,J12Fam)
I42Da Coffey Marvel(K10A,J12Faf)
I42Daf Coffey Smith (K9A,I19Ba)
I42Dam Boone Hannah (K9Aa,I19B)

[I-43] McGRIFF I41Ba
  William/Nancy E Boone
I43A   WILLIAM D
I43B   MARTHA
I43Ba Lewis —

[I-44] VAUGHAN I41Bb
  Herod/Nancy E Boone
I44A   MARIONA
I44B   WILSON
I44C   ALICE
I44Ca Bodendick W. T.
I44D   AMANDA
I44Da Dodds Ben
I44E   NANCY E (J27Fa)

I44Ea Graham William P (J27F)

[I-45] BOONE I42A
John/ Unknown
I45A   WILLIAM
I45B   DANIEL

[I-46] BOONE I42B
  Israel/Julia Ann Gelette
I46A   SARAH (I53Ba)
I46Aa Ellis George G (I53B)
I46Aaf Ellis James (I52E,G15Gaf)
I46Aam Pearson - (I52Ea,G15Gam)
I46B   ELIZA J (G12Aa)
I46Ba Copeland Francis Marion (G12A)
I46Baf Copeland John (G11A,U16Aaf)
I46Bam Wiseman Mary A (G11Aa,U16Aam)
I46C   MARY
I46Ca Cansler Nathan Henderson Jr
I46Caf Cansler John
I46D   WILLIAM (Babe)
I46E   ALBERT

[I-47] BOONE I42C
  Jesse/Anna Cansler
I47A   MARTHA
I47B   ELIZABETH (Hettie)
I47Ba Vaughan A.C. "Brud"
I47Baf Vaughan "Cat"
I47C   HENDERSON —I48—
I47Ca Harris Luvicey
I47Caf Harris Nathan
I47Cb Barnes Ella
I47Cbf Barnes Dr.

[I-48] BOONE I47C
  Henderson/Luvicey Harris
I48A   EVA
I48Aa Hight —
I48B   ANNA
I48Ba Ramsey Charles
I48C   MATTIE
I48Ca Blackmore — —I50—
I48D   ANDREW

266

I48E   JESSE
I48F   DANIEL
        (2)Ella Barnes
I48G   FRANK
I48H   UNKNOWN
I48Ha   unknown
I48I   WILLARD
I48J   UNKNOWN
I48Ja   Paddock Roy

[I-50] BLACKMORE I48Ca
        Unknown/Mattie Boone
I50A   GRACE
I50B   LOIS
I50C   EARL
I50D   WILLIAM
I50E   LELA
I50Ea   Williams Frank

[I-51] ELLIS unknown
        unknown/unknown
I51A   WILLIAM -I52- (J26Caf)
I51Aa   Lacy Phoebe (J26Cam)

[I-52] ELLIS I51A
        William/Phoebe Lacy
I52A   JOHN G
I52B   PHILLIP
I52C   ALLAN
I52D   LUCRETIA
I52Da   Lambeth Lytle(G11Ja,J12Caf,
                     T18Aaf)
I52Daf Lambeth Samuel (G11Jaf)
I52E   JAMES -I53- (G15Gaf,I46Aaf)
I52Ea   Pearson — (G15Gam,I46Aam)
I52F   LOUIS FRANK -I54- (J26Ca)
I52Fa   Graham Eliza (J26C)
I52G   GEORGE
I52H   MARTHA
I52Ha   Shelton John
I52I   SARAH ESTHER
I52Ia   Shelton Lee
I52J   T. JEFF -I55- (V25Da)
I52Ja   Hoops Susan N (V25D)

[I-53] ELLIS I52E
        James/ — Pearson
I53A   THOMAS G (G15Ga)
I53Aa   Copeland Martha Luella (G15G)
I53Aaf Copeland Solomon Jr (G11E)
I53B   GEORGE G (I46Aa)
I53Ba   Boone Sarah (I46A)
I53Baf Boone Israel (I42B,G12Aaf)
I53Bam Gelette Julia(I42Ba,I42Cb,G12Aam

[I-54] ELLIS I52F
        Louis Frank/Eliza Graham
I54A   ORA ALNETTA
I54Aa   Vaughan Mark
I54Aaf Vaughan John W (T14Ba,G58Caf)
I54Aam Crismon Mary (T14B)
I54B   MARY E
I54Ba   Barnett Isaac
I54C   RAMER
I54Ca   Martin Louisa M
I54D   JUDSON
I54Da   Parker Addie

[I-55] ELLIS I52J
        T. Jeff/Susan Hoops
I55A   HARRIET N
I55B   AUSTIN R
I55C   MILLIE L
I55Ca   Strong J. R.
I55D   WILLIAM R
I55Da   Smith Josephine
I55E   DON M
I55Ea   Rowan William A
I55F   OLLIE B
I55Fa   Followill Rob
I55G   JAMES M
I55H   JOHN E
I55Ha   Webb Maud Wilma
I55I   LUCRETIA A

[I-56] BOONE I15H
        Jesse/Cloe Van Hibler
I56A   ALONZO
I56B   ALBERT G

I56C JAMES M
I56D VAN D
I56E HARRIET
I56F MINERVA
I56G PANTHA
I56H EMILY

[I-57] BOONE I15J
  Nathan/Olive Van Bibber
I57A JAMES
I57B HOWARD
I57C JOHN
I57D DELINDA
I57E MALINDA
I57F MARY
I57G SUSAN
I57H NANCY
I57I JEMIMA
I57J LAVINIA
I57K OLIVE
I57L MELCINA
I57M MAHALEY

[I-58] BOONE I11A
  George IV/Deborah Howell
I58A GEORGE
I58B MARY
I58Ba Hope Thomas
I58C HANNAH
I58Ca Hughws —
I58D DEBORAH
I58Da Bennett Joseph
I58E DIANA
I58Ea Coles —
I58F WILLIAM
I58G JOSIAH -I59-
I58Ga Hite Hannah
I58H JEREMIAH
I58I ABIGAIL
I58J HEZEKIAH

[I-59] BOONE I58G
  Josiah/Hannah Hite
I59A GEORGE
I59B NOAH
I59C JOSIAH Jr.
I59Ca Ellender Mrs
I59D REHUMA
I59E RUTH
I59Ea Sisk Pluright
I59F JEREMIAH
I59Fa Nevell Joyce
I59G HANNAH
I59Ga Vurger George
I59Gb Barnhill James
I59H REHUMA 2nd
I59I ALLISON

[I-60] BRYAN Unknown
  unknown/unknown
I60A MORGAN Sr -I61-
I60Aa Strode Martha

[I-61] BRYAN I60A
  Morgan Sr./Martha Strode
I61A JAMES -I62-
I61Aa Enochs Rebecca
I61B MORGAN Jr. Capt.
I61Ba Forbush —
I61C WILLIAM
I61Ca Boone Mary
I61D JOSEPH (I12Faf)
I61E SAMUEL
I61F ELEANOR
I61Fa Linville William
I61G THOMAS
I61Ga Hunt Sarah

[I-62] BRYAN I61A
   James/Rebecca Enochs
I62A   DAVID
I62Aa Poor Mary
I62B   SUSAN
I62C   JONATHAN
I62Ca Ooshow Mary
I62D   POLLY
I62E   HENRY
I62Ea Sparks Elizabeth
I62F   REBECCA (I12Fa)
I62Fa Boone Daniel (I12F)

J-10 EADS(Edds) unknown
unknown/unknown
J10A   JOHN -J11- (L11Ba,E53Caf)
J10Aa   Simpson Nancy (L11B,E53Cam)

J-11 EADS J10A
John/ Nancy Simpson
J11A   BENJAMIN -J12- (E53Ca,K11Caf,
                T13Caf,T16Aaf,J26Bbf)
J11Aa   Hughes Mary (E53C,K11Cam,
                T13Cam,
J11Ab   Taff Mahala (J26Bbm)
J11Abf Taff Peter(G10Aaf,G50Abf,I42Abf)
J11B   MARY ALICE
J11Ba   Laughlin William

J-12 EADS J11A
Benjamin/Mary Hughes
J12A   FRANCES (T13Ca,E20Abm,J27Aam)
J12Aa   Crismon James(T13C,E20Abf,J27Aaf
J12B   LEWIS -J14- (L15Ba,P14Baf,
                Z13Eaf,Z13Haf)
J12Ba   Simpson Jane (L15B,P14Bam,
                Z13Eam,Z13Ham)
J12Baf Simpson William (L12E,J12Daf)
J12C   PERRY F
J12Ca   Lambeth Mary
J12Caf Lambeth Lytle(G11Ja,I52Da,T18Aaf
J12Cam Copeland Sallie (G11J,T18Aam)
J12D   GEORGE WASHINGTON -J15- (L15Ca,
                D32Baf,G31Baf)
J12Da   Simpson Frances (L15C,D32Bam,
                G31Bam
J12Daf Simpson William Jr (L12E,J12Baf)
J12E   WILLIAM M
J12Ea   Finn Elizabeth
J12Eaf Finn Barnett(E20Aaf,G34Aaf,
                K27Baf)
J12F   CAROLINE (K11Ca,G32Dam,G32Eam,
                K26Cbm,K32Cbm)
J12Fa   Coffey Campbell (K11C,G32Daf,
                G32Eaf,K26Cbf,K32Cbf)
J12Faf Coffey Marvel (K10A,I42Da)
J12Fam Boone Rachel (K10Aa,I42D)

    (2)Martha Taff
J12G   LORENZO DOW
J12Ga   Reed Lucinda Penelope
J12H   MYRA (T16Aa)
J12Ha   Crismon Gilbert -J16- (T16A)
J12Haf Crismon William W Sr (T13J)
J12Ham Whrattles Margaret (T13Ja)
J12I   BENJAMIN S
J12J   AMANDA (J26Bb)
J12Ja   Graham Michael(J26B,T18Ba,T15Ecf
J12Jaf Graham George W -J26- (T18Baf)
J12Jam Hickle Harriett (T18Bam)
J12K   JENNIE
J12Ka   Hawkins Barney
J12L   LOUISA
J12La   Tackett J Perry -J17-
J12Laf Tackett Willis M (S11Ba,
                J14Caf,J20Aaf,Z13Faf)
J12Lam Briggs Zylphia (S11B.J14Cam,
                J20Aam,Z13Fam)

J-14 EADS J12B
Lewis/Jane Simpson
J14A   SERENA (Z13Ea)
J14Aa   Nelson James S
J14Ab   Hughes George H (Z13E)
J14B   MARY SARAH FRANCES Z13Ha
J14Ba   Hughes Hiram -J18- (Z13H)
J14Baf Hughes McKamy Z12A,S11Gaf)
J14Bam Davidson Elizabeth(Z12Aa,S11Gam
J14C   LYDIA
J14Ca   Tackett J.I. -J19-
J14Caf Tackett Willis M (S11Ba,J12Laf
                J20Aaf,Z13Faf)
J14Cam Briggs Zylphia (S11B,J12Lam,
                J20Aam,Z13Fam)
J14D   BENJAMIN F
J14Da   Duncan Amanda
J14Daf Duncan Riley
J14Dam Roberson Jane
J14E   WILLIAM S -J20- (D33Haf,P14Daf)
J14Ea   Helton Lydia (D33Ham,P14Dam)
J14Eaf Helton James
J14Eam Vaughan Bursetta

J14F   MALINDA S15Aa
J14Fa   Briggs John H -J21- (S15A)
J14Faf Briggs Daniel B. W.(S11G,Z13Ba)
J14Fam Hughes Melvina J (S11Ga,Z13B)
J14G   MOSES W -J22- (P14Ba)
J14Ga   Carnes Louisa (P14B)
J14Gaf Carnes John (P11I,G11Ha,J20Eaf)
J14Gam Copeland M (G11H,P11Ia,J20Eam)

[J-15] EADS J12D
    George W/Frances Simpson
J15A   MARY A
J15Aa   Keeney —
J15B   SAMUEL P
J15C   GUS (D32Ba)
J15Ca   Shockley Bettie (D32B)
J15Caf Shockley Joseph (D25E)
J15Cam Russell Nancy (D25Ea)
J15D   MARION A
J15E   ELIZABETH S
J15Ea   Bassett George
J15F   JAMES C -J23- K15Daf)
J15Fa   Wiles Sarah (K15Dam)
J15Faf Wiles Thomas L (U13Caf)
J15Fam Johnson Catherine (U13Cam)
J15G   JOSEPH T -J24- (G31Ba)
J15Ga   Gremp Fannie Isabelle (G31B)
J15Gaf Gremp Karl Ludwig (G29Ia)

[J-16] CRISMON J12Ha
    Gilbert/Myra Eads
J16A   BEN
J16B   JEFF
J16C   DOW
J16D   NORA
J16Da   Shelton James
J16E   AUGUSTA
J16Ea   Roberds Charles
J16F   ELISE
J16Fa   Williams Joseph
J16G   MARY
J16Ga   Patrick Henry
J16H   MONROE

[J-17] TACKETT J12La
    J. Perry/Louisa Eads
J17A   ELLA
J17B   BERTHA
J17Ba   Frey P.C.
J17C   FRANK

[J-18] HUGHES J14Ba
Hiram/Mary Eads
J18A   BETTIE JANE
J18Aa   Kinion Charles B
J18B   NANCY E
J18Ba   Helton William T
J18C   JAMES (Newt)
J18Ca   Krone Mabel
J18D   A. B.

[J-19] TACKETT J14Ca
    J. I./Lydia Eads
J19A   MARTIN M
J19B   LUCY
J19Ba   Curtis W. A.
J19C   LEONA
J19Ca   Terry Floyd

[J-20] EADS J14E
    . WilliamS/Lydia Helton
J20A   JOSEPHINE
J20Aa   Tackett G. H.
J20Aaf Tackett Willis M (S11Ba,
                J12Laf,J14Caf,Z13Faf)
J20Aam Briggs Zylphia (S11B,J12Lam,
                J14Cam,Z13Fam)
J20B   LOUISA
J20Ba   Briggs James
J20C   B. F. Jr (D33Ha)
J20Ca   Shockley Millie O (D33H)
J20Caf Shockley Thomas R (D25H,Y19Ga)
J20Cam McGee Sarah (Y19G,D25Ha)
J20D   WELDON W
J20E   LEWIS JEFFERSON -J25- (P14Da)
J20Ea   Carnes Jennie L (P14D)
J20Eaf Carnes John (P11I,G11Ha,J14Gaf)
J20Eam Copeland M E (G11H,P11Ia,J14Gam)

J20F   J. MICK
J20Fa   Emory Laura
J20Faf Emery Louis
J20Fam Martin Mary

[J-21] BRIGGS J14Fa
     John H/Malinda Eads
J21A   BONEY
J21Aa   Boulware —
J21B   WHERRY
J21C   EWELL
J21D   MABEL
J21E   EFFIE

[J-22] EADS J14G
     Moses W/Louisa Carnes
J22A   LOUIS J
J22B   BUNYAN
J22C   EVERETT E
J22Ca   Adkins Maude
J22Caf Adkins J. P.
J22D   MAUDE
J22Da   Juergens John Adam

[J-23] EADS J15F
     James C/Sarah Wiles
J23A   RAY
J23B   LULA
J23Ba   Weatherby —
J23C   MARY
J23Ca   Burton —
J23D   CHARLES
J23E   DELLA (K15Da)
J23Ea   Coffey Squire (K15D)
J23Eaf Coffey John (K12A)
J23Eam Vanderpool Susan (K12Aa)
J23F   WALTER
J23G   THOMAS WASHINGTON
J23Ga   Brandel Sallie E
J23Gaf Brandel Mike

[J-24] EADS J15G
     Joseph T/Fannie Gremp
J24A   J. ALPHA

J24B   GEORGE L
J24C   STELLA
J24Ca   Roberson Glen
J24D   MYRTLE
J24Da   Hall William
J24E   ELLORA
J24Ea   Groff Chester A

[J-25] EADS J20E
     Lewis J/Jennie Carnes
J25A   ALICE
J25Aa   Stites John
J25B   MILFORD
J25C   KATE
J25Ca   Sollenberger —
J25D   CORA
J25Da   Duffin F. M.
J25E   LYDIA
J25Ea   Veasman Joseph
J25F   AMANDA
J25Fa   Duffin Hugh
J25G   GERTRUDE
J25Ga   Kellis —
J25H   EUGENE

[J-26] GRAHAM J12Jaf
     George W/Harriett Hickle
J26A   JOHN CALVIN
J26Aa   Miller Elizabeth
J26B   MICHAEL SPESSARD -J27-
          J12Ja,T18Ba,T15Ecf)
J26Ba   Skaggs Jane (T18B,T15Ecm)
J26Bb   Eads Amanda (J12J)
J26Bbf Eads Benjamin (J11A,E53Ca,
          K11Caf,T13Caf,T16Aaf)
J26Bbm Taff Mahala (J11Ab)
J26C   ELIZA (I52Fa)
J26Ca   Ellis Louis Frank (I52F)
J26Caf Ellis William (I51A)
J26Cam Lacy Phoebe (I51Aa)
J26D   MARY JANE
J26Da   Meltabarger James (T15Ja)

[J-27] GRAHAM J26B
  Michael S/Jane Skaggs
J27A   CLORAH BELL (T15Ec)
J27Aa   Crismon Robert E (T15E)
J27Aaf Crismon James(T13C,J12Aa,E20Abf
J27Aam Eads Frances(J12A,T13Ca,E20Abm)
J27B   MARUSIA
    2)Amanda Eads
J27C   HARRIET MATILDA
J27D   ORLEANA
J27E   LEONA MAY
J27Ea   Martin Benjamin
J27F   WILLIAM PRESTON (I44Ea)
J27Fa   Vaughan Nancy E (I44E)
J27G   JOHN CLEMENS
J27Ga   Vaughan Roberta
J27Gaf Vaughan Richard W
J27Gam Crismon Mary
J27H   GEORGE EMERSON
J27Ha   Barnett Ollie
J27I   JAMES WADE
J27Ia   Cross Lena
J27J   SARAH NEPPIE
J27Ja   Dodds John

[K-08] COFFEY unknown
unknown/unknown
K8A   WILLIAM -K9- (I13Ca,I19Baf)
K8Aa   Boone Anne (I13C,I19Bam)

[K-09] COFFEY K8A
William/Anna Boone
K9A   SMITH -K10- (I19Ba,I42Daf)
K9Aa   Boone Hannah (I19B,I42Dam)
K9Aaf   Boone Jesse (I13A)
K9Aam   McMahan Sarah (I13Aa)

[K-10] COFFEY K9A
Smith/Hannah Boone
K10A   MARVEL -K11- (I42Da,J12Faf)
K10Aa   Boone Rachel (I42D,J12Fam)
K10Aaf Boone Johnathan (I40B)

[K-11] COFFEY K10A
Marvel/Rachel Boone
K11A   IRVIN -K12-
K11Aa   Hughes Nancy
K11B   SQUIRE -K13- (K34Ca,K26Baf)
K11Ba   Parker Drusilla (K34C,K26Bam)
K11Baf Parker Henry -K34-
K11Bam — Martha
K11C   CAMPBELL -K14- J12Fa,G32Daf,
        G32Eaf,K26Cbf,K32Cbf)
K11Ca   Eads Caroline (J12F,G32Dam,
        G32Eam,K26Cbm,K32Cbm)
K11Caf Eads Benjamin (J11A,E53Ca,
        J26Bbf,T13Caf,T16Aaf)
K11Cam Hughes Mary(J11Aa,T13Cam,E53C)
K11D   LAVINA
K11Da   Odom Isaac W
K11Daf Odom Jacob
K11E   ELIZABETH
K11Ea   Petty William
K11F   TEMPERANCE
K11Fa   Orr James
K11G   WILLIAM BRAZEAL
K11Ga   unknown
K11H   UNKNOWN
K11Ha   Moss William

[K-12] COFFEY K11A
Irvin/Nancy Hughes
K12A   JOHN -K15- (J23Eaf)
K12Aa   Vanderpool Susan (J23Eam)
K12B   ALEXANDER -K16-
K12Ba   Doyle Martha Ann
K12C   WILLIAM -K17-
K12Ca   Whitton Belle
K12D   SQUIRE -K18-
K12Da   Gibson Jane
K12E   MARTHA
K12Ea   Mahaney E.P.
K12F   SAMUEL -K19-
K12Fa   Vaughan Sarah
K12G   JAMES -K20-
K12Ga   Crafton Maggie

[K-13] COFFEY K11B
Squire/Drusilla Parker
K13A   MARTHA
K13Aa   Swicegood John
K13B   ISABELLE
K13Ba   Fields John
K13C   DOVE
K13Ca   Davis John
K13D   MATILDA (K26Ba)
K13Da   Moss James (K26B)
K13Daf Moss Edward Rev.(K25A,K14Eaf)
K13Dam Roberson —(K25Ab,K14Eam)
K13E   WILLIAM DANIEL BOONE -K21-
K13Ea   Cox Lavina
K13Eaf Cox David (K34Da)
K13Eam Parker Emeline (K34D)
K13F   NELLIE
K13Fa   Wells Jerry
K13G   JOHN RICHARD -K22-
K13Ga   Wells Hodge

[K-14] COFFEY K11C
Campbell/Caroline Eads
K14A   JAMES S
K14B   ISABELLE (G32Ea,K32Cb)
K14Ba   Ballance Thomas Monroe (K32C)
K14Baf Balance William D (K31Aa)

274

K14Bam Davis Martha (K31A)
K14Bb Copeland John Henry (G32E)
K14Bbf Copeland John (G29K,K14Caf)
K14Bbm Doyle Nancy (G29Ka,K14Cam)
K14C MARY F (G32Da)
K14Ca Copeland W. Noah (G32D)
K14Caf Copeland John (G29K,K14Bbf)
K14Cam Doyle Nancy (G29Ka,K14Bbm)
K14D JOHN
K14E BENJAMIN I (K26Cb)
K14Ea Moss Martha (K26C)
K14Eaf Moss Edward Rev (K25A,K13Daf)
K14Eam Roberson Hutton (K25Ab,K13Dam)
K14F HIRAM KIMZEY -K23-
K14Fa Evans Mary Ann
K14Faf Evans Jesse

[K-15] COFFEY K12A
    John/Susan Vanderpool
K15A IRVIN
K15B ELIZABETH
K15Ba Sudheimer William
K15C OLIVER
K15D SQUIRE (J23Ea)
K15Da Eads Della (J23E)
K15Daf Eads James C (J15F)
K15Dam Wiles Sarah (J15Fa)

[K-16] COFFEY K12B
    Alexander/Martha Doyle
K16A IRVIN E
K16B MARTHA R
K16C WILLIAM M
K16D NANCY C
K16Da Mahaney —
K16E JAMES H
K16F MARY E
K16Fa Sharp —
K16G LILLIE E
K16Ga Knight —
K16H ARTHUR B
K16I ESTELLE P

[K-17] COFFEY K12C
    William/Belle Whitton
K17A JOHN
K17B COSY

[K-18] COFFEY K12D
    Squire/Jane Gibson
K18A ARTHUR
K18B ERNEST
K18C CARNEY

[K-19] COFFEY K12F
    Samuel/Sarah Vaughan
K19A BERTIE
K19B ALTHA

[K-20] COFFEY K12G
    James/Maggie Crafton
K20A LAWRENCE
K20B FLORENCE
K20C BELVIA

[K-21] COFFEY K13E
    William Danial/Lavina Cox
K21A UNKNOWN
K21Aa Leach Levi
K21B ARLIE
K21C JESSE
K21D UNKNOWN
K21Da Durnell Everett
K21E UNKNOWN
K21Ea Selvidge Homer
K21F ROY
K21G CECIL

[K-22] COFFEY K13G
    John Richard/Hodge Wells
K22A GEORGE

[K-23] COFFEY K14F
    Hiram Kimzey/Mary Evans
K23A EARL
K23B SHERMAN
K23C JESSE

K23D   THOMAS
K23E   LENNIE
K23Ea   Snodgrass J. S.
K23F   LIZZIE
K23Fa   Behm —
K23G   SIDNEY –K24–
K23Ga   Weidinger Kate

[K-24] COFFEY K23G
   Sidney/Kate Weidinger
K24A   CELLUS
K24B   BERNICE

[K-25] MOSS unknown
   unknown/unknown
K25A   EDWARD –K26– K13Daf,K14Eaf)
K25Aa   Boone Mary
K25Ab   Roberson — (K13Dam,K14Eam)

[K-26] MOSS K25A
   Edward/— Roberson
K26A   LUCINDA (K14Ea)
K26Aa   Burgess W. Thomas –K27–
K26B   JAMES (K13Da)
K26Ba   Coffey Matilda (K13D)
K26Baf Coffey Squire (K11B,K34Ca)
K26Bam Parker Drusilla (K34C,K11Ba)
K26C   MARTHA (K14Ea)
K26Ca   Murphy William C
K26Caf Murphy W. A. (Lannie)
K26Cam Crismon Judith
K26Cb   Coffey Benjamin I (K14E)
K26Cbf Coffey Campbell (K11C,J12Fa,
           G32Daf,G32Eaf,K32Cbf)
K26Cbm Eads Caroline (J12F,K11Ca,
           G32Dam,G32Eam,K32Cbm)

[K-27] BURGESS K26Aa
   W. Thomas/Lucinda Moss
K27A   EDWARD
K27B   OCTAVIA
K27Ba   Finn George Wesley –K28–
K27Baf FinnBarnett(J12Eaf,G34Aaf,E20Aaf
K27Bam Orton Malinda

K27C   CHESLEY

[K-28] FINN K27Ba
   George Wesley/Octavia Burgess
K28A   BELMA
K28Aa   Rice —
K28B   LEE
K28C   BURGESS
K28D   ROBERT
K28E   RUTH
K28Ea   Shackleford —
K28F   GLADYS
K28Fa   Shackleford —
K28G   EDNA
K28Ga   Fann —
K28H   MALINDA
K28Ha   Albeitz —
K28I   JESSIE
K28Ia   Curtis —

[K-30] DAVIS unknown
   unknown/unknown
K30A   WILLIAM Sr –K31–
K30Aa   Brown Harriet

[K-31] DAVIS K30A
   William Sr/Harriett Brown
K31A   MARTHA (K14Bam)
K31Aa   Ballance Willliam –K32– (K14Baf)
K31B   FREDERICK
K31Ba   —— Sarah J
K31C   WILLIAM Jr (H13Baf,Y34Baf)
K31Ca   Tennyson Eliza (H13Bam,Y34Bam)
K31Caf Tennyson William B
K31D   THOMAS –K33–(H13Ba,Y29Baf,Y29Caf
K31Da   Light Temperance C. (H13B,
                              Y29Bam,Y2
K31Daf Light Enoch (H12A)
K31Dam unknown (H12Aa)

[K-32] BALLANCE K31Aa
   William D/Martha Davis
K32A   WILLIAM E
K32Aa   Lee Mary

276

K32B   GEORGE W
K32Ba   Honse Lottie
K32C   THOMAS MONROE (K14Ba)
K32Ca   Fenton Sarah
K32Cb   Coffey Isabelle (K14B,G32Ea)
K32Cbf Coffey Campbell (K11C,J12Fa,
            G32Daf,G32Eaf,K26Cbf)
K32Cbm Eads Caroline (J12F,K11Ca,
            G32Dam,G32Eam,K26Cbm)
K32D   MARY JANE
K32Da   Reynolds William J
K32E   JOHN WESLEY
K32Ea   Snodgrass —
K32Eaf Snodgrass George W (Y15E,K33Aaf,
            K33Caf,K33Daf,Y63Daf)
K32Eb   Giesler Nancy L
K32F   MARTHA ANN
K32Fa   Gaddy Harm
K32G   ELIZA
K32Ga   Walker Robert

[K-33] DAVIS K31D
    Thomas Sr/Temperance Light
K33A   ELIZABETH (Y29Ab)
K33Aa   Snodgrass James D (Y29A,Y63Da)
K33Aaf Snodgrass George W (Y15E,K32Eaf,
            K33Caf,K33Daf,Y63Daf)
K33B   ANDY J
K33C   SARAH JOSEPHINE (Y29Ba)
K33Ca   Snodgrass Ebenezer (Y29B)
K33Caf Snodgrass George W (Y15E,K32Eaf,
            K33Aaf,K33Daf,Y63Daf)
K33D   MARTHA C (Y29Ca,Y57Aam)
K33Da   Snodgrass Archibald(Y29C,Y57Aaf)
K33Daf Snodgrass George W (Y15E,K32Eaf,
            K33Aaf,K33Caf,Y63Daf)
K33E   CLARA H
K33Ea   Feeler Michael Sr (E20Ba)
K33Eaf Feeler Simon (E20Cb,E20Baf)
K33Eam Daley Deborah E (E20Bam)
K33F   CATHERINE ELLEN
K33Fa   Pelikan Julius
K33G   LEWIS E
K33Ga   Love Clara H

K33Gaf Love James

[K-34] PARKER K11Baf
    Henry/ Martha —
K34A   JAMES -K35- (Y28Aa)
K34Aa   Lane Catherine (Y28A)
K34Aaf Lane Charles C (Y15Da)
K34Aam Snodgrass Matilda (Y15D)
K34B   WILLIAM
K34C   DRUSILLA (K11Ba,K26Bam)
K34Ca   Coffey Squire (K11B,K26Baf)
K34D   EMELINE (K13Eam)
K34Da   Cox David (K13Eaf)
K34E   UNKNOWN
K34Ea   Johnson Myscal
K34F   POLLY
K34Fa   Myers Joseph
K34Faf Myers Gabriel (Y15Fc,Y30Aaf)
K34Fam Ricker —
K34G   MALINDA (G18Bam)
K34Ga   Spratley William H (G18Baf)

[K-35] PARKER K34A
    James/Catherine Lane
K35A   AMANDA (K37Ca)
K35Aa   Rogers Isaac D (K37C)
K35Aaf Rogers Valentine (K36A)
K35Aam Durbin Malissa (K36Aa)
K35B   MYRA

[K-36] ROGERS unknown
    unknown/unknown
K36A   VALENTINE -K37- (K35Aaf)
K36Aa   Durbin Malissa (K35Aam)
K36Ab   Greenstreet Elizabeth

277

[K-37] ROGERS K36A
   Valentine/Malissa Durbin
K37A MALISSA
K37Aa McQueen James J
K37Aaf McQueen James (S18Db)
K37Aam Poe Eliza Backues (S18D)
K37B .LUCY
K37Ba Liston Isaac
K37C ISAAC D (K35Aa)
K37Ca Parker Amanda (K35A)
K37D .EMELINE
K37Da Collier Hiram
K37E CYNTHIA
K37Ea Wilson Herod
    (2)Elizabeth Greenstreet
K37F JOHN C
K37Fa Crider Ann
K37G ALEX M
K37H JOSEPH H
K37Ha Thompson Lula

[L-11] SIMPSON unknown
  unknown/unknown
L11A   WILLIAM Sr -L12-
L11Aa unknown
L11B   NANCY (J10Aa,E53Cam)
L11Ba Eads John (J10A,E53Caf)

[L-12] SIMPSON L11A
  William Sr/unknown
L12A   SAMUEL -L13- (L15Daf)
L12Aa unknown
L12B   DANIEL -L14-
L12Ba unknown
L12C   BENJAMIN
L12D   JAMES
L12E   WILLIAM Jr -L15- (J12Daf,J12Baf)
L12Ea Archer Elizabeth Serena

[L-13] SIMPSON L12A
  Samuel/unknown
L13A   MARTHA (L15Da)
L13Aa Simpson Barney H (L15D)

[L-14] SIMPSON L12B
  Daniel/unknown
L14A   WILLIAM (Snurl)
L14Aa Ramsey Diana
L14Aaf Ramsey Robert L

[L-15] SIMPSON L12E
  William Jr/Elizabeth S Archer
L15A   MAHALA
L15Aa Strickland Joseph
L15Aaf Strickland Samuel
L15Aam Crismon Rachel
L15B   JANE(J12Ba,P14Bam,Z13Eam,Z13Ham)
L15Ba Eads Lewis (J12B, P14Baf,
               Z13Eaf,Z13Haf)
L15C   FRANCES   (J12Da,D32Bam,
               G31Bam)
L15Ca Eads George W (J12D,D32Baf,
               G31Baf)
L15D   BARNEY (L13Aa)
L15Da Simpson Martha (L13A)

L15Daf Simpson Samuel (L12A)
L15E   MOSES L
L15Ea Rice Catherine
L15F   MARY
L15Fa Lee Louis
L15G   CAROLINE
L15Ga Scott Henry
L15Gaf Scott George (E23Eaf)
L15Gam Doyel Mary (E23Eam)
L15H   LOUISA
L15Ha Miller Joseph
L15I   SAMUEL -L16-
L15Ia Powers Lydia Angeline
L15Iaf Powers John Thompson Rev(S11Caf)
L15Iam Ferrier Elizabeth (S11Cam)

[L-16] SIMPSON L15I
  Samuel/Lydia Angeline Powers
L16A   MATILDA
L16Aa Roberts James H
L16B   TINE
L16Ba Copeland Steve
L16C   DIORA (Z34Aa)
L16Ca Henderson Victor C (Z34A)
L16Caf Henderson Albert Smith (Z30Aa)
L16Cam Miller Sarah E (Z30A)
L15D   THOMAS
L16Da Wilson Zilphia
L16Daf Wilson Thomas
L16E   CALLIE
L16Ea Scott Henry -L17-
L16F   MAHALA EMELINE
L16Fa Keaton George M -L18-
L16G   LYDIA ANGELINE
L16Ga Bacon James H -L19-
L16H   JOSEPHINE
L16Ha Briggs Stephen
L16Haf Briggs Lafayette
L16I   JOHN W -L20-
L16Ia Copeland Basheba
L16Iaf Copeland Jehu (G29M)
L16Ib — Olive
L16J   WILLIAM T -L21-
L16Ja Copeland Lucy

L16Jaf Copeland John

[L-17] SCOTT L16Ea
   Henry/Callie Simpson
L17A   THOMAS
L17B   SAVANNAH
L17Ba York —

[L-18] KEATON L16Fa
   George M/Mahala Simpson
L18A   SAMUEL
L18B   NORA
L18Ba Wilder William
L18C   GRACE

[L-19] BACON L16Ga
   James H/Lydia Simpson
L19A   UNKNOWN
L19Aa Love W. E.
L19B   UNKNOWN
L19Ba Graham J. W.
L19C   SMALL

[L-20] SIMPSON L16I
   John W/Basheba Copeland
L20A   ANGELINE
L20B   UNKNOWN

[L-21] SIMPSON L16J
   William T/Lucy Copeland
L21A   EFFIE
L21B   EDNA
L21C   BASHEBA
L21D   VICTORIA
L21E   BLANCHE
L21F   BUNYAN
L21G   LEONARD
L21H   WILLIAM
L21I   BRYAN

[M-10] NOBLETT unknown
  unknown/unknown
M10A   WILLIAM THOMAS -M11-
M10Aa   unknown

[M-11] NOBLETT M10A
  William/unknown
M11A   IRA -M12-
M11Aa   Young Rebecca
M11Aaf Young Joseph
M11B   JOHN A -M13-
M11Ba   Dunnivan —
M11Bb   Boyd Mary
M11C   HENRY CLAY -M14-
M11Ca   Matlock Sophronia Adaline
M11Caf Matlock George W (G35Da,Y13Abf)
M11Cam Copeland Sarah (G35D,Y13Abm)
M11D   FRANK
M11E   WILLIAM BERRY
M11F   MARGARET ANN (P13Aam)
M11Fa   Bowman John -M15- (P13Aaf)
M11G   ANGELINE
M11Ga   Skaggs Asa -M16-
M11H   MYRA JANE
M11Ha   Jackson Spencer -M17-
M11Hb   Wright James -M18-
M11I   ELEANOR (Q31Da)
M11Ia   Moreland Anderson (Q31D)
M11Iaf Moreland George (Q30A,H52Eaf)

[M-12] NOBLETT M11A
  Ira/Rebecca Young
M12A   ELIZABETH ANN
M12Aa   Smallwood John
M12B   JEFF
M12C   WILL
M12D   IRA Jr.

[M-13] NOBLETT M11B
  John A/ — Dunnivan
M13A   L.E. -M20-
M13Aa   —— Edna
  (2)Mary Boyd
M13B   OLIVER

M13C   MINNIE
M13Ca   Beckman William -M21-
M13D   JULIA
M13Da   Fulton Frank
M13E   EDNA
M13Ea   Pelikan Frank T

[M-14] NOBLETT M11C
  Henry Clay/Sophronia Matlock
M14A   WILLIAM -M22-
M14Aa   Terrill Nellie
M14Aaf Terrill John R
M14B   IDA
M14Ba   Biles Charles
M14C   JOHN W
M14D   MARY J
M14Da   Bullock James
M14E   SARAH E
M14F   BARBARA A
M14Fa   Mizell C.W.

[M-15] BOWMAN M11Fa
  John/Margaret Noblett
M15A   MARY J
M15Aa   Collier William E Sr -M23-
M15B   MARGARET E
M15Ba   West Elijah M
M15C   HANNAH
M15Ca   Giesler John Henry
M15Caf Giesler Ely
M15Cam Skaggs Charlotte
M15D   SARAH (Y42Bbm)
M15Da   Giesler David -M24- (Y42Bbf)
M15Daf Giesler John
M15Db   Joyce Hezekiah
M15E   WILLIAM THOMAS -M25- (P13Aa)
M15Ea   Carnes Elizabeth (P13A)
M15Eaf Carnes William P (P11G E21Ba)
M15Eam Branson Ruth Ann(E21B,P11Ga)
M15Eb   unknown
M15F   DANIEL H -M26- (H55E)
M15Fa   Moreland Mary (H55Ea)
M15Faf Moreland William Sr (H55Eaf)
M15Fam Bennett Polly (H55Eam)

[M-16] SKAGGS M11Ga
   Asa/Angeline Noblett
M16A   MARGARET
M16B   HARVEY
M16C   ELI
M16D   JOHN
M16Da Schram Sallie
M16Db Engle Ann
M16E   BETTIE
M16Ea West William —M27—
M16Eb Blackwell Thomas

[M-17] JACKSON M11Ha
   Spencer/Myra Jane Noblett
M17A   HENRY
M17B   FRANCIS
M17C   ELIZABETH

[M-18] WRIGHT M11Hb
   James/Myra Jane Noblett
M18A   WILLIAM
M18B   JOHN
M18C   LYDIA
M18Ca Duncan John

[M-20] NOBLETT M13A
   L. E./ — Edna
M20A   RAYMOND
M20B   JOHN
M20C   CLAUDE
M20D   RHEA
M20Da Cox Nic
M20E   VERA
M20F   ELLIE
M20G   LEO

[M-21] BECKMAN M13Ca
   William/Minnie Noblett
M21A   DEWEY
M21B   WILLIAM Jr

[M-22] NOBLETT M14A
   William/Nellie Terrill
M22A   CLAY

M22B   CLARENCE
M22C   CHESTER

[M-23] COLLIER M15Aa
   William E Sr/Mary J Bowman
M23A   MARY A
M23Aa Tynes Thomas J
M23B   JOHN W
M23Ba Crabtree —
M23C   AMOS T
M23Ca Gibbons Martha
M23D   EDNA
M23E   WILLIAM E Jr
M23F   SIDNEY J
M23G   THOMAS J
M23H   BYRON
M23I   LOU
M23Ia O'Neill James H
M23J   DAVID D

[M-24] GIESLER M15Da
   David/Sarah Bowman
M24A   EDWARD LEE
M24Aa Mitchem Mollie
M24B   CARRIE L (Y42Bb)
M24Ba Jones Jerry (Y42B)
M24Baf Jones James A (Y23B)
M24Bam Young Rosanna (Y23Ba)
M24C   MARY
M24Ca West Jacob —M28—

[M-25] BOWMAN M15E
   William Thomas/Elizabeth Carnes
M25A   DELLA
M25Aa Krone Jack
       (2)unknown
M25B   EVERETT
M25C   RICHARD
M25D   EDWARD
M25E   JOHN
M25F   MAUD
M25Fa Campbell —

[M-26] BOWMAN M15F
  Daniel H/Mary Moreland
M26A   JOHN
M26B   MARGARET
M26Ba   Hunt —

[M-27] WEST M16Ea
  William/Bettie Skaggs
M27A   OLIVER
M27B   JESSE
M27C   HENRY
M27D   JOHN
M27E   VIOLA
M27F   MAMIE
M27Fa   Hatmaker —
M27G   MARY
M27Ga   Wilson Len

[M-28] WEST M24Ca
  Jacob/Mary Giesler
M28A   LOGAN —M29—
M28Aa   Mason Emily
M28B   GEORGE
M28C   CYNTHIA
M28Ca   Peters Jeff
M28D   ROBY
M28E   ROSA
M28Ea   Mason Hank
M28F   DELLA
M28Fa   McKinney Leslie
M28Fb   Joyce Hezekiah

[M-29] WEST M28A
  Logan/Emily Mason
M29A   ALFRED
M29B   DELMAR

[P-09] CARNES unknown
  unknown/unknown
P9A   JOSIAH -P10-
P9Aa   unknown

[P-10] CARNES P9A
  Josiah/unknown
P10A   JEHU -P11- (E21Baf,G11Faf,
                   G11Haf)
P10Aa Burton Nancy(E21Bam,G11Fam,G11Ham)

[P-11] CARNES P10A
  Jehu/NancyBurton
P11A   MATILDA
P11Aa Berry John -P12-
P11B   MARY
P11Ba Rowden Isaac N
P11C   NANCY J
P11Ca Brumble John
P11D   EDITH E
P11Da Laughlin Thomas M
P11E   ANN (G11Fa)
P11Ea Copeland Joseph Jr (G11F)
P11Eaf Copeland William Sr (G10A,
                 D17Faf,D25Gaf,P11Iaf)
P11Eam Taff Martha (G10Aa,D17Fam,
                      D25Gam,P11Iam)
P11F   THOMAS
P11Fa McKnight —
P11G   WILLIAM P -P13- (E21Ba,M15Eaf)
P11Ga Branson Ruth Ann (E21B,M15Eam)
P11Gaf Branson David
P11H   LEVI
P11Ha Rowden Margaret
P11Haf Rowden James
P11I   JOHN F -P14- (G11Ha,J14Gaf,
                     J20Eaf)
P11Ia Copeland Mary E (G11H,J14Gam,
                        J20Eam)
P11Iaf Copeland William (G10A,D17Faf,
                  D25Gaf,P11Eaf)
P11Iam Taff Martha (G10Aa,D17Fam,
                    D25Gam,P11Eam)
P11J   JOSIAH, Dr.

[P-12] BERRY P11Aa
  John/Matilda Carnes
P12A   JOHN JEHU
P12Aa Boyce Sarah Frances
P12B   MARGARET
P12Ba Williams John J
P12Baf Williams John W
P12Bam Hinton Mary
P12C   GEORGE
P12D   MARY
P12E   NANCY
P12F   SARAH ANN
P12G   ELIZABETH JANE

[P-13] CARNES P11G
  William P/Ruth Ann Branson
P13A   ELIZABETH (M15Ea)
P13Aa Bowman William Thomas (M15E)
P13Aaf Bowman John (M11Fa)
P13Aam Noblett Margaret Ann (M11F)
P13Ab Kinnard John R
P13B   MARY
P13Ba Adkins W. D.
P13C   NANCY
P13Ca Agee W. T.

[P-14] CARNES P11I
  John F/Mary E Copeland
P14A   LYDIA ANN
P14Aa Martin William C -P15-
P14Aaf Martin John
P14Aam Hill Malinda
P14B   LOUISA (J14Ga)
P14Ba Eads Moses W (J14G)
P14Baf Eads Louis J12B,L15Ba,
                   Z13Eaf,Z13Haf)
P14Bam Simpson Jane (L15B,J12Ba,
                      Z13Eam,Z13Ham)
P14C   MARY (G43Cam,G60Aam)
P14Ca Breeden James R -P16- G43Caf,
                             G60Aaf)
P14D   JENNIE L(J20Ea)
P14Da Eads Lewis Jefferson (J20E)
P14Daf Eads William S (J14E,D33Haf)

P14Dam Helton Lydia (J14Ea,D33Ham)
P14E   IDA M
P14Ea   Breeden William -P17-

[P-15] MARTIN P14Aa
    William C/Lydia Ann Carnes
P15A   IRWIN
P15B   WALTER
P15C   MOSES
P15D   GEORGE
P15E   IDA
P15Ea   Birmingham Walter
P15F   ELLA
P15Fa   Prater Richard
P15G   OLIVER
P15Ga   Barnett Cora

[P-16] BREEDEN P14Ca
    James R/Mary Carnes
P16A   ELMER (G60Aa)
P16Aa   Burns Edith (G60A)
P16B   JOHN (G43Ca)
P16Ba   Copeland Emma (G43C)
P16Baf   Copeland Martin M (G350)
P16Bam   Hazzard Livonia (G350a)
P16C   EVERETT
P16D   EUNICE
P16E   LAMON
P16Ea   Duncan Elizabeth
P16Eaf   Duncan Burl
P16F   ELIZABETH
P16Fa   Slats —
P16G   WILLARD
P16H   CHARLES
P16I   JACOB
P16J   LEVI
P16K   JESSE
P16L   OLLIE
P16M   MELVIA
P16Ma   White —
P16N   HESTER
P16Na   McDaniels Frank
P16O   ELLA
P16Oa   Grant Joe

P16P   EMMA

[P-17] BREEDEN P14Ea
    William/Ida M Carnes
P17A   STEPHEN
P17B   THOMAS
P17C   MARSHALL
P17D   LESLIE
P17E   NETTIE
P17Ea   Lock Jack
P17F   ALICE
P17Fa   Swafford —
P17G   ANNA
P17Ga   Connor James
P17H   DORA

[Q-30] MORELAND unknown
unknown/unknown
Q30A   GEORGE -Q31- (H52Eaf,M11Iaf)
Q30Aa   unknown

[Q-31] MORELAND Q30A
George/unknown
Q31A   ELIAS Sr -Q32- (R12Daf)
Q31Aa   Sewell Miriam
Q31B   THOMAS -Q33-
Q31Ba   James Elizabeth
Q31Baf James John
Q31Bb   Spencer Elizabeth
Q31C   JOHN (Jack) -Q40-
Q31Ca   Bennett Sarah
Q31D   ANDERSON -Q34- (M11Ia)
Q31Da   Noblett Eleanor (M11I)
Q31Db   unknown
Q31Dc   Briggs Sarah Jane
Q31E   ANN
Q31Ea   Renfro —
Q31F   SARAH
Q31Fa   McCann —
Q31G   NANCY (H52Ea)
Q31Ga   Bailey James R (H52E)
Q31Gaf Bailey James Sr (H51A)
Q31Gb   Husbands Joseph
Q31Gbf Husbands Herman

[Q-32] MORELAND Q31A
Elias Sr/Miriam Sewell
Q32A   ELIAS Jr
Q32B   GEORGE
Q32Ba   Shinkle Cynthia
Q32C   THOMAS
Q32Ca   Briggs Mary
Q32Caf Briggs James Y(S10A,D15Ca,Z13Baf)
Q32Cam ShockleyMartha(D15C,S10Aa,Z13Bam)
Q32D   PLEASANT
Q32Da   unknown
Q32E   ELIZA C (R12Da,G21Dam,R31Bam)
Q32Ea   Terrill Jackson (R12D,G21Daf,
                                R31Baf)
Q32Eaf Terrill Reuben (R10A)

Q32Eam Morton Susannah (R10Aa)
Q32F   MIRIAM (Y24Ba)
Q32Fa   Johnson William (Y24B)
Q32G   NANCY
Q32Ga   Butler Samuel Rev
Q32H   JANE
Q32Ha   Carter Lemuel
Q32Hb   Carter Lorenzo
Q32I   SEMANTHA
Q32Ia   Chappell —
Q32J   MARY CAROLINE (Q36Ba)
Q32Ja   Shinkle Leonard (Q36B)
Q32Jb   Carter Ransom
Q32Jc   Rhodes Isaac
Q32K   IRBY
Q32L   WILLIAM (Bucky)

[Q-33] MORELAND Q31B
Thomas/Elizabeth James
Q33A   SARAH E
Q33Aa   Southard Edward
Q33B   REBECCA JANE
Q33Ba   Hart Dennis
Q33Baf Hart Adam (Q33Caf)
Q33C   HANNAH
Q33Ca   Hart Lovick
Q33Caf Hart Adam (Q33Baf)
Q33D   MARY A
Q33Da   John Marcus
Q33Daf John William
Q33Dam Deatherage Rebecca
Q33E   JACOB
Q33Ea   Earhardt Susan
Q33F   THOMAS H
Q33Fa   Carrington Malinda
Q33G   J. R. (Shack)
Q33Ga   Love Margaret E
Q33Gaf Love John (R21Baf)
Q33Gb   Roberson Lucinda
Q33H   JAMES E
Q33Ha   John Cynthia
Q33I   R. H.
Q33Ia   Barnwell Laura
Q33Iaf Barnwell Julian F

(2)Elizabeth Spencer
Q33J   MALINDA
Q33Ja   Roberson T. H. B.
Q33Jb   Fisher William
Q33K   AVERY
Q33Ka   James Damarius
Q33L   MARGARET E
Q33La   Arnold Edward P -Q46-
Q33M   RACHEL H
Q33Ma   Nipp W. R.

[Q-34] MORELAND Q31D
    Anderson/Eleanor Noblett
Q34A   ANN
Q34B   ELIZABETH
Q34Ba   Giesler Acy
    (2)unknown
Q34C   JOHN
Q34D   GEORGE
Q34E   WILLIAM
Q34F   MALISSA
Q34G   MARGARET
Q34Ga   Shanks John
    (3)Sarah Jane Briggs
Q34H   NANCY
Q34I   MATTIE
Q34J   OLLIE
Q34K   ANDREW J

[Q-35] SHINKLE unknown
    unknown/unknown
Q35A   SAMUEL -Q36-
Q35Aa   Courtney Louvenia (Lucinda)

[Q-36] SHINKLE Q35A
    Samuel/Courtney Louvenia
Q36A   GEORGE W
Q36Aa   Wagner Emily
Q36B   LEONARD (Q32Ja)
Q36Ba   Moreland Mary Caroline (Q32J)
Q36C   JAMES STEPHEN (Q37Ha)
Q36Ca   Coppedge Eliza Ann (Q37H)
Q36Caf Coppedge George Sr-Q37- (Q43Baf)
Q36Cam unknown

Q36D   JOHN
Q36Da   John Rebecca

[Q-37] COPPEDGE Q36Caf
    George H/unknown
Q37A   ANTHONY K
Q37B   FIELDING TEED
Q37Ba   Roberson —
Q37C   GEORGE (Doss) -Q38-
Q37Ca   Davis Polly Ann
Q37Caf Davis John (G12Gaf)
Q37Cam Pigg Agnes (G12Gam)
Q37D   JAMES H -Q39- (Q44Haf)
Q37Da   Kennett Margaret (Q44Ham)
Q37E   NANCY
Q37Ea   Cock John
Q37F   LUCINDA
Q37Fa   Craig John R
Q37G   JANE (Q43Ba)
Q37Ga   Harrison John Milton (Q43B)
Q37H   ELIZA ANN (Q36Ca)
Q37Ha   Shinkle James Stephen (Q36C)
Q37I   MARGARET E
Q37Ia   Boggs James

[Q-38] COPPEDGE Q37C
    George (Doss)/Polly Ann Davis
Q38A   BELLE
Q38Aa   Imboden George W
Q38Aaf Imboden George Sr
Q38Aam Hughes Elizabeth Ann
Q38B   JOHN D
Q38C   JAMES
Q38D   JANE

[Q-39] COPPEDGE Q37D
    James H/Margaret Kennett
Q39A   MARY L (Q44Ha)
Q39Aa   Harrison Lewis Harvey (Q44H)
Q39Aaf Harrison Lewis Sr (Q42B,Y25Eaf)
Q39Aam Sellers Elizabeth Ann (Q42Bb)
Q39B   SAMUEL H
Q39Ba   Dillon Lola B
Q39Baf Dillon William Andrew Jackson

Q39Bam Hawkins Sarah P
Q39C BETTIE
Q39Ca Walker Alonzo D
Q39D GEORGE H
Q39E ETHEL
Q39Ea Dehn William
Q39F JAMES M Jr
Q39G JOSEPH M
Q39H ORA
Q39Ha Smith James E

[Q-40] MORELAND Q31C
 John/Sarah Bennett
Q40A JOHN P
Q40Aa Brown Ann
Q40Aaf Brown Robert
Q40Aam Walker Jemima

[Q-42] HARRISON unknown
 unknown/unknown
Q42A WILLIAM -Q43- (Y23Faf)
Q42Aa Shephard Nancy (Y23Fam)
Q42B LEWIS -Q44- (Q39Aaf,Y25Eaf)
Q42Ba Hutchison Esther G (Y25Eam)
Q42Baf Hutchison James
Q42Bb Sellers Elizabeth Ann (Q39Aam)
Q42Bc Jamison Nancy Jane
Q42C TYREE -Q45- (Y22Aaf)
Q42Ca Malone Frances (Y22Aam)
Q42D ELIZA
Q42Da Giesler Noah
Q42E MATILDA
Q42Ea Reeves —

[Q-43] HARRISON Q42A
 William/Nancy Shephard
Q43A WILLIAM JASPER
Q43Aa Mosier Anna
Q43Aaf Mosier Daniel
Q43B JOHN MILTON (Q37Ga)
Q43Ba Coppedge Jane (Q37G)
Q43Baf Coppedge George H Sr (Q36Caf)
Q43C MARY J
Q43Ca Clymer George W

Q43D PERMELIA
Q43Da Murry Lafayette
Q43Daf Murry Thomas
Q43E ELIZA M (Y23Fa)
Q43Ea Jones George Washington (Y23F)
Q43Eaf Jones Elijah (Y14Ca,Y21Baf,
 Y22Baf,Y25Baf,Y25Daf)
Q43Eam Johnson Sarah (Y14C,Y21Bam,
 Y22Bam,Y25Bam,Y25Dam)
Q43F ALICE
Q43Fa Stokes James

[Q-44] HARRISON Q42B
 Lewis/Esther Hutchison
Q44A WILLIAM ALEXANDER
Q44B CLARK MONROE
Q44C JOHN HENRY
Q44D LOADICEA NARCISSA
Q44Da Walker Robert J
Q44Daf Walker Moses
Q44Dam Meade Belinda
Q44E MALISSA JANE
Q44Ea Smithers —
Q44Eb Coppedge "Doss"
Q44Ec Stephenson —
Q44F THOMAS JEFFERSON (Y25Ea,R31Eaf)
Q44Fa Johnson Elizabeth (Y25E,R31Eam)
Q44Faf Johnson William (Y14E,Y66Aaf)
Q44Fam McGee Elizabeth (Y14Ea,Y66Aam)
Q44G MARSHALL
Q44Ga Hildebrand Mollie
Q44Gaf Hildebrand William W.
Q44Gb unknown
Q44Gc Gibson Mary J
Q44Gcf Gibson Robert (Q44Kaf)
 (2)Elizabeth Sellers
Q44H LEWIS HARVEY (Q39Aa)
Q44Ha Coppedge Mary L (Q39A)
Q44Haf Coppedge James M (Q37D)
Q44Ham Kennett Margaret (Q37Da)
 (3)Nancy Jane Jamison
Q44I BENJAMIN FRANKLIN
Q44J OLIVE MEDORA
Q44Ja Crum George Washington

Q44Jaf Crum Robert Sevier(G16Aaf,Y31Aaf
Q44Jam Hutchison Elizabeth(G16Aam,
                              Y31Aam)
Q44K   STERLING PRICE
Q44Ka   Gibson Anna B
Q44Kaf Gibson Robert (Q44Gcf)
Q44L   JOSEPH ALBERT
Q44La   Bray Dora A
Q44Laf Bray Thomas A

[Q-45] HARRISON Q42C
        Tyree/Frances Malone
Q45A   JOHN TYREE
Q45Aa   Haynes Eliza
Q45B   FRANCIS MARION
Q45Ba   Davis Ellen
Q45C   EMELINE
Q45Ca   Bullock Jackson
Q45D   SARAH JANE
Q45Da   Bullock James
Q45E   ELIZABETH
Q45Ea   Matlock G. W.
Q45F   LAVINA C (Y22Aa)
Q45Fa   Carroll Phillip H (Y22A)
Q45G   ARMINTA
Q45Ga   Francis W. R.

[Q-46] ARNOLD Q33La
        Edward P/Margaret E Moreland
Q46A   MAE
Q46B   CHARLES
Q46C   FRANK

[R-10] TERRILL unknown
unknown/unknown
R10A   REUBEN 1st —R11— (Q32Eaf)
R10Aa   Morton Susannah (Q32Eam)

[R-11] TERRILL R10A
Reuben 1st/Susannah Morton
R11A   REUBEN 2nd —R12—
R11Aa   Lacy Lucretia
R11B   WILLIAM
R11Ba   Sorrell Virginia
R11C   GEORGE
R11D   KETURAH
R11Da   Quisenberry William
R11E   JACKSON

[R-12] TERRILL R11A
Reuben 2nd/Lucretia Lacy
R12A   REUBEN 3rd —R13— (D40Baf,R20Aaf)
R12Aa   Lacy Frances (D40Bam,R20Aam)
R12B   HAMILTON —R14— (D40Aaf)
R12Ba   Terrill Martha (D40Aam)
R12Baf Terrill James
R12C   JOHN
R12Ca   Stockton Bettie
R12Cb   Pankey Caroline
R12Cbf Pankey Mack
R12D   JACKSON —R15— (Q32Ea,G21Daf,
                        R31Baf)
R12Da   Moreland Eliza C (Q32E,G21Dam,
                        R31Bam)
R12Daf Moreland Elias (Q31A)
R12E   KETURAH
R12F   NANCY
R12Fa   Campbell Morris K
R12G   BETSEY
R12Ga   Given Benjamin

[R-13] TERRILL R12A
Reuben 3rd/Frances Lacy
R13A   KETURAH (R20Aa)
R13Aa   Pinnell William R (R20A)
R13B   ELIZA C
R13Ba   Scantlin Henry M

R13C   JAMES O
R13Ca   Creekpaum Telitha E
R13D   MARY
R13Da   Price —
R13E   JOHN R
R13F   WILLIAM
R13G   GEORGE
R13H   CHARLES M (D40Ba)
R13Ha   Shockley Dena Rebecca (D40B)
R13Haf Shockley Francis A (D27D,D66Iaf)
R13Ham Matthews Amanda (D27Da,D66Iaf)
R13I   ROBERT W
R13J   MILLARD

[R-14] TERRILL R12B
Hamilton/Martha Terrill
R14A   CHARLES
R14Aa   Lemons Telitha
R14B   FRANCES
R14Ba   Smith William
R14Bb   Collins —
R14C   MARY
R14Ca   Shockley Thomas Barton
R14D   ELLEN
R14Da   Campbell James

[R-15] TERRILL R12D
Jackson/Eliza Moreland
R15A   JOHN W
R15B   LUCY
R15Ba   Crider John R
R15C   DeWITT C
R15D   EDWARD
R15E   SAMUEL Dr.
R15Ea   Matthews Mattie
R15Eb   Orr Mertie
R15F   A. JACK Dr (G21Da)
R15Fa   Atkins Elsie (G21D)
R15Faf Atkins John Hubbard (G12Fa)
R15Fam Copeland Telitha (G12F)
R15Fb   unknown
R15Fc   Evans Nellie
R15G   CARLOS
R15H   ELIZA C (R31Ba)

R15Ha Ridenhour Charles (R31B)
R15Haf Ridenhour John S (R30A,Y50Daf)
R15Ham Griffith Dorcas A (R30Aa,Y50Dam)

R21C   ELLA E
R21Ca Fritts Marion F
R21Caf Fritts Philip (R21Aaf)

[R-16] PINNELL unknown
  unknown/unknown
R16A   PETER -R17-
R16Aa unknown

[R-17] PINNELL R16A
  Peter/unknown
R17A   RICHARD -R18-
R17Aa unknown

[R-18] PINNELL R17A
  Richard/unknown
R18A   ASA -R19-
R18Aa Clemens Elizabeth

[R-19] PINNELL R18A
  Asa/Elizabeth Clemens
R19A   LUNSFORD LANE -R20-
R19Aa unknown
R19B   AUGUSTUS -R21-
R19Ba Shephard Millie
R19C   WILLIAM LEWIS -R22-
R19Ca Johnson Mary
R19Caf Johnson Disbury

[R-20] PINNELL R19A
  Lunsford L/ unknown
R20A   WILLIAM B (R13Aa)
R20Aa Terrill Keturah (R13A)
R20Aaf Terrill Reuben 3rd (R12A,D40Baf)
R20Aam Lacy Frances (R12Aa,D40Bam)

[R-21] PINNELL R19B
  Augustus/Millie Shephard
R21A   ELIZABETH
R21Aa Fritts Robert W
R21Aaf Fritts Philip (R21Caf)
R21B   CYNTHIA E
R21Ba Love John E
R21Baf Love John (Q33Gaf)

[R-22] PINNELL R19C
  William Lewis/Mary Johnson
R22A   ASA D -R23-
R22Aa Hawkins Permelia
R22Aaf Hawkins Robert
R22B   LUNSFORD LANE -R24-
R22Ba Oliver Martha Ellen
R22Bb Skaggs Vina
R22Bbf Skaggs George
R22C   WILLIAM BOWLES McCLELLAN -R32-
R22Ca Shockley Sarah A
R22Caf Shockley Vincent
R22Cam Arnett Louvica
R22D   IDA LEORA MAY
R22Da Lovelace James Adolphus
R22Daf Lovelace Thomas Jones
R22Dam Holman Mary Susannah
R22E   MARY E
R22Ea Moreland Jerry N

[R-23] PINNELL R22A
  Asa D/Permelia Hawkins
R23A   ROSALIA
R23Aa Martin —
R23B   LIDA
R23Ba Coen —
R23C   GREGORY
R23D   WALTER
R23E   EVERETT
R23F   LEILA
R23G   ERNEST

[R-24] PINNELL R22B
  Lunsford Lane/Martha E Oliver
R24A   BLUFORD
R24Aa Skaggs Julia
R24Ab Ellis Edna
R24B   CARRIE MARTILLA
R24Ba Skaggs Louis J
R24C   JAMES TILDEN

R24Ca   Hawkins Lou
R24Caf Hawkins George P
R24Cam Martin Sallie Louise
R24D   WILLIAM L
R24E   ELSIE MAUD
R24F   CLAUDE
    (2)Vina Skaggs
R24G   LUNSFORD SHELBY
R24Ga   Doyle Florida
R24H   GEORGE LOUIS
R24Ha   Fly Elma
R24I   IRA MARTIN
R24Ia   Kenney Mary
R24J   DELLA FEROL
R24Ja   Nikkelson Clarence
R24K   LESSIE LAVINA
R24Ka   Wallace William
R24L   WHEELER WARD
R24M   HALLEY HUNTER
R24Ma   Brown Fern
R24N   LESTER LEE
R24Na   Gosney Alice

[R-25] RIDENHOUR unknown
    unknown/unknown
R25A   JOHN -R26- (D22Aaf,D22Gaf)
R25Aa   Reed Elizabeth (D22Aam,D22Gam)

[R-26] RIDENHOUR R25A
    John/Elizabeth Reed
R26A   AMELIA
R26B   MARGARET CHRISTINA (D22Ga)
R26Ba   Shockley Alexander (D22G)
R26Baf Shockley Uriah(D16G,C11Fa,R26Eaf
R26Bam Barbarick Matilda (D16Gb,R26Eam)
R26C   THOMAS BENTON -R27-
R26Ca   Crider Julia Ann
R26Cb   Mitchell Luvicia
R26D   ADAM -R28-
R26Da   Groff Rachel
R26Db   Anderson Eliza Ann
R26E   REUBEN J (D22Aa)
R26Ea   Shockley Elizabeth(Hettie)(D22A)
R26Eaf Shockley Uriah(D16G,C11Fa,R26Baf

R26Eam Barbarick Matilda (D16Gb,R26Bam)
R26F   ELVIRA
R26Fa   Chambers William -R29-
R26G   ELIZABETH
R26Ga   Hawkins Samuel H
R26Gaf Hawkins William
R26H   MARTIN -R30- (S20Daf)
R26Ha   Mahon Sarah Ann Rebecca (S20Dam)

[R-27] RIDENHOUR R26C
    Thomas Benton/Julia A Crider
R27A   JOHN A
R27B   THOMAS M
R27C   WILLIAM A
R27D   MARGARET A
R27Da   Shockley Albert
R27E   MARY E
R27Ea   Kokenberger Sam
    (2)Luvicia Mitchell
R27F   FRED M
R27G   LEWIS J
R27H   ALBERT A
R27I   JAMES L
R27J   SUSAN M
R27Ja   Green John
R27K   LENNIE F
R27Ka   Headman Charles
R27L   SARAH F
R27La   Perrin Alonzo
R27M   POLLY
R27Ma   Pointer "Cap"
R27N   RHODA J
R27Na   Rogers Oscar

[R-28] RIDENHOUR R26D
    Adam/Eliza A Anderson
R28A   JOHN W
R28Aa   Harris Belle
R28B   MOLLIE
R28Ba   Ready Richard
R28C   LOUIS H
R28Ca   Pointer Polly
R28D   ALEXANDER
R28Da   Groff Belle

R28E   ROBERT R
R28Ea   Bledsoe Etha

[R-29] CHAMBERS R26Fa
    William/Elvira Ridenhour
R29A   WILLIAM
R29B   HESTER
R29Ba   Hutson Pat
R29C   SUSAN
R29Ca   Sharp Joseph K

[R-30] RIDENHOUR R26H
    Martin/Sarah A Mahon
R30A   JOHN SHEPHARD -R31- (R15Haf,
                              Y50Daf)
R30Aa   Griffith Dorcas (R15Ham,Y50Dam)
R30B   NANCY ELIZABETH (S20Da)
R30Ba   Backues Thomas M (S20D)
R30Baf Backues Thomas (S18B,S13Aaf,
                              Z31Daf,Z31Eaf)
R30Bam Keeney Malinda (S18Ba,Z31Dam,
                              Z31Eam)
R30C   MARY JANE
R30Ca   Wilson William Jr
R30Caf Wilson William Sr
R30Cam Rogers Louisa
R30D   MARTHA LOUISE
R30Da   Griffith William
R30E   WILLIAM ALEXANDER
R30F   SUSAN MARGARET CHRISTINA
R30Fa   Goodman William
R30G   SARAH FRANCES
R30Ga   Schweigler Julius
R30H   MARTIN ANDREW JACKSON
R30I   VIRGINIA HARRIETT
R30Ia   Groff James
R30J   THOMAS HUSTON
R30Ja   Keeney Barbara
R30K   DAVID JASPER
R30Ka   McQueen Emma
R30Kaf McQueen James J
R30L   ADAM LOUIS (ANDREW)
R30La   Price Nellie

[R-31] RIDENHOUR R30A
    John S/Dorcas A Griffith
R31A   JOHN O
R31Aa   Pointer — (R31Cb)
R31Aaf Pointer Charles (R31Caf)
R31B   CHARLES E (R15Ha)
R31Ba   Terrill Eliza C (R15H)
R31Baf TerrillJackson(R12D,Q32Ea,G21Daf
R31Bam Moreland Eliza(Q32E,R12Da,G21Dam
R31C   DECATUR
R31Ca   Pointer —
R31Caf Pointer Charles (R31Aaf)
R31Cb   Pointer — (R31Aa)
R31D   BRUCE
R31Da   Milam —
R31E   RAINEY (Y50Da)
R31Ea   Harrison Cecil (Y50D)
R31Eaf Harrison Thomas J (Q44F,Y25Ea)
R31Eam Johnson Elizabeth (Y25E,Q44Fa)
R31F   ELLA
R31Fa   Keonig Chris
R31G   SOPHIA
R31Ga   Tynes Ernest
R31H   CORA
R31Ha   Mason Gus

[R-32] PINNELL R22C
    William Bowles/Sarah A Shockley
R32A   ELVIN CECIL
R32B   MURIEL ETHELIND
R32Ba   Ackle J. Fred
R32C   RALPH E
R32Ca   McCutcheon Nora B
R32D   GLADYS
R32Da   Huhtala Oscar
R32E   GRETCHEN
R32Ea   Hoey James J
R32F   LESTER W
R32G   WILLIAM L
R32Ga   Fisk Oleta

[S-10] BRIGGS unknown
unknown/unknown
S10A   JAMES Y -S11- (D15Ca,Q32Caf,
                      Z13Baf)
S10Aa Shockley Martha (D15C,Q32Cam,
                      Z13Bam)

[S-11] BRIGGS S10A
James Y/Martha Shockley
S11A   SCOTT TERRY -S12- (G19Daf)
S11Aa Fennessey Bridget (G19Dam)
S11B   ZYLPHIA (J12Lam,J14Cam,
              J20Aam,Z13Fam)
S11Ba Tackett Willis M (J12Laf,J14Caf,
                        J20Aaf,Z13Faf)
S11Baf Tackett John
S11C   JOHN BURR -S13- (S20Haf)
S11Ca Powers Melissa (S20Ham)
S11Caf Powers John Thompson (L15Iaf)
S11Cam Ferrier Elizabeth (L15Iam)
S11D   JAMES LAFAYETTE
S11Da Murphy Nancy
S11E   MARY MINERVA
S11Ea Fennessey Dennis -S14-
S11F   SIDNEY
S11G   DANIEL BOONE -S15-(Z13Ba,J14Faf)
S11Ga Hughes Melvina J (Z13B,J14Fam)
S11Gaf Hughes McKamy W (Z12A,J14Baf)
S11Gam Davidson Elizabeth (Z12Aa,J14Bam)
S11H   SHARILDA

[S-12] BRIGGS S11A
Scott Terry/Bridget Fennessey
S12A   A MOSES
S12B   JAMES
S12C   TERRY
S12D   DENNIS
S12E   THOMAS
S12Ea Birmingham Catherine Agnes
S12Eaf Birmingham Walter

[S-13] BRIGGS S11C
John Burr/Melissa Powers
S13A   CHARLES -S16- (S20Ha)

S13Aa Backues Amanda (S20H)
S13Aaf Backues Thomas Sr (Z31Daf,
                  Z31Eaf,R30Daf,S18B)
S13Aam — Pattie(S18Bb)
S13B   STEPHEN
S13Ba Crismon Malinda
S13Baf Crismon "Slim Ike"
S13C   EUGENIA
S13Ca Juergens Herman
S13D   EMELIZA
S13Da Shelton Jesse
S13Daf Shelton George
S13Dam Burks Celia
S13E   JAMES T
S13Ea Hancock Malinda
S13Eaf Hancock Gilbert
S13F   NEWTON
S13Fa Rose Missouri
S13Faf Rose Marion
S13G   MARGARET

[S-14] FENNESSEY S11Ea
Dennis/Mary M Briggs
S14A   MARY
S14Aa Breeden William
S14B   KATE
S14Ba Breeden Stephen
S14C   THOMAS
S14D   ANDY
S14E   MARGARET
S14Ea Birmingham Walter
S14F   EVA
S14Fa Reichel Ulrich

[S-15] BRIGGS S11G
Daniel Boone W/Melvina Jane Hughes
S15A   JOHN H (J14Fa)
S15Aa Eads Malinda (J14F)
S15B   MARY
S15C   MARGARET

[S-16] BRIGGS S13A
Charles/Amanda Backues
S16A   EVA

294

S16B   MOLLIE
S16C   THOMAS
S16D   WALTER
S16E   JOHN

[S-17] BACKUES unknown
  unknown/unknown
S17A   SANFORD -S18-
S17Aa   — Mary A

[S-18] BACKUES S17A
  Sanford/ Mary A —
S18A   JOHN -S19-
S18Aa   Keeney —
S18B   THOMAS SR -S20- (R30Baf,S13Aaf,
                        Z31Daf,Z13Eaf)
S18Ba   Keeney Malinda (R30Bam,Z31Dam.
                        Z31Eam)
S18Bb   — Pattie (S13Aam)
S18C   ISAAC C -S21-
S18Ca   — Susan
S18D   ELIZA (K37Aam)
S18Da   Poe Barnabas Madison
S18Db   McQueen James (K37Aaf)
S18E   ROWENA
S18F   SALLIE
S18G   CENA O
S18Ga   Keeney Michael

[S-19] BACKUES S18A
  John/— Keeney
S19A   SANFORD 2nd
S19B   JOHN KEENEY

[S-20] BACKUES S18B
  Thomas Sr/Malinda Keeney
S20A   EMELINE (Z31Da)
S20Aa   James Thomas P (Z31D)
S20B   SUSAN H (Z31Ea)
S20Ba   James Alonzo (Z31E)
S20Bb   Hutchison Alexander Hamilton
S20Bbf Hutchison John
S20Bbm Nanney Lucy
S20C   MARY ANN (V13Eam)

S20Ca   Harris William H (V13Eaf)
S20D   THOMAS M -S22- (R30Ba)
S20Da   Ridenhour Nancy Elizabeth (R30b)
S20Daf Ridenhour Martin (R26H)
S20Dam Mahon Sarah Ann Rebecca (R26Ha)
     (2)Pattie —
S20E   JOHN
S20Ea   Santee Nancy
S20F   MALINDA
S20Fa   Bacon John F
S20G   ELIZA
S20Ga   Copeland John
S20H   AMANDA (S13Aa)
S20Ha   Briggs Charles (S13A)
S20Haf Briggs John Burr (S11C)
S20Ham Powers Malissa (S11Ca)
S20I   VIRGINIA
S20Ia   Rowden Louis A
S20Iaf Rowden William N (V18E,G57Jaf)
S20Iam Carnes Mary (V18Ea,G57Jam)

[S-21] BACKUES S18C
  Isaac C/Susan —
S21A   ANDREW J
S21Aa   Keeney Hannah M (D65Ga)
S21Aaf Keeney Sylvester (D65Gaf)

[S-22] BACKUES S20D
  Thomas M/Nancy E Ridenhour
S22A   MARTIN (Y56Aaf)
S22Aa   Shanks Martha (Y56Aam)
S22B   EMELINE
S22Ba   Cox Rafe
S22C   LYDIA
S22Ca   Wendt George
S22D   RAY
S22E   JOHN H
S22Ea   Krewson Nora
S22Eaf Krewson Jacob
S22F   MORRIS S
S22Fa   Griffith Ida
S22G   ANDREW J
S22Ga   Franklin —
S22Gaf Franklin Robert

S22H   ADAM
S22Ha Elrod —
S22I   SARAH
S22Ia Walker W. A.
S22J   EVE
S22Ja Hutchison Henry
S22Jaf Hutchison Perry
S22Jam Krewson Josephine

[T-10] CRISMON unknown
  unknown/unknown
T10A   GEORGE -T11-
T10Aa   unknown

[T-11] CRISMON T10A
  George/unknown
T11A   CAMPBELL -T12-
T11Aa   unknown

[T-12] CRISMON T11A
  Campbell/unknown
T12A   GILBERT -T13- (D17Laf,E17Baf)
T12Aa   unknown
T12B   UNKNOWN (U10Aa,E53Aam,U16Bam,
                U53Bam,E53Bam)
T12Ba   Helton James (U10A,E53Aaf,
                U16Baf,U53Baf)

[T-13] CRISMON T12A
  Gilbert/unknown
T13A   JOHN -T14- (T27Aaf)
T13Aa   Brashears Flavilla M (T27Aam)
T13Aaf Brashears Joseph Rev
T13B   ISAAC ("Oregon Ike")
T13Ba   Miller —
T13Bb   Murphy Louisiana K (T30Da)
T13C   JAMES -T15-(J12Aa,E20Abf,J27Aaf)
T13Ca   Eads Frances (J12A,E20Abm)
T13Caf Eads Benjamin (J11A,E53Ca,
                J26Bbf,K11Caf,T16Aaf)
T13Cam Hughes Mary (E53C,J11Aa,
                K11Cam,)
T13Cb   unknown
T13D   ARCH
T13E   PLEASANT
T13F   MOSES
T13G   STEPHEN
T13H   BETSEY
T13I   SALLIE CUMILE
T13Ia   Thompson Flem
T13J   WILLIAM W -T16- (J12Haf
T13Ja   Whrattles Margaret (J12Ham)
T13K   SARAH (E17Ba)

T13Ka   Branson Reuben (E17B)
T13L   MAHALA (D17La)
T13La   Shockley Henry (D17L)
T13Laf Shockley Meredith Sr(D14F,G11Iaf
T13Lam Worrell Sarah (D14Fa,G11Iam)
T13M   POLLY

[T-14] CRISMON T13A
  John/Flavilla M Brashears
T14A   AMANDA
T14Aa   Vaughan William Hood (T14Baf)
T14Aaf Vaughan William Sr (I41Bbf)
T14Aam — Margaret (I41Bbm)
T14B   MARY (I54Aam)
T14Ba   Vaughan John W (G58Caf,I54Aaf)
T14Baf Vaughan William Hood (T14Aa)
T14C   GILBERT Jr.
T14Ca   Jones Nancy
T14D   HUGH
T14Da   Rowden Ann
T14Daf Rowden John Hardin
T14E   JOSEPH
T14Ea   Lawson Caroline
T14Eaf Lawson Andrew
T14F   MARK (T30Hc)
T14Fa   Woods Nancy (T30H)
T14Faf Woods Samuel -T30- (G29Gaf)
T14Fam Vaughan Sarah (G29Gam)
T14G   WILLIAM W Jr
T14Ga   unknown
T14Gb   Basham Nancy
T14H   MYRA
T14Ha   Wiles George
T14I   NANCY (T27Aa)
T14Ia   Whitaker Archeleus A (T27A)
T14Ib   Arendall James

[T-15] CRISMON T13C
  James/Frances Eads
T15A   JESSE H
T15Aa   Elsey Margaret L
T15Aaf Elsey John
T15B   JAMES MUNRO
T15Ba   Elkins Bathsheba

SIBLING GROUP T

T15C BENJAMIN F
T15Ca Taff Amanda (Annette)
T15Caf Taff John (G46A,Y25Iaf)
T15Cam Anderson Mahala (G46Aa,Y25Iam)
T15D GILBERT O
T15Da Juergens Launa
T15E ROBERT E (J27Aa)
T15Ea Shelton Josie
T15Eaf Shelton William
T15Eam Lawson Polly Ann
T15Eb Meltabarger Josie
T15Ebf Meltabarger Lafayette
T15Ebm Vaughan Bettie
T15Ec Graham Clorah Belle (J27A)
T15Ecf Graham Michael(J26B,J12Ja,T18Ba)
T15Ecm Skaggs Jane (T18B,J26Ba)
T15F LOUISA J
T15G NANCY J
T15Ga Cole W. C.
T15H MARGARET (E20Ab)
T15Ha Lowder Duncan M
T15Hb Branson William G (E20A,U12Naf)
T15I MALINDA
T15Ia (Incorrect name in 1st Printing
T15Iaf   "   "   " "   ")
T15Iam Huskey —
T15J MATILDA
T15Ja Meltabarger James (J26Da)
T15K MARY
T15Ka Richmond Joseph

[T-16] CRISMON T13J
    William W/Margaret Whrattles
T16A GILBERT (J12Ha) -J16-
T16Aa Eads Myra (J12H)
T16Aaf Eads Benjamin (J11A,E53Ca,
             K11Caf.J26Bbf,T13Caf)
T16B WILLIAM W Jr.
T16Ba Morrow Eliza
T16Baf Morrow James
T16Bam Powers Lydia
T16C ISAAC A (V12Ga)
T16Ca Rowden Susan (Sarah) (V12G)

T16Caf Rowden Asa (V11A) -V12-
T16Cam Hannah Margaret (V11Aa)
T16D STEPHEN (U13Aaf)
T16Da Breeding —
T16Db Miller Jane (U13Aam)
T16Dc Ezell Sallie
T16E GABRIEL
T16F ELIZA E
T16G RACHEL
T16H MARY

[T-17] SKAGGS unknown
    unknown/unknown
T17A FREEMAN -T18-
T17Aa unknown

[T-18] SKAGGS T17A
    Freeman/unknown
T18A GIDEON P -T19- (T28Baf)
T18Aa Lambeth Lucinda Jane (T28Bam)
T18Aaf Lambeth Lytle(G11Ja,I52Da,J12Caf)
T18Aam Copeland Polly C (G11J,J12Cam)
T18B JANE (J26Ba,T15Ecm)
T18Ba Graham Michael(J26B,J12Ja,T15Ecf)
T18Baf Graham George Washington (J12Jaf)
T18Bam Hickle Harriett (J12Jam)
T18C W. P.
T18D GORDON
T18E JEFFERSON D -T20-
T18Ea Arendall Alice
T18F JAMES
T18G NEWTON
T18H UNKNOWN
T18Ha Murphy T. A.

[T-19] SKAGGS T18A
    Gideon P/Lucinda J Lambeth
T19A MINNIE
T19Aa Wilson G. W.
T19B MARY
T19Ba Skelton Emmett (T19Fa)
T19C ALICE
T19Ca Skelton Perry

T19D   GEORGE W
T19E   LAUNA J
T19Ea   Sholl —
T19F   MATILDA E
T19Fa   Skelton Emmett (T19Ba)
T19G   SALLIE (T28Ba)
T19Ga   West Daniel M -T21- (T28B)
T19Gaf West John (T24D)
T19Gam Burd Mary (T24Da)

[T-20] SKAGGS T18E
    Jefferson D/Alica Arendall
T20A   BENNETT
T20Aa   Irwin Beulah
T20Ab   Copeland Myrtle

[T-21] WEST T19Ga
    Daniel M/Sallie Skaggs
T21A   VEVA
T21Aa   Dunlap —
T21B   IVA
T21Ba   Barnhart Isaac
T21C   CLARENCE
T21D   GORDON
T21E   PAUL

[T-22] WEST unknown
    unknown/unknown
T22A   WILLIAM -T23-
T22Aa   unknown

[T-23] WEST T22A
    William/unknown
T23A   HARDIN -T24-
T23Aa   Williams Katherine
T23Ab   — Sarah
T23B   WOODSON -T25-
T23Ba   Reynolds —
T23C   WILLIAM JR -T26-
T23Ca   unknown
T23Cb   Whitaker —
T23D   SARAH
T23Da   Whitaker Thomas Benton -T27-

[T-24] WEST T23A
    Hardin/Katherine Willliams
T24A   WILLIAM
T24B   DAVID
T24C   RICHARD
T24Ca   Burd Ailsie
T24Caf Burd Daniel (T24Daf,T24Eaf)
T24D   JOHN -T28- (T19Gaf)
T24Da   Burd Mary (T19Gam)
T24Daf Burd Daniel (T24Caf,T24Eaf)
T24E   THOMAS
T24Ea   Burd Anna
T24Eaf Burd Daniel (T24Caf,T24Daf)
T24F   MARK -T29-
T24Fa   Holmes Lucy
T24Faf Holmes Oliver
T24Fb   Perkins Isabelle
T24Fbf Perkins Isaac
T24G   JANE
T24Ga   Barnhart Thomas
T24H   SALLIE
T24Ha   Green "Doc" (T24Ja)
T24I   ANGELINE
T24J   EMELINE
T24Ja   Green "Doc" (T24Ha)
    (2)unknown
T24K   DEE
T24L   MARION
T24M   "DOC"
T24N   LUCY

[T-25] WEST T23B
    Woodson/ — Reynolds
T25A   SARAH
T25Aa   Pearson —
T25B   ARZILLA
T25Ba   Hedge —
T25C   THOMAS
T25D   UNKNOWN
T25Da   Burnett James
T25E   MARK
T25Ea   Livingston —
T25F   JOHN H
T25Fa   Thompson Peggy Jane

T25Faf Thompson William S (T26Aaf)

[T-26] WEST T23C
   William Jr/unknown
T26A   WARREN A "Doc"
T26Aa   Thompson Nancy
T26Aaf Thompson William S (T25Faf)

[T-27] WHITAKER 23Da
   Thomas Benton/Sarah West
T27A   ARCHELAUS (T14Ia)
T27Aa   Crismon Nancy (T14I)
T27Aaf Crismon John (T13A
T27Aam Brashears Flavilla M (T13Aa)
T27B   JAMES
T27C   WILLIAM
T27D   GAY
T27Da   Shelton Mary O
T27Daf Shelton William
T27E   JOHN
T27F   MARK
T27Fa   Rothwell Mary
T27G   MATILDA (V18Aa)
T27Ga   Rowden James (V18A)
T27H   "BABE"
T27Ha   Skaggs William

[T-28] WEST T24D
   John/Mary Burd
T28A   KATE
T28Aa   Burns George
T28B   DANIEL M "Doc" (T19Ga)
T28Ba   Skaggs Sallie (T19G)
T28Baf Skaggs Gideon P (T18A)
T28Bam Lambeth Lucinda Jane (T18Aa)

[T-29] WEST T24F
   Mark/Lucy Holmes
T29A   CAROLINE
T29Aa   Sherrill George
T29B   HARRIET
T29Ba   McWhorter —
T29C   ELLA
T29Ca   Pickering Alex

T29D   DAVID H
T29Da   Williams —
T29E   JANE
T29Ea   Norris —
T29F   MARY
T29Fa   Street Richard A
      (2)Isabelle Perkins
T29G   A. C.

[T-30] WOODS T14Faf
   Samuel Major/Sarah Vaughan
T30A   JOHN HENRY
T30B   AMANDA
T30C   SOPHIA (E27Aam)
T30Ca   Holmes William W (E27Aaf)
T30Caf Holmes Oliver Perry (T30Gaf)
T30Cam — Mary
T30D   RICHARD
T30Da   Murphy Louisiana K (T13Bb)
T30E   SARAH
T30Ea   Murphy Kelley
T30F   ELIZABETH
T30Fa   Shaw George W
T30G   MYRA
T30Ga   Holmes Albert
T30Gaf Holmes Oliver Perry (T30Caf)
T30H   NANCY (T14Fa)
T30Ha   Keith William
T30Hb   Southerland —
T30Hc   Crismon Mark (T14F)
T30I   LUCINDA (G29Ga)
T30Ia   Copeland Martin (G29G)
T30J   VIRGINIA
T30Ja   Courtwright John

[T-31] WEST T25F
   John H/Peggy Jane Thompson
T31A ANDY
T31B OLIVER
T31C FRANCIS
T31D ROSE
T31E LENA
T31F ELSIE
T31G LETTIE

[U-10] HELTON unknown
    unknown/unknown
U10A   JAMES Sr.-U11- (T12Ba,
        E53Aaf,E53Baf,U16Baf)
U10Aa   Crismon —(T12B,E53Aam,
        E53Bam,U16Bam)

[U-11] HELTON U10A
    James,Sr/—Crismon
U11A · ISAAC Sr -U12- (E53Ba,U16Ba,
        E25Caf,G12Iaf,V13Caf,V15Daf)
U11Aa   Hughes Elizabeth (E53B,V13Cam,
        V15Dam)
U11Ab   Cowan Mary A (U16B,E25Cam,G12Iam)
U11Abf Cowan David Sr -U16- (G12Baf)
U11Abm Martin Telitha (G12Bam)
U11B   WILLIAM TODD -U13- (E18Aaf)
U11Ba   Washam Julia Ann (E18Aam)
U11Bam — Nancy
U11C   CRISMON (G19Haf)
U11Ca   Pryor Louisa Jane (G19Ham)
U11Caf Pryor Stephen
U11D   JAMES
U11E   PETER
U11Ea   Anderson Emeline
U11F   POLLY
U11Fa   Hughes John
U11G   JANE (E53Aa)
U11Ga   Hughes Stephen (E53A)
U11Gaf Hughes John (E52A)
U11Gam Bilyeu — (E52Aa)
U11H   ELIZABETH (Betsey)
U11Ha   Miller David
U11I   LOUISA
U11Ia   Anderson William

[U-12] HELTON U11A
    Isaac Sr/Eizabeth Hughes
U12A   LOUISA J
U12Aa   Breeden William
U12Aaf Breeden John (D25Gbf,U12Baf)
U12B   NANCY
U12Ba   Breeden Abraham R (D25Gb)
U12Baf Breeden John (D25Gbf,U12Aaf)

U12C   PERRY
U12Ca   Ready Martha J
U12Caf Ready Thomas
U12D   JAMES -U14-
U12Da   Taff Jeanette
U12Daf unknown
U12Dam Copeland Sarah(Y25Iam)
U12Db   Belk Amanda
U12Dbf Belk John (U12Dcf)
U12Dc   Belk Julia Ann
U12Dcf Belk John (U12Dbf)
U12E   JESSE -U15-
U12Ea   Sherrill Matilda
U12F   STEPHEN (V13Ca)
U12Fa   Rowden Sarah Corretta (V13C)
U12Faf Rowden Robert (V12A)
U12Fam Tyree Nancy (V12Aa)
U12G   ISAAC C
U12Ga   Breeding —
U12Gaf Breeding Elijah
U12Gb   Lee Cynthia
        (2)Mary Ann Cowan
U12H   RACHEL
U12Ha   Curtman George Dr (E12Maf)
U12Haf Curtman Charles Otto
U12Ham Wilson Elizabeth Jane
U12I   DAVID (G12Ia)
U12Ia   Copeland Matilda Roberta (G12I)
U12Iaf Copeland John (G11A)
U12J   ROBERT
U12Ja   Stokes Mina
U12K   JUDITH
U12Ka   Fitzpatrick Bernard
U12L   MARY
U12La   Krone Monroe
U12M   AMANDA (V15Da)
U12Ma   Rowden Asa (V15D)
U12Maf Rowden Rufus (V12D)
U12Mam Massey Polly (V12Da)
U12N   MARTIN (E25Ca)
U12Na   Branson Nancy (E25C)
U12Naf Branson William (E20A,T15Hb)
U12Nam Finn Martha A (E20Aa)
U12O   CHARLES

301

U120a Finn Leona
U120af Finn William D (G32Ebf)
U120am Russell Malinda (G32Ebm)

[U-13] HELTON U11B
  William Todd/Julia Ann Washam
U13A   JAMES REUBEN
U13Aa Crismon Martha J
U13Aaf Crismon Stephen (T16D)
U13Aam Miller Jane (T16Db)
U13B   JOHN
U13Ba Pryor Lottie
U13Bb Wittkop Kate
U13Bc Hughes Rachel
U13C   RICHARD
U13Ca Wiles Jane
U13Caf Wiles Thomas (J15Faf)
U13Cam Johnson Catherine (J15Fam)
U13D   MARY (Polly) (E18Aa)
U13Da Branson William(Red Head)(E18A)
U13E   NANCY
U13Ea Hughes Stephen
U13F   MARGARET J
U13Fa Prewett Moses "Doc"
U13G   ELIZABETH
U13Ga Wiles James

[U-14] HELTON U12D
  James/Jeanette Taff
U14A   ISAAC
U14B   HENRY
U14Ba Moss Eliza
U14Baf Moss Johnathan
U14Bam Tyree Mary D
U14C   JOHN
U14Ca Johnson —
U14D   MARY
U14Da Gardner John

[U-15] HELTON U12E
  Jesse/Matilda Sherrill
U15A   MOSES
U15B   OLIVER
U15C   BEN

U15D   GEORGE
U15E   JESSE Jr
U15F   WILLIAM
U15G   BERTIE
U15Ga Vaughan George
U15H   LOUISA
U15Ha Woody Archie D
U15Haf Woody John Jefferson
U15Ham Barnhart Martha Sarilda
U15I   ELMEDA
U15Ia Briggs A. M.

[U-16] COWAN U11Abf
  David Sr./Telitha Martin
U16A   LOUISA EVALINE (G12Ba)
U16Aa Copeland William M (G12B)
U16Aaf Copeland John (G11A,I46Baf)
U16Aam Wiseman Mary A (G11Aa,I46Bam)
U16B   MARY ANN (U11Ab,E25Cam,G12Iam)
U16Ba Helton Isaac Sr (U11A,E53Ba,
           E25Caf,G12Iaf,V13Caf,V15Daf)
U16Baf Helton James (U10A,T12Ba,E53Aam,
                     E53Bam)
U16Bam Crismon — (T12B,U10Aa,E53Aam,
                     E53Bam)
U16C   ELIZABETH
U16Ca Connor John –U17–
U16D   ELIZA (G51Iam)
U16Da Barnhart E. P. (G51Iaf)
U16E   ADELINE
U16F   JOHN
U16Fa Martin —
U16Faf Martin John Y
U16G   DAVID Jr –U18–
U16Ga Pendleton Eliza
U16Gaf Pendleton George
U16H   WILLIAM –U19–
U16Ha unknown
U16I   GEORGE

[U-17] CONNOR U16Ca
  John/Elizabeth Cowan
U17A   THOMAS
U17B   JAMES

302

U17C   MICHAEL
U17D   JOHN
U17E   EDWARD
U17F   WILLIAM
U17G   MARY
U17Ga   Birmingham Thomas

[U-18] COWAN U16G
        David Jr/Eliza Pendleton
U18A   FRANK
U18Aa   Barnhart Fannie
U18Aaf Barnhart Mat
U18B   AZARIAH
U18C   ETTA
U18D   LOTTIE

[U-19] COWAN U16H
        William/unknown
U19A   AUSTIN
U19B   OSCAR

[V-10] ROWDEN unknown
    unknown/unknown
V10A   ABRAM -V11-
V10Aa   unknown

[V-11] ROWDEN V10A
    Abram/unknown
V11A   ASA -V12- (T16Caf)
V11Aa   Hannah Margaret (T16Cam)
V11B   NATHANIEL -V17-
V11Ba   unknown
V11C   H. BENTON

[V-12] ROWDEN V11A
    Asa/Margaret Hannah
V12A   ROBERT -V13- (U12Faf,V21Baf)
V12Aa   Tyree Nancy (U12Fam)
V12Aaf Tyree Satterthwaite
V12Aam Stanford Elizabeth
V12B   AKE E -V14- (V25Aaf)
V12Ba   Hill Catherine (V25Aam)
V12Baf Hill George
V12Bb   Greever Emma L
V12C   WILLIAM A
V12Ca   Wiseman Matilda
V12Caf Wiseman Thomas D
V12D   RUFUS -V15- (U12Maf)
V12Da   Massey Mary (U12Mam)
V12Daf Massey William
V12Dam Hill Elizabeth
V12E   JAMES H -V16-
V12Ea   Powers Emeline
V12Eaf Powers John Dr.
V12F   RACHEL
V12Fa   Elzey John
V12G   SARAH (SUSAN) (T16Ca)
V12Ga   Crismon Isaac (Ike) (T16C)

[V-13] ROWDEN V12A
    Robert/Nancy Tyree
V13A   SATTERWAITE
V13Aa   Miller Alma California
V13B   CORDELIA (V21Ba)
V13Ba   Breeden John W (V21B)

V13C   SARAH CORRETTA (U12Fa)
V13Ca   Helton Stephen (U12F)
V13Caf Helton Isaac Sr (U11A,E53Ba,
            U16Ba,E25Caf,G12Iaf,V15Daf)
V13Cam Hughes Elizabeth(E53B,U11Aa,
            V15Dam)
V13D   LOUIS CLINTON
V13Da   Felker Jennie
V13Daf Felker John
V13E   NINA ANN
V13Ea   Harris B. F.
V13Eaf Harris William H (S20Ca)
V13Eam Backues Mary Ann (S20C)
V13F   ROBERT L
V13Fa   Given Angeline
V13Faf Given H. E.

[V-14] ROWDEN V12B
    Ake E/Catherine Hill
V14A   MALINDA (G31Eam)
V14Aa   Cansler James H (G31Eaf)
V14Aaf Cansler Nathan Henderson
V14Aam Reynolds Hannah C
V14B   MARY (V25Aa)
V14Ba   Hoops George (V25A)
V14C   MARGARET
V14Ca   Benage A. L.
V14D   BENTON
V14E   WILLIAM D
V14Ea   West Caroline

[V-15] ROWDEN V12D
    Rufus/Mary Massey
V15A   CHARLOTTE
V15B   MARGARET
V15Ba   Martin James O
V15Baf Martin John
V15C   GEORGE
V15D   ASA (U12Ma)
V15Da   Helton Amanda (U12M)
V15Daf Helton Isaac Sr (U11A,E53Ba,
            U16Ba,E25Caf,G12Iaf,V13Caf)
V15Dam Hughes Elizabeth (E53B,U11Aa,
            V13Cam)

SIBLING GROUP V

[V-16] ROWDEN V12E
   James H/Emeline Powers
V16A   ROBERT
V16B   ELIZABETH
V16Ba Krone Robert
V16Bb Myers W. C.

[V-17] ROWDEN V11B
   Nathaniel/unknown
V17A   ISAAC D
V17B   HARRISON
V17C   WILEY
V17D   JAMES E -V18-
V17Da Lawson Margaret
V17Daf Lawson Nathan
V17E   ALONZO LONNIE
V17F   JACOB
V17G   ANDREW
V17H   JOHN
V17I   LINDA BRANHAM
V17J   CAROLINE HICKMAN
V17K   SALLY
V17L   MARTHA PARKS
V17M   NANCY DIAL
V17N   SUSAN LAWSON
V17O   ANN CLARK

[V-18] ROWDEN V17D
   James/Margaret Lawson
V18A   JAMES (T27Ga)
V18Aa Whitaker Matilda (T27G)
V18B   JOHN G
V18Ba Davidson Tabitha
V18C   ABRAM
V18Ca Lawson Delilah Ann
V18Caf Lawson George
V18Cam Blankenship Elmina
V18Cb Whitaker Margaret J
V18D   JOHN
V18E   WILLIAM N (G57Jaf,S20Iaf)
V18Ea Carnes Mary (G57Jam,S20Iam)
V18F   NANCY
V18Fa Blankenship Jessee
V18Fb Healey Thomas

V18G   ELIZABETH
V18Ga Nelson George
V18H   EMELINE
V18Ha Ogle William
V18Hb Clark William
V18I   MALINDA
V18Ia Martin James
V18J   MARY
V18Ja Barr George

[V-19] BREEDEN UNKNOWN
   unknown/unknown
V19A   JOHN -V20-
V19Aa unknown

[V-20] BREEDEN V19A
   John/unknown
V20A   JOSEPH -V21-
V20Aa Williams Margaret
V20Ab Wherry Mary
V20Abf Wherry Daniel Boone

[V-21] BREEDEN V20A
   Joseph/Margaret Williams
V21A   LOUIS ROLAND
V21Aa Forrester Elizabeth Malissa
V21Aaf Forrester Thomas
V21B   JOHN WILLIAM (V13Ba)
V21Ba Rowden Cordelia (V13B)
V21Baf Rowden Robert (V12A)
V21C   HANNAH
V21D   SARAH

[V-22] HOOPS Unknown
   unknown/unknown
V22A   DAVID -V23-
V22Aa — Lucy Ann

[V-23] HOOPS V22A
   David/Lucy Ann —
V23A   GEORGE
V23Aa Walton Amanda
Y23B   JOHN -V24-
Y23Ba Walton —

V23Bb   Kinsey —
V23C   DAVID –V25–
V23Ca   Walton Louisiana
V23Cb   —— Sarah
V23D   MARTHA
V23Da   Smith Benjamin
V23Daf Smith Wyatt (V23Eaf,V23Faf)
V23E   MARY ANN
V23Ea   Smith Alfred
V23Eaf Smith Wyatt (V23Daf,V23Faf)
V23F   RACHEL
V23Fa   Smith Moses
V23Faf Smith Wyatt (V23Daf,V23Eaf)

[V-24] HOOPS V23B
        John/— Walton
V24A   LOUISIANA ANN
V24Aa   Goodman David M
V24B   AMANDA M
V24Ba   Reed Samuel W –V26–
V24C   MARTHA
V24Ca   Strickland William
V24Cam Henderson Abiel
V24D   DAVID –V27–
V24Da   Mahan Fannie
V24Daf Mahan John

[V-25] HOOPS V23C
        David/Louisiana Walton
V25A   GEORGE (V14Ba)
V25Aa   Rowden Mary (V14B)
V25Aaf Rowden Ake E (V12B)
V25Aam Hill Catherine (V12Ba)
V25B   ELIZABETH
V25Ba   Mosby Joseph –V28–
V25Baf Mosby Williamson
V25C   HARRIETT E
V25Ca   Anderson Richard W
V25Caf Anderson Thomas (V25Eaf,Z17Caf)
                            Y23Eaf)
V25Cam Wiseman Myra (V25Eam,Z17Cam)
        (2)—Sarah
V25D   SUSAN N (I52Ja)

V25Da   Ellis T. Jeff (I52J)
V25E   NANCY A
V25Ea   Anderson James Monroe
V25Eaf Anderson Thomas (V25Caf,Y23Eaf,
                            Z17Caf)
V25Eam Wiseman Myra (V25Cam,
                            Z17Cam)

[V-26] REED V24Ba
        Samuel W/Amanda M Hoops
V26A   ADELE D
V26Aa   Haskell Charles W
V26B   THERESE H
V26Ba   McNaghten Frank M
V26Bb   Brown —
V26C   ANNA M
V26Ca   Pierson William A
V26D   BERTIE R
V26Da   Rowden Arthur M
V26Db   Coomrod —
V26E   AUSTIN M
V26Ea   Colmer Lenore
V26F   SAMUEL B
V26Fa   Tyner Cora B
V26G   CASSIUS M

[V-27] HOOPS V24D
        David/Fannie Mahan
V27A   JOHN
V27B   IDA E
V27C   RACHEL A
V27D   VIRGINIA
V27E   FRANCES

[V-28] MOSBY V25Ba
        Joseph/Elizabeth Hoops
V28A   JOSEPH H
V28Aa   McDaniel Zetta
V28B   SAMUEL L
V28C   BETTIE
V28Ca   Peggs J. D.
V28D   GEORGE
V28E   DAVID S
V28F   ANNA

[Y-11] JOHNSON unknown
  unknown/unknown
Y11A   THOMAS Sr -Y12-
Y11Aa   unknown
Y11B   ROBERT

[Y-12] JOHNSON Y11A
  Thmoas Sr/unknown
Y12A   THOMAS Jr -Y13- (Z12Baf)
Y12Aa   unknown
Y12B   JAMES -Y14-
Y12Ba   unknown
Y12C   UNKNOWN
Y12Ca   Snodgrass George Sr -Y15-
Y12D   UNKNOWN

[Y-13] JOHNSON Y12A
  Thomas Jr/unknown
Y13A   JAMES -Y16- (Z12Ia)
Y13Aa   Hughes Elvira (Z12I)
Y13Aaf Hughes William (Z11A)
Y13Aam Bilyeu Priscilla (Z11Aa)
Y13Ab   Medlock Harriet
Y13Abf Medlock Wash (G35Da,M11Caf)
Y13Abm Copeland Sarah (G35D,M11Cam)
Y13B   MARY
Y13Ba   Coyle James
Y13C   WILLIAM
Y13Ca   Clements Ellen
Y13D   ABRAHAM -Y17-
Y13Da   Avery Emeline
Y13Db   McGee Nancy (Y15Ba)
Y13Dbf McGee Henry(Y13Gaf,Y14Eaf,Y15Baf)
Y13Dc   Dunivin Didamia E
Y13E   JOHN MYSCAL -Y18-
Y13Ea   unknown
Y13Eb   Clements Mary
Y13F   LUCINDA (Z12Ba)
Y13Fa   Bowen Thomas
Y13G   SARAH (D25Ham,D25Iam)
Y13Ga   McGee John -Y19- (D25Haf,D25Iaf)
Y13Gaf McGee Henry(Y13Dbf,Y14Eaf,Y15Baf)
Y13H   ELIZABETH (Y39Aam)
Y13Ha   Hawkins Zion R -Y20- (Y39Aaf)

[Y-14] JOHNSON Y12B
  James/unknown
Y14A   JOHN -Y21-
Y14Aa   unknown
Y14B   ELIZABETH (Y23Jam,Y71Aam,Y71Dam)
Y14Ba   Carroll John -Y22- (Y23Jaf,
                    Y71Aaf,Y71Daf)
Y14Bb   Smithers "Cad"
Y14C   SARAH (Q43Eam,Y21Bam,Y22Bam,
                    Y25Bam,Y25Dam)
Y14Ca   Jones Elijah -Y23- (Q43Eaf,
            Y21Baf,Y22Baf,Y25Baf,Y25Daf)
Y14D   THOMAS JEFFERSON -Y24- (Y72Eaf)
Y14Da   Thompson Martha (Y72Eam)
Y14Daf Thompson Israel
Y14E   WM. S-Y25-(Q44Faf,Y66Aaf,Y23Gaf)
Y14Ea   McGee Elizabeth(Q44Fam,Y66Aam
Y14Eaf McGee Henry(Y13Dbf,Y13Gaf,Y15Baf
Y14F   PHILLIP -Y26-
Y14Fa   Ammerman Sarah Ann
Y14Fb   Hutchison Elizabeth

[Y-15] SNODGRASS Y12Ca
  George Sr/unknown
Y15A   JAMES
Y15Aa   Tennison —
Y15B   ARCH
Y15Ba   McGee Nancy (Y13Db)
Y15Baf McGee Henry(Y13Dbf,Y13Gaf,Y14Eaf
Y15C   POLLY
Y15Ca   West Thomas -Y27-
Y15D   MATILDA (K34Aam)
Y15Da   Lane Charles C -Y28- (K34Aaf)
Y15E   GEORGE W -Y29- (K32Eaf,K33Aaf,
            K33Aaf,K33Caf,K33Daf,Y63Daf)
Y15Ea   unknown
Y15Eb   Daniels Julia Ann (Y63Dam)
Y15Ebf Daniels Thomas
Y15F   SARAH
Y15Fa   Davidson William -Y30-
Y15Fb   Malone William -Y31-
Y15Fc   Myers Gabriel-Y32-(K34Faf,Y30Aaf
Y15Fcf Myers George
Y15Fd   German Zachariah

[Y-16] JOHNSON Y13A
   James/Elvira Hughes
Y16A   ISAAC N -Y33-
Y16Aa Cox —
Y16B   EMILY C
Y16Ba Stroud Robert

[Y-17] JOHNSON Y13D
   Abraham/Emeline Avery
Y17A   MONROE -Y34-
Y17Aa Fleming Naomi O

[Y-18] JOHNSON Y13E
   John M/ unknown
Y18A   HARRIET
Y18Aa Miller Henry B
   (2)Mary Clements
Y18B   BARDNEY
Y18Ba Skyles —
Y18C   JOHN BUNYAN
Y18Ca Gaines —
Y18D   MARY BELLE
Y18E   CHARLES MYSCAL
Y18F   T. FRANCIS
Y18Fa Davis —
Y18Faf Davis William

[Y-19] McGEE Y13Ga
   John/Sarah Johnson
Y19A   LUCINDA
Y19Aa Followill Milton
Y19B   WILLIAM RILEY -Y35-
Y19Ba Kinkeade Elizabeth
Y19C   HENRY
Y19D   THOMAS
Y19E   ELIZABETH
Y19F   LEONA (Z31Fa,D37Cam)
Y19Fa James John Burton (Z31F,D37Caf)
Y19G   SARAH JANE (D25Ha,J20Cam)
Y19Ga Shockley Thomas R (D25H,J20Caf)
Y19Gaf Shockley William R (D17F,
          G11Ia,G11Daf)
Y19Gam — Ruth (D17Fb,G11Dam)
Y19H   JAMES B

Y19I   J ELLEN (D25Ia)
Y19Ia Shockley Amos (D25I)
Y19Iaf Shockley William (D17F,G11Ia,
                G11Daf)
Y19Iam — Ruth (D17Fb,G11Dam)

[Y-20] HAWKINS Y13Ha
   Zion R/Elizabeth Johnson
Y20A   WILLIAM L -Y36- (Y39Aa)
Y20Aa Johnson Mary E (Y39A)
Y20Aaf JohnsonWilliam(Y21B,Y23Ia,Y66Ba
Y20Aam JonesElizabeth(Y23I,Y21Ba,Y66Ba
Y20B   MARY E
Y20Ba Robinson Ison H -Y37-
Y20C   THOMAS R -Y38-
Y20Ca Waddle Jennie
Y20D   SALLIE

[Y-21] JOHNSON Y14A
   John/unknown
Y21A   GEORGE
Y21Aa Moreland —
Y21Aaf Moreland Elias
Y21B   WILLIAM -Y39- (Y23Ia,Y20Aaf,
               Y66Baf)
Y21Ba Jones Elizabeth (Y23I,Y20Aam,
                Y66Bam)
Y21Baf Jones Elijah (Y14Ca,Q43Eaf,
         Y22Baf,Y25Baf,Y25Daf)
Y21Bam Johnson Sarah (Y14C,Q43Eam,
          Y22Bam,Y25Bam,Y25Dam)

[Y-22] CARROLL Y14Ba
   John/Elizabeth Johnson
Y22A   PHILIP H -Y40- (Q45Fa)
Y22Aa Harrison Lavina (Q45F)
Y22Aaf Harrison Tyree (Q42C)
Y22Aam Malone Frances (Q42Ca)
Y22B   JAMES J -Y41- (Y23Ja)
Y22Ba Jones Lydia Ann (Y23J)
Y22Baf Jones Elijah (Y14Ca,Q43Eaf,
         Y21Baf,Y25Baf,Y25Daf)
Y22Bam Johnson Sarah (Y14C,Q43Eam,
          Y21Bam,Y25Bam,Y25Dam

Y22C   ELIZA Ann (Y71Da)
Y22Ca   Ammerman John (Y71D)
Y22D   SARAH ANN (Y71Aa,Y24Cam,Y74Bam)
Y22Da   Ammerman Philip Hibler (Y71A,
                          Y24Caf,Y74Baf)
Y22Daf Ammerman Isaac (Y70A)
Y22Dam Johnson Jane (Y70Aa)

[Y-23] JONES Y14Ca
        Elijah/Sarah Johnson
Y23A   GABRILLA
Y23B   JAMES A -Y42- (M24Baf)
Y23Ba   Young Rosanna (M24Bam)
Y23C   THOMAS J
Y23Ca   Luster Mary
Y23D   CLAYTON D.P. (Y25Ba)
Y23Da   Johnson Sarah (Y25B)
Y23Daf Johnson William S
Y23E   IRVINE JACKSON -Y43-
Y23Ea   Anderson Emily J
Y23Eaf Anderson Thomas (V25Caf,V25Eaf,
                          Z17Caf)
Y23F   GEORGE WASHINGTON -Y44- (Q43Ea)
Y23Fa   Harrison Eliza M (Q43E)
Y23Faf Harrison William (Q42A)
Y23Fam Shephard Nancy (Q42Aa)
Y23G   FRANCIS MARION -Y45- (Y25Da)
Y23Ga   Johnson Lucinda C (Y25D)
Y23Gaf Johnson William S (Y14E,Q44Faf,
                          Y66Aaf)
Y23H   NAPOLEON B Dr -Y46-
Y23Ha   Arendall Augustan Elizabeth
Y23Haf Arendall Joseph Jones
Y23Ham Winston Elvira Elizabeth
Y23I   ELIZABETH (Y20Aam,Y66Bam,Y21Ba)
Y23Ia   Johnson Wm(Y21B,Y66Baf,Y20Aaf)
Y23J   LYDIA ANN (Y22Ba)
Y23Ja   Carroll James J (Y22B)
Y23Jaf Carroll John(Y14Ba,Y71Aaf,Y71Daf)
Y23Jam Johnson Elizabeth (Y14B,Y71Aam,
                          Y71Dam)

[Y-24] JOHNSON Y14D
        Thomas J/Martha Thompson
Y24A   JOHN
Y24B   WILLIAM (Q32Fa)
Y24Ba   Moreland Miriam (Q32F)
Y24C   JAMES (Y72Ea)
Y24Ca   Ammerman Jane (Y72E)
Y24Caf Ammerman P (Y71A,Y22Da,Y74Baf)
Y24Cam Carroll Sarah Ann(Y22D,Y71Aa,
                          Y74Bam)
Y24D   LYDIA
Y24Da   Moreland W.W.
Y24E   JANE
Y24Ea   Moreland Elias
Y24F   NARCISSUS
Y24Fa   Tennison William G
Y24G   THOMAS
Y24Ga   Renick Ann
Y24Gb   Brittain Jennie
Y24H   CAL F -Y47-
Y24Ha   — Mary J

[Y-25] JOHNSON Y14E
        William G/Elizabeth McGee
Y25A   JULIA A
Y25Aa   Wofford Alex -Y48-
Y25Aaf Wofford Charles P (Y48C,E43Baf)
Y25Aam Ammerman Ida May (Y48Ca,E43Bam)
Y25B   SARAH (Y23Da)
Y25Ba   Jones Clayton D.P. (Y23D)
Y25Baf Jones Elijah (Y14Ca,Q43Eaf,
                  Y21Baf,Y22Baf,Y25Daf)
Y25Bam Johnson Sarah (Y14C,Q43Eam,
                  Y21Bam.Y22Bam,Y25Dam)
Y25C   JOHN MARION -Y49- (Y59Caf)
Y25Ca   — Martha
Y25D   LUCINDA CATHERINE (Y23Ga)
Y25Da   Jones Francis Marion (Y23G)
Y25Daf Jones Elijah (Y14Ca,Q43Eaf)
                  Y21Baf,Y22Baf,Y25Daf)
Y25Dam Johnson Sarah (Y14C,Q43Eam
                  Y21Bam,Y22Bam,Y25Bam)
Y25E   ELIZABETH MISOURI (Q44Fa,R31Eam)

Y25Ea   Harrison Thomas Jefferson -Y50-
              (Q44F,R31Eaf)
Y25Eaf Harrison Lewis Sr (Q42D,Q39Aaf)
Y25Eam Hutchison Esther G (Q42Ba)
Y25F   JAMES HARRISON (Y66Aa)
Y25Fa   Burchard Mary Ellen (Y66A)
Y25Faf Burchard Nathan -Y66- (Y39Daf)
Y25Fam Sorrell Martha (Y39Dam)
Y25G   MARY E (Y73Ca)
Y25Ga   Sherman James M (Y73C)
Y25Gaf Sherman Charles W (Y71Ba)
Y25Gam Ammerman Nancy (Y71B)
Y25H   WILLIAM HENRY -Y51-
Y25Ha   Nieweg Minnie
Y25I   ALFRED B
Y25Ia   Taff Minnie Lee
Y25Iaf Taff John (G46A,T15Caf)
Y25Iam Anderson Mahala (G46Aa,T15Cam)

[Y-26] JOHNSON Y14F
    Phillip/Sarah A Ammerman
Y26A   WILLIAM JEFFERSON
Y26Aa   Moman Mary Jane
Y26B   JAMES K POLK
Y26Ba   unknown
Y26C   JOHN SANFORD
Y26Ca   Basham Elizabeth
Y26Caf Basham Edward
Y26D   ELIZA JANE
Y26Da   Moman Hiram J

[Y-27] WEST Y15Ca
    Thomas/Polly Snodgrass
Y27A   WILLIAM (G27Ia)
Y27Aa   Elrod Lucinda (G27I)
Y27Aaf Elrod Thomas Benton Jr (G25Ba)
Y27Aam Copeland Casandra (G25B)
Y27B   JAMES
Y27Ba   Slater Hariett
Y27C   THOMAS
Y27Ca   Halslip —

[Y-28] LANE Y15Da
    Charles C/Matilda Snodgrass
Y28A   CATHERINE (K34Aa)
Y28Aa   Parker — (K34A)
Y28B   MAHALA
Y28Ba   Followill William Jr

[Y-29] SNODGRASS Y15E
    George W/(2)Julia Ann Daniels
Y29A   JAMES DAVID -Y52- (K33Aa,Y63Da)
Y29Aa   Ferrell Olivia (Y63D)
Y29Aaf Ferrell John Meade (Y61G)
Y29Aam Fitzgerald Elvira (Y61Ga)
Y29Ab   Davis Elizabeth (K33A)
Y29B   EBENEZER J -Y53- (K33Ca)
Y29Ba   Davis Sarah Josephine (K33C)
Y29Baf Davis Thomas (K31D,H13Ba,Y29Caf)
Y29Bam Light Temperance Caroline (H13B
                         K31Da,Y29Cam)
Y29C   ARCHIBALD (K33Da,Y57Aaf)
Y29Ca   Davis Martha C (K33D,Y57Aam)
Y29Caf Davis Thomas (K31D,H13Ba,Y29Baf)
Y29Cam Light Temperance Caroline (H13B
                         K31Da,Y29Bam)
Y29D   SIMON
Y29Da   Carney Edna
Y29E   GEORGE W Jr
Y29F   SARAH A
Y29Fa   Goggin Charles
Y29G   JULIA A
Y29Ga   Poor Barton
Y29H   WILLIAM R -Y54-
Y29Ha   Feeler Mary
Y29Haf Feeler Jackson (Y52Aaf)
Y29Ham Elder Rebecca (Y52Aam)
Y29I   MARIA E

[Y-30] DAVIDSON Y15Fa
    William/Sarah Snodgrass
Y30A   MARY
Y30Aa   Myers William
Y30Aaf Myers Gabriel (K34Faf,Y15Fc)

[Y-31] MALONE Y15Fb
   William/Sarah Snodgrass
Y31A   JAMES (Z24Aaf)
Y31Aa   Crum Rachel Jane (Z24Aam)
Y31Aaf Crum Robert Sevier(G16Aaf,Q44Jaf)
Y31Aam Hutchison Elizabeth (G16Aam,
                              Q44Jam)

Y31B   HANNAH
Y31Ba   Follcwill William
Y31Bb   Prewett John

[Y-32] MYERS Y15Fc
   Gabrial/Sarah Snodgrass
Y32A   C. C. (G27Faf)
Y32Aa   unknown
Y32Ab   Coates Ellen

[Y-33] JOHNSON Y16A
   Isaac N/— Cox
Y33A   CHARLES
Y33Aa   Brittain Maria
Y33B   DAVID -Y55-
Y33Ba   Bartle Roena
Y33Baf Bartle Warren
Y33C   ELIZABETH
Y33Ca   McDaniel Samuel

[Y-34] JOHNSON Y17A
   Monroe/Naomi Fleming
Y34A   JAMES OLIVER
Y34B   MARY E
Y34Ba   Davis Perry E
Y34Baf Davis William Jr (K31C,H13Baf)
Y34Bam Tennyson Eliza A (K31Ca,H13Bam)
Y34C   WILLIAM
Y34D   CLARENCE
Y34Da   Love Elnore I
Y34E   CORA E
Y34Ea   Bassett Elmer
Y34F   NAOMI E
Y34G   EDNA F
Y34Ga   Copeland William
Y34H   AVERY N
Y34Ha   Branson Cora

Y34Haf Branson William

[Y-35] McGEE Y19B
   William Riley/Elizabeth Kinkeade
Y35A   THOMAS S
Y35B   EDNA J
Y35Ba   Crider Ed -Y56-

[Y-36] HAWKINS Y20A
   William L/Mary E Johnson
Y36A   DORA
Y36Aa   Humphrey Paris
Y36B   OMA
Y36Ba   Duncan Edward
Y36Baf Duncan Thomas B
Y36Bam Walker Eliza L
Y36C   BERTHA
Y36Ca   Evans John
Y36D   OBEDIENCE (Bedie)
Y36Da   Burcham Herbert
Y36E   LUCY
Y36Ea   Baker Sam
Y36F   MABEL
Y36Fa   Zeusch, Professor
Y36G   RAY

[Y-37] ROBINSON Y20Ba
Ison H/Mary Hawkins
Y37A   ALICE
Y37Aa   Hadley Sam
Y37B   OBEDIENCE
Y37Ba   Root Howard

[Y-38] HAWKINS Y20C
   ThomasR/Jennie Waddle
Y38A   THOMAS A
Y38B   ANNA
Y38Ba   Stevenson Robert

[Y-39] JOHNSON Y21B
   William/Elizabeth Jones
Y39A   MARY E (Y20Aa)
Y39Aa   Hawkins William L (Y20A)
Y39Aaf Hawkins Zion R (Y13Ha)

Y39Aam Johnson Elizabeth (Y13H)
Y39B   JANE
Y39Ba   Ragan George M -Y57-
Y39C   LOUISA
Y39Ca   Romine Lee
Y39D   W. D. P. (Y66Ba)
Y39Da   Burchard Virginia (Y66B)
Y39Daf Burchard Nathan (Y25Faf)
Y39Dam Sorrell Martha (Y25Fam)

[Y-40] CARROLL Y22A
    Philip H/Lavina Harrison
Y40A   LAURA
Y40Aa   Letterman Peter F
Y40B   LIDA
Y40Ba   Letterman James
Y40C   WILLIAM R
Y40Ca   Stockton Jane
Y40Caf Stockton Joseph (D71Ea,D26Haf)
Y40Cam Travis Eliza (D71E,D26Ham)

[Y-41] CARROLL Y22B
    James J/Lydia A Jones
Y41A   WILLIAM R
Y41B   FRANK E
Y41C   ROBERT L
Y41D   JOSE
Y41Da   Elkins L. C.
Y41E   MARY
Y41Ea   Goodman Alfred
Y41F   HUMBOLT
Y41G   JENNIE
Y41Ga   Denton —
Y41H   JOHN H
Y41Ha   Gillispie Malissa

[Y-42] JONES Y23B
    James A/Rosanna Young
Y42A   WILLIAM CLAYTON -Y58-
Y42Aa   Rogers Rachel M
Y42Aaf Rogers Elisha
Y42Aam Wallace —
Y42B   JERRY (M24Ba)
Y42Ba   unknown

Y42Bb   Giesler Carrie (M24B)
Y42Bbf Giesler David (M15Da)
Y42Bbm Bowman Sarah (M15D)
Y42C   JAMES A Jr
Y42Ca   Rogers Susan
Y42Caf Rogers John A (E34Caf)
Y42Cam Cummings Mildred (E34Cam)
Y42D   LEONA F (G27Czm)
Y42Da   Fann Joseph M -Y59- (G27Caf)
Y42Daf Fann George
Y42Dam Hutchison Delila
Y42E   ELIZABETH JANE
Y42Ea   Hutchison Luther
Y42Eaf Hutchison William
Y42Eam Nanney Martha E

[Y-43] JONES Y23E
    Irvine J/Emily Anderson
Y43A   AMANDA
Y43Aa   Haynes William
Y43B   GEORGIA ANN
Y43Ba   Adkins Butler
Y43C   IDA I
Y43Ca   Knight James M
Y43D   WILLIAM T

[Y-44] JONES Y23F
    George Washington/Eliza Harrison
Y44A   IDA
Y44Aa   Bray Edward
Y44B   GERTRUDE
Y44Ba   Westphalen Charles
Y44Bb   Schneider Frank

[Y-45] JONES Y23G
    Francis Marion/Lucinda Johnson
Y45A   LAURA
Y45Aa   Nieweg August
Y45B   LYDIA
Y45C   JOAN
Y45Ca   Bradshaw Mart
Y45D   CLAUDE O
Y45E   OMER H Dr
Y45F   RALPH Dr

SINLING GROUP Y

[Y-46] JONES Y23H
  Napoleon/Augustan E Arendall
'46A OLLIE
'46Aa Branson C.S. Dr
'46B Myrtle

[Y-47] JOHNSON Y24H
  Cal F/Mary J —
'47A WILLIAM
'47Aa Ryan Maggie
'47B OCTAVIA
'47Ba Glenn L.A.
'47C CHARLES W
'47D AUSTIN L
'47E THOMAS L
'47F WALDO P

[Y-48] WOFFORD Y25Aa
  Alex/Julia Johnson
'48A ANDREW J
'48B JOHN
'48C CHARLES PERRY (E43Baf,Y25Aaf)
'48Ca Ammerman Ida May (E43Bam,Y25Aam)
'48Caf Ammerman John Carroll (Y72F)
'48Cam Henderson Jane (Y72Fa)

[Y-49] JOHNSON Y25C
  John Marion/Martha —
Y49A MOLLIE E
Y49Aa Tackett Fielding
Y49B WILLIAM E Dr
Y49Ba Skouby Leanora
Y49C EDWARD
Y49D LEE
Y49E ELLA (Y59Ca)
Y49Ea Fann Clayton (Y59C)
Y49F GROVER C Dr
Y49Fa Morhaus Emily

[Y-50] HARRISON Y25Ea
  Thomas Jefferson/Elizabeth M Johnson
Y50A WILLIAM H
Y50B ADOLPHEUS
Y50C GRACE

Y50Ca Travis Oliver
Y50D CECIL (R31Ea)
Y50Da Ridenhour Rainey (R31E)
Y50Daf Ridenhour John S (R30A,R15Haf)
Y50Dam Griffith Dorcas A (R30Aa,R15Ham)

[Y-51] JOHNSON Y25H
  William H/Minnie Nieweg
Y51A CLAY
Y51B JAMES
Y51C EARL
Y51D MYRTLE
Y51Da Guffey H.B.
Y51E CLYDE

[Y-52] SNODGRASS Y29A
  James D/(2)Elizabeth Davis
Y52A OLIVIA
Y52Aa Feeler James Arthur
Y52Aaf Feeler Jackson (Y29Haf)
Y52Aam Elder Rebecca (Y29Ham)
Y52Ab Gillispie Jesse
Y52B NANNIE
Y52Ba James Alonzo
Y52C EBENEZER
Y52Ca Satterfield Ollie
Y52D JESSE J
Y52Da Stewart Gertrude
Y52Daf Stewart Lazarus
Y52Dam Mahon Malinda
Y52Db Hart Ethel
Y52Dbf Hart John Avery
Y52Dbm Merriwether Belle
Y52E GEORGE W
Y52Ea Walls Phoebe
Y52Eaf Walls Thomas
Y52F CHARLES D
Y52Fa Cordsmeyer —
Y52Faf Cordsmeyer G.W. Judge (Y62Daf)
Y52G THOMAS EDWARD
Y52Ga Vaughan Zaddie
Y52Gaf Vaughan John

313

[Y-53] SNODGRASS Y29B
   Ebenezer/Sarah J Davis
Y53A   OMA
Y53Aa   Knight William
Y53B   CLARA
Y53Ba   Dambach Albert
Y53C   LOLA
Y53Ca   Allen Kenneth
Y53D   CLEVE
Y53E   BESSIE
Y53F   LOUIS

[Y-54] SNODGRASS Y29H
   William R/Mary B Feeler
Y54A   LOYD
Y54Aa   Davis Adeline
Y54Aaf Davis Joseph
Y54B   INA
Y54Ba   James Thomas
Y54C   CLARICE
Y54Ca   James Richard
Y54D   ROY
Y54Da   Hutson Della
Y54E   LELA
Y54Ea   Hart Clarence
Y54Eaf Hart John (Y54Iaf)
Y54Eam James Elizabeth (Y54Iam)
Y54F   CHESTER
Y54Fa   Copeland Ruby
Y54Faf Copeland Ollie
Y54G   WASH
Y54Ga   Parker Olive
Y54Gaf Parker John F
Y54H   HOLLY
Y54I   ERNESTINE
Y54Ia   Hart Everett
Y54Iaf Hart John (Y54Eaf)
Y54Iam James Elizabeth (Y54Eam)
Y54J   RAYMOND
Y54K   LESLIE
Y54Ka   Birdsong —
Y54L   HARRY

[Y-55] JOHNSON Y33B
   David/Roena Bartle
Y55A   FRANCIS
Y55B   EDWARD
Y55C   MARIE
Y55Ca   Campbell—
Y55D   CHARLES
Y55E   LULA
Y55Ea   Metz Charles
Y55F   AMANDA
Y55Fa   Watson —
Y55G   MABEL
Y55Ga   Watson —
Y55H   RAY

[Y-56] CRIDER Y35Ba
   Ed/Edna J McGee
Y56A   THURMAN
Y56Aa   Backues Minnie
Y56Aaf Backues Martin (S22A)
Y56Aam Shanks Martha (S22Aa)

[Y-57] RAGAN Y39Ba
   George M/Jane Johnson
Y57A   DOLPH
Y57Aa   Snodgrass Nellie
Y57Aaf Snodgrass Archibald (Y29C,K33Da)
Y57Aam Davis Martha C (K33D,Y29Ca)
Y57B   CHARLES
Y57C   JOHN
Y57Ca   Gillispie Tillie
Y57D   MAUD
Y57Da   Tune David

[Y-58] JONES Y42A
   William Clayton/Rachel M Rogers
Y58A   JAMES EDGAR
Y58B   JOHN C THURMAN
Y58C   ALFRED BURTON
Y58D   BOLEY ANDERSON
Y58E   IDA
Y58Ea   Murphy L.J.
Y58F   EFFIE
Y58Fa   Bishop John Bunyan

Y58Fat Bishop John(G12Eaf,G20Caf,Y58Gaf
Y58Fam Elrod Martha Serilda (G12Eam,
              G20Cam,Y58Gam
Y58G   MAUD
Y58Ga   Bishop Adam
Y58Gaf Bishop John(G12Eaf,G20Caf,Y58Faf
Y58Gam Elrod Martha Serilda (G12Eam,
              G20Cam,Y58Fam
Y58Gb   Moss Edward

[Y-59] FANN Y42Da
    Joseph M/Leona Jones
Y59A   GERTRUDE
Y59Aa   Elrod Colonel
Y59B   BERTHA (G27Ca)
Y59Ba   Elrod Tony (G27C)
Y59C   CLAYTON (Y49Ea)
Y59Ca   Johnson Ella (Y49E)
Y59Caf Johnson John Marion (Y25C
Y59D   RAINEY
Y59E   CLAUDE

[Y-60] FERRELL unknown
    unknown/unknown
Y60A   ENOCH Sr -Y61-
Y60Aa   Meade Katherine

[Y-61] FERRELL Y60A
    Enoch Sr/Katherine Meade
Y61A   WILLIAM ROWAN
Y61Aa   Forester Mary
Y61B   CATHERINE
Y61Ba   Davis James
Y61C   LUCINDA
Y61Ca   Copeland Jasper
Y61D   POLLY HARRIETT
Y61Da   Appley William Dr
Y61E   ROBERT
Y61F   THOMAS JEFFERSON -Y62-
Y61Fa   Baker Louemma
Y61G   JOHN MEADE -Y63- (Y29Aaf)
Y61Ga   Fitzgerald Elvira (Y29Aam)
Y61H   ENOCH PARKER -Y64-
Y61Ha   — Emma

Y61I   RHODES
Y61J   ANGIRONA
Y61Ja   Hogue John
Y61Jb   Schneider Martin
Y61K   NANCY CAROLINE
Y61Ka   Slater Silas
Y61L   HUSTON LAFAYETTE -Y65-
Y61La   Jarvis Martha F

[Y-62] FERRELL Y61F
    ThomasJefferson/Louemma Baker
Y62A   JOHN J Dr
Y62Aa   Brittain Stella
Y62B   CATHERINE
Y62Ba   Sughrue George
Y62C   THOMAS ENOCH Dr
Y62Ca   Travis Della May
Y62Caf Travis William James(D71A,Y74Lat
Y62Cam Hull Elizabeth A (D71Aa,Y74Eam)
Y62D   HUSTON E Dr
Y62Da   Cordsmeyer Mary
Y62Daf Cordsmeyer G.W. Judge (Y52Faf)

[Y-63] FERRELL Y61G
    John Meade/Elvira Fitzgerald
Y63A   THOMAS
Y63B   OPHELIA
Y63C   WARREN
Y63D   OLIVIA (Y29Aa)
Y63Da   Snodgrass James D (Y29A,K33Aa)
Y63Daf Snodgrass George W (Y15E,K32Eaf,
                    (K33Aaf,K33Caf,K33Daf)
Y63Dam Daniels Julia Ann (Y15Eb)
Y63E   JOHN APPLEY
Y63Ea   Lugabill Emma

[Y-64] FERRELL Y61H
    EnochP/Emma —
Y64A   LYDA
Y64Aa   Elliott William
Y64Ab   Walker Ellis
Y64B   LOU
Y64Ba   Wynn Lee
Y64C   WILLIAM

Y64Ca Evans Rose
Y64D   CARRIE
Y64Da Hull C.A.
Y64E   AMANDA
Y64Ea Shinneman Bert
Y64F   THOMAS J
Y64Fa Wagner Emma

[Y-65] FERRELL Y61L
   Huston L/Martha Jarvis
Y65A WILLIAM RHODES Dr
Y65B OLLIE
Y65C EMMA
Y65Ca Peters Edwin
Y65D EUNICE
Y65Da Heide Charles

[Y-66] BURCHARD Y25Faf
   Nathan/Martha Sorrell
Y66A MARY ELLEN (Y25Fa)
Y66Aa Johnson James Harrison (Y25F)
Y66Aaf Johnson William S (Y14E,Q44Faf)
Y66Aam McGee Elizabeth (Y14Ea,Q44Fam)
Y66B VIRGINIA (Y39Da)
Y66Ba Johnson W.D.P. (Y39D)
Y66Baf Johnson William (Y21B,Y23Ia,
                Y20Aaf)
Y66Bam Jones Elizabeth (Y23I,Y21Ba,
                Y20Aam)
Y66C BARBARA
Y66Ca Huffman James T
Y66D MALISSA J
Y66Da Edwards G.W.
Y66E FANNIE

[Y-70] AMMERMAN unknown
   unknown/unknown
Y70A ISAAC -Y71- (Y22Daf)
Y70Aa Johnson Jane (Y22Dam)
Y70Aaf Johnson Robert

[Y-71] AMMERMAN Y70A
   Isaac/Jane Johnson
Y71A   PHILIP HIBLER -Y72- (Y22Da,
                    Y24Caf,Y74Baf)
Y71Aa Carroll Sarah(Y22D,Y24Cam,Y74Bam)
Y71Aaf Carroll John(Y14Ba,Y23Jaf,Y71Daf)
Y71Aam Johnson Elizabeth (Y14B,Y23Jam,
                    Y71Dam)
Y71B   NANCY (Y25Gam)
Y71Ba Sherman Charles W -Y73- (Y25Gaf)
Y71C   JENNIE
Y71Ca Johnson Philip
Y71D   JOHN (Y22Ca)
Y71Da Carroll Eliza (Y22C)
Y71Daf Carroll John (Y14Ba,Y23Ja,Y71Aaf)
Y71Dam Johnson Elizabeth (Y14B,Y23Jam,
                    Y71Aam)
Y71E   SAMUEL
Y71Ea Smithers —
Y71F   ISAAC
Y71G   WILLIAM
Y71Ga Newberry Lydia
Y71H   JOSEPH
Y71I   SANFORD
Y71Ia Newberry Susan Rebecca

[Y-72] AMMERMAN Y71A
   Philip H/Sarah Ann Carroll
Y72A WILLARD B
Y72B JOSEPH
Y72C JAMES
Y72Ca Sprewell —
Y72D CONRAD (Y74Ba)
Y72Da Wallace Irene (Y74B)
Y72Daf Wallace John G -Y74-
Y72Dam Winston Laura
Y72E JANE (Y24Ca)
Y72Ea Johnson James (Y24C)
Y72Eaf Johnson Thomas Jefferson (Y14D)
Y72Eam Thompson Martha (Y14Da)
Y72F JOHN CARROLL (Y48Caf)
Y72Fa Henderson Jane (Y48Cam)
Y72Faf Henderson William Wallace Dr
Y72Fam Smith Charlotta

[Y-73] SHERMAN Y71Ba
   Charles W/Nancy Ammerman
Y73A   MARGARET
Y73Aa   Hammond Bert
Y73B   JOSEPH
Y73Ba   Graham Katherine
Y73C   JAMES M (Y25Ga)
Y73Ca   Johnson Mary E (Y25G)
Y73Caf Johnson William S

[Y-74] WALLACE Y72Daf
   John G/Laura Winston
Y74A   ROBERT L
Y74Aa   Summers —
Y74Ab   — Belle
Y74B   IRENE (Y72Da)
Y74Ba   Ammerman Conrad (Y72D)
Y74Baf Ammerman Philip Hibler (Y71A,
                     Y22Da,Y24Caf)
Y74Bam Carroll Sarah(Y22D,Y71Aa,Y24Cam)
Y74Bb   Smith William
Y74C   EUNICE
Y74Ca   Ramey Robert
Y74D   EMMA
Y74Da   Williams James
Y74E   CHARLES -Y75- (D72Ha)
Y74Ea   Travis Minnie (D72H)
Y74Eaf Travis William James(D71A,Y62Caf
Y74Eam Hull Elizabeth A (D71Aa,Y62Cam)
Y74F   EDWARD DOUGLAS -Y76-
Y74Fa   Price Linda
Y74Faf Price Jack

[Y-75] WALLACE Y74E
   Charles/Minnie Travis
Y75A   AUSTIN Dr
Y75B   ALVA
Y75C   ETHEL
Y75Ca   Dehn Julius A
Y75D   EDITH
Y75Da   Davis —
Y75E   ARMINTA

[Y-76] WALLACE Y74F
   Edward D/Linda Price
Y76A   LILLIE
Y76B   MINNIE
Y76Ba   Manicke John C
Y76C   JOHN O
Y76Ca   Brown Minniw
Y76D   WILLIAM J
Y76Da   Clemmons Lillie
Y76E   RUTH
Y76Ea   Martin Ollie
Y76F   NELLIE
Y76Fa   Waggoner Otis
Y76G   OMA
Y76Ga   Glenn Carl
Y76H   ORA
Y76Ha   Threewit Charles
Y76I   JEWEL
Y76Ia   Woodruff Dow

[Z-10] HUGHES unknown
unknown/unknown
Z10A   WILLIAM -Z11-
Z10Aa   unknown

[Z-11] HUGHES Z10A
William/unknown
Z11A   WILLIAM -Z12- (Y13Aaf)
Z11Aa   Bilyeu Priscilla (Y13Aam)
Z11B   JAMES
Z11C   ROLAND
Z11D   JOSEPH
Z11E   JOHN
Z11F   MARY
Z11Fa   Bilyeu William -Z35-

[Z-12] HUGHES Z11A
William/Priscilla Bilyeu
Z12A   McKAMY WILSON -Z13- (J14Baf,
                            S11Gaf)
Z12Aa   Davidson Elizabeth(J14Bam,S11Gam)
Z12B   HIRAM -Z14-
Z12Ba   Johnson Lucinda (Y13F)
Z12Baf Johnson Thomas Sr (Y12A)
Z12C   ELISHA -Z15-
Z12Ca   Coleman Mary
Z12D   DAVID T
Z12E   STEPHEN
Z12F   JOHN
Z12G   REBECCA
Z12Ga   Tucker — -Z16-
Z12Gb   Tyler John Hunter -Z17-
Z12H   ELIZABETH
Z12Ha   Shobe — -Z18-
Z12Hb   Wright —
Z12I   ELVIRA (Y13Aa)
Z12Ia   Johnson James (Y13A)
Z12J   MELVIN
Z12K   PRISCILLA

[Z-13] HUGHES Z12A
McKamy Wilson/Elizabeth Davidson
Z13A   HARRIETT E
Z13Aa   Crane Larkin

Z13B   MELVINA JANE (S11Ga,J14Fam)
Z13Ba   Briggs Daniel B W (S11G,J14Faf)
Z13Baf Briggs James Y(S10A,D15Ca,Q32Caf)
Z13Bam ShockleyMartha(D15C,S10Aa,Q32Cam)
Z13C   LUCINDA C
Z13Ca   Knight J.M.
Z13D   NANCY PRISCILLA
Z13Da   Ramsey — (Z20A)
Z13E   GEORGE H (J14Ab)
Z13Ea   Eads Serena (J14A)
Z13Eaf Eads Lewis (J12B,L15Ba,P14Baf,
                            Z13Haf)
Z13Eam Simpson Jane (L15B,J12Ba,P14Bam,
                            Z13Ham)
Z13F   JOHN P -Z22-
Z13Fa   Tackett Mary M
Z13Faf Tackett Willis M (S11Ba,
                  J12Laf,J14Caf,J20Aaf)
Z13Fam Briggs Zylphia (S11B,J12Lam,
                        J14Cam,J20Aam)
Z13G   ELISHA D
Z13Ga   Roach Rachel J
Z13H   HIRAM (J14Ba)
Z13Ha   Eads Sarah Frances (Mary) (J14B)
Z13Haf Eads Lewis (J12B,L15Ba,P14Baf,
                            Z13Eaf)
Z13Ham Simpson Jane (L15B,J12Ba,P14Bam,
                            Z13Eam)

[Z-14] HUGHES Z12B
Hiram/Lucinda Johnson
Z14A   LOUISA JANE
Z14Aa   Carber Joel -Z23-
Z14B   THOMAS
Z14C   NAPOLEON BONAPARTE
Z14Ca   Gorsig Laura
Z14Cb   McKany Fannie

[Z-15] HUGHES Z12C
Elisha/MaryColeman
Z15A   JOHN
Z15B   FRANCES
Z15Ba   Colbert John
Z15Bb   Fabrette —

SIBLING GROUP Z

[Z-16] TUCKER Z12Ga
  unknown/Rebecca Hughes
Z16A   FANNIE
Z16B   MYRA
Z16Ba   Davis Henry

[Z-17] TYLER Z12Gb
  .John Hunter/Rebecca Hughes
Z17A   NANCY
Z17B   ELISHA
Z17C   CYNTHIA A
Z17Ca   Anderson Thomas Bickerton -Z24-
Z17Caf Anderson Thomas (V25Caf,V25Eaf,
                                    Y23Eaf)
Z17Cam Wiseman Myra (V25Cam,V25Eam)
Z17D   THOMAS
Z17E   ARIZONA
Z17Ea   Parker W.C.
Z17F   RUTH
Z17Fa   Logan Enos S

[Z-18] SHOBE Z12Ha
  unknown/Elizabeth Hughes
Z18A   MARY JANE (Z26Ab)
Z18Aa   Huffman Henry (Z26A)

[Z-20] RAMSEY unknown
  unknown/unknown
Z20A   UNKNOWN -Z21- (Z13Da)
Z20Ab   unknown

[Z-21] RAMSEY Z20A
  unknown/(2)unknown
Z21A   RUTHERFORD

[Z-22] HUGHES Z13F
  John P/Mary M Tackett
Z22A   OLIVER
Z22Aa   Tackett Louisa
Z22B   ETTA
Z22Ba   Whisenant Marion

[Z-23] CARBER Z14Aa
  Joel/Louisa Jane Hughes
Z23A   ALEXANDER
Z23B   LUCINDA JANE
Z23C   HENRY JEFFERSON
Z23D   ROSE
Z23E   MELVINA D
Z23F   ANNA LOUISE
Z23G   JOHN C

[Z-24] ANDERSON Z17Ca
  Thomas Bickerton/Cynthia Tyler
Z24A   LOIS
Z24Aa   Malone George W
Z24Aaf Malone James (Y31A)
Z24Aam Crum Rachel Jane (Y31Aa)
Z24B   ADDIE
Z24Ba   Hughes Newton
Z24C   PAUL
Z24D   MILDRED
Z24Da   Rogers Ernie
Z24E   GRACE

[Z-25] HUFFMAN unknown
  unknown/unknown
Z25A   UNKNOWN -Z26-
Z25Aa   unknown

[Z-26] HUFFMAN Z25A
  unknown/unknown
Z26A   HENRY -Z27- (Z18Aa)
Z26Aa   Davis Elizabeth Ann
Z26Aaf Davis John
Z26Ab   Shobe Mary Jane (Z18A)
Z26B   JACOB -Z28-
Z26Ba   unknown
Z26C   JAMES -Z29-
Z26Ca   Davis Lucy
Z26Caf Davis James
Z26D   ELIZABETH
Z26Da   Miller Nelson -Z30-
Z26E   BARBARA
Z26Ea   James David -Z31-
Z26F   UNKNOWN (Z41Ca)

Z26Fa Green Henry (Z41C)
Z26G   UNKNOWN
Z26Ga Larrick —

[Z-27] HUFFMAN Z26A
   Henry/Elizabeth Ann Davis
Z27A   PHILLIP NEWTON
Z27Aa Gaines Susan
Z27Aaf Gaines Willian
Z27B   ANNA ELIZABETH
Z27Ba Crider Martin Jackson –Z32–
   (2) Mary Jane Shobe
Z27C   FRANCES
Z27Ca Haynes William
Z27D   MARGARET (MARY) E
Z27Da Ridenhour John Clark
Z27Daf Ridenhour John Sartain
Z27Dam unknown
Z27E   WILLIAM
Z27Ea McDaniel Emma
Z27F   MALISSA
Z27Fa Gaines Thomas

[Z-28] HUFFMAN Z26B
   Jacob/unknown
Z28A   WILLIAM R –Z33–
Z28Aa West —
Z28Ab unknown
Z28Ac Haislip Della
Z28B   DELILA
Z28C   JOHN N
Z28D   JAMES T
Z28E   L.L.

[Z-29] HUFFMAN Z26C
   James/Lucy Davis
Z29A   JOHN H
Z29B   JEFFERSON D
Z29C   MARY E
Z29Ca Murphy Joseph

[Z-30] MILLER Z26Da
   Nelson/Elizabeth Huffman
Z30A   SARAH E (L16Cam)

Z30Aa Henderson Albert –Z34– (L16Ca

[Z-31] JAMES Z26Ea
   David/Barbara Huffman
Z31A   COLUMBUS
Z31B   CATHERINE
Z31C   AMERICUS
Z31D   THOMAS P (S20Aa)
Z31Da Backues Emeline (S20A)
Z31Daf Backues Thomas Sr (S18B,R30Ba
                      S13Aaf,Z31Ea
Z31Dam Keeney Malinda (S18Ba,R30Bam,
                      Z31Ea
Z31E   ALONZO (S20Ba)
Z31Ea Backues Susan H (S20B)
Z31Eaf Backues Thomas Sr (S18B,R30Ba:
                      S13Aaf,Z31Da
Z31Eam Keeney Malinda (S18Ba,R30Bam,
                      Z31Da
Z31F   JOHN BURTON Sr (Y19Fa,D37Caf)
Z31Fa McGee Leona (Y19F,D37Cam)
Z31G   MARY A
Z31Ga Stewart Vincent

[Z-32] CRIDER Z27Ba
   Martin Jackson/Ann Elizabeth Huffr
Z32A   NEWTON M
Z32Aa McCabe Iva P
Z32B   JOHN R
Z32Ba Bagwell Inez
Z32C   MYRTLE
Z32Ca Allen Alexander
Z32D   GEORGE W
Z32E   NANCY JANE
Z32Ea Matlock Wesley R
Z32F   WILLIAM H
Z32Fa McCabe Lula
Z32G   OLIVER B
Z32Ga Smiley Dora

[Z-33] HUFFMAN Z28A
   William R/— West
Z33A   NELSON
Z33Aa Rogers Louemma

SIBLING GROUP Z

Z33Aaf Rogers Morgan
Z33Aam Birdsong Malissa
Z33B   MARY
Z33Ba   Curtis Jacob
Z33C   ROWENA ANN
Z33Ca   Smith James
    (2)unknown
Z33D   LOUIS
Z33Da   Rucker Mamie
Z33E   JAMES
Z33Ea   Burgess Barbara
    (3)Della Haislip
Z33F   JOHN
Z33G   WILL
Z33H   CHARLES

[Z-34] HENDERSON Z30Aa
    Albert Smith/Sarah E Miller
Z34A   VICTOR C (L16Ca)
Z34Aa   Simpson Diora (L16C)
Z34B   CHARLES
Z34C   MARY LEE
Z34Ca   Holienbeck Homer
Z34D   DORA
Z34Da   Hawkins Price
Z34E   LILLIE
Z34Ea   Bodendick Fred E
Z34F   HELEN A
Z34Fa   Spratley James H
Z34G   JAMES ALTON
Z34Ga   Honse Mayme
Z34H   FLORENCE
Z34Ha   Camp Elmer

[Z-35] BILYEU Z11Fa
    William/Mary Hughes
Z35A   JAMES
Z35B   MONROE
Z35C   RUTH ANN
Z35Ca   Swim John
Z35D   STEPHEN
Z35Da   Anderson Rebecca Ann
Z35Daf Anderson William
Z35E   CYNTHIA ANN

Z35Ea   Short — -Z36-
Z35Eb   Stewart James -Z37-

[Z-36] SHORT Z35Ea
    unknown/Cynthia A Bilyeu
Z36A   MARY
Z36Aa   Burgess Elijah -Z38-

[Z-37] STEWART Z35Eb
    James/Cynthia A Bilyeu
Z37A   ALVA
Z37B   BERT
Z37C   BEN
Z37D   JANE
Z37E   JOSEPH -Z39-
Z37Ea   Thompson Mamie
Z37F   CORA

[Z-38] BURGESS Z36Aa
    Elijah/Mary Short
Z38A   BERTHA
Z38Aa   Putnam —
Z38B   CHARLES
Z38C   ELIZABETH
Z38Ca   Bennett —
Z38D   LOU
Z38Da   Bradford —
Z38E   ARCH
Z38F   TONY
Z38G   FRANK
Z38H   ETTA

[Z-39] STEWART Z37E
    Joseph/Mamie Thompson
Z39A   IRENE
Z39B   MARIE
Z39C   GEORGIA

[Z-40] GREEN unknown
    unknown/unknown
Z40A   ELISHA -Z41- (C14Daf)
Z40Aa   unknown

[Z-41] GREEN Z40A
   Elisha/unknown
Z41A DILLARD -Z42-
Z41Aa unknown
Z41Ab Eads Polly
Z41B SARAH ANN (E17Aam)
Z41Ba David William (E17Aaf)
Z41C HENRY (Z26Fa)
Z41Ca Huffman — (Z26F)
Z41D MARY JANE (C14Da)
Z41Da Cox Joshua (C14D)
Z41Daf Cox Andrew (C11D,D16Ia)
Z41E DAVID
Z41F UNKNOWN
Z41Fa Medlock John

[Z-42] GREEN Z41A
   Dillard/unknown
Z42A WESLEY
Z42Aa Searcy —
Z42B BEE ANN
Z42Ba Johnson Peter
Z42C JANE
Z42Ca Cox Dorsey
Z42D SARAH
Z42Da David —
Z42E CAROLINE
Z42Ea Ryno George
Z42F SARAH JANE
Z42Fa West William -Z43-
Z42G HARRIET
Z42Ga West Newman
Z42H BARBARA
Z42Ha Moon Wood
Z42Haf Moon Elwood (G27Ha)
Z42Ham Elrod Nancy (G27H)
Z42I MARY ANN
Z42Ia Taylor J.W.

[Z-43] WEST Z42Fa
   William/Sarah Jane Green
Z43A JOSEPH
Z43B DILLARD

Z43C UNKNOWN
Z43Ca Barnes Joseph

PART IV
CHARTS

USING CHARTS

These Charts respresent more than 7100 inter-related individuals, and 800 family groups. It is not feasible space-wise to show all of them by their Serial Numbers. However they are all included.

This is accomplished by two methods:
1. Where the Sibling Group appears in brackets, this symbol represents all members of that group. For example: [A25] represents all members of the group, and also indicates that no descendants of that group are listed.
2. Since it is essential to show any individual of a group in cases where the descendants of that individual are shown, any individual or individuals of a Sibling Group shown on the chart designates the Chart position for all others of that group, since they all have common ancestors.

Because of the extreme condensation of these charts and their extensive range, the spotting of Sibling Groups require some searching. To expedite this, an index is provided showing which chart or charts contain a Sibling Group.

The charts augment Parts II and III. Their most valued use is in providing quickly a broad scope in kinship study. Nothing is contained in the charts that cannot be obtained by use of the Index and Sibling Groups.

INDEX TO LOCATION OF SIBLING
GROUPS ON THE CHARTS

SIB.GROUP	CHART
E89	E/3
E90-E93	E/2
E94,E95	E/3

FAM. GROUP F

F2-F10	F
F10	A
F11-F12	F
F12	B/1
F13	F
F14-F18	B/1,F
F18	B/2
F19	A,B/1,F
F20-F23	B/1,F
F24,F25	A,B/1,F
F26-F30	B/1.F
F31	F
F32	A,F
F33-F47	F
F49-F61	F
F61	B/1
F62-F71	A

FAM.GROUP G

G10	G/1,G/2
G11-G34	G/1
G35-G45	G/2
G47,G47	G/1,G/2
G48	G/2
G49-G61	G/1
G62-G66	G/2

FAM. GROUP H
ALL ON CHART H

FAM. GROUP I
ALL ON CHART I

FAM. GROUP J
ALL ON CHART J

FAM. GROUP K
ALL ON CHART K

SIB.GROUP	CHART

FAM. GROUP L
ALL ON CHART L

FAM. GROUP M
ALL ON CHART M

FAM. GROUP P
ALL ON CHART P

FAM. GROUP Q
ALL ON CHART Q

FAM. GROUP R
ALL ON CHART R

FAM. GROUP S
ALL ON CHART S

FAM. GROUP T
ALL ON CHART T

FAM. GROUP U
ALL ON CHART U

FAM. GROUP V
ALL ON CHART V

FAM. GROUP Y

Y11-Y12	Y/1,Y/2
Y13	Y/1
Y14-Y15	Y/2
Y16-Y20	Y/1
Y21-Y32	Y/2
Y33-Y38	Y/1
Y39-Y54	Y/2
Y55-Y56	Y/1
Y58-Y76	Y/2

FAM. GROUP Z
ALL ON CHART Z

```
   No.1                No.2        No.3                    No.4
  BURGESS            BURGESS      BURGESS                  OSBORN
    B4H                B5F         B6A   STRIBLING          B72C
     :              B5Fa-A87A       :      A85A              :
     :               FOWLER         :       :               :
 ─────────                          :      A86F            [A82]
 A88C    A88A                       :   A37D=A86Fa
 A88Ca    :         See B/1  A37C  :      :      ───────HUNTER───────
 OFFUTT  A99A  A99B       :      :      :    A81A          A81B
   :      :    A99Ba      :      :   A38A=A81Aa             :
   :      :    SMITH      :    [A35]  :                     :
 A93A   F10D    :      ───────────  :────────────────  ─────────
   :      :    F62A    A39C  A39D  A39E  A39F A39J  A83B
 A94A   [F32]   :       :     :     :     :    :   A83Ba
 A94Aa          F63C   A66B  A67J  [A68] A69A A70A  HUDGENS
 WADE            :     A66Ba  :              :    :    ;
   :            F64F   ALLISON :            A76G A78A [A84]
 A95A           F64Fa   :     :              :    :
 A95Aa          RAMEY    :     :           [A77]A79K
 COCHRANE         :     A73C   :              :
   :            F65A     :     :            [A80]
 A96A             :      :     :
 A96Aa          F66A   [A74]  A71B  A71I
 NOLEN          F66Aa           :     :
   :            McCUNE        [A75]  [A72]
 A97A             :
   :            F67F         No.7
 [A98]          F67Fa        NOBLE                No.8
                RICHEY       A10A               (FILLIGIM)
                  :            :                FILLINGHAM
 ──────────────────────     A11H              A40A              VILLINES
 F68D     F68C   F68A       | TATE              :                A52A
 F68Da    F68Ca   :         :    :              :   YOUNG          :
 NISLEY  STRIBLING [F70]    A12E  :            A41A A46A A48A     :
   :        :              :   A60A  JONES  |      :    :   A53A
 [F71]    [F69]            A13A  :   A55A A42A     : A49A   :
                           :   A61A    :     :A42Aa=A47A  :  A54A
                           A14B  :   A56A    :         A50A==A54Aa
                           :   A62D=A56Aa:  A43A              :
   No.5          No.6      A15J    :     : A43Aa======A51A
  ──BURGESS──   BURGESS    :      A57A    :
  B7A     B7G    B8G       A16B     :    A44A
   :       :      :        :      : A58A=A44Aa:
 A64F A34A A34F  A90A      A17E              :
   :    :    :    :        :           B19Ga=A45A
 [F19][F24][F25] ─────     B19Aa=A18B        :
                 F30C F30D                 [B53]
                  :    :
                [A92] [A91]
                      326
```

FAMILY GROUP CHART B/1

```
Gen                              BURGESS
 1                                B3A
                                   :
 2              B4A See #10  B4B            B4H See #1
                B4Aa : Chart F   :          :  Chart A
                        :        :          :
  See*2                 :        :          :
3 ChartA B5F   B5A    B5E      [F12]        A88
    B5Fa :      :      :
         :      :      :
         :      :      :
         :      :      :
4  B6A  B6E [F13] B7A    B7C    B7D   B7G    B7H    B7I    B7J
    :    :      :     :      :     :     :      :      :      :
    :    :      :     :      :     :     :      :      :      :
    :    :      :     :      :     :     :      :      :      :
    :    :      :     :      :     :     :      :      :      :
    :    :      :     :      :     :     :      :      :      :
5  A37   :    A64F  F14C  F14D   :  A34A A34F  F15D  F16C  F16E  F17B
  See*3 F18C          :      :      :     :      :     :      :      :
  ChartA Cont'd on    :      :      :     :      :     :      :      :
         B/2          :      :      :     :      :     :      :      :
                      :      :      :     :      :     :      :      :
                      :      :      :     :      :     :      :      :
6           [F19] [F20] [F21I]  :  [F24] [F25] [F33] [F26] [F27] [F28]
                             :   :
7                         [F29]  :
     Gen                         :
      5           B8C    B8D           B8G
                   :      :             :
                   :      :             :
      6          F22E   [F23]          A90A
                   :                    :
                   :                    :
      7          [F61]                [F30]
```

GENERATION BIRTH DATE AVERAGES: (Includes B,A and F groups)

Gen	Av.	Gen	Av.	To nearest 5 years
-1	1570*	7	1810	
0	1600	8	1835	
1	1625	9	1870	
2	1660	10	1900	
3	1695	11	1925	
4	1730	12	1950	
5	1755	13	1975	
6	1780			* Projected from Gen. 0

```
Gen                              BURGESS
4                            B6E      B6D              : BURGESS Gen
                              :    SEE  No.21          :   B3A    1
5                  See B/1 F18C        B/3            :    :
                              :                        :   B4A    2
6                            B9A                       :    :
                              :                        :   B5F    3
                              :                        :    :
7              B10A                    B10D See No.17  :   B6E    4
                :                        :    Chart F  :    :
8               :                       F34            :   F18C   5
                :                                      :    :
                :                                      :   B9A    6
                :
B11A              B11B               B11D B11J B11E  :
B11Aa             :   B70A    B80A   B11Da  :    .:
SHOCKLEY          :    :       :     McKay  :    :
  :               :   B71J             :    :    :
  :               :  :B71Ja=B81A       :    :    :
9  B12A  B12B     :    :              [B14] [B55] :
B12Aa B12Ba       :  B72F B72C
KORN  KORN  B13A B13E=B72Fa :  B15B   B15C  B15E B15F  B15G  B15I  B15J
  :     :    :   :          :  B15Ba  B15Ca B15Ea  :   B15Ga  :    B15Ja
  :     :    :   :          :  GREEN SIDDENS GOOD  :   REDD   :    DeWHIT
  :     :    :   :          :    :     :     :     :    :     :     :
10 B16C [B17] B18B :   [A82] [B20] [B21]   :  [B23] [B24] [B25] [B26.
B16Ca       :   :                          :
GARRETT     :   :              B22A  B22C  B22D  B22F
  :         :   :               :     :     :     :
  :         :   :             [B34] [B35] [B36] [B37]
  :         :   :
  :         :  :B19A       B19C       B19D    B19E    B19F      B19G
  :         :   :   :       :          :   See No.22: SEE No.20 B19Ga
11 :      [B28]:           :          :    B/3 :        B/3 FILLINGHA
   :          :           :          :          :           :
[B27] B29B  B29C  B30A  B30B  B30C B31A  B32A    B32B      B33A
      B29Ba B29Ca B30Aa B30Ba  :     :  B32Aa     :       B33Aa
      WISE  WILLEY KRAUSE DAVIS :     :  LOGAN     :       COOPER
        :     :     :     :     :     :    :       :         :
12 B38A B38B    :     :     :     :     :    :       :
     :  B38Ba B39A  B40A [B41] B42A [B43] B44A  B45A  B45B  [B46]
     : BAZEMORE B39Aa B40Aa     B42Aa     B44Aa   :   B45Ba
     :      : BRADLEY MORRIS    YARYAN    ABBIATTI  :  GATNEY
     :      :     :     :          :        :     :      :
13 [B47] [B48] [B49] [B50]       [B51]    [B52] [B53] [B54]
```

```
                              No.20
Gen                                   LAZARUS
 5                                     B56A
                       GIRTON           :
 6                     B65A            B57A
                        :               :               BURGESS
            FISHER     : HARTMAN        :               B9A
 7          B63A  B66A  B60A  B58A                       :
             :     :     :     :                        B10A
 8           :     :    B61D    :                        :
             :    B67A   :B61Da=B59A                     B11B
          B64A=B67Aa:    :                               :
 9                 :    B62F                             B13E
             B68A=B62Fa:                                  :
                        :                                 :
10                _____:_____                          B19F  See B/2
            B69A       B69B  B69C ===============B19Fa
             :         B69Ba
             :         LYNCH
             :          :
             :          :
11          B73B      B74A  B74B
            B73Ba     B74Aa   :
            HANCOCK   BECKER   :
             :          :      :
12         [B75]     [B76]  B77A                       No.22
                              :
                              :                        ALEXANDER
12                          [B78]                      B86A
           No.21                           BLANTON       :
                                           B93A   B87A  McBRIDE
                                            :      :    B91A
           BURGESS                         B94A   B88A    :
           B3A                BURGESS        :      :   :B88Aa=B92A
            :                 B13E         B95A     :
           B4A                 :            :      B89A
            : WASHINGTON      See B/2 B19E  :   B96A=B89Aa:
           B5F  B97A                       B19Ea===========B90A
            :    :
   See B/2 B6E  B6D  B98E
           B6Da  :
            :    :
            : B99A
           B99Aa
```

FAMILY GROUP CHART C

```
Gen.                          COX(COCKS)                    OWSLEY(UUSLEY)
 1                              C10A                              C34A
                                 :                                 :
                                 :                                 :
                                COX              COOPER            :
 2    C11A            C11D  C11G            C11B  C27A            C35A
       :                :    :               :     :               :
       :                :    :               :     :               :
       :                :    :               :     :               :
 3    C12A            C14D  C15E  C13C  C13D  C13Oa═C28G* C28C      :
       :                :    :      :   C13Da══════════════:══C36C **
       :                :    :      :                             :
      COX               :    :      :                             :     :
 4  C16Ca C16C C16H C16Ha C17E  [C32] [C26]                    C29D C37C
    GILSTRAP        WILLARD  :                                   :     :
      :              :       :                                   :     :
      :              :       :                                   :     :
      :              :       :                                   :     :
 5  C18F─C18Fa C19Da C19D C40A                                 C30A C38C
     COGBILL  WINN         :                                    :     :
       :        :          :                                    :     :
       :        :        C41A                        FOOTE      :     :
 6     :     [C21]         :                         C31Ea C31E [C39]
       :                 [C42]                                  :
       :                                                        :
     ────────                                                   :
 6  ──C20A──      C20B   C20C                                    :
    C20Aa  C20Ab COGBILL COGBILL                                :
    EDMUNDS BOWERS  :       :                                   :
      :       :     :       :                                   :
 7  [C22]  [C23]  [C24]  [C25]                              [C33]
```

* COOPER FAMILY: Related to Cox family in C13 Sibling Group
               C28G Thomas McCuin Cooper married
               C13O Martha Jane Cox
**OWSLEY FAMILY: Related to Cox family in C13 Sibling Group
               C36C Emmanuel Owsley married
               C13D Sarah Malinda Cox
AVERAGE DATES OF BIRTH USING KNOWN DATES IN THIS GROUP
       GENERATION 1: 1770   5: 1891
                   2: 1805   6: 1929
                   3: 1838   7: 1945
                   4: 1859

330

```
Gen                         SHOCKLEY
 1                           D10A
                              :
                              :
 2                  ┌────────────────┐
                    D11E          D11G
                     :              :
 3                 [D12]          D13E
                                    :
    DAVID         ┌────────────────────────────────────────┐
 4  D73A              D14D              D14H   D14B      D14F
     :                :                D14Ha    :          :
     :                :                SHOCKLEY :         D17
     :                :      To other groups  :    :    SEE D/2
     :                :           :            :    :
 5   :  ┌────┬────┬────┬──────────┐       D58D  ┌─────┐
     : D16J D16C D16D D16G      D16F            D15B D15C
  D74A=D16Ja :    :    :          :          :  : To other groups
     :   :    :    :    :          :          :    :
     :   :    :    :    :     ┌────┴───┐      :    :
 6  D75C  D19D D20F D22L  D21E    D21G  D82A  D18G
     :    :    :   D22La D21Ea   D21Ga   :     :
     :    :    : HAYNES CAMPBELL OWENS   :     :
     :    :    :   :      :       :      :     :
     :    :    :   :      :       :      :     :
 7  D76C [D30] [D59] [D81] :     D89A   D83A [D29]
     :               :      :      :     :
     :               :      :      :     :
     :               :      :      :     :
 8   :         ┌────────┐ ┌────┐   :  [D84]
     :         D85A     D85B D90C
    D77B       D85Aa     :    :
    D77Ba      LOCKWOOD  :    :
    RODGERS      :       :    :
     :           :       :    :
     :           :       :    :
 9  D78B        D86A   [D88] [D91]
    D78Ba        :
    BASTIAN      :
     :           :
     :           :
10  D79B        [D87]
    D79Ba
    GAUSMAN
     :
     :
11  [D80]
```

GENERATION BIRTH DATE AVERAGES			
Gen	Av.	Gen	Av.
1	1650	7	1865
2	1685	8	1885
3	1720	9	1905
4	1760	10	1925
5	1800	11	1950
6	1825		

331

```
Gen                                              SHOCKLEY
 1                                               D10A
                                                  :
 2                                               D11G
                                                  :
 3                                               D13E
                                                  :
 4            (D14B,D,H SEE D/1                   D14F
                                                  :
                                                  :
                                                  :
 5   D17G  D17A  D17D                             D17F        (D17H,D17J)
      :     :     :                                :           SEE  D/3
      :     :     :              TRAVIS            :
      :     :     :              D70A              :
      :     :     :               :               :
      :     :     :               :               :
      :     :     :              D71E  D71A        :
      :     :     :        D26Haf=D71Ea   :        :
      :     :     :            :       :           :
 6    :    [D23]  [D24]        :      [D72] D25D  D25E  D25H  D25I
      :                        :            D25Da   :     :     :
 _____   :            SKEEN    :     :     :
 D26B    D26F    D26H   :                     :      :     :     :
 D26Ba   D26Fa  :D26Ha                        :      :     :     :
 POOL    CARTER  :                            :      :     :     :
  :       :      :                            :      :     :     :
 7 [D35]  D36A   :                          [D31] D32D [D33] [D34]
          D36Aa  :
          ALLDRIDGE :
           :      :
 8        [D49]  D37C                              [D48]
                 D37Ca
                 JAMES
                  :
                  :
                  :
 9               D50A
                 D50Aa
                 GILLISPIE
                  :
                  :
10               [D55]
```

332

```
Gen                                                    SHOCKLEY
 1                                                       D10A
                                                          :
 2                                                       D11G
                                                          :
 3                                                       D13E
                                                          :
 4                                  B14B,D,H      D14F
                                    SEE D/1         :
         WALLACE                                    :
 5        D64A                      D17A,D,F,G    D17H  D17J
           :                        SEE D/2        :   D17Ja
           :                                       :   ATKINS
 6   D65E  D65F  D65G  D65H                         :    :
      :     :     :     :                          :    :
 7    :   [D67] [D68] [D69]                         :    :
      :                                             :    :
      :                                             :    :
 6    :          D27D  D27I  D27A  D27B D27G D27H  D27J  :
      :           :     :     :   D27Ba  :  D27Ha   :    :
      :           :     :     :   DURBIN :  BRANSON  :   :
      :           :     :     :    :    :    :      :    :
 7  D66I _____:    D43D D38A [D39] [D41] [D42] [D44]  :
    D66Ia=D40E D40B D40A    :    :    :                        :
         : (Tie to :       :    :    :      Gen _____:
         : group R) :      :    :    :       6  D28A  D28C   D28D    D28G
         :          :    [D54]  :            :  D28Ca  D28Da  D28Ga
 8     [D53]  D52G  D52F      [D51]           :  HOLMAN CRIDER  CAHILL
              D52Ga D52Fa                     :    :     :       :
              STEWART PURCELL                7 [D45] [D46]  :   [D63]
                 :     :                             :
 9             [D57] [D56]                           :
                                             _____:
                                           8  D47E          D47F
                                              D47Ea   D47Fa  D47Fb
                                              SAMPLES THOMPSON MITCHEM
                                                :      :       :
                                           9  [D60]  [D61]   [D62]
```

333

```
Gen                    BRANSON
 1                      E7A
         _____:_____
 2   E8A    E8C                        E8H                   E8K
     :      :                          :                     E8Ka
     :      :                          :                     ROGERS
     :      :                          :                      :
 3   E80B  E9E          E9A            E77C                  [E76]
     :     E9Ea         :              :
 4   :     FAWCETT      :              [E78]
     :     :            :
    [E81] [E79]  E10A          E10D  See E/2
                   :
    HUGHES  _____:_____
 5  E52A      E11C      E11A                    E11D               E11
    :         :         :                       :                  :
    :         :         :                       :                  :
 6  E53A     [E13]     E12A    McMILLIAN       SEE E/2             E14
    :                   :      E16Eaf                              :
    :_____:_____:_____:_____:_____:
 7  E54F  E54G  E54A  E16A  E16E    :
    :     :     :     :     E16Ea=E67A                     E67C E18
    :     :     :     :                                      :    :
 8 [E56] [E57] E55D   :          Branson                      :    :
               E55Da=E20D  E20A           E20B   E20C  E20D [E68] [E2
                            :             E20Ba  E20Ca  :
                            :             FEELER SOUDER- :
                            :                    MEYER   :
                            :                     :      :    :
 9  E25B   E25C  E25D  E25L  E25M   E25N  E25K  [E26] [E27] [E28]
    E25Ba  E25Ca  :    E25La E25Ma  E25Na  :
    WILLIAMS HELTON : DUNCAN CURTMAN SCOTT  :
    :       :     :     :     :      :      :
10 [E35]  [E36] [E37] [E38] [E39]  [E40]  E85F
                                            :
```

GENERATION BIRTH DATE AVERAGES   E86B Gen 11
Gen Average Gen Average   Gen Average   :
 1   1680   6   1800   11   1940   [E87] Gen 12
 2   1705   7   1825   12   1970
 3   1730   8   1855   (Insufficient
 4   1750   9   1885   data for good
 5   1770   10   1910   averages)

FAMILY GROUP CHART E/2

```
en                              BRANSON
3                                ED9A
                                   :
4                               ┌──────────────┐
                                E10A          E10D
                                  :             :
5           ┌─────────────────┐    ┌─────┐      :
           E11A    E11C        E11B            :
           SEE E/1             SEE E/1         :
                                               :
                                               :
6     ┌─────────┬──────────────────────┬───────:──────┐
     E15D      E15A                    E15C          E15B
      :          :                       :           SEE E/3
      :          :                       :
      :          :                       :
7   [E90]       E19A                     E61A
                 :                       E61Aa
                 :                       CARROLL
                 :                         :
                 :                         :
                 :─────────────┐           :
8     ┌──────┬──────┬──────┬───┘           :
     E24A   E24C   E24H   E24K   E62A
      :      :      :      :      :
      :      :      :      :      :
      :      :      :      :      :
9     ;    [E60]  [E58]  E65I   E63B
      :                   :      :
  ┌───────┬──────┬────────:      :
 E34A    E34B   E34C    E34D     :      :
 E34Aa   E34Ba    :     E34Da    :      :
 BRAY    WALKER    :    FORTUNE   :      :
  :       :       :      :        :      :
  :       :       :      :        :      :
10 [E42]  [E43]  [E44]  [E45]   [E66]   E88A
                                          :
                                          :
11                                ┌───────:──────┐
                                 E91A         E91B
                                  :             :
12                              [E92]         [E93]
```

335

FAMILY GROUP CHART E3

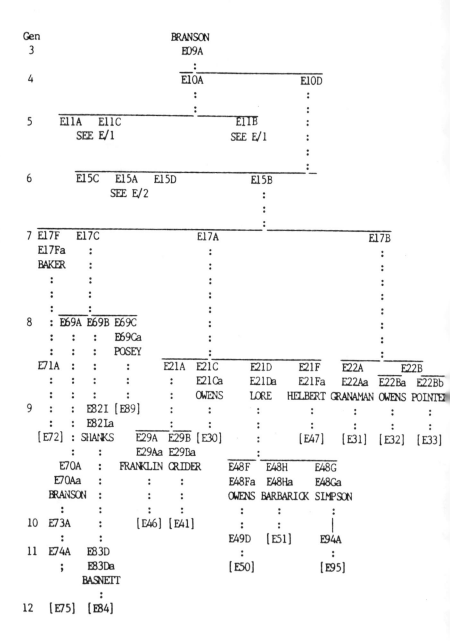

```
Gen                       BRANSON
 3                        E09A
                            :
 4                        E10A                    E10D
                            :                       :
                            :                       :
 5   E11A    E11C            E11B                    :
         SEE E/1        SEE E/1                      :
                                                    :
                                                    :
 6   E15C   E15A   E15D          E15B               :
         SEE E/2                   :
                                   :
                                   :
 7  E17F   E17C          E17A                      E17B
    E17Fa    :             :                         :
    BAKER    :             :                         :
      :      :             :                         :
      :      :             :                         :
      :      :             :                         :
 8    :  E69A E69B E69C     :                         :
      :    :    :   E69Ca   :                         :
      :    :    :   POSEY   :                         :
    E71A   :    :    :    E21A  E21C   E21D   E21F   E22A      E22B
      :    :    :    :      :   E21Ca  E21Da  E21Fa  E22Aa  E22Ba  E22Bb
      :    :    :    :      :   OWENS   LORE   HELBERT GRANAMAN OWENS POINTE?
 9    :    :  E82I [E89]    :    :      :       :      :      :      :
      :    :  E82Ia         :    :      :       :      :      :      :
   [E72] : SHANKS  E29A E29B [E30]      :     [E47]  [E31]  [E32]  [E33]
         :    :  E29Aa E29Ba            :
      E70A    :  FRANKLIN CRIDER   E48F  E48H   E48G
      E70Aa   :     :     :        E48Fa E48Ha  E48Ga
      BRANSON :     :     :        OWENS BARBARICK SIMPSON
         :    :     :     :          :     :       :
10    E73A   :   [E46] [E41]         :     :       |
         :    :                   E49D  [E51]    E94A
         :    :                     :              :
11    E74A   E83D                 [E50]          [E95]
         ;   E83Da
             BASNETT
               :
12   [E75]  [E84]
```

336

FAMILY GROUP CHART F
Note: This Chart is a Supplement to the B Group

No.9	**No.10**	**No.11**	**No.12**	**No.13**	**No.14**
GAITHER	CHEW	ROBINS			
F2A	F40A	F43A	B4B	B5A	B6E
:	:		:	:	:
F3A	F41A	F44A=B3Aaf	[F12]	[F13]	[F13]
:	:				
F4A	F42A	**No.15**		**No.16**	

F42Aa=B4A
See B/1

		B4H	

B5Ha=F5A	F5C	A88B	A88A	:	B8C	B8D	B8G
:	:	:	:		F22E	[F23]	A90A
F6D	[F46]	F11B	A99A		:		:
:		:	:		[F61]		[F30]

F7A	F7F		[F31]	F10D
:	:			
F8H	[F45]			[F32]
:				
[F9]				

No.17
B10D See B/2

		F34A				F34H	F34B
		:				F34Ha	:
		:				McLAMBETH	:
		:				:	:

F35A	F35D	F35E	F35H		F38A	F38B	F56H
F35Aa	:	F35Ea	:		:	:	:
LANKENAU	:	FRANCIS	:		:	:	:
:	:	;	:		:	:	:
F36A	F51B	[F55]	[F54]		[F39]	[F52]	F57A
F36Aa	:						F57Aa
MILLER	:						TOLBERT
:	:						:

F37A	F37B	[F53]					F58C
F37Aa	:						:
RITTERBUSCH	:						F59A
:	:						:
[F49]	[F50]						[F60]

No.19

B7I	B7A		B7G		B7B	B7C		B7H	B7J
:	:		:		:	:		:	:
F16C	F16E	A64F	A34A	A34F	[F47]	F14C	F14D	F15D	F17B
:	:	:	:	:		:	:	:	:
[F26]	[F27]	[F19]	[F24]	[F25]		[F20]	[F211]	[F33]	[F28]
						:			
						[F29]			

337

FAMILY GROUP CHART G/1

```
Gen                                        COPELAND
 1                        G10A         G10C           G10B        G10E
                                    SEE BELOW          :      G10Ea  G10Eb
                           :                           :      TAFT  BLANTON
                           :                           :        :      :
 2            G11A         G11B G11D G11E  G11G  G25A G25B G25C  :      :
              :             :    :    :    :      :  G25Ba :  [G46]  [G47]
              :             :    :    :    :      :  ELROD  :
              :             :    :    :    :      :    :    :
 3 G12A G12B G12C  G12F  G12D G13C [G14][G15] G16B [G26][G27][G28]
    :    :    :   G12Fa   :    :                :
    :    :    :   ADKINS  :    :                :
    :    :    :     :     :    :                :
 4 [G17] G18L [G19] [G21]  :  [G22]          [G23]
         :                 :
 5     [G24]               :
                           :_____
                           :        :   Gen          COPELAND
Gen   BURNS                :        :    1 G10A,B   G10C  G10D,G10E
 1    G49A                 :        :      SEE ABOVE  :   SEE G/2
       :                   :        :                :
 2 G50B G50C G50D  G50E  G50A       :       _____:
    :    :  G50Da G50Ea   :         :    2 G29G  G29I    G29K
    :    : DAVIDSON WILSON :         :       :   G29Ia    :
    :    :    :     :      :         :       :   GREMP     :
 3 [G52][G53][G54] [G55]   :         :       :    :     __:__
                           :         :    3 [G30] [G31] G32C G32D
       _____:         :                   :    :
       G51B G51F G51G G51H G51I G51C :    4             [G33][G34]
        :    :    :    :    :    :  :
        :    :    :    :    :    : G20E
 4   [G56][G58][G59][G60][G61] G57C=G20Ea

        GENERATION BIRTH DATE AVERAGES
           Gen    Av
            1    1795
            2    1835
            3    1860
            4    1885
            5    No data
```

```
Gen _____COPELAND_____
 1   G10A,B,C                        G10D                           G10E
     SEE G/1                          :                        _____
                                      :        ·              G10Ea    G10Eb
                                      :                        TAFF    BLANTON
                                      :                         :        :
 2  ___G35A___  G35G   G35I   G35J   G35K   G35L   G35M   G35O   [G46]   G47B
         :      G35Ga  G35Ia    :      :      :      :      :               :
         :      BERRY  BECKHAM  :      :      :      :      :               :
         :        :      :      :      :      :      :      :               :
 3       :      [G37]  [G38]  [G39]  [G40]  [G41]  [G42]  [G43]           [G43]
         :
     ___G36D G36E G36C_____BELL_____
        :     :    G36Ca=G62C G62A G62B G62D
        :     :          :     :    :    :
        :     :          :     :    :    :
 4  [G44][G45]         [G65][G63][G64][G66]
```

```
Gen.
 1                        LIGHT                    BAILEY
                          H11A                     H51A
                           ⋮                        ⋮
                           ⋮                        ⋮
                           ⋮                        ⋮
 2  ‾H12A‾   ‾H12C‾    ‾H12B‾   H12Ba══H52A   ‾H52C‾  ‾H52E‾  ‾H52G‾
       ⋮        ⋮         ⋮                      ⋮       ⋮       ⋮
       ⋮        ⋮         ⋮                      ⋮       ⋮       ⋮
       ⋮      [H15]       ⋮                      ⋮       ⋮       ⋮
 3  ‾H13C‾  H13D     ‾H14G‾  H14H             H53B  [H54]   H55E
    H13Ca   H13Da       ⋮      ⋮                ⋮             ⋮
    REEVES  RHODES      ⋮      ⋮                ⋮             ⋮
      ⋮       ⋮         ⋮      ⋮                ⋮             ⋮
      ⋮       ⋮         ⋮      ⋮                ⋮             ⋮
 4  [H16]   [H17]     [H18]  [H19]            [H56]         [H57]
```

GENERATION BIRTH DATE AVERAGES
The following dates are poorly documented, and should
be used with caution:

Generation	Average Birth Dates
1	1790
2	1815
3	1835
4	1860

FAMILY GROUP CHART I

```
Gen                              BOONE            BRYAN
1                                I10A             I60A
                                  :                :
                                  :                :
2  I11A                          I11C             I61A
    :                             :                :
    :                             :                :
3  I58G  I12B  I12C      I12H    I12I I12J I12F     :
    :     :     :         :       :    :    : I12Fa=I62F
    :     :     :         :       :    :    :
4 [I59]  I13A [I14]  I16A I16C I16D I17A [I18]  :
              :     :    :    :    :           I15C  I15D  I15H  I15J
              :     :    :    :    :           I15Ca I15Da   :     :
              :     :    :    :    :          HAYES CALLAWAY [I56] [I57]
              :     :    :    :    :            :     :
              :     :    :    :    :            :     :
5          I19A   [I22] [I23] [I24] [I25] [I20] [I21]
              :
              :
              :
                                 ELLIS
6      I40A          I40B        I51A
        :             :           :
        :             :           :
7      I41B           :           :
    I41Ba I41Bb  I42A I42C I42B  I52E I52F I52J
   McGriff Vaughan  :    :    :    :    :    :
     :     :     :    :    :    :    :    :
     :     :     :    :    :    :    :    :
8  [I43]  [I44] [I45] I47C I46A  :    :    :
                       :   I46Aa= I53B [I54] [I55]
                       :
                       :
9                     I48C
                      I48Ca
                     BLACKMORE
                       :
10                   [I50]
```

	Gen	Av.	Gen	Av.
GENERATION BIRTH DATE AVERAGES:	1	1675	6	1810
	2	1710	7	1835
(Adjusted slightly to	3	1730	8	1855
obtain better separation)	4	1765	9	No data
	5	No data	10	No data

```
Gen                                        EADS (Edds)
1                                            J10A
                                              :
                                              :
                                              :
2                                            J11A
                                              :
                                              :
                                              :
3            J12B                                      J12D      J12H    J12L    J
              :                                         :        J12Ha   J12La   J
              :                                         :        CRISMON TACKETT G
              :                                         :           :       :
              :                                         :           :       :
4             :                                         :         [J16]   [J17]   J
              :                                         :
              :                                         :
              :                                         :
    J14B  J14C  J14E  J14F   J14G          J15F   J15G
    J14Ba J14Ca   :   J14Fa    :             :      :
    HUGHES TACK-  :   BRIGGS   :             :      :
      :    ETT    :     :      :             :      :
      :     :     :     :      :             :      :
5 [J18] [J19]  J20E  [J21]  [J22]         [J23]  [J24]                        [J
                 :
                 :
                 :
6             [J25]
```

GENERATION BIRTH DATE AVERAGES:
Generation	Average Birth Dates
1	1775
2	1805
3	1835
4	1860
5	1885
6	1910

FAMILY GROUP CHART K

                                              Gen

Gen   COFFEY   3   DAVIS
 1   K8A   K30A
                                 :   :
                                 :   :
                                 :   4   K31D   K31A
 2   K9A   :   K31Aa
                                 :   :   BALLANCE
                                 :   :   :
          ROGERS   :   5   K33   K32C
 3   K36A   K10A   K32Cb=K14B See K14B below
            :   :
            :   :
    MOSS   :   PARKER   :
 4 K25A   :   K11B   K11A   K11C
     :   :   K34A K34O=K11Ba :   :   :
     :   :   :   :   :   :
     :   :   :   :   :   :
 5   :   :   K35A   :   :   :
     :   K37O=K35Aa   :   :   :
     :   :   :   :   :
     :   :   :   :   :
     :   K13D K13E K13G K12A K12B K12C K12D K12F K12G   K14F K14B
 5 K26A K26B= K13Da :   :   :   :   :   :   :   :   : See
    K26Aa   :   :   :   :   :   :   :   :   : Above
    BURGESS   :   :   :   :   :   :   :   :   :
     :   :   :   :   :   :   :   :   :   :
 6 K27B   [K21] [K22] [K15] [K16] [K17] [K18] [K19] [K20] K23G
    K27Ba   :
    FINN   :
     :   :
     :   :
 7 [K28]   [K24]
       GENERATION BIRTH DATE AVERAGES;
          Generation Average Birth Dates
               1   No data
               2   No data
               3   1805
               4   1830
               5   1855
               6   1875
               7   No data

FAMILY GROUP CHART L

Gen.				SIMPSON		
1				L11A		
				:		
				:		
				:		
2	L12A	L12B		:	L12E	
	:	:			:	
	:	:			:	
	:	:			:	
3	[L13]	[L14]			L15I	
					:	
					:	
					:	
4		L16G	L16E	L16F	L16J	L16I
		L16Ga	L16Ea	L16Fa	:	:
		BACON	SCOTT	KEATON	:	:
		:	:	:	:	:
		:	:	:	:	:
5		[L19]	[L17]	[L18]	[L21]	[L20]

GENERATION BIRTH DATE AVERAGES:

Generation	Average Birth Dates
1	No data
2	1810
3	1830
4	1860
5	No data

```
Gen                              NOBLETT
 1                               M10A
                                  :
                                  :
                                  :
 2   M11B    M11C    M11A         M11F      M11G    ——————M11H——————
      :       :       :           M11Fa     M11Ga   M11Ha    M11Hb
      :       :       :           BOWMAN    SKAGGS  JACKSON  WRIGHT
      :       :       :             :         :       :        :
      :       :       :             :         :       :        :
 3  M13A M13C M14A   [M12]           :         :     [M17]    [M18]
     : M13Ca   :                     :         :
     : BECKMAN :                     :         :
     :   :     :   M15A   M15D M15E  M15F   M16E
     :   :     :   M15Aa  M15Da  :     :    M16Ea
     :   :     :   COLLIER GIESLER :    :    WEST
     :   :     :     :      :    :     :      :
     :   :     :     :      :    :     :      :
 4 [M20] [M21] [M22] [M23] M24C [M25] [M26] [M27]
                          M24Ca
                          WEST
                            :
                            :
                            :
 5                        M28A
                            :
                            :
                            :
 6                        [M29]
```

GENERATION BIRTH DATE AVERAGES:(Based on only 3 dates total)

Generation	Average birth dates
1	No data
2	1825
3	1865
4	No data
5	No data
6	No data

```
Gen                        CARNES
 1                          P9A
                             :
                             :
                             :
 2                          P10A
                             :
                             :
                             :
     _____:_____
 3   P11A                   P11G                   P11I
     P11Aa                   :                      :
     BERRY                   :                      :
       :                     :                      :
       :                     :                      :
       :                     :                      :
 4   [P12]                 [P13]    _____:_____
                                    P14A        P14C        P14E
                                    P14Aa       P14Ca       P14Ea
                                    MARTIN      BREEDEN     BREEDEN
                                      :            :           :
                                      :            :           :
 5                                  [P15]        [P16]       [P17]
```

GENERATION BIRTH DATE AVERAGES: Data for one generation only

Generation	Average birth date
1	No data
2	No data
3	No data
4	1857
5	No data

```
Gen                                                MORELAND
 1                                                   Q30A
                                                      :
      HARRISON                                        :
                                         SHINKLE      :
 2  Q42C Q42B Q42A                         Q35A    Q31A Q31C Q31D  Q31B
      :    :    :                            :       :    :    :     :
      :    :    :                            :       :    :    :     :
      :    :    :          COPPEDGE          :       :    :    :     :
 3  [Q45][Q44] Q43B                        Q36C Q36B  :    :    :   Q33L
            Q43Ba=Q37G Q37D Q37C  Q37H=Q36Ca Q36Ba=Q32J [Q40] [Q34] Q33La
                        :    :                                    ARNOLD
                        :    :                                       :
                        :    :                                       :
 4                    [Q39] [Q38]                                  [Q46]
```

GENERATION BIRTH DATE AVERAGES

Generation	Average birth dates
1	No data
2	1810
3	1845
4	1870

FAMILY GROUP CHART R

```
Gen              PINNELL
 1               R16A
                  :
                  :
                                   TERRILL              RIDENHOUR
 2               R17A               R10A                 R25A
                  :                  :                    :
                  :                  :                    :
                  :                  :                    :
 3               R18A               R11A         R26H R26C R26D R26F
                  :                  :            :    :    :   R26Fa
                  :                  :            :    :    :   CHAMBER
                  :                  :            :    :    :    :
 4  R19B      R19C      R19A    R12A R12B R12D   R30A [R27] [R28] [R29]
     :          :        :       :    :    :     :
     :          :        :       :    :    :     :
     :          :        :       :    :    :     :
 5  [R21]  R22A R22B R22C  R20A   :  [R14] R15H   :
            :    :    :   R20Aa =R13A      R15Ha =R31B
            :    :    :
            :    :    :
 6         [R23] [R24] [R32]
```

GENERATION BIRTH DATE AVERAGES

Generation	Average Birth Dates
1	No data
2	1790
3	1825
4	1845
5	No data
6	No data

```
Gen                    BRIGGS                              BACKUES
 1                     S10A                                 S17A
                        :                                    :
                        :                                    :
                        :                                    :
     _____      _____
 2   S11A      S11E      S11G      S11C           S18B      S18C      S18A
      :        S11Ea      :         :              :         :         :
      :       FENNESSEY   :         :             _____    :
      :          :        :         :            S20H   S20D  [S21]  [S19]
 3   [S12]     [S14]     [S15]    S13A══S20Ha      :
                                    :              :
                                    :              :
 4                                [S16]          [S22]
```

GENERATION BIRTH DATE AVERAGES

Generation	Average birth date
1	No data
2	1835
3	1860
4	No data

FAMILY GROUP CHART T

```
Gen                                                              CRISMON
 1                                                                 T10A
                                                                    :
                                                                    :
                                                                    :
 2                                                                 T11A
                                                                    :
                                                                    :
                                                                    :
                                              WEST                  :
 3                                            T22A                 T12A
                                               :                    :
                                               :                    :
           SKAGGS                              :                    :
 4          T17A        ‾T23A‾ ‾T23B‾ T23C  T23D      ‾T13A‾      T13C  T13J
             :            :      :      :   T23Da        :          :     :
             :            :      :      :  :WHITAKER     :          :     :
             :            :      :      :   :            :          :     :
 5    ‾‾‾‾‾‾:‾‾‾‾‾‾  T24D T24F T25F [T26]  :   ‾T14I‾ ‾T14F‾ WOODS [T15][T16]
      T18E        T18A  :    :    :       T27A =T14Ia  T14Fa= T30H
       :           :    :    :    :
       :           :    :    :    :
 6     :         T19G   :    :  [T31]
     [T20]    T19Ga=T28B [T29]
              WEST
               :
               :
 7           [T21]
```

GENERATION BIRTH DATE AVERAGES

Generation	Average birth date
1	No data
2	No data
3	No data
4	1815
5	1850
6	1870
7	No data

350

```
Gen        HELTON
 1         U10A
              :
              :
              :                          COWAN
 2    U11B      U11A
       :          :U11Ab=U16B    U16C        U16G       U16H
       :          :              U16Ca        :          :
       :          :              CONNOR       :          :
       :          :                :          :          :
       :          :                :          :          :
 3   [U13]   U12D  U12E          [U17]      [U18]      [U19]
              :     :
              :     :
              :     :
              :     :
 4         [U14]  [U15]
```

GENERATION BIRTH DATE AVERAGES

Generation	Averages birth dates
1	No data
2	1830
3	1850
4	No data

FAMILY GROUP CHART V

```
Gen                              ROWDEN
 1                               V10A
                                  :
                                  :
      BREEDEN                _____:_____                      HOOPS
 2    V19A          V11A                     V11B                   V22A
       :             :                        :                      :
       :             :                        :                      :
       :             :                        :                      :
 3    V20A V12A   V12D    V12E    V12B      V17D        V23C              V23B
       :    :      :       :       :          :          :                :
       :    :      :       :       :          :          :                :
       :    :      :       :       :          :          :                :
 4     :    :      :       :       :        [V18]        :        _____:_____
       :  V13B  [V15]   [V16]   V14B                     :        V24B       V24D
      V21B=V13Ba              V14Ba=V25A    _____     :        V24Ba       :
                                         V25B           V25B      REED        :
                                                        V25Ba     :           :
                                                        MOSBY     :           :
                                                         :        :           :
                                                         :        :           :
 5                                                     [V28]    [V26]       [V27]
```

GENERATION BIRTH DATE AVERAGES

Generation	Birth Date Averages
1	No data
2	1790
3	1820
4	1845
5	1865

```
Gen                                    JOHNSON
 1                                      Y11A
                                          :
                                          :
 2                          Y12A        Y12B       Y12C
                             :                SEE Y/2
                             :
                             :
                             :
                             :
                             :
 3      Y13A    Y13D    Y13E    Y13G              Y13H
         :       :       :      Y13Ga            Y13Ha
         :       :       :      McGEE            HAWKINS
         :       :       :       :                 :
         :       :       :       :                 :
         :       :       :       :                 :
 4      Y16A    Y17A   [Y18]   Y19B    Y20A   Y20B      Y20C
         :       :              :       :    Y20Ba       :
         :       :              :       :    ROBINSON    :
         :       :              :       :     :          :
         :       :              :       :     :          :
 5      Y33B   [Y34]          Y35B    [Y36]  [Y37]     [Y38]
         :                    Y35Ba
         :                    CRIDER
         :                      :
         :                      :
 6     [Y55]                  [Y56]
```

GENERATION BIRTH DATE AVERAGES	Gen	Average
	1	No data
	2	1790
(Includes Y12A,Y12B and Y12C)	3	1825
	4	1850
	5	1870
	6	1891

FAMILY GROUP CHART Y/2

```
Gen                                          JOHNSON
 1                                            Y11A
                                               :
 2                                  Y12A  Y12B  Y12C  (SEE BELOW)
                                               :
       AMMERMAN                                :
 3      Y70A    Y14B  Y14F   Y14A Y14D          Y14E                    Y14C
         :      Y14Ba  :      :    :            :                       Y14Ca
         :      CARROLL :     :    :            :                       JONES
 4       :        :   [Y26]   :    :   Y25A Y25C Y25E Y25H Y25F           :
         :        :           :    :   Y25Aa  :  Y25Ea  :  Y25Fa=Y66A    :
         :        :           :    :  :WOFFORD :HARRISON :               :
         :        :           :    :    :    :    :    :    :            :
         :        :           :    :    :    :    :    :    :            :
         :      Y22D Y22A Y22B   Y21B Y24H [Y48][Y49][Y50][Y51]          :
     Y71B Y71A=Y22Da :    :       :    :                                 :
     Y71Ba    :      :    :       :    :     Y23B    Y23E Y23F Y23G Y23H
     SHERMAN  :      :    :       :    :      :       :    :    :    :
 5     :      :   [Y40][Y41]      :  [Y47]    :       :    :    :    :
       :      :                   :           :     [Y43] [Y44] [Y45] [Y46]
       :      : Y74B Y74E Y74F  Y39B        Y42A Y42D
    [Y73] Y72D =Y74Ba  :    :   Y39Ba         :   Y42Da
                       :    :   RAGAN         :   FANN
                       :    :    :            :    :
 6              [Y75][Y76][Y57]        [Y58] [Y59]
```

```
Gen                    JOHNSON
 1                     Y11A
                        :
                                                    FERRELL
 2            Y12A  Y12B  Y12C                       Y60A
                          Y12Ca                       :
                          SNODGRASS                   :
                            :                         :
 3   Y15C   Y15D         Y15F              Y15E      Y61G Y61H  Y61L Y61F
     Y15Ca  Y15Da Y15Fa   Y15Fb Y15Fc       :        :    :     :    :
     WEST   LANE  DAVIDSON MALONE MYERS      :        :    :     :    :
      :      :     :        :      :         :        :    :     :    :
      :      :     :        :      :         :       Y63D [Y64][Y65][Y62]
 4  [Y27]  [Y28]  [Y30]   [Y31]  [Y32]    Y29H Y29B Y29A=Y63Da
                                            :    :    :
                                            :    :    :
 5                                        [Y54] [Y53] [Y52]
```

```
Gen                                          HUGHES
 1                                           Z10A
                                              :
                                             `:
                                              :
 2                     _____Z11A_____            Z11F
                               :                                       Z11Fa
                               :                                       BILYEU
                               :                                         :
 3      ____Z12A____ Z12B Z12C____Z12G____ ___Z12H___ Z25A ____Z35E____
                :      :    :   Z12Ga Z12Gb Z12Ha      :   Z35Ea Z35Eb
                :      :    :   TUCKER TYLER  SHOBE     :   SHORT STEWART
                :      :    :     :     :      :        :     :      :
                :      :    :     :     :      :        :     :      :
     RAMSEY  Z13D Z13F Z14A [Z15] [Z16] Z17C   :      Z26A Z36A   Z37E
 4   Z20A= Z13Da   :  Z14Aa              Z17Ca Z18A= Z26Ab Z36Aa    :
        :          : CARBER             ANDERSON See below BURGESS  :
        :          :    :                 :                  :      :
        :          :    :                 :                  :      :
 5    [Z21]     [Z22] [Z23]             [Z24]              [Z38]  [Z39]
```

```
Gen                        HUFFMAN                          GREEN
 3                          Z25A                            Z40A
                             :                               :
                             :                               :
 4        ____Z26A____ Z26B Z26C Z26D ___Z26E___ Z26F        :
      Z18A=Z26Ab  :     :    :  Z26Da  Z26Ea  Z26Fa = __Z41C__ Z41A
      See above   :     :    :  MILLER JAMES              :     :
                  :     :    :    :      :                :     :
 5              Z27B  Z28A [Z29] Z30A  [Z31]            Z42F
                Z27Ba   :       Z30Aa                  Z42Fa
                CRIDER  :       HENDERSON              WEST
                  :     :         :                     :
                  :     :         :                     :
 6             [Z32]  [Z33]    [Z34]                  [Z43]
```

GENERATION BIRTH DATE AVERAGES:	Gen	Average	Gen	Average
	1	No data	4	1835
(Insufficient data)	2	No data	5	1870
	3	1810	6	1885

APPENDIX

DATE	NAME	DATE	NAME	DATE	NAME	DATE	NAME
1817	Agee	1819	Clements	1311	Henry	1812	Reynolds
1309	Allen	1806	Cole	1321	Hinton	1319	Richardson
1821	Ammerman	1803	Coleman	1318	Hoops	1799	Ridenhour
1304	Anderson	1801	Collins	1812	Howard	1798	Roberts
1320	Arnold	1820	Compton	1789	Huffman	1814	Robinson
1319	Bacon	1794	Connor	1794	Hughes	1801	Rogers
1818	Bailey	1804	Cooper	1820	Humphrey	1818	Rose
1796	Baker	1318	Copeland	1806	Hutton	1809	Russell
1815	Barbarick	1799	Cowan	1799	James	1795	Scholl
1310	Barnes	1303	Cox	1800	Johnson	1309	Scott
1808	Bell	1812	Crider	1779	Jones	1319	Shelton
1320	Bennett	1314	Cross	1817	King	1318	Shobe
1319	Berry	1802	Crow	1321	Kinsey	1812	Shockley
1313	Bilyeu	1319	David	1311	Lane	1309	Simpson
1814	Blackwell	1801	Davidson	1808	Laughlin	1821	Skaggs
1794	Boone	1800	Davis	1310	Lee	1799	Smith
1809	Boyd	1308	Dodds	1806	Lewis	1808	Sparks
1800	Boyle	1809	Duncan	1314	Lore	1302	Spencer
1821	Branson	1801	Eads	1803	Martin	1798	Stewart
1319	Bray	1811	Edwards	1804	Massey	1300	Strickland
1318	Breeding	1811	Elliott	1818	Matlock	1821	Strong
1313	Briggs	1808	Ellis	1311	Matthews	1813	Tackett
1809	Brooks	1302	Evans	1804	Miller	1810	Taylor
1796	Brown	1799	Ferrell	1806	Moss	1797	Thomas
1800	Bryan	1818	Fitzgerald	1796	Murphy	1809	Thompson
1320	Bumpass	1800	Gibson	1809	Myers	1309	Tipton
1804	Burchard	1315	Glenn	1808	Nichols	1818	Todd
1811	Burgess	1308	Graham	1812	Ogle	1806	Travis
1798	Burns	1797	Green	1812	Owens	1805	Tucker
1797	Butler	1806	Greenstreet	1809	Palmer	1773	Tyler
1303	Caldwell	1797	Hall	1321	Parker	1800	Walker
1309	Callaway	1810	Hamilton	1812	Perkins	1312	Wallace
1799	Campbell	1808	Hammond	1320	Pierce	1812	West
1311	Cannon	1797	Hancock	1813	Pinnell	1812	Wheeler
1821	Carroll	1811	Harris	1810	Pointer	1799	Wherry
1312	Carter	1789	Harrison	1300	Poor	1794	Williams
1311	Caton	1809	Hart	1814	Prater	1800	Wilson
1798	Chambers	1790	Hawkins	1798	Price	1800	Wood
1804	Chandler	1801	Hayes	1319	Pryor	1809	Woods
1797	Clark	1818	Helton	1800	Ramsey	1821	Wright
1809	Clay	1810	Henderson	1811	Reed	1804	Young

PROOF OF KINSHIPS OF ALL IN INDEX

<u>CLANS</u>   Individuals are divided into two clans:
BOONE AND SHOCKLEY
They are also divided into Family Groups:
BOONE GROUP   SHOCKLEY GROUP
FAMILIES   FAMILIES
G,H,I,K,L,M,P,T,U,V,Y   A,B,C,D,E,F,J,Q,R,S,Z

KINSHIP OF THE TWO CLANS: They are related in many
ways. One is shown:
Peter Copeland G11D married Nancy Shockley D25G
KINSHIP BETWEEN FAMILY GROUPS OF A CLAN: Family
 Groups of Boone Clan are shown as related to
 Family Group G of that clan, and Groups of the
 Shockley clan are shown as related to Family
 Group D of that clan.
Numbers shown are primary and secondary numbers
 for the same individual

BOONE CLAN

FAM.GR.				FAM.GR.			
G	All related			P	P11Ea	=	G11F
H	H55Aa	=	G38D	T	T30Ia	=	G29G
I	I46Ba	=	G12A	U	U12Ia	=	G12I
K	K14Ca	=	G32D	V	V18E	=	G57Jaf
L	L16Iaf	=	G29M	Y	Y27Aa	=	G27I
M	M11Cam	=	G35D				

SHOCKLEY CLAN

FAM.GR.				FAM.GR.			
A	Supplement to B:	A18Ba	= B19A(Many others)				
B	B10Ba	=	D16F	Q	Q32Cam	=	D15C
C	C11Aa	=	D16E	R	R13Ha	=	D40B
D	All related			S	S10Aa	=	D15C
E	E16Ia	=	D75C	Z	Z13Bam	=	D15C
F	Supplement to B:	F05A	= B05Ha(Many others)				
J	J20Ca	=	D33H		Q,S,Z Same person		

KINSHIP BETWEEN INDIVIDUALS IN A FAMILY GROUP:
 To establish kinship within a Family Group, see
 the Family Group Charts, PART IV.

AUTHENTICITY

Genealogical compilations, especially those of the magnitude of this work, should always be viewed with caution. Where data is derived from many sources covering a date span of more than 350 years, it is impossible to state with certainity that errors do not exist.

Even public records can be in error, for many reasons, particularly in transcribing original documents. The information may not have been directly received from public record, and may have passed through many hands before reaching the researcher.

Data obtained from bible records, from personal memory, or from a source where erroneous conclusions have been made by individuals who have not revealed the fact that good documentation was lacking, may cause a compiler to unsuspectantly accept data that is in error.

These are only a few of the good alibis for error. About the only defense any compiler may have to prevent errors is to be the advance agent, weighing all information received with a demand for good evidence. This, I have diligently made a condition of acceptance.

Only in a very few instances have I reluctantly accepted what I considered inadequate documentation. In such isolated cases, I have considered the probability of an erroneous assumption to be minimal. I contend that a compilation of this type, when reviewed with a realization that it is unrealistic to assume that it is perfect, can be a valuable foundation on which an individual may build his or her family tree.

BIBLIOGRAPHY

Am.Hist.Co. : Colonial and Revolutionary Lineages
American History Co of America 1939

Bailey Thos A: The American Pageant D.C. Heath & Co
Boston 1961

Baldwin Leland D: Survey of American History Am.Book Co N.Y
1955

Balasco,Milton J: Topics In Am.History Cambridge Book Co
Bronxville NY 1959

Bryan W.S./Rose Robert:Pioneer Families of Missouri 1876

Burgess,James Z.: Burgess History Crown Graphics Inc. Cooks-
ville, Tenn 1976

Burgess,M.R.: The House of Burgesses The Borge Press SanBer-
nardino Ca 1983

Burke Co.N.C.HistSoc: Burke County N.C. Heritage Burke Co Hist
Soc. Morganton, N.C. 1981

Canfield,Wilder: The Making of Modern America Houghton Mifflin
Co. Cambridge Mass 1950

Carman,Kimmel,Walker:Historical Currents In Changing Am. John
C Winston Co.Philadelphia 1942

Chitwood, Oliver P.: A History of Colonial America Harper and
Row Pub. N.Y. 1931

Clemens Wm M: American Marriage Records Biblio Co. Pompton
Lakes N.J. 1926

Clement Claude C:History of Pittsylvania Va J.P. Bell Co.
Lynchburg Va 1929

Daughters of Am Rev. Mag: Missouri, The Cross Road State 1964

Daughters of Am Rev:Service Index Nat. Soc. Dau. Am Rev 1966
and supplements

Eckert, Allen W.: The Frontiersmen Little Brown and Co Boston
1967

Elliott Lawrence:The Long Hunter Readers Digest Press 1976

Ellsberry,Elizabeth Prather:Early Will Records No. Central
Missouri Chillicothe Mo 1960

Encyclopedia Brittanica:

Everton Handbook for Genealogists Logan Utah 1971

Fisher Dorothy Canfield: Our Independence and the Constitution
Random House NY 1950

Foster Genevieve:Abraham Lincoln's World Chas Scribner's Sons
New York 1944

Furnas, J.C.:The Americans G.P. Putnam Sons NY 1969

Gavian,Ruth and Hamm, Wm: The American Story D.C.Heath &
Co. Boston 1959

Gebler,Ernest: The Plymouth Adventure Doubleday and Co Inc
Garden City NY. 1950

Goodspeed and Co:Hist. of SE Missouri 1888

Goodspeed and Co:Hist.of Franklin,Jefferson,Washington,Craw-
ford and Gasconade Cos Mo 1888

Goodspeed and Co: History of Cole,Manteau,Morgan,Benton,Miller
Maries and Osage Cos Mo 1889

Griffin,Frances C.: Dillards of Virginia

Hamlin,Chas. Hughes:They Went Thataway Gen. Pub Co Baltimore
1974

Hamm, William A: The American People D.C. Heath & Co Boston
1939

Higginson, Thos Wentworth: History of The United States Lee
and Shepard Pub Boston 1881

Hotten,John Camden: Lists of Emigrants to America Geneal.Pub
Co. Baltimore Md 1974

King,Everett Marshall History of Maries Co Mo Ramfre Press
Cape Girardeau Mo 1963

Lansing,Marion:Makers of the Americas D.C. Heath & Co Boston
1955

Leckie,Robert:The Wars of America Harper and Row Pub. NY 1968

Livingston, Joel T.: History of Jasper Co Mo. The Lewis Pub Co
Chicago 1912

Mace,Willliam H: A Primary History. Stories of Heroism Rand
McNally & Co NY 1909

McGuire,Edna: Daniel Boone Wheeler Pub Co Chicago 1945

Miller, William: A History of the United States. Dell Pub. Co
N.Y.1958

Moody,Ralph: Stagecoach West Promontory Press 1967

Mormon Gen. Soc:International Genealogical Index Salt Lake
City Utah

Morton, Olen F: History of Rockbridge Co Va. Baltimore Regional
Pub Co Staunton Va 1973

Newman,Harry Wright: Anne Arundel Co.,Maryland Gentry
Printed in Scotland 1970

North,F.A.: History of Jasper County Mo Mills & Co.,
DesMoines, Iowa. 1883

Nugent,Nell Marion:Cavaliers and Pioneers of Virginia
Baltimore Genealogical Pub Co Baltimore 1969

Paxton, Frederic L.: History of the American Frontier Houghton
Mifflin Co Boston 1924

Phifer,Edmund W: History of No. Car. County Burke 1977

Seale,Rev. Monroe: History of White County Tennessee 1935

Smith,Mellcene Thurman,Lewis Jessymin Thurman Hist. and

Lineage Book,Nat.Soc. Daughters of Am.Colonists in Mo. 1936

Strode,Hudson: Jefferson Davis,American Patriot Harcourt,Brace and World Inc NY 1955

Swinton,William: Condensed History of The United States Ivison Blakeman Co.,New York 1871

Todd,Lewis P and Curti, Merle: America´s History Harcourt Brace and Co New York 1950

Tripp,Mrs David A: Early Shockley Families. 1970

U.S.Census Reports: 1790 to 1900

Vaughan,James L:American History, Part II Cambridge Book Co Bronxville NY 1963

Vineyard John, Woodruff,Howard, Hodges Nadine: Public Land Claims Missouri 1967

Warfield, J.D.: The Founders of Anne Arundel and Howard Counties,Maryland. Reginal Pub Co. Balt.

Wayland,John W: Virginia Valley Records Genealogical Pub Co Baltimore 1973

Wells H.G.: The Outline of History Garden City Books NY 1920

West,Willis Mason and West Ruth: American People Norwood Press, Norwood Mass 1928

Williams,O.P.:History of Gentry and Worth Cos Mo 1882

Williams,O.P.:History of St.Charles,Montgomery and Warren Cos Mo 1885

Works Progress Administratio:Early Missouri Archives

Wulfeck:Marriages of Some Virginia Residents.